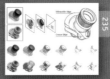

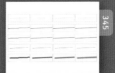

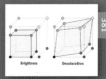
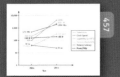

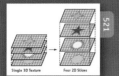
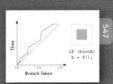
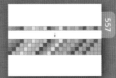
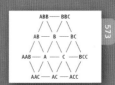
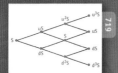
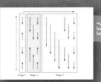

GENERAL-PURPOSE COMPUTATION ON GPUs: A PRIMER

GPU Gems 2

GPU Gems 2

Programming Techniques for High-Performance Graphics and General-Purpose Computation

Edited by Matt Pharr

Randima Fernando, Series Editor

✦ Addison-Wesley

Upper Saddle River, NJ • Boston • Indianapolis • San Francisco
New York • Toronto • Montreal • London • Munich • Paris • Madrid
Capetown • Sydney • Tokyo • Singapore • Mexico City

About the Cover: The Nalu character was created by the NVIDIA Demo Team to showcase the rendering power of the GeForce 6800 GPU. The demo shows off advanced hair shading and shadowing algorithms, as well as iridescence and bioluminescence. Soft shafts of light from the water surface are blocked by her body, and her skin is lit by the light refracted through the water's surface, with her body and hair casting soft shadows on her as she swims.

Many of the designations used by manufacturers and sellers to distinguish their products are claimed as trademarks. Where those designations appear in this book, and Addison-Wesley was aware of a trademark claim, the designations have been printed with initial capital letters or in all capitals.

The authors and publisher have taken care in the preparation of this book, but make no expressed or implied warranty of any kind and assume no responsibility for errors or omissions. No liability is assumed for incidental or consequential damages in connection with or arising out of the use of the information or programs contained herein.

NVIDIA makes no warranty or representation that the techniques described herein are free from any Intellectual Property claims. The reader assumes all risk of any such claims based on his or her use of these techniques.

The publisher offers excellent discounts on this book when ordered in quantity for bulk purchases or special sales, which may include electronic versions and/or custom covers and content particular to your business, training goals, marketing focus, and branding interests. For more information, please contact:

U.S. Corporate and Government Sales
(800) 382-3419
corpsales@pearsontechgroup.com

For sales outside of the U.S., please contact:

International Sales
international@pearsoned.com

Visit Addison-Wesley on the Web: www.awprofessional.com

Library of Congress Cataloging-in-Publication Data
GPU gems 2 : programming techniques for high-performance graphics and general-purpose computation / edited by Matt Pharr ; Randima Fernando, series editor.
    p. cm.
  Includes bibliographical references and index.
  ISBN 0-321-33559-7 (hardcover : alk. paper)
  1. Computer graphics. 2. Real-time programming. I. Pharr, Matt. II. Fernando, Randima.

  T385.G688 2005
  006.66—dc22

                         2004030181

GeForce™ and NVIDIA Quadro® are trademarks or registered trademarks of NVIDIA Corporation.
Nalu, Timbury, and Clear Sailing images © 2004 NVIDIA Corporation.
mental images and mental ray are trademarks or registered trademarks of mental images, GmbH.

ISBN 0-321-33559-7

Text printed in the United States on recycled paper at Quebecor World Taunton in Taunton, Massachusetts.

First printing, March 2005

*To everyone striving to make
today's best computer graphics
look primitive tomorrow*

Contents

PART I   GEOMETRIC COMPLEXITY   1

Chapter 1
Toward Photorealism in Virtual Botany 7
David Whatley, Simutronics Corporation

Chapter 4
Segment Buffering 69
Jon Olick, 2015

Chapter 5
Optimizing Resource Management with Multistreaming. 75
Oliver Hoeller, Piranha Bytes
Kurt Pelzer, Piranha Bytes

Chapter 6
Hardware Occlusion Queries Made Useful 91
Michael Wimmer, Vienna University of Technology
Jiří Bittner, Vienna University of Technology

Chapter 7
Adaptive Tessellation of Subdivision Surfaces with Displacement Mapping

Michael Bunnell, NVIDIA Corporation

Chapter 8
Per-Pixel Displacement Mapping with Distance Functions 123
William Donnelly, University of Waterloo

PART II   SHADING, LIGHTING, AND SHADOWS   137

Chapter 9
Deferred Shading in *S.T.A.L.K.E.R.* 143
Oles Shishkovtsov, GSC Game World

Chapter 13
Implementing the mental images Phenomena Renderer on the GPU

Martin-Karl Lefrançois, mental images

Chapter 14
Dynamic Ambient Occlusion and Indirect Lighting

Michael Bunnell, NVIDIA Corporation

Chapter 15
Blueprint Rendering and "Sketchy Drawings" 235
Marc Nienhaus, University of Potsdam, Hasso-Plattner-Institute
Jürgen Döllner, University of Potsdam, Hasso-Plattner-Institute

Chapter 16
Accurate Atmospheric Scattering 253
Sean O'Neil

Chapter 17
Efficient Soft-Edged Shadows Using Pixel Shader Branching 269
Yury Uralsky, NVIDIA Corporation

Chapter 18
Using Vertex Texture Displacement for Realistic Water Rendering 283
Yuri Kryachko, 1C:Maddox Games

Chapter 19
Generic Refraction Simulation 295
Tiago Sousa, Crytek

PART III   HIGH-QUALITY RENDERING   307

Chapter 20
Fast Third-Order Texture Filtering 313
Christian Sigg, ETH Zurich
Markus Hadwiger, VRVis Research Center

Chapter 21
High-Quality Antialiased Rasterization 331
Dan Wexler, NVIDIA Corporation
Eric Enderton, NVIDIA Corporation

Chapter 27
Advanced High-Quality Filtering 417
Justin Novosad, discreet

Chapter 28
Mipmap-Level Measurement 437
Iain Cantlay, Climax Entertainment

Chapter 33
Implementing Efficient Parallel Data Structures on GPUs 521

Aaron Lefohn, University of California, Davis
Joe Kniss, University of Utah
John Owens, University of California, Davis

Chapter 34
GPU Flow-Control Idioms 547

Mark Harris, NVIDIA Corporation
Ian Buck, Stanford University

Chapter 38
High-Quality Global Illumination Rendering Using Rasterization

Toshiya Hachisuka, The University of Tokyo

Chapter 39
Global Illumination Using Progressive Refinement Radiosity

Greg Coombe, University of North Carolina at Chapel Hill
Mark Harris, NVIDIA Corporation

Chapter 42
Conservative Rasterization

Jon Hasselgren, Lund University
Tomas Akenine-Möller, Lund University
Lennart Ohlsson, Lund University

PART VI   SIMULATION AND NUMERICAL ALGORITHMS   691

Chapter 43
GPU Computing for Protein Structure Prediction

Paulius Micikevicius, Armstrong Atlantic State University

Chapter 44
A GPU Framework for Solving Systems of Linear Equations

Jens Krüger, Technische Universität München
Rüdiger Westermann, Technische Universität München

Foreword

Before the advent of dedicated PC graphics hardware, the industry's first 3D games used CPU-based software rendering. I wrote the first Unreal Engine in that era, inspired by John Carmack's pioneering programming work on *Doom* and *Quake*. Despite slow CPUs and low resolutions, the mid-1990s became a watershed time for graphics and gaming. New visual effects appeared almost monthly, marked by milestones like *Quake's* light mapping and shadowing and Unreal's colored lighting and volumetric fog. That era faded away as fixed-function 3D accelerators appeared. Deprived of the programmability that drove innovation and differentiation, 3D games grew indistinct.

Today, a new Renaissance in 3D graphics is under way, driven by fully programmable GPUs—*graphics processing units*—that deliver thousands of times the graphics power available just ten years ago. Combining incredible parallel computing power with modern, high-level programming languages, today's GPUs have unleashed a Cambrian Explosion of innovation and creativity. Real-time soft shadowing, accurate lighting models, and realistic material interactions are readily achievable. But the most important gain of programmability is that you can do *anything* with a GPU so long as you can find an algorithm to express your idea. *GPU Gems 2* demonstrates many such ideas-turned-algorithms.

Let us take a moment to review the set of resources available to today's graphics programmer. First, you have access to a GPU that can perform tens of billions of floating-point calculations per second in programmable shading algorithms. It's your workhorse; if you can move your problem into the realm of pixels and vertices, then you can harness the GPU's immense power. Second, you have a CPU, the system's general-purpose computing engine. The CPU sends commands to the graphics processing unit, manages resources, and interacts with the outside world. Finally, you have access to artistic content—texture maps, meshes, and other multimedia data that the GPU can combine, filter, and procedurally modify during rendering.

The Gems in this book employ these resources in novel ways to render realistic scenes, process images, and produce special effects. In doing so, many of the previous era's

graphics rules may be broken. GPUs are fast and flexible enough that you may render a given object many times, decomposing a scene into its components—lighting, shadowing, reflections, post-processing effects, and so on. You can employ the GPU for decidedly non-graphics tasks like collision detection, physics, and numerical computation; and within texture maps you can encode arbitrary data, such as vectors, positions, or lookup tables used by shader programs. And while visual realism is now achievable on GPUs, it is not your only option: nonphotorealistic rendering techniques are available, such as cel shading, exaggerated motion blur and light blooms, and other effects seen frequently in Hollywood productions.

Seven years after I wrote Unreal's original software renderer, my company began developing a new game engine, Unreal Engine 3, designed for the capabilities of today's modern GPUs. It has been an incredible experience! Where we once built 300-polygon scenes with static lighting and texture maps, we now combine dynamic per-pixel lighting and shadowing with realistic material effects in million-polygon scenes. We've seen an explosive

growth in the power and flexibility available to programmers and artists alike. But while much has changed in graphics development, several truths have remained: that graphics requires a unique combination of engineering, artistry, and invention unmatched in other fields; that innovation moves at an incredible pace as hardware performance increases exponentially; and that graphics programming is *a heck of a lot of fun!*

Here in *GPU Gems 2*, you'll find a wealth of knowledge and insight, plus many just plain neat ideas, which can be readily applied on today's graphics hardware. But the techniques here are only a starting point on your adventure—the real fun and opportunity lie in finding new ways to customize and combine these Gems and to invent new ones.

Tim Sweeney
Founder and Technical Director, Epic Games

Screenshots from Unreal Engine 3 Technology Demo, http://www.unrealtechnology.com

Preface

The first volume of *GPU Gems* was conceived in the spring of 2003, soon after the arrival of the first generation of fully programmable GPUs. The resulting book was released less than a year later and quickly became a best seller, providing a snapshot of the best ideas for making the most of the capabilities of the latest programmable graphics hardware.

GPU programming is a rapidly changing field, and the time is already ripe for a sequel. In the handful of years since programmable graphics processors first became available, they have become faster and more flexible at an incredible pace. Early programmable GPUs supported programmability only at the vertex level, while today complex per-pixel programs are common. A year ago, real-time GPU programs were typically tens of instructions long, while this year's GPUs handle complex programs hundreds of instructions long and still render at interactive rates. Programmable graphics has even transcended the PC and is rapidly spreading to consoles, handheld gaming devices, and mobile phones.

Until recently, performance-conscious developers might have considered writing their GPU programs in assembly language. These days, however, high-level GPU programming languages are ubiquitous. It is extremely rare for developers to bother writing assembly for GPUs anymore, thanks both to improvements in compilers and to the rapidly increasing capabilities of GPUs. (In contrast, it took many more years before game developers switched from writing their games in CPU assembly language to using higher-level languages.)

This sort of rapid change makes a "gems"-style book a natural fit for assembling the state of the art and disseminating it to the developer community. Featuring chapters written by acknowledged experts, *GPU Gems 2* provides broad coverage of the most exciting new ideas in the field.

Innovations in graphics hardware and programming environments have inspired further innovations in how to use programmability. While programmable shading has long been a staple of offline software rendering, the advent of programmability on GPUs has led to the invention of a wide variety of new techniques for programmable shading. Going far beyond procedural pattern generation and texture composition, the state of the art of using shaders on GPUs is rapidly breaking completely new ground, leading to novel techniques for animation, lighting, particle systems, and much more.

Indeed, the flexibility and speed of GPUs have fostered considerable interest in doing computations on GPUs that go beyond computer graphics: general-purpose computation on GPUs, or "GPGPU." This volume of the *GPU Gems* series devotes a significant number of chapters to this new topic, including an overview of GPGPU programming techniques as well as in-depth discussions of a number of representative applications and key algorithms. As GPUs continue to increase in performance more quickly than CPUs, these topics will gain in importance for more and more programmers because GPUs will provide superior results for many computationally intensive applications.

With this background, we sent out a public call for participation in *GPU Gems 2*. The response was overwhelming: more than 150 chapters were proposed in the short time that submissions were open, covering a variety of topics related to GPU programming. We were able to include only about a third of them in this volume; many excellent submissions could not be included purely because of constraints on the physical size of the book. It was difficult for the editors to whittle down the chapters to the 48 included here, and we would like to thank everyone who submitted proposals.

The accepted chapters went through a rigorous review process in which the book's editors, the authors of other chapters in the same part of the book, and in some cases additional reviewers from NVIDIA carefully read them and suggested improvements or changes. In almost every case, this step noticeably improved the final chapter, due to the high-quality feedback provided by the reviewers. We thank all of the reviewers for the time and effort they put into this important part of the production process.

Intended Audience

We expect readers to be familiar with the fundamentals of computer graphics and GPU programming, including graphics APIs such as Direct3D and OpenGL, as well as GPU languages such as HLSL, GLSL, and Cg. Readers interested in GPGPU programming may find it helpful to have some basic familiarity with parallel programming concepts.

Developers of games, visualization applications, and other interactive applications, as well as researchers in computer graphics, will find *GPU Gems 2* an invaluable daily resource. In particular, those developing for next-generation consoles will find a wealth of timely and applicable content.

Trying the Examples

GPU Gems 2 comes with a CD-ROM that includes code samples, movies, and other demonstrations of the techniques described in the book. This CD is a valuable supplement to the ideas explained in the book. In many cases, the working examples provided by the authors will provide additional enlightenment. You can find sample chapters, updated CD content, supplementary materials, and more at the book's Web site, **http://developer.nvidia.com/GPUGems2/**.

Acknowledgments

An enormous amount of work by many different people went into this book. First, the contributors wrote a great collection of chapters on a tight schedule. Their efforts have made this collection as valuable, timely, and thought provoking as it is.

The section editors—Kevin Bjorke, Cem Cebenoyan, Simon Green, Mark Harris, Craig Kolb, and Matthias Wloka—put in many hours of hard work on this project, working with authors to polish their chapters and their results until they shone, consulting with them about best practices for GPU programming, and gently reminding them of deadlines. Without their focus and dedication, we'd still be working through the queue of submissions. Chris Seitz also kindly took care of many legal, logistical, and business issues related to the book's production.

Many others at NVIDIA also contributed to *GPU Gems 2*. We thank Spender Yuen once again for his patience while doing a wonderful job on the book's diagrams, as well as on the cover. Helen Ho also helped with the illustrations as their number grew to more than 150. We are grateful to Caroline Lie and her team for their continual support of our projects. Similarly, Teresa Saffaie and Catherine Kilkenny have always been ready and willing to provide help with copyediting as our projects develop. Jim Black coordinated communication with a number of developers and contributors, including Tim Sweeney, to whom we are grateful for writing a wonderfully focused and astute Foreword.

At Addison-Wesley Professional, Peter Gordon, Julie Nahil, and Kim Boedigheimer oversaw this project and helped to expedite the production pipeline so we could release this book in as timely a manner as possible. Christopher Keane's copyediting skills and Jules Keane's assistance improved the content immeasurably, and Curt Johnson helped to market the book when it was finally complete.

The support of several members of NVIDIA's management team was instrumental to this project's success. Mark Daly and Dan Vivoli saw the value of putting together a second volume in the *GPU Gems* series and supported this book throughout. Nick Triantos allowed Matt the time to work on this project and gave feedback on a number of the GPGPU chapters. Jonah Alben and Tony Tamasi provided insightful perspectives and valuable feedback about the chapter on the GeForce 6 Series architecture. We give sincere thanks to Jen-Hsun Huang for commissioning this project and fostering the innovative, challenging, and forward-thinking environment that makes NVIDIA such an exhilarating place to work.

Finally, we thank all of our colleagues at NVIDIA for continuing to push the envelope of computer graphics day by day; their efforts make projects like this possible.

Matt Pharr
NVIDIA Corporation

Randima (Randy) Fernando
NVIDIA Corporation

Contributors

Tomas Akenine-Möller, Lund University

Tomas Akenine-Möller is an associate professor in the department of computer science at Lund University in Sweden. His main interests lie in real-time rendering, graphics on mobile devices, and shadows.

Arul Asirvatham, Microsoft Research

Arul Asirvatham is a Ph.D. student in the School of Computing, University of Utah. He received a B.Tech. in computer science and engineering in 2002 from the Indian Institute of Information Technology in India. His primary research interest is digital geometry processing; he has been working on mesh parameterization techniques. He is also interested in real-time computer graphics. Currently he is focusing on rendering huge terrain data sets interactively.

Jiří Bittner, Vienna University of Technology

Jiří Bittner is currently affiliated with the Institute of Computer Graphics and Algorithms of the Vienna University of Technology. He received his Ph.D. in 2003 from the department of computer science and engineering of the Czech Technical University in Prague. His research interests include visibility computations, efficient real-time rendering techniques, global illumination, and computational geometry.

Kevin Bjorke, NVIDIA Corporation

Kevin Bjorke is a member of the Developer Technology group at NVIDIA. He was a section editor and authored several chapters for *GPU Gems*. He has an extensive and award-winning production background in live-action and computer-animated films, television, advertising, theme park rides, and, of course, games. Kevin has been a regular speaker at events such as Game Developers Conference (GDC) and ACM SIGGRAPH since the mid-1980s. His current work at NVIDIA involves exploring and harnessing the power of programmable shading for high-quality real-world applications.

Ian Buck, Stanford University

Ian Buck is completing his Ph.D. in computer science at the Stanford Computer Graphics Lab, researching general-purpose computing models for GPUs. He received a B.S.E. in computer science from Princeton University in 1999 and received fellowships from the Stanford School of Engineering and NVIDIA. His research focuses on programming language design for graphics hardware as well as general-computing applications that map to graphics hardware architectures.

Michael Bunnell, NVIDIA Corporation

Michael Bunnell graduated from Southern Methodist University with degrees in computer science and electrical engineering. He wrote the Megamax C compiler for the Macintosh, Atari ST, and Apple IIGS before cofounding what is now LynuxWorks. After working on real-time operating systems for nine years, he moved to Silicon Graphics, focusing on image-processing, video, and graphics software. Next, he worked at Gigapixel, then at 3dfx, and now at NVIDIA, where, interestingly enough, he is working on compilers again—this time, shader compilers.

Iain Cantlay, Climax Entertainment

Iain Cantlay is currently a senior engineer at Climax, where he was responsible for the graphical aspects of the *Leviathan* MMO engine and *Warhammer Online*. His current projects include *MotoGP 3* (to be published for Xbox and PC by THQ in 2005). Iain is passionate about exploiting the best visuals from the latest technology, but natural phenomena interest him most: terrain, skies, clouds, vegetation, and water.

Francesco Carucci, Lionhead Studios

Francesco Carucci graduated from the Politecnico di Torino in Italy with a degree in software engineering. When he was eight, rather than make pizza (like every good Italian), he decided to make video games, and he tried to animate a running character in BASIC on an Intellivision. He is now writing code to animate running characters at Lionhead, working on the latest rendering technology for *Black & White 2*. He contributed to various Italian technical 3D sites and to *ShaderX2*. His main interests include lighting and shadowing algorithms, 3D software construction, and the latest 3D hardware architectures. And when he needs help, he writes shaders for food.

Cem Cebenoyan, NVIDIA Corporation

Cem Cebenoyan is a software engineer working in the Developer Technology group at NVIDIA. He was an author and section editor for *GPU Gems*. He spends his days researching graphics techniques and helping game developers get the most out of graphics hardware. He has spoken at past Game Developer Conferences on character animation, graphics performance, and nonphotorealistic rendering. Before joining NVIDIA, he was a student and research assistant in the Graphics, Visualization, and Usability Lab at the Georgia Institute of Technology.

Eric Chan, Massachusetts Institute of Technology

Eric Chan is a Ph.D. student in the Computer Science and Artificial Intelligence Laboratory at M.I.T. He fiddles with graphics architectures, shading languages, and real-time rendering algorithms. He has recently developed efficient methods for rendering hard and soft shadows. Before attending graduate school, Eric was a research staff member in the Stanford Computer Graphics Laboratory. As part of the Real-Time Programmable Shading team, he wrote compiler back ends for the NV30 and R300 fragment architectures and developed a pass-decomposition algorithm for virtualizing hardware resources. Eric enjoys photography and spends an unreasonable amount of his free time behind the camera.

Greg Coombe, The University of North Carolina at Chapel Hill

Greg Coombe is a graduate student at the University of North Carolina at Chapel Hill. He received a B.S. in mathematics and a B.S. in computer science from the University of Utah in 2000. Greg's research interests include global illumination, graphics hardware, nonphotorealistic rendering, virtual environments, and 3D modeling. During the course of his graduate studies, he has worked briefly at Intel, NVIDIA, and Vicious Cycle Software. Greg was the recipient of the NVIDIA Graduate Fellowship in 2003 and 2004.

Jürgen Döllner, University of Potsdam, Hasso-Plattner-Institute

Jürgen Döllner, a professor at the Hasso-Plattner-Institute of the University of Potsdam, directs the computer graphics and visualization division. He has studied mathematics and computer science and received a Ph.D. in computer science. He researches and teaches in real-time computer graphics and spatial visualization.

William Donnelly, NVIDIA Corporation and University of Waterloo

William Donnelly is a fourth-year undergraduate in computer science and mathematics at the University of Waterloo in Ontario. He interned with Okino Computer Graphics, where he worked on global illumination and volumetric rendering; and with NVIDIA's Demo Team, where he worked on the "Last Chance Gas" and "Nalu" demos. He has been destined for greatness in computer graphics since mastering the art of the Bezier spline at age ten.

Frédo Durand, Massachusetts Institute of Technology

Frédo Durand received a Ph.D. from Grenoble University in France in 1999, where he worked on both theoretical and practical aspects of 3D visibility. From 1999 until 2002, he was a postdoc in the M.I.T. Computer Graphics Group, where he is now an assistant professor. His research interests span most aspects of picture generation and creation, including realistic graphics, real-time rendering, nonphotorealistic rendering, and computational photography. He received a Eurographics Young Researcher Award in 2004. *(Digital drawing courtesy of Victor Ostromoukhov)*

Eric Enderton, NVIDIA Corporation

Eric Enderton is a senior engineer at NVIDIA, where he is working on the Gelato film renderer. After studying computer science at the University of California, Berkeley, Eric spent a decade developing rendering and animation software at Industrial Light & Magic, and he later consulted at other studios. His film credits include *Terminator 2*; *Jurassic Park*; and *Star Wars, Episode I: The Phantom Menace*.

Zhe Fan, Stony Brook University

Zhe Fan is a Ph.D. candidate in the computer science department at Stony Brook University. He received a B.S. in computer science from the University of Science and Technology of China in 1998 and an M.S. in computer science from the Chinese Academy of Sciences in 2001. His current research interests include GPU clusters for general-purpose computation, parallel graphics and visualization, and modeling of amorphous phenomena.

Randima Fernando, NVIDIA Corporation

Randima (Randy) Fernando has loved computer graphics since age eight. Working in NVIDIA's Developer Technology group, he helps teach developers how to take advantage of the latest GPU technology. Randy has a B.S. in computer science and an M.S. in computer graphics, both from Cornell University. He has published research in SIGGRAPH and is coauthor, with Mark Kilgard, of *The Cg Tutorial: The Definitive Guide to Programmable Real-Time Graphics*. He edited *GPU Gems: Programming Techniques, Tips, and Tricks for Real-Time Graphics* and is the *GPU Gems* series editor.

Nathaniel Fout, University of California, Davis

Nathaniel Fout received a B.S. in chemical engineering and an M.S. in computer science from the University of Tennessee in 2002 and 2003, respectively. He is a Ph.D. student in computer science at the University of California, Davis, where he is a member of the Institute for Data Analysis and Visualization. His research interests include volumetric compression for rendering, multivariate and comparative visualization, and tensor visualization.

James Fung, University of Toronto

James Fung is completing his Ph.D. in engineering. He received a B.A.Sc. in engineering science and an M.S. in electrical engineering from the University of Toronto. His research interests include wearable computing, mediated reality, and exploring new types of musical instrument interfaces based on EEG brain-wave signal processing. His most recent work has been the development of the GPU-based computer vision and mediated reality library called OpenVIDIA.

Simon Green, NVIDIA Corporation

Simon Green is a senior software engineer in the Developer Technology group at NVIDIA. He started graphics programming on the Sinclair ZX-81, which had 1 kB of RAM and a screen resolution of 64×48 pixels. He received a B.S. in computer science from the University of Reading, in the United Kingdom, in 1994. Since 1999 Simon has found a stable home at NVIDIA, where he develops new rendering techniques and helps application developers take maximum advantage of GPU hardware. He is a frequent presenter at GDC, has written for *Amiga Shopper* and *Wired* magazines, and was a section editor for *GPU Gems*. His research interests include cellular automata, general-purpose computation on GPUs, and analog synthesizers.

Toshiya Hachisuka, University of Tokyo

Toshiya Hachisuka is an undergraduate in the Department of Systems Innovation at the University of Tokyo. He also works as a programmer for MagicPictures, integrating cutting-edge research results into current computer graphics software. He has studied computer graphics since age ten. His current research interests are physically based rendering, physically based modeling, real-time rendering techniques, and general-purpose computation on GPUs.

Markus Hadwiger, VRVis Research Center

Markus Hadwiger received his Ph.D. in computer science from the Vienna University of Technology in 2004, where he concentrated on high-quality real-time volume rendering and texture filtering with graphics hardware, in cooperation with the VRVis Research Center. He has been a researcher at VRVis since 2000, working in the Basic Research on Visualization group and the Medical Visualization group (since 2004). From 1996 to 2001, he was also the lead programmer of the cross-platform 3D space-shooter game *Parsec*, which is now an open source project.

Mark Harris, NVIDIA Corporation

Mark Harris received a B.S. from the University of Notre Dame in 1998 and a Ph.D. in computer science from the University of North Carolina at Chapel Hill (UNC) in 2003. At UNC, Mark's research covered a wide variety of computer graphics topics, including real-time cloud simulation and rendering, general-purpose computation on GPUs, global illumination, nonphotorealistic rendering, and virtual environments. Mark is now a member of NVIDIA's Developer Technology team based in the United Kingdom.

Jon Hasselgren, Lund University

Jon Hasselgren received an M.Sc. from Lund University. He now pursues graduate studies in the computer science department, where he researches graphics for mobile phones.

Oliver Hoeller, Piranha Bytes

Oliver Hoeller is a senior software engineer at Piranha Bytes, which developed the RPGs *Gothic I* and *Gothic II*. Previously he was director of development at H2Labs/Codecult, where he was responsible for development and architecture design of the Codecreatures game system. He was an active member of the German demo scene in the 1980s and early 1990s. After exploring different areas—developing music software, creating a security program, and working as a Web services consultant—Oliver returned to his roots and now guarantees a high level of visual quality for Piranha Bytes' forthcoming *Gothic III*.

Hugues Hoppe, Microsoft Research

Hugues Hoppe is a senior researcher in the Computer Graphics Group at Microsoft Research. His primary interests lie in the acquisition, representation, and rendering of geometric models. He received the 2004 ACM SIGGRAPH Achievement Award for his pioneering work on surface reconstruction, progressive meshes, geometry texturing, and geometry images. His publications include twenty papers at ACM SIGGRAPH, and he is associate editor of *ACM Transactions on Graphics*. He received a B.S. in electrical engineering in 1989 and a Ph.D. in computer science in 1994 from the University of Washington.

Daniel Horn, Stanford University

Daniel Horn is a Ph.D. candidate at the Stanford Computer Graphics Lab; he received his B.S. from the University of California, Berkeley. While Daniel focuses on programming graphics hardware and real-time graphics, theory and compilers have always interested him deeply, and he tries to incorporate knowledge from those fields into his graphics research. In his spare time, Daniel enjoys hacking with his brother, Patrick, on their open source space sim, *Vega Strike*. He also enjoys roaming with friends in the Bay Area's many natural parks, from Palo Alto's Foothills Park to Berkeley's Tilden Park.

Samuel Hornus, GRAVIR/IMAG–INRIA

Samuel Hornus is a Ph.D. candidate at INRIA in Grenoble, France: He is a former student of the Ecole Normale Supérieure de Cachan. His research focuses on 3D visibility problems, as well as other aspects of computer graphics, such as texture authoring, interactive walkthroughs, real-time shadows, realistic rendering, implicit surfaces, and image-based modeling.

Arie Kaufman, Stony Brook University

Arie Kaufman is the director of the Center for Visual Computing, a distinguished professor and chair of the Computer Science Department, and distinguished professor of radiology at Stony Brook University. He received a B.S. in mathematics and physics from the Hebrew University of Jerusalem in 1969; an M.S. in computer science from the Weizmann Institute of Science, Rehovot, Israel, in 1973; and a Ph.D. in computer science from the Ben-Gurion University, Israel, in 1977. Kaufman has conducted research and consulted for more than thirty years, with numerous publications in volume visualization; graphics architectures, algorithms, and languages; virtual reality; user interfaces; and multimedia.

Jan Kautz, Massachusetts Institute of Technology

Jan Kautz is a postdoctoral researcher at M.I.T. He is particularly interested in realistic shading and lighting, hardware-accelerated rendering, textures and reflection properties, and interactive computer graphics. He received his Ph.D. in computer science from the Max-Planck-Institut für Informatik in Germany; a diploma in computer science from the University of Erlangen in Germany; and an M.Math. from the University of Waterloo in Ontario.

Emmett Kilgariff, NVIDIA Corporation

Emmett Kilgariff is a director of architecture in the GPU group at NVIDIA, where he has contributed to the design of many GeForce chips, including the GeForce 6 and GeForce 7 Series. He has more than twenty years of experience designing graphics hardware, at Sun Microsystems, Silicon Graphics, 3dfx, and many small companies whose memories have faded over time.

Gary King, NVIDIA Corporation

Unscrupulous. Unconventional. Uncouth. Unkempt. All are accurate adjectives for the worst thing to happen to the graphics industry since Execute Buffers. A master of GPU arcana, lore, and the occult, he spends his days at NVIDIA crafting increasingly ingeniously nefarious rendering techniques, imbuing next-generation architectures with unholy energies, worshipping the Dark Lord, and kicking puppies.

Peter Kipfer, Technische Universität München

Peter Kipfer is a postdoctoral researcher in the Computer Graphics and Visualization Group at the Technische Universität München. He received his Ph.D. from the University of Erlangen-Nürnberg in 2003 for his work on parallel and distributed visualization and rendering within the KONWIHR supercomputing project. His current research focuses on general-purpose computing and geometry processing on the GPU.

Joe Kniss, University of Utah

Joe Kniss is a Ph.D. student in computer science at the University of Utah, where he is a member of the Scientific Computing and Imaging Institute. His research interests include nonpolygonal rendering, light transport in participating media, user-interface design, and all things GPU. He is a Department of Energy High-Performance Computer Science graduate fellow.

Craig Kolb, NVIDIA Corporation

Craig Kolb has been interested in computer graphics since he began writing games on his high school's sub-megaflop PDP-11. He received a B.A. and an M.Sc. from Princeton, where he wrote the first version of rayshade, a popular ray tracer, as part of his senior thesis. He spent the 1990s waiting for frames to render: first as a research assistant to Benoit Mandelbrot at Yale, then as a Ph.D. candidate researching camera and rendering systems at Princeton and Stanford, and later as head of rendering development at Pixar Animation Studios. In 2000 he cofounded Exluna and now works in the Software Architecture group at NVIDIA finding novel ways to push multi-gigaflop GPUs to their limits.

Jens Krüger, Technische Universität München

Jens Krüger is a Ph.D. student in the Computer Graphics and Visualization Group at the Technische Universität München. Jens's current research focuses on GPU solutions to numerical problems, often arising in physically based simulations. He has published papers on GPU programming at conferences such as ACM SIGGRAPH and IEEE Visualization. In 2004 he received an ATI Fellowship, which honors outstanding graduate students in areas related to computer graphics and graphics systems.

Yuri Kryachko, 1C:Maddox Games

Yuri Kryachko is the 3D graphics and effects programmer on *IL-2 Sturmovik*, *WW2*, *IL-2 Sturmovik: Forgotten Battles*, *AEP*, and *Pacific Fighters*. He has been at Maddox Games since 1996, and he's been playing and creating PC games since writing his first 2D game in 1987. He received an M.S. from the department of applied mathematics of the Moscow State Engineering Physics Institute (Technical University). Previous game projects include *City3D–Drive Simulator (ELF)* in 1995 and *Helicopter Simulator* from 1995 to 1996.

Sylvain Lefebvre, GRAVIR/IMAG–INRIA

Sylvain Lefebvre is a final-year Ph.D. student at INRIA in Grenoble, France. He received an M.S. in computer science from the INPG University, Grenoble, in 2001. His research focuses on developing new texturing methods for creating, storing, and rendering highly detailed textures for real-time applications. Recently he has worked on landscape texturing, direct painting on meshes, and the progressive loading of texture maps. He is also interested in many aspects of game programming.

Aaron Lefohn, University of California, Davis

Aaron Lefohn is a Ph.D. student in the computer science department at the University of California, Davis, and a graphics software engineer at Pixar Animation Studios. His current research focuses on data-parallel data structures and programming models and their application to high-quality interactive rendering. Aaron completed his M.S. in computer science at the University of Utah in 2003; he received an M.S. in theoretical chemistry from the University of Utah in 2001 and a B.A. in chemistry from Whitman College in 1997. Aaron is a National Science Foundation graduate fellow in computer science.

Martin-Karl Lefrançois, mental images

Martin-Karl Lefrançois is senior graphics software engineer at mental images in Berlin, maker of the mental ray renderer and other graphics software products. Under his lead, his team at mental images delivered automatic GPU support in mental ray 3.3 and is responsible for GPU acceleration support in all mental images products. After graduating with a degree in computer science and mathematics from the University of Sherbrooke in Quebec, he worked as a graphics developer for nearly ten years at Softimage in Montreal and Tokyo before leading the core game engine team at A2M.

Wei Li, Siemens Corporate Research

Wei Li is a research scientist at Siemens Corporate Research in Princeton, New Jersey. His current research focuses on texture-based volume rendering and general-purpose computation on the GPU. He received an M.S. and a Ph.D. in computer science from Stony Brook University in 2001 and 2004, respectively. He also received a B.S. and an M.S. in electrical engineering from Xi'an Jiaotong University in China in 1992 and 1995, respectively.

Donald Liu, Siemens Medical Solutions USA

Donald Liu received a B.Eng. from Qinghua University in Beijing in 1984; he received an M.Eng. and a D.Eng. from the University of Tokyo in 1988 and 1991, respectively. He was an assistant professor at Sophia University in Tokyo for a year before joining the faculty of the electrical engineering department at the University of Rochester in New York. Since 1997 he has been with the Siemens Medical Solutions Ultrasound Group in Issaquah, Washington, where he is currently a senior staff systems engineer. He is a senior member of IEEE and a recipient of the National Institutes of Health FIRST award. His research interests include analysis and correction of ultrasonic wavefront distortion, efficient image formation, and digital signal processing.

Paulius Micikevicius, Armstrong Atlantic State University
Paulius Micikevicius received a B.S. in computer science from Midwestern State University in 1998 and a Ph.D. in computer science from the University of Central Florida (UCF) in 2002. He is an assistant professor at Armstrong Atlantic State University in Savannah, Georgia, as well as a research associate at the Media Convergence Laboratory at UCF. His research interests include real-time graphics, graphics processing for mixed/augmented reality experiences, and parallel computing and graph theory.

Fabrice Neyret, GRAVIR/IMAG–INRIA
Fabrice Neyret has worked on the R&D teams of several companies, including TDI in Paris and Alias|Wavefront in Toronto. He received a master's degree in applied mathematics, an engineering degree from Telecom Paris (ENST), and a Ph.D. in computer science. He did his postdoctoral work at the University of Toronto. He is currently a full-time CNRS researcher at GRAVIR lab in Grenoble, France. His research interests include natural phenomena (especially water and clouds), highly complex scenes (such as landscapes covered by forest), textures, local illumination and shaders, alternate representations (such as volumetric textures), phenomenological approaches, and, of course, getting the most out of GPUs. He is also involved in pedagogic software (such as MobiNet), scientific popularization, and writing short stories.

Hubert Nguyen, NVIDIA Corporation
Hubert Nguyen is a software engineer on the NVIDIA Demo Team. He spends his time searching for novel effects that show off the features of NVIDIA's latest GPUs. He most recently worked on "Nalu," NVIDIA's mermaid. Before joining NVIDIA, Hubert was at 3dfx interactive, the creators of Voodoo Graphics. Prior to 3dfx, Hubert was part of the R&D department of Cryo Interactive in Paris. Hubert started to develop 3D graphics programs when he was involved in the European demo scene. He holds a degree in computer science.

Marc Nienhaus, University of Potsdam, Hasso-Plattner-Institute
Marc Nienhaus is a Ph.D. candidate at the Hasso-Plattner-Institute of the University of Potsdam. He studied mathematics and computer science and has worked as a software engineer focusing on computer graphics. His research interests include real-time rendering, nonphotorealistic rendering, and depiction strategies for symbolizing dynamics.

Justin Novosad, discreet

Justin Novosad is a software developer for discreet (a division of Autodesk). He received a bachelor's degree in computer engineering and a master's degree in medical imaging, both from École Polytechnique de Montréal, in 2001 and 2003, respectively. Justin is a member of the "effects" team at discreet, working on the Inferno, Flame, and Flint visual effects and digital compositing products. Before joining discreet in 2004, he was a research engineer at Sainte-Justine Hospital in Montreal, where he developed computer vision algorithms for the study of spinal deformities from X-ray data. His fields of interest include computer graphics, computer vision, machine learning, image processing, and applied mathematics. He is a cofounder of the ACM SIGGRAPH Montreal Professional Chapter.

Lennart Ohlsson, Lund University

Lennart Ohlsson is an assistant professor in the computer science department at Lund University. His primary research interest is software architecture for computer graphics.

Jon Olick, 2015

Jon Olick has been creating games since age 11. He is a senior software engineer specializing in graphics technology and engine design at 2015, where he has worked on titles such as *Medal of Honor: Allied Assault* and *Men of Valor: Vietnam*. He is now developing engine technology for future products.

Sean O'Neil

Sean O'Neil graduated from Georgia Tech in 1995 with a B.S. in computer science. He lives in Atlanta with his wife and two wonderful children. All of his full-time positions have been in the telecommunications industry, so for now graphics programming is just a hobby.

John Owens, University of California, Davis

John Owens is an assistant professor of electrical and computer engineering at the University of California, Davis, where he leads research projects in graphics hardware/software and wireless sensor networks. Prior to his appointment at Davis, he earned an M.S. and a Ph.D. in electrical engineering from Stanford University in 1997 and 2002, respectively. At Stanford he was an architect of the Imagine Stream Processor and a member of the Concurrent VLSI Architecture Group and the Computer Graphics Laboratory. He received a B.S. in electrical engineering and computer science from the University of California, Berkeley, in 1995.

Kurt Pelzer, Piranha Bytes

Kurt Pelzer is a senior software engineer at Piranha Bytes, where he worked on the PC game *Gothic*, the top-selling *Gothic II* (awarded RPG of the Year in Germany during 2001 and 2002, respectively), and the add-on *Gothic II: The Night of the Raven*. Previously he was a senior programmer at Codecult and developed several real-time simulations and technology demos built on Codecult's 3D engine. Kurt has published in *GPU Gems*, *ShaderX2*, and *Game Programming Gems 4*.

Matt Pharr, NVIDIA Corporation

Matt Pharr is a senior software developer in the Software Architecture group at NVIDIA, where he works on Cg and interactive rendering techniques. He is coauthor, with Greg Humphreys, of *Physically Based Rendering: From Theory to Implementation*. Previously he was a cofounder of Exluna and a Ph.D. student in the Stanford Computer Graphics Lab, where he researched systems issues for rendering and theoretical foundations of rendering; he published a series of SIGGRAPH papers on these topics.

Jeremy Selan, Sony Pictures Imageworks

Jeremy Selan currently pioneers color and lighting tools at Sony Pictures Imageworks. His work has been utilized on numerous motion pictures, most recently on *Spider-Man 2*. Professionally, he maintains an active interest in colorimetry and digital cinema. He is a graduate of the Program of Computer Graphics and the School of Electrical and Computer Engineering at Cornell University. In his free time—drawn by a climate markedly superior to that of his hometown, Skokie, Illinois—Jeremy is an aspiring Santa Monica beach bum.

Oles Shishkovtsov, GSC Game World

Oles Shishkovtsov became interested in programming and graphics at age 13; by age 17 he had won two national competitions in programming and enrolled at the Junior Academy of Science in Ukraine. At 19 he started working for White Lynx as a software developer/graphics programmer, where he successfully completed three projects. Since 2000 he has worked for GSC Game World as an engine architect/team leader and has continued doing R&D in his free time. He has spent the last three years working on *S.T.A.L.K.E.R.: Shadows of Chernobyl*.

Christian Sigg, ETH Zurich

Christian Sigg received his degree in computational science and engineering from the Swiss Federal Institute of Technology Zurich. He became interested in computer graphics during a semester abroad at the University of Texas at Austin, where he worked on parallel volume rendering at the Computational Visualization Center. He is working on his Ph.D. at the ETH Zurich Computer Graphics Laboratory. His research interests lie in the area of algorithms for implicit surface representations using graphics hardware.

Tiago Sousa, Crytek

Tiago Sousa is a self-taught game and graphics programmer who has worked at Crytek as an R&D software engineer for the last two years. He has contributed to most of the special effects in Crytek's games. In 1999, before joining Crytek, he cofounded a pioneering game development team in Portugal and studied computer science at a local university. He spends most of his time researching real-time and non-real-time graphics and reading all kinds of technical books.

Thilaka Sumanaweera, Siemens Medical Solutions USA

Thilaka Sumanaweera has been having fun with first GL and then OpenGL since the late 1980s, creating 2, 3, and 4D applications in computer vision, image processing, and medical imaging. He received his Ph.D. in electrical engineering from Stanford University in 1992. He then joined the Radiological Sciences Laboratory at Stanford's Radiology Department as a postdoc and a research associate developing CT/MRI image fusion and image-guided neurosurgery. Currently he is a Fellow in the Siemens Medical Solutions Ultrasound Division, working in the areas of volume rendering, motion detection and compensation, and image segmentation. He holds 24 patents for techniques related to medical imaging and visualization, and he has published extensively in medical journals.

Yury Uralsky, NVIDIA Corporation

Yury Uralsky became interested in games and computer graphics when the ZX Spectrum 48K was a dream machine and writing software rasterizers in assembly language was fun. He received an M.S. in computer science from the Moscow State Technical University in 2001. He worked as a graphics engine programmer for Eagle Dynamics, creating graphics for the flight simulator *LockOn: Modern Air Combat*. He joined the NVIDIA Developer Technology group in March 2004 and enjoys pushing 3D graphics forward in the NVIDIA Moscow office.

Pete Warden, Apple Computer

Pete Warden has worked as a graphics engine programmer on PC, PSX, PS2, GameCube, and Xbox titles, specializing in low-level assembler and vector unit programming on the PS2. He has also published 45 open source video filters that run in a variety of real-time video applications on Windows, Linux, and OS X, including After Effects, and helped to create the Freeframe open plug-in standard. Pete is now part of the team working on Apple's Motion video effects package, a fully GPU-based image-processing application. He has written many of its original video filters and also works on the rendering engine.

Li-Yi Wei, NVIDIA Corporation

Li-Yi Wei is a 3D graphics architect at NVIDIA Corporation. He received a B.S. in electrical engineering from the National Taiwan University in 1993 and a Ph.D. in electrical engineering from Stanford University in 2001. He spends 1 percent of his time designing next-generation graphics hardware and the remaining 99 percent verifying that the design actually works. When not wreaking havoc on NVIDIA's chips, he enjoys researching various fields of computer graphics. He is a frequent contributor to SIGGRAPH and other academic conferences.

Xiaoming Wei, Stony Brook University

Xiaoming Wei is an assistant professor of computer science at Iona College in New Rochelle, New York. She received her Ph.D. in computer science from Stony Brook University in 2004. She received a B.Sc. from the Beijing University of Aeronautics and Astronautics in 1995 and an M.Sc. in computer science from Tsinghua University in Beijing in 1998. Her research interests include physically based modeling, natural phenomena modeling, and computer animation.

Rüdiger Westermann, Technische Universität München

Rüdiger Westermann studied computer science at the Technical University Darmstadt, Germany. He received a Ph.D. in computer science from the University of Dortmund, Germany. In 2002 he was appointed the chair of Computer Graphics and Visualization at the Technische Universität München. His research interests include general-purpose computing on GPUs, hardware-accelerated visualization and image synthesis, hierarchical methods in scientific visualization, volume rendering, flow visualization, and parallel graphics algorithms.

Daniel Wexler, NVIDIA Corporation

Daniel Wexler attended the University of California, Berkeley, where he studied with the graphics research group before leaving school to work at Sun Microsystems. He worked at Xaos Tools before joining the R&D team at Pacific Data Images (PDI) in 1995. After spending six years writing a new renderer and shading system for PDI, which was used on a variety of feature film projects including *Antz* and *Shrek*, he joined NVIDIA to work on hardware-based rendering systems with Larry Gritz and the rest of the NVIDIA architecture team.

David Whatley, Simutronics Corporation

David Whatley is president and CEO of Simutronics Corporation and a developer and publisher of online games. His passion for online gaming led him to found Simutronics in 1987, when he was 20 years old. David—chief designer and technology architect of most of the company's games—has won numerous awards, including Computer Gaming World's first Online Game of the Year award for *CyberStrike*. His current focus is on alternate techniques for more photorealistic rendering of 3D environments in games.

Michael Wimmer, Vienna University of Technology

Michael Wimmer is an assistant professor at the Institute of Computer Graphics and Algorithms of the Vienna University of Technology, where he received an M.Sc. in 1997 and a Ph.D. in 2001. His current research interests are real-time rendering, virtual and augmented reality, computer games, and real-time visualization of urban environments; he has coauthored several scientific papers in these fields. He also teaches courses on 3D computer games and real-time rendering.

Matthias Wloka, NVIDIA Corporation

Matthias Wloka is a software engineer in the Developer Technology group at NVIDIA. His primary responsibility is to collaborate with game developers to enhance image quality and graphics performance of their games; he is also a regular contributor at game developer conferences, such as GDC. Matthias's passion for computer gaming started at age 15 when he discovered that his school's Commodore PET 2001 computers could also play Black Jack. He started writing his own games soon thereafter and continues to use the latest graphics hardware to explore the limits of interactive real-time rendering. Before joining NVIDIA, Matthias was a game developer at GameFX/THQ. He received an M.Sc. in computer science from Brown University in 1990 and a B.Sc from Christian-Albrechts-University in Kiel, Germany, in 1987.

Cliff Woolley, University of Virginia

Cliff Woolley is a Ph.D. student in computer science at the University of Virginia. His research interests include interactive rendering techniques, sparse sample reconstruction, and general-purpose computation using programmable graphics hardware. He received an M.C.S. in computer graphics from the University of Virginia in 2003 and a B.A. in computer science and theater at Washington and Lee University in 1999.

Vertex Position

Vertex Normal

Vertex Diffuse Color (Color 0)

Vertex Specular Color (Color 1)

Texture Coordinate Set 0

Additional Texture Coordinate Sets

Tangent Vector for Tangent-Space Normal Maps

Bone Weight

Additional Animation Data
(Bone Weights and Influence)

Stream G

Stream T

Stream

Vertex Assembly

Vertex

PART I
GEOMETRIC
COMPLEXITY

Today's games are visually more interesting and complex than ever before. Geometric complexity—how many objects are visible and how detailed each looks—is one of the dimensions in which games are making leaps and bounds.

Advances in technology are partly responsible for these leaps and bounds: CPUs, memory, and buses all have become faster, but specifically GPUs are undergoing significant change and are becoming ever more powerful—at a rate faster than Moore's Law.

These GPU changes include incorporating fixed-function processing for the vertex- and pixel-shading units, then generalizing those to be fully programmable. GPUs also have gained more units to process pixels and vertices in parallel: the GeForce 6800 Ultra, for example, incorporates 6 vertex shader units and 16 pixel pipelines.

Despite these performance advances, rendering complex scenes is still more difficult than simply dumping all geometry onto the GPU and forgetting about it. The simple approach tends to fail either because the generated GPU workload turns out to be excessive, or because the associated CPU overhead is prohibitive. This part of the book discusses the challenges today's games face in rendering complex geometric scenes.

Chapter 1, "Toward Photorealism in Virtual Botany" by **David Whatley** of Simutronics Corporation, provides a holistic view on how to render nature scenes. It explains the multitude of different techniques, from scene management and rendering various plant layers to post-processing effects, that Simutronics' *Hero's Journey* employs to generate complex and stunning visuals.

Rendering terrain is a good example of why simply dumping all available data to the GPU cannot work: the horizon represents a near-infinite amount of vertex data and thus workload. **Arul Asirvatham** and **Hugues Hoppe** of Microsoft Research use vertex texture fetches for a new highly efficient terrain-rendering algorithm. Their technique avoids overloading the GPU even as it shifts most work onto the GPU and away from the CPU, which too often is the bottleneck in modern games. **Chapter 2, "Terrain Rendering Using GPU-Based Geometry Clipmaps,"** provides all the implementation details.

As already mentioned, another way to increase geometric complexity is to increase the number of visible objects in a scene. The straightforward solution of drawing each object independently of the others, however, quickly bogs down even a high-end system. It is much easier to efficiently draw ten objects that are one million triangles each, than it is to draw one million objects that are ten triangles each. **Francesco Carucci** of Lionhead Studios faces this very problem while developing *Black & White 2*, the sequel to Lionhead's critically acclaimed *Black & White*. **Chapter 3, "Inside Geometry Instancing,"** describes his solution: a framework of instancing techniques that applies to legacy GPUs as well as to GPUs supporting DirectX 9's instancing API. **Jon Olick** of 2015 provides further optimizations to the instancing technique that prove beneficial for 2015's title *Men of Valor: Vietnam*. Jon describes his findings in **Chapter 4, "Segment Buffering."**

Also, as games incorporate more and more data—more complex scenes of more complex meshes rendered in multiple, disparate passes supporting the gamut of differing functionality from legacy to current high-end GPUs—managing this glut of data efficiently becomes paramount. **Oliver Hoeller** and **Kurt Pelzer** of Piranha Bytes are currently working on Piranha Bytes' *Gothic III* engine. They share their solutions in **Chapter 5, "Optimizing Resource Management with Multistreaming."**

The best way to render lots of geometry to create geometric complexity is to avoid rendering the occluded parts. **Michael Wimmer** and **Jiří Bittner** of the Vienna University of Technology explore how best to apply that idea in **Chapter 6, "Hardware Occlusion Queries Made Useful."** Occlusion queries are a GPU feature that provides high-latency feedback on whether an object is visible or not after it is rendered. Unlike earlier occlusion-query culling techniques, Michael and Jiří's algorithm is pixel-perfect. That is, it introduces no rendering artifacts, generates a near-optimal set of visible objects to render, does not put unnecessary load on the GPU, and has minimal CPU overhead.

Similarly, increasing geometric detail only where visible and simplifying it when and where it isn't visible is a good way to avoid excessive GPU loads. View-dependent and adaptive subdivision schemes are an appealing solution that the offline-rendering world already employs to render their highly detailed models to subpixel geometric accuracy. Subdivision surfaces have not yet found a place in today's real-time applications, partly because they are not directly supported in graphics hardware. Rendering subdivision surfaces thus seems out of reach for real-time applications. Not so, says **Michael Bunnell** of NVIDIA Corporation. In **Chapter 7**, Michael shows how his implementation of **"Adaptive Tessellation of Subdivision Surfaces with Displacement Mapping"** is already feasible on modern GPUs and results in movie-quality geometric detail at real-time rates.

Finally, faking geometric complexity with methods that are cheaper than actually rendering geometry allow for higher apparent complexity at faster speeds. Replacing geometry with textures that merely depict it used to be an acceptable trade-off—and in the case of grates and wire-mesh fences, often still is. Normal mapping is a more sophisticated fake that properly accounts for lighting information. Parallax mapping is the latest craze that attempts to also account for intra-object occlusions. **William Donnelly** of the University of Waterloo one-ups parallax mapping: he describes **"Per-Pixel Displacement Mapping with Distance Functions"** in **Chapter 8**. Displacement mapping provides correct intra-object occlusion information, yet minimally increases computation cost. His technique gives excellent results while taking full advantage of the latest programmable pixel-shading hardware. Even better, it is practical for applications today.

Matthias Wloka, NVIDIA Corporation

Chapter 1

Toward Photorealism in Virtual Botany

David Whatley
Simutronics Corporation

Rendering natural scenes in real time, while leaving enough CPU and GPU resources for other game-engine requirements, is a difficult proposition. Images of botany require a great deal of visual depth and detail to be convincing. This chapter describes strategies for rendering more photorealistic natural scenes in a manner that is friendly to real-time game engines. The methods presented here work together to create a convincing illusion of grassy fields teeming with plants and trees, while not overwhelming either the CPU or the GPU. These techniques are used in Simutronics' *Hero's Journey*, as shown in Figure 1-1.

We begin by describing the foundation for managing scene data in large outdoor environments. Next, we provide details on how to maximize throughput of the GPU to achieve the required visual density in grass. Then we expand on these techniques to add ground clutter and larger-scale botany, such as trees. Finally, we tie the visuals together with shadowing and environmental effects.

1.1 Scene Management

Game engines must manage their rendering techniques to match the scope of the environment they hope to visualize. Game levels that feature nature scenes, made up of thousands of trees and bushes and perhaps millions of blades of grass, present significant data management problems that must be solved to allow rendering at interactive frame rates.

Figure 1-1. Babbling Brook: A Nature Scene from *Hero's Journey*

Rendering a virtual nature scene convincingly is both an artistic and a technical challenge. We can approach the rendering of nature much like a painter: break down the elements into layers and treat each layer independently to ultimately create a unified whole. For example, a layer of grass, a layer of ground clutter, a layer of trees, and so on. All these layers share some common properties, which we can leverage to compress our data representation.

Our goal is to travel the game camera over long distances of convincing outdoor scenes without having to dedicate excessive memory resources to managing the task. With guided deterministic random-number generation, we have an algorithm that can "plant" all of the elements of nature in a reasonable manner while achieving the same visual results each time we revisit the same spot on the map. In an online game, everyone would see the same thing right down to the placement of a blade of grass without this placement being permanently stored in memory.

1.1.1 The Planting Grid

We establish a world-space fixed grid around the camera to manage the planting data for each layer of plants and other natural objects. Each grid cell contains all of the data to render its layer in the physical space it occupies. In particular, the cell data structure stores the corresponding vertex and index buffers, along with material information to represent what is drawn.

For each layer of botany, we establish a distance from the camera that the layer needs to generate visuals; this determines the size of our virtual grid. As the camera moves, the virtual grids travel with it. When a grid cell is no longer in the virtual grid, we discard it and add new cells where needed to maintain our full grid structure. As each cell is added, a planting algorithm is used to fill in the layer with the appropriate data for rendering. See Figure 1-2.

1.1.2 Planting Strategy

For each cell that is filled with natural objects, we need to pick suitable spots on the ground where those objects are placed. The heuristic used to choose these spots depends on the type of object being placed. Generally, we would like to pick random spots, at some desired density, and then see if the corresponding points on the ground are acceptable for what we are planting. In our implementation, a ground polygon's material determines what layers are applicable.

The obvious approach is to randomly cast rays straight down at the ground within the volume of the cell. Each time we hit a polygon, we check to see if it is suitable (Can grass be planted here? Is the slope too severe?). If we succeed, then we have a planted point. We continue until we reach the proper density.

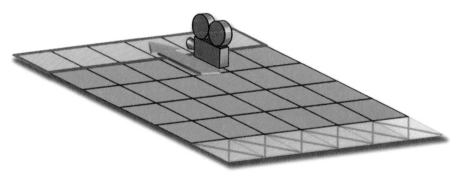

Figure 1-2. The Virtual Grid
Each layer consists of a fixed-size grid that is world-space aligned. The dark green cells represent active cells. The camera is moving forward, and the cells marked with an X are being discarded as new cells (shown in light green) are added to maintain our virtual grid size. A useful improvement in the implementation is to pool the grid cells and simply recycle them, because a new cell is always added when an old one is discarded.

This approach yields good results but has significant problems. First, in grid cells where there are few suitable places to plant (for example, just the top of a polygon that is marked for grass), we can burn inordinate amounts of CPU time trying to randomly achieve our density requirement. So in the worst case, we must abandon our search if we reach some maximum limit of planting attempts. Second, we cannot handle overlapping terrain (such as a land bridge) with this approach.

A better approach is to collect all of the polygons that intersect the cell, discard all polygons inappropriate for planting, and then scan-convert them to find suitable spots for planting. This is similar to rasterizing a polygon for rendering, but instead each "pixel" of our traversal is a world-space potential planting point. We must be careful to keep the scan conversion rate appropriate to the density, while not exceeding the boundaries of the triangle. Further, at each planting point we select, it is important to offset along the plane of the polygon by some suitable random distance to eliminate repeating patterns. All of these values are adjustable coefficients that should be determined during design time. In our implementation, the designer can interactively tweak these values to achieve the desired result for the layer.

Finally, when scan-converting we also must take care to clip to the polygon edges (when offsetting) as well as to the cell's border, because the polygon may extend beyond it (and another cell is managing the planting there).

Planting in this manner can take place in real time or as part of offline level preprocessing. In the latter case, the grass planting spots should be stored in a highly compressed form; the data should be uncompressed at run time as each cell is added to the set of potentially visible cells by the moving camera.

1.1.3 Real-Time Optimization

If this planting operation is done in real time, care must be taken to ensure that planting is a fast operation. Collecting polygons in a grid cell can be done quickly by using an AABB tree or a similar data structure. Because many cells may need to be planted suddenly due to continuous camera movement, it is also effective to queue up this task so that we spend only a relatively fixed amount of CPU on the task for each frame. By extending the size of the grid, we can be reasonably sure that all the appropriate planting will take place before the contents of the cell come into view.

1.2 The Grass Layer

Achieving interactive frame rates for endless fields of grass requires a careful balance of GPU techniques and algorithms. The key challenge is to create a visual that has high apparent visual complexity at relatively low computational and rendering cost. Doing so creates a convincing volume of grass. Here we introduce a technique similar to the one presented by Pelzer (2004) in "Rendering Countless Blades of Waving Grass." Our technique yields higher-quality and more-robust results at a reduced GPU and CPU burden. Figure 1-3 shows a scene rendered with our technique.

Obviously, drawing each grass blade is out of the question. But we can create such an illusion with clumps of grass, which are best represented by camera-facing quads with a suitable grass texture. Billboards of this nature create the illusion of volume at a minimal cost. However, a large field of grass can still require an excessive number of draw calls, so we must carefully structure our usage of the GPU to achieve sufficient volume and density.

Figure 1-3. A Convincing Grass Layer
To be convincing, the illusion of volume must be maintained even though the grass is drawn using camera-facing quads.

GPUs work best when they are presented with large batch sizes to draw at once. Therefore, our goal is to figure out how to draw fields of grass with a relatively small number of draw calls to the API. The naive approach is to draw one billboard at a time. Instead, what we want is to draw as many as is practical in one draw call.

To achieve this, we use a technique whereby we create a vertex and an index buffer and fill it with a large number of grass billboards. We then draw all these billboards in one call. This algorithm is similar to speeding up a CPU loop by unrolling it.

For our purposes, each layer of grass—that is, all grass that uses the same texture and other parameters—is represented by a vertex and an index buffer pair per grid cell, as shown in Figure 1-4. For each clump of grass (or billboard) we plant, we write its positions into the vertex buffer and update the index buffer accordingly. We need four vertices and six indices per billboard. For each vertex, we set the position to the point where we have planted the grass clump. This means that all four vertices of a billboard have an identical position, but we offset this position in the vertex shader to create the proper camera-facing quad shape. Alternatively, if the grass texture fits within a triangular shape, we can save processing one vertex each. Even better, at this point, indices become unnecessary and can be skipped altogether without loss of performance; no vertex is ever reused out of the post-transformation-and-lighting cache when rendering this sort of triangle soup.

Once the vertex buffer is created and sent to video memory, we can draw each grid cell's worth of botany with a single draw call. On the GPU, we use a vertex shader to

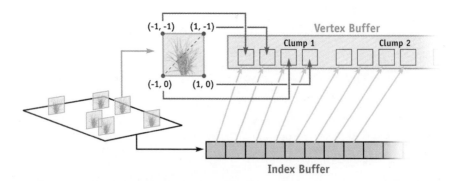

Figure 1-4. Structures for Drawing Each Grid Cell
Each grid cell contains a vertex and an index buffer into which we unroll our grass quads. The position of each of the quad's four vertices is set to the planting point (where the grass roots enter the ground) and the vertex shader moves the vertices into proper position. The entire grid cell's worth of grass can now be drawn in one call.

offset each of the vertices so that they form a screen-aligned quad. Since each vertex moves in a different direction, we have to identify which vertex forms what corner of the quad. To do this, we augment our vertex data with two additional floats that contain -1, 0, or 1. The first float is for the x direction on the screen, and the second is for the y. We multiply this factor by our scale in x and y to offset as necessary. Additionally, we can randomly set all -1 and 1 values to slightly different values (such as 0.98 or -1.2) to add size variety to each grass clump.

Though we intend to move the vertex in screen space, we do all our work in world space so that we get the perspective effect for free. To do this, we provide our vertex shader with a vector that points to the right of the camera and another that points up from the camera. Simple math moves the vertex into the correct position:

```
// For each vertex, we pass a -1, 0, 1 value for x, y, which determines
// how it is moved by the right and up vectors of the camera. This
// we pass in as a texture coordinate (inTexCoord2).

Out.Pos = Input.inPos + (Input.inTexCoord2.x * RightVector) +
                        (Input.inTexCoord2.y * UpVector);
```

Our approach differs from Pelzer's because we use camera-facing billboards instead of having three quads per clump and doing no screen alignment. The screen-facing billboards create a constant depth at all view angles (even when looking down), whereas the three-quad clump approach progressively breaks down as the camera looks more directly down at the grassy field. In a third-person camera view, typical of many types of games and simulations, this is not an uncommon camera angle.

1.2.1 Simulating Alpha Transparency via Dissolve

When rendering grass, we want to use transparency to improve the visual blending and fade out at a distance near the boundary of our virtual grid. However, alpha-based transparency is far from ideal because it requires sorting, which is slow. Although there are techniques that take advantage of the chaotic nature of grass to minimize some of the sorting (Pelzer 2004), we can actually eliminate it altogether.

To do this, we adopt a dissolve effect (also called the screen-door effect) instead of alpha blending to simulate translucency. We accomplish this by modulating the alpha channel of our grass texture with a noise texture. Then we use alpha test to eliminate pixels from rendering. By sliding the alpha test value from 0 to 1, the texture appears to dissolve. The process is shown in Figure 1-5. SpeedTreeRT, a commercial package for real-time foliage creation, was the first to use this technique to blend between levels of detail

Figure 1-5. Components of the Grass Texture

Grass texture with (a) the diffuse texture, (b) the artist-created alpha channel, (c) the Perlin noise texture, and (d) the result of multiplying the artist alpha by the Perlin noise. This can be done in the pixel shader, or the fixed-function pipeline, or as part of the authoring process by generating mip levels that have a progressively more transparent pattern, to create fade with a fixed alpha-test value.

with alpha testing enabled. Simutronics has licensed IDV's SpeedTreeRT for *Hero's Journey*, and techniques drawn or adapted from this commercial foliage toolkit are noted as such in this chapter.

The benefit of this technique is that the alpha test is a fast operation and order-independent. We no longer need to sort, yet grass appears to fade out at a distance. Although a dissolve does not look nearly as good as true alpha translucency under normal circumstances, we can exploit the fractal properties of nature to completely mask any visual artifacts of the screen-door technique. Experimentally, we have found that if we use a Perlin noise texture (Perlin 2002) rather than a random noise texture, the dissolve effect matches the environment well enough to be nearly as good as alpha translucency.

One problem we have, however, is that the alpha test value we select needs to be based on the distance of each billboard from the camera. However, we can only use exactly one alpha test value for each batch (each grid cell) even though the batch is filled with grass clumps at varying distances; this is because we are rendering the entire grid cell in one draw call. Because we want each grass billboard to fade out precisely based on its distance from the camera, we select a fixed alpha test value and instead manipulate the alpha channel in the shaders, linearly interpolating them toward full alpha based on the distance from the camera and the maximum range at which we want grass to start being visible. We do this by adjusting the alpha component of the output color of the vertex shader, which then attenuates the alpha of the texel in the pixel shader (this can also be done with the fixed-function pipeline).

An additional pass can be made over grid cells nearest the camera, drawing with alpha blending to feather the edges of the grass blades into the scene, thus eliminating any harsh edges from blades of grass close to the camera. This can achieve marginally better compositing at the expense of another pass. But because alpha test is still used, relatively few pixels are written to the back buffer (just the edges of the blades, at most). Alpha blending and alpha testing work well together; it is often a good idea to experiment with both to achieve the best illusion of depth and volume.

1.2.2 Variation

To increase the realism of our grass, we want to introduce as much variety as we can without impeding frame rate. One approach is to use a variety of images for grass, but our batching approach limits us to one texture per draw call. Fortunately, we can use a larger texture with different variations of grass arranged on them. During the vertex building, we can adjust the UV coordinates to select different subregions of the texture (that is, we can build a texture atlas; see NVIDIA 2004 for more on this technique). It is easy to have, for instance, four different grass clump variations on one texture. Plus, as we unroll grass quads into the vertex buffer, we can randomly flip the U coordinate to mirror the image. Be sure to allow space between your images so that mipmapping does not introduce texel-bleed artifacts.

Each billboard can also carry along color information. This is very useful for tinting a grayscale texture or doing subtle color shifting in the vertex shader, if you also establish a color for each cluster when planting. We have found that Perlin noise works here as well. It is easy, for example, to tint grass from a healthy green to a dying brown to impart broad color variations and break up the repetitiveness of the grass. See Figure 1-6.

1.2.3 Lighting

Lighting plays an important role in how grass looks. For billboard grass, we want to make sure that our grass is lit like the ground underneath. Because the ground naturally undulates, and thus picks up different angles of sunlight, we want to simulate this by attenuating the brightness of the grass. To do so, we need to know the angle of the

Figure 1-6. Using RGB Information to Increase Realism
Each planting of grass carries RGB information in the vertices. In this scene, the color values are derived from a Perlin noise function to simulate grass that is greener and patches that are a less-healthy brown.

ground on which the grass is sitting. An easy solution is to pass along this information in the vertex definition as another vector. During planting, we determine the normal of the polygon on which we are planting grass and carry this along in our grass billboard definition. With this approach, the vertex shader can do the same lighting calculation as for the polygon underneath the grass and attenuate its color to match. On hilly terrain, this causes the grass to have the subtle angle-to-the-light cues that the ground has.

Unfortunately, this approach leads to a faceted shading of the grass even though the ground polygons are likely smooth shaded (such as with Gouraud shading). To get around this discrepancy, the normal that is passed through the vertex shader must itself be smoothly interpolated during the planting process.

If the sun angle is dynamic, a simplification is to assume that the ground normal is roughly straight up and then carry out the lighting based on this normal and the light angle. In this way, we do not have to compute or carry the ground polygon normal in the vertex definition. There is a quality trade-off here, but this approach was good enough for our application.

1.2.4 Wind

Grass comes alive when wind affects it. Offsetting the top two vertices of the grass quad each frame causes the quad to wave in the wind. We compute this offset by using a sum of sines approximation, similar to computing surface undulation for water (Finch 2004). The trick to this is to carry a blend weight in the vertex definition, where the top two vertices of the grass quad are set to 1 and the bottom two to 0. Then we multiply our wind scale factor by this value, so that the bottom vertices remain firmly planted in the ground. For additional variation, we can randomize the top two vertex weights somewhat during planting. This simulates some grass being more or less rigid.

Grass blades often change their orientation to the light as they wave in the wind, causing them to brighten and darken. We can use the wind term to augment the lighting to simulate this effect. This greatly improves the visual effect of the wind, even for grass clumps at a distance where the physical waving deformation becomes subpixel in size.

Note, however, that the wind factors should not be allowed to deform the grass quads too much. If they do, the resulting deformation will appear comical rather than realistic. Subtlety is the key.

1.3 The Ground Clutter Layer

Ground cover consists of more than just waving fields of grass. Twigs, small plants, rocks, and other debris complete the illusion of natural complexity. Some of these can be represented as billboards just as grass is, but the richness of the environment is enhanced when we mix in an assortment of geometric objects, as well.

Just as we did with grass billboards, we unroll our 3D mesh data into vertex and index buffers for each grid cell, which can then be drawn with a single call. We must group our ground clutter into layers that use the same textures and shaders. We can apply random transforms to vary their size and orientation as we pick our planting points, but the transforms must vary depending on the nature of the mesh: an upside-down rock is okay, but an upside-down bush is not. For additional variety, we can pass RGB information to tint the objects just as we did with the grass polygons.

The dissolve technique for handling order-independent transparency effects works exactly the same for 3D meshes as it does for billboards. We modulate the alpha channel of the texture by our Perlin noise texture and use our distance from the camera to attenuate. Then alpha test dissolves the 3D meshes the same way it did with the grass billboards.

Each vertex can be given a weighting value, which allows us to apply the same wind math to the 3D as we did with the billboards. Obviously, we want objects such as rocks and twigs to be rigid, but leafy plants can have artist-driven weights to achieve the proper effect. Figure 1-7 shows an example of a scene with ground clutter.

Figure 1-7. Using Ground Clutter to Add Dense Detail
Here ground clutter is used to add dense detail to the shoreline of a river. The rocks, branches, and twigs are all 3D meshes unrolled into vertex buffers per grid cell. The reeds are rendered with the grass-rendering technique.

1.4 The Tree and Shrub Layers

The trunk and primary branches of a tree should be modeled as 3D meshes. Secondary branches can be simulated with billboards to add visual complexity. For trees that are leafy, we can use techniques similar to the one we used for grass to create clumps of leaves from camera-facing billboards.

The following approach to rendering trees and shrubs is based on SpeedTreeRT, which provides all of the real-time rendering information for tree assets and includes SpeedTreeCAD for parametric authoring of trees (IDV 2004). The actual rendering of trees is still the responsibility of the game engine, which gives developers a lot of flexibility in implementation.

Because trees need to maintain their basic volume over long distances but are expensive to render in great detail, a level-of-detail (LOD) strategy must be employed. As a tree recedes into the distance, larger but fewer leaf clump billboards can be used. For the larger billboards, we use a different texture that shows more but smaller leaves.

For efficiency, all of the textures related to a tree should be consolidated into a single texture, as shown in Figure 1-8. In fact, it is even preferable to have multiple tree textures packed into one texture, so we can draw more of them in one call.

At some suitable distance, we eventually want to represent a tree with a camera-facing billboard. This can be difficult when the tree's profile is asymmetrical. To get around

Figure 1-8. Storing Multiple Leaf Cluster Images in a Single Texture
A single texture contains many leaf cluster images, at different resolutions for level of detail, plus the billboards for a tree at a distance. Building a composite texture in this way makes it possible to draw many trees with fewer texture changes. This composite map was generated using SpeedTreeCAD.

the problem, we can produce tree images for the billboard at various angles and then blend between them based on the angle of the tree and the camera.

If trees are placed manually, we have found that it is best to give the level designer fine control over LOD transition points for each instance. In areas where trees are dense, you can get away with LOD transitions fairly near the camera. But in other places, with long lines of sight but fewer trees, it's easier to maintain their high detail and avoid visual artifacts.

Shrubs and fronds can be handled as just another type of tree using many of the same techniques. For example, a leafy bush is simply a tree with a small or nonexistent trunk. Further, you can turn a tree upside down, turn off the leaves, and get an elaborate exposed root system to marry up with a normal tree.

Trees can be authored in a standard modeling package, but artists need some mechanism to specify where leaf points and branch billboards go. This can complicate exporting. The actual rendering of the trees is still the responsibility of the game engine, which gives developers a lot of flexibility in implementation.

1.5 Shadowing

Because we pass an RGB tint for grass and ground clutter, we can choose a dark tint for areas in shadow. This requires us to know whether or not each planted item is in shadow. To be effective in natural environments, this sort of shadowing needs to only grossly approximate the correct shadowing. See Figure 1-9.

One approach is to make the shadow determination when the planting occurs. Simply cast a shadow feeler ray from the planting position toward the dominant light source (the sun) and see if there is an intersection. If so, adjust the RGB values toward the scene's ambient color. Remember that a shadow feeler ray cast is concerned only about any intersection (not just the closest) so it can be much more efficient than a standard collision ray cast.

Soft shadows (technically called *antialiased* shadows in this context) can be achieved by casting more than one shadow feeler. Figure 1-10 shows how this works. By offsetting each ray start position slightly, three or five ray casts from a given spot can be performed. The fraction of hits is used to attenuate the light between the diffuse sun lighting and the scene's ambient lighting. Widening the offsets increases the softness of the shadowing.

Figure 1-9. Grass Shadowed by a Tree Root
In this scene, grass is shadowed by an object (an oversized tree root). Having multiple shadow feelers per grass clump helps soften the transitions between shadowed and illuminated areas.

These sorts of shadows are not dynamic, but they can be recomputed fairly quickly at intervals for slow-moving light sources (such as the traveling sun). In general, they provide sufficient visual cues to cause the scenery to seem more lifelike.

Special approximation techniques can be used to cause shadow feeler hits when casting through the bulk of a tree. Instead of looking for intersections with individual leaves, simply collide with the spherical volume of the leafy part of the tree or the cylinder of the trunk. For the leafy part, use a random function to determine if rays intersect based on the density of the leaves. Although this shadowing technique is crude, accurate solutions are not visually distinct.

If planting is precomputed as an offline process, then shadow fidelity can be greatly enhanced. One possibility beyond shadow feelers is to look at the texel of a light map to determine shadowing. This can be difficult in real time if the light map is not in system memory.

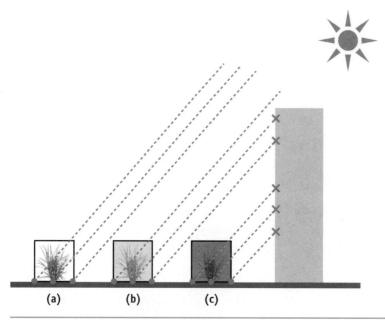

Figure 1-10. Visibility Testing Using Ray Casts
Shadow feeler ray casts are projected from the planting point toward the light source (which is directional in this case). Any collision indicates that the point is in shadow. To get a softer shadow, project additional offset shadow feelers and use the fraction of hits to determine how much to tint toward the ambient lighting. Care must be taken so that the shadow feelers do not immediately intersect the ground plane at the planting point.

1.6 Post-Processing

Natural environments react to sunlight in ways that are hard to simulate in real time. Like most interactive techniques, the goal is to find methods that achieve a reasonable, if not accurate, result. Using post-processing effects, we can tie the visuals together to achieve a superior environment.

Full-scene post-processing glow is useful for magical and high-tech effects in games, and extending this simple technique for natural effects has proven effective. Real-time glow techniques provide a way to simulate blooming—as well as create a natural softening effect (brought about by a Gaussian blur)(James and O'Rorke 2004). However, because glow is an additive effect, care must be taken to account for this when authoring textures. It is easy to get carried away and overbrighten a scene. As with all effects, just because a little is good, more isn't necessarily better.

1.6.1 Sky Dome Blooming

A textured sky dome provides a rich opportunity to use glow to our advantage. We can set aside the alpha channel of the sky dome for the artist to define areas that are more luminous. This allows the artist to have a lot of control over how the sun and the clouds interact. When rendering the sky dome, simply apply the alpha layer to the glow channel. Figure 1-11 shows an example.

A sky dome with a good amount of glow blooms around the delicate structure of tree leaves and branches. This yields a particularly realistic touch that is almost immediately noticeable, as shown in Figure 1-12. Because the sky glow is controlled by the artist, this technique is particularly effective and finely tuned at no additional cost.

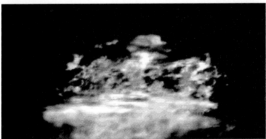

Figure 1-11. Sky Dome Diffuse Texture and Glow Component

Figure 1-12. Varying Amounts of Sky Dome Glow
From left to right, no glow, moderate glow, and a lot of glow. Notice that it glows only in the areas of the sky designated by the artist in the alpha channel of the sky dome texture.

1.6.2 Full-Scene Glow

Cinematography of natural environments is often enhanced by a technique in which diffusing gauze (cheesecloth) is placed over the camera lens. If post-processing glow is being used, we can simply clear the glow channel to an adjustable, nonzero value to create a full-scene glow. Because the glow is a simulation based on a Gaussian blur, this causes the whole scene to appear to be diffused; also, bright areas bloom slightly without having to resort to more expensive HDR effects. For natural outdoor scenes, this approach can greatly mitigate the harsh computer-generated look of polygons for no extra GPU cost (because full-scene glow processing is already occurring). See Figure 1-13.

Figure 1-13. The Effect of Full-Scene Glow
The scene on the left is rendered with no glow; the scene on the right has a large amount of full-scene glow. Besides the obvious brightening effect, the glow's Gaussian blur causes the scene to appear softer and diffused.

1.7 Conclusion

Rendering nature in a convincing way always adds visual drama to a game. Figure 1-14 illustrates how these techniques can be very effective at conveying a sense of the inherent complexity and grandeur of natural scenery.

1.8 References

Finch, Mark. 2004. "Effective Water Simulation from Physical Models." In *GPU Gems*, edited by Randima Fernando, pp. 5–29. Addison-Wesley.

IDV. 2004. SpeedTreeRT API and SpeedTreeCAD Windows application. **http://www.idvinc.com/html/speedtreert.htm**

James, Greg, and John O'Rorke. 2004. "Real-Time Glow." In *GPU Gems*, edited by Randima Fernando, pp. 343–362. Addison-Wesley.

Figure 1-14. Creating the Illusion of a Lush Landscape
Here all techniques work together to produce a suitable illusion of a lush landscape. As the camera travels over this expansive game level, the level of detail remains high near the camera at interactive frame rates.

NVIDIA Corporation. 2004. "Improve Batching Using Texture Atlases." SDK white paper. **http://download.nvidia.com/developer/NVTextureSuite/Atlas_Tools/Texture_Atlas_Whitepaper.pdf**

Pelzer, Kurt. 2004. "Rendering Countless Blades of Waving Grass." In *GPU Gems*, edited by Randima Fernando, pp. 107–121. Addison-Wesley.

Perlin, Ken. 2002. "Improving Noise." *ACM Transactions on Graphics (Proceedings of SIGGRAPH 2002)* 21(3), pp. 681–682. **http://mrl.nyu.edu/~perlin/paper445.pdf**

I would like to thank the entire Simutronics Hero's Journey *art and programming team for their invaluable contributions to this effort, especially 3D artists Richard Amsinger and Kyle Knight, whose work is featured in this chapter. Additionally, I would like to thank Dave Dean and Bryan Cool for their programming wizardry, which contributed a great deal to the techniques presented in this chapter. Last, I want to thank our art director, Tracy Butler, for providing the illustrations that help clarify many of the concepts in this chapter.*

Chapter 2

Terrain Rendering Using GPU-Based Geometry Clipmaps

Arul Asirvatham
Microsoft Research

Hugues Hoppe
Microsoft Research

The geometry clipmap introduced in Losasso and Hoppe 2004 is a new level-of-detail structure for rendering terrains. It caches terrain geometry in a set of nested regular grids, which are incrementally shifted as the viewer moves. The grid structure provides a number of benefits over previous irregular-mesh techniques: simplicity of data structures, smooth visual transitions, steady rendering rate, graceful degradation, efficient compression, and runtime detail synthesis. In this chapter, we describe a GPU-based implementation of geometry clipmaps, enabled by vertex textures. By processing terrain geometry as a set of images, we can perform nearly all computations on the GPU itself, thereby reducing CPU load. The technique is easy to implement, and allows interactive flight over a 20-billion-sample grid of the United States stored in just 355 MB of memory, at around 90 frames per second.

2.1 Review of Geometry Clipmaps

In large outdoor environments, the geometry of terrain landscapes can require significant storage and rendering bandwidth. Numerous level-of-detail techniques have been developed to adapt the triangulation of the terrain mesh as a function of the view. However, most such techniques involve runtime creation and modification of mesh structures (vertex and index buffers), which can prove expensive on current graphics architectures. Moreover, use of irregular meshes generally requires processing by the CPU, and many applications such as games are already CPU-limited.

The geometry clipmap framework (Losasso and Hoppe 2004) treats the terrain as a 2D elevation image, prefiltering it into a mipmap pyramid of L levels as illustrated in Figure 2-1. For complex terrains, the full pyramid is too large to fit in memory. The geometry clipmap structure caches a square window of $n \times n$ samples within each level, much like the texture clipmaps of Tanner et al. 1998. These windows correspond to a set of nested regular grids centered about the viewer, as shown in Figure 2-2. Note that the finer-level windows have smaller spatial extent than the coarser ones. The aim is to maintain triangles that are uniformly sized in screen space. With a clipmap size $n = 255$, the triangles are approximately 5 pixels wide in a 1024×768 window.

Only the finest level is rendered as a complete grid square. In all other levels, we render a hollow "ring," which omits the interior region already rendered at finer resolutions.

As the viewer moves, the clipmap windows are shifted and updated with new data. To permit efficient incremental updates, the clipmap window in each level is accessed toroidally, that is, with 2D wraparound addressing (see Section 2.4).

One of the challenges with the clipmap structure is to hide the boundaries between successive resolution levels, while at the same time maintaining a watertight mesh and avoiding temporal popping artifacts. The nested grid structure of the geometry clipmap provides a simple solution. The key idea is to introduce a transition region near the outer perimeter of each level, whereby the geometry and textures are smoothly morphed to interpolate the next-coarser level (see Figure 2-3). These transitions are efficiently implemented in the vertex and pixel shaders, respectively.

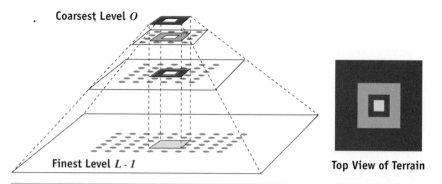

Figure 2-1. How Geometry Clipmaps Work
Given a filtered terrain pyramid of L levels, the geometry clipmap caches a square window at each resolution level. From these windows, we extract a set of L nested "rings" centered about the viewer. The finest-level ring is filled in.

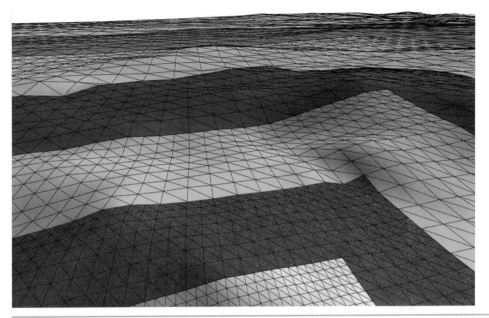

Figure 2-2. Terrain Rendering Using a Coarse Geometry Clipmap
Illustration of terrain rendering using a coarse geometry clipmap (size n = 31, L = 10). Each colored ring is formed from a different clipmap level.

The nested grid structure of the geometry clipmap also enables effective compression and synthesis. It allows the prediction of the elevation data for each level by upsampling the data from the coarser level. Thus, one need only store or synthesize the residual detail added to this predicted signal.

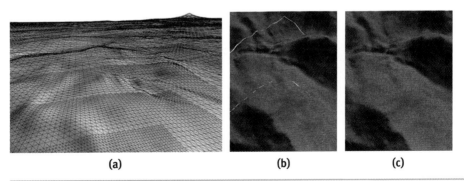

(a)	(b)	(c)

Figure 2-3. Achieving Visual Continuity by Blending Within Transition Regions
(a) Transition regions (in purple). (b) Without blending. (c) With blending.

2.2 Overview of GPU Implementation

The original implementation of geometry clipmaps presented in Losasso and Hoppe 2004 represents each clipmap level as a traditional vertex buffer. Because the GPU currently lacks the ability to modify vertex buffers, that implementation required significant intervention by the CPU to both update and render the clipmap (see Table 2-1).

In this chapter, we describe an implementation of geometry clipmaps using vertex textures. This is advantageous because the 2D grid data of each clipmap window is much more naturally stored as a 2D texture, rather than being artificially linearized into a 1D vertex buffer.

Recall that the clipmap has L levels, each containing a grid of $n \times n$ geometric samples. Our approach is to split the (x, y, z) geometry of the samples into two parts:

- The (x, y) coordinates are stored as constant vertex data.

- The z coordinate is stored as a single-channel 2D texture—the *elevation map*. We define a separate $n \times n$ elevation map texture for each clipmap level. These textures are updated as the clipmap levels shift with the viewer's motion.

Because clipmap levels are uniform 2D grids, their (x, y) coordinates are regular, and thus constant up to a translation and scale. Therefore, we define a small set of *read-only*

Table 2-1. Comparison with Original CPU Implementation
Our implementation of geometry clipmaps using vertex textures moves nearly all operations to the GPU.

	Original Implementation[1]	GPU-Based Implementation
Elevation Data	In vertex buffer	In 2D vertex texture
Vertex Buffer	Incrementally updated by CPU	Constant!
Index Buffer	Generated every frame by CPU	Constant!
Upsampling	CPU	GPU
Decompression	CPU	CPU
Synthesis	CPU	GPU
Adding Residuals	CPU	GPU
Normal-Map Update	CPU	GPU
Transition Blends	GPU	GPU

1. Losasso and Hoppe 2004.

vertex and index buffers, which describe 2D "footprints," and repeatedly instance these footprints both within and across resolution levels, as described in Section 2.3.2.

The vertices obtain their z elevations by sampling the elevation map as a vertex texture. Accessing a texture in the vertex shader is a new feature in DirectX 9 Shader Model 3.0, and is supported by GPUs such as the NVIDIA GeForce 6 Series.

Storing the elevation data as a set of images allows direct processing using the GPU rasterization pipeline (as noted in Table 2-1). For the case of synthesized terrains, all runtime computations (elevation-map upsampling, terrain detail synthesis, normal-map computation, and rendering) are performed entirely within the graphics card, leaving the CPU basically idle. For compressed terrains, the CPU incrementally decompresses and uploads data to the graphics card (see Section 2.4).

2.2.1 Data Structures

To summarize, the main data structures are as follows. We predefine a small set of constant vertex and index buffers to encode the (x, y) geometry of the clipmap grids. And for each level $0 \ldots L-1$, we allocate an elevation map (a 1-channel floating-point 2D texture) and a normal map (a 4-channel 8-bit 2D texture). All these data structures reside in video memory.

2.2.2 Clipmap Size

Because the outer perimeter of each level must lie on the grid of the next-coarser level (as shown in Figure 2-4), the grid size n must be odd. Hardware may be optimized for texture sizes that are powers of 2, so we choose $n = 2^k-1$ (that is, 1 less than a power of 2) leaving 1 row and 1 column of the textures unused. Most of our examples use $n = 255$.

The choice of grid size $n = 2^k-1$ has the further advantage that the finer level is never exactly centered with respect to its parent next-coarser level. In other words, it is always offset by 1 grid unit either left or right, as well as either top or bottom (see Figure 2-4), depending on the position of the viewpoint. In fact, it is necessary to allow a finer level to shift while its next-coarser level stays fixed, and therefore the finer level must sometimes be off-center with respect to the next-coarser level. An alternative choice of grid size, such as $n = 2^k-3$, would provide the possibility for exact centering, but it would still require the handling of off-center cases and thus result in greater overall complexity.

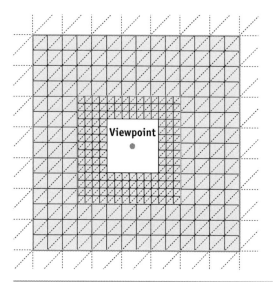

Figure 2-4. Two Successive Clipmap Rings
Note that vertices of the coarser level are coincident with those of the finer level at the interlevel boundary. This property is crucial for avoiding cracks in the rendered terrain.

2.3 Rendering

2.3.1 Active Levels

Although we have allocated L levels for the clipmap, we often render (and update) only a set of *active levels* $0 \ldots L'-1$, where the number of levels $L' \leq L$ is based on the height of the viewpoint over the underlying terrain. The motivation is that when the viewer is sufficiently high, the finest clipmap levels are unnecessarily dense and in fact result in aliasing artifacts. Specifically, we deactivate levels for which the grid extent is smaller than $2.5h$, where h is the viewer height above the terrain. Since all the terrain data resides in video memory, computing h involves reading back one point sample (immediately below the viewpoint) from the elevation map texture of the finest active level ($L'-1$). This readback incurs a small cost, so we perform it only every few frames. Of course, we render level $L'-1$ using a complete square rather than a hollow ring.

The implementation described in Losasso and Hoppe 2004 allows "cropping" of a level if its data was not fully updated during viewer motion. To simplify our GPU implementation, we have decided to forgo this feature. We instead assume that a level is either fully updated or declared inactive.

2.3.2 Vertex and Index Buffers

As explained earlier, we represent the grid (x, y) values as vertex data, while storing the z elevation values as a one-channel floating-point texture. A brute-force approach would be to define a single vertex buffer containing the (x, y) data for the entire ring within a level. To both reduce memory costs and enable view frustum culling, we instead break the ring into smaller 2D footprint pieces, as illustrated in Figure 2-5.

Most of the ring is created using 12 blocks (shown in gray) of size $m \times m$, where $m = (n + 1)/4$. Since the 2D grid is regular, the (x, y) geometries of all blocks within a level are identical up to a translation. Moreover, they are also identical across levels up to a uniform scale. Therefore, we can render the (x, y) geometries of all terrain blocks using a single read-only vertex buffer and index buffer, by letting the vertex shader scale and translate the block (x, y) geometry using a few parameters.

For our default clipmap size $n = 255$, this canonical block has 64×64 vertices. The index buffer encodes a set of indexed triangle strips whose lengths are chosen for optimal vertex caching. We use 16-bit indices for the index buffer, which allows a maximum block size of $m = 256$ and therefore a maximum clipmap size of $n = 1023$.

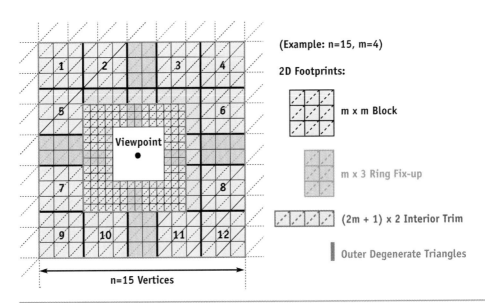

Figure 2-5. Partitioning a Clipmap Ring
Each clipmap ring is partitioned into a set of 2D footprints: 12 block instances, ring fix-up, and interior trim.

However, the union of the 12 blocks does not completely cover the ring. We fill the small remaining gaps using a few additional 2D footprints, as explained next. Note that in practice, these additional regions have a very small area compared to the regular $m \times m$ blocks, as revealed in Figure 2-6. First, there is a gap of $(n - 1) - ((m - 1) \times 4) = 2$ quads at the middle of each ring side. We patch these gaps using four $m \times 3$ fix-up regions (shown in green in Figures 2-5 and 2-6). We encode these regions using one vertex and index buffer, and we reuse these buffers across all levels. Second, there is a gap of one quad on two sides of the interior ring perimeter, to accommodate the off-center finer level. This L-shaped strip (shown in blue) can lie at any of four possible locations (top-left, top-right, bottom-left, bottom-right), depending on the relative position of the fine level inside the coarse level. We define four vertex and one index buffer for this interior trim, and we reuse these across all levels.

Also, we render a string of degenerate triangles (shown in orange) on the outer perimeter. These zero-area triangles are necessary to avoid mesh T-junctions. Finally, for the finest level, we fill the ring interior with four additional blocks and one more L-shaped region.

Because the footprint (x, y) coordinates are local, these do not require 32-bit precision, so we pack them into a `D3DDECLTYPE_SHORT2`, requiring only 4 bytes per vertex. In the future, it may be possible to compute the (x, y) coordinates within the $m \times m$ block from the vertex index i itself as (`fmod(i, m), floor(i/m)`).

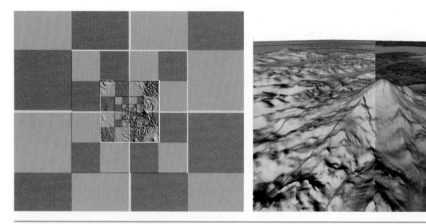

Figure 2-6. Visualizing the Nested Grid Structure
For practical clipmap sizes, most of the terrain is rendered using instances of the m×m block. Left: top view of terrain, showing each nested grid composed of 12 blocks. Right: forward view, showing nested grid structure and final shaded terrain.

2.3.3 View Frustum Culling

View frustum culling is done at the block level on the CPU. Each block is extruded by $[z_{min}, z_{max}]$ and intersected with the view frustum in 3D. It is rendered only if this intersection is nonempty. Depending on the view direction, the rendering load is reduced by a factor of 2 to 3 for a 90-degree field of view, as shown in Figure 2-7.

2.3.4 DrawPrimitive Calls

For each level, we make up to 14 DrawPrimitive (DP) calls: 12 for the blocks, 1 for the interior trim, and 1 for the remaining triangles. With view frustum culling, on average only 4 of the 12 blocks are rendered each frame. The finest level requires 5 more calls to fill the interior hole. Thus, overall we make $6L + 5$ (71 for $L = 11$) DP calls per frame on average. This total number could be further reduced to $3L + 2$ (35) by instancing all blocks rendered in each level using a single DP call.

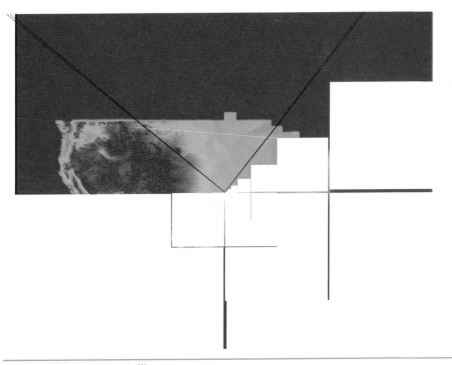

Figure 2-7. View Frustum Culling

2.3.5 The Vertex Shader

The same vertex shader is applied to the rendering of all 2D footprints described previously. First, given the footprint (x, y) coordinates, the shader computes the world (x, y) coordinates using a simple scaling and translation. Next, it reads the z value from the elevation map stored in the vertex texture. No texture filtering is necessary because the vertices correspond one-to-one with the texture samples.

For smooth transitions, the vertex shader blends the geometry near the outer boundary of each level with that of the next-coarser level. It computes the blending parameter α based on the (x, y) location relative to the continuous viewer position (v_x, v_y). Specifically, $\alpha = \max(\alpha_x, \alpha_y)$, with

$$\alpha_x = \text{clamp}\left(\left(\left|x - v_x\right| - \left(\frac{n-1}{2} - w - 1\right)\right)\Big/w, \; 0, \; 1\right),$$

and similarly for α_y.

Here, all coordinates are expressed in the $[0 \ldots n-1]$ range of the clipmap grid, and w is the transition width (chosen to be $n/10$). The desired property is that α evaluates to 0 except in the transition region, where it ramps up linearly to reach 1 at the outer perimeter. Figure 2-3a (on page 29) shows the evaluation of the parameter α within the transition regions in purple.

For geometric blending, we linearly interpolate between the current (fine-level) elevation z_f and the elevation z_c at the same (x, y) location in the next-coarser level:

$$z' = (1 - \alpha)z_f + \alpha z_c$$

In the general case, the sample location lies on an edge of the coarser grid, and z_c is obtained by averaging the two coarse samples on the edge endpoints. We could perform this computation at runtime, but it would require a total of three vertex-texture lookups (one for z_f and two for $z_c = (z_{c1} + z_{c2})/2$) and vertex-texture reads are currently expensive (Gerasimov et al. 2004).

Instead, we compute z_c as part of the clipmap update, and pack both z_f and z_c into the same 1-channel floating-point texture. We achieve this by storing z_f into the integer part of the float, and the difference $z_d = z_c - z_f$ (scaled) into the fractional part. The packing is done in the pixel shader of the upsampling stage (see Section 2.4.1).

Listing 2-1 is the High-Level Shader Language (HLSL) vertex program for clipmap rendering.

Listing 2-1. Vertex Shader Code for Rendering a Clipmap Level

```
struct OUTPUT {
  vector pos   : POSITION;
  float2 uv    : TEXCOORD0; // coordinates for normal-map lookup
  float  z     : TEXCOORD1; // coordinates for elevation-map lookup
  float  alpha : TEXCOORD2; // transition blend on normal map
};

uniform float4 ScaleFactor, FineBlockOrig;
uniform float2 ViewerPos, AlphaOffset, OneOverWidth;
uniform float  ZScaleFactor, ZTexScaleFactor;
uniform matrix WorldViewProjMatrix;

// Vertex shader for rendering the geometry clipmap
OUTPUT RenderVS(float2 gridPos: TEXCOORD0)
{
  OUTPUT output;
  // convert from grid xy to world xy coordinates
  //   ScaleFactor.xy: grid spacing of current level
  //   ScaleFactor.zw: origin of current block within world
  float2 worldPos = gridPos * ScaleFactor.xy + ScaleFactor.zw;

  // compute coordinates for vertex texture
  //   FineBlockOrig.xy: 1/(w, h) of texture
  //   FineBlockOrig.zw: origin of block in texture
  float2 uv = gridPos * FineBlockOrig.xy + FineBlockOrig.zw;

  // sample the vertex texture
  float zf_zd = tex2Dlod(ElevationSampler, float4(uv, 0, 1));

  // unpack to obtain zf and zd = (zc - zf)
  //   zf is elevation value in current (fine) level
  //   zc is elevation value in coarser level
  float zf = floor(zf_zd);
  float zd = frac(zf_zd) * 512 - 256; // (zd = zc - zf)
```

```
// compute alpha (transition parameter) and blend elevation
float2 alpha = clamp((abs(worldPos - ViewerPos) -
                      AlphaOffset) * OneOverWidth, 0, 1);
alpha.x = max(alpha.x, alpha.y);
float z = zf + alpha.x * zd;
z = z * ZScaleFactor;

output.pos = mul(float4(worldPos.x, worldPos.y, z, 1),
                  WorldViewProjMatrix);
output.uv = uv;
output.z = z * ZTexScaleFactor;
output.alpha = alpha.x;
return output;
}
```

2.3.6 The Pixel Shader

The pixel shader accesses the normal map and shades the surface. We let the normal map have twice the resolution of the geometry, because one normal per vertex is too blurry. The normal map is incrementally computed from the geometry whenever the clipmap is updated (see Section 2.4.3).

For smooth shading transitions, the shader looks up the normals for the current level and the next-coarser level and blends them using the α value computed in the vertex shader. Normally this would require two texture lookups. Instead, we pack the two normals as $(N_x, N_y, N_{cx}, N_{cy})$ in a single four-channel, 8-bit-per-channel texture, implicitly assuming $N_z = 1$ and $N_{cz} = 1$. We must therefore renormalize after unpacking.

Shading color is obtained using a lookup into a z-based 1D texture map.

Listing 2-2 shows the HLSL pixel program for clipmap rendering.

Listing 2-2. Pixel Shader Code for Rendering a Clipmap Level

```
// Parameters uv, alpha, and z are interpolated from vertex shader.
// Two texture samplers have min and mag filters set to linear:
//    NormalMapSampler:   2D texture containing normal map,
//    ZBasedColorSampler: 1D texture containing elevation-based color

uniform float3 LightDirection;
```

```
// Pixel shader for rendering the geometry clipmap
float4 RenderPS(float2 uv    : TEXCOORD0,
                float  z     : TEXCOORD1,
                float  alpha : TEXCOORD2) : COLOR
{
  float4 normal_fc = tex2D(NormalMapSampler, uv);
  // normal_fc.xy contains normal at current (fine) level
  // normal_fc.zw contains normal at coarser level
  // blend normals using alpha computed in vertex shader
  float3 normal = float3((1 - alpha) * normal_fc.xy +
                  alpha * (normal_fc.zw), 1);

  // unpack coordinates from [0, 1] to [-1, +1] range, and renormalize
  normal = normalize(normal * 2 - 1);
  // compute simple diffuse lighting
  float s = clamp(dot(normal, LightDirection), 0, 1);
  // assign terrain color based on its elevation
  return s * tex1D(ZBasedColorSampler, z);
}
```

2.4 Update

As the viewer moves through the environment, each clipmap window translates within its pyramid level so as to remain centered about the viewer; thus, the window must be updated accordingly. Because viewer motion is coherent, generally only a small L-shaped region of the window needs to be incrementally processed each frame. Also, the relative motion of the viewer within the windows decreases exponentially at coarser levels, so coarse levels seldom require updating.

We update the active clipmap levels in coarse-to-fine order. Recall that each clipmap level stores two textures: a single-channel floating-point elevation map, and a four-channel, 8-bit-per-channel normal map. During the update step, we modify regions of these textures by rendering to them using a pixel shader.

To avoid having to translate the existing data, we perform all accesses toroidally as illustrated in Figure 2-8. That is, we use wraparound addressing to position the clipmap window within the texture image. Under this toroidal access, the L-shaped update region

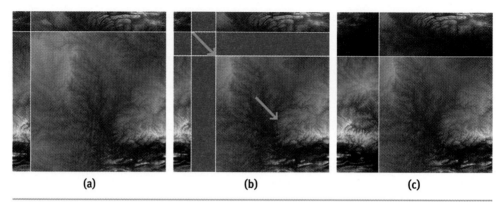

Figure 2-8. Processing a Toroidal Update
(a) Elevation map before update. (b) Viewer motion in green and update region in red. (c) Elevation map after update.

usually becomes a + shape, shown in red in Figure 2-8. We write to this region by rendering two quads. Note that three or four quads may be needed if the update region wraps across the texture boundary.

To facilitate terrain compression and synthesis, elevation data in the update region is first predicted by upsampling the coarser level, and a residual signal is then added to provide the detail. The next sections describe the three basic steps of the update process: upsampling the coarser-level elevation data, adding the residuals, and computing the normal map.

2.4.1 Upsampling

The finer-level geometry is predicted from the coarser one using an interpolatory subdivision scheme. We use the tensor-product version of the well-known four-point subdivision curve interpolant, which has mask weights $(-\frac{1}{16}, \frac{9}{16}, \frac{9}{16}, -\frac{1}{16})$ (Kobbelt 1996). This upsampling filter has the desirable property of being C^1 smooth.

Depending on the position of the sample in the grid (even-even, even-odd, odd-even, odd-odd), a different mask is used. For an even-even pixel, only 1 texture lookup is needed because the sample is simply interpolated; for an odd-odd pixel, 4×4 texture lookups are needed; the remaining two cases require 4 texture lookups. On the CPU, the mask to be used can be easily deduced using an "if" statement. However, branch statements are expensive in the pixel shader. Hence, we always do 16 texture lookups but apply a different mask based on a lookup in a 2×2 texture.

The HLSL code for the upsampling shader appears in Listing 2-3. Code for the missing functions Upsample and ZCoarser is included on the accompanying CD.

Listing 2-3. Pixel Shader Code for Creating/Updating a Clipmap Elevation Map

```
// residualSampler: 2D texture containing residuals, which can be
//   either decompressed data or synthesized noise
// p_uv: coordinates of the grid sample

uniform float2 Scale;

// Pixel shader for updating the elevation map
float4 UpsamplePS(float2 p_uv : TEXCOORD0) : COLOR
{
  float2 uv = floor(p_uv);

  // the Upsample() function samples the coarser elevation map
  //   using a linear interpolatory filter with 4x4 taps
  // (depending on the even/odd configuration of location uv,
  //   it applies 1 of 4 possible masks)
  float z_predicted = Upsample(uv);  // details omitted here

  // add the residual to get the actual elevation
  float residual = tex2D(residualSampler, p_uv * Scale);
  float zf = z_predicted + residual;

  // zf should always be an integer, since it gets packed
  //   into the integer component of the floating-point texture
  zf = floor(zf);

  // compute zc by linearly interpolating the vertices of the
  //   coarse-grid edge on which the sample p_uv lies
  float zc = ZCoarser(uv);   // details omitted here
  float zd = zc - zf;
  // pack the signed difference zd into the fractional component
  float zf_zd = zf + (zd + 256)/512;

  return float4(zf_zd, 0, 0, 0);
}
```

2.4.2 Residuals

The residuals added to the upsampled coarser data can come from either decompression or synthesis.

In the compressed representation, the residual data is encoded using image compression. We use a particular lossy image coder called PTC because it supports efficient region-of-interest decoding (Malvar 2000). The CPU performs the decompression and stores the result into a residual texture image.

Alternatively, we synthesize fractal detail by letting the residuals be uncorrelated Gaussian noise (Fournier et al. 1982). This synthesis is made extremely fast on the GPU by reading a small precomputed 2D texture containing Gaussian noise. We enable texture wrapping to extend the Gaussian texture infinitely, and apply a small magnification to the texture coordinates to break the regular periodicity. The superposition of noise across the many resolution levels gives rise to a terrain without any visible repetitive patterns, as Figure 2-9 shows.

2.4.3 Normal Map

The shader that updates the normal map for a level takes as input the elevation map at the same level. It computes the current normal as the cross product of two grid-aligned tangent vectors. Additionally, it does a texture lookup to gather the normal from the coarser level. Finally, it packs $(N_x, N_y, N_{cx}, N_{cy})$ into the four-channel texture. The code is included in the accompanying CD.

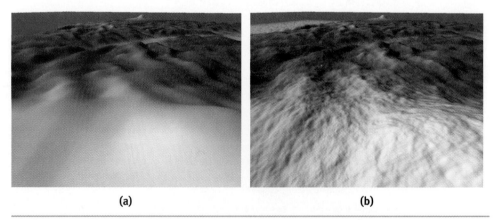

(a)   (b)

Figure 2-9. On-the-Fly Terrain Synthesis
(a) Coarse geometry plus zero residuals. (b) Coarse geometry plus synthesized noise.

2.5 Results and Discussion

Our main data set is a $216,000 \times 93,600$ height map of the conterminous United States at 30-meter spacing and 1.0-meter vertical resolution. It compresses by a factor of more than 100 and therefore fits in only 355 MB of system memory. We render this terrain into a 1024×768 window on a PC with a 2.4 GHz Pentium 4, 1 GB system memory, and an NVIDIA GeForce 6800 GT.

Rendering rate: For $L = 11$ levels of size $n = 255$, we obtain 130 frames/sec with view frustum culling, at a rendering rate of 60 million triangles/sec. The use of a vertex-texture lookup is a bottleneck, since removing the lookup increases rendering rate to 185 frames/sec. (For $n = 127$, the rate with vertex textures is 298 frames/sec.)

Update rate: Table 2-2 shows the processing times for the various steps of the update process, for the extreme case of updating a whole level at once. Decompression on the CPU is clearly the bottleneck of the update process.

Final frame rate: For decompressed terrains, the system maintains a rate of around 87 frames/sec during viewer motion, and for synthesized terrains, the frame rate is about 120 frames/sec.

Table 2-2. Update Times for Processing an Entire 255×255 Level
These are worst-case numbers because, in general, during smooth viewer motions, only small fractions of a full level need be updated per frame.

	Previous Implementation*	GPU-Based Implementation
Upsampling	3 ms	1.0 ms
Decompression	8 ms	8 ms**
Synthesis	3 ms	~0 ms
Normal-Map Computation	11 ms	0.6 ms

* Losasso and Hoppe 2004.
**Still on the CPU.

2.6 Summary and Improvements

We have presented a GPU implementation of the geometry clipmap framework. The representation of geometry using regular grids allows nearly all computation to proceed on the graphics card, thereby offloading work from the CPU. The system supports interactive flight over a 20-billion-sample grid of the U.S. data set stored in just 355 MB of memory at around 90 frames/sec.

2.6.1 Vertex Textures

Geometry clipmaps use vertex textures in a very special, limited way: the texels are accessed essentially in raster-scan order, and in one-to-one correspondence with vertices. Thus, we can hope for future mechanisms that would allow increased rendering efficiency.

2.6.2 Eliminating Normal Maps

It should be possible to directly compute normals in the pixel shader by accessing four filtered samples of the elevation map. At present, vertex texture lookups require that the elevation maps be stored in 32-bit floating-point images, which do not support efficient bilinear filtering.

2.6.3 Memory-Free Terrain Synthesis

Fractal terrain synthesis is so fast on the GPU that we can consider regenerating the clipmap levels during every frame, thereby saving video memory. We allocate two textures, T_1 and T_2, and toggle between them as follows. Let T_1 initially contain the coarse geometry used to seed the synthesis process. First, we use T_1 as a source texture in the update pixel shader to upsample and synthesize the next-finer level into the destination texture T_2. Second, we use T_1 as a vertex texture to render its clipmap ring. Then, we swap the roles of the two textures and iterate the process until all levels are synthesized and rendered. Initial experiments are extremely promising, with frame rates of about 59 frames/sec using $L = 9$ levels.

2.7 References

Fournier, Alain, Don Fussell, and Loren Carpenter. 1982. "Computer Rendering of Stochastic Models." *Communications of the ACM* 25(6), June 1982, pp. 371–384.

Gerasimov, Philip, Randima Fernando, and Simon Green. 2004. "Shader Model 3.0: Using Vertex Textures." NVIDIA white paper DA-01373-001_v00, June 2004. Available online at **http://developer.nvidia.com/object/using_vertex_textures.html**.

Kobbelt, Leif. 1996. "Interpolatory Subdivision on Open Quadrilateral Nets with Arbitrary Topology." In *Eurographics 1996*, pp. 409–420.

Losasso, Frank, and Hugues Hoppe. 2004. "Geometry Clipmaps: Terrain Rendering Using Nested Regular Grids." *ACM Transactions on Graphics (Proceedings of SIGGRAPH 2004)* 23(3), pp. 769–776.

Malvar, Henrique. 2000. "Fast Progressive Image Coding without Wavelets." In *Data Compression Conference (DCC '00)*, pp. 243–252.

Tanner, Christopher, Christopher Migdal, and Michael Jones. 1998. "The Clipmap: A Virtual Mipmap." In *Computer Graphics (Proceedings of SIGGRAPH 98)*, pp. 151–158.

Chapter 3

Inside Geometry Instancing

Francesco Carucci
Lionhead Studios

A great way to enrich the user experience in an interactive application is to present a credible world, full of small, interesting features and objects. From countless blades of grass, to trees, to generic clutter: it all improves the final perception and helps maintain the user's "suspension of disbelief." If the user can believe the world he is immersed in, he is more likely to be emotionally connected to that world—the Holy Grail of game development.

From a rendering point of view, achieving this richness translates into rendering many small objects, often each one similar to the next, with only small differences such as color, position, and orientation. For example, every tree in a big forest might be geometrically very similar, but all may be different in terms of their color or height. The user perceives a forest made of many unique trees and believes the world to be credible, enriching his or her game experience.

However, rendering a large number of small objects, each made from a few polygons, imposes a big strain on today's GPUs and rendering libraries. Graphics APIs such as Direct3D and OpenGL are not designed to efficiently render a small number of polygons thousands of times per frame (Wloka 2003).

This chapter addresses the problem of rendering many unique instances of the same geometry in Direct3D. Figure 3-1 shows an example from *Black & White 2*, a game in development at Lionhead Studios.

Figure 3-1. Geometry Instancing in *Black & White 2*

3.1 Why Geometry Instancing?

Submitting triangles to the GPU for rendering in Direct3D is a relatively slow operation. Wloka 2003 shows that a 1 GHz CPU can render only around 10,000 to 40,000 batches per second in Direct3D. On a more modern CPU, we can expect this number to be between 30,000 and 120,000 batches per second (around 1,000 to 4,000 batches per frame at 30 frames/sec). That's not much! It means that if we want to render a forest of trees, and we submit one tree per batch, we cannot render more than 4,000 trees, regardless of how many polygons are in a tree—with no CPU time left for the rest of the game. This situation is clearly not ideal. We would like to be able to minimize the number of state and texture changes in our application and render the same triangles multiple times within the same batch in a single call to Direct3D. Thus, we would minimize CPU time spent in submitting batches and free up that time for other systems, such as physics, artificial intelligence, and game logic.

3.2 Definitions

We first define concepts behind geometry instancing, to make clear the kinds of objects that are part of the problem.

3.2.1 Geometry Packet

A geometry packet is a description of a packet of geometry to be instanced, a collection of vertices and indices. A geometry packet can be described in terms of vertices—with position, texture coordinates, normal, possibly tangent space and bones information for skinning, and per-vertex colors—and in terms of indices into the vertex stream. This kind of description directly maps to the most efficient way to submit geometry to the GPU.

A geometry packet is an abstract description of a piece of geometry, where the geometric entities are expressed in model space without any explicit reference to the context in which they will be rendered.

Here's a possible description in code of a geometry packet; it includes both the geometric information for the object as well as its bounding sphere:

```
struct GeometryPacket
{
   Primitive mPrimType
   void* mVertices;
   unsigned int mVertexStride;

   unsigned short* mIndices;

   unsigned int mVertexCount;
   unsigned int mIndexCount;

   D3DXVECTOR3 mSphereCentre;
   float mSphereRadius;
};
```

3.2.2 Instance Attributes

Typical attributes per instance are the model-to-world transformation matrix, the instance color, and an animation player providing the bones used to skin the geometry packet.

```
struct InstanceAttributes
{
  D3DXMATRIX mModelMatrix;
  D3DCOLOR mInstanceColor;
  AnimationPlayer* mAnimationPlayer;
  unsigned int mLOD;
};
```

3.2.3 Geometry Instance

A geometry instance is a geometry packet with the attributes specific to the instance. It directly connects a geometry packet and the instance attributes packet with which it's going to be rendered, giving an almost complete description of the entity ready to be submitted to the GPU.

Here's how a geometry instance structure might look in code:

```
struct GeometryInstance
{
  GeometryPacket* mGeometryPacket;
  InstanceAttributes mInstanceAttributes;
};
```

3.2.4 Render and Texture Context

The render context is the current state of the GPU in terms of render states (such as alpha blending and testing states, active render target, and more). The texture context tracks the currently active textures. Render context and texture context are usually modeled with classes, as shown in Listing 3-1.

3.2.5 Geometry Batch

A batch is a collection of geometry instances and the render states and texture context to be used to render the collection. It always directly maps to a single DrawIndexed-Primitive() call, to simplify the design of the class.

Listing 3-2 is an abstract interface for a geometry batch class.

Listing 3-1. Render and Texture Context Classes

```
class RenderContext
{
public:

  // Begin the render context and make its render state active
  //
  void Begin(void);

  // End the render context and restore previous render state,
  // if necessary
  //
  void End(void);

private:

  // Any description of the current render state and pixel
  // and vertex shaders.
  // D3DX Effect framework is particularly useful.
  //
  ID3DXEffect* mEffect;

  // Application-specific render states
  // . . .
};

class TextureContext
{
public:

  // Set current textures to the appropriate texture stages
  //
  void Apply(void) const;

private:
  Texture mDiffuseMap;
  Texture mLightMap;

  // . . .
};
```

Listing 3-2. GeometryBatch Class

```
class GeometryBatch
{
public:

  // Remove all instances from the geometry batch
  //
  virtual void ClearInstances(void);

  // Add an instance to the collection and return its ID.
  // Return -1 if it can't accept more instances.
  //
  virtual int AddInstance(GeometryInstance* instance);

  // Commit all instances, to be called once before the
  // render loop begins and after every change to the
  // instances collection
  //
  virtual unsigned int Commit(void) = 0;

  // Update the geometry batch, eventually prepare GPU-specific
  // data ready to be submitted to the driver, fill vertex and
  // index buffers as necessary, to be called once per frame
  //
  virtual void Update(void) = 0;

  // Submit the batch to the driver, typically implemented
  // with a call to DrawIndexedPrimitive
  //
  virtual void Render(void) const = 0;

private:
  GeometryInstancesCollection  mInstances;

  // . . .
};
```

3.3 Implementation

The engine's renderer can see geometry instancing only in terms of the abstract interface of a GeometryBatch, which hides the specifics of the instancing implementation and provides services for managing instances, updating, and rendering a batch. This way, the engine can concentrate on sorting batches to minimize render state and texture changes, while the GeometryBatch takes care of the actual implementation and communication protocol with Direct3D.

Listing 3-3 shows a simple implementation of a render loop in pseudocode, sorting GeometryBatches first by render context and then by texture context, thus minimizing the number of render-state changes.

Listing 3-3. Render Loop in Pseudocode

```
// Update phase
Foreach GeometryBatch in ActiveBatchesList
  GeometryBatch.Update();

// Render phase
Foreach RenderContext
Begin
  RenderContext.BeginRendering();
  RenderContext.CommitStates();

  Foreach TextureContext
  Begin
    TextureContext.Apply();
    Foreach GeometryBatch in the texture context
      GeometryBatch.Render();
  End
End
```

The update and render phases can be kept separate in case we want to update all batches once and render several times: this idea is extremely useful when implementing shadow mapping or water reflection and refraction, for example.

In this chapter, we discuss four implementations of GeometryBatch and analyze their performance characteristics, with a particular interest in the memory footprint and flexibility of each technique.

Here's a brief summary:

- **Static batching.** The fastest way to instance geometry. Each instance is transformed once to world space, its attributes are applied, and then it's sent already transformed to the GPU with every frame. Although simple, static batching is the least flexible technique.

- **Dynamic batching.** The slowest way to instance geometry. Each instance is streamed to GPU memory every frame, already transformed and with attributes applied. Dynamic batching seamlessly supports skinning and provides the most flexible implementation.

- **Vertex constants instancing.** A hybrid implementation in which multiple copies of the geometry for each instance are copied once into GPU memory. Instance attributes are then set every frame through vertex constants, and a vertex shader completes geometry instancing.

- **Batching with Geometry Instancing API.** Using the Geometry Instancing API provided by DirectX 9 and fully supported in hardware by GeForce 6 Series GPUs, this implementation offers a flexible and fast solution to geometry instancing. Unlike all other methods, this does not require geometry packet replication in the Direct3D vertex stream.

3.3.1 Static Batching

In static batching, we want to transform all instances once and copy them to a static vertex buffer. The most noticeable advantages of static batching are its rendering efficiency and its compatibility with any GPU on the market, regardless of age.

To implement static batching, we first create a vertex buffer object (with its associated index buffer) to fill with the transformed geometry. This object must be big enough to accept the maximum number of instances we decide to handle. Because we fill the buffer once and never touch it again, we can create it with the D3DUSAGE_WRITEONLY flag, giving a useful hint to the driver to put the buffer in the fastest memory available:

```
HRESULT res;

res = lpDevice->CreateVertexBuffer(
  MAX_STATIC_BUFFER_SIZE,
  D3DUSAGE_WRITEONLY,
  0,
  D3DPOOL_MANAGED,
  &mStaticVertexStream,
  0);

ENGINE_ASSERT(SUCCEEDED(res));
```

Whether to choose `D3DPOOL_MANAGED` or `D3DPOOL_DEFAULT` to create the buffer depends on the particular application and especially on the memory management strategy of the engine.

The next step is to implement the `Commit()` method to actually fill the vertex and index buffers with the transformed geometry that needs to be rendered.

Here is the `Commit()` method in pseudocode:

```
Foreach GeometryInstance in Instances
Begin
  Transform geometry in mGeometryPacket to world space
    with instance mModelMatrix
  Apply other instance attributes (like instance color)
  Copy transformed geometry to the Vertex Buffer
  Copy indices (with the right offset) to the Index Buffer
  Advance current pointer to the Vertex Buffer
  Advance current pointer to the Index Buffer
End
```

From now on, it's just a matter of submitting the instances we have already prepared with a simple call to `DrawIndexedPrimitive()`. The actual implementation of the `Update()` and `Render()` methods is trivial.

Static batching is the fastest way to render many instances, and it supports instances of different geometry packets inside the same geometry batch, but it has a few serious limitations:

- **Large memory footprint.** Depending on the size of each geometry packet and the number of instances being rendered, the memory footprint might become too big; for large worlds, it's easy to spend the video memory budget reserved for geometry. Falling back to AGP memory is possible, but that makes this technique slower and thus less appealing.
- **No support for different levels of detail.** Because all instances are copied once into the vertex buffer at commit time, choosing a level of detail valid for all situations is not easy and leads to suboptimal usage of the polygon budget. A semi-static solution is possible, in which all the levels of detail of a particular instance are instanced in the vertex buffer, while indices are streamed every frame, picking up the right level of detail for each instance. But this makes the implementation clumsier, defeating the purpose of this solution: simplicity and efficiency.

- **No support for skinning.**
- **No direct support for moving instances.** Implementing moving instances requires vertex shader logic with dynamic branching in order to be efficient. This can be prohibitive on older graphics cards. The end result would essentially be vertex constants instancing.

These limitations are addressed with the next technique, trading off rendering speed for additional flexibility.

3.3.2 Dynamic Batching

Dynamic batching overcomes the limitations of static batching at the cost of reducing rendering efficiency. A major advantage of dynamic batching is, like static batching, that it can be implemented on any GPU without support for advanced programmable pipelines.

The first step is to create a vertex buffer (and its associated index buffer) as dynamic by using the D3DUSAGE_DYNAMIC and D3DPOOL_DEFAULT flags. These flags ensure that the buffer is placed in the best possible memory location, given that we intend to dynamically update its contents.

```
HRESULT res;

res = lpDevice->CreateVertexBuffer(
  MAX_DYNAMIC_BUFFER_SIZE,
  D3DUSAGE_DYNAMIC | D3DUSAGE_WRITEONLY,
  0,
  D3DPOOL_DEFAULT,
  &mDynamicVertexStream,
  0);
```

Choosing the right value for MAX_DYNAMIC_BUFFER_SIZE is vital in this implementation. Two choices dictating the actual value are possible:

- Choosing a value large enough to contain geometry for all instances that might be needed in a frame
- Choosing a value large enough to contain geometry for a certain number of instances

The first approach ensures a proper separation between updating and rendering a batch. Updating a batch means streaming all instances into the dynamic buffer; rendering just submits the geometry with a call to DrawIndexedPrimitive(). But this approach typically requires a large amount of graphics memory (that is, either video or AGP memory) and is less reliable in the worst case if we can't ensure that the buffer is always big enough during the life of the application.

The second solution requires interleaving between streaming geometry and rendering it: when the dynamic buffer is full, its geometry is submitted for rendering and the content of the buffer is discarded, ready for more instances to be streamed. For optimal performance, it is important to use the proper protocol, that is, locking the dynamic buffer with `D3DLOCK_DISCARD` at the beginning of a new batch of instances and with `D3DLOCK_WRITEONLY` for each new instance to be streamed. The drawback of this solution is that it requires locking the buffer and streaming geometry again each time the batch needs to be rendered, for example, when implementing shadow mapping.

The choice depends on the particular application and its requirements. In this chapter, we choose the first solution, for its simplicity and clarity, but we add a slight complication: dynamic batching naturally supports skinning, and we address this in our implementation.

The `Update()` method is very similar to the `Commit()` method we have already described in Section 3.3.1, but it is executed every frame. Here it is in pseudocode:

```
Foreach GeometryInstance in Instances
Begin
  Transform geometry in mGeometryPacket to world space with
    instance mModelMatrix
  If instance needs skinning, request a set of bones from
    mAnimationPlayer and skin geometry
  Apply other instance attributes (like instance color)
  Copy transformed geometry to the Vertex Buffer
  Copy indices (with the right offset) to the Index Buffer
  Advance current pointer to the Vertex Buffer
  Advance current pointer to the Index Buffer
End
```

In this case, the `Render()` method is a trivial call to `DrawIndexedPrimitive()`.

3.3.3 Vertex Constants Instancing

In vertex constants instancing, we take advantage of vertex constants to store instancing attributes. Vertex constants batching is very fast in terms of rendering performance, and it supports instances moving from frame to frame, but it pays in terms of flexibility.

The main limitations are these:

- Limited number of instances per batch, depending on the number of constants available; usually no more than 50 to 100 instances can be batched in a single call. However, this can be enough to significantly reduce the CPU load from draw calls.
- No skinning; vertex constants are already used to store instance attributes.
- Need graphics hardware support for vertex shaders.

The first step is to prepare a static vertex buffer (with its associated index buffer) to store multiple copies of the same geometry packets, stored in model space, one for each instance in the batch.

The vertex buffer layout is illustrated in Figure 3-2.

The source vertex format must be updated to add an integer index to each vertex, which is constant per instance, indicating which instance the geometry packet belongs

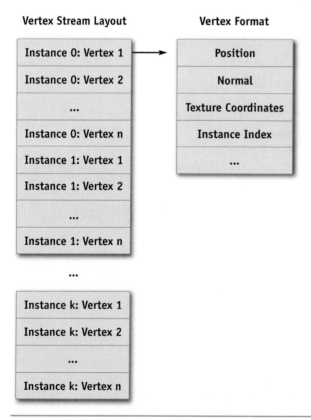

Figure 3-2. Vertex Buffer Layout

to. This is similar to palette skinning, in which each vertex contains an index to the bone (or multiple bones) affecting it.

The updated vertex format is this:

```
struct InstanceVertex
{
  D3DXVECTOR3  mPosition;

  // Other vertex properties, such as normal and texture
  // coordinates

  WORD  mInstanceIndex[4]; // Direct3D requires SHORT4

};
```

The `Commit()` method prepares the vertex buffer with the proper layout after all instances have been added to the geometry batch.

The next step is to upload attributes for each instance being rendered. Suppose we have only the model matrix, describing instance position and orientation, and the instance color.

When using a DirectX 9-class GPU, we can use a maximum of 256 vertex constants; we can reserve 200 for instancing attributes. In our example, each instance requires 4 constants for the model matrix and 1 constant for instance color, for a total of 5 constants per instance, leading to a maximum of 40 instances per batch.

Listing 3-4 shows the `Update()` method. The actual instancing is done in the vertex shader, shown in Listing 3-5.

Listing 3-4. The `Update()` Method

```
D3DXVECTOR4 instancesData[MAX_NUMBER_OF_CONSTANTS];

unsigned int count = 0;

for (unsigned int i = 0; i < GetInstancesCount(); ++i)
{
  // write model matrix
  instancesData[count++] = *(D3DXVECTOR4*)
      &mInstances[i].mModelMatrix.m11;
  instancesData[count++] = *(D3DXVECTOR4*)
      &mInstances[i].mModelMatrix.m21;
```

Listing 3-4 *(continued)*. The `Update()` Method

```
instancesData[count++] = *(D3DXVECTOR4*)
    &mInstances[i].mModelMatrix.m31;
instancesData[count++] = *(D3DXVECTOR4*)
    &mInstances[i].mModelMatrix.m41;

// write instance color
instanceData[count++] = ConvertColorToVec4(mInstances[i].mColor));
}


lpDevice->SetVertexConstants(
  INSTANCES_DATA_FIRST_CONSTANT,
  instancesData,
  count);
```

Listing 3-5. Vertex Shader for Vertex Constants Instancing

```
// vertex input declaration
struct vsInput
{
  float4 position : POSITION;
  float3 normal   : NORMAL;

  // other vertex data
  int4 instance_index : BLENDINDICES;
};


vsOutput VertexConstantsInstancingVS(
  in vsInput input)
{
  // get the instance index; the index is premultiplied
  // by 5 to take account of the number of constants
  // used by each instance
  int instanceIndex = ((int[4]) (input.instance_index))[0];

  // access each row of the instance model matrix
  float4 m0 = InstanceData[instanceIndex + 0];
  float4 m1 = InstanceData[instanceIndex + 1];
  float4 m2 = InstanceData[instanceIndex + 2];
  float4 m3 = InstanceData[instanceIndex + 3];

  // construct the model matrix
  float4x4 modelMatrix = { m0, m1, m2, m3 };
```

Listing 3-5 *(continued)*. Vertex Shader for Vertex Constants Instancing

```
// get the instance color
float4 instanceColor = InstanceData[instanceIndex + 4];

// transform input position and normal to world space with
// the instance model matrix
float4 worldPosition = mul(input.position, modelMatrix);
float3 worldNormal = mul(input.normal, modelMatrix);

// output position, normal, and color
output.position = mul(worldPosition, ViewProjectionMatrix);
output.normal = mul(worldNormal, ViewProjectionMatrix);
output.color = instanceColor;

// output other vertex data
}
```

The `Render()` sets the view projection matrix and submits all instances with a `DrawIndexedPrimitive()` call.

A possible optimization in production code is to store the rotational part of the model matrix as a quaternion, saving two vertex constants and increasing the maximum number of instances to around 70. A uniform scaling value can be stored in the *w* component of the translation vector. The model matrix is then reconstructed in the vertex shader, increasing its complexity and execution time.

3.3.4 Batching with the Geometry Instancing API

The last technique we present in this chapter is batching with the Geometry Instancing API exposed by DirectX 9 and fully implemented in hardware on GeForce 6 Series GPUs. As more hardware starts supporting the Geometry Instancing API, this technique will become more interesting, because it elegantly solves limitations imposed by vertex constants instancing, has a very limited memory footprint, and requires little intervention by the CPU. The only drawback of this technique is that it can only handle instances of the same geometry packet.

DirectX 9 provides the following call to access the Geometry Instancing API:

```
HRESULT SetStreamSourceFreq(
  UINT StreamNumber,
  UINT FrequencyParameter);
```

StreamNumber is the index of the source stream and *FrequencyParameter* indicates the number of instances each vertex contains.

We first create two vertex buffers: a static one to store geometry for the single geometry packet we want to instance multiple times, and a dynamic one to store instance data. The two vertex streams are shown in Figure 3-3.

The `Commit()` method ensures that all instances are using only one geometry packet and copies its geometry to the static buffer.

The `Update()` method simply copies all instance attributes into the second stream. Even though this method looks very similar to the `Update()` method of a dynamic batch, CPU intervention and graphics bus (AGP or PCI Express) bandwidth are minimal. Moreover, we can choose to allocate a vertex buffer big enough to accept attributes for all instances without worrying about graphics memory consumption, because each instance attribute uses only a fraction of the memory consumed by a whole geometry packet.

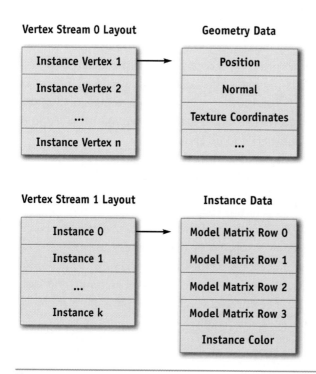

Figure 3-3. Vertex Streams for Instancing with the Geometry Instancing API

The Render() method sets up two streams with the correct stream frequency and issues a DrawIndexedPrimitive() call to render all instances in one batch, as shown in Listing 3-6.

The GPU takes care of virtually duplicating vertices of the first stream and packing them together with the second stream. The vertex shader sees as input a vertex with its position in model space and an additional instance attribute giving the model matrix to transform it to world space.

Listing 3-6. Setting Up Two Streams for Batching with the Geometry Instancing API

```
unsigned int instancesCount = GetInstancesCount();

// set up stream source frequency for the first stream
// to render instancesCount instances
// D3DSTREAMSOURCE_INDEXEDDATA tells Direct3D we'll use
// indexed geometry for instancing
lpDevice->SetStreamSourceFreq(
  0,
  D3DSTREAMSOURCE_INDEXEDDATA | instancesCount);

// set up first stream source with the vertex buffer
// containing geometry for the geometry packet
lpDevice->SetStreamSource(
  0,
  mGeometryInstancingVB[0],
  0,
  mGeometryPacketDecl);

// set up stream source frequency for the second stream;
// each set of instance attributes describes one instance
// to be rendered
lpDevice->SetStreamSourceFreq(
  1,
  D3DSTREAMSOURCE_INSTANCEDATA | 1);

// set up second stream source with the vertex buffer
// containing all instances' attributes
pd3dDevice->SetStreamSource(
  1,
  mGeometryInstancingVB[0],
  0,
  mInstancesDataVertexDecl);
```

The vertex shader code appears in Listing 3-7.

Listing 3-7. Vertex Shader for Batching with the Geometry Instancing API

```
// vertex input declaration
struct vsInput
{
  // stream 0
  float4 position : POSITION;
  float3 normal   : NORMAL;

  // stream 1
  float4 model_matrix0 : TEXCOORD0;
  float4 model_matrix1 : TEXCOORD1;
  float4 model_matrix2 : TEXCOORD2;
  float4 model_matrix3 : TEXCOORD3;

  float4 instance_color : D3DCOLOR;
};

vsOutput GeometryInstancingVS(
  in vsInput input)
{
  // construct the model matrix
  float4x4 modelMatrix =
  {
    input.model_matrix0,
    input.model_matrix1,
    input.model_matrix2,
    input.model_matrix3
  };

  // transform input position and normal to world space
  // with the instance model matrix
  float4 worldPosition = mul(input.position, modelMatrix);
  float3 worldNormal = mul(input.normal, modelMatrix);

  // output position, normal, and color
  output.position = mul(worldPosition, ViewProjectionMatrix);
  output.normal = mul(worldNormal, ViewProjectionMatrix);
  output.color = input.instance_color;

  // output other vertex data
}
```

With minimal CPU overhead and memory footprint, this technique can efficiently render many copies of the same geometry and is therefore the ideal solution in many scenarios. The only drawback is that it requires special hardware capabilities and doesn't easily support skinning.

To implement skinning, it would be possible to store all bones for all instances into a texture and fetch the right bones of the right instance with the texture fetch available in Shader Model 3.0 (which is required by the Geometry Instancing API). If this solution seems attractive, the performance impact of using texture fetches with this kind of access pattern is uncertain and should be tested.

3.4 Conclusion

This chapter defined the concepts behind geometry instancing and described four different techniques to achieve the goal of efficiently rendering the same geometry multiple times. Each technique has pros and cons, and no single technique clearly represents the ideal choice for every scenario. The best choice depends mainly on the application and on the type of objects being rendered.

Some scenarios and proposed solutions:

- An indoor scene with many static instances of the same geometry, which rarely or never move (such as walls or furniture). This is an ideal case for static batching.
- An outdoor scene with many instances of animated objects, as in a strategy game with big battles involving hundreds of soldiers. In this scenario, dynamic batching is probably the best solution.
- An outdoor scene with lots of vegetation and trees, many of which tend to modify their attributes (for example, trees and grass swaying in the wind), and lots of particle systems. This is probably the best scenario for the Geometry Instancing API.

Often the same application needs to rely on two or more techniques. Figures 3-4 and 3-5 show two examples. In such cases, hiding the implementation behind an abstract geometry batch concept makes the engine more modular and easier to maintain. As a result, the costs of implementing all the geometry-instancing techniques are greatly reduced for the entire application.

Figure 3-4. Combining Static Batching and Geometry Instancing in a Real Scene
Buildings in this screenshot are rendered with static batching, while trees use the Geometry Instancing API.

Figure 3-5. Combining GPU and CPU Animation in a Real Scene
Close soldiers are animated on the GPU, while distant soldiers are batched in few dynamic batches and animated on the CPU.

3.5 References

Cebenoyan, Cem. 2004. "Graphics Pipeline Performance." In *GPU Gems*, edited by Randima Fernando, pp. 473–486. Addison-Wesley. Available online at **http://developer.nvidia.com/object/GPU_Gems_Samples.html**

O'Rorke, John. 2004. "Managing Visibility for Per-Pixel Lighting." In *GPU Gems*, edited by Randima Fernando, pp. 245–257. Addison-Wesley.

Wloka, Matthias. 2003. "Batch, Batch, Batch: What Does It Really Mean?" Presentation at Game Developers Conference 2003. **http://developer.nvidia.com/docs/IO/8230/BatchBatchBatch.pdf**

Chapter 4

Segment Buffering

Jon Olick
2015

As graphical requirements evolve to include more polygons, more clutter, and better lighting to create more realistic-looking scenes, we are forced to produce more art to meet those requirements. One technique that helps to conserve development time is an instancing approach. For example, a single chair is modeled and placed all around the game world (see Figure 4-1). Instancing helps immensely to shrink development time. It is, however, all too common for modern games to become limited by the number of draw calls (Wloka 2003). If each instance used in a scene leads to one more batch, it may not be possible to realize the benefits of instancing: batches become the bottleneck. Segment buffering is a technique that collects multiple instances that are close to each other in the scene and merges them into "über-instances," thus reducing the number of batches and providing a simple and elegant solution to the batch bottleneck.

4.1 The Problem Space

Figure 4-1 shows a scene containing many static objects of the same material. Most GPUs cannot efficiently render scenes like this for more than a thousand instances; each instance potentially requires a render-state change, such as transform changes, light map texture changes, or vertex stream changes. These render-state changes cause driver and thus CPU overhead, ultimately resulting in poor performance. Although we

Figure 4-1. A Scene with Many Instances of the Same Object
From Men of Valor: Vietnam

could work around this problem on the content side by merging multiple models to create new models to instance around the world (thereby reducing the total number of instances), such an approach would require making a fair amount of custom art and could cause the maps to look repetitious.

4.2 The Solution

Segment buffering automates the merging of similar instances while maintaining most of the benefits of rendering separate instances. The primary benefits of segment buffering are thus a nonrepetitious look and the ability to not draw some of the original instances, as if they were removed from the visibility set.

4.3 The Method

Let's assume that we have a list of instances of a specific model. The next step is to spatially organize the instances such that in a 1D array, objects that are near each other spatially are also near each other in the array. With this new, organized list, the final step is to stitch all of the individual instances together as if they were one big instance, recording which parts in the new vertex/index buffers belong to the individual instances. We call each record in this list a segment. To render objects inside the segment buffer, simply generate a list of segments to be rendered while merging sequential segments in the list. This procedure thus generates a new list of optimally merged sections of the vertex/index buffer to render. Segments are rendered as static batches (see Chapter 3 of this book, "Inside Geometry Instancing").

4.3.1 Segment Buffering, Step 1

The key to making segment buffering work and work well is in the spatial organization of the segments inside the segment buffer. For this, we can use any spatial organization structure. K-d trees (Samet 1989, 1990), where k is 3, perform well for 2015's game *Men of Valor: Vietnam*. Octrees (Suter 1999) or any other spatial data structures would probably work just as well.

The tree is generated from a list of points that represent the locations of the instances for which we are creating a segment buffer. Once we have this tree, we do a depth-first traversal, always branching left first at every interior tree node. When we hit a leaf, we add all the points contained in the leaf to the new ordered list. When the traversal is complete, we have a spatially ordered list of instances.

The segment buffers and the spatially ordered list of instances need to be generated only when a new list of instances is introduced. In the majority of cases, then, the segment buffers and ordered list of instances need to be created only at load time.

4.3.2 Segment Buffering, Step 2

Given a spatially ordered list of instances, we iterate through the list and construct a single vertex/index buffer containing all of the instances. We make sure to transform each instance's vertex buffer components into world space before the instance is written into the big vertex buffer. Also, we need to record what parts of the big vertex/index buffer belong to each instance, for later reference during rendering. Again, this big vertex/index buffer needs to be created only in the event a new list of instances is introduced, typically at load time.

4.3.3 Segment Buffering, Step 3

When rendering, instead of immediately drawing an instance that is segmented, we generate a list of all these instances that need to be rendered. Instances outside the view frustum, for example, need not be rendered and should be omitted. Then we translate this list of instances into the parts of the big vertex/index buffer we previously generated for segment buffering. While doing this, we can merge segments adjacent to one another in the big vertex/index buffer to achieve an optimal list of the pieces of those buffers to be rendered. The result is the exact same output as if the instance list was rendered individually without segment buffering.

4.4 Improving the Technique

To make segment buffering a viable technique for a game that uses light mapping extensively, we need to implement automatic texture-atlas generation (NVIDIA 2004). This is because we cannot segment instances together that require render-state changes in between the rendering of each instance. In scenes where every instance has its own light map, a texture change is required between the rendering of each instance. Automatic texture-atlas generation is fairly easy to implement in the context of segment buffering because every instance inside the big vertex buffer has a unique section. Thus, the texture coordinates can be directly modified without affecting any other instance. This is in contrast to the traditional method of modifying the texture coordinates inside a vertex or pixel shader.

4.5 Conclusion

In this chapter, we have described a technique to significantly reduce the number of batches rendered in a single displayed frame. In doing so, the technique enables us to create a much richer and more realistic-looking environment. In addition to segment buffering, we described enhancements that make it applicable in situations where it normally would not be appropriate.

4.6 References

NVIDIA Corporation. 2004. "Improve Batching Using Texture Atlases." SDK white paper. **http://download.nvidia.com/developer/NVTextureSuite/Atlas_Tools/ Texture_Atlas_Whitepaper.pdf**

Samet, Hanan. 1989. *Applications of Spatial Data Structures.* Addison-Wesley.

Samet, Hanan. 1990. *The Design and Analysis of Spatial Data Structures.* Addison-Wesley.

Suter, Jaap. 1999. "Introduction to Octrees." Flipcode Web site. **http://www.flipcode.com/tutorials/tut_octrees.shtml**

Wloka, Matthias. 2003. "Batch, Batch, Batch: What Does It Really Mean?" Presentation at Game Developers Conference 2003. **http://developer.nvidia.com/docs/IO/8230/BatchBatchBatch.pdf**

Chapter 5

Optimizing Resource Management with Multistreaming

Oliver Hoeller
Piranha Bytes

Kurt Pelzer
Piranha Bytes

One of the most difficult problems in modern real-time graphics applications is the massive amount of data that must be managed. Complex scenes with complex meshes combined with multiple render passes—as are needed for high-quality shadows and additional reflection and refraction effects, for example—are expensive to render. Finding ways to feed the GPU with optimally formatted data is crucial for successfully rendering complex scenes.

This chapter addresses this issue and focuses on a flexible model to resolve the problem of handling the gamut of graphics hardware found in current PCs. A PC game must be able to run and run well on the latest high-end GPU all the way down to last year's "value" GPU—and on everything in between. We introduce a solution that handles the massive amount of data and is careful to transmit only the currently needed vertex components for each pass. This system, which has been implemented in the *Gothic III* engine, combines two powerful techniques: several vertex buffers are combined via multistreaming (a feature introduced with Microsoft DirectX 8.0), and each vertex buffer is controlled by an optimized resource manager. We present both the abstract concept as well as its implementation based on DirectX 9.0c.

5.1 Overview

Each vertex in a mesh has multiple components associated with it (position, normal, tangent, texture coordinates, and so on), but all of these entities aren't always necessary when rendering the object. We want an automated system that uses only the currently needed vertex components. To handle the task, we use vertex buffer streams specialized for certain subtasks. Depending on the current rendering pass, subsets of these streams are combined to assemble the vertices.

We need four basic types of streams, as shown in Figure 5-1. Here are the streams and their subtasks:

- **G—Vertex stream for geometry data.** Contains vertex position, normal, and vertex color(s).

- **T—Vertex stream for texture-mapping data.** Holds texture coordinate sets and additional information such as tangent vectors for tangent-space normal maps.

- **A—Vertex stream for animation data.** Holds animation data such as bone weights and influences.

- **I—Vertex stream for instancing data.** Contains data for vertex stream frequency instancing.

Subsets of these four streams combine to handle different tasks, as shown in Figure 5-2:

- **Render meshes without animation**
  Possible stream combinations: **G** *or* **G + T**

- **Render meshes with animation**
  Possible stream combinations: **G + A** *or* **G + T + A**

- **Render instanced meshes (optionally with animation)**
  Possible stream combinations: **G + I** *or* **G + T + I**
  (Optional: **G + A + I** *or* **G + T + A + I**)

- **Render pure z-pass (optionally with or without instancing, with or without animation)**
  Possible stream combinations: **G**
  (Optional: **G + A** *or* **G + I** *or* **G + A + I**)

The next section presents an implementation of this model.

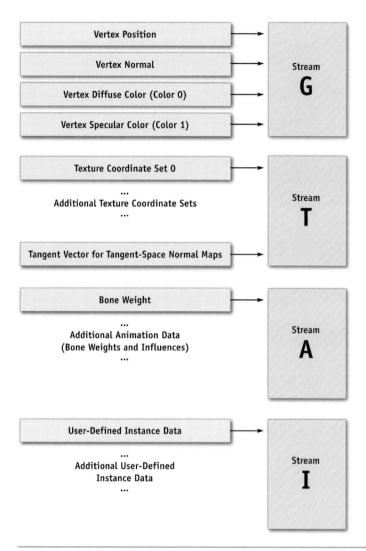

Figure 5-1. Four Types of Vertex Streams

5.2 Implementation

Now we show how to implement the abstract concept discussed in Section 5.1. First we examine some multistreaming example code based on DirectX 9.0c. Next we present the resource manager that handles the mesh resources. Finally, we show how to translate generic mesh data into the appropriate hardware structure.

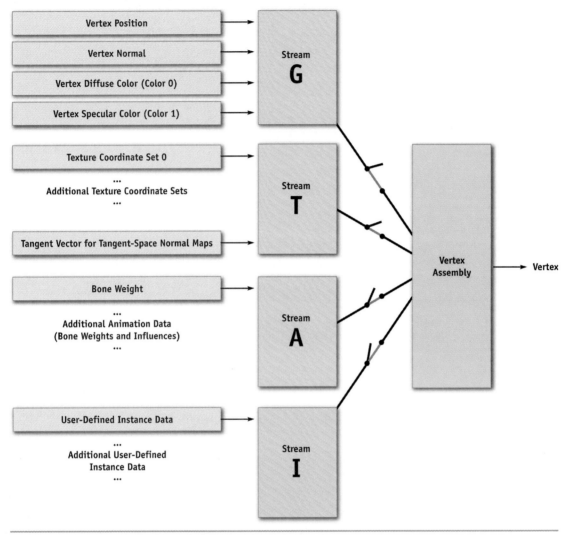

Figure 5-2. Combining Currently Needed Streams

5.2.1 Multistreaming with DirectX 9.0

Microsoft DirectX 8.0 introduced the notion of a stream to bind data to input registers. A stream is a uniform array of component data. Each component consists of one or more elements that represent a single entity, such as position, normal, color, texture coordinate set, and so on. With streams, GPUs are able to perform a direct memory access (DMA) from multiple vertex buffers in parallel. The Direct3D caps bit

`D3DCAPS9.MaxStreams` defines how many streams a GPU supports; modern hardware supports up to 16 streams, while older, DirectX 8.0-compliant GPUs are limited to 8 streams. Because multistreaming has some minor performance implications, it's advisable to minimize the number of active streams. Because our implementation uses only 1 to 4 streams, all GPUs with multistreaming support can be targeted, with minimal loss of performance.

Listing 5-1 shows our multistreaming example code. Using DirectX 9.0 for this task, we need only three simple components:

- A correct vertex declaration (an array of `D3DVERTEXELEMENT9`) and the `IDirect3DDevice9::CreateVertexDeclaration()` method to create a vertex declaration object.
- The `IDirect3DDevice9::SetVertexDeclaration()` method to set the vertex declaration object.
- The `IDirect3DDevice9::SetStreamSource()` method to bind a vertex buffer to a device data stream, creating an association between the vertex data and one of several data stream ports that feed the primitive processing functions.

Listing 5-1. A Set of Vertex Definitions and a Vertex Declaration

```
//
// Initializations:
//
// Here is a set of vertex definitions to support two streams.
// Vertex format:
//      stream 0 -> position + normal + color 0 + color 1
//      stream 1 -> 4 texture coordinate pairs
struct VTXSTREAM_0
{
  float fPosX, fPosY, fPosZ;
  float fNormX, fNormY, fNormZ;
  DWORD dwColor0, dwColor1;
};

struct VTXSTREAM_1
{
  float fTexU0, fTexV0;
  float fTexU1, fTexV1;
  float fTexU2, fTexV2;
  float fTexU3, fTexV3;
};
```

```
// Vertex declaration
D3DVERTEXELEMENT9 m_VtxDcl[] =
{
    {0, 0, D3DDECLTYPE_FLOAT3, D3DDECLMETHOD_DEFAULT,
     D3DDECLUSAGE_POSITION, 0}, // stream 0, position
    {0, 12, D3DDECLTYPE_FLOAT3, D3DDECLMETHOD_DEFAULT,
     D3DDECLUSAGE_NORMAL, 0},    // stream 0, normal
    {0, 24, D3DDECLTYPE_D3DCOLOR, D3DDECLMETHOD_DEFAULT,
     D3DDECLUSAGE_COLOR, 0},     // stream 0, color 0
    {0, 28, D3DDECLTYPE_D3DCOLOR, D3DDECLMETHOD_DEFAULT,
     D3DDECLUSAGE_COLOR, 1},     // stream 0, color 1
    {1, 0, D3DDECLUSAGE_FLOAT2, D3DDECLMETHOD_DEFAULT,
     D3DDECLUSAGE_TEXCOORD, 0}, // stream 1, tex coord set 0
    {1, 8, D3DDECLUSAGE_FLOAT2, D3DDECLMETHOD_DEFAULT,
     D3DDECLUSAGE_TEXCOORD, 1}, // stream 1, tex coord set 1
    {1, 16, D3DDECLUSAGE_FLOAT2, D3DDECLMETHOD_DEFAULT,
     D3DDECLUSAGE_TEXCOORD, 2}, // stream 1, tex coord set 2
    {1, 24, D3DDECLUSAGE_FLOAT2, D3DDECLMETHOD_DEFAULT,
     D3DDECLUSAGE_TEXCOORD, 3}  // stream 1, tex coord set 3
}

// Create a vertex declaration object
LPDIRECT3DVERTEXDECLARATION9 m_pVtxDeclObject;
m_pd3dDevice->CreateVertexDeclaration(m_VtxDcl,&m_pVtxDclObj);
```

In Listing 5-1, we present a set of vertex definitions and create a vertex declaration object m_pVtxDeclObject that describes the following vertex data layout:

- Vertex position data are found in stream 0 with a 0-byte offset. The data type is three-component float that expands to (float, float, float, 1).

- Vertex normal data are found in stream 0 with a 12-byte offset. The data type is three-component float that expands to (float, float, float, 1).

- Diffuse and specular color are found in stream 0 with offsets of 24 bytes (diffuse) and 28 bytes (specular). The data type is four-component, packed, unsigned bytes mapped to a range of 0 to 1.

- Texture coordinate data (sets 0 to 3) are found in stream 1 with offsets of 0 bytes (set 0), 8 bytes (set 1), 16 bytes (set 2), and 24 bytes (set 3). The data type is two-component float that expands to (float, float, 0, 1).

Before calling a draw method, we must set this vertex declaration object together with the vertex buffers bound to the correct device data streams, as shown in Listing 5-2.

Listing 5-2. Binding Vertex Buffers to Streams

```
//
// Each time we want to render primitives:
//

// Set the vertex declaration object
m_pd3dDevice->SetVertexDeclaration(m_pVtxDclObj);

// Bind vertex buffers to device data streams
m_pd3dDevice->SetStreamSource(0, m_pVtxBuf0, 0, sizeof(VTXSTREAM_0));
m_pd3dDevice->SetStreamSource(1, m_pVtxBuf1, 0, sizeof(VTXSTREAM_1));

// Render ..
m_pd3dDevice->DrawIndexedPrimitive( .. );
```

The actual references to the stream data do not occur until a drawing method, such as `IDirect3DDevice9::DrawIndexedPrimitive()`, is called.

5.2.2 Resource Management

In the *Gothic III* engine, we employ the concept of *resource management* to handle the administration of all data-intensive elements, such as vertex data (mesh information), textures, animation data (key frames and skinning data), sounds, and music. All these data structures use a uniform framework. It provides a simple interface so that other systems of the engine can access it.

All resources are packed into abstract data objects. We address these data objects by file name or by a globally unique identifier (GUID). The access of data containers is similarly organized like a database access. If you call a query, you get a referenceable data container with all necessary structures of the specified data.

The resource management system ensures the immediate and simultaneous availability of the data. It is also responsible for converting this proprietary data into the graphics hardware's preferred format.

As we mentioned, the resource management system makes it possible to store mesh data in specified file locations and to load these mesh objects only as needed. These structures must be stored in an efficient and flexible way, but vertex data layout can vary substantially from mesh to mesh.

The loaded resources should provide a reference counter, so that the same mesh can be used repeatedly in a scene. Geometry instancing is used to speed up rendering this type of mesh. (See Chapter 3 of this book, "Inside Geometry Instancing.")

The mesh information is generated by tools such as 3ds max or Maya. For this operation, a suitable importer has to be developed, as shown in Figure 5-3.

The Mesh Resource

One of the database containers provided by the resource management system is a mesh resource, which has all relevant structures, all vertex and index data arrays, and a link to an abstract material object (which is also a referenceable resource).

Note that the vertex structure wrapped into a resource class (as shown in Figure 5-3) isn't adapted to any specific graphics API (such as DirectX or OpenGL). We can therefore implement the whole resource system independent of the graphics API used.

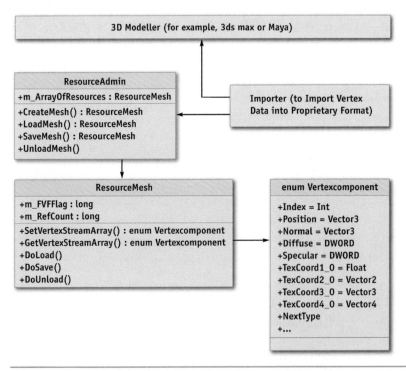

Figure 5-3. Structure of the Resource Framework

These structures consist of simple vertex streams (arrays) containing a single vertex component, such as position (an array of 3D vectors), normals (an array of 3D vectors), color (an array of DWORD values), or up to 16 texture coordinates (an array of 1D, 2D, 3D, or 4D vectors) and other customized data arrays such as weights for hardware skinning.

To complete this groundwork, we have developed a hardware-independent resource framework with a mesh class and its administrative interface. Furthermore, we have written a specified importer for the corresponding modeling tool.

5.2.3 Processing Vertices

The renderer takes over the task of changing the hardware-independent data into a format that is optimal for the graphics hardware.

First, the mesh resources are loaded into main memory at the start of the application. Alternatively, we use an on-demand approach to load the data into memory when needed, using a separate thread.

For the renderer, the mesh object is only a temporary container to build up the correct format. The generated hardware-dependent format is used by the application to draw the scene. The reason for this strict separation is the ability to tailor the data optimally for the GPU found in the PC on which the application is currently running. We use only the vertex data that are actually needed.

This separation becomes useful in the adaptation of needed texture coordinates: On less powerful hardware, many visual effects are turned off because the hardware is incapable of running them, or because the overall rendering load needs to be reduced. Because these effects are not rendered, the texture coordinates used by these effects need not be passed to the graphics hardware. They can simply be removed. So we reduce memory consumption and save processor power and bandwidth.

For this task, we provide a submodule, which we have named Vertexprocessor, that translates the generic mesh data into the specified hardware structure. The following steps are necessary for the data to be prepared for multistreaming:

- When a mesh resource is requested, Vertexprocessor loads this data into memory if the object isn't already available, or increments the reference counter of the mesh object if it is already loaded.
- The stored vertex format of the mesh object is determined. This can happen via the embedded FVF flag or with the implementation used in the resource class (hardware independent).

- The Vertexprocessor divides the single generic vertex arrays into the four hardware-specific vertex streams (that is, streams **G**, **T**, **A**, and **I**, discussed in Section 5.1). The vertex arrays are accessed by the `MeshResource::GetVertexStreamArray()` method, as shown in Figure 5-4, which translates or copies the arrays into the specific component of one of the four vertex buffers.

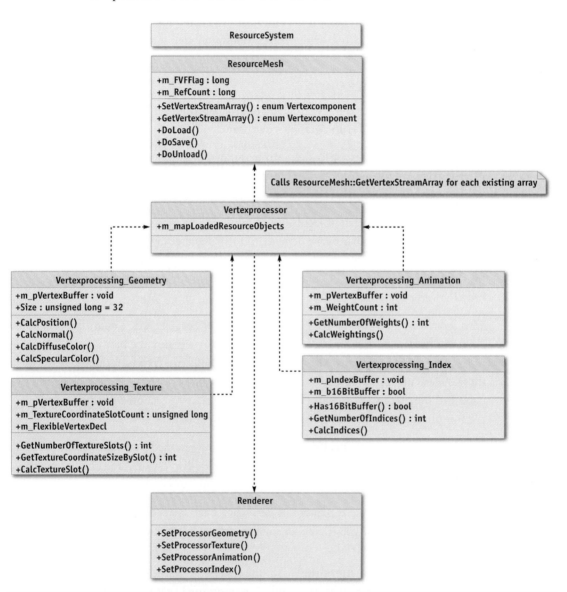

Figure 5-4. Query of Single Vertex Streams Used by Vertexprocessor

Geometry Data

The Vertexprocessor unit for geometry data seeks position, normals, and the two colors (if available) from a mesh object.

For illustration purposes, Listing 5-3 creates a vertex buffer that contains all this information and uses this specific vertex layout. The buffer should have a cache-friendly size of 32 bytes per entry, so the layout is fixed for this buffer type.

Listing 5-3. Creating a Vertex Buffer

```
D3DVERTEXELEMENT9 m_VtxDcl[] =
{
  {0, 0, D3DDECLTYPE_FLOAT3, D3DDECLMETHOD_DEFAULT,
   D3DDECLUSAGE_POSITION, 0}, // stream 0, position
  {0, 12, D3DDECLTYPE_FLOAT3, D3DDECLMETHOD_DEFAULT,
   D3DDECLUSAGE_NORMAL, 0},   // stream 0, normal
  {0, 24, D3DDECLTYPE_D3DCOLOR, D3DDECLMETHOD_DEFAULT,
   D3DDECLUSAGE_COLOR, 0},    // stream 0, color 0
  {0, 28, D3DDECLTYPE_D3DCOLOR, D3DDECLMETHOD_DEFAULT,
   D3DDECLUSAGE_COLOR, 0},    // stream 0, color 1
};


// Here comes the vertex definition.
// Vertex format:
//      stream 0 -> position + normal + color 0 + color 1
struct sVTXStreamGeometry
{
  float vecPos[ 3 ];
  float vecNorm[ 3 ];
  DWORD dwColor0, dwColor1;
};


// Data container Resourcemesh supports GetVertexStreamArray here.
// (See API methods above.)
cResourceMesh* m_pResourceMesh;


// Create the vertex declaration and create a specific vertex buffer.
// For clarity, we calculate the size of the buffer in the number of
// elements and the corresponding FVF flags. In our engine implementation,
// the geometry stream has a size of 32 bytes (cache-friendly), so we
// can easily create the sufficient memory size of the vertex buffer.
CreateVertexDeclaration( m_VtxDcl );
m_pVtxBuf0 = CreateVertexBuffer(NumVertices,
            FVF_XYZ | FVF_NORMAL | FVF_DIFFUSE | FVF_SPECULAR);
```

Listing 5-3 *(continued)*. Creating a Vertex Buffer

```
sVTXStreamGeometry* pBuffer = LockBuffer(m_pVtxBuf0);
for each vertexIndex in m_pResourceMesh
{
  pBuffer->m_vecPos =
   m_pResourceMesh->GetVertexStreamArray(enum_Position, vertexIndex);
  pBuffer->m_vecNorm =
   m_pResourceMesh->GetVertexStreamArray(enum_Normal, vertexIndex);
  pBuffer->m_dwColor0 =
   m_pResourceMesh->GetVertexStreamArray(enum_Diffuse, vertexIndex);
  pBuffer->m_dwColor1 =
   m_pResourceMesh->GetVertexStreamArray(enum_Specular, vertexIndex);
  pBuffer++;
}
```

Texture Data

The Vertexprocessor unit for texture data fetches the available texture coordinate slots from the mesh object and builds up a flexible vertex buffer with all necessary texture coordinates. At most, eight texture coordinate groups (with a 1D, 2D, 3D, or 4D vector per texture coordinate) are possible.

In addition, one of the slots can be encoded as tangent vectors for tangent-space normal maps; otherwise, it would be necessary to use a separate vertex buffer stream for this information. We omit this in Listing 5-4 for clarity. It is, however, straightforward to add this feature.

If light maps are available, we should use a separate Vertexprocessor unit (that is, a separate vertex buffer per mesh instance), because every instance must have unique UV pairs for light map textures. Light maps must be individually mapped, and their mapping coordinates depend on their world-space position, and so they can't be instantiated. This can be a big problem for the memory footprint and performance of your application. Consequently, light maps are useful for big meshes, such as terrain in outdoor scenarios or irregular wall meshes in dungeons, but not for small meshes or multi-instantiated objects.

Listing 5-4. A Vertex Buffer Stream for Texture Data

```
// Data container Resourcemesh supports GetVertexStreamArray here.
// (See API methods above.)
cResourceMesh* m_pResourceMesh;
```

Listing 5-4 *(continued)*. A Vertex Buffer Stream for Texture Data

```
// This is a template array structure to allocate a flexible amount
// of vtxDcl structures in one block
Array<D3DVERTEXELEMENT9> arrDeclVtx;

// We create a specific vertex buffer for textures. We use the FVF flag
// from Resourcemesh and filter the specific texture flags to create
// the specific buffer.
// For clarity, we use here a function that calculates the size of the
// buffer and the corresponding FVF flags. You can use an alternative
// implementation to calculate the correct size of the vertex buffer.
sVTXStreamTexture* pVtxBuf1 =
 CreateVertexBuffer(NumTextureEntries,
                    m_pResourceMesh->m_FVFFlag & TextureFlags);
// Lock buffer with unspecific byte pointer
char* pBuffer = LockBuffer( pVtxBuf1 );

// Current buffer position (in bytes) in locked data of vertex buffer
DWORD dwGlobalBufferPosition = 0;
for each textureIndex in m_pResourceMesh
{
  DWORD dwCurrentOffset = 0; // Current offset position for vtxDecl

  for (int i = 0; i<m_pResourceMesh->GetNumberOfTextureSlots(); i++)
  {
    // Array template allocates us a new structure at the end of the
    // structure block and returns a nonconstant reference of the block.
    // All structures allocated before remain unchanged (by realloc).
    D3DVERTEXELEMENT9& flexibleElement = arrDeclVtx.InsertNewEnd();

    flexibleElement.Stream = 1; // Is at 2nd position after Geometry
    flexibleElement.Usage  = D3DDECLUSAGE_TEXCOORD;

    // Current size in bytes of texture slots (u,v = 8 bytes)
    // r,s,t = 12 bytes, r,s,t,w = 16 bytes
    DWORD dwCurrentTextureSlotSize =
          m_pResourceMesh->GetTextureCoordinateSizeBySlot( i );

    // For specified slot, we look for what size (in bytes) we need
    // and add it to our global offset counter dwCurrentOffset
    flexibleElement.Offset = dwCurrentOffset;
```

Listing 5-4 (continued). A Vertex Buffer Stream for Texture Data

```
// Calculate stream position in Resourcemesh for specified
// texture slot
int enumStreamArraySlot =
    m_pResourceMesh->GetTextureSlotEnum( i );

// Now copy out the vertex information from the Resourcemesh
// stream into locked buffer
memcpy(&pBuffer[ dwGlobalBufferPosition + dwCurrentOffset ],
  m_pResourceMesh->GetVertexStreamArray(enumStreamArraySlot,
    textureindex), dwCurrentTextureSlotSize);

dwCurrentOffset += dwCurrentTextureSlotSize;

// Calculate types of vtxDecl (D3DDECLTYPE_FLOAT2 = 8 bytes,
// D3DDECLTYPE_FLOAT3 = 12 bytes, D3DDECLTYPE_FLOAT4 = 16 bytes)
flexibleElement.Type =
    CalculateDataSizeType(dwCurrentTextureSlotSize);

  }
  // Add new position offset to global position in buffer
  dwGlobalBufferPosition += dwCurrentOffset;
}
```

Animation Data

The Vertexprocessor unit for animation data builds up weights for animation skinning with bones in hardware. A varying number of weights per bone can be used, so it is not necessary to waste more memory than is really needed. In *Gothic III*, we use up to six weights per bone for our animation system.

Index Data

An index buffer corresponding to the above vertex buffers is also built up. Indices are stored into a mesh object as a separate stream of information. The bit size of index entries (whether 16 or 32 bit) depends on the number of vertices. Having more than 65,535 entries necessitates using DWORDs as index entries. Otherwise, WORD (16-bit) indices suffice. Choosing the smallest possible data type helps reduce an application's memory footprint.

The Vertexprocessor has the responsibility to create all the previously described vertex buffers in an optimal manner for hardware (typically they are created as `Pool_Managed` and `WriteOnly`)(Ashida 2004).

Rendering the Streams

Once all the streams are built up properly, they are available for rendering and drawing.

As an example of using streams separately, we execute the **G**-stream (that is, the geometry stream) as a separate z-pass, to achieve fast z-rejects in hardware and to use this buffer in conjunction with an occlusion query system implemented in the render system. (See Chapter 6 of this book, "Hardware Occlusion Queries Made Useful," for an example of such a system.)

It is possible to add the **A**-stream (the animation stream) in the calculation, but the effort isn't worthwhile in most cases. The number of pixels that differ because of the animation is typically small and thus out of proportion to the additional rendering cost of adding animation.

Individual streams are activated depending on the view (whether solid rendering or z-pass) by the renderer.

5.3 Conclusion

In this chapter, we have shown how current applications can overcome problems caused by the growing amount of geometry data in scenes. We've discussed a flexible model that gives the application more control over the data and drives the detected hardware optimally by combining two powerful techniques:

- Several vertex buffers are combined via multistreaming.
- Each vertex buffer is controlled by an optimized resource manager.

A nice side benefit: we efficiently handle the bandwidth for data, which sometimes can be limited because of data duplication/redundant data transmission across the bus from system memory to the GPU.

5.4 References

Ashida, Koji. 2004. "Optimising the Graphics Pipeline." NVIDIA presentation.
http://developer.nvidia.com/docs/IO/10878/
ChinaJoy2004_OptimizationAndTools.pdf

Cebenoyan, Cem. 2004. "Graphics Pipeline Performance." In *GPU Gems*, edited by Randima Fernando, pp. 473–486. Addison-Wesley. Available online at http://developer.nvidia.com/object/GPU_Gems_Samples.html

For additional information about programming one or more streams in DirectX, see the Microsoft Web site:
http://msdn.microsoft.com/directx

Chapter 6

Hardware Occlusion Queries Made Useful

Michael Wimmer
Vienna University of Technology

Jiří Bittner
Vienna University of Technology

6.1 Introduction

Hardware occlusion queries were one of the most eagerly awaited graphics hardware features in a long time. This feature makes it possible for an application to ask the 3D API (OpenGL or Direct3D) whether or not any pixels would be drawn if a particular object were rendered. With this feature, applications can check whether or not the bounding boxes of complex objects are visible; if the bounds are occluded, the application can skip drawing those objects. Hardware occlusion queries are appealing to today's games because they work in completely dynamic scenes.

However, although this feature has been available for more than two years (via the `NV/ARB_occlusion_query` OpenGL extension and by the `IDirect3DQuery9` interface in Direct3D), there is not yet widespread adoption of this feature for solving visibility culling in rendering engines. This is due to two main problems related to naive usage of the occlusion query feature: the overhead caused by issuing the occlusion queries themselves (since each query adds an additional draw call), and the latency caused by waiting for the query results.

In this chapter, we present a simple but powerful algorithm that solves these problems (Bittner et al. 2004): it minimizes the number of issued queries and reduces the impact of delays due to the latency of query results.

To achieve this, the algorithm exploits the spatial and temporal coherence of visibility by reusing the results of occlusion queries from the previous frame in order to initiate and schedule the queries in the current frame. This is done by storing the scene in a hierarchical data structure (such as a k-d tree or octree [Cohen-Or et al. 2003]), processing nodes of the hierarchy in a front-to-back order, and interleaving occlusion queries with the rendering of certain previously visible nodes.

The algorithm is smart about the queries it actually needs to issue: most visible interior nodes of the spatial hierarchy and many small invisible nodes are not tested at all. Furthermore, previously visible nodes are rendered immediately without waiting for their query result, which allows filling the time needed to wait for query results with useful work.

6.2 For Which Scenes Are Occlusion Queries Effective?

Let's recap briefly for which scenes and situations the algorithm presented in this chapter is useful.

Occlusion queries work best for large scenes where only a small portion of the scene is visible each frame—for example, a walkthrough in a city. More generally, the algorithm presented here works if in each frame there are large occluded interior nodes in the hierarchy. These nodes should contain many objects, so that skipping them if they are occluded saves geometry, overdraw, and draw calls (which are a typical bottleneck in today's rendering systems [Wloka 2003]). An important advantage the algorithm has over most other techniques used nowadays in games (such as portal culling) is that it allows completely dynamic environments.

Some games—for example, shader-heavy ones—use a separate initial rendering pass that writes only to the depth buffer. Subsequent passes test against this depth buffer, and thus expensive shading is done only for visible pixels. If the scenes are complex, our occlusion-culling algorithm can be used to accelerate establishing the initial depth buffer and at the same time to obtain a complete visibility classification of the hierarchy. For the subsequent passes, we skip over objects or whole groups of objects that are completely invisible at virtually no cost.

Finally, if there is little or no occlusion in a scene—for example, a flyover of a city—there is no benefit to occlusion culling. Indeed, occlusion queries potentially introduce an overhead in these scenes and make rendering slower, no matter how the occlusion queries are used. If an application uses several modes of navigation, it will pay to switch off occlusion culling for modes in which there is no or only very little occlusion.

6.3 What Is Occlusion Culling?

The term *occlusion culling* refers to a method that tries to reduce the rendering load on the graphics system by eliminating (that is, culling) objects from the rendering pipeline if they are hidden (that is, occluded) by other objects. There are several methods for doing this.

One way to do occlusion culling is as a preprocess: for any viewpoint (or regions of viewpoints), compute ahead of time what is and is not visible. This technique relies on most of the scene to be static (so visibility relationships do not change) and is thus not applicable for many interactive and dynamic applications (Cohen-Or et al. 2003).

Portal culling is a special case of occlusion culling; a scene is divided into cells (typically rooms) connected via portals (typically door and window openings). This structure is used to find which cells (and objects) are visible from which viewpoint—either in a preprocess or on the fly (Cohen-Or et al. 2003). Like general preprocess occlusion culling, it relies on a largely static scene description, and the room metaphor restricts it to mostly indoor environments.

Online occlusion culling is more general in that it works for fully dynamic scenes. Typical online occlusion-culling techniques work in image space to reduce computation overhead. Even then, however, CPUs are less efficient than, say, GPUs for performing rasterization, and thus CPU-based online occlusion techniques are typically expensive (Cohen-Or et al. 2003).

Fortunately, graphics hardware is very good at rasterization. Recently, an OpenGL extension called `NV_occlusion_query`, or now `ARB_occlusion_query`, and Direct3D's occlusion query (`D3DQUERYTYPE_OCCLUSION`) allow us to query the number of rasterized fragments for any sequence of rendering commands. Testing a single complex object for occlusion works like this (see also Sekulic 2004):

1. Initiate an occlusion query.
2. Turn off writing to the frame and depth buffer, and disable any superfluous state. Modern graphics hardware is thus able to rasterize at a much higher speed (NVIDIA 2004).
3. Render a simple but conservative approximation of the complex object—usually a bounding box: the GPU counts the number of fragments that would actually have passed the depth test.
4. Terminate the occlusion query.

5. Ask for the result of the query (that is, the number of visible pixels of the approximate geometry).

6. If the number of pixels drawn is greater than some threshold (typically zero), render the complex object.

The approximation used in step 3 should be simple so as to speed up the rendering process, but it must cover at least as much screen-space area as the original object, so that the occlusion query does not erroneously classify an object as invisible when it actually is visible. The approximation should thus be much faster to render, and does not modify the frame buffer in any way.

This method works well if the tested object is really complex, but step 5 involves waiting until the result of the query actually becomes available. Since, for example, Direct3D allows a graphics driver to buffer up to three frames of rendering commands, waiting for a query results in potentially large delays. In the rest of this chapter, we refer to steps 1 through 4 as "issuing an occlusion query for an object."

If correctness of the rendered images is not important, a simple way to avoid the delays is to check for the results of the queries only in the following frame (Sekulic 2004). This obviously leads to visible objects being omitted from rendering, which we avoid in this chapter.

6.4 Hierarchical Stop-and-Wait Method

As a first attempt to use occlusion queries, we show a naive occlusion-culling algorithm and extend it to use a hierarchy. In the following section, we show our coherent hierarchical culling algorithm, which makes use of coherence and other tricks to be much more effective than the naive approach.

6.4.1 The Naive Algorithm, or Why Use Hierarchies at All?

To understand why we want to use a hierarchical algorithm, let's take a look at the naive occlusion query algorithm first:

1. Sort objects front to back.

2. For each object

    a. Issue occlusion query for the object (steps 1–4 from previous section).

    b. Stop and wait for result of query.

    c. If number of visible pixels is greater than 0, render the object.

Although this algorithm calculates correct occlusion information for all of our objects, it is most likely slower than just rendering all the objects directly. The reason is that we have to issue a query and wait for its result for every object in the scene!

Now imagine, for example, a walkthrough of a city scene: We typically see a few hundred objects on screen (buildings, streetlights, cars, and more). But there might be tens of thousands of objects in the scene, most of which are hidden by nearby buildings. If each of these objects is not very complex, then issuing and waiting for queries for all of them is more expensive than just rendering them.

6.4.2 Hierarchies to the Rescue!

We need a mechanism to group objects close to one another so we can treat them as a single object for the occlusion query. That's just what a spatial hierarchy does. Examples of spatial hierarchies are k-d trees, BSP trees, and even standard bounding-volume hierarchies. They all have in common that they partition the scene recursively until the cells of the partition are "small" enough according to some criterion. The result is a tree structure with interior nodes that group other nodes, and leaf nodes that contain actual geometry.

The big advantage of using hierarchies for occlusion queries is that we can now test interior nodes, which contain much more geometry than the individual objects. In our city example, hundreds or even thousands of objects might be grouped into one individual node. If we issue an occlusion query for this node, we save the tests of all of these objects—a potentially huge gain!

If geometry is not the main rendering bottleneck, but rather the number of draw calls issued (Wloka 2003), then making additional draw calls to issue the occlusion queries is a performance loss. With hierarchies, though, interior nodes group a larger number of draw calls, which are all saved if the node is occluded using a single query. So we see that in some cases, a hierarchy is what makes it possible to gain anything at all by using occlusion queries.

6.4.3 Hierarchical Algorithm

The naive hierarchical occlusion-culling algorithm works like this—it is specified for a node within the hierarchy and initially called for the root node:

1. Issue occlusion query for the node.
2. *Stop and wait* for the result of the query.

3. If the node is visible:

    a. If it is an interior node:

        i. Sort the children in front-to-back order.

        ii. Call the algorithm recursively for all children.

    b. If it is a leaf node, render the objects contained in the node.

This algorithm can potentially be much faster than the basic naive algorithm, but it has two significant drawbacks.

6.4.4 Problem 1: Stalls

This approach shares the first drawback with the naive algorithm. Whenever we issue an occlusion query for a node, we cannot continue our algorithm until we know the result. But waiting until the query result becomes available may be prohibitive. The query has to be sent to the GPU. There it sits in a command queue until all previous rendering commands have been issued (and modern GPUs can queue up more than one frame's worth of rendering commands!). Then the bounding box associated with the query must be rasterized, and finally the result of the query has to travel back over the bus to the driver.

During all this time, the CPU sits idle, and we have caused a CPU stall. But that's not all. While the CPU sits idle, it doesn't feed the GPU any new rendering commands. Now when the result of the occlusion query arrives, and the CPU has finally figured out what to draw and which commands to feed the GPU next, the command buffer of the GPU has emptied and it has become idle for some time as well. We call this GPU starvation. Obviously, we are not making good use of our resources. Figure 6-1 sums up these problems.

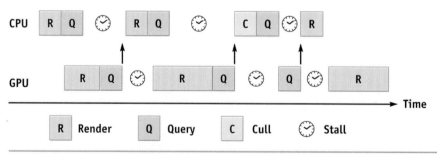

Figure 6-1. CPU Stalls and GPU Starvation Caused by Occlusion Queries

6.4.5 Problem 2: Query Overhead

The second drawback of this algorithm runs contrary to the original intent of the hierarchical method. We wanted to reduce the overhead for the occlusion queries by grouping objects together. Unfortunately, this approach increases the number of queries (especially if many objects are visible): in addition to the queries for the original objects, we have to add queries for their groupings. So we have improved the good case (many objects are occluded), but the bad case (many objects are visible) is even slower than before.

The number of queries is not the only problem. The new queries are for interior nodes of the hierarchy, many of which, especially the root node and its children, will have bounding boxes covering almost the entire screen. In all likelihood, they are also visible. In the worst case, we might end up filling the entire screen tens of times just for rasterizing the bounding geometry of interior nodes.

6.5 Coherent Hierarchical Culling

As we have seen, the hierarchical stop-and-wait method does not make good use of occlusion queries. Let us try to improve on this algorithm now.

6.5.1 Idea 1: Being Smart and Guessing

To solve problem 1, we have to find a way to avoid the latency of the occlusion queries. Let's assume that we could "guess" the outcome of a query. We could then react to our guess instead of the actual result, meaning we don't have to wait for the result, eliminating CPU stalls and GPU starvations.

Now where does our guess come from? The answer lies, as it so often does in computer graphics, in temporal coherence. This is just another way of expressing the fact that in real-time graphics, things don't move around too much from one frame to the next. For our occlusion-culling algorithm, this means that if we know what's visible and what's occluded in one frame, it is very likely that the same classification will be correct for most objects in the following frame as well. So our "guess" is simply the classification from the previous frame.

But wait—there are two ways in which our guess can go wrong: If we assume the node to be visible and it's actually occluded, we will have processed the node needlessly. This can cost some time, but the image will be correct. However, if we guess that a node is occluded and in reality it isn't, we won't process it and some objects will be missing from the image—something we need to avoid!

So if we want to have correct images, we need to verify our guess and rectify our choice in case it was wrong. In the first case (the node was actually occluded), we update the classification for the next frame. In the second case (the node was actually visible), we just process (that is, traverse or render) the node normally. The good news is that we can do all of this later, whenever the query result arrives. Note also that the accuracy of our guess is not critical, because we are going to verify it anyway. Figure 6-2 shows the different cases.

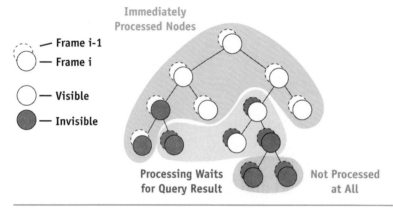

Figure 6-2. Processing Requirements for Various Nodes

6.5.2 Idea 2: Pull Up, Pull Up

To address problem 2, we need a way to reduce overhead caused by the occlusion queries for interior nodes.

Luckily, this is easy to solve. Using idea 1, we are already processing previously visible interior nodes without waiting for their query results anyway. It turns out that we don't even need to issue a query for these nodes, because at the end of the frame, this information can be easily deduced from the classification of its children, effectively "pulling up" visibility information in the tree. Therefore, we save a number of occlusion queries and a huge amount of fill rate.

On the other hand, occlusion queries for interior nodes that were occluded in the previous frame are essential. They are required to verify our choice not to process the node, and in case the choice was correct, we have saved rendering all the draw calls, geometry, and pixels that are below that node (that is, inside the bounding box of the node).

What this boils down to is that we issue occlusion queries only for previously visible leaf nodes and for the largest possible occluded nodes in the hierarchy (in other words, an occluded node is not tested if its parent is occluded as well). The number of queries issued is therefore linear in the number of visible objects. Figure 6-3 illustrates this approach.

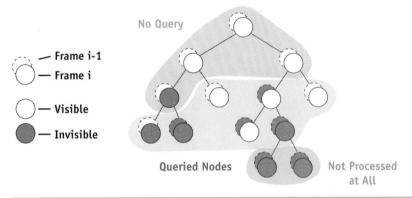

Figure 6-3. Occlusion Query Requirements for Various Nodes

6.5.3 Algorithm

We apply these two ideas in an algorithm we call "coherent hierarchical culling." In addition to the hierarchical data structure for the front-to-back traversal we already know, we need a "query queue" that remembers the queries we issued previously. We can then come back later to this queue to check whether the result for a query is already available.

The algorithm is easy to incorporate into any engine as it consists of a simple main traversal loop. A queue data structure is part of the C++ standard template library (STL), and a hierarchical data structure is part of most rendering libraries anyway; for example, for collision detection.

The algorithm visits the hierarchy in a front-to-back order and immediately recurses through any previously visible interior node (idea 1). For all other nodes, it issues an occlusion query and stores it in the query queue. If the node was a previously visible leaf node, it also renders it immediately, without waiting for the query result.

During the traversal of the hierarchy, we want to make sure that we incorporate the query results as soon as possible, so that we can issue further queries if we encounter a change in visibility.

Therefore, after each visited node, we check the query queue to see if a result has already arrived. Any available query result is processed immediately. Queries that verify our guess to be correct are simply discarded and do not generate additional work. Queries that contradict our guess are handled as follows: Nodes that were previously visible and became occluded are marked as such. Nodes that were previously occluded and became visible are traversed recursively (interior nodes) or rendered (leaf nodes). Both of these cases cause visibility information to be pulled up through the tree. See Figure 6-4, which also depicts a "pull-down" situation: a previously occluded node has become visible and its children need to be traversed.

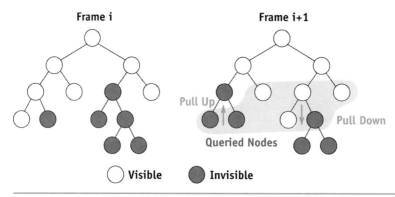

Figure 6-4. Visibility of Hierarchy Nodes in Two Consecutive Frames

6.5.4 Implementation Details

The algorithm is easy to follow using the pseudocode, which we show in Listing 6-1. Let's discuss some of the details in the code.

To maintain the visibility classification for all nodes over consecutive frames, we use a `visible` flag and a `frameID`, which increments every frame. Nodes visible in the previous frame are easily identified through `lastVisited = frameID - 1` and `visible = true`; all other nodes are assumed invisible. This way, we don't have to reset the visibility classification for each frame.

Listing 6-1. Algorithm Pseudocode

```
TraversalStack.Push(hierarchy.Root);
while ( not TraversalStack.Empty() or
        not QueryQueue.Empty() )
{
  //- PART 1: process finished occlusion queries
  while ( not QueryQueue.Empty() and
          (ResultAvailable(QueryQueue.Front()) or
           TraversalStack.Empty()) )
  {
    node = QueryQueue.Dequeue();
    // wait if result not available
    visiblePixels = GetOcclusionQueryResult(node);
    if ( visiblePixels > VisibilityThreshold )
    {
      PullUpVisibility(node);
      TraverseNode(node);
    }
  }

  //- PART 2: hierarchical traversal
  if ( not TraversalStack.Empty() )
  {
    node = TraversalStack.Pop();
    if ( InsideViewFrustum(node) )
    {
      // identify previously visible nodes
      wasVisible = node.visible and
                   (node.lastVisited == frameID - 1);
      // identify nodes that we cannot skip queries for
      leafOrWasInvisible = not wasVisible or IsLeaf(node);
      // reset node's visibility classification
      node.visible = false;
      // update node's visited flag
      node.lastVisited = frameID;
      // skip testing previously visible interior nodes
      if ( leafOrWasInvisible )
      {
        IssueOcclusionQuery(node);
        QueryQueue.Enqueue(node);
      }
```

Listing 6-1 (continued). Algorithm Pseudocode

```
            // always traverse a node if it was visible
            if ( wasVisible )
              TraverseNode(node);
        }
      }
    }

TraverseNode(node)
{
  if ( IsLeaf(node) )
    Render(node);
  else
    TraversalStack.PushChildren(node);
}

PullUpVisibility(node)
{
  while (not node.visible)
  {
    node.visible = true;
    node = node.parent;
  }
}
```

To establish the new visibility classification for the current frame, we set all nodes we encounter during the traversal to invisible by default. Later, when a query identifies a node as visible, we "pull up" visibility; that is, we set all its ancestors to visible as well.

Interior nodes that were visible in the previous frame (that is, not `leafOrWasInvisible`) are nodes for which we skip occlusion queries altogether.

Traversing a node means rendering the node for leaf nodes or pushing its children onto the traversal stack so that they get rendered front to back.

We also assume that the `Render()` call renders an object only if it hasn't been rendered before (this can be checked using the `frameID`). This facilitates the code for previously visible objects: when we finally get the result of their visibility query, we can just process them again without introducing a special case or rendering them twice (since they have already been rendered immediately after their query was issued).

Another advantage is that we can reference objects in several nodes of the hierarchy, and they still get rendered only once if several of these nodes are visible.

Furthermore, we have to be careful with occlusion tests for nodes near the viewpoint. If the front faces of a bounding box get clipped by the near plane, no fragments are generated for the bounding box. Thus the node would be classified as occluded by the test, even though the node is most likely visible. To avoid this error for each bounding box that passes the view-frustum test, we should check whether any of its vertices is closer than the near plane. In such a case, the associated node should be set visible without issuing an occlusion query. Finally, note that for the occlusion queries, the actual node bounding boxes can be used instead of the (usually less tight) nodes of the spatial hierarchy.

6.5.5   Why Are There Fewer Stalls?

Let's take a step back and see what we have achieved with our algorithm and why.

The coherent hierarchical culling algorithm does away with most of the inefficient waiting found in the hierarchical stop-and-wait method. It does so by interleaving the occlusion queries with normal rendering, and avoiding the need to wait for a query to finish in most cases.

If the viewpoint does not move, then the only point where we actually might have to wait for a query result is at the end of the frame, when all the visible geometry is already rendered. Previously visible nodes are rendered right away without waiting for the results.

If the viewpoint does move, the only dependency occurs if a previously invisible node becomes visible. We obviously need to wait for this to be known in order to decide whether to traverse the children of the node. However, this does not bother us too much: most likely, we have some other work to do during the traversal. The query queue allows us to check regularly whether the result is available while we are doing useful work in between.

Note that in this situation, we might also not detect some occlusion situations and unnecessarily draw some objects. For example, if child A occludes child B of a previously occluded interior node, but the query for B is issued before A is rendered, then B is still classified as visible for the current frame. This happens when there is not enough work to do between issuing the queries for A and B. (See also Section 6.5.7, where we show how a priority queue can be used to increase the chance that there is work to do between the queries for A and B.)

6.5.6 Why Are There Fewer Queries?

We have already seen that a hierarchical occlusion-culling algorithm can save a lot of occlusion queries if large parts of the scene are occluded. However, this is paid for by large costs for testing interior nodes.

The coherent hierarchical culling algorithm goes a step further by obviating the need for testing most interior nodes. The number of queries that need to be issued is only proportional to the number of visible objects, not to the total number of objects in the scene. In essence, the algorithm always tests the largest possible nodes for occluded regions.

Neither does the number of queries depend on the depth of the hierarchy, as in the hierarchical stop-and-wait method. This is a huge win, because the rasterization of large interior nodes can cost more than occlusion culling buys.

6.5.7 How to Traverse the Hierarchy

We haven't talked a lot about traversing the hierarchy up to now. In principle, the traversal depends on which hierarchy we use, and is usually implemented with a traversal stack, where we push child nodes in front-to-back order when a node is traversed. This basically boils down to a depth-first traversal of the hierarchy.

However, we can gain something by not adhering to a strict depth-first approach. When we find nodes that have become visible, we can insert these nodes into the traversal, which should be compatible with the already established front-to-back order in the hierarchy.

The solution is not to use a traversal stack, but a priority queue based on the distance to the observer. A priority queue makes the front-to-back traversal very simple. Whenever the children of a node should be traversed, they are simply inserted into the priority queue. The main loop of the algorithm now just checks the priority queue, instead of the stack, for the next node to be processed.

This approach makes it simple to work with arbitrary hierarchies. The hierarchy only needs to provide a method to extract its children from a node, and to compute the bounding box for any node. This way, it is easy to use a sophisticated hierarchy such as a k-d tree (Cohen-Or et al. 2003), or just the bounding volume hierarchy of the scene graph for the traversal, and it is easy to handle dynamic scenes.

Note also that an occlusion-culling algorithm can be only as accurate as the objects on which it operates. We cannot expect to get accurate results for individual triangles if we only test nodes of a coarse hierarchy for occlusion. Therefore, the choice of a hierarchy plays a critical role in occlusion culling.

6.6 Optimizations

We briefly cover a few optimizations that are beneficial in some (but not all) scenes.

6.6.1 Querying with Actual Geometry

First of all, a very simple optimization that is always useful concerns previously visible leaf nodes (Sekulic 2004). Because these will be rendered regardless of the outcome of the query, it doesn't make sense to use an approximation (that is, a bounding box) for the occlusion query. Instead, when issuing the query as described in Section 6.3, we omit step 2 and replace step 3 by rendering the actual geometry of the object. This saves rasterization costs and draw calls as well as state changes for previously visible leaf nodes.

6.6.2 Z-Only Rendering Pass

For some scenes, using a z-only rendering pass can be advantageous for our algorithm. Although this entails twice the transformation cost and (up to) twice the draw calls for visible geometry, it provides a good separation between occlusion culling and rendering passes as far as rendering states are concerned. For the occlusion pass, the only state that needs to be changed between an occlusion query and the rendering of an actual object is depth writing. For the full-color pass, visibility information is already available, which means that the rendering engine can use any existing mechanism for optimizing state change overhead (such as ordering objects by rendering state).

6.6.3 Approximate Visibility

We might be willing to accept certain image errors in exchange for better performance. This can be achieved by setting the `VisibilityThreshold` in the algorithm to a value greater than zero. This means that nodes where no more than, say, 10 or 20 pixels are visible are still considered occluded. Don't set this too high, though; otherwise the algorithm culls potential occluders and obtains the reverse effect.

This optimization works best for scenes with complex visible geometry, where each additional culled object means a big savings.

6.6.4 Conservative Visibility Testing

Another optimization makes even more use of temporal coherence. When an object is visible, the current algorithm assumes it will also be visible for the next frame. We can even go a step further and assume that it will be visible for a number of frames. If we do that, we save the occlusion queries for these frames (we assume it's visible anyway). For example, if we assume an object remains visible for three frames, we can cut the number of required occlusion queries by almost a factor of three! Note, however, that temporal coherence does not always hold, and we almost certainly render more objects than necessary.

This optimization works best for deep hierarchies with simple leaf geometry, where the number of occlusion queries is significant and represents significant overhead that can be reduced using this optimization.

6.7 Conclusion

Occlusion culling is an essential part of any rendering system that strives to display complex scenes. Although hardware occlusion queries seem to be the long-sought-after solution to occlusion culling, they need to be used carefully, because they can introduce stalls into the rendering pipeline.

We have shown an algorithm that practically eliminates any waiting time for occlusion query results on both the CPU and the GPU. This is achieved by exploiting temporal coherence, assuming that objects that have been visible in the previous frame remain visible in the current frame. The algorithm also reduces the number of costly occlusion queries by using a hierarchy to cull large occluded regions using a single test. At the same time, occlusion tests for most other interior nodes are avoided.

This algorithm should make hardware occlusion queries useful for any application that features a good amount of occlusion, and where accurate images are important. For example, Figure 6-5 shows the application of the algorithm to the walkthrough of a city model, with the visibility classification of hierarchy nodes below. The orange nodes were found visible; all the other depicted nodes are invisible. Note the increasing size of the occluded nodes with increasing distance from the visible set. For the viewpoint shown, the algorithm presented in this chapter provided a speedup of about 4 compared to rendering with view-frustum culling alone, and a speedup of 2.6 compared to the hierarchical stop-and-wait method.

Figure 6-5. Visualizing the Benefits of Occlusion Queries for a City Walkthrough

6.8 References

Bittner, J., M. Wimmer, H. Piringer, and W. Purgathofer. 2004. "Coherent Hierarchical Culling: Hardware Occlusion Queries Made Useful." *Computer Graphics Forum (Proceedings of Eurographics 2004)* 23(3), pp. 615–624.

Cohen-Or, D., Y. Chrysanthou, C. Silva, and F. Durand. 2003. "A Survey of Visibility for Walkthrough Applications." *IEEE Transactions on Visualization and Computer Graphics* 9(3), pp. 412–431.

NVIDIA Corporation. 2004. *NVIDIA GPU Programming Guide.*
http://developer.nvidia.com/object/gpu_programming_guide.html

Sekulic, D. 2004. "Efficient Occlusion Culling." In *GPU Gems*, edited by Randima Fernando, pp. 487–503. Addison-Wesley.

Wloka, M. 2003. "Batch, Batch, Batch: What Does It Really Mean?" Presentation at Game Developers Conference 2003.
http://developer.nvidia.com/docs/IO/8230/BatchBatchBatch.pdf

Chapter 7

Adaptive Tessellation of Subdivision Surfaces with Displacement Mapping

Michael Bunnell
NVIDIA Corporation

In this chapter we describe how to perform view-dependent, adaptive tessellation of Catmull-Clark subdivision surfaces with optional displacement mapping. We use the GPU to do the tessellation calculations, which saves graphics bus bandwidth and is many times faster than using the CPU. The first part of this chapter explains how to tessellate subdivision surfaces to polygons for rendering high-quality curved surfaces without visible polygon artifacts. The second part of this chapter describes how to add displacement-mapping support for rendering highly detailed models that can be animated in real time.

This chapter takes a repeated subdivision approach to tessellation, implemented by rendering into 2D textures. The subdivision, flatness test, and final vertex attribute calculations are done using fragment programs (pixel shaders). This method assumes that the vertex data of the subdivision surface control mesh are stored in a texture map. Intermediate results are also rendered to and read from texture maps, and the final tessellation results (position, normal, and so on) are rendered to a vertex array ready to be used by a render-primitives call such as `glDrawElements()`.

7.1 Subdivision Surfaces

Subdivision surfaces are arguably the most popular curved-surface representation used in computer graphics today. Specifically, Catmull-Clark subdivision surfaces are supported in practically every 3D modeling and animation application. Introduced to the big screen by Pixar with *A Bug's Life*, they have been used in all of Pixar's movies since, including *Finding Nemo* and *The Incredibles*. Subdivision surfaces are often combined with displacement mapping to add extra detail for computer-generated characters in live-action movies. The most striking example of a displacement-mapped subdivision surface model is probably the creature Gollum from the recent *Lord of the Rings* movies.

Subdivision surfaces are curved surfaces (or higher-order surfaces) described by a simple polygon control mesh and some subdivision rules. The subdivision rules define how to perform one subdivision step on the surface. Each subdivision step creates a new mesh with more geometry and a smoother appearance than the previous mesh. Figure 7-1 illustrates such rules applied to a cube.

7.1.1 Some Definitions

- **Limit surface**—the hypothetical surface created after an infinite number of subdivision steps
- **Valence (of a vertex)**—the number of edges connected to a vertex
- **Extraordinary point**—a vertex with a valence other than 4 (for a quad-based subdivision scheme, such as Catmull-Clark)

7.1.2 Catmull-Clark Subdivision

We use Catmull-Clark subdivision surfaces in this chapter, and so we use the Catmull-Clark subdivision rules (Catmull and Clark 1978). Catmull-Clark subdivision works on meshes of arbitrary manifold topology. However, it is considered a quad-based subdivision scheme because it works best on four-sided polygons (quads) and because all

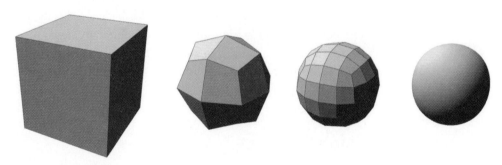

Figure 7-1. Catmull-Clark Subdivision of a Cube
From left to right: Original control mesh, mesh after one subdivision step, mesh after two steps, and the limit surface.

the polygons in the mesh after the first subdivision step are quads. Our implementation is limited to control meshes consisting only of quads. This implies that the source models have to be created as all-quad models, a task familiar to artists with a NURBS modeling background or experience using Lightwave SubPatches.

The Catmull-Clark rules to subdivide an all-quad mesh are simple. Split each face of the control mesh into four faces by adding a vertex in the middle of the face and a vertex at each edge. The positions of these new vertices and the new positions of the original vertices can be computed from the pre-subdivided mesh vertex positions using the weight masks in Figure 7-2. We show only the weight masks for calculating the new positions of original vertices of valence 3, 4, and 5. The weight masks for higher valences follow the same progression.

If we examine a couple of subdivision steps of a single face, we notice that subdivision is very similar to scaling a 2D image. The only differences are the filtering values used and that the vertex position data is generally stored as floating point, while most images are stored as integer or fixed point. Figure 7-3 shows a single face of a mesh being subdivided two times. One thing to note about this figure is that we need a ring of vertices around the faces that are being subdivided to perform the subdivision. Also, the extraordinary point (the vertex of valence 5) at the upper-left corner of the face in the original mesh is present in the subdivided meshes too.

7.1.3 Using Subdivision for Tessellation

One obvious way to tessellate subdivision surfaces is to apply a fixed number of subdivision steps on the original control mesh to create a list of quads to render. In fact, that is how pre-tessellated surfaces are created with most 3D-modeling packages. The disadvantage of this method is that parts of a model are over-tessellated and other parts under-tessellated. Also, it leaves the burden of selecting the number of subdivisions on the application program. Under-tessellation leads to visible polygon artifacts. Over-tessellation creates too

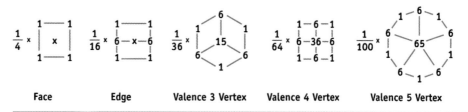

Figure 7-2. Catmull-Clark Subdivision Masks
Used for calculating new vertex positions from pre-subdivided mesh vertex positions.

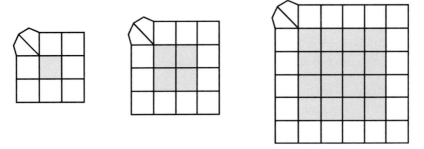

Figure 7-3. Subdividing a Face of a Subdivision Surface

many small triangles that can severely affect rendering performance. Too much geometry causes the GPU to become vertex-transform or triangle-setup limited. Worse, having many tiny triangles that are just a few pixels in size can significantly reduce rasterizer efficiency.

Adaptive Subdivision

We use a flatness-test-based adaptive subdivision algorithm to avoid the problems with the fixed subdivision method. Instead of blindly subdividing a fixed number of steps, we test the surface for flatness first. In this way, the subdivision adapts to the surface curvature and the viewpoint. The closer the surface is or the more curved it is, the more it gets subdivided. See Figure 7-4. We measure flatness as the distance from the polygonal mesh to the limit surface measured in screen pixels. For example, a flatness value of 0.5 means the maximum distance from the polygon approximation of the surface to the limit surface is half a pixel.

7.1.4 Patching the Surface

We need to store the subdivision control mesh vertex data in a format that allows for efficient processing. We do this by breaking up the original control mesh into smaller meshes that can be represented as regular 2D grids and therefore stored in 2D arrays. See Figure 7-5. Now we can infer the mesh connectivity by the location of vertices in the array. Vertices next to each other are assumed to be connected by edges. Control points arranged this way, in a 2D array or matrix, are generally referred to as *patches*, so that is what we call them. Our patches are different in that we allow extraordinary points at the patches' corners.

The obvious way to divide the control mesh into patches is to create a patch for each face of the mesh. This method requires a lot of duplicated vertices because we need to include the vertices from neighboring faces so we can subdivide the patch. We can improve on this situation by creating patches with more faces when possible.

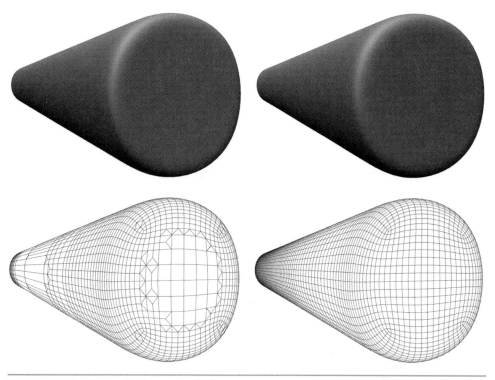

Figure 7-4. Adaptive vs. Uniform Tessellation
The long, cylindrical object on the left is adaptively tessellated and consists of about one-third as many polygons as the uniformly tessellated one on the right.

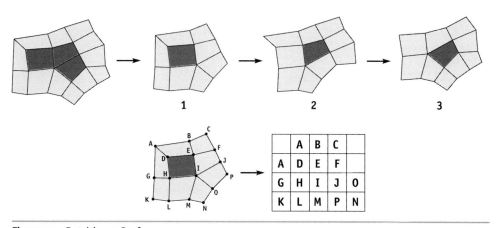

Figure 7-5. Patching a Surface
Top: A mesh is broken up into meshes 1, 2, and 3. Bottom: Mesh 1 is converted to a patch.

Patching a surface is not a trivial process, but fortunately it can be done in a preprocessing step. Even animated meshes generally do not change topology, so the vertex locations in each patch can be precalculated and stored in a 2D texture. The texture can be passed to the tessellation code along with the list of patch information, which includes the size of the patch and the valences of any extraordinary vertices. The demo program available on the book's Web site shows one possible implementation of patching an arbitrary quad model.

7.1.5 The GPU Tessellation Algorithm

The tessellation algorithm works as follows. First, we copy the vertex data of the control mesh (positions) into the patch buffer texture. The flatness test assumes the vertex coordinates are in eye space. If they are not in eye space, they can be transformed before or during this copy. Next, we check each patch for flatness (see "The Flatness Test," later in this section). Then we compute vertex attribute data, such as positions and normals, for the patches that are flat and write them to the vertex array, writing the index information to a primitive index buffer. Patches that are not flat are subdivided into another patch buffer. Then we swap patch-buffer pointers and go back to the flatness test step. This section describes each step in the tessellation process in more detail.

CPU Processing

We use the CPU to do buffer management and to create the list of vertex indices that form part of the tessellation result. The CPU does not have to touch the vertex data, but it does read the flatness test results (using `glReadPixels`) and decides which patches need further tessellation. It assigns patch locations in the buffers, and it uses a simple recursive procedure to build the primitive index list based on the edge flatness results computed by the shaders.

Creating the Patches

Patches are created by rendering a quad per patch at the appropriate location in the patch buffer, to copy the control mesh vertex position data from a texture. The program executed at the quad's fragments uses a precomputed texture to index the control mesh vertices discussed in Section 7.1.4. If there are more vertex attributes to subdivide, such as texture coordinates, they are copied into a different location in the patch buffer. Vertex attributes other than position are bilinearly interpolated for performance.

The Flatness Test

The flatness of each edge in the patch is calculated by rendering a quad of appropriate size into the flatness buffer using the FlatTest1.cg or the FlatTest2.cg shaders. (All of the shaders mentioned here can be found with the SubdViewer demo program.) Unlike the other buffers used for tessellation, this buffer is not floating point. It is an 8-bit-per-component buffer.

The two flat-test shaders measure the flatness at each edge of the control mesh. Both shaders treat the four control points along an edge as a b-spline curve and measure the flatness of the curve. One shader is used before the first subdivision step because it can handle s-type curves, which are curves whose first derivatives change sign. The second, faster test is used thereafter, because there are only c-type curves after the first subdivision. (C-type curves have first derivatives that do not change sign and thus are c-shaped.)

As shown in Figure 7-6, the first shader's flatness test calculates the distance from the control point 2 to the midpoint of control points 1 and 3, as well as the distance of control point 3 to the midpoint of control points 2 and 4. The second flatness test calculates the distance from the midpoint of control points 1 and 4 to the midpoint of control points 2 and 3. Both tests compare the calculated distance to the flatness value given in pixels, scaled appropriately. The flatness value is prescaled to account for the distance of the b-spline control points from the limit curve, and it is doubled so the midpoint calculations can be done with only an add. Because the control points are assumed to be in eye space, the flatness distance is scaled by the z value of the midpoint of control points 2 and 3 to handle perspective projection.

The flatness test also needs to handle z-scale values that are less than the near render plane to avoid over-tessellating meshes that cross the near plane. It does so by reflecting z values less than the near plane to the other side of the plane. This technique results in good tessellation for patches that cross the near plane without creating too much geometry that would be clipped later.

Results of the flatness test are copied to host memory, so that the CPU can decide which patches are flat. The results are also saved for each level of subdivision except the last (we know all edges are flat after the last subdivision), so they can be used to build

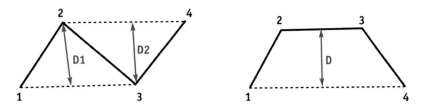

Figure 7-6. Comparing Flatness Tests
Left: Flatness test 1 measures two distances. Right: Flatness test 2 measures only one.

the array of primitive indices. This data is packed to save bandwidth and averages about 200 times fewer bytes of data than the description of the patch itself.

Subdivision

Subdivision is performed by rendering a quad for each patch into the destination patch buffer using the Subdiv.cg shader shown in Listing 7-1. The render works similar to a 2× scaled image blit, but it uses the weights for Catmull-Clark subdivision, as discussed in Section 7.1.2. The source coordinate for rendering is offset from the patch's origin by (0.75, 0.75), to account for the ring of extra vertices around the faces that are being subdivided and to create a similar ring in the destination. See Figure 7-7. The size of the result patch is twice that of the source patch, minus 3. The Subdiv.cg shader uses the fractional part of the source coordinates to determine which subdivision mask to use: the face mask, the edge mask, or the valence-4 vertex mask. Attributes other than position are interpolated bilinearly in Normal.cg.

Listing 7-1. Subdiv.cg—Subdividing a Regular Mesh Using Catmull-Clark Rules

```
float4 main(float4 srcCoord,
            uniform samplerRECT srcTexMap : TEXUNIT0) : COLOR
{
  float3 wh, wv;      // weight values
  float3 s1, s2, s3;
  float2 f;

  // calculate weights based on fractional part of
  // source texture coordinate
  //
  // x == 0.0, y == 0.0 use face weights (1/4, 1/4, 0)
  //                                     (1/4, 1.4, 0)
  //                                     (  0,   0, 0)
  // x == 0.5, y == 0.0 use edge weights (horizontal)
  //                                     (1/16, 6/16, 1/16)
  //                                     (1/16, 6/16, 1/16)
  //                                     (  0,    0,    0)
  // x == 0.0, y == 0.5 use edge weights (vertical)
  //                                     (1/16, 1/16, 0)
  //                                     (6/16, 6/16, 0)
  //                                     (1/16, 1/16, 0)
  // x == 0.5, y == 0.5 use valence 4 vertex weights
  //                                     (1/64,  6/64, 1/64)
  //                                     (6/64, 36/64, 6/64)
  //                                     (1/64,  6/64, 1/64)
```

```
wh = float3(1.0/8.0, 6.0/8.0, 1.0/8.0);
f = frac(srcCoord.xy + 0.001) < 0.25; // account for finite precision
if (f.x != 0.0) {
  wh = float3(0.5, 0.5, 0.0);
  srcCoord.x += 0.5; // fraction was zero — move to texel center
}
wv = float3(1.0/8.0, 6.0/8.0, 1.0/8.0);
if (f.y != 0) {
  wv = float3(0.5, 0.5, 0.0);
  srcCoord.y += 0.5;  // fraction was zero — need to move to texel center
}

// calculate the destination vertex position by using the weighted
// sum of the 9 vertex positions centered at srcCoord

s1 = texRECT(srcTexMap, srcCoord.xy + float2(-1, -1)).xyz * wh.x +
     texRECT(srcTexMap, srcCoord.xy + float2(0, -1)).xyz * wh.y +
     texRECT(srcTexMap, srcCoord.xy + float2(1, -1)).xyz * wh.z;

s2 = texRECT(srcTexMap, srcCoord.xy + float2(-1, 0)).xyz * wh.x +
     texRECT(srcTexMap, srcCoord.xy + float2(0, 0)).xyz * wh.y +
     texRECT(srcTexMap, srcCoord.xy + float2(1, 0)).xyz * wh.z;

s3 = texRECT(srcTexMap, srcCoord.xy + float2(-1, 1)).xyz * wh.x +
     texRECT(srcTexMap, srcCoord.xy + float2(0, 1)).xyz * wh.y +
     texRECT(srcTexMap, srcCoord.xy + float2(1, 1)).xyz * wh.z;

  return float4(s1 * wv.x + s2 * wv.y + s3 * wv.z, 0);
}
```

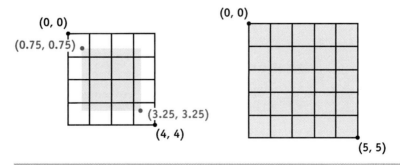

Figure 7-7. Resampling a Patch
The blue 2.5×2.5-pixel square portion of the patch (left) is sampled to create a 5×5-pixel patch (right).

If there are any extraordinary points at the corners of the patch, they are copied and adjusted using the extraordinary-point subdivision shader, EPSubdiv.cg. This shader does not really subdivide per se, because no more data is created. It only adjusts the positions based on the subdivision rules, using a table lookup to get the appropriate filter weights. It calculates the coordinates of the weights in the lookup table based on the valence of the extraordinary point and the relative position of the control point that it is calculating. This shader is much slower than the regular subdivision shader, but it runs at many fewer pixels. Each corner of the patch (that has an extraordinary point) is handled by rendering a separate, small quad. The extraordinary-point shader is run after the regular subdivision shader and overwrites the control points in the destination that were calculated incorrectly.

Limit Positions and Normals

We use the limit shaders and normal shaders to create the vertex attributes that are written to the vertex array for rendering, including the attributes that are bilinearly interpolated, which are copied in the normal shader. The limit shader calculates the position on the limit surface corresponding to the vertices of the patch. It uses a weighted average of each vertex and its eight neighbors (Halstead et al. 1993). The control points themselves are often not close enough to the limit surface to be substituted for the limit surface points, especially for neighboring patches that are subdivided to different depths. The EPLimit.cg shader is used to calculate the limit position for extraordinary points.

The normal shader calculates two tangents for each control point and then uses their cross product to calculate the surface normal of the limit surface at that point. The EPNormal.cg shader does the same for extraordinary points. Both shaders calculate the tangents using a weighted average of the control vertex's neighbors. Because the normal shaders use the same control points as the limit shaders, it is a good idea to combine them in a single shader and use multiple render targets to write out the position and normal at the same time.

7.1.6 Watertight Tessellation

Watertight tessellation means that there are no gaps between polygons in the tessellation output. Even tiny gaps can lead to missing pixels when rendering the surface. One source of these gaps is the fact that floating-point operations performed in different orders do not always give the exact same result. Ordering shader calculations so that they are identical for neighboring patches costs a lot of performance. Therefore, we do not rely on positions or flatness data at the edge of a patch to match its neighbor's. The index list-building code ensures watertightness by using only one patch's data for shared corners and edges.

Another watertight tessellation problem that must be avoided is T-junctions. T-junctions often crop up with adaptive tessellation schemes. They occur if a patch is split even though one or more of its edges is flat. If the patch sharing the flat edges is not also split, then a T-junction is created. There are different methods for avoiding T-junctions during tessellation, some of which are quite complicated. Our tessellator has the advantage that index values of all the vertices of a patch are known when building the index list. The tessellator simply replaces the index of the vertex at the junction with one that is farther from the edge and fills the gap with a triangle, as illustrated in Figure 7-8. Moving the vertex at the T-junction avoids zero-area triangles, which can cause artifacts when rendering alpha-blended surfaces.

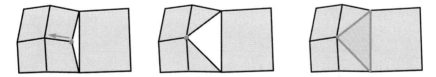

Figure 7-8. Handling T-Junctions
Left: A T-junction causes a crack in the mesh. Middle: The vertex at the T-junction is replaced with one away from the edge. Right: The crack is filled with a triangle.

7.2 Displacement Mapping

Displacement mapping is a method for adding geometric complexity to a simple, lightweight model. A displacement map is a texture map containing a scalar value per texel that describes how much the surface to which it is applied should be displaced in the direction of its normal. Unlike bump or normal maps, displacement maps change the actual geometry of the surface, not just the surface normal.

There are several reasons to add displacement mapping to subdivision surfaces. First, subdivision surfaces provide a nice, smooth surface from which to displace, even when animated. Second, they are very compact. The control mesh does not need any normal and tangent data, like polygon models, because they are derived during tessellation. Third, it is easy to modify our subdivision surface shaders to support adaptive displacement mapping.

7.2.1 Changing the Flatness Test

The trick to efficient displacement mapping is adding geometry where it is really needed. We can modify our flatness test so that more geometry is added if the maximum displacement is greater than the flatness threshold. Because the flatness is tested per edge, we create a table using the displacement map containing the maximum displacement on either side of each edge. Figure 7-9 shows a 2D representation of how the maximum distance is calculated for each level of subdivision. Note that all the low-resolution mesh points are located on the displaced surface, because that is where the tessellated vertices are positioned. In the flatness-test shaders, we add the edge's maximum displacement value to the error distance before comparing it to the flatness threshold. All that is left to do geometry-wise is to add the displacement from the displacement map to the vertex position in the limit shaders.

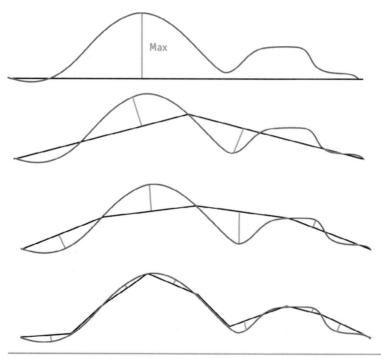

Figure 7-9. Four Steps of the Maximum Displacement Calculation

7.2.2 Shading Using Normal Mapping

We use normal mapping to take the displacement into account when shading the surface, instead of adjusting the vertex normals. See Figure 7-10 for an example. This technique has a couple of advantages. First, normal mapping is done per pixel, so it generally allows more detailed shading than is possible with vertex normals. More important, the surface does not appear to pop when animated, as the amount of geometry changes due to adaptive tessellation. Normal mapping requires some extra attributes from the tessellator: a tangent, and normal map texture coordinates.

Figure 7-10. An Example of Displacement Mapping
The displacement and normal maps (top) were used to change the appearance of the low-resolution model from smooth (left) to detailed (right). Creature model courtesy of Bay Raitt, Boxrocket Entertainment.

7.3 Conclusion

We have described a method to tessellate subdivision surfaces on the GPU using subdivision with a breadth-first recursion algorithm. We described the shaders necessary to perform flatness testing, to carry out the subdivision, and to compute the limit surface attributes. We also explained how to modify the shaders to add displacement-mapping support for increasing the geometric detail of subdivision surface models.

7.4 References

Catmull, E., and J. Clark. 1978. "Recursively Generated B-Spline Surfaces on Arbitrary Topology Meshes." *Computer Aided Design* 10(6), pp. 350–355.

DeRose, T., M. Kass, and T. Truong. 1998. "Subdivision Surfaces in Character Animation." In *Computer Graphics (Proceedings of SIGGRAPH 98)*, pp. 85–94.

Halstead, M., M. Kass, and T. DeRose. 1993. "Efficient, Fair Interpolation Using Catmull-Clark Surfaces." In *Computer Graphics (Proceedings of SIGGRAPH 93)*, pp. 35–44.

Chapter 8

Per-Pixel Displacement Mapping with Distance Functions

William Donnelly
University of Waterloo

In this chapter, we present distance mapping, a technique for adding small-scale displacement mapping to objects in a pixel shader. We treat displacement mapping as a ray-tracing problem, beginning with texture coordinates on the base surface and calculating texture coordinates where the viewing ray intersects the displaced surface. For this purpose, we precompute a three-dimensional distance map, which gives a measure of the distance between points in space and the displaced surface. This distance map gives us all the information necessary to quickly intersect a ray with the surface. Our algorithm significantly increases the perceived geometric complexity of a scene while maintaining real-time performance.

8.1 Introduction

Cook (1984) introduced displacement mapping as a method for adding small-scale detail to surfaces. Unlike bump mapping, which affects only the shading of surfaces, displacement mapping adjusts the positions of surface elements. This leads to effects not possible with bump mapping, such as surface features that occlude each other and nonpolygonal silhouettes. Figure 8-1 shows a rendering of a stone surface in which occlusion between features contributes to the illusion of depth.

The usual implementation of displacement mapping iteratively tessellates a base surface, pushing vertices out along the normal of the base surface, and continuing until

Figure 8-1. A Displaced Stone Surface
Displacement mapping (top) gives an illusion of depth not possible with bump mapping alone (bottom).

the polygons generated are close to the size of a single pixel. Michael Bunnell presents this approach in Chapter 7 of this book, "Adaptive Tessellation of Subdivision Surfaces with Displacement Mapping."

Although it seems most logical to implement displacement mapping in the vertex shading stage of the pipeline, this is not possible because of the vertex shader's inability to generate new vertices. This leads us to consider techniques that rely on the pixel shader. Using a pixel shader is a good idea for several reasons:

- **Current GPUs have more pixel-processing power than they have vertex-processing power.** For example, the GeForce 6800 Ultra has 16 pixel-shading pipelines to its 6 vertex-shading pipelines. In addition, a single pixel pipeline is often able to perform more operations per clock cycle than a single vertex pipeline.

- **Pixel shaders are better equipped to access textures.** Many GPUs do not allow texture access within a vertex shader; and for those that do, the access modes are limited, and they come with a performance cost.

- **The amount of pixel processing scales with distance.** The vertex shader always executes once for each vertex in the model, but the pixel shader executes only once per pixel on the screen. This means work is concentrated on nearby objects, where it is needed most.

A disadvantage of using the pixel shader is that we cannot alter a pixel's screen coordinate within the shader. This means that unlike an approach based on tessellation, an approach that uses the pixel shader cannot be used for arbitrarily large displacements. This is not a severe limitation, however, because displacements are almost always bounded in practice.

8.2 Previous Work

Parallax mapping is a simple way to augment bump mapping to include parallax effects (Kaneko et al. 2001). Parallax mapping uses the information about the height of a surface at a single point to offset the texture coordinates either toward or away from the viewer. Although this is a crude approximation valid only for smoothly varying height fields, it gives surprisingly good results, particularly given that it can be implemented with only three extra shader instructions. Unfortunately, because of the inherent assumptions of the technique, it cannot handle large displacements, high-frequency features, or occlusion between features.

Relief mapping as presented by Policarpo (2004) uses a root-finding approach on a height map. It begins by transforming the viewing ray into texture space. It then performs a linear search to locate an intersection with the surface, followed by a binary search to find a precise intersection point. Unfortunately, linear search requires a fixed step size. This means that in order to resolve small details, it is necessary to increase the number of steps, forcing the user to trade accuracy for performance. Our algorithm does not have this trade-off: it automatically adjusts the step size as necessary to provide fine detail near the surface, while skipping large areas of empty space away from the surface.

View-dependent displacement mapping (Wang et al. 2003) and its extension, generalized displacement mapping (Wang et al. 2004), treat displacement mapping as a ray-tracing problem. They store the result of all possible ray intersection queries within a three-dimensional volume in a five-dimensional map indexed by three position coordinates and two angular coordinates. This map is then compressed by singular value decomposition, and decompressed in a pixel shader at runtime. Because the data is five-dimensional, it requires a significant amount of preprocessing and storage.

The algorithm for displacement rendering we present here is based on sphere tracing (Hart 1996), a technique developed to accelerate ray tracing of implicit surfaces. The concept is the same, but instead of applying the algorithm to ray tracing of implicit surfaces, we apply it to the rendering of displacement maps on the GPU.

8.3 The Distance-Mapping Algorithm

Suppose we want to apply a displacement map to a plane. We can think of the surface as being bounded by an axis-aligned box. The conventional displacement algorithm would render the bottom face of the box and push vertices upward. Our algorithm instead renders the top plane of the box. Then within the shader, we find which point on the displaced surface the viewer would have really seen.

In a sense, we are computing the inverse problem to conventional displacement mapping. Displacement mapping asks, "For this piece of geometry, what pixel in the image does it map to?" Our algorithm asks, "For this pixel in the image, what piece of geometry do we see?" While the first approach is the one used by rasterization algorithms, the second approach is the one used by ray-tracing algorithms. So we approach distance mapping as a ray-tracing problem.

A common ray-tracing approach is to sample the height map at uniformly spaced locations to test whether the viewing ray has intersected the surface. Unfortunately, we encounter the following problem: as long as our samples are spaced farther apart than a single texel, we cannot guarantee that we have not missed an intersection that lies between our samples. This problem is illustrated in Figure 8-2. These "overshoots" can cause gaps in the rendered geometry and can result in severe aliasing. Thus we have two options: either we accept artifacts from undersampling, or we must take a sample for each texel along the viewing ray. Figure 8-3 shows that our algorithm can render objects with fine detail without any aliasing or gaps in geometry.

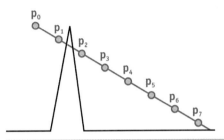

Figure 8-2. A Difficult Case for Displacement Algorithms
An algorithm that takes fixed-size steps misses an important piece of geometry.

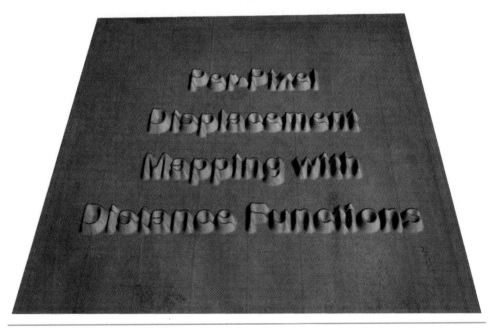

Figure 8-3. Rendering Displaced Text
Because of the fine detail, text is a difficult case for some per-pixel displacement algorithms, particularly those based on uniformly spaced sampling. Note that our algorithm correctly captures occlusion between letters without aliasing.

We can draw two conclusions from the preceding example:

1. We cannot simply query the height map at fixed intervals. It either leads to undersampling artifacts or results in an intractable algorithm.

2. We need more information at our disposal than just a height field; we need to know how far apart we can take our samples in any given region without overshooting the surface.

To solve these problems, we define the distance map of the surface. For any point p in texture space and a surface S, we define a function $\text{dist}(p, S) = \min\{d(p, q) : q \text{ in } S\}$. In other words, $\text{dist}(p, S)$ is the shortest distance from p to the closest point on the surface S. The distance map for S is then simply a 3D texture that stores, for each point p, the value of $\text{dist}(p, S)$. Figure 8-4 shows a sample one-dimensional height map and its corresponding distance map.

This distance map gives us exactly the information we need to choose our sampling positions. Suppose we have a ray with origin p_0 and direction vector $\mathbf{d}$, where $\mathbf{d}$ is normalized to unit length. We define a new point $p_1 = p_0 + \text{dist}(p_0, S) \times \mathbf{d}$. This point has the important property that if p_0 is outside the surface, then p_1 is also outside the surface. We then apply the same operation again by defining $p_2 = p_1 + \text{dist}(p_1, S) \times \mathbf{d}$, and so on. Each consecutive point is a little bit closer to the surface. Thus, if we take enough samples, our points converge toward the closest intersection of the ray with the surface. Figure 8-5 illustrates the effectiveness of this algorithm.

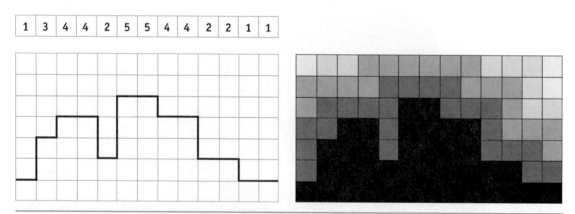

Figure 8-4. A Sample Distance Map in Two Dimensions
Left, top: A one-dimensional height map as an array. Left, bottom: The height map visualized in two dimensions. Right: The corresponding two-dimensional distance map.

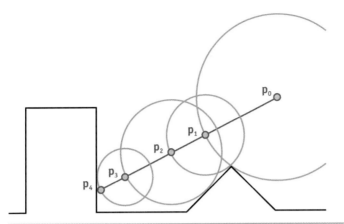

Figure 8-5. Sphere Tracing

A ray begins at point p_0. We then determine the distance to the closest point on the surface. Geometrically we can imagine expanding a sphere S_0 around p_0 until it intersects the surface. Point p_1 is then the intersection between the ray and the sphere. We repeat this process, generating points $p_2..p_4$. We can see from the diagram that point p_4 is effectively the intersection point with the surface, and so in this case the algorithm has converged in four iterations.

It is worth noting that distance functions do not apply only to height fields. In fact, a distance map can represent arbitrary voxelized data. This means that it would be possible to render small-scale detail with complex topology. For example, chain mail could be rendered in this manner.

8.3.1 Arbitrary Meshes

Up to this point, we have discussed applying distance mapping only to planes. We would like to apply distance mapping to general meshes. We do so by assuming the surface is locally planar. Based on this assumption, we can perform the same calculations as in the planar case, using the local tangent frame of the surface. We use the local surface tangents to transform the view vector into tangent space, just as we would transform the light vector for tangent space normal mapping. Once we have transformed the viewing ray into tangent space, the algorithm proceeds exactly as in the planar case.

Now that we know how to use a distance map for ray tracing, we need to know how to efficiently compute a distance map for an arbitrary height field.

8.4 Computing the Distance Map

Computing a distance transform is a well-studied problem. Danielsson (1980) has presented an algorithm that runs in $O(n)$ time, where n is the number of pixels in the map. The idea is to create a 3D map where each pixel stores a 3D displacement vector to the nearest point on the surface. The algorithm then performs a small number of sequential sweeps over the 3D domain, updating each pixel's displacement vector based on neighboring displacement vectors. Once the displacements have been calculated, the distance for each pixel is computed as the magnitude of the displacement. An implementation of this algorithm is on the book's CD.

When the distance transform algorithm is finished, we have computed the distance from each pixel in the distance map to the closest point on the surface, measured in pixels. To make these distances lie in the range [0, 1], we divide each distance by the depth of the 3D texture in pixels.

8.5 The Shaders

8.5.1 The Vertex Shader

The vertex shader for distance mapping, shown in Listing 8-1, is remarkably similar to a vertex shader for tangent-space normal mapping, with two notable differences. The first is that in addition to transforming the light vector into tangent space, we also transform the viewing direction into tangent space. This tangent-space eye vector is used in the vertex shader as the direction of the ray to be traced in texture space. The second difference is that we incorporate an additional factor inversely proportional to the perceived depth. This allows us to adjust the scale of the displacements interactively.

8.5.2 The Fragment Shader

We now have all we need to begin our ray marching: we have a starting point (the base texture coordinate passed down by the vertex shader) and a direction (the tangent-space view vector).

The first thing the fragment shader has to do is to normalize the direction vector. Note that distances stored in the distance map are measured in units proportional to pixels; the direction vector is measured in units of texture coordinates. Generally, the distance map is much higher and wider than it is deep, and so these two measures of distance are quite different. To ensure that our vector is normalized with respect to the measure of distance used by the distance map, we first normalize the direction vector, and then

Listing 8-1. The Vertex Shader

```
v2fConnector distanceVertex(a2vConnector a2v,
  uniform float4x4 modelViewProj,
  uniform float3 eyeCoord,
  uniform float3 lightCoord,
  uniform float invBumpDepth)
{
  v2fConnector v2f;

  // Project position into screen space
  // and pass through texture coordinate
  v2f.projCoord = mul(modelViewProj, float4(a2v.objCoord, 1));
  v2f.texCoord = float3(a2v.texCoord, 1);

  // Transform the eye vector into tangent space.
  // Adjust the slope in tangent space based on bump depth
  float3 eyeVec = eyeCoord - a2v.objCoord;
  float3 tanEyeVec;
  tanEyeVec.x = dot(a2v.objTangent, eyeVec);
  tanEyeVec.y = dot(a2v.objBinormal, eyeVec);
  tanEyeVec.z = -invBumpDepth * dot(a2v.objNormal, eyeVec);
  v2f.tanEyeVec = tanEyeVec;

  // Transform the light vector into tangent space.
  // We will use this later for tangent-space normal mapping
  float3 lightVec = lightCoord - a2v.objCoord;
  float3 tanLightVec;
  tanLightVec.x = dot(a2v.objTangent, lightVec);
  tanLightVec.y = dot(a2v.objBinormal, lightVec);
  tanLightVec.z = dot(a2v.objNormal, lightVec);
  v2f.tanLightVec = tanLightVec;

  return v2f;
}
```

multiply this normalized vector by an extra "normalization factor" of (*depth*/*width*, *depth*/*height*, 1).

We can now proceed to march our ray iteratively. We begin by querying the distance map, to obtain a conservative estimate of the distance we can march along the ray without intersecting the surface. We can then step our current position forward by that distance to obtain another point outside the surface. We can proceed in this way to generate a sequence of points that converges toward the displaced surface. Finally, once we have the texture coordinates of the intersection point, we compute normal-mapped lighting in tangent space. Listing 8-2 shows the fragment shader.

8.5.3 A Note on Filtering

When sampling textures, we must be careful about how to specify derivatives for texture lookups. In general, the displaced texture coordinates have discontinuities (for example, due to sections of the texture that are occluded). When mipmapping or anisotropic filtering is enabled, the GPU needs information about the derivatives of the texture coordinates. Because the GPU approximates derivatives with finite differences, these derivatives have incorrect values at discontinuities. This leads to an incorrect choice of mipmap levels, which in turn leads to visible seams around discontinuities.

Instead of using the derivatives of the displaced texture coordinates, we substitute the derivatives of the base texture coordinates. This works because displaced texture coordinates are always continuous, and they vary at approximately the same rate as the base texture coordinates.

Because we do not use the GPU's mechanism for determining mipmap levels, it is possible to have texture aliasing. In practice, this is not a big problem, because the derivatives of the base texture coordinates are a good approximation of the derivatives of the displaced texture coordinates.

Note that the same argument about mipmap levels also applies to lookups into the distance map. Because the texture coordinates can be discontinuous around feature edges, the texture unit will access a mipmap level that is too coarse. This in turn results in incorrect distance values. Our solution is to filter the distance map linearly without any mipmaps. Because the distance map values are never visualized directly, aliasing does not result from the lack of mipmapping here.

8.6 Results

We implemented the distance-mapping algorithm in OpenGL and Cg as well as in Sh (http://www.libsh.org). The images in this chapter were created with the Sh implementation, which is available on the accompanying CD. Because of the large number of dependent texture reads and the use of derivative instructions, the implementation works only on GeForce FX and GeForce 6 Series GPUs.

Listing 8-2. The Fragment Shader

```
f2fConnector distanceFragment(v2fConnector v2f,
  uniform sampler2D colorTex,
  uniform sampler2D normalTex,
  uniform sampler3D distanceTex,
  uniform float3 normalizationFactor)
{
  f2fConnector f2f;

  // Normalize the offset vector in texture space.
  // The normalization factor ensures we are normalized with respect
  // to a distance which is defined in terms of pixels.
  float3 offset = normalize(v2f.tanEyeVec);
  offset *= normalizationFactor;

  float3 texCoord = v2f.texCoord;

  // March a ray
  for (int i = 0; i < NUM_ITERATIONS; i++) {
    float distance = f1tex3D(distanceTex, texCoord);
    texCoord += distance * offset;
  }

  // Compute derivatives of unperturbed texcoords.
  // This is because the offset texcoords will have discontinuities
  // which lead to incorrect filtering.
  float2 dx = ddx(v2f.texCoord.xy);
  float2 dy = ddy(v2f.texCoord.xy);

  // Do bump-mapped lighting in tangent space.
  // 'normalTex' stores tangent-space normals remapped
  // into the range [0, 1].
  float3 tanNormal = 2 * f3tex2D(normalTex, texCoord.xy, dx, dy) - 1;
  float3 tanLightVec = normalize(v2f.tanLightVec);
  float diffuse = dot(tanNormal, tanLightVec);

  // Multiply diffuse lighting by texture color
  f2f.COL.rgb = diffuse * f3tex2D(colorTex, texCoord.xy, dx, dy);
  f2f.COL.a = 1;

  return f2f;
}
```

In all examples in this chapter, we have used a 3D texture size of $256 \times 256 \times 16$, but this choice may be highly data-dependent. We also experimented with maps up to $512 \times 512 \times 32$ for complex data sets. We set the value of NUM_ITERATIONS to 16 iterations for our examples. In most cases, this was more than sufficient, with 8 iterations sufficing for smoother data sets.

Our fragment shader, assuming 16 iterations, compiles to 48 instructions for the GeForce FX. Each iteration of the loop takes 2 instructions: a texture lookup followed by a multiply-add. GeForce FX and GeForce 6 Series GPUs can execute this pair of operations in a single clock cycle, meaning that each iteration takes only one clock cycle. It should be noted that each texture lookup depends on the previous one; on GPUs that limit the number of indirect texture operations, this shader needs to be broken up into multiple passes.

We tested our distance-mapping implementation on a GeForce FX 5950 Ultra and on a GeForce 6800 GT with several different data sets. One such data set is pictured in Figure 8-6. On the GeForce FX 5950 Ultra, we can shade every pixel at 1024×768 resolution at approximately 30 frames per second. If we reduce the number of iterations to 8, we obtain approximately 75 frames per second at the same resolution. On the GeForce 6800 GT, we were able to run at a consistent 70 frames per second, even shading every pixel at 1280×1024 resolution with 16 iterations.

8.7 Conclusion

We have presented distance mapping, a fast iterative technique for displacement mapping based on ray tracing of implicit surfaces. We show that the information contained in a distance function allows us to take larger steps when rays are farther from the surface, while ensuring that we never take a step so large that we create gaps in the rendered geometry. The resulting implementation is very efficient; it converges in a few iterations, and each iteration costs only a single cycle on GeForce FX and GeForce 6 Series GPUs.

In the future we would like to use the dynamic branching capabilities of Shader Model 3 GPUs to improve the performance of our technique by taking "early outs" for pixels that converge quickly. This would allow us to increase the quality of the technique by devoting more computing power to pixels that converge more slowly.

We would also like to adapt our technique to curved surfaces. Although our algorithm can be used on any model with appropriate tangents, it results in distortion in regions

Figure 8-6. A Grating Rendered with Displacement Mapping

of high curvature. In particular, generalized displacement mapping (Wang et al. 2004) uses a type of tetrahedral projection to account for curved surfaces, and this method can also be applied to our algorithm. Such a tetrahedral projection can be accomplished in a vertex shader (Wylie et al. 2002).

8.8 References

Cook, Robert L. 1984. "Shade Trees." In *Computer Graphics (Proceedings of SIGGRAPH 84)* 18(3), pp. 223–231.

Danielsson, Per-Erik. 1980. "Euclidean Distance Mapping." *Computer Graphics and Image Processing* 14, pp. 227–248.

Hart, John C. 1996. "Sphere Tracing: A Geometric Method for the Antialiased Ray Tracing of Implicit Surfaces." *The Visual Computer* 12(10), pp. 527–545.

Kaneko, Tomomichi, Toshiyuki Takahei, Masahiko Inami, Naoki Kawakami, Yasuyuki Yanagida, Taro Maeda, and Susumu Tachi. 2001. "Detailed Shape Representation with Parallax Mapping." In *Proceedings of the ICAT 2001 (The 11th International Conference on Artificial Reality and Telexistence)*, Tokyo, December 2001, pp. 205–208.

Policarpo, Fabio. 2004. "Relief Mapping in a Pixel Shader Using Binary Search." **http://www.paralelo.com.br/arquivos/ReliefMapping.pdf**

Wang, Lifeng, Xi Wang, Xin Tong, Stephen Lin, Shimin Hu, Baining Guo, and Heung-Yeung Shum. 2003. "View-Dependent Displacement Mapping." *ACM Transactions on Graphics (Proceedings of SIGGRAPH 2003)* 22(3), pp. 334–339.

Wang, Xi, Xin Tong, Stephen Lin, Shimin Hu, Baining Guo, and Heung-Yeung Shum. 2004. "Generalized Displacement Maps." In *Eurographics Symposium on Rendering 2004*, pp. 227–234.

Wylie, Brian, Kenneth Moreland, Lee Ann Fisk, and Patricia Crossno. 2002. "Tetrahedral Projection Using Vertex Shaders." In *Proceedings of IEEE Volume Visualization and Graphics Symposium 2002*, October 2002, pp. 7–12.

Special thanks to Stefanus Du Toit for his help implementing the distance transform and writing the Sh implementation.

PART II
SHADING, LIGHTING, AND SHADOWS

The subject of shading, lighting, and shadows is a broad one, which touches many areas of real-time 3D applications, from the low-level instructions that determine how a pixel is colored or a vertex is positioned, to the higher-level ideas that govern the content creation and art pipeline.

Each year, GPUs with more and more features and higher performance become available; much of that extra power and flexibility is poured into "solving" the problem of creating realistic shading, lighting, and shadows. But we are decidedly not there yet, and we may never be. Every current algorithm for real-time shadows, for example, has artifacts in certain cases, or performance problems in others, or most likely both. Similarly with lighting: you often have to trade interactivity or scene complexity for quality. This part of the book is all about making good choices among these trade-offs and creating great-looking and fast real-time renderings.

In **Chapter 9, "Deferred Shading in *S.T.A.L.K.E.R.*," Oles Shishkovtsov** of GSC Game World details the deferred shading architecture developed for the game *S.T.A.L.K.E.R.* Deferred shading has gained popularity lately, but there are a number of nonobvious pitfalls when one goes to implement this approach. This chapter covers solutions to these problems and explains how to create a robust, flexible, and fast deferred renderer.

Irradiance environment maps enable fast, high-quality diffuse and specular lighting, with one significant caveat: the lighting environment must be static. **Gary King** of NVIDIA shows how to avoid this limitation in **Chapter 10, "Real-Time Computation of Dynamic Irradiance Environment Maps"** by using newer GPU features to dramatically accelerate irradiance map creation, making it feasible in real time for use with dynamic scenes.

Accurately rendering complex materials such as denim and wool is a tricky business; the usual texture-mapping approaches don't give realistic results for such materials. In **Chapter 11, "Approximate Bidirectional Texture Functions," Jan Kautz** of the Massachusetts Institute of Technology presents a method for approximating BTFs (which are a very general description of a material's properties) using precomputation combined with a runtime calculation that is just a fairly simple pixel shader looking up into a volume texture.

The amount of texture detail possible in a scene often has the single greatest impact on the overall visual quality; however, texture detail is often fundamentally limited by hardware texture-size constraints and texture memory space issues. In **Chapter 12, "Tile-Based Texture Mapping," Li-Yi Wei** of NVIDIA works around these restrictions by synthesizing larger virtual textures at runtime from a smaller set of texture tiles using pixel shaders.

The increased flexibility of modern GPUs is rapidly narrowing the gap between renderings that traditionally could only be done using software algorithms and those that are fully hardware-accelerated. In **Chapter 13, "Implementing the mental images Phenomena Renderer on the GPU," Martin-Karl Lefrançois** of mental images introduces the architecture of the mental ray renderer, used in the production of numerous feature films, and describes the implementation of its GPU-accelerated components.

The algorithms usually employed for ambient occlusion and indirect lighting are confined to limited environments that cannot be animated, thus limiting their usefulness. In **Chapter 14, "Dynamic Ambient Occlusion and Indirect Lighting," Michael Bunnell** of NVIDIA describes a technique for accelerating the computation of ambient occlusion and indirect lighting using the GPU, turning the algorithms into real-time solutions.

When visualizing complex objects and architectures, perfect photorealism is often not ideal for understanding structures and object relationships, and non-photorealistic techniques are necessary to aid comprehension. **Marc Nienhaus** and **Jürgen Döllner** of the University of Potsdam explain some techniques that make good use of the latest features of modern GPUs for achieving this goal in real time in **Chapter 15, "Blueprint Rendering and 'Sketchy Drawings.'"**

In **Chapter 16, "Accurate Atmospheric Scattering," Sean O'Neil** presents a flexible real-time hardware-accelerated technique for simulating atmospheric scattering that works as well on the ground as it does from space, producing some truly gorgeous visuals.

In *GPU Gems* (Addison-Wesley, 2004), efficient, high-quality soft shadows were the focus of a number of chapters. **Yury Uralsky** of NVIDIA shows there's still a lot of life left in the topic in **Chapter 17, "Efficient Soft-Edged Shadows Using Pixel Shader Branching."** Yury covers techniques for rendering high-quality soft shadow edges as well as optimization techniques based on using pixel shader early-outs to minimize shadow computation cost.

Yuri Kryachko of 1C:Maddox Games presents an overview of the water effect from the game *Pacific Fighters* in **Chapter 18, "Using Vertex Texture Displacement for Realistic Water Rendering."** The technique uses the ability of newer GPUs to perform texture fetches at the vertices of a mesh to do true displacement mapping on the water surface, resulting in very high quality and efficient animated water that looks incredibly realistic.

Finally, **Tiago Sousa** of Crytek introduces a technique for simulating refractive surfaces such as water or glass in **Chapter 19, "Generic Refraction Simulation."** This technique is a generalization of an effect used in the popular game *Far Cry*.

Looking back on the year since writing my introduction to the Lighting and Shadows section of the original *GPU Gems*, it's clear that the pace of innovation has not slowed. Indeed, many of the techniques in this section were simply impossible to achieve a year ago, and many others were impractical. I, for one, can't wait to see what new techniques people come up with in the year ahead!

Cem Cebenoyan, NVIDIA

Chapter 9

Deferred Shading in *S.T.A.L.K.E.R.*

Oles Shishkovtsov
GSC Game World

This chapter is a post-mortem of almost two years of research and development on a renderer that is based solely on deferred shading and 100 percent dynamic lighting, targeted at high-end GPUs. Because no single solution can suit all needs, this chapter should not be considered a comprehensive guide to performing deferred shading.

9.1 Introduction

For those who are not familiar with the concepts of deferred shading, we recommend Hargreaves and Harris 2004. This presentation is a good introduction to the basics, and it briefly showcases a number of techniques originally developed for and used in the game *S.T.A.L.K.E.R.* With deferred shading, during scene-geometry rendering, we don't have to bother with any lighting; instead, we just output lighting properties such as the position and normal of each pixel. Later we apply lighting as a 2D post-process using this intermediate buffer—usually called a *G-buffer* (Saito and Takahashi 1990)—as input to the lighting shader.

When most people first think about deferred shading, they envision nice algorithmic properties such as perfect depth complexity for lighting, predictable performance proportional to the lights' screen-space areas, simplified scene management, and more. One additional crucial fact is usually missed: the ability to cut down on large numbers of batches, which are inevitable when dynamic shadows come into the game. Ask a representative of your favorite IHV, who will say that many games are still CPU-limited. Reduced CPU usage was one of the main reasons we chose deferred shading in *S.T.A.L.K.E.R.* Another factor was that forward shading engines (with traditional immediate shading architectures, such as those in *Doom 3* or *Far Cry*) usually unnecessarily pay the high cost of repeating the same work—vertex transform, anisotropic texture filtering, parallax mapping, normal map decompression, detail texturing, and so on. In the case of *S.T.A.L.K.E.R.*, where we were limited both by CPU and by vertex processing and had moderate overdraw, we had almost the ideal case for deferred shading. So, to meet our goal and to raise the visual bar—rendering high-quality, high-polygon content with fully dynamic lighting and shadowing—deferred shading was the inevitable choice. Figures 9-1 and 9-2 show examples of a scene generated by our forward shading and deferred shading renderers, respectively.

Figure 9-1. Screenshot from the First, Forward Shading Renderer
The original renderer was based on DirectX 8.

Figure 9-2. Screenshot from the Second, Deferred Shading Renderer
The second renderer targets DirectX 9-class hardware.

9.2 The Myths

The first myth—"Deferred shading is slow on current hardware"—arises mostly from the fact that the current generation of games tries to load-balance most of the lighting work between the vertex and pixel pipelines. When all the calculations are performed at pixel level (this is the only possible way to go with deferred shading), performance will be similar, because lighting pixel shaders for deferred renderers are not that much more complicated than those for forward renderers. The only added work is G-buffer sampling and, possibly, unpacking. But your application is much less likely to become bottlenecked by the CPU or the vertex pipe. The actual mileage will vary depending on the data set and, more important, on your rendering engine's actual *overdraw*, measured as the number of pixels passing the z-test divided by the screen area.

Another myth is that deferred shading is useless for rendering directional lights. In *S.T.A.L.K.E.R.*'s case, this is true for scenes with a few unshadowed directional lights; but it's false even for a single, shadow-casting directional light (such as the sun). A more detailed explanation appears in Section 9.3.2, on the optimization of the lighting phase.

Because deferred renderers process each object only once, conventional techniques for handling multiple material types (such as changing shaders per-object) do not translate well. However, by using DirectX 9 multiple render targets (MRT), we can render up to 16 material attributes during the G-buffer creation phase (four render targets of four floating-point numbers each). Ten are used to perform basic diffuse and specular lighting (three each for albedo, normal, and position, plus one for gloss), but this leaves six components for controlling the lighting functions. In *S.T.A.L.K.E.R.*, we stored material and object IDs in the spare components and defined functions in each light shader (accelerated using 2D and 3D texture lookup tables) that depended on these values. This freed us from a specific material reflection model, while also allowing us to define a huge number of light shader primitives without the combinatorial increase in the number of shaders that affects forward renderers. In addition to the traditional point, spot, and directional light primitives, we also had special light sources such as wrapped hemispherical sources and volumetric fog. This approach can be considered an inversion of the shaders in forward renderers: instead of using light properties to modify material shaders, we used material properties to modify light shaders. By adapting our material system to take advantage of the benefits of deferred shading and using textures to efficiently avoid some of the limitations, we created a deferred rendering engine in which the only limits on the types of materials were the artists' and programmers' imaginations.

During the writing of this chapter, *S.T.A.L.K.E.R.* was in the process of synchronizing the material look between two renderers: the first one targeted at DirectX 8-class hardware, and a second one targeted at high-end DirectX 9-class hardware. An interesting discovery was that more than 90 percent of materials used in the first renderer were just simple modifiers to the base albedo and emissive terms, plus a few that affected the position and surface normal. Examples are the waving of trees or grass under the wind, or different sorts of detail texturing. These modifications were performed identically in every rendering pass, so there was almost a direct mapping to the forward phase of the second renderer, the G-buffer creation phase.

9.3 Optimizations

Delivering a product that pushes the newest graphics hardware to its limits while still offering a playable game requires a great deal of planning. Both technical and artistic decisions must consider the target audience and the target hardware. Failing to do so may result in significant wasted effort. This happened to us when we changed the target for *S.T.A.L.K.E.R.*'s first renderer from fixed-function T&L (DirectX 7-class) GPUs to first-generation pixel shading (DirectX 8-class) GPUs; we had to rewrite much of our tool set and engine to accommodate the change. Our goals for *S.T.A.L.K.E.R.*'s second (deferred) renderer were for it to be a drop-in replacement for the first renderer (so it would work on the same data set and content, except for the lighting environment), and for it to run with "maximal eye candy" at 30 frames per second on a GeForce 6800 Ultra at 1024×768 resolution. We encouraged our designers to complicate the second renderer's lighting environment whenever the performance exceeded this target.

9.3.1 What to Optimize

Given the structure of a deferred renderer, the obvious places that are likely to be performance bottlenecks are deferring, lighting, and post-processing. Our *S.T.A.L.K.E.R.* performance testing confirmed this:

- Average number of lights per frame in closed spaces: 50
- Average number of lights per pixel in closed spaces: 5
- Average number of lights per pixel in open spaces: less than 1
- Average geometric depth complexity: 2.5

Because one of the primary features of the second renderer is real-time shadowing, shadow creation was a significant bottleneck; in fact, in some scenes it turned out to be the largest individual bottleneck. Given this, our optimization goals were obvious:

- Limit the number of lights drawn to just those that affect the rendered image.
- Convert shadow-casting lights to unshadowed lights where possible.
- Simplify the lighting shaders as much as possible.
- Optimize post-processing and deferring passes, but not at the expense of quality.

We decided to favor quality over performance for the G-buffer creation and post-processing (G-buffer shading) passes because these have tightly bounded costs, whereas a game player is free to drop multiple torches in the same place, making lighting arbitrarily expensive. Also, most artists are comfortable optimizing for forward renderers (by reducing the number of polygons or the resolution of textures, adding good occluders, and so on), and these optimizations also benefit the deferring pass.

9.3.2 Lighting Optimizations

The most important optimization for the lighting pass is to render only those lights that actually affect the final image, and for those lights, render only the affected pixels. For *S.T.A.L.K.E.R.*, we used a hierarchical occlusion-culling system that utilized both the CPU and the GPU. Our coarsest test was sector-portal culling followed by CPU-based occlusion culling (similar to the hierarchical z-buffer [Greene et al. 1993]). In a typical closed-space frame, this reduced the number of lights by up to 30 to 50 percent. Then we used DirectX 9's occlusion query to eliminate the completely occluded lights. Finally, we used a stencil mask to tag affected pixels for each light. All together, these culling optimizations resulted in a twofold or even larger performance increase.

Even with perfect culling, though, lighting is still the most expensive aspect of a deferred renderer. Therefore, it is important to make sure that the shaders and artistic properties of the light sources are optimized as much as possible. About half of the time we spent creating *S.T.A.L.K.E.R.*'s deferred renderer was devoted to searching for ways to squeeze additional cycles out of our lighting shaders. The primary artistic decisions we made were these:

- **Does the light need to cast shadows?**
  - Many lights are needed only to mimic a global illumination-style look, and shadows just ruin the illusion.
- **Does the light need a projective image?**
  - If so, maybe the projection is the same as the shadow-map projection (which saves a few dp4s)?
- **Does the light need to cast shadows from translucent surfaces?** See Figure 9-3.
  - If so, are there any translucent surfaces that exist in the light's frustum?
  - If both projective image and translucent color-modifier are required, maybe we can combine them into one image?
- **Does the light need to contribute to glossy specular reflection?**
  - Many lights in *S.T.A.L.K.E.R.* were added to mimic global illumination. For these lights, we used very simple diffuse-only lighting.

Figure 9-3. Cast Shadows from Translucent Objects

- **Does the light move?**
  - If it doesn't, we precomputed shadow-caster visibility to make shadow generation more efficient, by incrementally testing visibility for primitives that are found to be static to each other in a particular light configuration, thus forming a conservative potentially visible set (PVS) with a set of rules that can invalidate parts of it.

Additionally, we made some special optimizations for directional lights (such as the sun).

Optimizing the Sun

Although large-scale shadow mapping from directional light sources is a quite interesting and difficult problem, it is beyond the scope of this chapter. We used a single 2048×2048-pixel shadow map for most of the sun lighting, using a perspective shadow map-style projection transform to maximize area near the viewer. A demo showcasing a variety of related techniques can be found in King 2004. Sun shadows need very careful filtering and therefore have a relatively high per-pixel cost, so we want to skip as much work as possible; this is where deferred shading comes in. The first optimization comes from the fact that the sky box doesn't need to be shaded, and it occupies a significant part of the screen (30 to 40 percent is common in a typical outdoor environment). Also, in average configurations of the viewer and sun direction, approximately 50 percent of pixels face away from the sun and don't need to have complex shading applied. Finally, the pixels that have an ambient occlusion term of zero cannot be reached by sun rays, so they can also be excluded from processing. We use a shader to quickly determine these conditions per-pixel, and store the results in a stencil mask so that the GPU's hierarchical culling hardware can avoid applying complex shading on these pixels.

The final algorithm for sunlight accumulation is shown in Listing 9-1.

Note: There is an option to use a single-sample shadow term in pass 0 to avoid the lighting and shadow filtering cost for points in shadow. This doesn't work in practice because (1) the performance was lower, and (2) a single sample is insufficient, because the percentage-closer filtering (PCF) kernel in pass 1 is quite large.

This idea is more useful for Pixel Shader 3.0 dynamic branching, because it has high screen-space coherence and because these shadow samples can be utilized in the final computation. This is left as an exercise for the reader.

We can compute the theoretical performance increase due to this stencil mask: assuming that 15 percent of pixels have an ambient occlusion of zero, and 30 percent of the frame is occupied by the sky, the expected percentage of pixels that will be shaded is $(1 - 0.3) \times 0.5 \times (1 - 0.15) \approx 30$ percent, or about a $3\times$ increase in frames per second. The actual performance increase measured in *S.T.A.L.K.E.R.* was close to $2\times$.

Listing 9-1. Pseudocode for Sunlight Accumulation

```
Pass 0: Render full-screen quad only where 0x03==stencil count
        (where attributes are stored)
  If ((N dot L) * ambient_occlusion_term > 0)
    discard fragment
  Else
    color = 0, stencil = 0x01
Pass 1: Render full-screen quad only where 0x03==stencil count
  Perform light accumulation / shading
```

9.3.3 G-Buffer-Creation Optimizations

The biggest individual step you can take to improve the performance of creating the G-buffer is selecting the appropriate format for the buffer itself.

Contrary to a common misconception, you don't need a feature-rich GPU to do deferred shading. All you need is DirectX 9 Pixel Shader 2.0 support; no fancy surface formats or even MRT are strictly required. All of these extras can be considered optimizations for performance and quality. Implementations exist for other platforms as well, such as the Microsoft Xbox and the Sony Playstation 2 (Geldreich et al. 2004).

First we have to define the space in which we work. Due to the limited range of components, we are forced to work in a tight, restricted space. The obvious candidates are view space and post-projection space. Then comes the question: How much performance can we dedicate to unpacking?

The drawback of any fat-format encoding (that is, having buffers larger than 32 bits per texel) is the reading speed. For example, a 64-bit texel can take twice as much time to load as a 32-bit one, even when the entire surface fits inside the texture cache (and 128-bit texels are even slower).

So let's start with the assumption (which is not the case, in fact) that we are limited by MRT surface count. We outline the major features of the most practical solutions first for position encoding and then for normal encoding. See Table 9-1.

Depth encoding is usually done in one of two ways:

1. **Storing z/w of the visible surface at each pixel.** Along with the (x, y) pixel coordinates and information from the perspective projection, this is enough information to reconstruct the 3D eye-space position.

2. **Storing distance from the near plane, thus avoiding the division in the G-buffer-creation phase.** Along with interpolated ray direction (from the eye position to the center of the pixel on the near plane), this is enough to find the exact point of intersection.

There is no row labeled "Precision of the Method" in Table 9-1 because the methods are all similar in this respect. There may be differences due to hardware precision, but assuming fp32-capable hardware, we can build the following list, from best to worst:

- Depth, encoded as R32F (single-component, 32-bit floating point)
- Post-projection space, integer encoding, all three components (x, y, z) stored
- Depth, encoded in 24-bit R8G8B8
- Eye-space, fp16 encoding, all three components (x, y, z) stored

Table 9-1. Storage Options for the Position Buffer

	Depth Only (32 bits per pixel)		Full (x, y, z) Position (64 bits per pixel)	
	R32F	A8R8G8B8	Post-Projection Space	Eye Space
Hardware Support	GeForce FX or better	All	GeForce FX or better	GeForce FX or better
	Radeon 9500 or better		Radeon 9500 or better	Radeon 9500 or better
G-Buffer Creation Cost	Single mov	Three texs	One rcp	Single mov
	Low bandwidth	Three muls	One mul	
		One mov	One mov	
Decoding Cost	One mov	Same as the R32F, plus one dp3	Four dp4s	None
	Four dp4s		One rcp	
	One rcp		One mul	
	One mul for screen-space reconstruction			
	Similar cost for ray-based reconstruction			
Sampling and Storage	32 bits	32 bits	64 bits	64 bits
Virtual Position Support	Limited	Limited	Arbitrary, but expensive	Arbitrary
Free Components	0	1	1	1

This ordering depends, of course, on the application, but the differences are not significant enough to worry about in a typical open-space, first-person shooter view.

The options for storing the normals (stored in eye space, which has obvious benefits for lighting calculations) are shown in Table 9-2.

Interestingly enough, *S.T.A.L.K.E.R.* was actually working using each of the encodings shown in Table 9-2 at different times during development, and on quite different hardware, with combinations limited only by the fact that rendering targets must have the same bit depth on current hardware when using MRT. The only interesting exception was the NVIDIA GeForce FX line of GPUs, where deferring was performed via DirectX 9 multi-element textures (MET), instead of multiple render targets, but was then decompressed into ordinary surfaces, mostly because of sampling performance and latency issues.

We can make quality and performance trade-offs using the options enumerated in these tables and some basic renderer statistics. Because many lights affect every pixel in *S.T.A.L.K.E.R.*, sampling and decoding affects performance more than any other properties. On the other hand, the quality of the stored normals, and the ability to support virtual position (more about this later) greatly influence the resulting image quality. Free components can be used to improve performance, too, but only in limited cases.

Table 9-2. Storage Options for the Normal Buffer

	A8R8G8B8	A2R10G10B10	R16G16F	A16R16G16B16F
Hardware Support	All	Radeon 9500 or better	GeForce FX or better Radeon 9500 or better	GeForce FX or better Radeon 9500 or better
Deferring Cost	One mad	One mad	None	None
Decoding Cost	One mad One nrm	One mad One nrm	One mov One dp2a One rsq One rcp	None
Sampling and Storage	32 bits	32 bits	32 bits	64 bits
Quality	Poor	Good for rough surfaces	Excellent	Excellent
Free Components	1	1 Very low precision	0	1

In addition to position and normal, *S.T.A.L.K.E.R.*'s pipeline required three other attributes: gloss mask, an ambient occlusion term, and material index. The ideal configuration for us became: material (FX8), ambient-occlusion (FX8), gloss-mask (FX8), position (3xFP16), and normal (3xFX16). The closest configuration we were able to achieve, using DirectX-supported formats, was eye-space position and ambient occlusion stored in A16R16G16B16F, eye-space normal and material ID stored in another A16R16G16B16F, and RGB albedo and gloss stored in A8R8G8B8. Because of a limitation of current graphics hardware that requires the same bit depth for surfaces used in the MRT operation, the albedo-gloss surface was expanded to full A16R16G16B16F. This encoding could be seen as a waste of video memory bandwidth—and it is indeed. However, this "wasteful" configuration was actually the fastest on a GeForce 6800 Ultra, even when compared to smaller, lower-quality alternatives, because of its much simpler decoding. That is why *S.T.A.L.K.E.R.* dropped support for any other layout, although we do check for MRT_INDEPENDENT_BITDEPTH to try to utilize a 32-bit format for albedo and gloss, even if no hardware capable of doing so currently exists in the market.

9.3.4 Shadowing Optimizations

Stencil shadows and shadow maps both work well within deferred renderers. For artistic reasons, we chose to use shadow maps exclusively in *S.T.A.L.K.E.R.* This allowed us to cast shadows from semitransparent geometry and adjust the shadow boundary based on each pixel's virtual position. However, most important, we were able to generate smooth, soft shadow transitions, which is not possible with stencil shadows.

We implemented only the basic types of shadowed light sources, because highly specialized implementations allowed us to optimize them greatly. The next section briefly touches on spotlights, but our main focus is on omnidirectional lights, which are the most difficult light sources from which to cast shadows, especially if you're concerned about performance.

Efficient Omni Lights

There are three major options for omnidirectional shadow mapping in deferred renderers:

- Using a cube map for storing distance from the light center, R32F or A8R8G8B8 packed.

- Using a 2D surface with "unrolled" cube-map faces, with reindexing done through a small cube map (called *virtual shadow depth* cube texture [King and Newhall 2004]).

- Treating the point light as six spotlights and rendering each separately.

There is another technique, called "dual-paraboloid shadow maps," but it is not generally applicable to deferred shading, because a nonlinear projection applied first at the vertex level and then at the pixel level can lead to major artifacts.

Let's outline the major benefits and drawbacks, as shown in Table 9-3. Here, by *scalability* we mean using different sizes for different faces, which can enable packing shadow maps for many lights on one surface. *Continuity* means we are able to change the resolution smoothly from, say 1024×1024 to 16×16 in one-pixel decrements.

Treating point lights like six spotlights is difficult for forward shading engines due to the amount of retransformed geometry for every face, but for deferred shading, it is probably the best choice. *S.T.A.L.K.E.R.* was doing a lot of shadow-filtering work, so that was the option we chose. One nuance to keep in mind: leave a small border around each spotlight (small, but larger than the filter-kernel radius) to avoid filtering glitches at frustum edges.

9.4 Improving Quality

The architecture of a deferred renderer can greatly affect the final image quality, as can the decisions made on what to store in the G-buffer. This section briefly outlines a few decisions and tricks we used in *S.T.A.L.K.E.R.* to achieve the level of visual quality we needed.

Table 9-3. Comparison of Omni Lighting Techniques

	Cube Map	Virtual Shadow Depth Cube Texture	Six Spotlights
Scalability and Continuity	Low	Moderate	Excellent
	Few fixed sizes	Faces can be of different sizes, but only from a few fixed sets	Any variation of sizes is possible
	All faces are the same		
Hardware Filtering Support	No	Yes	Yes
Cost of Filtering	Moderate	Excellent for bilinear	Excellent
		Moderate for arbitrary percentage-closer filtering	
Render Target Switches	Six	One	One
Packing Support	No	Yes	Yes
Cost of Screen Space Stencil Masking	Low	Low	Moderate
			Some stencil overdraw
Memory Cost and Bandwidth Usage	High	Moderate	Excellent
	Surface is almost unusable for everything else	Few fixed sizes limits packing ability	

9.4.1 The Power of "Virtual Position"

Simulated displacement mapping is extremely popular in next-generation engines. (See Chapter 8 of this book, "Per-Pixel Displacement Mapping with Distance Functions," for a related technique.) The simplest (and most popular) of these approaches is parallax mapping (Kaneko et al. 2001, Welsh 2004). It works reasonably well with most lighting models, except when it comes to shadows. It looks really strange when the shadows are still, but the underlying surface changes due to different eye position or lighting conditions. Our trick to hide such objectionable effects was to move the eye-space position slightly away from the surface in the direction of the per-pixel normal, in proportion to the height map value at the original sampling point, as shown in Figures 9-4 and 9-5. Doing so adds a greater sense for the bumpiness of the surface close to shadow boundaries or really close to light sources. Another, unintended, effect of this trick was alleviating most of the biasing problems associated with shadow maps. The reason why this works is simple: with good filtering, the worst "surface acne" appears in areas with low heights—which is almost desirable, because in real life, pits are usually darker from self-occlusion.

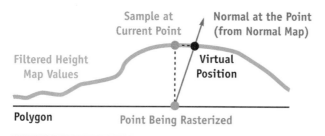

Sample at
Current Point

Normal at the Point
(from Normal Map)

Filtered Height
Map Values

Virtual
Position

Polygon

Point Being Rasterized

Figure 9-4. The Virtual Position Trick
This technique simulates parallax effects in bump-mapped geometry. It offsets the point being shaded based on the bump map's normal and the height of the bump map surface at the point.

Figure 9-5. The Virtual Position Trick in Action
Note how the shadow follows the bump on the fence in the lower right.

9.4.2 Ambient Occlusion

Our most ambitious goal in writing *S.T.A.L.K.E.R.*'s second renderer was to create a purely dynamic renderer that didn't depend on any precalculation, especially for the lighting environment. We met the goal, with two exceptions:

1. The sector-portal structure and low-polygonal geometry used for occlusion culling was already available from the data set created for the first renderer.

2. The ambient occlusion term was available too, but it was stored mostly in light maps, used by the first renderer.

Using visibility data may seem like a compromise, but this data doesn't require much preprocessing (we don't use any sort of PVS and mostly rely on occlusion culling). On the other hand, using light maps for the ambient occlusion term seemed to be a big waste of both memory and designer time. Instead, we stored the occlusion term in an unused per-vertex component, and this worked well enough for *S.T.A.L.K.E.R.* The way we handle it: tessellating original geometry up to a constant edge length (0.5 meters in our case), then applying adaptive tessellation, estimating both edge error and the triangle-middle-point error up to a minimum edge length (0.1 meters in our case). The next step was simplification based on the Quadric Error Metric algorithm (see Garland and Heckbert 1998 and Hoppe 1999) with intermediate errors recomputed at each iteration with a simple placement policy of three variants: edge middle, first, or second vertex. We allow no more than a 10 percent increase in vertex count and use a fixed maximal error limit, but in practice we did not reach this limit on vertices in any of our levels. Although we still allowed the usage of light maps to store the ambient occlusion term, we encouraged our artists to shift to a vertex-based solution. The result: our first renderer was changed to use the vertex-based ambient occlusion, too.

9.4.3 Materials and Surface-Light Interaction

The generic way of doing materials in a deferred renderer—store all the information the light-shader needs—is the right way to go in the future, because "Hey! The real world is shaded by the same shader." The alternative is to use something like material index and to apply different fragment programs to different materials branching on this index—this is fairly questionable on today's hardware though.

To maintain the target frame rate, we limited ourselves to a material index into a light-response lookup table. After many experiments to find an optimal re-parameterization for this texture, we settled on the simplest and most intuitive way: indexing the volume texture by ($N \cdot L$, $N \cdot H$, *material*). This allows a fairly large range of materials to be simulated, from dimmed surfaces to glossy reflecting ones, and even a faux-anisotropic reflection model. Figure 9-6 shows an example.

The beauty of this solution is that materials that come from adjacent layers in the texture can be blended by the texture-sampling unit for free. We also discovered that when

Figure 9-6. Metallic Material Forced for All Surfaces

the layers are ordered by increasing shininess (or decreasing roughness), we needed only four layers to represent almost everything in *S.T.A.L.K.E.R.* So, the result was a $64 \times 256 \times 4$, A8L8 texture summing up to a 128 K table with fairly coherent access from the pixel shader. We left the diffuse lookup at this relatively high resolution (64 samples), because the function it stores may not be linear, and linear filtering that is done by hardware isn't always acceptable.

9.5 Antialiasing

A deferred renderer is just incompatible with current hardware-assisted antialiasing, unfortunately (Hargreaves and Harris 2004). Thus, antialiasing becomes solely the responsibility of the application and the shader; we cannot rely on the GPU alone. Because aliasing itself arises from the mismatched frequencies of the source signal and of the destination discrete representation, a good approximation of an antialiasing filter is just a low-pass filter, which is simple blurring. This is a zero-cost operation in the console world, where any TV display works like a low-pass filter anyway. In the PC world, we need an alternative. Our solution was to trade some signal frequency at the discontinuities for smoothness, and to leave other parts of the image intact. This was performed in a way similar to the edge-detection filters used in nonphotorealistic applications: We detect discontinuities in both depth and normal direction by taking $8 + 1$ samples of depth and finding how depth at the current pixel differs from the ideal line passed through opposite corner points. The normals were used to fix issues such as a wall perpendicular to the floor, where the depth forms a perfect line (or will be similar at all samples) but an aliased edge exists. The normals were processed in a similar cross-filter manner, and the dot product between normals was used to determine the presence of an edge. Listing 9-2 shows the code.

The two detectors were then multiplied to produce a single value indicating how much the current pixel "looks like an edge." This value was used to offset four bilinear texture lookups into the composited (near-final) back buffer. The result was automatic weighting of samples with a very strong edge-detection policy that seamlessly handles edge and alpha-test/texkill aliasing without blurring other parts of the image. See Figure 9-7 for a sample result.

Listing 9-2. Edge-Detection Shader Used for Antialiasing

```
struct v2p
{
  float4 tc0: TEXCOORD0;   // Center
  float4 tc1: TEXCOORD1;   // Left Top
  float4 tc2: TEXCOORD2;   // Right Bottom
  float4 tc3: TEXCOORD3;   // Right Top
  float4 tc4: TEXCOORD4;   // Left Bottom
  float4 tc5: TEXCOORD5;   // Left / Right
  float4 tc6: TEXCOORD6;   // Top / Bottom
};

//////////////////////////////////////////////////////////////////////
uniform sampler2D s_distort;
uniform half4 e_barrier;  // x=norm(~.8f), y=depth(~.5f)
uniform half4 e_weights;  // x=norm, y=depth
uniform half4 e_kernel;   // x=norm, y=depth

//////////////////////////////////////////////////////////////////////
half4 main(v2p I) : COLOR
{
```

Listing 9-2 (continued). Edge-Detection Shader Used for Antialiasing

```
// Normal discontinuity filter
half3 nc = tex2D(s_normal, I.tc0);
half4 nd;
nd.x =  dot(nc, (half3)tex2D(s_normal, I.tc1));
nd.y =  dot(nc, (half3)tex2D(s_normal, I.tc2));
nd.z =  dot(nc, (half3)tex2D(s_normal, I.tc3));
nd.w =  dot(nc, (half3)tex2D(s_normal, I.tc4));
nd -= e_barrier.x;
nd = step(0, nd);
half ne = saturate(dot(nd, e_weights.x));

// Opposite coords
float4 tc5r = I.tc5.wzyx;
float4 tc6r = I.tc6.wzyx;

// Depth filter : compute gradiental difference:
// (c-sample1)+(c-sample1_opposite)
half4 dc = tex2D(s_position, I.tc0);
half4 dd;
dd.x = (half)tex2D(s_position, I.tc1).z +
       (half)tex2D(s_position, I.tc2).z;
dd.y = (half)tex2D(s_position, I.tc3).z +
       (half)tex2D(s_position, I.tc4).z;
dd.z = (half)tex2D(s_position, I.tc5).z +
       (half)tex2D(s_position, tc5r).z;
dd.w = (half)tex2D(s_position, I.tc6).z +
       (half)tex2D(s_position, tc6r).z;
dd = abs(2 * dc.z - dd)- e_barrier.y;
dd = step(dd, 0);
half de = saturate(dot(dd, e_weights.y));

// Weight
half w = (1 - de * ne) * e_kernel.x;  // 0 - no aa, 1=full aa

// Smoothed color
// (a-c)*w + c = a*w + c(1-w)
float2 offset = I.tc0 * (1-w);
half4 s0 = tex2D(s_image, offset + I.tc1 * w);
half4 s1 = tex2D(s_image, offset + I.tc2 * w);
half4 s2 = tex2D(s_image, offset + I.tc3 * w);
half4 s3 = tex2D(s_image, offset + I.tc4 * w);
return (s0 + s1 + s2 + s3)/4.h;
}
```

Figure 9-7. Weight Computed by the Edge-Detection Shader

There is one side note to this approach: the parameters/delimiters tweaked for one resolution do not necessarily work well for another; even worse, they often do not work at all. That is because the lower the resolution, the more source signal is lost during discretization, and blurring becomes a worse approximation of an antialiasing filter. Visually, you get more and more false positives, and the picture becomes more blurred than necessary. However, lowering the blur radius according to resolution works fine.

9.5.1 Efficient Tone Mapping

Both high-dynamic-range lighting and automatic exposure control are natural, easy, and relatively cheap extensions to deferred renderers. But the way *S.T.A.L.K.E.R.* handles this is somewhat different.

The main difference is that we estimate scene luminance based only on the luminance of a blurred bloom surface. So the desired luminance should be set really low, to something like 0.01.

When building the bloom target, we blend information from the current frame into the previous frame's bloom target. This gives sharper highlights near the really bright parts and allows use of a smaller filter kernel; we used a simple 2×2 cross filter. The side effect of this approach is the appearance of a slight motion blur, but this was even desired by our artists.

After the final average luminance was determined, we blended it into a 1×1 R32F render target to perform adaptation (as in the DirectX 9 SDK sample); however, the blend speed needed to be significantly lower than the bloom's blend speed to avoid resonance effects.

Our initial implementation used the classical tone-map operator similar to the log-average one described in the DirectX SDK. We changed this to a simple linear scale and linear average luminance estimation, because our artists complained that the original one reduced contrast. This works better for us because our data set was designed around the low-dynamic-range rendering used in the first renderer.

The result is spectacular and extremely efficient: enabling tone mapping with automatic exposure control has less than a 1 percent impact on frame rate.

9.5.2 Dealing with Transparency

Unfortunately, deferred renderers are incompatible with any sort of alpha blending. Depth peeling (Everitt 2001) is not an option, given current GPU performance levels.[1] We handled transparency with a straightforward hack: we used forward rendering for transparent primitives with lighting but without shadows. This was done by copying-and-pasting from the first renderer's source tree.

9.6 Things We Tried but Did Not Include in the Final Code

Because of our goal to raise the visual bar higher than any game ever written, even without deep content modification (content was almost fixed at the time of writing, except for constant small changes required by gameplay flow), we tried a few ideas that didn't make it into the actual commercial game.

---

1. There is another option, usually called "screen-door transparency," but its use is fairly questionable as a generic solution. See Foley et al. 1990.

9.6.1 Elevation Maps

The concept of elevation maps can be found in Dietrich 2000. The first assumption was that because the layers are drawn only in the first (attribute-deferring) phase, they should not greatly affect performance. Another assumption was that with little position modification (perhaps 1 cm total), we should be able to hide layering with a relatively small number of layers, something like three to five layers.

After implementation of this scheme, we found the following:

- To make 1 cm of displacement, we need at least 32 layers at 1024×768 resolution, so that layering becomes invisible, but even then, the algorithm fails around the sharp edges, where it produces something like "fur."
- Deferring even 4 layers costs an incredible amount of fill and shading power (especially including `texkill`, which can work against early-z), dropping the frame rate by up to 30 percent.
- The antialiasing method described earlier proved to be quite good at masking out artifacts between layers.

Although we decided to drop the scheme altogether, it was fun to see adaptive displacement mapping in almost real time, approximately 3 frames per second with 64 layers. The idea can still be useful for an application with a cheaper G-buffer creation phase.

9.6.2 Real-Time Global Illumination

An old dream for the author of this chapter was to see global illumination in an interactive application, which doesn't depend on any precomputation and works with 100 percent dynamic lighting conditions and a similarly dynamic environment. The algorithm we chose is similar to photon mapping (Jensen 2001), but without any sort of "final gathering." (Although not strictly related, one may want to read a paper of Ingo Wald's, such as Wald 2003.) All the lights were modified to track the changes in their local environment by casting hundreds of rays (on the CPU) in random directions; selecting the fixed amount of the brightest secondary, indirect lights; adding them to the database; and then repeating the same process on them until the minimal threshold was reached or the fixed number of iterations ended. Then everything continued as usual, up to the end of render-frame, where all the secondary lights were just destroyed (cached, in fact).

The first results were at least strange from a visual standpoint: lots of bright spots everywhere, crossed by weird shadows. Then the secondary light was modified to be more like a hemispherical spot, with the major contribution along the primary axis (parent reflection vector) and gradually lowering power to the sides. The shadows were disabled altogether, but CPU-based rays were increased several times to provide some sense of occlusion. For the sake of optimization, the specular contribution from the secondary lights was dropped; also the lights used no material information at all—they were pure Blinn-style. The result really looks like a global illumination and was obtained almost in real time: up to 10 frames per second with up to 500 indirect lights, where direct-only lighting runs at around 50 to 60 frames per second on our target hardware.

Although this frame rate is unacceptable for a real-time game application, one can extrapolate the performance growth curve of current GPUs—approximately doubling in performance every year—to hope that in two years, this approach could be practical.

9.7 Conclusion

Deferred shading, although not appropriate for every game, proved to be a great rendering architecture for accomplishing our goals in *S.T.A.L.K.E.R.* It gave us a rendering engine that leverages modern GPUs and has lower geometry-processing requirements, lower pixel-processing requirements, and lower CPU overhead than a traditional forward shading architecture. And it has cleaner and simpler scene management to boot. Once we worked around the deficiencies inherent in a deferred shader, such as a potentially restricted material system and the lack of antialiasing, the resulting architecture was both flexible and fast, allowing for a wide range of effects. See Figure 9-8 for an example. Of course, the proof is in the implementation. In *S.T.A.L.K.E.R.,* our original forward shading system, despite using significantly less complex and interesting shaders, actually ran slower than our final deferred shading system in complex scenes with a large number of dynamic lights. Such scenes are, of course, exactly the kind in which you need the most performance!

9.8 References

Dietrich, Sim. 2000. "Elevation Maps."
http://www.nvidia.com/object/Elevation_Maps_Paper.html

Everitt, C. 2001. "Interactive Order-Independent Transparency." NVIDIA technical report. http://developer.nvidia.com/object/Interactive_Order_Transparency.html

Figure 9-8. *S.T.A.L.K.E.R.* in Action

Foley, James D., Andries van Dam, Steven K. Feiner, and John F. Hughes. 1990. *Computer Graphics: Principles and Practice.* Addison-Wesley.

Garland, M., and P. Heckbert. 1998. "Simplifying Surfaces with Color and Texture Using Quadric Error Metrics." In *IEEE Visualization 98*, October 1998, pp. 263–269.

Geldreich, Rich, Matt Pritchard, and John Brooks. 2004. "Deferred Lighting and Shading." Presentation at Game Developers Conference 2004. **http://www.gdconf.com/archives/2004/pritchard_matt.ppt**

Greene, Ned, Michael Kass, and Gavin Miller. 1993. "Hierarchical Z-Buffer Visibility." In *Computer Graphics (Proceedings of SIGGRAPH 93)*, pp. 231–238.

Hargreaves, Shawn, and Mark Harris. 2004. "Deferred Shading." Presentation. **http://download.nvidia.com/developer/presentations/2004/6800_Leagues/ 6800_Leagues_Deferred_Shading.pdf**

Hoppe, H. 1999. "New Quadric Metric for Simplifying Meshes with Appearance Attributes." In *IEEE Visualization 99*, October 1999, pp. 59–66.

Jensen, Henrik Wann. 2001. *Realistic Image Synthesis Using Photon Mapping*. AK Peters.

Kaneko, Tomomichi, Toshiyuki Takahei, Masahiko Inami, Naoki Kawakami, Yasuyuki Yanagida, Taro Maeda, and Susumu Tachi. 2001. "Detailed Shape Representation with Parallax Mapping." In *Proceedings of the ICAT 2001 (The 11th International Conference on Artificial Reality and Telexistence)*, Tokyo, December 2001, pp. 205–208.

King, Gary. 2004. Practical Perspective Shadow Mapping demo. **http://download.nvidia.com/developer/SDK/Individual_Samples/DEMOS/Direct3D9/PracticalPSM.zip**

King, Gary, and William Newhall. 2004. "Efficient Omnidirectional Shadow Maps." In *ShaderX 3*, edited by Wolfgang Engel. Charles River Media.

Saito, T., and T. Takahashi. 1990. "Comprehensible Rendering of 3-D Shapes." In *Computer Graphics (Proceedings of SIGGRAPH 90)* 24(4), August 1990, pp. 197–206.

Wald, Ingo. 2003. Instant Global Illumination, Version II. **http://www.openrt.de/Gallery/IGI2/**

Welsh, Terry. 2004. "Parallax Mapping with Offset Limiting: A Per-Pixel Approximation of Uneven Surfaces." **http://www.infiscape.com/doc/parallax_mapping.pdf**

Chapter 10

Real-Time Computation of Dynamic Irradiance Environment Maps

Gary King
NVIDIA Corporation

Environment maps are a popular image-based rendering technique, used to represent spatially invariant[1] spherical functions. This chapter describes a fully GPU-accelerated method for generating one particularly graphically interesting type of environment map, *irradiance environment maps*, using DirectX Pixel Shader 3.0 and floating-point texturing. This technique enables applications to quickly approximate complex global lighting effects in dynamic environments (such as radiosity from dynamic lights and dynamic objects). For brevity, this chapter assumes that the reader has working knowledge of environment maps, particularly cube maps (Voorhies and Foran 1994) and dual-paraboloid maps (Heidrich and Seidel 1998).

10.1 Irradiance Environment Maps

Imagine a scene with k directional lights, with directions $d_1..d_k$ and intensities $i_1..i_k$, illuminating a diffuse surface with normal n and color c. Given the standard OpenGL and DirectX lighting equations, the resulting pixel intensity B is computed as:

$$B = c \sum_{j=1..k} \max\left(0, d_j \cdot n\right) i_j.$$

Equation 10-1. Diffuse Reflection

---

1. Kevin Bjorke's chapter in *GPU Gems* (Bjorke 2004) describes a technique to use environment maps in spatially varying ways by applying a spatially varying function to the input texture coordinate.

In this context, an environment map with k texels can be thought of as a simple method of storing the intensities of k directional lights, with the light direction implied from the texel location. This provides an efficient mechanism for storing arbitrarily complex lighting environments; however, the cost of computing B increases proportionally to the number of texels in the environment map. What we would like is a mechanism for precomputing the diffuse reflection, so that the per-pixel rendering cost is independent of the number of lights/texels.

Looking at Equation 10-1, we notice a few things: First, all surfaces with normal direction n will return the same value for the sum. Second, the sum is dependent on just the lights in the scene and the surface normal. What this means is that we can compute the sum for any normal n in an offline process executed once per environment map, and store the result in a second environment map, indexed by the surface normal. This second environment map is known as the *diffuse irradiance environment map* (or just the diffuse environment map), and it allows us to illuminate objects with arbitrarily complex lighting environments with a single texture lookup. (This includes natural lighting environments generated from photographs, created by Miller and Hoffman [1984], popularized by Paul Debevec [1998], and demonstrated in Figure 10-1.) Some simple pseudocode for generating diffuse environment maps[2] is shown in Listing 10-1. Figure 10-2b shows an example of a diffuse environment map.

Figure 10-1. An Image Generated Using Irradiance Environment Maps
Comparison of an object lit by a single directional light (left) and a real-time irradiance environment map (right).

---

2. For simplicity, this pseudocode does not properly weight the texels in the input environment map (to account for the sampling rate differences across environment maps). The example code included on the book's CD properly handles this.

Listing 10-1. Diffuse Convolution Pseudocode

```
diffuseConvolution(outputEnvironmentMap, inputEnvironmentMap)
{
  for_all {T_0: outputEnvironmentMap}
    sum = 0
    N = envMap_direction(T_0)
    for_all {T_1: inputEnvironmentMap}
      L = envMap_direction(T_1)
      I = inputEnvironmentMap[T_1]
      sum += max(0, dot(L, N)) * I
    T_0 = sum
  return outputEnvironmentMap
}
```

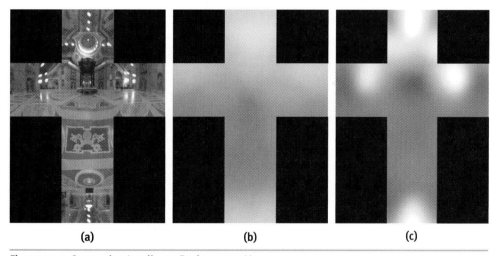

| (a) | (b) | (c) |

Figure 10-2. Comparing Irradiance Environment Maps
(a) A cube environment map of St. Peter's Basilica. The resulting (b) diffuse and (c) specular maps. St. Peter's light probe © 1999 Paul Debevec, http://www.debevec.org/Probes/.

This concept can be trivially extended to handle popular symmetric specular functions, such as the Phong reflection model. Instead of creating an irradiance environment map indexed by the surface normal, we create one indexed by the view-reflection vector R; and instead of computing `max(0, dot(L, N))` for each input texel, we compute `pow(max(0, dot(R, L)), s)`. These are known as *specular irradiance environment maps*.

10.2 Spherical Harmonic Convolution

Although rendering with irradiance environment maps is extremely efficient (just one lookup for a diffuse reflection or two for diffuse and specular), generating them using the algorithm in Listing 10-1 is not. For M input texels and N output texels, generating a single irradiance map is an $O(MN)$ operation. In more concrete terms, if we want to generate a diffuse cube map with an edge length of just 32 texels, from an input cube map with an edge length of 64 texels, the cost is $32 \times 32 \times 6 \times 64 \times 64 \times 6 \approx 151$ million operations. Even with CPU speeds approaching 4 GHz, real-time generation of irradiance environment maps cannot be achieved using such a brute-force algorithm.

At SIGGRAPH 2001, a technique was presented that reduced the cost of computing irradiance environment maps from $O(MN)$ to $O(MK)$, with $N >> K$ (Ramamoorthi and Hanrahan 2001b). The key insight was that diffuse irradiance maps vary extremely slowly with respect to the surface normal, so they could be generated and stored more efficiently by using the frequency-space representation of the environment map. To convert a spherical function (such as an environment map) into its frequency-space representation, we use the *real spherical harmonic transform*[3]:

$$L_l^m = \int_S L(\theta, \phi)\, y_l^m(\theta, \phi) \sin\theta\, d\theta\, d\phi.$$

Equation 10-2. Spherical Harmonic Transform

For N discrete samples (such as an environment map), Equation 10-2 becomes:

$$L_l^m = \sum_{i=0}^{N-1} L(i)\, y_l^m(i)\, d\omega(i),$$

Equation 10-3. Discrete Spherical Harmonic Transform

where

$$\sum_{i=0}^{N-1} d\omega(i) = 4\pi$$

is the solid angle subtended by each sample,[4] and definitions for y_l^m (the spherical harmonic basis functions) can be found in Ramamoorthi and Hanrahan 2001b, Green 2003, or any spherical harmonics reference.

---

3. For those with signal-processing backgrounds, the spherical harmonic transform is analogous to the Fourier transform in Cartesian coordinate systems.

4. The definition of $d\omega$ will depend on the type of environment map used, because the different projections

While a detailed discussion of spherical harmonics is outside the scope of this chapter, the References section lists a number of excellent articles that provide in-depth explanations (and other applications) of spherical harmonics. In order to use spherical harmonics for computing irradiance maps, all we need to know are some basic properties:

- Any band l has $2l + 1$ coefficients m, defined from $-l..l$. Therefore, an lth-order projection has $(l + 1)^2$ total coefficients.

- The basis functions are linear and orthonormal.

- Convolving two functions in the spatial domain is equivalent to multiplying them in the frequency domain.

The last property (known as the *convolution theorem* in signal-processing parlance) is an extremely powerful one, and the reason why we can use spherical harmonics to efficiently generate irradiance maps: Given two functions that we want to convolve (the Lambertian BRDF and a sampled lighting environment, for example), we can compute the convolved result by separately projecting each function into an lth-order spherical harmonic representation, and then multiplying and summing the resulting $(l + 1)^2$ coefficients. This is more efficient than brute-force convolution because for diffuse lighting (and low-exponent specular), the L_l^m coefficients (Equation 10-3) rapidly approach 0 as l increases, so we can generate very accurate approximations to the true diffuse convolution with a very small number of terms. In fact, Ramamoorthi and Hanrahan (2001a) demonstrate that $l = 2$ (9 coefficients) is all that is required for diffuse lighting, and $l = \sqrt{s}$ is sufficient for specular lighting (where s is the Phong exponent). This reduces the runtime complexity of the example convolution to just $9 \times 64 \times 64 \times 6 \approx 221$ thousand operations per function (442 thousand total, 1 for the lighting environment, and 1 for the reflection function), compared to the 151 million operations using the brute-force technique.

We can further improve the spherical harmonic convolution performance by noticing that the reflection function coefficients are constant for each function (Lambert, Phong, and so on). Therefore, each function's coefficients can be computed once (in a preprocess step) and be reused by all convolutions. This optimization reduces the runtime complexity of the example convolution to just 221 thousand operations.

---

used by different environment map types (such as spherical, cubic, and azimuth-angle) will cause the relative sampling densities to vary uniquely across the unit sphere. Therefore, to generate a correct result, we need to use the correct solid angle subtended by each texel. The included demo has functions that calculate $d\omega$ for both dual-paraboloid and cubic environment maps.

The only remaining detail is that our diffuse environment map is now stored in a spherical harmonic representation. To convert it back into its spatial representation,[5] we generate a new environment map by using the inverse spherical harmonic transform (the tilde indicates that the reconstructed function is an approximation):

$$\tilde{L}\left(\theta, \phi\right) = \sum_{l=0}^{n-1} \sum_{m=-l}^{l} L_l^m \, y_l^m \left(\theta, \phi\right).$$

Equation 10-4. Inverse Spherical Harmonic Transform

Application of this formula is trivial: for every texel in the output environment map, multiply the spherical harmonic basis function by the coefficients. This is an $O(KN)$ process, so the total runtime complexity for generating irradiance environment maps is $O(KN + KM)$.

10.3 Mapping to the GPU

With Pixel Shader 3.0 and floating-point textures (features supported on GeForce 6 Series GPUs), mapping spherical harmonic convolution to the GPU becomes a trivial two-pass operation[6]: one pass to transform the lighting environment into its spherical harmonic representation, and one to convolve it with the reflection function and transform it back into the spatial domain.

10.3.1 Spatial to Frequency Domain

To transform a lighting environment into its spherical harmonic representation, we need to write a shader that computes Equation 10-3. This equation has some interesting properties that can be exploited to make writing a shader a very straightforward process:

- The output is $(l + 1)^2$ three-vector floats (one for each of red, green, and blue).
- The input is N three-vector floats, N scalar $d\omega$ values, and N scalar y_l^m values.
- For any input texel i from any environment map L, $y_l^m(i) \, d\omega(i)$ is a scalar constant.

The last point is the important one: it means that we can generate one texture per (l, m) pair as an offline process. This can then be mapped onto the GPU using $(l + 1)^2$

---

5. Ramamoorthi and Hanrahan (2001b) also demonstrate how to apply the spherical harmonic coefficients directly, without generating an output environment map.

6. For a sufficiently motivated programmer, the convolution could be performed in multiple Pixel Shader 2.0 passes; however, this distinction does not apply to the author of this chapter.

rendering passes, where each pass generates a three-vector of spherical harmonic coefficients by looping over all N texels in the input environment map, and multiplying each by the corresponding texel in the appropriate lookup table. We can reduce this to a single pass by tiling the lookup tables, and rendering all of the $(l + 1)^2$ three-vector coefficients at once, as separate pixels in an output texture. Using Pixel Shader 3.0's VPOS input register, we can trivially map the output pixel location to a tile in the lookup table, allowing each of the output pixels to project the input environment map onto the appropriate spherical harmonic basis function (scaled by $d\omega$). This is shown in HLSL pseudocode in Listing 10-2 and demonstrated in Figure 10-3.

Listing 10-2. Spherical Harmonic Projection Pseudocode

```
float2 map_to_tile_and_offset( tile, offsetTexCoord )
{
  return (tile / numTiles) +
         (offsetTexCoord / (numTiles * numSamples))
}


float3 SH_Projection( inputEnvironmentMap,
                      dωY_lm,
                      currentL_lm : VPOS ) : COLOR
{
   sum = 0
   for_all {T_0: inputEnvironmentMap}
     T_1 = map_to_tile_and_offset(currentL_lm, T_0)
     weighted_SHbasis = dωY_lm[T_1]
     radiance_Sample = inputEnvironmentMap[T_0]
     sum += radiance_Sample * weighted_SHbasis
   return sum
}
```

Note that for simplicity, you may want a separate lookup table for each face in the environment map. The included demo uses dual-paraboloid environment maps for input, so two weight lookup tables are generated.

10.3.2 Convolution and Back Again

As described in Section 10.2, the convolution operator in frequency space is just multiplying the L_l^m coefficients generated in Section 10.3.1 with a set of precomputed coefficients for the desired reflection function (for clarity, we refer to these as the A_l^m coefficients), and then evaluating Equation 10-4 for each texel in the output environment map. This is very

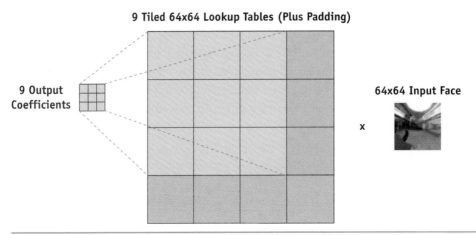

9 Tiled 64x64 Lookup Tables (Plus Padding)

9 Output Coefficients

x

64x64 Input Face

Figure 10-3. Mapping Output Coefficients to Input Lookup Table Tiles for One Face

similar to the process we used with Equation 10-3, and we can use tiling to execute this operation in a single shader pass, too. Because $A_l^m y_l^m$ is a scalar constant for any given (l, m) pair and texel location, we can precompute $(l + 1)^2$ environment maps that store these values. If the desired output environment map is a cube map, we can instead precompute six weighting textures (one for each cube-map face), tile the (l, m) coefficients inside each face, and generate the final cube map by iteratively setting each face as the active render target, binding the appropriate weight texture, and executing the pixel shader.

The pixel shader used to perform the convolution plus inverse transformation is very similar to the one used in Section 10.3.1; however, instead of executing an N-element loop over K output values, we execute a K-element loop over M output values. Pseudocode is provided in Listing 10-3.

Listing 10-3. Convolution and Evaluation Pseudocode

```
float3 SH_Evaluation( L₁ₘ,
                      A₁ₘY₁ₘ,
                      thetaPhi : VPOS ) : COLOR
{
   sum = 0
   for_all {T₀: L₁ₘ}
     T₁ = map_to_tile_and_offset(T₀, thetaPhi)
     weighted_BRDF = A₁ₘY₁ₘ[T₁]
     light_environment = inputEnvironmentMap[T₀]
     sum += light_environment * weighted_BRDF
   return sum
}
```

As mentioned in footnote 5, Ramamoorthi and Hanrahan (2001b) demonstrate an alternative method for performing diffuse convolution by generating a 4×4 matrix from the first nine L_l^m terms and using this to transform the normal vector. When per-vertex lighting is sufficient, this approach may be more efficient than the one described in this chapter; however, because the convolved cube-map resolution is generally much lower than the screen resolution, the approach described here offers significant performance advantages when per-pixel lighting is desired, or in scenes with high polygon counts.

10.4 Further Work

So far, we've managed to show how to use GPUs to accelerate what is traditionally an offline process. However, because this operation executes in milliseconds on modern GPUs, by using render-to-texture functionality to generate the input environment maps, applications can practically generate diffuse and specular cube maps for dynamic environments. The accompanying demo generates irradiance maps in excess of 300 frames per second on a GeForce 6800 GT. Flat ambient lighting can be replaced with a cube-map lookup that varies as the sun moves through the sky, or as flares are tossed into a small room.

One of the deficiencies of using irradiance environment maps for scene lighting is that correct shadowing is extremely difficult, if not impossible. One technique that offline renderers use to compensate for this is computing a global shadowing term (called *ambient occlusion*) that is used to attenuate the illumination from the environment map (Landis 2002). For static objects, the ambient occlusion value can be precomputed and stored; however, for dynamic objects, this is not possible. In Chapter 14 of this book, "Dynamic Ambient Occlusion and Indirect Lighting," Mike Bunnell provides a method for efficiently approximating ambient occlusion values, so that this same technique can be applied to dynamic characters.

Also, spherical harmonics have a number of valuable properties not explored in this chapter. For example, component-wise linear interpolation between two sets of spherical harmonic coefficients is equivalent to linear interpolation of the spatial representations. Component-wise addition of two sets of coefficients is equivalent to addition of the spatial representations. These two properties (combined with the convolution theorem) provide a powerful set of primitives for approximating numerous complex, global lighting effects. This concept is described in detail in Nijasure 2003.

10.5 Conclusion

Rendering dynamic, complex lighting environments is an important step for interactive applications to take in the quest for visual realism. This chapter has demonstrated how one method used in offline rendering, irradiance maps, can be efficiently implemented on modern GPUs. By cleverly applying and extending the techniques presented here, real-time applications no longer need to choose between complex static lighting and simple dynamic lighting; they can have the best of both.

10.6 References

Bjorke, K. 2004. "Image-Based Lighting." In *GPU Gems*, edited by Randima Fernando, pp. 307–321. Addison-Wesley. *This chapter describes a technique to use environment maps to represent spatially variant reflections.*

Debevec, P. 1998. "Rendering Synthetic Objects into Real Scenes: Bridging Traditional and Image-Based Graphics with Global Illumination and High Dynamic Range Photography." In *Computer Graphics (Proceedings of SIGGRAPH 98)*, pp. 189–198.

Green, R. 2003. "Spherical Harmonic Lighting: The Gritty Details." **http://www.research.scea.com/gdc2003/spherical-harmonic-lighting.pdf**

Heidrich, W., and H.-P. Seidel. "View-Independent Environment Maps." *Eurographics Workshop on Graphics Hardware 1998*, pp. 39–45.

Kautz, J., et al. 2000. "A Unified Approach to Prefiltered Environment Maps." *Eurographics Rendering Workshop 2000*, pp. 185–196.

Landis, H. 2002. "Production-Ready Global Illumination." Course 16 notes, SIGGRAPH 2002.

Miller, G., and C. Hoffman. 1984. "Illumination and Reflection Maps: Simulated Objects in Simulated and Real Environments." **http://athens.ict.usc.edu/ReflectionMapping/illumap.pdf**

Nijasure, M. 2003. "Interactive Global Illumination on the GPU." **http://www.cs.ucf.edu/graphics/GPUassistedGI/GPUGIThesis.pdf**

Ramamoorthi, R., and P. Hanrahan. 2001a. "A Signal-Processing Framework for Inverse Rendering." In *Proceedings of SIGGRAPH 2001*, pp. 117–128.

Ramamoorthi, R., and P. Hanrahan. 2001b. "An Efficient Representation for Irradiance Environment Maps." In *Proceedings of SIGGRAPH 2001*, pp. 497–500.

Voorhies, D., and J. Foran. 1994. "Reflection Vector Shading Hardware." In *Proceedings of SIGGRAPH 94*, pp. 163–166.

Chapter 11

Approximate Bidirectional Texture Functions

Jan Kautz
Massachusetts Institute of Technology

In this chapter we present a technique for the easy acquisition and rendering of realistic materials, such as cloth, wool, and leather. These materials are difficult to render with previous techniques, which mostly rely on simple texture maps. The goal is to spend little effort on acquisition and little computation on rendering but still achieve realistic appearances.

Our method, which is based on recent work by Kautz et al. (2004), arises from the observation that under certain circumstances, the material of a surface can be acquired with very few images, yielding results similar to those achieved with full *bidirectional texture functions* (or BTFs—we give a full definition in the first section). Rendering with this approximate BTF amounts to evaluating a simple shading model and performing a lookup into a volume texture. Rendering is easily possible using graphics hardware, where it achieves real-time frame rates. Compelling results are achieved for a wide variety of materials.

11.1 Introduction

One of the long-sought goals in computer graphics is to create photorealistic images. To this end, realistic material properties are a necessity. It is especially important to capture the fine spatial variation and mesostructure of materials, because they convey a lot of information about the material. Figure 11-1 compares a rendering of a piece of cloth using only a single diffuse texture map and using our method, which preserves spatial variation and self-shadowing. The comparison shows how important the mesostructure of a material is, and it demonstrates that for many materials, simple texture mapping or even bump mapping is not sufficient to render it realistically.

Unfortunately, the acquisition of such material properties is fairly tedious and time-consuming (Dana et al. 1999, Lensch et al. 2001, Matusik et al. 2002). This is because material properties are specified by the four-dimensional *bidirectional reflectance distribution function* (BRDF), which depends on the local light and viewing directions; the Phong model is an example of a BRDF. If spatial variation across a surface is to be captured, this function (which is the bidirectional texture function we mentioned earlier [Dana et al. 1999]) becomes six-dimensional. Obviously, the acquisition of such a high-dimensional function requires taking many samples, resulting in large acquisition times (and storage requirements), which is the reason why BTF measurements are not readily available.

The benefit of capturing all this data is that BTFs generate very realistic renderings of materials, because they capture not only the local reflectance properties for each point on a surface, but also all nonlocal effects, such as self-shadowing, masking, and inter-reflections within a material, as seen in Figure 11-1.

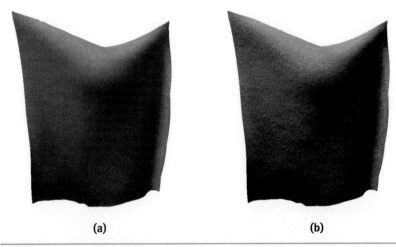

(a)   (b)

Figure 11-1. Comparing Simple Diffuse Texture Mapping and Our Method
(a) Simple diffuse texture map. (b) Our BTF method, preserving detail.

Instead of acquiring a full BTF and rendering with that, we show that it is sufficient to acquire only some slices of the BTF. This allows for a simple acquisition setup (which can be done manually) and an even simpler rendering method, which runs in real time on GPUs even a few years old. An artist can also easily manipulate an acquired material, for example, making it more or less specular by manipulating a few parameters. To make this work, we assume that the captured material patch is isotropic (that is, its appearance does not depend on its orientation) and has only small-scale features (that is, no large self-shadowing and masking effects). Later on, we discuss in more detail why this is necessary.

11.2 Acquisition

The acquisition and preprocessing steps are very simple, resulting in a fast acquisition procedure.

11.2.1 Setup and Acquisition

The setup is illustrated in the top of Figure 11-2. A camera is looking orthographically at the material to be acquired. The material is assumed to be planar, so it is best to place the material patch on a flat surface. We then illuminate the surface with a parallel light source (a distant point light source works fine) at different incident elevation angles. The light source is moved only along an arc; that is, it is not rotated around the surface normal. With the light source moving along an arc, the material reveals small self-shadowing effects, which are very characteristic of many materials.

The light source elevation angles are (roughly) spaced in 10-degree steps; that is, we acquire ten images for every material. For real-time rendering, low-dynamic-range images work fine, as shown in Section 11.4; however, high-dynamic-range images can also be acquired.

In Figure 11-2, you can see the acquired images for a few different light source angles. We acquire all images manually, but even then the acquisition of a material takes only a few minutes, a big advantage over other methods (Dana et al. 1999, Matusik et al. 2002, Sattler et al. 2003).

11.2.2 Assembling the Shading Map

We now assemble our acquired images as a stack of images. To this end, we first compute the average radiance (or intensity) a_k of each acquired image k. Because we want to index efficiently into this stack of images later on, it is useful to resample the stack so

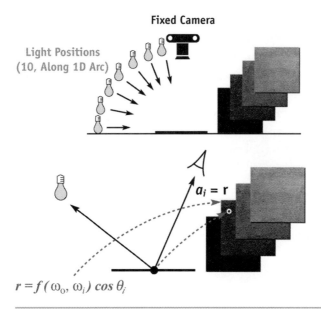

Fixed Camera

Light Positions (10, Along 1D Arc)

$a_i = r$

$r = f(\omega_o, \omega_i) \cos \theta_i$

Figure 11-2. An Overview of the Capture Methodology
Top: We capture images for different light directions and for a fixed orthogonal view, resulting in the shading map. Bottom: For each image, we compute the average reflected radiance (that is, the average intensity). During rendering, we compute the value r based on some user-defined lighting model (such as Phong) and use this value to do a per-fragment lookup into our stack of images according to the average intensity. Finally, we scale the value with the intensity of the light source.

that the average radiance increases linearly. This is done by first computing what the average radiance for slice i should be, where i refers to a slice in the resampled stack:

$$r_i = \frac{i \times a_{\max}}{N - 1}, \qquad i = 0..N - 1 \tag{1}$$

Here r_i denotes the desired radiance for slice i, $a_{\max}$ is the maximum acquired average radiance, and N is the number of slices. For each resampled slice i we now take the two original images whose average radiances a_{k1} and a_{k2} are above and below the desired radiance r_i and linearly interpolate between those two images accordingly. The resulting stack of new images is called the *shading map*, as shown in Figure 11-3. From now on, the values stored in the shading map are interpreted as BRDF times cosine value, as explained in the next section.

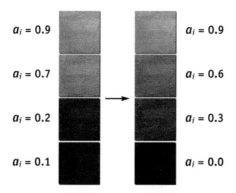

Figure 11-3. Creating a Shading Map
The input images are resampled and form the shading map, in which the average intensity increases linearly for every image.

11.3 Rendering

As stated before, rendering with our data is fairly simple. First we give a high-level description and then go into more details.

Consider shading a fragment with an ordinary lighting model—such as the Phong model—and a point light source. In that case, we compute the amount of reflected light by evaluating the lighting model with the current view and light direction and a set of parameters such as diffuseness, specularity, and so on. This value gives us a rough idea of how bright the pixel should be. Now that we have figured out its brightness, we can use our stack of images to shade it better. We select the image in our stack that has the same average brightness as our pixel. We now look up the appropriate texel from that image and use this value instead. This will introduce the fine detail such as self-shadowing, which we have captured in our image stack, and make the rendering much more realistic.

11.3.1 Detailed Algorithm

Here we describe the computation necessary for one fragment only; obviously, it has to be repeated for every fragment. We assume that for a fragment, we are given local view and light directions (ω_o, ω_i), as well as a set of texture coordinates (s, t).

First, we compute the value r by evaluating a lighting model, that is, the BRDF f_r (which can be any BRDF model) multiplied by the cosine of the incident angle:

$$r\left(\omega_o, \omega_i\right) = \sigma f_r\left(\omega_o, \omega_i\right) \cos \theta_i.$$

The value σ is used to fine-tune the shade of the material. It is needed if the acquisition is not done with a unit light source or if only low-dynamic-range images are captured.

For example, for the simple Phong model, this computation boils down to the following formula:

$$r\left(\omega_o, \omega_i\right) = \sigma\left(k_d \cos \theta_i + k_s\left(\omega_o \times \omega_{i,\,reflected}\right)^E\right),$$

where k_d and k_s are the diffuse and specular coefficients, respectively, and E is the specular exponent.

Now we compute the amount of reflected light by multiplying the intensity of the incident light with the value $S(r)$ from our shading map:

$$L_0\left(\omega_o\right) = S\left(r\left(\omega_o, \omega_i\right)\right) I\left(\omega_i\right),$$

where $I(\omega_i)$ is the intensity of the light source (coming from ω_i). Using the value $r(\omega_o, \omega_i)$, we do a lookup into our shading map using the operator $S()$. It performs the lookup with the coordinates $(s, t, r/a_{max} \times (N-1))$, where (s, t) signifies the position in the map, and $r/a_{max} \times (N-1)$ is the layer to be chosen (as before, a_{max} is the maximum acquired value and N is the number of slices). Trilinear filtering of the shading map samples should be used to avoid blockiness and contouring artifacts.

One special case needs to be treated. If the required value r is higher than the maximum average value a_{max} in our shading map, we can either clamp the result at a_{max} or scale the brightest image in our shading map to the desired level r_i. The smallest average radiance r_0 is always zero (see Equation 1), and no special treatment is required.

11.3.2 Real-Time Rendering

The algorithm for real-time rendering using graphics hardware is straightforward. We load the shading map as a 3D (volume) texture onto the graphics hardware. In a vertex shader, we compute $r(\omega_o, \omega_i)$ (for a single-point light source). The result of the vertex shader is a set of texture coordinates $(s, t, r/a_{max})$, which is then used to look up into the shading map. A fragment shader performs the multiplication with the intensity of the light source. See Listing 11-1 for a vertex and fragment shader performing this operation.

Newer graphics hardware supports dependent texture lookups in the fragment shaders. With this feature, it is possible to compute the BRDF (times the cosine) on a per-fragment basis and then do a dependent texture lookup into the shading map, which avoids undersampling artifacts that may occur when using a vertex shader.

Listing 11-1. The Vertex and Pixel Shaders Needed for Rendering
In this example, we used the enhanced Phong shading model.

```
// Vertex Shader
void btfv( float4 position : POSITION,
           float3 normal   : NORMAL,
           float3 tex      : TEXCOORD0,
       out float4 HPOS     : POSITION,
       out float3 TEX      : TEXCOORD0,
       out float4 COL0     : TEXCOORD1,
           uniform float4x4 mvp,
           uniform float3 lightpos, uniform float3 eye,
           uniform float lightintensity, uniform float Ka,
           uniform float Kd, uniform float Ks, uniform float N )
{
  // compute light direction
  float3 L = lightpos - (float3)position;
  L = normalize( L );

  // compute reflected direction
  float3 R = (2.0f * dot(eye, normal) * normal - eye);

  // lighting (enhanced, physically correct Phong model)
  const float pi = 3.14159265;
  float costh = dot(normal, L);
  float specular = pow(dot(R, L), N);
  float intensity = Kd/pi + Ks * (N + 2.0) * specular/(2.0 * pi);
  intensity *= costh; // * cos(th)

  // check boundaries
  if ( diffuse < 0.0 || intensity < 0.0 ) intensity = 0.0;
  if ( intensity > 1.0 ) intensity = 1.0;

  // add ambient
  intensity += Ka;

  // set coordinates for lookup into volume
  TEX.z = intensity;  // based on lighting, a_max assumed to be 1
  TEX.xy = tex.xy;    // copy the 2D part from application
```

```
  // set light source intensity for scaling in fragment shader
  COL0.rgb = lightintensity;

  // transform position
  HPOS = mul(mvp, position);
}


// Fragment Shader
float3 btfp( float3 tc    : TEXCOORD0,
             float3 color : TEXCOORD1,
             uniform sampler3D material : TEXUNIT0) : COLOR
{
  float3 r = (float3)tex3D( material, tc ).xyz; // lookup into volume
  return r * color;                             // scale by intensity
}
```

11.4 Results

We will show several renderings with acquired materials. All materials were acquired using ten different light source positions. The images were cropped to 1024×1024 and then downscaled to 512×512. In order to be compatible with graphics hardware, which usually requires power-of-two texture sizes, we resampled these ten images down to eight images during linearization. The linearization takes about 5 seconds for each set of images. For all renderings, we have used the Phong model.

In Figure 11-4, you can see different renderings done with our real-time implementation. The materials shown are jeans (Stanford bunny and pants), suede (Stanford bunny), leather (cat), pressed wood (head), wax (head), nylon (pants), cloth (piece of cloth), and wool (piece of knit cloth).

Figure 11-5 shows a rendering of a sweater made of wool. The left image was done with a full BTF (6,500 images, compressed using principal components analysis with 16 components). The right image was done with our technique. Differences are visible mainly at grazing angles, where masking effects become important, which cannot be reproduced by our technique. This also results in slight color differences (although some color difference is also caused by the compression). Considering that wool is one of the materials that violates our initial assumptions (it has a larger-scale structure and is anisotropic), our method does fairly well.

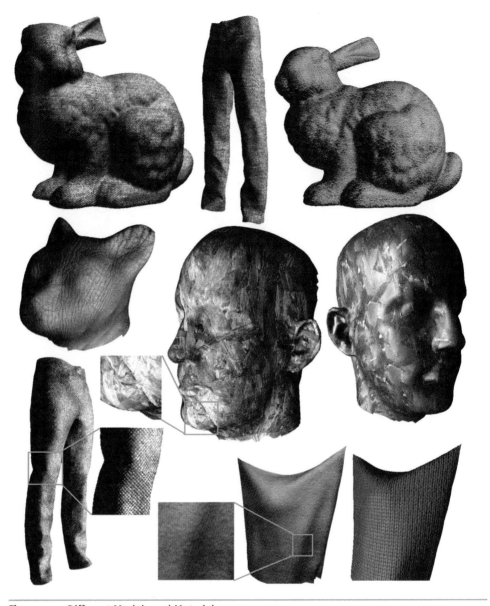

Figure 11-4. Different Models and Materials
The materials shown are jeans, suede, leather, pressed wood, wax, nylon, cloth, and wool. All models are rendered in real time.

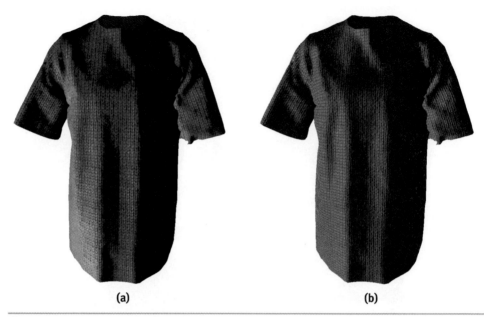

(a)   (b)

Figure 11-5. A Sweater Made of Wool
(a) Full BTF. (b) New method.

11.4.1 Discussion

Why is it sufficient to acquire images for a fixed view and only several incident illumination directions? As stated earlier, we are acquiring only the change in illumination due to a material's surface structure, and for this purpose our method suffices. The artist supplies the actual BRDF.

We believe that this technique works so well because a human observer expects a certain kind of variation in materials. Judging from the results, this variation is captured by our technique and gives a good impression of the actual materials.

Generally speaking, materials with small-scale variations, such as the cloth, suede, jeans, and other materials shown, work best. Materials with spatially varying reflectance properties (such as different specularities, and so on) are captured well, too, as can be seen in the candle wax and pressed wood in Figure 11-4.

For certain materials, though, this technique works less well. For example, the acquisition of highly specular materials is problematic, mainly because of our use of a point light source as an approximation to a parallel light source. Our method assumes materials with a fine-scale structure. This is because our technique models variation with the incidence angle only, not with the azimuth. Therefore, shadows from larger structures cannot be captured or represented well, because they always appear in the same direction. Furthermore, the materials are assumed to be isotropic.

Even for materials violating these assumptions, our technique might still be suitable for a fast preview, because it is much better than regular texturing, as Figure 11-1 shows.

11.5 Conclusion

We have presented a method that enables acquisition and rendering of complex spatially varying materials using only a few images. This empirical method does not capture the actual BRDF but only how illumination changes due to fine surface structure; the BRDF can be adapted later. Real-time rendering using the technique can be easily implemented.

11.6 References

Dana, K., B. van Ginneken, S. Nayar, and J. Koenderink. 1999. "Reflectance and Texture of Real-World Surfaces." *ACM Transactions on Graphics* 18(1), January 1999, pp. 1–34.

Kautz, J., M. Sattler, R. Sarlette, R. Klein, and H.-P. Seidel. 2004. "Decoupling BRDFs from Surface Mesostructures." In *Proceedings of Graphics Interface 2004*, May 2004, pp. 177–184.

Lensch, H., J. Kautz, M. Goesele, W. Heidrich, and H.-P. Seidel. 2001. "Image-Based Reconstruction of Spatially Varying Materials." In *12th Eurographics Workshop on Rendering*, June 2001, pp. 103–114.

Matusik, W., H. Pfister, A. Ngan, P. Beardsley, and L. McMillan. 2002. "Image-Based 3D Photography Using Opacity Hulls." *ACM Transactions on Graphics (Proceedings of SIGGRAPH 2002)*, July 2002, pp. 427–437.

Sattler, M., R. Sarlette, and R. Klein. 2003. "Efficient and Realistic Visualization of Cloth." In *Eurographics Symposium on Rendering 2003*, June 2003, pp. 167–178.

Chapter 12

Tile-Based Texture Mapping

Li-Yi Wei
NVIDIA Corporation

Many graphics applications such as games and simulations frequently use large textures for walls, floors, or terrain. There are several issues with large textures. First, they can consume significant storage, in either disk space, system memory, or graphics memory. Second, they can consume significant bandwidth, during either initial texture loading or rendering. Third, most graphics cards impose an upper limit on individual texture sizes. For example, the GeForce 6800 has an upper resolution limit of $4{,}096 \times 4{,}096$ for RGBA8 textures, and many other GPUs have stricter limitations.

One possible solution to address these problems is texture compression. However, existing GPU texture-compression techniques such as DXT have a limited compression ratio. In addition, texture compression cannot handle the problem of texture size limit.

An alternative approach is texture tiling, as shown in Figure 12-1. For example, if we have a large wall or floor consisting of repeating tiles, then obviously we don't have to store all the tiles. Instead, we could have just one tile and repeat it on the wall. For more complex patterns, we can dice up the wall or floor into smaller polygons and apply different texture tiles or texture coordinate transformations for each polygon. The advantage of this approach is that we can achieve infinite compression ratio in theory, because we can produce an arbitrarily large output from a few tiles. The disadvantage, however, lies in the complication of application code and data.

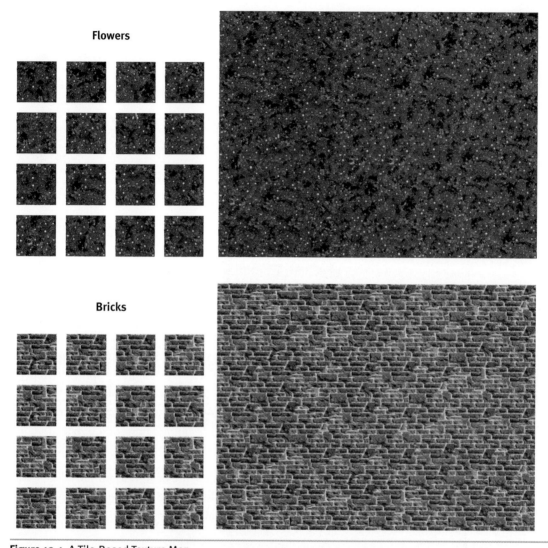

Flowers

Bricks

Figure 12-1. A Tile-Based Texture Map
Given a small set of input texture tiles (left), our system provides a large virtual texture map (right) without storing the entire texture. Our approach supports native hardware texture filtering and does not require modifying the geometry or texture coordinates of the application.

Our goal is to present a tile-based texture-mapping scheme that is transparent to the application. Specifically, we do not require changing the original geometry or texture coordinates in order to use texture tiles. Instead, we implement the texture tiling as a fragment program that handles the details of accessing and filtering the tiled texture.

12.1 Our Approach

We represent a large texture as a small set of tiles and assemble the tiles into a large virtual texture on the fly for answering texture requests. To minimize visual repetition, we assemble the tiles nonperiodically. There is a huge literature on nonperiodic tiling, but for our method, we chose Wang tiles for their simplicity (Cohen et al. 2003). Wang tiles are square tiles in which each tile edge is encoded with a color. A valid tiling requires all shared edges between tiles to have matching colors. When a set of Wang tiles is filled with texture patterns that are continuous across matching tile edges, a valid tiling from such a set can produce an arbitrarily large texture without pattern discontinuity. A sample Wang tiling is shown in Figure 12-2.

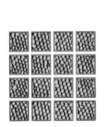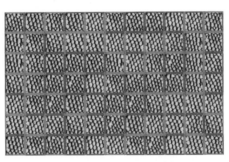

Figure 12-2. Texture Tiling Using Wang Tiles
The input tiles are shown on the left, and a sample tiling is shown on the right. In this example, we have two vertical and horizontal tile edge colors, represented as red and green, respectively. In the output, note that adjacent tiles share identical edge colors.

We extend the Wang tiling approach to a GPU-friendly implementation. Given a texture request (s, t), we first figure out on which tile it lands, based on the (s, t) location. We then fetch the corresponding texels from that input texture tile. Figure 12-3 illustrates the procedure. We carefully pack the texture tiles into a single texture map so that we can perform texture fetching and filtering on this single texture via texturing hardware.

12.2 Texture Tile Construction

There are several methods to construct the Wang tile set. One possibility is to draw the tiles manually; all we need to do is to ensure that the drawings are continuous across tile boundaries while producing sufficiently interesting tiling results. Figures 12-5 and 12-6, later in this chapter, show a tile set drawn by me and the tiling results, respectively. This manual approach works only for line art.

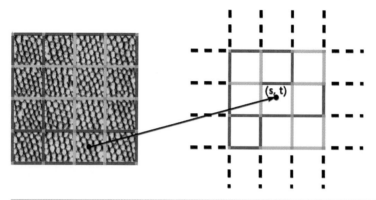

Figure 12-3. An Overview of Tile-Based Texture Mapping
Left: The packed input tiles. Right: The output virtual texture. Given a texture request (s, t), our algorithm first determines on which tile the request lands. The algorithm then fetches the corresponding texels from that input tile.

For natural texture patterns such as those from photographs, there are algorithmic ways to build the tile set, as described in Cohen et al. 2003, Section 3.2. We have found that this approach works well for many natural texture patterns, and we provide the source code on the accompanying CD. The sample tiles previously shown in Figure 12-1 were generated with this approach.

There are additional methods for constructing the tiles; we refer readers to Cohen et al. 2003 for more details.

12.3 Texture Tile Packing

One common problem with previous texture tiling or atlas approaches is the filtering issue. Specifically, given a collection of tiles, how do we perform filtering for the output virtual texture, especially when the sample is on the tile border and requires texels from multiple tiles for bilinear or trilinear filtering?

There are several possible solutions, among them performing texture filtering in the fragment program, or packing all tiles into a single texture and adding boundary padding between the tiles so that bilinear filtering would be correct. The first of these is computationally expensive, and the second consumes a large amount of texture memory.

In our approach, we pack all the texture tiles into a single texture map without any boundary padding, in a way that makes it possible to perform the texture filtering directly via the texturing hardware without fragment program emulation. We achieve this by packing a set of Wang tiles into a single texture map, ensuring that any tile edges shared between two tiles have identical edge color encoding. Because the tiles are built with a continuous pattern across identical edge colors, bilinear filtering directly across adjacent tiles produces the correct result. It is possible to prove that, for a complete tile set (that is, with all possible edge color combinations), it is always possible to pack the tiles in such a way. In addition, each tile is used only once, so there is no wasted texture memory.

Here we describe how the packing can be done, without going into detailed mathematical proofs, which can be found in Wei 2004. For clarity, we begin with packing in one dimension. We assume that we have a set of tiles with only one horizontal edge color and that we would like to pack them horizontally. The packing can be achieved with the following equation:

$$TileIndex1D\left(e_1, e_2\right) = \begin{cases} 0, & e_1 = e_2 = 0 \\ e_1^2 + 2 \times e_2 - 1, & e_1 > e_2 > 0 \\ 2 \times e_1 + e_2^2, & e_2 > e_1 \geq 0 \\ \left(e_1 + 1\right)^2 - 2, & e_1 = e_2 > 0 \\ \left(e_1 + 1\right)^2 - 1, & e_1 > e_2 = 0 \end{cases} \quad (1)$$

Basically, given a tile with left edge e_1 and right edge e_2, where e_1 and e_2 are integer indices starting from 0, this function computes the horizontal location of this tile within the packing. A sample 1D packing with three vertical edge colors can be found in Figure 12-4a.

The packing in 2D can be performed by computing vertical and horizontal indices separately using Equation 1. In other words, the horizontal tile location is computed from the left and right edges only, and the vertical tile location is computed from the top and bottom edges only. A 2D sample packing with three vertical and horizontal edge colors can be found in Figure 12-4b. The computation can be expressed in Cg-like code as shown in Listing 12-1.

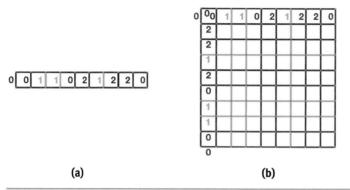

(a)   (b)

Figure 12-4. Examples of Tile Packing
(a) 1D packing with three colors. (b) 2D packing with three vertical and horizontal colors.

Listing 12-1. Code for Tile Packing

```
float TileIndex1D(const float e1, const float e2)
{
  float result;
  if (e1 < e2) result = (2 * e1 + e2 * e2);
  else if (e1 == e2)
    if (e1 > 0) result = ((e1 + 1) * (e1 + 1) - 2);
    else result = 0;
  else
    if (e2 > 0) result = (e1 * e1 + 2 * e2 - 1);
    else result = ((e1 + 1) * (e1 + 1) - 1);
  return result;
}


float2 TileIndex2D(const float4 e)
{
  float2 result;
  // orthogonally compute the horizontal and vertical locations
  // the x, y, z, w components of e store
  // the south, east, north, and west edge coding
  result.x = TileIndex1D(e.w, e.y);
  result.y = TileIndex1D(e.x, e.z);
  return result;
}
```

12.4 Texture Tile Mapping

Given that the output virtual texture is composed from the tile set, we need to know which tile is used for each region of the texture. Specifically, for each texture coordinate (s, t), we need to be able to determine efficiently on which tile it lands.

There are two possible solutions for mapping tiles into the output texture. The first approach is simply to precompute the mapping and store the result into an index texture map. For example, if the output is composed of 128×128 tiles, then we use a 128×128 index texture to store the (*row, column*) location of each tile as in the input pack. Because the index texture map will have limited size, this approach isn't able to handle arbitrarily large textures. However, it is more than enough for most applications, and it is very efficient. Note that this index map does not require a mipmap pyramid because we do not require mipmap filtering for the (*row, column*) locations.

The second approach does not need this index texture at all; instead, the tile for each output region can be computed on the fly via a special fragment program with hashing. This approach has the advantage that it does not consume an extra texture map, and it does not suffer from the restriction on index texture map size, as in the first approach. However, in our current implementation, we have found the second approach too slow for real-time applications; so for the rest of this chapter, we discuss only the first approach. However, the second approach might be faster in future-generation GPUs, and we refer interested readers to Wei 2004 for more details.

Given that we have a precomputed index texture, the process for our tile-based texture mapping is actually pretty simple, and is best explained by the actual Cg program, as shown in Listing 12-2. Given the input coordinate, we first scale it with respect to the number of tiles in the output. We then use this scaled value to fetch the index texture, which will tell us which input tile to use. Finally, we use the fractional part of the scaled texture coordinate to fetch the final texel from the selected input tile. Note that in the final texture fetch, we need to specify the derivatives ddx and ddy to ensure the correct level-of-detail computation.

Listing 12-2. Code for Tile Mapping

```
struct FragmentInput
{
  float4 tex : TEX0;
  float4 col : COL0;
};
```

Listing 12-2 *(continued)*. Code for Tile Mapping

```
struct FragmentOutput
{
  float4 col : COL;
};

float2 mod(const float2 a, const float2 b)
{
  // emulate integer mod operations in a float-only environment
  return floor(frac(a/b) * b);
}

FragmentOutput fragment(FragmentInput input,
    uniform sampler2D tilesTexture,
    uniform samplerRECT indexTexture)
{
  FragmentOutput output;

  // osizeh and osizev are the number of output tiles
  // they are compile-time constants
  float2 mappingScale = float2(osizeh, osizev);
  // the scaling is required for RECT textures
  // we will also need its fractional part in the final tex read
  float2 mappingAddress = input.tex.xy * mappingScale;
  // figure out which input tile to use
  float4 whichTile = texRECT(indexTexture,
                             mod(mappingAddress, mappingScale));

  // isizeh and isizev are the number of input tiles
  // they are compile-time constants
  float2 tileScale = float2(isizeh, isizev);
  // this is to ensure the correct input mipmap level is accessed
  float2 tileScaledTex = input.tex.xy * float2(osizeh/isizeh,
                                               osizev/isizev);

  // fetch the final texel color
  // note we need to specify ddx/ddy explicitly
  output.col = tex2D(tilesTexture,
                     (whichTile.xy + frac(mappingAddress))/tileScale,
                     ddx(tileScaledTex), ddy(tileScaledTex));
  return output;
}
```

12.5 Mipmap Issues

An inherent limitation of any tile-based texturing system is that mipmaps at lower resolutions are incorrect. There are actually several issues with mipmaps.

First, the maximum number of mipmap levels is constrained by the input tiles, which are of much smaller size than the output. For example, assuming we pack 4×4 tiles each with 32×32 pixels into a single 128×128 texture map, then the maximum number of mipmap levels is 8. Obviously, for any output texture larger than 128×128, we will not be able to access the coarser resolutions. In our experience, this is usually not a problem, because the tiles would reduce to a homogeneous void at lower resolutions anyway.

We also need to be careful when constructing the mipmap texture for the packed input. If you just use the automatic mipmap generation, chances are that the tiles will not be legal Wang tiles at lower mipmap resolutions. This can produce annoying aliasing artifacts when filtering across the tile boundary. Figure 12-5 demonstrates such a case.

As shown in Figure 12-5, in the output we have two tiles, ▮ and ▢, adjacent to each other. If we have a request (s, t) that lands on the right edge of ▮, and assuming the filter kernel is sufficiently large, as can happen in lower-resolution mipmap levels, then a correct filtering should involve a majority of the tile ▢. Unfortunately, because we always perform filtering in the input packing, the filtering would involve a majority of ◗ instead, and this is obviously incorrect. A more serious problem occurs when the filter footprint just crosses the boundary between ▮ and ▢. In this case, the filtering result would change discontinuously in the input, with an abrupt switch from filtering tiles ▮ and ◗ to ◖ and ▢. And this artifact could exhibit itself both spatially and temporally.

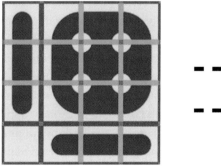 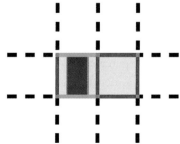

Figure 12-5. Artifacts Caused by Filtering
Involving tiles ▮, ▢, ◗, and ◖. Left: Packed input tiles. Right: Output virtual texture.

To remove these artifacts, we have to sanitize the tiles at all lower-resolution mipmap levels to ensure that they are legal Wang tiles. We achieve this by averaging all tile edges with the same color ID across all tiles. This does not produce a theoretically correct result (unless you store the entire lower-resolution mipmap levels for the output), but it at least eliminates popping visual artifacts. An implementation of this algorithm is available on the accompanying CD.

Figure 12-6 demonstrates the sanitization effects on the rendering. Without tile correction, the rendering would contain noticeable discontinuity, as shown in case (a). With correction on tile edges, the results look much better, as shown in case (b). A more correct approach would be to sanitize both edges and corners, but we have found that this usually produces over-blurry results, as case (c) demonstrates. In our experience, because most textures are homogeneous at lower mipmap resolutions, it is usually sufficient to sanitize edges only.

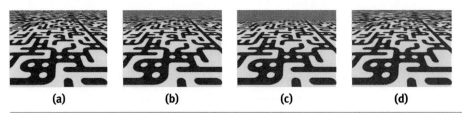

Figure 12-6. Filtering Results at Lower-Resolution Mipmap Levels
(a) Incorrect lower-resolution tiles. (b) Corrected tile edges only. (c) Corrected tile edges and corners. (d) Traditional texture mapping.

12.6 Conclusion

We have presented a tile-based texture-mapping system that generates a large virtual texture from a small set of tiles. We have described a Cg program implementation that does not require changing geometry or texture coordinates in the application. Our implementation requires two texture reads to emulate one large virtual texture, and is roughly 50 to 25 percent slower than a single-texture program (as measured on a GeForce 6800 GT, depending on various factors such as filtering mode and original program complexity). However, the speed is still fast enough for most applications, and the savings in texture memory is substantial. There are quality limitations of our approach at lower-resolution mipmap levels, but as long as the tile set is built correctly, the result looks reasonable despite being theoretically incorrect.

12.7 References

Cohen, Michael F., Jonathan Shade, Stefan Hiller, and Oliver Deussen. 2003. "Wang Tiles for Image and Texture Generation." *ACM Transactions on Graphics (Proceedings of SIGGRAPH 2003)* 22(3), pp. 287–294.

Glanville, R. Steven. 2004. "Texture Bombing." In *GPU Gems*, edited by Randima Fernando, pp. 323–338. Addison-Wesley.

Lefebvre, Sylvain, and Fabrice Neyret. 2003. "Pattern Based Procedural Textures." In *Proceedings of SIGGRAPH 2003 Symposium on Interactive 3D Graphics*, pp. 203–212.

Losasso, Frank, and Hugues Hoppe. 2004. "Geometry Clipmaps: Terrain Rendering Using Nested Regular Grids." *ACM Transactions on Graphics (Proceedings of ACM SIGGRAPH 2004)* 23(3), pp. 769–776.

Tanner, Christopher, Christopher Migdal, and Michael Jones. 1998. "The Clipmap: A Virtual Mipmap." In *Proceedings of SIGGRAPH 98*, pp. 151–158.

Wei, Li-Yi. 2004. "Tile-Based Texture Mapping on Graphics Hardware." In *Proceedings of Graphics Hardware 2004*, pp. 55–63.

I would like to thank the people who helped me in my original paper (Wei 2004), Hugues Hoppe for pointing out the mipmap issue, Shaun Ho for recommending the submission of this technique for this book, and my NVIDIA colleagues for their help and support.

Chapter 13

Implementing the mental images Phenomena Renderer on the GPU

Martin-Karl Lefrançois
mental images

13.1 Introduction

mental images' rendering software mental ray is the rendering component of many leading 3D content-creation tools, including industrial CAD, product design, and architectural design software packages. mental ray is widely used for the creation of visual effects and feature animation films, as well as for high-quality visualization and lighting simulation in industrial and architectural design. Now that modern GPUs can execute complex programs to compute the color of each shaded pixel, there is an opportunity to apply this power to rendering complex scenes that previously could be handled only by a CPU-based renderer. Given the substantial floating-point computational power available on GPUs, doing these computations on the GPU can be much faster than on the CPU. This chapter describes some of the work that mental images has done to add support for GPU-based rendering to mental ray.

Because the per-fragment mathematical computation done by a GPU can now be identical to the computation done by a software renderer, it is possible to use the GPU to accelerate rendering of the final image. Although some techniques, such as software ray tracing, cannot yet be replaced with an efficient GPU-based solution due to the limitations of current hardware, there are many scenes that do not require these techniques. Such scenes can be entirely rendered by the GPU. In some cases, we still have to combine software and hardware rendering to achieve the final image, but hardware technology evolves so fast that we will see more and more of the work shifting to the GPU.

One of the main difficulties with rendering high-quality imagery on the GPU is making it possible to use the same shaders on the GPU as on the CPU. Production companies use a carefully developed set of shaders that they combine to create the final effect they want. With most GPU programming languages, it is difficult to efficiently combine shaders, because the languages are designed for monolithic programs that implement a complete effect. However, the release of Cg 1.2 was a breakthrough for the creation of complex shaders on the GPU: with the addition of shader interfaces and unsized arrays to the language, it became possible to combine shaders at runtime to generate GPU programs that render the desired final effect.

In this chapter, we briefly review mental ray's 3.3/3.4 shading architecture and describe how we convert combinations of mental ray shaders to GPU programs. The techniques we use provide a powerful and flexible means of creating complex visual effects. We are now able to accelerate rendering of final images with the GPU without sacrificing quality or visual richness.

13.2 Shaders and Phenomena

For high-quality offline rendering, the concept of a "shader" is a slightly different one than for interactive rendering on GPUs. On the GPU, vertex shaders and fragment shaders operate on the input geometry to compute the color of each pixel. In mental ray, shaders are plug-in modules that are used in materials, light sources, cameras, and other elements to control a wide range of effects, from surface material, volume, and camera lens properties to compositing. High-end visual effects and feature animation production companies keep separate effect components in separate shaders that are combined automatically at runtime; it often makes more sense to divide particular visual effects into smaller elements that separately represent the environment and what interacts with it. As an example, objects carry surface shaders that define the response of the surface to incident light (that is, the BRDF). Lights are separate scene elements that carry light shaders that define the light emission characteristics. Both need to be combined at runtime to perform shading. Additionally, there are volume shaders; lens shaders attached to cameras; texture, environment, and other shaders that all contribute to shading and must be collected to create the fragment program.

When a software renderer renders a scene, different shaders are called in different stages of the pipeline. In the following example, the first shader to be called is the material shader, which defines the color of the illuminated surface. Then the light shaders of all of the lights illuminating this surface will be called in order to determine how much illumination they shine on the surface. Light shaders behave differently depending on whether they are point, spot, or area lights. If the surface is reflective, the environment shader may be called to add its contribution to the surface. If ray tracing is enabled, a ray might hit another object, whose material shader will then be called. If the object is transparent, the material and light shaders will be called again until full opacity is achieved. In addition to all those shaders, volume shaders, such as fog, can affect the final image. The volume shader, if attached to the camera, will be called for every sample. Figure 13-1 illustrates these basic concepts.

The mental ray renderer further extends this idea to include Phenomenon components (Driemeyer 2005). These look like shaders when they are applied to the scene, but their functionality is implemented in a different way. Whereas shaders usually function as standalone components, Phenomena encapsulate sets of subshader nodes connected to form graphs, as well as associated rendering options, geometry, material, volumes, and other elements that are automatically integrated at appropriate points in the scene. (Phenomena are a superset of Maya's Hypershade graphs, for example.) Both shaders

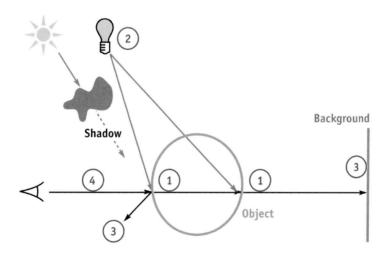

Shaders: (1) Material, (2) Light, (3) Environment, (4) Volume

Figure 13-1. Shaders in a Scene

and Phenomena have *interface parameters* that feed data into them and *result parameters* that return the result of their evaluation. In the case of Phenomena, the result parameters of the Phenomenon are taken from a specific shader that is called the *main root shader* of the Phenomenon.

Once defined, the shader can be used to control the surface properties of a material. Shaders and Phenomena can be connected to form shader graphs. In mental ray, users can assign the result parameter of another shader to an interface parameter.

Figure 13-2 shows an example of a Phenomenon. It uses three input parameter values to compute the result. These parameter values in turn may be computed by other shaders, may be constants set by the user, may be the results of texture lookups, and so on. Note that in this case, the final result value is computed by another "sub" Phenomenon in the blue box. This ability to "wire up" Phenomenon graphs in many different ways, using modular pieces, makes them a powerful paradigm for artists and designers.

In the schematic diagrams in this chapter, boxes represent shaders or Phenomena; their interface parameters (such as "ambient," "diffuse," or "specular") are on the left side and the result parameters are on the right side. Phenomenon instances are useful as prepackaged effects: a wood Phenomenon, for example, may have parameters that define colors and wood grain turbulence, and different predefined instances of it can supply parameter values to make it look like oak, redwood, birch, or other variations.

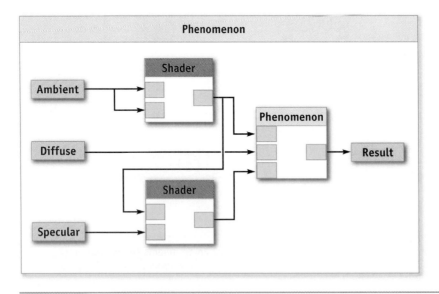

Figure 13-2. An Example of a Phenomenon

When using shaders or Phenomena in a scene, you need to know three properties:

- The name of the shader or Phenomenon
- Its interface parameters
- Its result parameter

The shader name is identical to the name of the Cg structure type that implements it. The interface parameters are a set of named values passed to the shader or Phenomenon when it runs. For example, a shader implementing Phong shading could have three interface parameters of type `color` named `ambient`, `diffuse`, and `specular` and one of type `scalar` named `exponent`. Finally, the result parameters of a shader represent the values returned by the shaders. Most of the time, this is a single value of type `color`, but other types and structures of multiple values are also possible.

13.3 Implementing Phenomena Using Cg

Because GPUs do not support loading multiple shaders and then having one shader call another shader at runtime, mental ray must collect the Phenomenon—including all subshaders that feed its input parameters, root shaders, and assigned shaders (such as light shaders that illuminate the surface)—into a single fragment program that can be downloaded to the GPU. The shader interfaces feature introduced in Cg 1.2 (Pharr 2004) facilitates this process.

In our system, we have predefined an abstract Cg interface type for each of the parameter types that may be passed as input, or computed as output, by a shader component. Shaders and Phenomena are written to use these abstract interface types when declaring input and output parameters. At runtime, concrete instances of each subshader are created using the Cg runtime library, and the outputs of each internal subshader are connected to the proper inputs, as shown in Figure 13-3.

The rest of this section provides details on the GPU programs we use, the interface types we define, and how output parameters are connected to the inputs of other shaders to form graphs.

13.3.1 The Cg Vertex Program and the Varying Parameters

We have found that for the majority of effects we want to achieve, we can use the same vertex program. This vertex program primarily serves as a simple pass-through for the

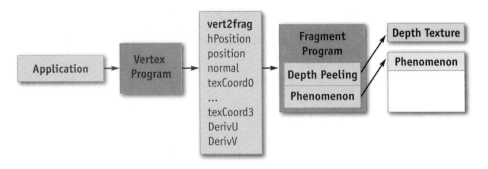

Figure 13-3. How a Phenomenon Fits into the Graphics Pipeline

data coming from the application. The most common varying parameters are transformed in the vertex shader and passed to the fragment shader.

In addition to the homogeneous position, the following varying parameters are sent to the fragment programs: the position, the normal, four texture coordinates, and the surface's parametric derivatives in U and V for bump mapping. All data, except texture coordinates, are transformed to camera space for simplicity. For example, the position in the fragment corresponds to the vector from the camera to the rendered pixel in eye space, and the length of the vector corresponds to the distance from the camera. In the fragment program, transformation matrices are available to convert from one space to another if needed. The varying parameters from the vertex program to the fragment program are stored in a structure called vert2frag, shown in Listing 13-1.

Listing 13-1. The Varying Parameters Sent to the Fragment Program

```
struct vert2frag
{
    float4 hPosition : POSITION;   // Homogeneous position
    float2 texCoord0 : TEXCOORD0;  // Texture coordinates
    float2 texCoord1 : TEXCOORD1;  // Texture coordinates
    float2 texCoord2 : TEXCOORD2;  // Texture coordinates
    float2 texCoord3 : TEXCOORD3;  // Texture coordinates
    float3 position  : TEXCOORD4;  // Eye-space position
    float3 normal    : TEXCOORD5;  // Eye-space normal
    float3 derivU    : TEXCOORD6;  // Derivative U
    float3 derivV    : TEXCOORD7;  // Derivative V
    float2 screen    : WPOS;       // Screen space
    float4 face      : COLOR0;     // 1 front, -1 back
};
```

13.3.2 The `main()` Entry Point for Fragment Shaders

All fragment programs composed from component shaders by mental ray must start with an entry function. To be able to translate Phenomena to the GPU, we had to come up with a common main entry point. For all shader graphs, we create a `main()` function that calls the appropriate Phenomenon root shader, which triggers the evaluation of the entire graph of shaders.

This main entry point also handles some general operations required in all shaders. For example, it includes a test for discarding pixels nearer than the z-depth texture, which is used for order-independent transparency.

13.3.3 The General Shader Interfaces

Support for interfaces was introduced in Cg 1.2. These interfaces provide a way to abstract how member functions in structures are implemented. We use them heavily to implement the value returned to a parameter of a shader. To be able to connect the output of one shader with the input parameters of other shaders, we have to define general Cg interface types that are used by all shaders. These default Cg interface types and their implementation are automatically inserted in each program. For each *parameter type* found in the description of the shader, an equivalent interface exists. As an example, if an input parameter is of type `scalar` in the declaration of the shader, it needs to be declared `miiScalar` in the Cg implementation of the shader.

Table 13-1 shows the corresponding parameter and interface types.

Table 13-1. mental ray Basic Type and Corresponding Cg Interfaces

mental ray Type	Cg Interface Type	Return Value
light	miiLight	misLightOut
boolean	miiBoolean	bool
integer	miiInteger	int
scalar	miiScalar	float
vector	miiVector	float3
color	miiColor	float4
color texture	miiColorTexture	float4
matrix	miiMatrix	float4x4

Each Cg interface type defines a single evaluation method, named `eval()`, that returns a value of the corresponding concrete type. For example:

```
// integer
interface miiInteger (
  int eval(vert2frag params);
);

// vector
interface miiVector (
  float3 eval(vert2frag params);
);
```

To write a shader that serves as a concrete implementation of an interface type, we simply define a struct that implements the appropriate `eval()` method. This allows us to "plug in" the struct wherever the corresponding interface type is called for.

As an example, the following case shows the implementation of `miiScalar`, in which we want a simple constant value to be assigned to an interface parameter. We create and connect a simple implementation of the interface, which causes a constant value to be returned by the `eval()` method:

```
// base scalar implementation
struct miScalar : miiScalar {
  float s;
  float eval(vert2frag params) {
    return s;
  }
};
```

13.3.4 Example of a Simple Shader

mental ray needs to know how shaders are defined to properly call them and assign values to the shader's parameter. Here is an example of a shader declaration as it can be found when parsing a mental ray scene:

```
declare shader
  color "mib_illum_phong" (
    color "ambience",
    color "ambient",
    color "diffuse",
    color "specular",
```

```
      scalar "exponent",   # phong exponent
      integer "mode",      # light selection mode 0..2
      array light "lights"
   )
 end declare
```

When writing fragment shaders, we follow a simple rule: in the Cg file implementing the shader, we define a structure that implements the interface corresponding to the return value of the shader as required by the declaration of the shader. The structure should also have the input parameters of the shader and an eval() method for the return interface.

The name of the structure is the same name found in the declaration of the shader. It must implement the return type interface also found in the shader declaration. All of the shader's required input parameters must be defined using their equivalent type interfaces. They also must have the same name as found in the shader declaration.

For a single shader, an instance of the shader will be created and connected to the main root of the Phenomenon. And when no shaders are attached to the input parameters, a simple interface that evaluates to a constant is connected, the variability of which is set to CG_LITERAL using the Cg runtime. Setting the variability to CG_LITERAL allows the Cg compiler to optimize the resulting fragment shader (by using constant folding) to a greater degree than if a uniform value were used.

As shown in Listing 13-2, the name of the structure is the same as the shader declaration. The structure implements the interface miiColor, which corresponds to the output parameter. Not all input parameters are needed; for example, the parameter mode is ignored in the Cg shader.

The graph in Figure 13-4 shows an example of the connection of values in the shader. Some parameters are omitted for clarity.

Listing 13-2. Cg Implementation of the Phong Illumination Model

```
struct mib_illum_phong : miiColor
{
  miiColor  ambience, ambient, diffuse, specular;
  miiScalar exponent;
  miiLight  lights[];

  // Implementation of miiColor
  float4 eval(vert2frag p) {
    float4 result;
```

```
float4 ldiffuse = diffuse.eval(p);
float4 lspecular = specular.eval(p);
float lexponent = exponent.eval(p)

result = ambience.eval(p) * ambient.eval(p);

// Material calculation for each light
for ( int i = 0; i < lights.length; i++ ){
// Light shader evaluation
  misLightOut light = lights[i].eval(p);

  // Lambert's cosine law
  float d = max(0, light.dot_nl);
  result += d * ldiffuse * light.color;

  // Phong's cosine power
  if (d > 0) {
    float s = mi_phong_specular(lexponent, light.dir,
                                vdir, p.normal);
    result += s * lspecular * light.color;
  }
}

return result;
  }
};
```

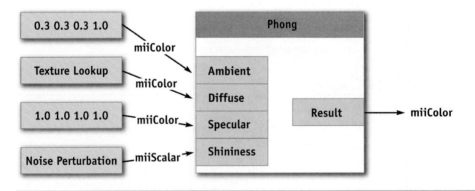

Figure 13-4. An Example of a Simple Shader

13.3.5 Global State Variables

Shaders may need additional information that is not passed to them via interface parameters. For example, it might be important to know the current object being rendered or the resolution of the final image. Also, many shaders need to convert from one coordinate space to another, which requires access to various transformation matrices. Our system uses specific global state variables to provide these values. For example, when creating a program, our system iterates through its global parameters looking for any named "miToWorld". If the program contains this parameter name and if the type corresponds to float4x4, it is initialized with the appropriate transformation matrix. Table 13-2 shows the variables that can be used.

These state variables are created as shared parameters using the Cg runtime. When we find a known state parameter as a program's global parameter, we just connect it to the corresponding global uniform parameter. When the value changes during a frame, we only have to update the value of the shared parameter to have the value updated in each shader that has a parameter bound to it. This use of uniform values is illustrated in Figure 13-5.

13.3.6 Light Shaders

Light shaders implement the characteristics of a light source. For example, a spotlight shader would use the illumination direction to attenuate the amount of light emitted within a cone. A light shader is called whenever a material shader uses the light interface to evaluate a light. In production scenes, we often find a lot of different lights illuminating a model. In our implementation, all light shaders must return a structure containing the amount of contributed color from the light, the direction to the light, and the dot product of the light direction and the normal. Because surface shaders are written to call out to the abstract light interface to get these values back, it is easy to use any type of light that implements this interface with any type of surface shader.

Light shaders are also responsible for shadow casting, as illustrated in Figure 13-6. In the light shader, we can compute whether or not the fragment is currently visible to the light source, using a shadow map rendered in a previous pass or a software-generated one. If the fragment is not visible, the light will typically return a black color, meaning there will be no light contribution to the illumination of the material.

Listing 13-3 is a sample implementation of a spotlight.

Table 13-2. mental ray Global State Variables

Usage	State Variable Name	Cg Type	Description
Material	`miToWorld`	`float4x4`	Matrix for transforming camera-space coordinates found in `vert2frag.position` to world space.
	`miFromWorld`	`float4x4`	Matrix for transforming world-space coordinates to camera space.
	`miToObject`	`float4x4`	Matrix for transforming camera-space coordinates to object space.
	`miFromObject`	`float4x4`	Matrix for transforming object-space coordinates to camera space.
Light Shaders Only	`miLightOrigin`	`float3`	Position of the light in camera space.
	`miLightDir`	`float3`	Direction of the light in camera space.
	`miLightSpread`	`float`	Spread angle for spotlights.
	`miLightType`	`int`	Type of the light: 0 = point, 1 = spot, 2 = directional
	`miLightFace`	`int`	Lighting face: 1 = front, 2 = back, 0 = both
	`miToLight`	`float4x4`	Matrix for transforming camera-space coordinates to light space.
	`miFromLight`	`float4x4`	Matrix for transforming light-space coordinates to camera space.
Camera	`miCameraAspect`	`float`	Aspect ratio: height $\times$ aspect = width
	`miCameraAperture`	`float`	Aperture size: atan(focal/aperture) = field of view
	`miCameraFocal`	`float`	Focal length: atan(focal/aperture) = field of view
	`miCameraClip`	`float2`	Clip plane: x = near, y = far
	`miCameraRes`	`float2`	Resolution of the window.
	`miCameraOrtho`	`bool`	Is the camera orthographic?
Shadow Map (Light Shaders Only)	`miShadowMap`	`bool`	If true, the global shadow map option is on.
	`miShadowMapTex`	`samplerRECT[1|6]`	Shadow map textures. 1 for spot and directional lights, 6 for point lights.
	`miShadowMapTransform`	`float4x4`	Matrix for transforming `vert2frag.position` to light space.
	`miShadowMapWindow`	`float2`	The transformation to apply to UV coordinates.
	`miShadowMapSize`	`float2`	The resolution of the shadow map.
	`miShadowMapBias`	`float`	The bias applied to the shadow map.
Shader	`miRayEnvironment`	`miiColor`	Connection to the environment shader.

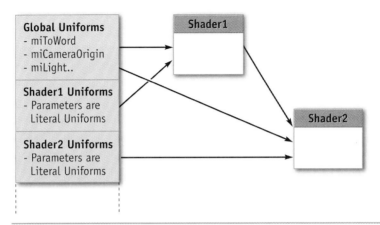

Figure 13-5. How Global Uniforms Are Shared

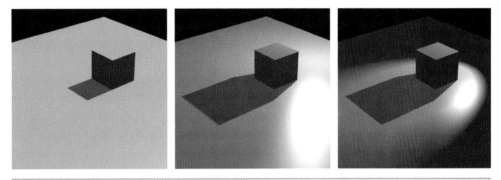

Figure 13-6. Directional, Point, and Spotlight Illumination and Shadow Map

Listing 13-3. Partial Cg Implementation of the mental ray Base Spotlight

```
struct mib_light_spot : miiLight {
  // parameters of the shader
  miiColor color;
  miiBoolean shadow;
  miiScalar factor;
  miiBoolean atten;
  miiScalar start;
  miiScalar stop;
  miiScalar cone;

  // Information from the light instance
  // position of the light
  float3 miLightOrigin;
```

```
  // direction of the light
  float3 miLightDir;
  // cos angle of the spread
  float miLightSpread;

  bool miShadowMap;                    // Shadow active or not?
  samplerRECT miShadowMapTex[1];   // light shadow map
  float4x4 miShadowMapTransfo;     // From camera to light space
  float2 miShadowMapWindow;        // size of the window
  float2 miShadowMapSize;          // size of the shadow map
  float miShadowMapBias;

  // Evaluation of the light
  misLightOut eval(vert2frag p) {
    misLightOut ret_val;
    float4 lcolor = color.eval(p);

    // vector to light
    ret_val.dir = normalize(miLightOrigin - p.position);
    ret_val.dot_nl = dot(p.normal, ret_val.dir);

    // shadow
    if (shadow.eval(p) && miShadowMap) {
      float lfactor = factor.eval(p);
      . . .
      lcolor.rgb *= lerp(lfactor, 1, map_z/4);
    }

    // cone
    . . .

    // dist attenuation
    . . .

    ret_val.color = lcolor;
    return ret_val;
  }
};
```

13.3.7 Texture Shaders

Texture shaders typically return a color from a texture image. They can also be procedural, like the classic marble or wood shaders. When a shader input parameter is attached to a texture image, an explicit `miColorTexture` parameter is created and its texture ID is mapped to the `sampler2D` parameter. By enabling automatic Cg runtime texture parameter management with a call to `cgGLSetManageTextureParameters()`, we do not have to handle the activation of the texture when the program is bound. This way we can load all textures and simply use `cgSetTextureParameter()` to access the image in the shader.

All evaluation methods of the basic interface need only one parameter, the `vert2frag` structure, except for the `miiColorTexture` interface. In addition to the usual varying parameters, we also add a `float2` parameter to pass the UV coordinates.

One nice thing about texture shaders is the ability to generate procedural texture coordinates. Usually UVs are attached to each vertex and are often generated from texture projections. These projections can be created in fragment programs, which can resolve all the artifacts that often arise when applying spherical mappings or other parametric projections at the vertex level.

Figure 13-7 (on the next page) shows a texture shader output, connected to the diffuse parameter of the Phong shader. The texture coordinates are calculated per fragment with a spherical projection.

Listing 13-4 is an example of a simple texture-lookup shader that returns a color.

Listing 13-4. Cg Implementation of the mental ray Texture Lookup Shader

```
struct mib_texture_lookup : miiColor
{
  miiColorTexture tex;
  miiVector coord;
  float4 eval(vert2frag p) {
    // Evaluation of the spherical projection shader
    float3 lcoord = coord.eval(p);
    // Evaluate to a simple tex2D call
    float4 ret_val = tex.eval(p, lcoord.xy);
    return ret_val;
  }
};
```

Figure 13-7. A Texture Shader Connected to the Diffuse Parameter of `mib_illum_phong`

13.3.8 Bump Mapping

In Figure 13-8, the normal vector used for the illumination of a material is perturbed by the bump-map shader. To apply bump mapping to a material shader, we have to modify the varying state normal before the evaluation of the material shader. We do this by adding an extra shader node to our graph, as illustrated in Figure 13-9. The interface of this node takes two parameters: the first one calls the normal modifier and returns the value to the varying state normal; the second parameter calls the material shader. Because the normal used by the material shader has been modified before its evaluation, the lighting is appropriately affected by the bump.

Because this is a shader returning a vector, the shader implementing the normal modifier can be of any type. It can be a normal texture lookup, it can modify the normal based on multiple texture lookups, or it can be procedural. The derivatives sent through the varying parameter ensure that you always sample in the same direction and that the bumps rotate appropriately with the object.

Figure 13-8. `mib_illum_phong` with the Normal Modified Using a Bump-Map Shader

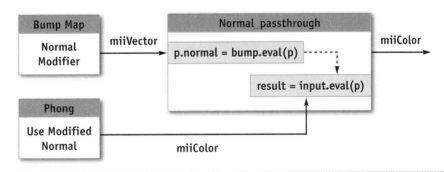

Figure 13-9. The Structure of a Bump Map Shader

13.3.9 Environment and Volume Shaders

The environment shader is an optional extra root of Phenomena that is evaluated if a ray goes to infinity. It can be called for reflective or transparent surfaces, or simply when there are no objects visible in a particular pixel. To make sure we are calling the environment shader for all such pixels of the rendered image, we draw a plane at epsilon in front of the camera's far clip plane.

Because fully general ray tracing is not yet supported on the GPU, reflective or refractive materials do not have the option of sending rays and hitting other objects or themselves. Therefore, they can only reflect their environment. To call the global environment shader graph from another shader, we must define a global state variable. In Figure 13-10, we show the connection between the graph and the global state variable `miRayEnvironment` of type `miiColor`.

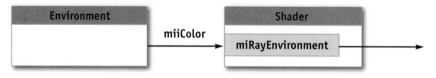

Figure 13-10. The Structure of an Environment Shader

Volume shaders are another Phenomenon root. These shaders need to be called for every rendered fragment. The volume shader attached to the camera affects the rendered color depending on different factors. One simple volume model is fog, which attenuates the color based on the distance to the camera. Because volume shaders need to be called for every fragment, the shader node is placed automatically on top of the main Phenomenon root, as illustrated in Figure 13-11.

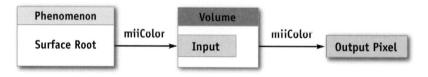

Figure 13-11. The Structure of a Volume Shader

In Figure 13-12, the blue shader for the spikes does not need to be modified due to the fog effect applied in this scene. The layer fog shader attached to the camera modifies the output of each of the scene's shaders, giving an atmospheric effect to the scene.

13.3.10 Shaders Returning Structures

Shaders are not limited to returning a single value; they can have multiple results. The values computed in such shaders are returned as a structure. A shader input parameter

Figure 13-12. Image Rendered Using a Volume Shader

might connect to one of the members of the structure. Because Cg cannot connect interfaces of different types, we must implement converters.

First, the shader that returns the structure must implement the interface of this structure. This interface is needed to connect to a converter. All members of the structure must have a converter node in order to be connected to a shader parameter. A shader returning a color and a vector will have to implement two converters: a structure `mystruct_outColor` implementing `miiColor` and a structure `mystruct_outVector` implementing `miiVector`. The converter has its input parameter connected to the output of the shader and returns a member of that structure. The resulting structure member can now be connected to the destination shader parameter.

Converters can be used by many shaders. To avoid duplicating them, we simply include the converter code using an `#include` statement. Figure 13-13 shows the conversion from an output structure containing a vector to an `miiVector`.

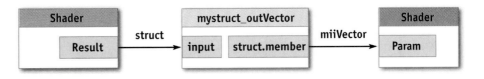

Figure 13-13. A Shader that Returns a Structure

13.3.11 Rendering Hair

In mental ray, hairs are rendered as Bezier curves. Hair width can be specified using a global radius, a per-hair radius, or a per-vertex radius. The approximation of the curves can generate millions of triangles when rendered with the GPU, each often smaller than a fragment. Because hairs are converted to triangles, they can be treated like any other geometry. We can attach a Phenomenon and use the varying parameter to follow the tangent of the hair, the distance from the root relative to the tip, and so on. This information is sufficient to implement any lighting model, because there is no fundamental difference between a hair Phenomenon and any other material Phenomenon. Figure 13-14 shows an example.

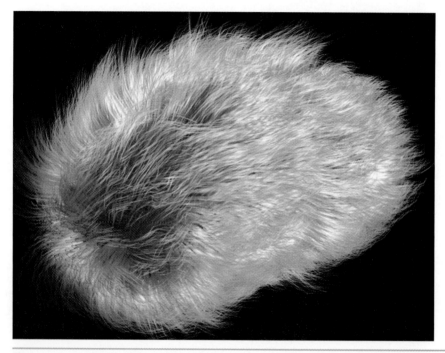

Figure 13-14. A Rendered Hairy Bean

13.3.12 Putting It All Together

When rendering a scene, we start collecting all the lights that need to cast shadow maps. mental ray also uses a Cg shader for evaluating the distance to the light, and the result is stored in a floating-point pbuffer.

We then convert all Phenomena to Cg and construct a unique tree from the different roots. If the resulting shader tree compiles successfully for the profile of the graphics card, the object is drawn by the GPU; otherwise, software renders it.

Because some materials are transparent, we draw the entire scene using an order-independent-transparency technique, also known as depth peeling (Everitt 2001). The shaders know the distance between each level and adjust the color contribution to the frame buffer. This is, for example, how we render hair primitives.

When all render passes are completed in hardware, the frame buffer is merged using the z-depth value and alpha to blend with the software pass.

During this process, a number of things can go wrong. For example, there might not be enough video or texture memory, or the Cg shader may not compile because of hardware limitations. In any of these cases, the objects in which errors occurred are rendered with software.

13.4 Conclusion

Phenomena converted to Cg and Phenomena evaluated by software produce the same result, and in the end, the hardware-rendered image is not noticeably different from the software-rendered version, which was our original goal. With hardware multisampling and supersampling, we can achieve comparable image quality as with software, and rendering on the GPU takes just a small fraction of the time needed for software to render a frame.

In complex production scenes, compiling the numerous shaders takes some time during preprocessing of the scene. Sometimes the Cg compiler overhead can reduce the overall gain from high-speed hardware rendering. But when shaders are compiled and all textures reside in video memory, there is no doubt that using the GPU to render the scene is far faster than using the CPU. With numerous test scenes, we have found that GPUs consistently render an order of magnitude or more faster than CPUs.

GPUs are now so fast that we can push the limit on the numbers of triangles in a scene. Because all triangles do not need to be resident in memory, we can render scenes that are very expensive to render in software. On the other hand, mental ray's software renderer provides functionality that cannot yet be achieved by hardware. Knowing the limitations of the hardware, we can create scenes to exploit its strengths and reduce rendering time by one or two orders of magnitude.

At the time this chapter was written, we noticed that the time to render a frame was being cut by more than a factor of two per year. Each new generation of GPUs provides more power and more memory, and overcomes more limitations. In the near future, current hardware limitations will disappear and will make the usage of GPUs even more common. We think that by 2010, almost all rendering will be GPU based.

13.5 References

Driemeyer, Thomas, ed. 2005. *Rendering with Mental Ray*, 3rd ed. Springer.

Everitt, Cass. 2001. "Order-Independent Transparency." Technical report. NVIDIA Corporation. Available online at **http://developer.nvidia.com/view.asp?IO=order_independent_transparency**

Pharr, Matt. 2004. "An Introduction to Shader Interfaces." In *GPU Gems*, edited by Randima Fernando, pp. 537–550. Addison-Wesley.

Chapter 14

Dynamic Ambient Occlusion and Indirect Lighting

Michael Bunnell
NVIDIA Corporation

In this chapter we describe a new technique for computing diffuse light transfer and show how it can be used to compute global illumination for animated scenes. Our technique is efficient enough when implemented on a fast GPU to calculate ambient occlusion and indirect lighting data on the fly for each rendered frame. It does not have the limitations of precomputed radiance transfer (PRT) or precomputed ambient occlusion techniques, which are limited to rigid objects that do not move relative to one another (Sloan 2002). Figure 14-1 illustrates how ambient occlusion and indirect lighting enhance environment lighting.

Our technique works by treating polygon meshes as a set of surface elements that can emit, transmit, or reflect light and that can shadow each other. This method is so efficient because it works without calculating the visibility of one element to another. Instead, it uses a much simpler and faster technique based on approximate shadowing to account for occluding (blocking) geometry.

14.1 Surface Elements

The first step in our algorithm is to convert the polygonal data to surface elements to make it easy to calculate how much one part of a surface shadows or illuminates another. Figure 14-2 illustrates the basic concept. We define a surface element as an oriented disk with a position, normal, and area. An element has a front face and a back

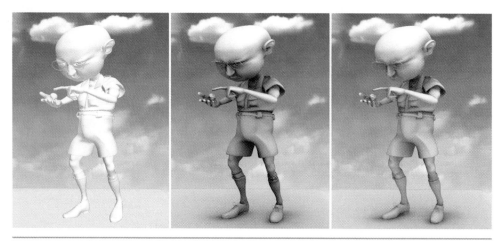

Figure 14-1. Adding Realism with Ambient Occlusion and Indirect Lighting
The scene on the left uses only environment lighting and looks very flat. The middle scene adds soft shadows using ambient occlusion. The scene on the right adds indirect lighting for an extra level of realism.

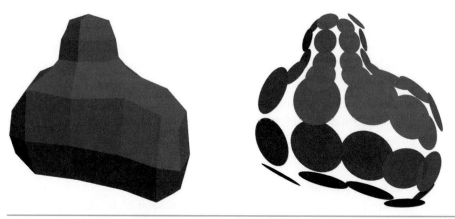

Figure 14-2. Converting a Polygonal Mesh to Elements
Left: A portion of a polygonal mesh. Right: The mesh represented as disk-shaped elements.

face. Light is emitted and reflected from the front-facing side. Light is transmitted and shadows are cast from the back. We create one element per vertex of the mesh. Assuming that the vertices are defined with a position and normal already, we just need to calculate the area of each element. We calculate the area at a vertex as the sum of one-third of the area of the triangles that share the vertex (or one-fourth of the area for quads). Heron's formula for the area of a triangle with sides of length a, b, and c is:

$$\sqrt{s(s-a)(s-b)(s-c)},$$

where s is half the perimeter of the triangle: $(a + b + c)/2$.

We store element data (position, normal, and area) in texture maps because we will be using a fragment program (that is, a pixel shader) to do all the ambient occlusion calculations. Assuming that vertex positions and normals will change for each frame, we need to be able to change the values in the texture map quickly. One option is to keep vertex data in a texture map from the start and to do all the animation and transformation from object space to eye (or world) space with fragment programs instead of vertex programs. We can use render-to-vertex-array to create the array of vertices to be sent down the regular pipeline, and then use a simple pass-through vertex shader. Another, less efficient option is to do the animation and transformation on the CPU and load a texture with the vertex data each frame.

14.2 Ambient Occlusion

Ambient occlusion is a useful technique for adding shadowing to diffuse objects lit with environment lighting. Without shadows, diffuse objects lit from many directions look flat and unrealistic. Ambient occlusion provides soft shadows by darkening surfaces that are partially visible to the environment. It involves calculating the accessibility value, which is the percentage of the hemisphere above each surface point not occluded by geometry (Landis 2002). In addition to accessibility, it is also useful to calculate the direction of least occlusion, commonly known as the *bent normal*. The bent normal is used in place of the regular normal when shading the surface for more accurate environment lighting.

We can calculate the accessibility value at each element as 1 minus the amount by which all the other elements shadow the element. We refer to the element that is shadowed as the *receiver* and to the element that casts the shadow as the *emitter*. We use an approximation based on the solid angle of an oriented disk to calculate the amount by which an emitter element shadows a receiver element. Given that A is the area of the emitter, the amount of shadow can be approximated by:

$$1 - \frac{r \cos \theta_E \max\left(1, \, 4 \cos \theta_R\right)}{\sqrt{\dfrac{A}{\pi} + r^2}}.$$

Equation 14-1. Shadow Approximation

As illustrated in Figure 14-3, θ_E is the angle between the emitter's normal and the vector from the emitter to the receiver. θ_R is the corresponding angle for the receiver element. The max$(1, 4 \times \cos \theta_R)$ term is added to the disk solid angle formula to ignore emitters that do not lie in the hemisphere above the receiver without causing rendering artifacts for elements that lie near the horizon.

Here is the fragment program function to approximate the element-to-element occlusion:

```
float ElementShadow(float3 v, float rSquared, float3 receiverNormal,
                    float3 emitterNormal, float emitterArea)
{
// we assume that emitterArea has already been divided by PI
    return (1 - rsqrt(emitterArea/rSquared + 1)) *
            saturate(dot(emitterNormal, v)) *
            saturate(4 * dot(receiverNormal, v));
}
```

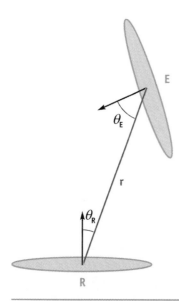

Figure 14-3. The Relationship Between Receiver and Emitter Elements
Receiver element R receives light or shadow from emitter E with r as the distance between the centers of the two elements.

14.2.1 The Multipass Shadowing Algorithm

We calculate the accessibility values in two passes. In the first pass, we approximate the accessibility for each element by summing the fraction of the hemisphere subtended by every other element and subtracting the result from 1. After the first pass, some elements will generally be too dark because other elements that are in shadow are themselves casting shadows. So we use a second pass to do the same calculation, but this time we multiply each form factor by the emitter element's accessibility from the last pass. The effect is that elements that are in shadow will cast fewer shadows on other elements, as illustrated in Figure 14-4. After the second pass, we have removed any double shadowing. However, surfaces that are triple shadowed or more will end up being too light. We can use more passes to get a better approximation, but we can approximate the same answer by using a weighted average of the combined results of the first and second passes. Figure 14-5 shows the results after each pass, as well as a ray-traced solution for comparison. The bent normal calculation is done during the second pass. We compute the bent normal by first multiplying the normalized vector between elements and the form factor. Then we subtract this result from the original element normal.

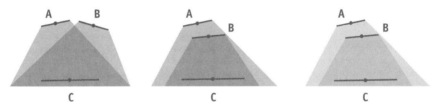

Figure 14-4. Correcting for Occlusion by Overlapping Objects
Left: Elements A and B correctly shadow C after the first pass. Middle: In this arrangement, B casts too much shadow on C. Right: B's shadow is adjusted by the second pass to shadow C properly.

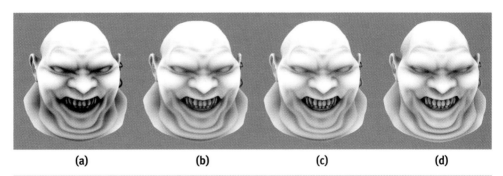

Figure 14-5. Comparing Models Rendered with Our Technique to Reference Images
Model rendered with ambient occlusion accessibility value calculated after (a) one pass, (b) two passes, and (c) three passes of the shader. (d) Image made by tracing 200 random rays per vertex for comparison. Model courtesy of Bay Raitt.

We calculate the occlusion result by rendering a single quad (or two triangles) so that one pixel is rendered for each surface element. The shader calculates the amount of shadow received at each element and writes it as the alpha component of the color of the pixel. The results are rendered to a texture map so the second pass can be performed with another render. In this pass, the bent normal is calculated and written as the RGB value of the color with a new shadow value that is written in the alpha component.

14.2.2 Improving Performance

Even though the element-to-element shadow calculation is very fast (a GeForce 6800 can do 150 million of these calculations per second), we need to improve our algorithm to work on more than a couple of thousand elements in real time. We can reduce the amount of work by using simplified geometry for distant surfaces. This approach works well for diffuse lighting environments because the shadows are so soft that those cast by details in distant geometry are not visible. Fortunately, because we do not use the polygons themselves in our technique, we can create surface elements to represent simplified geometry without needing to create alternate polygonal models. We simply group elements whose vertices are neighbors in the original mesh and represent them with a single, larger element. We can do the same thing with the larger elements, creating fewer and even larger elements, forming a hierarchy. Now instead of traversing every single element for each pixel we render, we traverse the hierarchy of elements. If the receiver element is far enough away from the emitter—say, four times the radius of the emitter—we use it for our calculation. Only if the receiver is close to an emitter do we need to traverse its children (if it has any). See Figure 14-6. By traversing a hierarchy in this way, we can improve the performance of our algorithm from $O(n^2)$ to $O(n \log n)$ in practice. The chart in Figure 14-7 shows that the performance per vertex stays consistent as the number of vertices in the hierarchy increases.

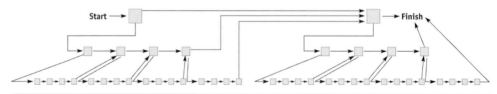

Figure 14-6. Hierarchical Elements
Elements are traversed in a hierarchy; child elements are traversed only if necessary.

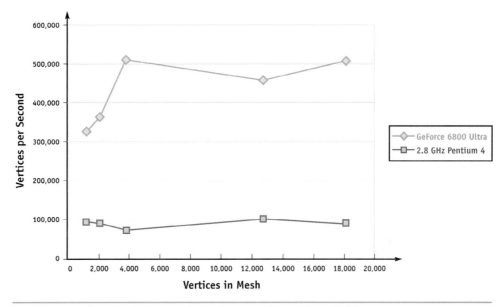

Figure 14-7. Ambient Occlusion Shader Performance for Meshes of Different Densities

We calculate a parent element's data using its direct descendants in the hierarchy. We calculate the position and normal of a parent element by averaging the positions and normals of its children. We calculate its area as the sum of its children's areas. We can use a shader for these calculations by making one pass of the shader for each level in the hierarchy, propagating the values from the leaf nodes up. We can then use the same technique to average the results of an occlusion pass that are needed for a following pass or simply treat parent nodes the same as children and avoid the averaging step. It is worth noting that the area of most animated elements varies little, if at all, even for nonrigid objects; therefore, the area does not have to be recalculated for each frame.

The ambient occlusion fragment shader appears in Listing 14-1.

Listing 14-1. Ambient Occlusion Shader

```
float4 AmbientOcclusion(
  float4 position : WPOS,
  float4 normOffset : TEX1,
  uniform samplerRECT lastResultMap : TEXUNIT0,
  uniform samplerRECT positionMap : TEXUNIT1,
  uniform samplerRECT elementNormalMap : TEXUNIT2,
  uniform samplerRECT indexMap : TEXUNIT3) : COL
{
```

Listing 14-1 *(continued)*. Ambient Occlusion Shader

```
float eArea;       // emitter area
float4 ePosition;  // emitter position
float4 eNormal;    // emitter normal
float3 rPosition = texRECT(positionMap, position.xy).xyz;
float3 rNormal = texRECT(elementNormalMap, position.xy).xyz;
float3 v;          // vector from receiver to emitter
float total = 0;   // used to calculate accessibility
float4 eIndex = float2(0.5, 0.5); // index of current emitter
float3 bentNormal = rNormal;       // initialize with receiver normal
float value;
float d2;          // distance from receiver to emitter squared

while (emitterIndex.x != 0) { // while not finished traversal
  ePosition = texRECT(positionMap, emitterIndex.xy);
  eNormal = texRECT(elementNormalMap, emitterIndex.xy);
  eArea = emitterNormal.w;
  eIndex = texRECT(indexMap, emitterIndex.xy); // get next index
  v = ePosition.xyz - rPosition; // vector to emitter
  d2 = dot(v, v) + 1e - 16;    // calc distance squared, avoid 0
  // is receiver close to parent element?
  if (d2 < -4*emitterArea) {   // (parents have negative area)
    eIndex.xy = eIndex.zw;     // go down hierarchy
    emitterArea = 0;           // ignore this element
  }
  v *= rsqrt(d2);              // normalize v
  value = SolidAngle(v, d2, rNormal, eNormal.xyz, abs(eArea)) *
          texRECT(resultMap, position.xy).w; // modulate by last result
  bentNormal -= value * v;     // update bent normal
  total += value;
}
if (!lastPass)                 // only need bent normal for last pass
  return saturate(1 - total); // return accessibility only
else return float4(normalize(bentNormal), 1 - total);
}
```

14.3 Indirect Lighting and Area Lights

We can add an extra level of realism to rendered images by adding indirect lighting caused by light reflecting off diffuse surfaces (Tabellion 2004). We can add a single bounce of indirect light using a slight variation of the ambient occlusion shader. We replace the solid angle function with a disk-to-disk radiance transfer function. We use one pass of the shader to transfer the reflected or emitted light and two passes to shadow the light.

For indirect lighting, first we need to calculate the amount of light to reflect off the front face of each surface element. If the reflected light comes from environment lighting, then we compute the ambient occlusion data first and use it to compute the environment light that reaches each vertex. If we are using direct lighting from point or directional lights, we compute the light at each element just as if we are shading the surface, including shadow mapping. We can also do both environment lighting and direct lighting and sum the two results. We then multiply the light values by the color of the surface element, so that red surfaces reflect red, yellow surfaces reflect yellow, and so on. Area lights are handled just like light-reflective diffuse surfaces except that they are initialized with a light value to emit.

Here is the fragment program function to calculate element-to-element radiance transfer:

```
float FormFactor(float3 v, float d2, float3 receiverNormal,
                 float3 emitterNormal, float emitterArea)
{
  // assume that emitterArea has been divided by PI
  return emitterArea * saturate(dot(emitterNormal, v)) *
    saturate(dot(receiverNormal, v)) / (d2 + emitterArea);
}
```

$$\frac{A \cos \theta_E \cos \theta_R}{\pi r^2 + A}$$

Equation 14-2. Disk-to-Disk Form Factor Approximation

We calculate the amount of light transferred from one surface element to another using the geometric term of the disk-to-disk form factor given in Equation 14-2. We leave off the visibility factor, which takes into account blocking (occluding) geometry. Instead we use a shadowing technique like the one we used for calculating ambient occlusion— only this time we use the same form factor that we used to transfer the light. Also, we multiply the shadowing element's form factor by the three-component light value instead of a single-component accessibility value.

We now run one pass of our radiance-transfer shader to calculate the maximum amount of reflected or emitted light that can reach any element. Then we run a shadow pass that subtracts from the total light at each element based on how much light reaches the shadowing elements. Just as with ambient occlusion, we can run another pass to improve the lighting by removing double shadowing. Figure 14-8 shows a scene lit with direct lighting plus one and two bounces of indirect lighting.

Figure 14-8. Combining Direct and Indirect Lighting
Top, left to right: Scene lit with direct lighting, with direct lighting plus one bounce of indirect lighting, and with direct lighting plus two bounces of indirect lighting. Bottom, left to right: Indirect lighting after one pass, after two passes (one bounce), and after two bounces (four passes total).

14.4 Conclusion

Global illumination techniques such as ambient occlusion and indirect lighting greatly enhance the quality of rendered diffuse surfaces. We have presented a new technique for calculating light transfer to and from diffuse surfaces using the GPU. This technique is suitable for implementing various global illumination effects in dynamic scenes with deformable geometry.

14.5 References

Landis, Hayden. 2002. "Production-Ready Global Illumination." Course 16 notes, SIGGRAPH 2002.

Pharr, Matt, and Simon Green. 2004. "Ambient Occlusion." In *GPU Gems*, edited by Randima Fernando, pp. 279–292. Addison-Wesley.

Sloan, Peter-Pike, Jan Kautz, and John Snyder. 2002. "Precomputed Radiance Transfer for Real-Time Rendering in Dynamic, Low-Frequency Lighting Environments." *ACM Transactions on Graphics (Proceedings of SIGGRAPH 2002)* 21(3), pp. 527–536.

Tabellion, Eric, and Arnauld Lamorlette. 2004. "An Approximate Global Illumination System for Computer Generated Films." *ACM Transactions on Graphics (Proceedings of SIGGRAPH 2004)* 23(3), pp. 469–476.

Chapter 15

Blueprint Rendering and "Sketchy Drawings"

Marc Nienhaus
University of Potsdam, Hasso-Plattner-Institute

Jürgen Döllner
University of Potsdam, Hasso-Plattner-Institute

In this chapter, we present two techniques for hardware-accelerated, image-space non-photorealistic rendering: blueprint rendering and sketchy drawing.

Outlining and enhancing visible and occluded features in drafts of architecture and technical parts are essential techniques for visualizing complex aggregate objects and for illustrating the position, layout, and relation of their components. Blueprint rendering is a novel multipass rendering technique that outlines visible and nonvisible visually important edges of 3D objects. The word *blueprint* in its original sense is defined by Merriam-Webster as "a photographic print in white on a bright blue ground or blue on a white ground used especially for copying maps, mechanical drawings, and architects' plans." Blueprints consist of transparently rendered features, represented by their outlines. Thus, blueprints make it easy to understand the structure of complex, hierarchical object assemblies such as those found in architectural drafts, technical illustrations, and designs.

In this sense, blueprint rendering can become an effective tool for interactively exploring, visualizing, and communicating spatial relations. For instance, they can help guide players through dungeon-like environments and highlight hidden chambers and components in a computer game, or they can make it easier for artists to visualize and design game levels in a custom level editor.

In contrast, rendering in a "sketchy" manner can be used to communicate visual ideas and to illustrate drafts and concepts, especially in application areas such as architectural and product designs. In particular, sketchy drawings encourage the exchange of ideas when people are reconsidering drafts.

Sketchy drawing is a real-time rendering technique for sketching visually important edges as well as inner color patches of arbitrary 3D geometries even beyond their geometrical boundary. Generally speaking, with sketchy drawing we sketch the outline of 3D geometries to imply vagueness and "crayon in" inner color patches exceeding the sketchy outline as though they have been painted roughly. Combining both produces sketchy, cartoon-like depictions that can be applied to enhance the visual attraction of characters and 3D scenery.

Because of the way they're implemented (with depth sprite rendering) and the fact that they work on a per-object basis, both blueprint and sketchy rendering can easily be integrated into any real-time graphics application.

15.1 Basic Principles

Blueprint and sketchy renderings are both built on three basic principles: (1) to preserve images of intermediate renderings of the scene's geometry, (2) to implement an edge enhancement technique, and (3) to apply depth sprite rendering. We briefly describe these concepts in the following sections.

15.1.1 Intermediate Rendering Results

We denote 2D data derived from 3D geometry and rendered into textures as *intermediate rendering results*. In doing so, we implement G-buffers (Saito and Takahashi 1990) that store geometric properties of 3D geometry. (See also Chapter 9 of this book, "Deferred Shading in *S.T.A.L.K.E.R.*," for application of this idea to realistic rendering.) In particular, we generate a normal buffer and a z-buffer by rendering encoded normal and z-values of 3D geometry directly into 2D textures, as shown in Figure 15-1. In a multipass rendering technique, we generate intermediate rendering results once and can reuse them in subsequent rendering passes. Technically, we use render-to-texture capabilities of graphics hardware. Doing so also allows us to render high-precision (color) values to high-precision buffers (such as textures).

15.1.2 Edge Enhancement

To extract visually important edges from 3D geometry on a per-object basis, we implement an image-space edge enhancement technique (Nienhaus and Döllner 2003).

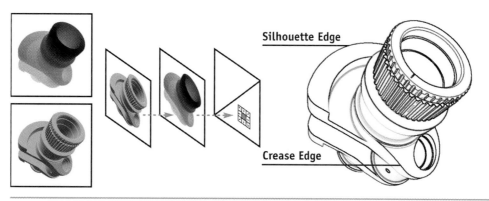

Figure 15-1. Steps in Creating an Edge Map
We texture a screen-aligned quad with the normal buffer and z-buffer and sample neighboring texture values to detect discontinuities, which are then represented as edge intensities. The resulting edge map contains visually important edges that are applicable to distinguish single components from each other in an overall composition.

Visually important edges include silhouette, border, and crease edges. We obtain these edges by detecting discontinuities in the normal buffer and z-buffer. For that purpose, we texture a screen-aligned quad that fills in the viewport of the canvas using these textures and calculate texture coordinates (s, t) for each fragment produced for the quad in such a way that they correspond to window coordinates. Sampling neighboring texels allows us to extract discontinuities that result in intensity values. The assembly of intensity values constitutes edges that we render directly into a single texture, called an *edge map*. Figure 15-2 depicts the normal and z-buffer and the resulting edge map.

15.1.3 Depth Sprite Rendering

Conceptually, depth sprites are 2D images that provide an additional z-value at each pixel for depth testing. For our purposes, we implement depth sprite rendering as follows:

1. We render a screen-aligned quad textured with a high-precision texture containing z-values.

2. We apply a specialized fragment shader that replaces fragment z-values of the quad (produced by the rasterizer) with z-values derived from accessing the texture. For optimizing fill rate, we additionally discard a fragment if its z-value equals 1—which denotes the depth of the far clipping plane. Otherwise, the fragment shader calculates RGBA color values of that fragment.

3. Rendering then proceeds with the ordinary depth test. If fragments pass the test, the frame buffer will be filled with the color and z-values of the depth sprite.

Figure 15-2. The Z-Buffer, Normal Buffer, and Edge Map for Each Layer
The z-buffer (first row) and the normal buffer (second row) of each depth layer (column) form the basis for constructing the edge map (third row) for each layer.

As an example in 3D scenes, depth sprite rendering can correctly resolve the visibility of image-based renderings derived from 3D geometries by considering their z-values. In particular, we can combine blueprints and sketchy drawings with other 3D geometric models in arbitrary order.

15.2 Blueprint Rendering

For blueprint rendering, we extract both visible and nonvisible edges of 3D geometry. Visible edges are edges directly seen by the virtual camera; nonvisible edges are edges that are occluded by faces of 3D geometry; that is, they are not directly seen. To extract these edges, we combine the depth-peeling technique (Everitt 2001) and the edge enhancement technique. Once generated, we compose visible and nonvisible edges as blueprints in the frame buffer.

15.2.1 Depth Peeling

Depth peeling is a technique that operates on a per-fragment basis and extracts 2D layers of 3D geometry in depth-sorted order. Generally speaking, depth peeling successively "peels away" layers of unique depth complexity.

In general, fragments passing an ordinary depth test define the minimal z-value at each pixel. But we cannot determine the fragment that comes second (or third, and so on) with respect to its depth complexity. Thus, we need an additional depth test to extract those fragments that form a layer of a given ordinal number (with respect to depth complexity) (Diefenbach 1996). We thus can extract the first n layers using n rendering passes.

We refer to a layer of unique depth complexity as a *depth layer* and a high-precision texture received from capturing the associated z-buffer contents as a *depth layer map*. Accordingly, we call the contents of the associated color buffer captured in an additional texture a *color layer map*. In particular, color layer maps can later be used in depth-sorted order to compose the final rendering, for example, for order-independent transparency (Everitt 2001).

The pseudocode in Listing 15-1 outlines our implementation of depth peeling. It operates on a set G of 3D geometries. We render G multiple times, whereby the rasterizer produces a set F of fragments. The loop terminates if no fragment gets rendered (*termination condition*); otherwise, we continue with the next depth layer. That is, if the number of rendering passes has reached the maximum depth complexity, the condition is satisfied.

Listing 15-1. Pseudocode for Combining Depth Peeling and Edge Enhancement for Blueprint Rendering

```
procedure depthPeeling(G ← 3DGeometry) begin
  i=0
  do
    F ← rasterize(G)
    /* Perform single depth test in the first rendering pass */
    if(i==0) begin
      for all fragment ∈ F begin
        bool test ← performDepthTest(fragment)
        if(test) begin
          fragment.depth → z-buffer
          fragment.color → color buffer
        end
        else reject fragment
      end
    end
    else begin
      /* Perform two depth test */
      for all fragment ∈ F begin
        if(fragment.depth > fragment.value_depthLayerMap(i-1)) begin
```

```
            /* First test */
            bool test ← performDepthTest(fragment)
            if(test) begin
              /* Second test */
              fragment.depth → z-buffer
              fragment.color → color buffer
            end
            else reject fragment
          end
          else reject fragment
        end
      end
      depthLayerMap(i) ← capture(z-buffer)
      colorLayerMap(i) ← capture(color buffer)
      /* Edge intensities */
      edgeMap(i) ← edges(depthLayerMap(i),colorLayerMap(i))
      i++
    while(occlusionQuery() ≠ 0 )   /* Termination condition */
  end
```

Performing Two Depth Tests

In the first rendering pass ($i = 0$), we perform an ordinary depth test on each fragment. We capture the contents of the z-buffer and the color buffer in a depth layer map and a color layer map for further processing.

In consecutive rendering passes ($i > 0$), we perform an additional depth test on each fragment. For this test, we use a texture with the depth layer map of the previous rendering pass ($i - 1$). We then determine the texture coordinates of a fragment in such a way that they correspond to canvas coordinates of the targeted pixel position. In this way, a texture access can provide a fragment with the z-value stored at that pixel position in the z-buffer of the previous rendering pass.

Now, the two depth tests work as follows:

- If the current z-value of a fragment is greater than the texture value that results from accessing the depth layer map, the fragment proceeds and the second ordinary depth test is performed.

- Otherwise, if the test fails, the fragment is rejected.

When we have processed all fragments, the contents of the z-buffer and the color buffer form the new depth layer map and color layer map. We can efficiently implement the additional depth test using a fragment program. Furthermore, we utilize the occlusion query extension (Kilgard 2004) to efficiently implement the termination condition.

15.2.2 Extracting Visible and Nonvisible Edges

We complement depth peeling with edge map construction for each depth layer. Because discontinuities in the normal buffer and z-buffer constitute visible edges, we must construct both for a rendering pass. We encode fragment normals as color values to generate the normal buffer as a color layer map. Then we can directly construct the edge map because the depth map already exists.

Furthermore, nonvisible edges become visible when depth layers are peeled away successively. Consequently, we can also extract nonvisible edges using the modified depth peeling technique (already shown in Listing 15-1).

As a result, our blueprint rendering technique preserves visible and nonvisible edges as edge maps for further processing. Figure 15-2 shows z-buffers, normal buffers, and resulting edge maps of successive depth layers.

Note that edges in edge maps of consecutive depth layers appear repeatedly because local discontinuities remain if we peel away faces of 3D geometry. Consider the following cases:

1. Two connected polygons share the same edge. One polygon occludes the other one. The discontinuity in the z-buffer that is produced along the shared edge will remain if we peel away the occluding polygon.

2. A polygon that partially occludes another polygon produces discontinuities in the z-buffer at the transition. If we peel away the occluding polygon and the nonoccluded portions, a discontinuity in the z-buffer will be produced at the same location.

Figure 15-3 illustrates both cases. However, the performance of edge map construction is virtually independent of the number of discontinuities.

15.2.3 Composing Blueprints

We compose blueprints using visible and nonvisible edges stored in edge maps in depth-sorted order. For each edge map, we proceed as follows:

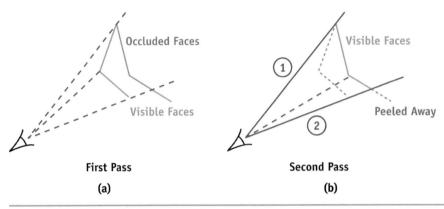

Figure 15-3. Two Possibilities When Peeling Away 3D Geometry
Rays are cast to discontinuities that are produced by the composition of polygons and that are visible from the camera position. (a) The first rendering pass. (b) The same composition with faces peeled away. The solid blue rays indicate edges that exist in both edge maps.

- We texture a screen-aligned quad that fills in the viewport with the edge map and its associated depth map.

- We further apply a fragment program that (1) performs depth sprite rendering using the appropriate depth layer map as input; (2) calculates the fragment's RGB value using the edge intensity value derived from accessing the edge map and, for instance, a bluish color; and (3) sets the fragment's alpha value to the edge intensity.

- We then use color blending by considering edge intensity values as blending factors for providing depth complexity cues while keeping edges enhanced.

We have found that in practice, it is sufficient to blend just the first few color layer maps to compose blueprints. The remaining layer maps have less visual impact on the overall composition because only a few (often isolated) pixels get colored. To alter the termination conditions for blueprint rendering and thus optimize rendering speed, we specify a desired minimal fraction of fragments (depending on the window resolution) to pass the depth test. In this way, we decrease the number of rendering passes while we maintain the visual quality of blueprints. To implement the trade-off between speed and quality, we configure the occlusion query extension appropriately. Figure 15-4a shows the resulting blueprint of the crank model.

15.2.4 Depth Masking

Depth masking is a technique that peels away a minimal number of depth layers until a specified fraction of a single, occluded component becomes visible. In fact, depth

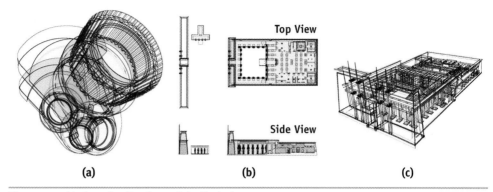

Figure 15-4. Various Applications of the Technique
(a) Blueprint rendering applied to the model of a crank to outline its design. (b) With blueprint rendering, we can generate plan views of the Temple of Ramses II automatically. (Model provided by ART+COM, Berlin. Used with permission.) (c) Depth masking applied to the temple and its statues.

masking provides a termination condition for blueprint rendering to dynamically adapt the number of rendering passes. For depth masking, we proceed as follows:

1. We derive a depth texture as the *depth mask* of the designated component in a preceding rendering pass.

2. In successive rendering passes, we render the depth mask as a depth sprite whenever we have peeled away a depth layer. If a specified fraction of the number of fragments passes the ordinary depth test (based on the z-buffer contents just produced), we terminate our technique. Otherwise, we must peel away more depth layers.

3. Finally, we simply integrate the designated component when composing blueprints.

The modifications to our technique are shown in pseudocode in Listing 15-2. Again, we use the occlusion query extension to implement the termination condition.

Listing 15-2. Pseudocode with Modified Termination Condition to Implement Depth Masking

```
procedure depthPeeling(G ← 3DGeometry,
                       C ← geometryOfOccludedComponent) begin
  depthMask ← depthTexture(C)
  quad ← createTexturedScreenAlignedQuad(depthMask)
  renderDepthSprite(quad)      /* Render quad as depth sprite */
  int Q = occlusionQuery()     /* Number of fragments of the components */
  . . .
```

```
do
    . . .
    renderDepthSprite(quad)
    int R = occlusionQuery()  /* Number of visible fragments of the
                                 component */
  while(R<fraction(Q))        /* Termination condition */
 end
```

15.2.5 Visualizing Architecture Using Blueprint Rendering

Blueprints can be used to outline the design of architecture. We apply blueprint rendering to generate plan views of architecture. Composing plan views using an orthographic camera is a straightforward task. In the visualization of the Temple of Ramses II in Abydos (Figure 15-4b), we can identify chambers, pillars, and statues systematically. Thus, blueprints increase the visual perception in these illustrations. The plan views are produced automatically.

A perspective view still provides better spatial orientation and conceptual insight in blueprints of architecture. Figure 15-4c visualizes the design of the entrance and the inner yard of the temple with its surrounding walls and statues. These are in front of the highlighted statues that guard the doorway to the rear part of the temple. With depth masking, we determine the number of depth layers that occlude the guarding statues and, therefore, must be peeled away. In this way, we can reduce the visual complexity of a blueprint if the structural complexity of the model is more than can be reasonably displayed.

15.3 Sketchy Rendering

Our sketchy drawing technique considers visually important edges and surface colors for sketching 3D geometry nonuniformly using uncertainty.

Our rendering technique proceeds as follows: As with blueprint rendering, we first generate intermediate rendering results that represent edges and surface colors of 3D geometry. Then we apply uncertainty values in image space to sketch these textures nonuniformly. Finally, we adjust depth information in such a way that the resulting sketchy drawing can be merged with general 3D scene contents.

15.3.1 Edges and Color Patches

We again use the edge enhancement technique to store edges of 3D geometry as an edge map for later usage, as shown in Figure 15-5a. In addition, we render surface colors of 3D geometry to texture to produce striking color patches that appear flat, cover all surface details, and emulate a cartoon-like style. We call that texture a *shade map*; see Figure 15-5b.

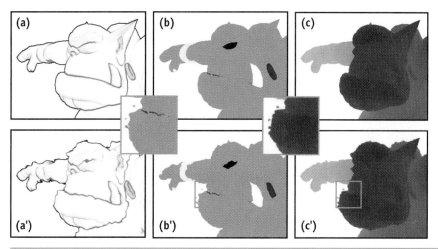

Figure 15-5. Applying Uncertainty Using Edge and Shade Maps
The edge map (a) and shade map (b) are two ingredients for sketchy drawings. Applying uncertainty results in perturbations of the edge map (a') and perturbations of the shade map (b'). Depth sprites use the depth map (c) to adjust z-values. For sketchy drawing, we reproduce the degrees of uncertainty applied to the edge and shade maps to perturb the depth map (c') for depth sprite rendering.

15.3.2 Applying Uncertainty

We apply uncertainty values to edges and surface colors in image space to simulate the effect of "sketching on a flat surface." For that purpose, we texture a screen-aligned quad (filling in the viewport of the canvas) using edge and shade maps as textures. Moreover, we apply an additional texture, whose texels represent uncertainty values. Because we want to achieve mostly continuous sketchy boundaries and frame-to-frame coherence, we opt for a noise texture whose texel values have been determined by the Perlin noise function (Perlin 1985); hence neighboring uncertainty values are correlated in image space. Once created (in a preprocessing step), the noise texture serves as an offset texture for accessing the edge and shade maps when rendering. That is, its texel values slightly perturb texture coordinates of each fragment of the quad that accesses the edge and shade maps.

In addition, we introduce a *degree of uncertainty* to control the amount of perturbation, for which we employ a user-defined 2×2 matrix. We multiply uncertainty values derived from the noise texture by that matrix to weight all these values uniformly and then use the resulting offset vector to translate the texture coordinates. Figure 15-6 illustrates the perturbation of the texture coordinates that access the shade map using the degree of uncertainty.

To enhance the sketchiness effect, we perturb texture coordinates for accessing the edge and shade maps differently. We thus apply two different 2×2 matrices, resulting in different degrees of uncertainty for each map. One degree of uncertainty shifts texture coordinates of the edge map, and one shifts texture coordinates of the shade map—that is, we shift them in opposite directions. Figure 15-5 shows the edge and shade maps after we have applied uncertainty.

We denote texture values that correspond to fragments of 3D geometry as *interior regions*; texture values that do not correspond to fragments of 3D geometry are called *exterior regions*. So in conclusion, by texturing the quad and perturbing texture coordinates using uncertainty, we can access interior regions of the edge and shade maps, whereas the initial texture coordinates would access exterior regions and vice versa (Figure 15-6). In this way, interior regions can be sketched beyond the boundary of 3D geometry, and exterior regions can penetrate interior regions. We can even produce spots beyond the boundary of the 3D geometry (Figure 15-5).

Finally, we combine texture values of the edge and the shade maps. We multiply the intensity values derived from perturbing the edge map with the color values derived from

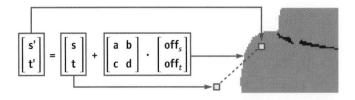

Figure 15-6. Applying Uncertainty in Image Space
We multiply the uncertainty value (off$_s$,off$_t$) derived from the noise texture by a 2×2 matrix (with weights a, b, c, and d) forming the degree of uncertainty that we apply to the texture coordinates (s, t) of a fragment to translate them in image space. In the figure, the perturbed texture coordinates (s', t') access a texture value of the interior region of the shade map even though the initial texture coordinates (s, t) would access the exterior region.

perturbing the shade map. For the sketchy drawing in Figure 15-7a, we determined uncertainty values (off_s, off_t) by using the turbulence function (based on Perlin noise):

$$off_s \leftarrow \texttt{turbulence(s, t);} \text{ and } off_t \leftarrow \texttt{turbulence(1 - s, 1 - t);}$$

15.3.3 Adjusting Depth

Up to now, we have merely textured a screen-aligned quad with a sketchy depiction. This method has significant shortcomings. When we render the quad textured with textures of 3D geometry, (1) z-values of the original geometry are not present in interior regions, and in particular, (2) no z-values of the original geometry are present in exterior regions when uncertainty has been applied. Thus the sketchy rendering cannot correctly interact with other objects in the scene.

To overcome these shortcomings, we apply depth sprite rendering by considering previous perturbations. That is, we additionally texture the quad with the high-precision depth map (already available) and access this texture twice using perturbed texture coordinates. As first perturbation, we apply the degree of uncertainty used for accessing the edge map; as second perturbation, we apply the degree of uncertainty used for accessing the shade map. The minimum value of both these texture values produces the final z-value of the fragment for depth testing. Figure 15-5c' shows the result of both perturbations applied to the depth map. The interior region of the perturbed depth map matches the combination of the interior regions of both the perturbed edge map and the perturbed shade map. Even those spots produced for the shade map appear in the perturbation of the depth map.

Thus, modifying depth sprite rendering allows us to adjust z-values for the textured quad that represents a sketchy depiction of 3D geometry. So, the z-buffer remains in a correct state with respect to that geometry, and its sketchy representation can be composed with further (for example, nonsketchy) 3D geometry. The accompanying video on the book's CD illustrates this feature.

15.3.4 Variations of Sketchy Rendering

We present two variations of sketchy rendering, both of which also run in real time.

Roughened Profiles and Color Transitions

Although we sketch edges and surface colors nonuniformly, the profiles and the color transitions of a sketchy depiction are precise as if sketched with pencils on a flat surface. We roughen the profiles and color transitions to simulate different drawing tools and

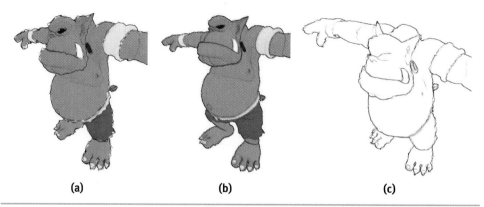

| (a) | (b) | (c) |

Figure 15-7. Different Styles of Sketchy Rendering
The combination of the perturbed edge, shade, and depth maps generates the final sketchy drawing in (a). Additionally, sketchy rendering can generate different styles of depiction, including (b) roughened profiles and color transitions and (c) repeated edge rendering.

media, such as chalk applied on a rough surface. We apply randomly chosen noise values; hence, adjacent texture values of the noise texture are uncorrelated. Consequently, the degrees of uncertainty that we apply to the texture coordinates of adjacent fragments are also uncorrelated. In this way, we produce sketchy depictions with softened and frayed edges and color transitions, as shown in Figure 15-7b. The roughness and granularity, in particular for edges, vary as though the pressure had varied as it does when drawing with chalk. This effect depends on the amount of uncertainty that we apply in image space.

Repeated Edges

A fundamental technique in hand drawings is to repeatedly draw edges to draft a layout or design. We sketch visually important edges only to simulate this technique. For that purpose, we exclude the shade map but apply the edge map multiple times using different degrees of uncertainty and possibly different edge colors. Edges will then overlap nonuniformly as if the edges of the 3D geometry have been sketched repeatedly, as in Figure 15-7c. We also have to adjust the depth information by accessing the depth map multiple times, using the corresponding degrees of uncertainty.

15.3.5 Controlling Uncertainty

Controlling uncertainty values, in general, enables us to configure the visual appearance of sketchy renderings. By providing uncertainty values based on a Perlin noise function for each pixel in image space, (1) we achieve frame-to-frame coherence, for instance, when interacting with the scene (because neighboring uncertainty values are correlated), and (2) we can access interior regions from beyond exterior regions and, vice versa, sketch beyond the boundary of 3D geometries. However, uncertainty values remain unchanged in image space and have no obvious correspondence with geometric properties of the original 3D geometry. Consequently, sketchy drawings tend to "swim" in image space (known as the *shower-door effect*) and we cannot predetermine their visual appearance.

To overcome these limitations, we seek to accomplish the following:

- Preserve geometric properties such as surface positions, normals, or curvature information to determine uncertainty values.
- Continue to provide uncertainty values in exterior regions, at least close to the 3D geometry.

Preserving Geometric Properties

To preserve geometric properties of 3D geometry to control uncertainty, we proceed as follows:

1. We render these geometric properties directly into a texture to generate an additional G-buffer.
2. Next we texture the screen-aligned quad with that additional texture, and then access geometric properties using texture coordinates (s, t).
3. Finally, we calculate uncertainty values based on a noise function, using the geometric properties as parameters.

Then we can use these uncertainty values to determine different degrees of uncertainty for perturbing texture coordinates resulting in (s', t'). Mathematically, we use the following function to determine the perturbed texture coordinates (s', t'):

$$f : (s, t) \rightarrow (s', t')$$
$$f(s, t) = p(s, t, g(s, t)),$$

where (s, t) represent texture coordinates of a fragment produced when rasterizing the screen-aligned quad, $g()$ provides the geometric properties available in the additional texture, and $p()$ determines the perturbation applied to (s, t) using $g()$ as input.

For sketchy rendering, we apply two functions $f(s, t)$ to handle perturbations for the edge ($f_{Edge}(s, t)$) and the shade ($f_{Shade}(s, t)$) maps differently.

Enlarging the Geometry

We enlarge the original 3D geometry to generate geometric properties in its surroundings in image space. We do this by slightly shifting each vertex of the mesh along its vertex normal in object space. For this technique to work as expected, the surface must at least form a connected component and each of its shared vertices must have an interpolated normal.

By enlarging the 3D geometry in this way, we can render the geometric properties into a texture for calculating uncertainty values in interior regions as well as in the exterior regions (nearby the original 3D geometry). That way, interior regions can be sketched beyond the boundary of the 3D geometry and exterior regions can penetrate interior regions. We can then apply perturbations based on uncertainty values that do have an obvious correspondence to the underlying 3D geometry.

15.3.6 Reducing the Shower-Door Effect

We now illustrate, by way of example, how to control sketchiness to reduce the shower-door effect for sketchy rendering.

We render enlarged 3D geometry with its object-space positions as color values into a texture. To do so, we determine the object-space positions for each of the displaced vertices and provide them as texture coordinates to the rasterization process. Then the rasterizer produces interpolated object-space positions for each fragment. A specialized fragment shader then outputs them as high-precision color values to a high-precision texture. Thus, $g(s, t)$ preserves object-space positions.

Based on $g(s, t)$, we can determine texture coordinates $f(s, t)$ using $p()$. In our example, the function $p()$ calculates the perturbation by a user-defined 2×2 matrix and by a Perlin noise function encoded into a 3D texture. Then we access the 3D texture using $g(s, t)$ as texture coordinates. We multiply the resulting texture value by the 2×2 matrix to obtain a degree of uncertainty. The function $f(s, t)$ then applies the degree of uncertainty to perturb (s, t), resulting in (s', t').

Calculating $f_{Edge}(s, t)$ and $f_{Shade}(s, t)$ using different matrices results in the sketchy depiction in Figure 15-8. The accompanying video on the book's CD illustrates that the shower-door effect has been significantly reduced. The overview in Figure 15-8 illustrates the process flow of sketchy rendering by considering the underlying geometric properties.

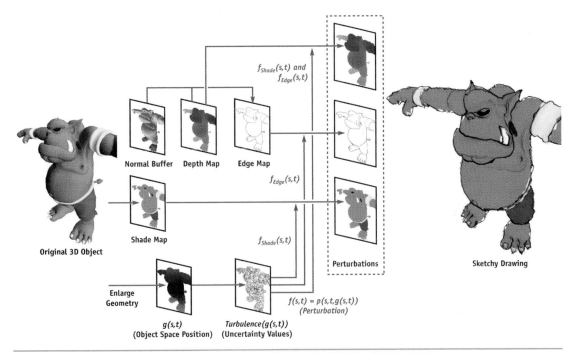

Figure 15-8. Buffers and Intermediate Rendering Results Involved in Sketchy Rendering

Although this example simply reduces the shower-door effect, it gives a clue as to how to control sketchy depictions using geometric properties. Using a higher-level shading language such as GLSL (Rost 2004) or Cg (Mark et al. 2003), one can further design and stylize sketchy drawings.

15.4 Conclusion

Blueprint rendering represents the first image-space rendering technique that renders visible and occluded edges of 3D geometries. In our future work, we aim at increasing visual perception of blueprints by combining edge maps based on techniques derived from volume rendering.

Sketchy drawing also represents the first image-space rendering technique that generates stylized edges of 3D geometries (Isenberg et al. 2003) for cartoon-like depictions. Because we produce and access the geometric properties and uncertainty values in exterior regions using intermediate rendering results, shaders written in higher-level shading languages alone are not enough to reproduce our technique for sketchy rendering. In our future work, we expect to reproduce artistically pleasing sketches.

15.5 References

Diefenbach, P. J. 1996. "Pipeline Rendering: Interaction and Realism Through Hardware-Based Multi-Pass Rendering." Ph.D. thesis. University of Pennsylvania.

Everitt, C. 2001. "Interactive Order-Independent Transparency." NVIDIA technical report. Available online at **http://developer.nvidia.com/object/Interactive_Order_Transparency.html**

Isenberg, T., B. Freudenberg, N. Halper, S. Schlechtweg, and T. Strothotte. 2003. "A Developer's Guide to Silhouette Algorithms for Polygonal Models." *IEEE Computer Graphics and Applications* 23(4), pp. 28–37.

Kilgard, M., ed. 2004. "NVIDIA OpenGL Extension Specifications." NVIDIA Corporation. Available online at **http://www.nvidia.com/dev_content/nvopenglspecs/nvOpenGLspecs.pdf**

Mark, W. R., R. S. Glanville, K. Akeley, and M. J. Kilgard. 2003. "Cg: A System for Programming Graphics Hardware in a C-like Language." *ACM Transactions on Graphics (Proceedings of ACM SIGGRAPH 2003)* 22(3), pp. 896–907.

Nienhaus, M., and J. Döllner. 2003. "Edge-Enhancement: An Algorithm for Real-Time Non-Photorealistic Rendering." *Journal of WSCG '03*, pp. 346–353.

Perlin, K. 1985. "An Image Synthesizer." In *Computer Graphics (Proceedings of SIGGRAPH 85)* 19(3), pp. 287–296.

Rost, R. J. 2004. *OpenGL Shading Language*. Addison-Wesley.

Saito, T., and T. Takahashi. 1990. "Comprehensible Rendering of 3-D Shapes." In *Computer Graphics (Proceedings of SIGGRAPH 90)* 24(4), August 1990, pp. 197–206.

The authors want to thank ART+COM, Berlin, for providing the model of the Temple of Ramses II; Amy and Bruce Gooch for the crank model; and Konstantin Baumann, Johannes Bohnet, Henrik Buchholz, Oliver Kersting, Florian Kirsch, and Stefan Maass for their contributions to the Virtual Rendering System.

Chapter 16

Accurate Atmospheric Scattering

Sean O'Neil

16.1 Introduction

Generating realistic atmospheric scattering for computer graphics has always been a difficult problem, but it is very important for rendering realistic outdoor environments. The equations that describe atmospheric scattering are so complex that entire books have been dedicated to the subject. Computer graphics models generally use simplified equations, and very few of them run at interactive frame rates. This chapter explains how to implement a real-time atmospheric scattering algorithm entirely on the GPU using the methods described in Nishita et al. 1993. Figure 16-1 shows screenshots from the scattering demo included on this book's CD.

Figure 16-1. Screenshots from the Scattering Demo

Many atmospheric scattering models assume that the camera is always on or very close to the ground. This makes it easier to assume that the atmosphere has a constant density at all altitudes, which simplifies the scattering equations in Nishita et al. 1993 tremendously. Refer to Hoffman and Preetham 2002 for an explanation of how to implement these simplified equations in a GPU shader. This implementation produces an attractive scattering effect that is very fast on DirectX 8.0 shaders. Unfortunately, it doesn't always produce very accurate results, and it doesn't work well for a flight or space simulator, in which the camera can be located in space or very high above the ground.

This chapter explains how to implement the full equations from Nishita et al. 1993 in a GPU shader that runs at interactive frame rates. These equations model the atmosphere more accurately, with density falling off exponentially as altitude increases. O'Neil 2004 describes a similar algorithm that ran on the CPU, but that algorithm was too CPU-intensive. It was based on a precalculated 2D lookup table with four floating-point channels. Calculating the color for each vertex required several lookups into the table, with extra calculations around each lookup. At the time that article was written, no GPU could support such operations in a shader in one pass.

In this chapter, we eliminate the lookup table without sacrificing image quality, allowing us to implement the entire algorithm in a GPU shader. These shaders are small and fast enough to run in real time on most GPUs that support DirectX Shader Model 2.0.

16.2 Solving the Scattering Equations

The scattering equations have nested integrals that are impossible to solve analytically; fortunately, it's easy to numerically compute the value of an integral with techniques such as the trapezoid rule. Approximating an integral in this manner boils down to a weighted sum calculated in a loop. Imagine a line segment on a graph: break up the segment into n sample segments and evaluate the integrand at the center point of each sample segment. Multiply each result by the length of the sample segment and add them all up. Taking more samples makes the result more accurate, but it also makes the integral more expensive to calculate.

In our case, the line segment is a ray from the camera through the atmosphere to a vertex. This vertex can be part of the terrain, part of the sky dome, part of a cloud, or even part of an object in space such as the moon. If the ray passes through the atmosphere to get to the vertex, scattering needs to be calculated. Every ray should have two points defined that mark where the ray starts passing through the atmosphere and where it stops passing through the atmosphere. We'll call these points *A* and *B*, and they are shown in Figure 16-2. When the camera is inside the atmosphere, *A* is the camera's position. When the vertex is inside the atmosphere, *B* is the vertex's position. When either point is in space, we perform a sphere-intersection check to find out where the ray intersects the outer atmosphere, and then we make the intersection point *A* or *B*.

Now we have a line segment defined from point *A* to point *B*, and we want to approximate the integral that describes the atmospheric scattering across its length. For now let's take five sample positions and name their points P_1 through P_5. Each point P_1 through P_5 represents a point in the atmosphere at which light scatters; light comes into the atmosphere from the sun, scatters at that point, and is reflected toward the camera. Consider the point P_5, for example. Sunlight goes directly from the sun to P_5 in a straight line. Along that line the atmosphere scatters some of the light away from P_5. At P_5, some of this light is scattered directly toward the camera. As the light from P_5 travels to the camera, some of it gets scattered away again.

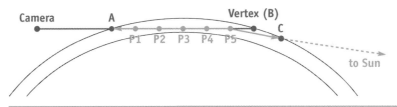

Figure 16-2. The Geometry of Atmospheric Scattering
The blue line represents the ray from the camera to the vertex. The green lines represent the rays from P_5 to the sun and to the camera.

16.2.1 Rayleigh Scattering vs. Mie Scattering

Another important detail is related to how the light scattering at the point *P* is modeled. Different particles in the atmosphere scatter light in different ways. The two most common forms of scattering in the atmosphere are *Rayleigh scattering* and *Mie scattering*. Rayleigh scattering is caused by small molecules in the air, and it scatters light more heavily at the shorter wavelengths (blue first, then green, and then red). The sky is blue because the blue light bounces all over the place, and ultimately reaches your eyes from every direction. The sun's light turns yellow/orange/red at sunset because as light travels far through the atmosphere, almost all of the blue and much of the green light is scattered away before it reaches you, leaving just the reddish colors.

Mie scattering is caused by larger particles in the air called aerosols (such as dust and pollution), and it tends to scatter all wavelengths of light equally. On a hazy day, Mie scattering causes the sky to look a bit gray and causes the sun to have a large white halo around it. Mie scattering can also be used to simulate light scattered from small particles of water and ice in the air, to produce effects like rainbows, but that is beyond the scope of this chapter. (Refer to Brewer 2004 for more information.)

16.2.2 The Phase Function

$$F(\theta, g) = \frac{3 \times \left(1 - g^2\right)}{2 \times \left(2 + g^2\right)} \times \frac{1 + \cos^2 \theta}{\left(1 + g^2 - 2 \times g \times \cos \theta\right)^{\frac{3}{2}}}$$

The phase function describes how much light is scattered toward the direction of the camera based on the angle θ (the angle between the two green rays in Figure 16-2) and a constant g that affects the symmetry of the scattering. There are many different versions of the phase function. This one is an adaptation of the Henyey-Greenstein function used in Nishita et al. 1993.

Rayleigh scattering can be approximated by setting g to 0, which greatly simplifies the equation and makes it symmetrical for positive and negative angles. Negative values of g scatter more light in a forward direction, and positive values of g scatter more light back toward the light source. For Mie aerosol scattering, g is usually set between -0.75 and -0.999. Never set g to 1 or -1, as it makes the equation reduce to 0.

16.2.3 The Out-Scattering Equation

$$t(P_a P_b, \lambda) = 4\pi \times K(\lambda) \times \int_{P_a}^{P_b} \exp\left(\frac{-h}{H_0}\right) ds$$

The out-scattering equation is the inner integral mentioned earlier. The integral part determines the "optical depth," or the average atmospheric density across the ray from point P_a to point P_b multiplied by the length of the ray. This is also called the "optical length" or "optical thickness." Think of it as a weighting factor based on how many air particles are in the path of the light along the ray. The rest of the equation is made up of constants, and they determine how much of the light those particles scatter away from the ray.

To compute the value of this integral, the ray from P_a to P_b will be broken up into segments and the exponential term will be evaluated at each sample point. The variable h is the height of the sample point. In my implementation, the height is scaled so that 0 represents sea level and 1 is at the top of the atmosphere. In theory, the atmosphere has no fixed top, but for practical purposes, we have to choose some height at which to render the sky dome. H_0 is the scale height, which is the height at which the atmosphere's average density is found. My implementation uses 0.25, so the average density is found 25 percent of the way up from the ground to the sky dome.

The constant λ is the wavelength (or color) of light and $K(\lambda)$ is the scattering constant, which is dependent on the density of the atmosphere at sea level. Rayleigh and Mie scattering each have their own scattering constants, including the scale height (H_0). Rayleigh and Mie scattering also differ in how they depend on wavelength. The Rayleigh scattering constant is usually divided by λ^4. In most computer graphics models, the Mie scattering constant is not dependent on wavelength, but at least one implementation divides it by $\lambda^{0.84}$. Wherever this equation depends on wavelength, it must be solved separately for each of the three color channels and separately for each type of scattering.

16.2.4 The In-Scattering Equation

$$I_v(\lambda) = I_s(\lambda) \times K(\lambda) \times F(\theta, g) \times \int_{P_a}^{P_b} \left[\exp\left(\frac{-h}{H_0}\right) \times \exp\left(-t\left(PP_c, \lambda\right) - t\left(PP_a, \lambda\right)\right) \right] ds$$

The in-scattering equation describes how much light is added to a ray through the atmosphere due to light scattering from the sun. For each point P along the ray from P_a to P_b, PP_c is the ray from the point to the sun and PP_a is the ray from the sample point to the camera. The out-scattering function determines how much light is scattered away along the two green rays in Figure 16-2. The remaining light is scaled by the phase function, the scattering constant, and the intensity of the sunlight, $I_s(\lambda)$. The sunlight intensity does not have to be dependent on wavelength, but this is where you would apply the color if you wanted to create an alien world revolving around a purple star.

16.2.5 The Surface-Scattering Equation

$$I_v'(\lambda) = I_v(\lambda) + I_e(\lambda) \times \exp\left(-t\left(P_a P_b, \lambda\right)\right)$$

To scatter light reflected from a surface, such as the surface of a planet, you must take into account the fact that some of the reflected light will be scattered away on its way to the camera. In addition, extra light is scattered in from the atmosphere. $I_e(\lambda)$ is the amount of light emitted or reflected from a surface, and it is attenuated by an out-scattering factor. The sky is not a surface that can reflect or emit light, so only $I_v(\lambda)$ is needed to render the sky. Determining how much light is reflected or emitted by a surface is application-specific, but for reflected sunlight, you need to account for the out-scattering that takes place before the sunlight strikes the surface (that is, $I_s(\lambda) \times \exp(-t(P_cP_b, \lambda)))$, and use that as the color of the light when determining how much light the surface reflects.

16.3 Making It Real-Time

Let's find out how poorly these equations will perform if they're implemented as explained in the preceding section, with five sample points for the in-scattering equation and five sample points for each of the integrals to compute the out-scattering equations. This gives $5 \times (5 + 5)$ samples at which to evaluate the functions for each vertex. We also have two types of scattering, Rayleigh and Mie, and we have to calculate each one for the different wavelengths of each of the three color channels (RGB). So now we're up to approximately $2 \times 3 \times 5 \times (5 + 5)$, or 300 computations per vertex. To make matters worse, the visual quality suffers noticeably when using only five samples for each integral. O'Neil 2004 used 50 samples for the inner integrals and five for the outer integral, which pushes the number of calculations up to 3,000 per vertex!

We don't need to go any further to know that this will not run very fast. Nishita et al. 1993 used a precalculated 2D lookup table to cut the number of calculations in half, but it still won't run in real time. Their lookup table took advantage of the fact that the sun is so far away that its rays can be considered parallel. (This idea is reflected in the in-scattering equation, in Section 16.2.4.) This makes it possible to calculate a lookup table that contains the amount of out-scattering for rays going from the sun to any point in the atmosphere. This table replaces one of the out-scattering integrals with a lookup table whose variables are altitude and angle to the sun. Because the rays to the camera are not parallel, the out-scattering integral for camera rays still had to be solved at runtime.

In O'Neil 2004, I proposed a better 2D lookup table that allows us to avoid both out-scattering integrals. The first dimension, x, takes a sample point at a specific altitude above the planet, with 0.0 being on the ground and 1.0 being at the top of the atmosphere. The second dimension, y, represents a vertical angle, with 0.0 being straight up and 1.0 being straight down. At each (x, y) pair in the table, a ray is fired from a point at altitude x to the top of the atmosphere along angle y. The lookup table had four channels, two reserved for Rayleigh scattering and two reserved for Mie scattering. One channel for each simply contained the atmospheric density at that altitude, or $\exp(-h/H_0)$. The other channel contained the optical depth of the ray just described. Because the lookup table was precomputed, I chose to use 50 samples to approximate the optical depth integral, resulting in very good accuracy.

As with the lookup table proposed in Nishita et al. 1993, we can get the optical depth for the ray to the sun from any sample point in the atmosphere. All we need is the height of the sample point (x) and the angle from vertical to the sun (y), and we look up (x, y) in the table. This eliminates the need to calculate one of the out-scattering integrals. In addition, the optical depth for the ray to the camera can be figured out in the same way, right? Well, almost. It works the same way when the camera is in space, but not when the camera is in the atmosphere. That's because the sample rays used in the lookup table go from some point at height x all the way to the top of the atmosphere. They don't stop at some point in the middle of the atmosphere, as they would need to when the camera is inside the atmosphere.

Fortunately, the solution to this is very simple. First we do a lookup from sample point P to the camera to get the optical depth of the ray passing through the camera to the top of the atmosphere. Then we do a second lookup for the same ray, but starting at the camera instead of starting at P. This will give us the optical depth for the part of the ray that we don't want, and we can subtract it from the result of the first lookup. Examine the rays starting from the ground vertex (B_1) in Figure 16-3 for a graphical representation of this.

There's only one problem left. When a vertex is above the camera in the atmosphere, the ray from sample point P through the camera can pass through the planet itself. The height variable is not expected to go so far negative, and it can cause the numbers in the lookup table to go extremely high, losing precision and sometimes even encountering a floating-point overflow. The way to avoid this problem is to reverse the direction of the rays when the vertex is above the camera. Examine the rays passing through the sky vertex (B_2) in Figure 16-3 for a graphical representation of this.

So now we've reduced 3,000 calculations per vertex to something closer to $2 \times 3 \times 5 \times (1 + 1)$, or 60 (assuming five samples for the out-scattering integral for the eye ray). Implemented in software on an Athlon 2500+ with an inefficient brute-force rendering method, I was able to get this method to run between 50 and 100 frames per second.

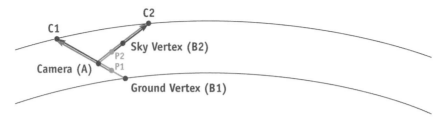

Figure 16-3. Problems with the Improved Lookup Table
This figure illustrates two issues with the lookup table when the camera is in the atmosphere. The lookup table can only return the optical depth for the blue and orange rays indicated. To get the optical depth from either sample point to the camera, the optical depth of each blue ray must be subtracted from the optical depth of its respective orange ray.

16.4 Squeezing It into a Shader

At this point, I felt that this algorithm had been squeezed about as much as it could, but I knew that I had to squeeze it even smaller to fit it into a shader. I didn't want this algorithm to require Shader Model 3.0, so having lookup tables in textures used by the vertex shaders wasn't possible. I decided to take a different approach and started to mathematically analyze the results of the lookup table. Even though I knew I couldn't come up with a way to simplify the integral equations, I had hoped that I might be able to simulate the results closely enough with a completely different equation.

16.4.1 Eliminating One Dimension

I started by plotting the results of the lookup table on a graph. I plotted height from 0.0 to 1.0 along the x axis and the lookup table result (optical depth) along the y axis. For various angles sampled from 0 to 1, I plotted a separate line on the graph. I noticed right away that each line dropped off exponentially as x went from 0 to 1, but the scale of each line on the graph varied dramatically. This makes sense, because as the angle of the ray goes from straight up to straight down, the length of the ray increases dramatically.

To make it easier to compare the shapes of the curves of each line, I decided to normalize them. I took the optical depth value at $x = 0$ (or height $= 0$) for each line and divided all of the values on that line by that value. This scaled all lines on the graph to start at $(x = 0, y = 1)$ and work their way down toward $(x = 1, y = 0)$. To my surprise, almost all of the normalized lines fell right on top of each other on the graph! The curve was almost exactly the same for every one, and that curve turned out to be $\exp(-4x)$.

This makes some sense, because the optical depth equation is the integral of $\exp(-h/H_0)$. I chose H_0 to be 0.25, so $\exp(-4h)$ is a common factor. It is still a bit puzzling, however, as the h inside the integral is not the same as the height x outside the integral, which is only the height at the start of the ray. The h value inside the integral does not vary linearly, and it has more to do with how it passes through a spherical space than with the starting height. There is some variation in the lines, and the variation increases as the angle increases. The variation gets worse exponentially as the angle increases over 90 degrees. Because we don't care about angles that are much larger than 90 degrees (because the ray passes through the planet), $\exp(-4x)$ works very well for eliminating the x axis of the lookup table.

16.4.2   Eliminating the Other Dimension

Now that the x dimension (height) of the lookup table is being handled by $\exp(-4x)$, we need to eliminate the y dimension (angle). The only part of the optical depth that is not handled by $\exp(-4x)$ is the scale used to normalize the lines on the graph explained previously, which is the value of the optical depth at $x = 0$. So now we create a new graph by plotting the angle from 0 to 1 on the x axis and the scale of each angle on the y axis. For lack of a better name, I call this the *scale function*.

The first time I looked at the scale function, I noticed that it started at 0.25 (the scale height) and increased on some sort of accelerating curve. Thinking that it might be exponential, I divided the scales by the scale height (to make the graph start at 1) and took the natural logarithm of the result. The result was another accelerating curve that I didn't recognize. I tried a number of curves, but nothing fit well on all parts of the curve. I ended up using graphical analysis software to find a "best fit" equation for the curve, and it came back with a polynomial equation that was not pretty but fit the values well.

One significant drawback to this implementation is that the scale function is dependent on the scale height and the ratio between the atmosphere's thickness and the planet's radius. If either value changes, you need to calculate a new scale function. In the demo included on this book's CD, the atmosphere's thickness (the distance from the ground to the top of the atmosphere) is 2.5 percent of the planet's radius, and the scale height is 25 percent of the atmosphere's thickness. The radius of the planet doesn't matter as long as those two values stay the same.

16.5 Implementing the Scattering Shaders

Now that the problem has been solved mathematically, let's look at how the demo was implemented. The C++ code for the demo is fairly simple. The `gluSphere()` function is called to render both the ground and the sky dome. The front faces are reversed for the sky dome so that the inside of its sphere is rendered. It uses a simple rectangular Earth texture to make it possible to see how the ground scattering affects colors on the ground, and it uses a simple glow texture billboard to render the moon. No distinct sun is rendered, but the Mie scattering creates a glow in the sky dome that looks like the sun (only when seen through the atmosphere).

I have provided shader implementations in both Cg and GLSL on the book's CD. The ground, the sky, and objects in space each have two scattering shaders, one for when the camera is in space and one for when the camera is in the atmosphere (this avoids conditional branching in the shaders). The ground shaders can be used for the terrain, as well as for objects that are beneath the camera. The sky shaders can be used for the sky dome, as well as for objects that are above the camera. The space shaders can be used for any objects outside the atmosphere, such as the moon.

The naming convention for the shaders is "*render_object*From*camera_position*". So the SkyFromSpace shader is used to render the sky dome when the camera is in space. There is also a common shader that contains some common constants and helper functions used throughout the shaders. Let's use SkyFromSpace as an example.

16.5.1 The Vertex Shader

As you can see in Listing 16-1, SkyFromSpace.vert is a fairly complex vertex shader, but hopefully it's easy enough to follow with the comments in the code and the explanations provided here. Kr is the Rayleigh scattering constant, Km is the Mie scattering constant, and ESun is the brightness of the sun. Rayleigh scatters different wavelengths of light at different rates, and the ratio is `1/pow(wavelength, 4)`. Referring back to Figure 16-2, v3Start is point *A* from the previous examples and v3Start + fFar * v3Ray is point *B*. The variable v3SamplePoint goes from P_1 to P_n with each iteration of the loop.

The variable fStartOffset is actually the value of the lookup table from point *A* going toward the camera. Why would we need to calculate this when it's at the outer edge of the atmosphere? Because the density is not truly zero at the outer edge. The density falls off exponentially and it is close to zero, but if we do not calculate this value and use it as an offset, there may be a visible "jump" in color when the camera enters the atmosphere.

You may have noticed that the phase function is missing from this shader. The phase function depends on the angle toward the light source, and it suffers from tessellation artifacts if it is calculated per vertex. To avoid these artifacts, the phase function is implemented in the fragment shader.

Listing 16-1. SkyFromSpace.vert, Which Renders the Sky Dome When the Camera Is in Space

```
#include "Common.cg"

vertout main(float4 gl_Vertex : POSITION,
    uniform float4x4 gl_ModelViewProjectionMatrix,
    uniform float3 v3CameraPos,      // The camera's current position
    uniform float3 v3LightDir,       // Direction vector to the light source
    uniform float3 v3InvWavelength,  // 1 / pow(wavelength, 4) for RGB
    uniform float fCameraHeight,     // The camera's current height
    uniform float fCameraHeight2,    // fCameraHeight^2
    uniform float fOuterRadius,      // The outer (atmosphere) radius
    uniform float fOuterRadius2,     // fOuterRadius^2
    uniform float fInnerRadius,      // The inner (planetary) radius
    uniform float fInnerRadius2,     // fInnerRadius^2
    uniform float fKrESun,           // Kr * ESun
    uniform float fKmESun,           // Km * ESun
    uniform float fKr4PI,            // Kr * 4 * PI
    uniform float fKm4PI,            // Km * 4 * PI
    uniform float fScale,            // 1 / (fOuterRadius - fInnerRadius)
    uniform float fScaleOverScaleDepth) // fScale / fScaleDepth
{
    // Get the ray from the camera to the vertex and its length (which
    // is the far point of the ray passing through the atmosphere)
    float3 v3Pos = gl_Vertex.xyz;
    float3 v3Ray = v3Pos - v3CameraPos;
    float fFar = length(v3Ray);
    v3Ray /= fFar;

    // Calculate the closest intersection of the ray with
    // the outer atmosphere (point A in Figure 16-3)
    float fNear = getNearIntersection(v3CameraPos, v3Ray, fCameraHeight2,
                            fOuterRadius2);

    // Calculate the ray's start and end positions in the atmosphere,
    // then calculate its scattering offset
    float3 v3Start = v3CameraPos + v3Ray * fNear;
    fFar -= fNear;
```

```
float fStartAngle = dot(v3Ray, v3Start) / fOuterRadius;
float fStartDepth = exp(-fInvScaleDepth);
float fStartOffset = fStartDepth * scale(fStartAngle);

// Initialize the scattering loop variables
float fSampleLength = fFar / fSamples;
float fScaledLength = fSampleLength * fScale;
float3 v3SampleRay = v3Ray * fSampleLength;
float3 v3SamplePoint = v3Start + v3SampleRay * 0.5;

// Now loop through the sample points
float3 v3FrontColor = float3(0.0, 0.0, 0.0);
for(int i=0; i<nSamples; i++) {
  float fHeight = length(v3SamplePoint);
  float fDepth = exp(fScaleOverScaleDepth * (fInnerRadius - fHeight));
  float fLightAngle = dot(v3LightDir, v3SamplePoint) / fHeight;
  float fCameraAngle = dot(v3Ray, v3SamplePoint) / fHeight;
  float fScatter = (fStartOffset + fDepth * (scale(fLightAngle) -
                                     scale(fCameraAngle)));
  float3 v3Attenuate = exp(-fScatter *
                      (v3InvWavelength * fKr4PI + fKm4PI));
  v3FrontColor += v3Attenuate * (fDepth * fScaledLength);
  v3SamplePoint += v3SampleRay;
}

// Finally, scale the Mie and Rayleigh colors
vertout OUT;
OUT.pos = mul(gl_ModelViewProjectionMatrix, gl_Vertex);
OUT.c0.rgb = v3FrontColor * (v3InvWavelength * fKrESun);
OUT.c1.rgb = v3FrontColor * fKmESun;
OUT.t0 = v3CameraPos - v3Pos;
return OUT;
}
```

16.5.2 The Fragment Shader

This shader should be fairly self-explanatory. One thing that is not shown in Listing 16-2 is that I commented out the math in the getRayleighPhase() function. The Rayleigh phase function causes the blue sky to be the brightest at 0 degrees and 180 degrees and the darkest at 90 degrees. However, I feel it makes the sky look too dark around 90 degrees. In theory, this problem arises because we are not implementing multiple scattering. Single scattering only calculates how much light is scattered coming directly from the sun. Light that is scattered out of the path of a ray just vanishes. Multiple scattering attempts to figure out where that light went, and often it is redirected back toward the camera from another angle. It is a lot like radiosity lighting, and it is not considered feasible to calculate in real time. Nishita et al. 1993 uses an ambient factor to brighten up the darker areas. I feel that it looks better to just leave out the Rayleigh phase function entirely. Feel free to play with it and see what you like best.

Listing 16-2. SkyFromSpace.frag, Which Renders the Sky Dome When the Camera Is in Space

```
#include "Common.cg"

float4 main(float4 c0 : COLOR0,
    float4 c1 : COLOR1,
    float3 v3Direction : TEXCOORD0,
    uniform float3 v3LightDirection,
    uniform float g,
    uniform float g2) : COLOR
{
    float fCos = dot(v3LightDirection, v3Direction) / length(v3Direction);
    float fCos2 = fCos * fCos;
    float4 color = getRayleighPhase(fCos2) * c0 +
                   getMiePhase(fCos, fCos2, g, g2) * c1;
    color.a = color.b;
    return color;
}
```

16.6 Adding High-Dynamic-Range Rendering

Atmospheric scattering doesn't look very good without high-dynamic-range (HDR) rendering. This is because these equations can very easily generate images that are too bright or too dark. See Figure 16-4. It looks much better when you render the image to a floating-point buffer and scale the colors to fall within the range 0..1 using an exponential curve with an adjustable exposure constant.

The exposure equation used in this demo is very simple: $1.0 - \exp(-fExposure \times color)$. The exposure constant works like the aperture of a camera or the pupils of your eyes. When there is too much light, the exposure constant is reduced to let in less light. When there is not enough light, the exposure constant is increased to let in more light.

Figure 16-4. The Importance of High Dynamic Range
The same scene rendered with HDR (left) and without HDR (right). Notice the extreme bright and dark regions in the image without HDR.

Without reasonable limits set on the exposure constant, daylight can look like moonlight and vice versa. Regardless, the relative brightness of each color is always preserved.

The HDR rendering implemented in this demo is also very simple. An OpenGL pbuffer is created with a floating-point pixel format and render-to-texture enabled. The same rendering code as before is used, but everything is rendered to the pbuffer's rendering context. Afterward, the main rendering context is selected and a single quad is rendered to fill the screen. The floating-point buffer is selected as a texture, and a simple exponential scaling shader is used to scale the colors to the normal 0–255 range. The exposure constant is set manually and can be changed at runtime in the demo, along with several of the scattering constants used.

Fortunately, modern GPUs support floating-point render targets. Some critical features such as alpha blending aren't available until you move up to GeForce 6 Series GPUs, so blending the sky dome with objects rendered in space won't work for older GPUs.

16.7 Conclusion

Although it took a fair number of simplifications to be able to interactively render scenes with the model described, the demo looks pretty sharp, especially with HDR rendering. Tweaking the parameters to the system can be a source of much entertainment; I had never imagined that the sky at the horizon would be orange at high noon if our atmosphere were a little thicker, or that sunsets would look that much more incredible. Red and orange skies produce sunsets of different shades of blue, and purple skies produce green sunsets. Once I even managed to find settings that produced a rainbow sunset.

In any case, the work is not done here. There are a number of improvements that could be made to this algorithm:

- Create an atmospheric-density scale function that is not hard-coded to a specific scale height and the ratio between the atmosphere thickness and the planetary radius.

- Split up the Rayleigh and Mie scattering so that they can have different scale depths.

- Provide a better way to simulate multiple scattering and start using the Rayleigh phase function again.

- Allow light from other sources, such as the moon, to be scattered, as well as sunlight. This would be necessary to create a moonlight effect with a halo surrounding the moon.

- Atmospheric scattering also makes distant objects look larger and blurrier than they are. The moon would look much smaller to us if it were not viewed through an atmosphere. It may be possible to achieve this in the HDR pass with some sort of blurring filter that is based on optical depth.

- Change the sample points taken along the ray from linear to exponential based on altitude. Nishita et al. 1993 explains why this is beneficial.

- Add other atmospheric effects, such as clouds, precipitation, lightning, and rainbows. See Harris 2001, Brewer 2004, and Dobashi et al. 2001.

16.8 References

Brewer, Clint. 2004. "Rainbows and Fogbows: Adding Natural Phenomena." NVIDIA Corporation. SDK white paper.
http://download.nvidia.com/developer/SDK/Individual_Samples/DEMOS/Direct3D9/src/HLSL_RainbowFogbow/docs/RainbowFogbow.pdf

Dobashi, Y., T. Yamamoto, and T. Nishita. 2001. "Efficient Rendering of Lightning Taking into Account Scattering Effects due to Clouds and Atmospheric Particles."
http://nis-lab.is.s.u-tokyo.ac.jp/~nis/cdrom/pg/pg01_lightning.pdf

Harris, Mark J., and Anselmo Lastra. 2001. "Real-Time Cloud Rendering." *Eurographics 2001* 20(3), pp. 76–84.
http://www.markmark.net/PDFs/RTClouds_HarrisEG2001.pdf

Hoffman, N., and A. J. Preetham. 2002. "Rendering Outdoor Scattering in Real Time." ATI Corporation.
http://www.ati.com/developer/dx9/ATI-LightScattering.pdf

Nishita, T., T. Sirai, K. Tadamura, and E. Nakamae. 1993. "Display of the Earth Taking into Account Atmospheric Scattering." In *Proceedings of SIGGRAPH 93,* pp. 175–182.
http://nis-lab.is.s.u-tokyo.ac.jp/~nis/cdrom/sig93_nis.pdf

O'Neil, Sean. 2004. "Real-Time Atmospheric Scattering." GameDev.net.
http://www.gamedev.net/columns/hardcore/atmscattering/

Chapter 17

Efficient Soft-Edged Shadows Using Pixel Shader Branching

Yury Uralsky
NVIDIA Corporation

Rendering realistic shadows has always been a hard problem in computer graphics. Soft shadows present an even greater challenge to developers, even when real-time performance is not required. Yet shadows are important visual clues that help us to establish spatial relationships between objects in a scene. In the past, artists understood the importance of shadows and used them to their advantage to emphasize certain objects and add depth to their pictures.

Real-world shadows always appear to have a certain amount of blurriness across their edges, and never appear strictly hard. Even on a bright, sunny day, when shadows are the sharpest, this is a noticeable effect. Even the sun, being a huge distance away from the Earth, can't be considered a point light source. Additionally, atmospheric scattering diffuses incoming light, blurring shadows from sunlight even more.

Recent advances in graphics hardware functionality and performance finally enable us to achieve real-time speeds when rendering soft shadows. This chapter discusses a method for rendering a high-quality approximation to real soft shadows at interactive frame rates. The method is based on adaptively taking multiple shadow-map samples in the fragment shader using a technique called *percentage-closer filtering* (PCF). With the branching capabilities of fragment shaders, this adaptive sampling approach provides increased visual quality while still maintaining high performance, compared to always taking a fixed number of samples.

17.1 Current Shadowing Techniques

The most well-known and robust techniques for rendering shadows are stencil shadow volumes and shadow maps. Both methods have their advantages and disadvantages.

Stencil shadow volumes work by classifying points on the scene surfaces with respect to frusta that encompass space where lighting is blocked by occluders. Sides of these frusta are formed by planes containing light-source position and edges in an object silhouette, as observed from the light source's point of view. The sides of the shadow volumes are rendered into a special off-screen buffer, "tagging" pixels in shadow. After that, normal scene rendering can color each pixel according to its tag value.

This method is simple and elegant, and it requires only minimal hardware support. It works well with both directional and point light sources, and it can be integrated pretty easily into any polygon-based rendering system such that every surface will be shadowed properly.

On the other hand, stencil shadow volumes depend heavily on how complex the geometry of a shadowing object is, and they burn a lot of fill rate. Most current implementations of the stencil shadow volumes algorithm require quite a bit of work on the CPU side, though that situation is likely to change in the future. Another downside of stencil shadow volumes is that the method is inherently multipass, which further restricts the polygon count of scenes with which it can be used.

Shadow maps are essentially z-buffers rendered as viewed from the light source's perspective. The entire scene is rendered into the shadow map in a separate pass. When the scene itself is rendered, the position of each pixel is transformed to light space, and then its z-value is compared to the value stored in the shadow map. The result of this comparison is then used to decide whether the current pixel is in shadow or not. Shadow mapping is an image-space algorithm, and it suffers from aliasing problems due to finite shadow-map resolution and resampling issues. Imagine we are looking at a large triangle positioned edge-on with respect to a light source such that the shadow stretches over it. As you can guess, its projection will cover only a handful of texels in the shadow map, failing to reproduce the shadow boundary with decent resolution. Another disadvantage of shadow maps is that they do not work very well for omnidirectional light sources, requiring multiple rendering passes to generate several shadow maps and cover the entire sphere of directions.

When their disadvantages can be avoided or minimized, shadow maps are great. Shadow maps are fully orthogonal to the rest of the rendering pipeline: everything that can be rendered and that can produce a z-value can be shadowed. Shadow maps scale very well as the triangle count increases, and they can even work with objects that have partially transparent textures. These properties have made this algorithm the method of choice for offline rendering.

Neither of these algorithms is able to produce shadows with soft edges "out of the box." Extensions to these algorithms exist that allow rendering of soft-edged shadows, but they rely on sampling the surface of the area light source and performing multiple shadow-resolution passes for each sample position, accumulating the results. This increases the cost of the shadows dramatically, and it produces visible color bands in the penumbrae of the shadows if the number of passes is not high enough.

However, it is possible to efficiently approximate soft shadows by modifying the original shadow-mapping algorithm. The percentage-closer filtering technique described by Reeves et al. (1987) takes a large number of shadow-map samples around the current point being shaded and filters their results to produce convincing soft shadows.

17.2 Soft Shadows with a Single Shadow Map

With PCF, instead of sampling the light source and rendering shadow maps at each sample position, we can get away with a *single* shadow map, sampling it several times in the area around the projected point in the shadow map, and then combining the results. This method does not produce physically correct soft shadows, but the visual effect is similar to what we see in reality.

17.2.1 Blurring Hard-Edged Shadows

Effectively, we are going to blur our hard-edged shadow so that it appears to have a softer edge. The straightforward way to implement this is to perform shadow-map comparisons several times using offset texture coordinates and then average the results. Intuitively, the amount of this offset determines how blurry the final shadow is.

Note that we cannot blur the actual contents of the shadow map, because it contains depth values. Instead, we have to blur the *results* of the shadow-map lookup when rendering a scene, which requires us to perform several lookups, each with a position offset slightly from the pixel's true position.

This approach resembles the traditional method for generating soft shadows by rendering multiple shadow maps. We just "rotate the problem 90 degrees" and replace expensive multiple shadow-map-generating passes with much less expensive multiple lookups into a single shadow map.

The GLSL code in Listing 17-1 demonstrates this idea.

Unfortunately, the naive approach only works well when the penumbra region is very small. Otherwise, banding artifacts become painfully obvious, as shown in Figure 17-1. When the number of shadow-map samples is small compared to the penumbra size, our "soft" shadow will look like several hard-edged shadows, superimposed over one another. To get rid of these banding artifacts, we would have to increase the number of shadow-map samples to a point where the algorithm becomes impractical due to performance problems.

Figure 17-1. A Naive Approach to Blurring Shadows
The image was rendered using 32 shadow-map samples. Notice the heavy banding in penumbra regions.

Listing 17-1. Implementing a Basic Algorithm for PCF

```
#define SAMPLES_COUNT 32
#define INV_SAMPLES_COUNT (1.0f / SAMPLES_COUNT)

uniform sampler2D decal;   // decal texture
uniform sampler2D spot;    // projected spotlight image
uniform sampler2DShadow shadowMap;   // shadow map

uniform float fwidth;
uniform vec2 offsets[SAMPLES_COUNT];

// these are passed down from vertex shader
varying vec4 shadowMapPos;
varying vec3 normal;
varying vec2 texCoord;
varying vec3 lightVec;
varying vec3 view;

void main(void)
{
  float shadow = 0;
  float fsize = shadowMapPos.w * fwidth;
  vec4 smCoord = shadowMapPos;

  for (int i = 0; i<SAMPLES_COUNT; i++) {
    smCoord.xy = offsets[i] * fsize + shadowMapPos;
    shadow += texture2DProj(shadowMap, smCoord) * INV_SAMPLES_COUNT;
  }

  vec3 N = normalize(normal);
  vec3 L = normalize(lightVec);
  vec3 V = normalize(view);

  vec3 R = reflect(-V, N);

  // calculate diffuse dot product
  float NdotL = max(dot(N, L), 0);

  // modulate lighting with the computed shadow value
  vec3 color = texture2D(decal, texCoord).xyz;

  gl_FragColor.xyz = (color * NdotL + pow(max(dot(R, L), 0), 64)) *
                      shadow * texture2DProj(spot, shadowMapPos) +
                      color * 0.1;
}
```

Let's find out how to implement this blurring in a more effective way without using too many shadow-map samples. To do this, we apply Monte Carlo methods, which are based on a probabilistic computation in which a number of *randomly placed* samples are taken of a function and averaged. In our context, that means we need to sample our shadow map *randomly*. This random placement of samples turns out to be a wise decision. The key point here is that the sequence of shadow-map sample locations is slightly different each time we calculate the shadowing value, so that the approximation error is different at different pixels. This effectively replaces banding with high-frequency noise, an artifact that the human visual system is trained to filter out very well. Note that the error is still there; it is just much better hidden from a human's eye.

If we carefully construct the sequence of offsets in a way that it has only a certain amount of randomness, we can get better results than if we use completely random offsets; this approach is called *stratified* or *jittered* sampling. To construct this distribution, we divide our domain into a number of subregions with equal areas, also known as *strata*, and randomly choose a sample location within each one. This subdivision provides even coverage of the domain, whereas each sample is still placed randomly within its cell.

If we assume that our sampling domain is a disk, stratification can be tricky. One possible solution is to stratify a square region and then warp it to a disk shape, preserving the area of the subregions. Generating a square grid of samples and then jittering it is straightforward, and for the area-preserving square-to-disk transformation, we use the following formulas:

$$x = \sqrt{v} \times \cos(2\pi u),$$
$$y = \sqrt{v} \times \sin(2\pi u),$$

where $u, v \in [0..1]$ and represent the jittered sample location within the square domain, and x, y are the corresponding sample position within the disk domain. Figure 17-2 illustrates the process. This way, the u dimension maps to angular position and the v dimension maps to radial distance from the disk center. The square roots compensate for the change in the cells' area as we move from the disk center outward, reducing the radial size of the cells.

17.2.2 Improving Efficiency

To achieve good shadow quality, we still need to take quite a few samples. We may need to take as many as 64 samples to have good-looking shadows with smooth penumbrae.

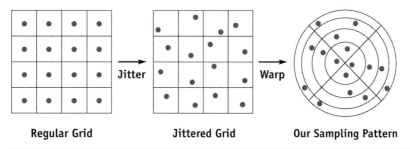

| Regular Grid | Jittered Grid | Our Sampling Pattern |

Figure 17-2. Jittering a Regular Grid and Warping to a Disk

Think about it: we need to sample the shadow map 64 times *per pixel*. This places significant pressure on texture memory bandwidth and shader processing.

Fortunately, most real-world shadows don't have a large penumbra region. The penumbra region is the soft part of the shadow, and it is where the most samples are needed. The other pixels are either completely in the shadow or completely out of the shadow, and for those pixels, taking one sample would give the same result as taking thousands of them.

Branching Like a Tree

Of course, we want to skip unnecessary computations for as many pixels as possible. But how do we know which pixels are in penumbrae and which are not? As you can guess, implementing this would require us to make decisions at the fragment level.

GeForce 6 Series GPUs finally enable true dynamic branching in fragment programs. This essentially means that now large blocks of code that do not need to be executed can be skipped completely, saving substantial computation.

Ideally, branch instructions would never have any overhead, and using them to skip code would only increase performance. Unfortunately, this is not the case. Modern GPUs have highly parallel, deeply pipelined architectures, calculating many pixels in concert. Pipelining allows GPUs to achieve high levels of performance, and parallelization is also natural for computer graphics, because many pixels perform similar computations. The consequence of using pipelining and parallel execution is that at any given time, a GPU processes several thousand pixels, but all of them run *the same* computations.

What does this have to do with branching, you say? Well, dynamic branching essentially enables pixels to choose their own execution paths. If two pixels follow different branches in their fragment program, you can no longer process those pixels together. That way, branching *hurts* parallelism to a certain extent.

For this reason, you want to make sure your branching is as *coherent* as possible. Coherence in this context means that pixels in some local neighborhood should always follow the same branch—that way, all of them can be processed together. The less coherent branching is, the less benefit you'll get from skipping code with branching.

Predict and Forecast

Now let's try to predict how much benefit we can expect from branching. Basically, we need to detect whether a pixel is in the penumbra and decide how many shadow-map samples it needs. If we could come up with an inexpensive "estimator" function that would tell us whether we need more samples for the current pixel, we could use it as our branch condition.

It is impossible to find out something about the shadow map at a given pixel without actually sampling the shadow map. It also seems obvious that one sample is not enough to determine if the current pixel is only partly in shadow. So, we need a way to determine that with a small number of samples.

Therefore, we take a small number of shadow-map samples and compare them. If they all happen to have the same value (that is, all of them are either ones or zeroes), then it is very likely that the rest of the samples within the same region will have the same value. This works because most shadows are "well behaved": changes between lit and shadowed areas are pretty infrequent compared to penumbra size. The smaller the number of samples we take to try to figure this out, the bigger the benefit we gain from branching.

The next question is how to place our estimation samples to make the penumbra prediction as precise as possible. If these samples have fixed locations within the sampling domain, once again we will suffer from banding. But we know how to deal with banding: jitter the samples again!

As it turns out, the best we can do is distribute the jittered samples in a circle near the edge of the disk, where they are most likely to catch the transition from light to shadow, as shown in Figure 17-3.

Of course, this placement of samples will fail to catch penumbrae for some pixels. But thanks to jittering, the next pixel will have a slightly different placement of estimation samples and will probably get it correct. That way, we again dissipate prediction error in high-frequency noise across adjacent pixels.

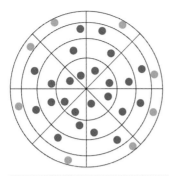
Figure 17-3. Estimation Samples (Shown in Green)

17.2.3 Implementation Details

For the shadow map itself, we use a depth texture and a "compare" texture application mode that are standard in OpenGL 1.4. Note that using floating-point formats for shadow maps is usually overkill and adds the unnecessary burden of having to manually perform comparisons in the fragment shader. As an additional benefit, NVIDIA hardware supports free four-sample bilinear percentage-closer filtering of depth textures, which helps to smooth out the penumbrae even more.

The bulk of our algorithm deals with jittered sampling. Because generating jittered offsets is a nontrivial task, it is best to precompute them and store them in a texture (jitter map).

To avoid the color-banding issue, pixels that are near each other need to use different sets of jittering offsets. It is not a problem if the offsets repeat due to tiling of the jitter map, as long as the noise frequency is high enough to keep the effect from being noticeable.

The most natural way to implement this is to use a 3D texture to store the jittered offsets. We store unique sequences of jittered offsets in "columns" of texels along the r texture dimension, and we tile the texture in screen space along the s and t dimensions. The texture extent in the s and t dimensions determines the size of the region where sequences are different, and its size in the r dimension depends on the maximum number of samples we intend to take. Conveniently for us, GLSL provides a built-in variable, `gl_FragCoord`, that contains current pixel position in screen space. This is exactly what we need to address this 3D texture in the s and t dimensions.

Because our offsets are two-dimensional and texels can have up to four channels, we can employ another optimization to reduce storage requirements for this 3D texture.

We store a pair of offsets per texel, with the first offset occupying the r and g components and the second one sitting in the b and a components of the texel. This way, the "depth" of our texture in texels is half the number of shadow-map samples we take per pixel. As an additional bonus, we save some amount of texture memory bandwidth, because we have to look up the texture only once for every two shadow-map samples.

Our offsets are stored in normalized form: if we distribute our samples within a disk with a radius of 1, then the center-relative offsets are always in the range $[-1..1]$. In a fragment program, we scale each offset by a blurriness factor to control how soft our shadows appear. Offsets don't need to be high precision, so we can get away with the signed four-component, 8-bit-per-component format for this texture.

Because our estimation samples need to be jittered too, we can use some of the offsets stored in the 3D texture for them. These should be located on the outer rings of the sampling disk. We fill our 3D texture in such a way that estimation sample offsets start at $r = 0$ within each column, with the rest of the offsets following. This simplifies addressing in the fragment program a bit.

To better understand the construction process for the jitter map, look at the function `create_jitter_lookup()` in the source code included on the accompanying CD.

Performance Notes

Shadow maps have another well-known problem related to sampling and precision. This problem is commonly called "shadow acne" and appears as shadow "leakage" on the lit side of the object, similar to z-fighting. It is usually avoided by rendering the object's back faces to the shadow map instead of its front faces. This moves the problem to the triangles facing away from the light source, which is not noticeable because those triangles are not lit by that light source and have the same intensity as shadowed surfaces.

This trick has certain performance implications with our soft shadow algorithm. Though not visible, the "acne" will have a significant impact on the branching coherence. To remedy this, we modulate our penumbra estimation result with the function `(dot(N, L) <= 0 ? 0 : 1)`. That is, if a pixel happens to belong to the shadowed side of the object, the function will resolve to 0, effectively invalidating potentially incorrect penumbra estimation and forcing it to return a "completely in shadow" result.

Another possible improvement is to use midpoint shadow maps instead of regular shadow maps. Midpoint shadow maps work by storing an averaged depth between front faces and back faces, as viewed from the light source. When shadowing objects are closed and have reasonable thickness, this reduces shadow-aliasing artifacts as well, at the expense of more complex shadow-map construction.

The GLSL fragment shader code in Listing 17-2 illustrates the adaptive sampling approach described in this chapter.

Listing 17-2. Implementing Adaptive Sampling for PCF of Shadow Maps

```
#define SAMPLES_COUNT 64
#define SAMPLES_COUNT_DIV_2 32
#define INV_SAMPLES_COUNT (1.0f / SAMPLES_COUNT)

uniform sampler2D decal;      // decal texture
uniform sampler3D jitter;     // jitter map
uniform sampler2D spot;       // projected spotlight image
uniform sampler2DShadow shadowMap;  // shadow map

uniform float fwidth;
uniform vec2 jxyscale;

// these are passed down from vertex shader
varying vec4 shadowMapPos;
varying vec3 normal;
varying vec2 texCoord;
varying vec3 lightVec;
varying vec3 view;

void main(void)
{
  float shadow = 0;
  float fsize = shadowMapPos.w * fwidth;
  vec3 jcoord = vec3(gl_FragCoord.xy * jxyscale, 0);
  vec4 smCoord = shadowMapPos;

  // take cheap "test" samples first
  for (int i = 0; i<4; i++) {
    vec4 offset = texture3D(jitter, jcoord);
    jcoord.z += 1.0f / SAMPLES_COUNT_DIV_2;

    smCoord.xy = offset.xy * fsize + shadowMapPos;
    shadow += texture2DProj(shadowMap, smCoord) / 8;

    smCoord.xy = offset.zw * fsize + shadowMapPos;
    shadow += texture2DProj(shadowMap, smCoord) / 8;
  }
```

```
vec3 N = normalize(normal);
vec3 L = normalize(lightVec);
vec3 V = normalize(view);

vec3 R = reflect(-V, N);

// calculate diffuse dot product
float NdotL = max(dot(N, L), 0);

// if all the test samples are either zeroes or ones, or diffuse dot
// product is zero, we skip expensive shadow-map filtering
if ((shadow - 1) * shadow * NdotL != 0) {
  // most likely, we are in the penumbra
  shadow *= 1.0f / 8;   // adjust running total

  // refine our shadow estimate
  for (int i = 0; i<SAMPLES_COUNT_DIV_2 - 4; i++) {
    vec4 offset = texture3D(jitter, jcoord);
    jcoord.z += 1.0f / SAMPLES_COUNT_DIV_2;

    smCoord.xy = offset.xy * fsize + shadowMapPos;
    shadow += texture2DProj(shadowMap, smCoord)* INV_SAMPLES_COUNT;

    smCoord.xy = offset.zw * fsize + shadowMapPos;
    shadow += texture2DProj(shadowMap, smCoord)* INV_SAMPLES_COUNT;
  }
}

// all done - modulate lighting with the computed shadow value
vec3 color = texture2D(decal, texCoord).xyz;

gl_FragColor.xyz = (color * NdotL + pow(max(dot(R, L), 0), 64)) *
                   shadow * texture2DProj(spot, shadowMapPos) +
                   color * 0.1;


}
```

17.3 Conclusion

We have described an efficient method for rendering soft-edged shadows in real time based on percentage-closer filtering in a fragment shader. Figure 17-4 shows sample results. This method is fully orthogonal with respect to other rendering techniques; for example, the stencil buffer can still be used for additional effects. Because most of the work is performed on the GPU, this method will demonstrate higher performance as new, more powerful GPU architectures become available.

Note that the approach described here may not work very well with unusual shadow-map projections such as perspective shadow maps. In such cases, more work is necessary to adjust the size of the penumbra on a per-pixel basis.

If used carefully, branching can provide significant performance benefits by allowing the GPU to skip unnecessary computations on a per-fragment basis. On a GeForce

Figure 17-4. Realistic Soft-Edged Shadows in Real Time

6800 GT GPU, our test implementation of adaptive shadow-map sampling showed more than twice the improvement in frame rate compared to the regular shadow-map sampling. The key point for achieving high performance with branching is to keep it as coherent as possible. This will become even more important for future hardware architectures, from which we can expect even more parallelism and deeper pipelining.

17.4 References

Akenine-Möller, Tomas, and Ulf Assarsson. 2002. "Approximate Soft Shadows on Arbitrary Surfaces Using Penumbra Wedges." In *Thirteenth Eurographics Workshop on Rendering,* pp. 297–306.

Assarsson, Ulf, Michael Dougherty, Michael Mounier, and Tomas Akenine-Möller. 2003. "An Optimized Soft Shadow Volume Algorithm with Real-Time Performance." In *Proceedings of the SIGGRAPH/Eurographics Workshop on Graphics Hardware 2003*, pp. 33–40.

Brabec, Stefan, and Hans-Peter Seidel. 2002. "Single Sample Soft Shadows Using Depth Maps." In *Proceedings of Graphics Interface 2002*, pp. 219–228.

Cook, Robert L. 1986. "Stochastic Sampling in Computer Graphics." *ACM Transactions on Graphics* 5(1), pp. 51–72.

Kirsch, Florian, and Jurgen Dollner. 2003. "Real-Time Soft Shadows Using a Single Light Sample." *WSCG* 11(1), pp. 255–262.

Reeves, William T., David H. Salesin, and Robert L. Cook. 1987. "Rendering Antialiased Shadows with Depth Maps." *Computer Graphics* 21(4), pp. 283–291.

Chapter 18

Using Vertex Texture Displacement for Realistic Water Rendering

Yuri Kryachko
1C:Maddox Games

Water surfaces are common in computer graphics, especially in games. They are a critical element that can significantly improve the level of realism in a scene. But depicting them realistically is a hard problem, because of the high visual complexity present in the motion of water surfaces, as well as in the way light interacts with water. This chapter describes techniques developed for rendering realistic depictions of the ocean for the game *Pacific Fighters*.

Modern graphics hardware provides a number of useful features with DirectX Shader Model 3.0 that can be used to aid the rendering of water surfaces. This chapter will discuss how one of these features, vertex texturing, can be used to increase the realism of rendered water surfaces. Figure 18-1 shows some sample results. In addition, we also use branching in order to improve the performance of our vertex programs.

18.1 Water Models

For water animation and rendering, a number of methods have been developed. The most remarkable and realistic-looking ones are those based on fluid dynamics and Fast Fourier Transforms (FFTs)(such as Tessendorf 2001). These methods provide very realistic results, but unfortunately they require substantial amounts of computation, making them inappropriate for interactive applications.

Figure 18-1. The Benefits of Displacement Mapping
Water surface rendered (left) with displacement mapping and (right) without displacement mapping.

At the other extreme, most games currently use very simple water models, most of which employ normal maps to create visual details. Unfortunately, these approaches cannot provide enough realism and do not faithfully reproduce waves on the surface.

We seek a technique that combines the speed of simple normal-mapped water-rendering methods with the visual quality of FFT-like approaches.

18.2 Implementation

Our implementation builds upon rendering algorithms that employ normal maps for lighting calculations. Because normal maps faithfully reproduce fine detail in high-frequency waves, we use them for our lighting calculations. However, in addition, we perturb the water mesh geometrically with lower-frequency waves with large amplitude.

18.2.1 Water Surface Model

Our model of a water surface is based on the superposition of several height maps, tiled in both space and time. Each texture represents one "harmonic" or "octave" of the spectrum, and the textures are added together as in Fourier synthesis. These textures are called *height maps* because each value represents the elevation of the corresponding point above the horizontal plane.

Height maps are great for artists: creating them is as simple as painting a grayscale image. See Figure 18-2. With height maps, artists can easily control the parameters of

Figure 18-2. A Height Map Used for Water Displacement

water animation down to individual waves by just painting their shapes. Height maps also work well as vertex textures: using them to displace vertex positions vertically is trivial.

By combining several height maps with different spatial and time scales, we can achieve complex and visually intricate animations:

$$H\left(x,\ y,\ t\right) = \sum_{i=0}^{N} h\left(A_i^x x + B_i^x,\ A_i^y y + B_i^y,\ A_i^t t + B_i^t\right).$$

The coefficients A and B and the number of terms under the sum are chosen heuristically to achieve the most aesthetically pleasing results while minimizing repeating-pattern artifacts. In *Pacific Fighters*, we sum four height maps for lighting calculations, and two of them with the largest scale are used for displacement mapping. This is sufficient for simulating moving ocean surfaces at scales from 10 cm up to 40 km.

18.2.2 Implementation Details

All of the computations we need to perform can be classified into two groups: geometric displacement computations and lighting computations. Because our water surface is finely tessellated, it is reasonable to perform lighting calculations at the fragment program level, offloading the displacement mapping to the vertex stage. Also, performing lighting calculations at the vertex stage can create visual artifacts, especially in the distance.

At the time of writing, the only hardware capable of doing vertex texturing were GeForce 6 Series GPUs and the latest NVIDIA Quadro FX GPUs. The vertex texture implementation on this hardware has certain restrictions; in particular, vertex textures must be 32-bit-per-component textures, floating point, and they can't use any filtering mode except nearest filtering. Nevertheless, they proved to be very useful for the techniques described in this chapter.

18.2.3 Sampling Height Maps

Our implementation samples the height maps per vertex and computes the resulting displacement value in the vertex program. For sampling, we use a radial grid, centered at the camera position. This grid is tessellated in such a way that it provides more detail closer to the viewer, as shown in Figure 18-3.

The following equations show how the vertex positions for the radial grid are computed.

$$r = a_0 + a_1 i^4$$
$$x_{i,j} = r \cos\left(2\pi j / M\right)$$
$$y_{i,j} = r \sin\left(2\pi j / M\right),$$

where $i = [0..N-1], j = [0..M-1]$. We choose a_0, a_1 so that

$$r_0 = a_0 = 10 \text{ cm}$$
$$r_{N-1} = a_0 + a_1\left(N-1\right)^4 = 40 \text{ km}.$$

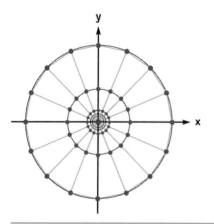

Figure 18-3. Radial Grid for Sampling Vertex Textures

With this approach, we naturally get distance-based tessellation, which provides a simple level-of-detail (LOD) scheme. Other approaches, such as the ROAM or SOAR terrain-rendering algorithms, could be used here, but they require a significant amount of work on the CPU side, which would eliminate all the benefits of using vertex textures. See Chapter 2 of this book, "Terrain Rendering Using GPU-Based Geometry Clipmaps," for another approach to rendering height fields on the GPU with adaptive tessellation.

Listing 18-1 shows the simple vertex shader that implements sampling from a single height map with a radial grid.

Listing 18-1. Vertex Shader for Sampling from a Height Map Using the Radial Grid Geometry

```
float4 main(float4 position : POSITION,
  uniform sampler2D tex0,
  uniform float4x4 ModelViewProj,
  uniform float4 DMParameters, // displacement map parameters
  uniform float4 VOfs) : POSITION
{
  // Read vertex packed as (cos(), sin(), j)
  float4 INP = position;

  // Transform to radial grid vertex
  INP.xy = INP.xy * (pow(INP.z, 4) * VOfs.z);

  // Find displacement map texture coordinates
  // VOfs.xy, DMParameters.x - Height texture offset and scale
  float2 t = (INP.xy + VOfs.xy) * DMParameters.x;

  // Fetch displacement value from texture (lod 0)
  float vDisp =  tex2D(tex0, t).x;

  // Scale fetched value from 0..1:
  // DMParameters.y - water level
  // DMParameters.z - wavy amplitude
  INP.z = DMParameters.y + (vDisp - 0.5) * DMParameters.z;

  // Displace current position with water height
  // and project it
  return mul(ModelViewProj, INP);
}
```

18.2.4 Quality Improvements and Optimizations

Packing Heights for Bilinear Filtering

Vertex texture fetch can be quite expensive. On GeForce 6 Series hardware, a single vertex texture fetch can introduce noticeable latency in the vertex program. So we want to minimize the number of texture fetches inside the vertex program. On the other hand, it is very desirable to perform some kind of filtering on the texture values; otherwise, visual quality will be significantly degraded.

Traditional well-known filtering methods are bilinear and trilinear filtering. Bilinear filtering computes the weighted average of four texels closest to the coordinates of the texture fetch. Trilinear filtering averages the results of bilinear lookups in adjacent mip levels, weighting each by the corresponding LOD fraction.

Because the current generation of graphics hardware doesn't support any form of filtering of vertex texture values, we have to emulate filtering in the shader with explicit math instructions. When implemented naively, even the simplest bilinear filter would require four texture lookups to calculate a single filtered value. A trilinear filter would require twice as many texture lookups.

To reduce the number of texture fetches necessary for filtering, we build our texture in a special way, so that each texel contains all the data necessary for a single bilinear texture lookup. This is possible because our height maps are essentially one-component textures, and we can pack four height values into a single texel of a four-component texture:

$$A_x^{i,j} = H^{i,j},$$
$$A_y^{i,j} = H^{i+1,j},$$
$$A_z^{i,j} = H^{i,j+1},$$
$$A_w^{i,j} = H^{i+1,j+1},$$
$$A_{filtered} = F\left(A_{x,y,z,w}^{i,j}\right),$$

where $i = 0..N - 1, j = 0..M - 1$. H is our height map value, F is a filtering function, and A is the packed output texture.

Listing 18-2 implements bilinear texture lookup into vertex texture, packed as shown previously.

Listing 18-2. Efficient Bilinear Texture Interpolation in Vertex Shaders
Based on fetching the appropriate four height components with a single texture fetch.

```
float tex2D_bilinear4x(uniform sampler2D tex,
  float4 t,
  float2 Scales)
{
  float size  = Scales.x;
  float scale = Scales.y;

  float4 tAB0 = tex2Dbias(tex, t);

  float2 f = frac(t.xy * size);
  float2 tAB  = lerp(tAB0.xz, tAB0.yw, f.x);
  return lerp(tAB.x, tAB.y, f.y);
}
```

We can extend this approach for trilinear filtering. Because trilinear filtering requires a fractional LOD value, we can use the distance from the camera as a good approximation of LOD. The code in Listing 18-3 implements trilinear texture lookup into the packed vertex texture.

Listing 18-3. Extending the Bilinear Filtering Technique to Trilinear Filtering

```
float tex2D_trilinear(uniform sampler2D tex,
  float4 t,
  float2 Scales)
{
  float fr = frac(t.z);
  t.z -= fr;  // floor(t.zw);
  float Res;
  if (fr < 0.30)
    Res =  tex2D_bilinear4x(tex, t.xyzz, Scales);
  else if (fr > 0.70)
    Res =  tex2D_bilinear4x(tex, t.xyzz + float4(0, 0, 1, 1),
                         Scales * float2(0.5, 2));
  else {
    Res = tex2D_bilinear4x(tex, t.xyzz, Scales);
    float Res1 = tex2D_bilinear4x(tex, t.xyzz + float4(0, 0, 1, 1),
                           Scales * float2(0.5, 2));
    fr = saturate((fr - 0.30) * (1 / (0.70 - 0.30)));
    Res = Res1 * fr + Res * (1 - fr);
  }
  return Res;
}
```

Note that we've further optimized trilinear texture fetch by performing two texture lookups only in the region where the influence of both mip levels is significant. In other regions, we "snap" the LOD value to the closest mip level, thus saving on texture bandwidth.

Avoiding Unnecessary Work with Branching

Even with optimized texture filtering, the number of texture fetches during water rendering can still be high, which significantly affects performance. We could reduce the total number of rendered vertices, but that would lower overall visual detail and increase aliasing.

Because we render our water with large batches of geometry, some of the triangles end up being completely off-screen. Note that even for such triangles, the vertex program is still executed, wasting precious computational resources. We can save a significant amount of per-vertex work if we skip computation for triangles falling outside the camera frustum.

The vertex program operates at one vertex at a time and has no access to topological information, so we can make decisions only on the per-vertex level, but not on the per-triangle level. This can create artifacts if some of the vertices within a triangle skip vertex texturing and others don't. We have found that in practice our triangles and our vertex texture displacements are small enough for this artifact not to be detectable.

The following pseudocode illustrates this idea:

```
float4 ClipPos = mul(ModelViewProj, INP);
float3 b0 = abs(ClipPos.xyz) < (ClipPos.www * C0 + C1);

if (all(b0)) {
  // Vertex belongs to visible triangle,
  // Perform texture sampling and displace vertex accordingly
}
```

In the preceding code, we use the clip-space vertex position to determine if the current vertex lies within the frustum, and then we perform the expensive computations only when necessary.

The values C0 and C1 are special "fudge" constants that control how much triangles need to extend beyond the camera frustum to trigger clipping. That way, we avoid artifacts caused by skipping texturing for out-of-frustum vertices whose triangles are still visible. Effectively, we are making our "clipping" frustum slightly wider, allowing for a certain amount of "guard-band" space along screen edges. Because our water plane is tessellated finely enough and the vertex texture displacements are reasonable, this simple method works well in practice.

Using Render-to-Texture

We can also improve the speed of our approach by first combining our height map textures into a single floating-point texture in a separate pass. It then becomes unnecessary to perform multiple expensive filtering operations in the vertex shader. Additionally, we can now use a more compact texture format, 16-bit floating point, for storage of the original height maps. We could also store a sequence of animated height maps as slices of a 3D texture, which would make animation smoother.

With this optimization, our rendering loop becomes two passes:

1. Combine the height maps using a special pixel shader by rendering a single quadrilateral into an fp32-texture. Texels in this texture map to the vertices of the radial mesh.

2. Use the generated height map as a vertex texture to displace the radial mesh vertices, as described previously.

Back Sides of Waves

Because our lighting computations are performed in the pixel shader under the assumption that the water surface is flat, this approximation can cause visual artifacts in certain cases.

In the case depicted in Figure 18-4, we see the back side of the wave, even though it is directed outward from the viewer due to geometrical displacement and shouldn't be visible in reality. This results in disturbing bright areas at the tops of the waves.

To minimize these artifacts, we adjust our normal vectors used for the lighting calculation by "tilting" them toward the viewer a bit, so that they correspond to the front faces of the wave more closely. You can find source code for this technique on the accompanying CD. Figure 18-5 shows a scene produced using the methods described in this chapter.

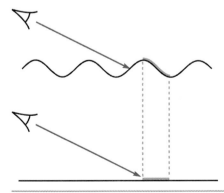

Figure 18-4. A Source of Rendering Artifacts
The back side of a wave (green) may be shaded even though it shouldn't be visible. Adjusting the normal vector used in the lighting calculation can significantly reduce this error.

Figure 18-5. Extremely Realistic Water Rendered with Techniques Presented Here

18.2.5 Rendering Local Perturbations

Sometimes it is desirable to render local choppiness caused by buoyant objects or by objects falling into the water. This is especially important for games, where it is necessary to generate explosions, ship trails, or the like. Because it is hard to integrate physically correct methods in our height-map-based model of the water surface, we discuss simpler methods, based on heuristics.

Analytical Deformation Model

The simplest way to achieve local choppiness is to disturb displaced vertex positions analytically, by combining them with the computed vertex position in the vertex shader. For explosions, we can use the following formula:

$$I(r) = \frac{I_0 \sin(kr + \omega t)e^{-bt}}{r^2},$$

where r is the distance from the explosion center in the water plane and b is a decimation constant. The values of I_0, ω, and k are chosen according to a given explosion and its parameters.

For rendering, we can use the same radial grid as the one used for regular water rendering, but centered at the explosion location.

Dynamic Displacement Mapping

Another option is to render all of the locally generated displacements directly into the vertex texture, essentially implementing a general-purpose programming on the GPU (GPGPU) type of approach. That way, we generate a vertex texture in the first pass and then use it in a subsequent pass for the actual water rendering. As an additional benefit, we can offload some work from the vertex shaders by filtering the base height map and summing "octaves" in the pixel shader.

To calculate displacements, we can either employ the above-mentioned analytical model or try using a cellular-automata approach, by evolving local displacements from frame to frame. Wind effects can also be taken into account by blurring the texture along the appropriate direction.

However, to cover 1 km of water surface with 50 cm resolution, it would be necessary to use a texture about 2048×2048 in size, which would create additional pressure on texture memory and shader execution speed. Also, quick transitions of the viewpoint would be problematic.

Nevertheless, we encourage the reader to experiment with these approaches.

Foam Generation

When choppiness is strong enough, we can generate foam to further increase realism. The simplest way to do this is to blend in a precreated foam texture at vertices displaced above a certain height H_0. Transparency of the foam texture is calculated according to the following formula:

$$Foam.a = \text{saturate}\left(\frac{H - H_0}{H_{max} - H_0}\right),$$

where H_{max} is the height at which the foam is at maximum, H_0 is the base height, and H is the current height.

The foam texture can be animated to show the evolution of foam creation and dissipation. The animation sequence can be either created manually by artists or generated programmatically.

18.3 Conclusion

By combining the flexibility of vertex texture fetch and the performance-saving features of dynamic branching, we were able to develop a practical method for rendering realistic-looking water surfaces at interactive speeds. The approach described here was successfully applied in the title *Pacific Fighters*, and it allowed us to create a realistic water surface across a significant range of distances—from 10 cm up to 40 km. This is acceptable for modern flight simulators. We were able to eliminate tiling artifacts across the whole visible region of the water surface.

Future hardware is likely to enable even more robust implementations of the technique, in particular eliminating the need to manually perform filtering of the texture values, as well as providing even more vertex shader performance.

The quality of our approach can be increased even further by employing advanced shading techniques, such as parallax mapping, to provide fine-grained details and bumps on the water surface. See Chapter 8, "Per-Pixel Displacement Mapping with Distance Functions," for one approach like this.

Finally, lighting calculations could greatly benefit from high-dynamic-range techniques, because highly reflective water surfaces can exhibit huge brightness variations.

18.4 References

Fournier, Alain, and William T. Reeves. 1986. "A Simple Model of Ocean Waves." In *Computer Graphics (Proceedings of SIGGRAPH 86)*, pp. 75-84.

Kryachko, Yuri. 2004. "Modelling Sea and River Water with Pixel Shader 2.0." Presentation. Available online at **http://www.kriconf.ru/2004/rec/KRI-2004.Programming_20.ppt**

Tessendorf, Jerry. 2001. "Simulating Ocean Water." In "Simulating Nature: Realistic and Interactive Techniques," *SIGGRAPH 2001* course notes, course 47.

Chapter 19

Generic Refraction Simulation

Tiago Sousa
Crytek

Refraction, the bending of light as it passes from a medium with one index of refraction to another (for example, from air to water, from air to glass, and so on), is challenging to achieve efficiently in real-time computer graphics. There are many well-known techniques for simulating light reflection (such as planar reflection maps and cubic environment maps), and these techniques work well in most situations. However, there aren't as many widely known and effective techniques for simulating refraction. This chapter describes an approach to refraction based on perturbing the texture coordinates used in a texture lookup of an image of the nonrefractive objects in the scene. This technique is very efficient and works well in many cases. The method presented here is an expansion of the techniques used in *Far Cry* for rendering water, heat haze, and the sniper-scope lens, among other effects.

There are several ways to simulate refraction: some are based on precomputing an environment map and then using it at runtime; others are based on computing the environment map on the fly. Drawbacks of these techniques are high texture memory usage and the performance penalty, especially if there are many refractive surfaces in the scene requiring different environment maps.

Another problem with current water refraction simulation techniques is that they require two rendering passes: one to generate the refraction map with geometry above the water plane clipped, and then another pass to render the water surface. This approach can also have poor performance, especially in complex rendering situations.

This chapter discusses a simple technique to overcome these problems. We start by introducing the basic technique, which is based on using the current back buffer as a refraction map and then adding displacement to the texture coordinates to simulate the refractive look. This basic approach can lead to artifacts, however, so we then discuss how to mask out geometry from the refraction map. Finally, we demonstrate some general techniques for rendering realistic water and glass using this refraction simulation technique. Figure 19-1 shows a simple example of refraction in a scene.

(a) (b)

Figure 19-1. An Example of Refraction in a Scene
*(a) Background scene (**S**). (b) Final composition with refractive meshes.*

19.1 Basic Technique

The first step of the basic refraction technique is to render the scene geometry into a texture, skipping all refractive meshes. This texture can be used to determine which objects are visible behind the refractive objects that will be rendered in a subsequent pass. We denote this texture as **S**.

The second step is to render the refractive meshes, looking up values from the texture **S** with a perturbation applied to simulate the refractive look. The perturbation can be achieved using a normal map **N**, where the normal-map red and green (XY) components are used and scaled by some small value to add a displacement into the projected texture coordinates. This approach is straightforward to implement in a shader: (1) fetch the texture **N**, (2) use the XY components scaled by a small value (such as 0.05), and (3) add this displacement value into the projected texture coordinates for **S**. Listing 19-1 shows a shader that demonstrates this approach; Figure 19-2 illustrates the three steps.

Listing 19-1. Shader for Basic Refraction Technique

```
half4 main(float2 bumpUV : TEXCOORD0,
    float4 screenPos : TEXCOORD1,
    uniform sampler2D tex0,
    uniform sampler2D tex1,
    uniform float4 vScale) : COLOR
{
    // fetch bump texture, unpack from [0..1] to [-1..1]
    half4 bumpTex=2.0 * tex2D(tex0, bumpUV.xy) - 1.0;

    // displace texture coordinates
    half2 newUV = (screenPos.xy/screenPos.w) + bumpTex.xy * vScale.xy;

    // fetch refraction map
    return tex2D(tex1, newUV);
}
```

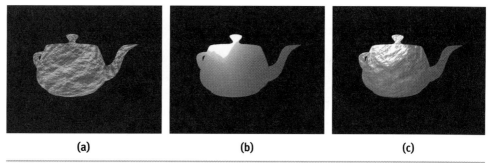

(a) (b) (c)

Figure 19-2. A Visualization of the Rendering Steps
*(a) Normal map (**N**). (b) Projected background texture (**S**). (c) Projected background texture with perturbation applied.*

19.2 Refraction Mask

The basic technique presented in the previous section will work reasonably well in a variety of situations, but it can be prone to artifacts if a bump with a large enough scale is used for perturbation when a mesh is in front of a refractive mesh. Figure 19-3 illustrates the problem: the brown sphere is inaccurately rendered as in the refraction in the teapot, even though it is in front of the teapot, not behind it.

These artifacts are visible because the texture **S** has all the scene geometry rendered into it, including objects in front of the refractive mesh, and we are indiscriminately applying

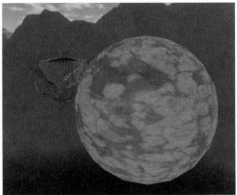

Figure 19-3. Artifacts Caused by the Technique

perturbation on every pixel. This leads to refraction "leakage" between objects in the scene. A straightforward solution is to decrease the amount of perturbation applied, until artifacts are reduced to an acceptable visual quality level. However, it is difficult to find a scale for the perturbation that works well in all circumstances, and this solution also has the negative side effect of capping how bumpy your refractive surfaces can be.

A better solution instead is to make sure that we actually don't add perturbation into the wrong pixels. To do so, we lay down a mask in the alpha channel of the S texture for all refractive meshes and use it to ensure that the perturbed coordinates are used only if they end up being inside a refractive object's area on the screen. See Figure 19-4 for an example.

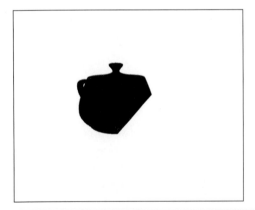

Figure 19-4. The Alpha Channel in the Frame Buffer
The refractive mesh is black.

For this approach to work, we need to change the rendering a bit: first we make sure that the alpha channel of texture **S** is cleared to white, and then we render refractive meshes as black only into texture **S**'s alpha channel. When rendering the refractive meshes, we make use of the extra information stored in **S**'s alpha channel, to discriminate which pixels will be processed. This is done by checking if alpha is white; if so, we do not add perturbation in that case. Only if alpha is black do we add perturbation. Thus, if perturbation would have included a pixel outside of the refractive object, we instead just use the original pixel, giving whatever geometry was directly behind the refractive object. Although this result is inaccurate—refraction may actually lead to objects that aren't directly behind the object becoming visible—it works well in practice and is quite efficient. Listing 19-2 shows the shader that implements this approach, and Figure 19-5 shows the results.

Listing 19-2. Improved Shader That Uses the Refraction Mask to Avoid Including Pixels from Objects in Front of the Refractive Object

```
half4 main(float2 bumpUV : TEXCOORD0,
    float4 screenPos : TEXCOORD1
    uniform sampler2D tex0,
    uniform sampler2D tex1,
    uniform float4 vScale) : COLOR
{
    // fetch bump texture
    half4 bumpTex=2.0 * tex2D(tex0, bumpUV.xy) - 1.0;

    // compute projected texture coordinates
    half2 vProj = (screenPos.xy/screenPos.w);

    // fetch refraction map
    half4 vRefrA = tex2D(tex1, vProj.xy + bumpTex.xy * vScale.xy);
    half4 vRefrB = tex2D(tex1, vProj.xy);

    return vRefrB * vRefrA.w + vRefrA * (1 - vRefrA.w);
}
```

It's simple in this way to remove the artifacts, making it possible to use this refraction simulation technique on every mesh type. Although almost not noticeable, some artifacts may be visible, because we're replacing occluder pixel colors with the background color.

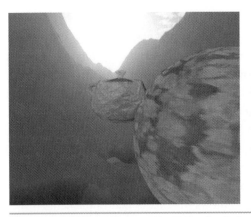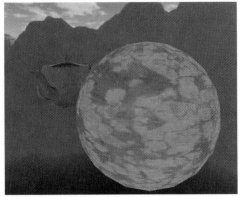

Figure 19-5. Artifacts Removed by Using the Refraction Mask

19.3 Examples

Many interesting effects can be achieved with the presented technique. For example, the normal map used may be an animated texture, or a transformation may be applied to its coordinates. In this section, we cover a few practical examples.

19.3.1 Water Simulation

Simulating refractive water is one of the applications in which the presented technique is particularly effective, as current methods use an extra pass to generate the refractive map, by rendering the scene again and clipping geometry above the water plane. With this technique, we can render water in just one pass, because the only extra work is to render the water plane into texture S's alpha channel for the refraction mask.

For *Far Cry*, we used an animated bump texture, which worked out really well. In later experiments, however, we achieved even better results by using multiple bump-map layers for animating water waves, then blending between reflection and refraction through a per-pixel Fresnel term. Figure 19-6 shows the rendering steps for water.

The water simulation rendering is done by rendering the scene as described in previous sections, with the water plane rendered into the back-buffer alpha for the refraction mask. Next we need to generate a water reflection map, by rendering the scene reflected through the water plane into the reflection map and clipping the geometry below the water surface. Finally, there's no need to do an extra rendering pass for the refraction map, because we can use texture S and its refraction mask on the alpha channel.

(a)   (b)   (c)

Figure 19-6. The Rendering Steps for Water
(a) Reflection. (b) Refraction. (c) Final composition.

Once the main texture input has been generated, we must render the water itself. In this example, we use four bump layers. The texture coordinates of the bump layers are scaled in the vertex shader by an increasing value for each, so that we have a nice mix of low-frequency and high-frequency details on the water waves. A translation is also added to the texture coordinates to simulate the motion of waves in the water. Listings 19-3 and 19-4 show the implementation.

Listing 19-3. Fresnel Approximation Computation for Water Rendering

```
half Fresnel(half NdotL, half fresnelBias, half fresnelPow)
{
  half facing = (1.0 - NdotL);
  return max(fresnelBias +
             (1.0 - fresnelBias) * pow(facing, fresnelPow), 0.0);
}
```

Listing 19-4. The Fragment Program for Refractive/Reflective Water

```
half4 main(float3 Eye : TEXCOORD0,
  float4 Wave0 : TEXCOORD1,
  float2 Wave1 : TEXCOORD2,
  float2 Wave2 : TEXCOORD3,
  float2 Wave3 : TEXCOORD4,
  float4 ScreenPos : TEXCOORD5,
  uniform sampler2D tex0,
  uniform sampler2D tex1,
  uniform sampler2D tex2) : COLOR
{
  half3 vEye = normalize(Eye);
```

```
// Get bump layers
half3 vBumpTexA = tex2D(tex0, Wave0.xy).xyz;
half3 vBumpTexB = tex2D(tex0, Wave1.xy).xyz;
half3 vBumpTexC = tex2D(tex0, Wave2.xy).xyz;
half3 vBumpTexD = tex2D(tex0, Wave3.xy).xyz;

// Average bump layers
half3 vBumpTex=normalize(2.0 * (vBumpTexA.xyz + vBumpTexB.xyz +
                          vBumpTexC.xyz + vBumpTexD.xyz) - 4.0);

// Apply individual bump scale for refraction and reflection
half3 vRefrBump = vBumpTex.xyz * half3(0.075, 0.075, 1.0);
half3 vReflBump = vBumpTex.xyz * half3(0.02, 0.02, 1.0);

// Compute projected coordinates
half2 vProj = (ScreenPos.xy/ScreenPos.w);
half4 vReflection = tex2D(tex2, vProj.xy + vReflBump.xy);
half4 vRefrA = tex2D(tex1, vProj.xy + vRefrBump.xy);
half4 vRefrB = tex2D(tex1, vProj.xy);

// Mask occluders from refraction map
half4 vRefraction = vRefrB * vRefrA.w + vRefrA * (1 - vRefrA.w);

// Compute Fresnel term
half NdotL = max(dot(vEye, vReflBump), 0);
half facing = (1.0 - NdotL);
half fresnel = Fresnel(NdotL, 0.2, 5.0);

// Use distance to lerp between refraction and deep water color
half fDistScale = saturate(10.0/Wave0.w);
half3 WaterDeepColor = (vRefraction.xyz * fDistScale +
                   (1 - fDistScale) * half3(0, 0.15, 0.115));

// Lerp between water color and deep water color
half3 WaterColor = half3(0, 0.15, 0.115);
half3 waterColor = (WaterColor * facing +
                   WaterDeepColor * (1.0 - facing));

half3 cReflect = fresnel * vReflection;

// final water = reflection_color * fresnel + water_color
return half4(cReflect + waterColor, 1);
}
```

19.3.2 Glass Simulation

Glass simulation is usually done using cube maps for both reflection and refraction, and then the results are blended using the Fresnel term. Some techniques go further and make refraction wavelength-dependent, to simulate chromatic aberration. In this example, we use only the texture **S** and a 2D reflection map to simulate the refraction and reflections on the glass. But this approach could be extended to include the previously mentioned techniques.

First we render the scene as usual to generate the **S** texture (with the refraction mask in alpha). The glass surface is then rendered by using environmental bump mapping blended with the refraction map using the per-pixel Fresnel term. The glass color comes from the diffuse texture modulated by the refraction. Figure 19-7 shows the three steps of this process.

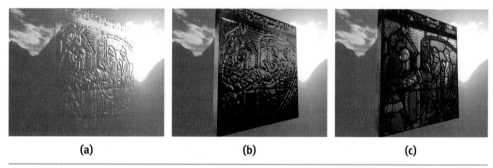

(a)   (b)   (c)

Figure 19-7. The Rendering Steps for Stained Glass
(a) Refraction. (b) Environmental bump mapping. (c) Final composition.

By changing the bump texture, diffuse texture, and environment map, it's simple to simulate the appearance of different types of glass without having to change the fragment program itself. Figure 19-8 shows two examples, and the shader appears in Listing 19-5.

Listing 19-5. Shader for Refractive/Reflective Glass Simulation

```
half4 main(float2 BaseUV : TEXCOORD0,
  float4 ScreenPos : TEXCOORD1,
  float3 Eye : TEXCOORD2,
  uniform sampler2D tex0,
  uniform sampler2D tex1,
  uniform sampler2D tex2,
  uniform sampler2D tex3) : COLOR
{
  half3 vEye = normalize(Eye.xyz);

  // Get bump and apply scale, then get diffuse
  half4 vBumpTex = 2.0 * tex2D(tex1, BaseUV.xy) - 1.0;
```

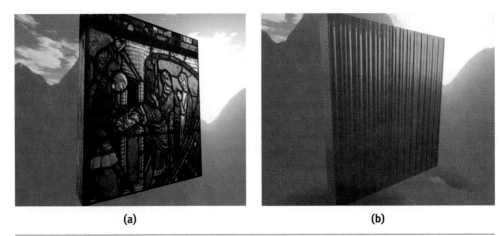

(a)   (b)

Figure 19-8. Different Glass Types
(a) Stained glass. (b) Partition glass.

Listing 19-5 *(continued).* Shader for Refractive/Reflective Glass Simulation

```
half3 vBump = normalize(vBumpTex.xyz * half3(0.2, 0.2, 1.0));
half4 vDiffuse = tex2D(tex0, BaseUV.xy);

// Compute reflection vector
half LdotN = dot(vBump.xyz, vEye.xyz);
half3 vReflect = 2.0 * LdotN * vBump.xyz - vEye;

// Reflection vector coordinates used for environmental mapping
half4 vEnvMap = tex2D(tex3, (vReflect.xy + 1.0) * 0.5);

// Compute projected coordinates and add perturbation
half2 vProj = (ScreenPos.xy/ScreenPos.w);
half4 vRefrA = tex2D(tex2, vProj.xy + vBump.xy);
half4 vRefrB = tex2D(tex2, vProj.xy);

// Mask occluders from refraction map
half4 vFinal = vRefrB * vRefrA.w + vRefrA * (1 - vRefrA.w);

// Compute Fresnel term
half fresnel = Fresnel(LdotN, 0.4, 5.0);

// Lerp between 1 and diffuse for glass transparency
vDiffuse.xyz = saturate(0.1 + vDiffuse.xyz * 0.9);

// Final output blends reflection and refraction using Fresnel term
return vDiffuse * vFinal * (1 - fresnel) + vEnvMap * fresnel;
}
```

19.4 Conclusion

In this chapter we have presented a technique to simulate refraction. The technique, though not physically based, produces results with good visual quality and is extremely efficient. The examples presented are just a few of the diverse effects that can be achieved.

One limitation of this technique is that, when applied to different-colored refractive surfaces, it will yield incorrect results where the surfaces overlap. As long as the refractive surfaces have a similar color, the visuals will look correct. One possible solution would be to sort refractive meshes from back to front and update the refraction map every time a refractive mesh is rendered. Alternatively, a less accurate solution would be to sort the refractive meshes from back to front and use alpha blending while rendering them.

The technique is also applicable to a range of target hardware: even though it's not demonstrated in this chapter, the technique can easily be expanded so that it works on lower-end hardware using pixel shader versions 1.1 to 1.4.

19.5 References

Akenine-Möller, Tomas, and Eric Haines. 2002. "Planar Reflections." In *Real-Time Rendering*, 2nd ed., pp. 239–243. A K Peters.

Everitt, Cass. 2001. "Projective Texture Mapping." NVIDIA Corporation. Available online at **http://developer.nvidia.com/object/Projective_Texture_Mapping.html**

Kilgard, Mark J. 2001. "Chromatic Aberration." NVIDIA Corporation. Available online at **http://developer.nvidia.com/object/chromatic_aberration.html**

Oliveira, Gustavo. 2000. "Refractive Texture Mapping, Part One." On Gamasutra Web site. Available online at
http://www.gamasutra.com/features/20001110/oliveira_01.htm

Vlachos, Alex, John Isidoro, and Chris Oat. 2002. "Rippling Reflective and Refractive Water." In *ShaderX*, edited by Wolfgang Engel. Wordware.

Wloka, Matthias. 2002. "Fresnel Reflection Technical Report." NVIDIA Corporation.

A special thanks to Martin Mittring and Carsten Wenzel for ideas and discussion about artifact minimization and to Márcio Martins for his model loader used in the chapter demos.

Wide Line

Filter

R

d

L

Sample Location

$w/2$

Mathematical Line L

R=0	R=85	R=171	R=255
G=0	G=85	G=171	G=255
B=0	B=85	B=171	B=255
A=0	A=85	A=171	A=255

Index (0, 3)

Index

Value (1.0,

Index (3, 0, 3)
Value (1.0, 0.0, 1.0)

Index (3, 0, 0)
Value (1.0, 0.0, 0.0)

PART III
HIGH-QUALITY
RENDERING

ROBOT IMAGE COURTESY OF FRANTIC FILMS

Every author of an interactive application is faced with a scale that must be balanced: deliver high-quality images, but deliver them at interactive speeds. While Moore's Law and the cleverness of GPU architects provide graphics programmers more raw horsepower with each generation of devices, fresh new techniques are also invented to get the most from the chips we have available today.

"High quality" is a slippery term, and one whose definition can change abruptly from year to year, with last year's innovative techniques being considered mundane by the next generation. What sorts of images could we achieve with the GPU's power if we were not constrained by real-time considerations? Horsepower never goes out of style—today's slow algorithm will eventually become tomorrow's fast one. Even in today's real-time applications, new GPUs are already capable of delivering image quality that would have been inaccessible only a year or two ago.

In **Chapter 20, "Fast Third-Order Texture Filtering,"** authors **Christian Sigg** of ETH Zurich and **Markus Hadwiger** of VRVis Research Center attack one of the fundamental challenges for all GPU-accelerated imaging: image filtering. They offer an efficient GPU-centric solution to complex filtering by leveraging the linear filtering already provided by GPUs. Their method delivers valid derivatives as well, with applications beyond simple 2D filtering into volume rendering and reconstruction of implicit surfaces.

Dan Wexler and **Eric Enderton** of NVIDIA, two of the authors of NVIDIA's GPU-accelerated final-film renderer Gelato, also confront both 2D image filtering and 3D imaging. In **Chapter 21, "High-Quality Antialiased Rasterization,"** they describe their method for filtering large, tiled images. Their method, as used in Gelato, is well suited to highly complex rendering that is performed in a large number of tiled pieces—and at resolutions that may be far higher than the rendering capacity of a single GPU pass.

In **Chapter 22, "Fast Prefiltered Lines,"** Eric Chan and **Frédo Durand** of the Massachusetts Institute of Technology present an accelerated method for improving the quality of an ubiquitous graphics entity that many users don't think about: simple lines. Chan and Durand draw lines using a CPU-prefiltered convolution that permits smooth line drawing from lookup table textures in the GPU, performed at interactive speeds. High-quality line drawing has application for game, CAD, and medical imaging, not just for 2D drawing but also for rendering such infamously problematic narrow 3D objects as telephone and power lines.

Hair-thin primitives come to the fore again with **Chapter 23, "Hair Animation and Rendering in the Nalu Demo,"** by **Hubert Nguyen** and **William Donnelly** of NVIDIA. They describe the breakthrough methods they employed for the animation and GPU rendering of "Nalu," a real-time demo whose innovative use of lighting and shadow techniques challenges the look of some of the best non-real-time character rendering from films and TV.

Rendering 3D images isn't the only application of GPUs in motion-picture production. In **Chapter 24, "Using Lookup Tables to Accelerate Color Transformations,"** **Jeremy Selan** of Sony Pictures Imageworks describes how complex color manipulations of 2D images—sourced from 3D renderings or live-action plates—can be performed in real time by GPUs for the purposes of compositing and real-time preview on a variety of output media.

In a similar vein, **Pete Warden** of Apple Computer describes in **Chapter 25, "GPU Image Processing in Apple's Motion,"** a program that faced many of the same challenges and provided powerful real-time solutions on the desktops of professional and amateur video users. Warden's experience with GPUs in a heterogeneous, media-rich environment may help lead the way to a graphics-intensive rethinking of the computer usage experience as a whole.

Simon Green of NVIDIA revisits and expands upon a topic from *GPU Gems*, revealing his methods in **Chapter 26, "Implementing Improved Perlin Noise."** This GPU-friendly algorithm has application in both 2D and 3D imaging and delivers higher quality than the simple texture noise currently in vogue among game programmers.

Justin Novosad of discreet takes yet another view of image filtering in **Chapter 27, "Advanced High-Quality Filtering."** He lays out a broad overview of the general problems of image reconstruction, and then he adds innovative ideas about image deblurring and even how to reduce live-action motion blur.

Finally, Climax Entertainment's **Iain Cantlay** brings high-quality issues to enlightened game programmers in **Chapter 28, "Mipmap-Level Measurement,"** providing ideas and tools to help programmers manage the complex balances between image quality, memory consumption, and rendering speed—not just for individual still images but also how they play out dynamically in an active, in-game environment.

Today's audiences—whether they are game players, movie watchers, or computer users—demand ever more rich, high-quality imagery, a trend that has been accelerating since at least the mid-1800s. It's in the interests of every GPU programmer to stay aware of these soon-to-be-standard methods for ensuring the best experiences in all media for today and tomorrow.

Kevin Bjorke, NVIDIA

Chapter 20

Fast Third-Order Texture Filtering

Christian Sigg
ETH Zurich

Markus Hadwiger
VRVis Research Center

Current programmable graphics hardware makes it possible to implement general convolution filters in fragment shaders for high-quality texture filtering, such as cubic filters (Bjorke 2004). However, several shortcomings are usually associated with these approaches: the need to perform many texture lookups and the inability to antialias lookups with mipmaps, in particular. We address these issues in this chapter for filtering with a cubic B-spline kernel and its first and second derivatives in one, two, and three dimensions.

The major performance bottleneck of higher-order filters is the large number of input texture samples that are required, which are usually obtained via repeated nearest-neighbor sampling of the input texture. To reduce the number of input samples, we perform cubic filtering building on linear texture fetches, which reduces the number of texture accesses considerably, especially for 2D and 3D filtering. Specifically, we are able to evaluate a tricubic filter with 64 summands using just eight trilinear texture fetches.

Approaches that perform custom filtering in the fragment shader depend on knowledge of the input texture resolution, which usually prevents correct filtering of mipmapped textures. We describe a general approach for adapting a higher-order filtering scheme to mipmapped textures.

Often, high-quality derivative reconstruction is required in addition to value reconstruction, for example, in volume rendering. We extend our basic filtering method to reconstruction of continuous first-order and second-order derivatives. A powerful application of these filters is on-the-fly computation of implicit surface curvature with tricubic B-splines, which have been applied to offline high-quality volume rendering, including nonphotorealistic styles (Kindlmann et al. 2003).

20.1 Higher-Order Filtering

Both OpenGL and Direct3D provide two different types of texture filtering: nearest-neighbor sampling and linear filtering, corresponding to zeroth and first-order filter schemes. Both types are natively supported by all GPUs. However, higher-order filtering modes often lead to superior image quality. Moreover, higher-order schemes are necessary to compute continuous derivatives of texture data.

We show how to implement efficient third-order texture filtering on current programmable graphics hardware. The following discussion primarily considers the one-dimensional case, but it extends directly to higher dimensions.

To reconstruct a texture with a cubic filter at a texture coordinate x, as shown in Figure 20-1a, we have to evaluate the convolution sum

$$w_0(x) \times f_{i-1} + w_1(x) \times f_i + w_2(x) \times f_{i+1} + w_3(x) \times f_{i+2} \qquad (1)$$

of four weighted neighboring texels f_i. The weights $w_i(x)$ depend on the filter kernel used. Although there are many types of filters, we restrict ourselves to B-spline filters in this chapter. If the corresponding smoothing of the data is not desired, the method can also be adapted to interpolating filters such as Catmull-Rom splines.

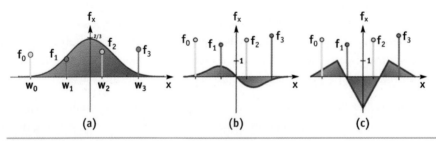

(a)   (b)   (c)

Figure 20-1. The Cubic B-Spline and Its Derivatives
(a) Convolution of input samples f_i with filter weights $w_i(x)$. First-order (b) and second-order (c) derivatives of the cubic B-spline filter for direct reconstruction of derivatives via convolution. (For purposes of illustration, the scale of the vertical axes varies.)

Note that cubic B-spline filtering is a natural extension of standard nearest-neighbor sampling and linear filtering, which are zeroth and first-degree B-spline filters. The degree of the filter is directly connected to the smoothness of the filtered data. Smooth data becomes especially important when we want to compute derivatives. For volume rendering, where derivatives are needed for shading, it has become common practice to store precomputed gradients along with the data. Although this leads to a continuous approximation of first-order derivatives, it uses four times more texture memory, which is often constrained in volume-rendering applications. Moreover, this approach becomes impractical for second-order derivatives because of the large storage overhead. On the other hand, on-the-fly cubic B-spline filtering yields continuous first-order and second-order derivatives without any storage overhead.

20.2 Fast Recursive Cubic Convolution

We now present an optimized evaluation of the convolution sum that has been tuned for the fundamental performance characteristics of graphics hardware, where linear texture filtering is evaluated using fast special-purpose units. Hence, a single linear texture fetch is much faster than two nearest-neighbor fetches, although both operations access the same number of texel values. When evaluating the convolution sum, we would like to benefit from this extra performance.

The key idea is to rewrite Equation 1 as a sum of weighted linear interpolations between every other pair of function samples. These linear interpolations can then be carried out using linear texture filtering, which computes convex combinations denoted in the following as

$$f_x = (1 - \alpha) \times f_i + \alpha \times f_{i+1}, \qquad (2)$$

where $i = \lfloor x \rfloor$ is the integer part and $\alpha = x - i$ is the fractional part of x. Building on such a convex combination, we can rewrite a general linear combination $a \times f_i + b \times f_{i+1}$ with general a and b as

$$(a + b) \times f_{(i+b)/(a+b)} \qquad (3)$$

as long as the convex combination property $0 \le b/(a + b) \le 1$ is fulfilled. Thus, rather than perform two texture lookups at f_i and f_{i+1} and a linear interpolation, we can do a single lookup at $i + b/(a + b)$ and just multiply by $(a + b)$.

The combination property is exactly the case when a and b have the same sign and are not both zero. The weights of Equation 1 with a cubic B-spline do meet this property, and therefore we can rewrite the entire convolution sum:

$$w_0(x) \times f_{i-1} + w_1(x) \times f_i + w_2(x) \times f_{i+1} + w_3(x) \times f_{i+2} =$$
$$g_0(x) \times f_{x-h_0(x)} + g_1(x) \times f_{x+h_1(x)}, \quad (4)$$

introducing new functions $g_0(x)$, $g_1(x)$, $h_0(x)$, and $h_1(x)$ as follows:

$$g_0(x) = w_0(x) + w_1(x) \quad h_0(x) = 1 - \frac{w_1(x)}{w_0(x) + w_1(x)} + x$$

$$g_1(x) = w_2(x) + w_3(x) \quad h_1(x) = 1 + \frac{w_3(x)}{w_2(x) + w_3(x)} - x \quad (5)$$

Using this scheme, the 1D convolution sum can be evaluated using two linear texture fetches plus one linear interpolation in the fragment program, which is faster than a straightforward implementation using four nearest-neighbor fetches. But most important, this scheme works especially well in higher dimensions; and for filtering in two and three dimensions, the number of texture fetches is reduced considerably, leading to much higher performance.

The filter weights $w_i(x)$ for cubic B-splines are periodic in the interval $x \in [0, 1]$: $w_i(x) = w_i(\alpha)$, where $\alpha = x - \lfloor x \rfloor$ is the fractional part of x. Specifically,

$$w_0(\alpha) = \frac{1}{6}\left(-\alpha^3 + 3\alpha^2 - 3\alpha + 1\right) \quad w_1(\alpha) = \frac{1}{6}\left(3\alpha^3 - 6\alpha^2 + 4\right)$$

$$w_2(\alpha) = \frac{1}{6}\left(-3\alpha^3 + 3\alpha^2 + 3\alpha + 1\right) \quad w_3(\alpha) = \frac{1}{6}\alpha^3 \quad (6)$$

As a result, the functions $g_i(x)$ and $h_i(x)$ are also periodic in the interval $x \in [0, 1]$ and can therefore be stored in a 1D lookup texture.

We now discuss some implementation details, which include (1) transforming texture coordinates between lookup and color texture and (2) computing the weighted sum of the texture fetch results. The Cg code of the fragment program for one-dimensional cubic filtering is shown in Listing 20-1. The schematic is shown in Figure 20-2.

Chapter 20   Fast Third-Order Texture Filtering

Listing 20-1. Cubic B-Spline Filtering of a One-Dimensional Texture

```
float4 bspline_1d_fp( float coord_source : TEXCOORD0,
  uniform sampler1D tex_source,   // source texture
  uniform sampler1D tex_hg,       // filter offsets and weights
  uniform float e_x,              // source texel size
  uniform float size_source       // source texture size
) : COLOR
{
  // calc filter texture coordinates where [0,1] is a single texel
  // (can be done in vertex program instead)
  float coord_hg = coord_source * size_source - 0.5f;

  // fetch offsets and weights from filter texture
  float3 hg_x = tex1D( tex_hg, coord_hg ).xyz;

  // determine linear sampling coordinates
  float coord_source1 = coord_source + hg_x.x * e_x;
  float coord_source0 = coord_source - hg_x.y * e_x;

  // fetch two linearly interpolated inputs
  float4 tex_source0 = tex1D( tex_source, coord_source0 );
  float4 tex_source1 = tex1D( tex_source, coord_source1 );
```

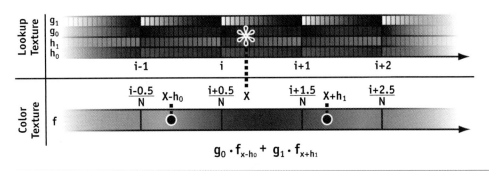

Figure 20-2. Cubic Filtering of a One-Dimensional Texture
To reconstruct a color texture of size N, we first perform a linear transformation of the reconstruction position x (∗). This gives us the texture coordinates for reading offsets $h_i(x)$ and weights $g_i(x)$ from a lookup texture. Second, two linear texture fetches of the color texture are carried out at the offset positions (●). Finally, the output color is computed by a linear combination of the fetched colors using the weights $g_i(x)$.

```
    // weight linear samples
    tex_source0 = lerp( tex_source0, tex_source1, tex_hg_x.z );

    return tex_source0;
}
```

As mentioned before, the functions $g_i(x)$ and $h_i(x)$ are stored in a lookup texture (called `tex_hg` in the listing) to reduce the amount of operations in the fragment program. In practice, a 16-bit texture of 128 samples is sufficient. Note that the functions are periodic in the sample positions of the input texture. Therefore, we apply a linear transformation to the texture coordinate and use a texture wrap parameter of GL_REPEAT for the lookup texture. In Listing 20-1, this linear transformation is incorporated into the fragment program for clarity. However, we would normally use a separate texture coordinate computed in the vertex shader.

After fetching the offsets and weights from the lookup texture, we compute the texture coordinate for the two linear texture fetches from the source color texture. Note that we need to scale the offset by the inverse of the texture resolution, which is stored in a constant-register shader parameter.

The rest of the program carries out the two color fetches and computes their weighted sum. Note that B-splines fulfill the partition of unity $\sum w_i(x) = 1$, and so do the two weights $g_0(x) + g_1(x) = 1$. Therefore, we do not need to actually store $g_1(x)$ in addition to $g_0(x)$ in this case, and the final weighting is again a convex combination carried out with a single `lerp()` instruction.

The fragment shader parameters of Listing 20-1 would be initialized as follows for a 1D source texture with 256 texels:

```
e_x = float( 1/256.0f );
size_source = float( 256.0f );
```

The `e_x` parameter corresponds to the size of a single source texel in texture coordinates, which is needed to scale the offsets fetched from the filter texture to match the resolution of the source texture. The `size_source` parameter simply stores the size of the source texture, which is needed to compute filter texture from source texture coordinates so that the size of the entire filter texture corresponds to a single texel of the source texture.

We now extend this cubic filtering method to higher dimensions, which is straightforward due to the separability of tensor-product B-splines. Actually, our optimization works even better in higher dimensions. Using bilinear or trilinear texture lookups, we can combine 4 or 8 summands into one weighted convex combination. Therefore, we are able to evaluate a tricubic filter with 64 summands using just eight trilinear texture fetches.

The offset and weight functions for multidimensional filtering can be computed independently for each dimension using Equation 5. In our implementation, this leads to multiple fetches from the same one-dimensional lookup texture. The final weights and offsets are then computed in the fragment program using

$$g_{\vec{i}}(\vec{x}) = \prod g_{i_k}(x_k) \qquad \vec{h}_{\vec{i}}(\vec{x}) = \sum \vec{e}_k \cdot h_{i_k}(x_k), \qquad (7)$$

where the index k denotes the axis and $\vec{e}_k$ are the basis vectors. Listing 20-2 shows an implementation that minimizes the number of dependent texture reads by computing all texture coordinates at once.

Listing 20-2. Bicubic B-Spline Filtering

```
float4 bspline_2d_fp( float2 coord_source : TEXCOORD0,
  uniform sampler2D tex_source,    // source texture
  uniform sampler1D tex_hg,        // filter offsets and weights
  uniform float2 e_x,              // texel size in x direction
  uniform float2 e_y,              // texel size in y direction
  uniform float2 size_source       // source texture size
) : COLOR
{
  // calc filter texture coordinates where [0,1] is a single texel
  // (can be done in vertex program instead)
  float2 coord_hg = coord_source * size_source - float2(0.5f, 0.5f);

  // fetch offsets and weights from filter texture
  float3 hg_x = tex1D( tex_hg, coord_hg.x ).xyz;
  float3 hg_y = tex1D( tex_hg, coord_hg.y ).xyz;

  // determine linear sampling coordinates
  float2 coord_source10 = coord_source + hg_x.x * e_x;
  float2 coord_source00 = coord_source - hg_x.y * e_x;

  float2 coord_source11 = coord_source10 + hg_y.x * e_y;
  float2 coord_source01 = coord_source00 + hg_y.x * e_y;
  coord_source10 = coord_source10 - hg_y.y * e_y;
  coord_source00 = coord_source00 - hg_y.y * e_y;
```

Listing 20-2 (continued). Bicubic B-Spline Filtering

```
    // fetch four linearly interpolated inputs
    float4 tex_source00 = tex2D( tex_source, coord_source00 );
    float4 tex_source10 = tex2D( tex_source, coord_source10 );
    float4 tex_source01 = tex2D( tex_source, coord_source01 );
    float4 tex_source11 = tex2D( tex_source, coord_source11 );

    // weight along y direction
    tex_source00 = lerp( tex_source00, tex_source01, hg_y.z );
    tex_source10 = lerp( tex_source10, tex_source11, hg_y.z );

    // weight along x direction
    tex_source00 = lerp( tex_source00, tex_source10, hg_x.z );

    return tex_src00;
}
```

The fragment shader parameters of Listing 20-2 would be initialized as follows for a 2D source texture with 256×128 texels:

```
e_x = float2( 1/256.0f, 0.0f );
e_y = float2( 0.0f, 1/128.0f );

size_source = float2( 256.0f, 128.0f );
```

The particular way the source texel size is stored in the e_x and e_y parameters allows us to compute the coordinates of all four source samples with a minimal number of instructions, because in this way we can avoid applying offsets along the x axis for all four samples, as shown in Listing 20-2. In three dimensions, the same approach makes it possible to compute all eight source coordinates with only 14 multiply-add instructions.

Filtering in three dimensions is a straightforward extension of Listing 20-2.

20.3 Mipmapping

For mipmapped textures, we run into the problem that the offset and scale operations of texture coordinates that correspond to the input texture resolution cannot be done with uniform fragment shader constants as shown in Listings 20-1 and 20-2. When a texture is mipmapped, the appropriate texture resolution changes on a per-fragment basis (for GL_*_MIPMAP_NEAREST filtering) or is even a linear interpolation between two adjacent texture resolutions (for GL_*_MIPMAP_LINEAR filtering).

In this chapter, we describe only the case of GL_*_MIPMAP_NEAREST filtering in detail. However, GL_*_MIPMAP_LINEAR filtering can also be handled with a slightly extended approach that filters both contributing mipmap levels with a bicubic filter and interpolates linearly between the two in the fragment shader.

For our filtering approach, we need to know the actual mipmap level and corresponding texture resolution used for a given fragment in order to obtain correct offsets (e_x, e_y, e_z) and scale factors (size_source). However, on current architectures, it is not possible to query the mipmap level in the fragment shader. We therefore use a workaround that stores mipmap information in what we call a *meta-mipmap*. The meta-mipmap is an additional mipmap that in each level stores the same information in all texels, such as the resolution of this level. A similar approach can be used to simulate derivative instructions in the fragment shader (Pharr 2004).

We use a floating-point RGB texture for the meta-mipmap, as follows:

```
// RGB meta-mipmap information for each texel of a given mipmap_level
metatexel = float3( 1/level_width, 1/level_height, mipmap_level );
```

The following code fragment shows how the size_source and e_x, e_y scales and offsets in Listings 20-1 and 20-2 (where they were uniform parameters) can then be substituted by a correct per-fragment adaptation to the actual mipmap level used by the hardware for the current fragment:

```
// fetch meta-mipmap information
float3 meta = tex2D( tex_meta, coord_source ).xyz;

// compute scales from offsets so we do not need to store them
float2 size_source = float2( 1.0f/meta.x, 1.0f/meta.y );

// filter texture coordinates
// where [0,1] is a single texel of the source texture
// (cannot be done in the vertex program anymore)
float2 coord_hg = coord_source * size_source - 0.5f;

// adjust neighbor sample offsets
e_x *= meta.x;
e_y *= meta.y;
```

Now e_x and e_y are initialized to unit vectors instead of being premultiplied with the texture dimensions:

```
e_x = float2( 1.0f, 0.0f );
e_y = float2( 0.0f, 1.0f );
```

For `GL_*_MIPMAP_NEAREST` filtering, we do not need the third component of the meta-mipmap (`meta.z`), which stores the mipmap level itself. However, to implement `GL_*_MIPMAP_LINEAR` filtering, we also need the interpolation weight between the two contributing mipmap levels. This weight can then be obtained as `frac(meta.z)` from the third meta-mipmap component as interpolated by the hardware.

An important consideration when using a meta-mipmap is its texture memory footprint, which can be quite high when used in a straightforward manner. Theoretically, we would need a meta-mipmap for each texture size and aspect ratio that an application is using in order to get the corresponding mipmap information. However, this memory overhead can be reduced considerably.

First, we use only a single meta-mipmap that matches the highest texture resolution used in the application (called `meta_baselevel_size`). To get correct mipmapping information for any resolution, we strip higher resolutions of the meta-mipmap on the fly by setting the `GL_TEXTURE_BASE_LEVEL` texture parameter to match the resolution of the current texture (called `target_size`):

```
glTexParameter( GL_TEXTURE_2D, GL_TEXTURE_BASE_LEVEL,
                log2( meta_baselevel_size / target_size ) );
```

Second, a meta-mipmap of height 1 can indeed be used for all aspect ratios and dimensions if the fragment shader profile supports the `ddx()` and `ddy()` functions for obtaining partial derivatives of texture coordinates with respect to screen coordinates. These functions, together with the variant of `tex2D()`, which accepts user-supplied derivatives, allow us to simulate all aspect ratios with respect to mipmap level selection even without knowing the actual mipmap level.

The texture fetch from the meta-mipmap is then performed with modified derivatives:

```
// fetch and modify derivatives
// requires uniform float2 meta_adjust; see below
float2 meta_ddx = ddx( coord_source ) * meta_adjust;
float2 meta_ddy = ddy( coord_source ) * meta_adjust;

// sample meta-mipmap with modified derivatives
float3 meta = tex2D( tex_meta, coord_src, meta_ddx, meta_ddy ).xyz;
```

The uniform parameter `meta_adjust` must be set in order to adapt the actual aspect ratio of the meta-mipmap to the aspect ratio of the target texture, where `cur_base_size` is the actual size of the current `GL_TEXTURE_BASE_LEVEL` of the meta-mipmap:

```
meta_adjust = float2( target_size_x/cur_base_size, target_size_y );
```

Because we supply modified derivatives that ultimately determine the mipmap level that the hardware will use, we effectively simulate a different aspect ratio of the meta-mipmap without requiring the corresponding storage.

In summary, the meta-mipmap texture memory footprint can be reduced to a *single 1D texture* with the highest texture resolution (of any axis) the application is using. This single meta-mipmap can then be used when filtering *any application texture* by setting the meta-mipmap's `GL_TEXTURE_BASE_LEVEL` and the `meta_adjust` uniform fragment shader parameter accordingly. Figure 20-3 shows the quality improvement using higher-order texture filtering of a 2D texture.

Bilinear   **Bicubic**

Figure 20-3. Comparing Texture-Filter Quality with Bilinear and Bicubic Reconstruction Filters
The source texture is a 128×64 image tiled on a plane. The bicubic filter incurs fewer staircase artifacts during reconstruction than the bilinear filter, which is especially visible on screen. Also note that the presented filtering approach accommodates perspective projection without extra effort.

20.4 Derivative Reconstruction

In addition to reconstructing the values in a texture map, the reconstruction of its derivatives also has many applications. For example, in volume rendering, the gradient of the volume is often used as a surface normal for shading. The gradient **g** of a scalar field *f*, in this case a 3D texture, is composed of its first partial derivatives:

$$g = \nabla f = \left(\frac{\partial f}{\partial x}, \frac{\partial f}{\partial y}, \frac{\partial f}{\partial z} \right)^T. \qquad (8)$$

The most common method for approximating gradient information is to use a simple central differencing scheme. However, for high-quality derivatives, we can also use convolution filters and apply the scheme illustrated previously for fast evaluation on GPUs. Figure 20-4 shows the quality improvement using higher-order gradients for Phong shading of isosurfaces. To reconstruct a derivative via filtering, we convolve the original data with the derivative of the filter kernel. Figures 20-1b and 20-1c (back on page 314) illustrate the first and second derivatives of the cubic B-spline. Computing the derivative becomes very similar to reconstructing the function value, just using a different filter kernel.

We can apply the fast filtering scheme outlined previously for derivative reconstruction with the cubic B-spline's derivative. The only difference in this case is that now all the

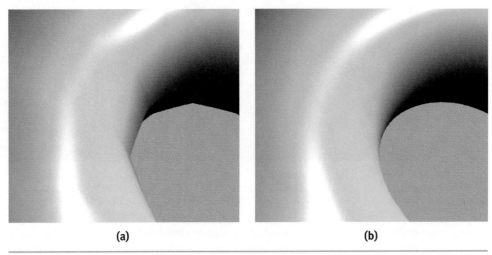

(a)   (b)

Figure 20-4. Comparing Shading Quality with Trilinear and Tricubic Reconstruction Filters
Isosurface rendering of a volumetric texture of size 163. Silhouette and highlights are much smoother if tricubic filtering is used for both the function value and the gradient reconstruction.

filter kernel weights sum up to zero instead of one: $\Sigma w_i(x) = 0$. Now, in comparison to Listing 20-1, where the two linear input samples were weighted using a single `lerp()`, we obtain the second weight as the negative of the first one; that is, $g_1(x) = -g_0(x)$, which can be written as a single subtraction and subsequent multiplication, as shown in Listing 20-3.

Listing 20-3. First-Derivative Cubic B-Spline Filtering of a One-Dimensional Texture

```
// . . . unchanged from Listing 20-1

  // weight linear samples
  tex_source0 = ( tex_source0 - tex_source1 ) * hg_x.z;

  return tex_source0;
}
```

To compute the gradient in higher dimensions, we obtain the corresponding filter kernels via the tensor product of a 1D derived cubic B-spline for the axis of derivation, and 1D (nonderived) cubic B-splines for the other axes.

In addition to first partial derivatives, second partial derivatives can also be computed very quickly on GPUs. All these second derivatives taken together make up the Hessian matrix **H**, shown here for the 3D case:

$$\mathbf{H} = \nabla\mathbf{g} = \begin{pmatrix} \dfrac{\partial^2 f}{\partial x^2} & \dfrac{\partial^2 f}{\partial x \partial y} & \dfrac{\partial^2 f}{\partial x \partial z} \\[2mm] \dfrac{\partial^2 f}{\partial y \partial x} & \dfrac{\partial^2 f}{\partial y^2} & \dfrac{\partial^2 f}{\partial y \partial z} \\[2mm] \dfrac{\partial^2 f}{\partial z \partial x} & \dfrac{\partial^2 f}{\partial z \partial y} & \dfrac{\partial^2 f}{\partial z^2} \end{pmatrix}. \tag{9}$$

The mixed derivatives in **H** (the off-diagonal elements) can be computed using the fast filtering approach for first derivatives that we have just described, because the 1D filter kernels are derived only once in this case.

For the diagonal elements of **H**, however, the derivative of the filter kernel itself has to be taken two times. Figure 20-1c shows the second derivative of the cubic B-spline, which is a piecewise linear function. The convolution sum with this filter is very simple to evaluate. Listing 20-4 shows how to do this using three linearly interpolated input samples. In this case, no filter texture is needed, due to the simple shape of the filter. The three input samples are simply fetched at unit intervals and weighted with a vector of (1, −2, 1).

Listing 20-4. Second-Derivative Cubic B-Spline Filtering of a One-Dimensional Texture

```
float4 bspline_dd_1d_fp( float coord_source : TEXCOORD0,
  uniform sampler1D tex_source,   // source texture
  uniform float e_x,              // source texel size
) : COLOR
{
  // determine additional linear sampling coordinates
  float coord_source1 = coord_source + e_x;
  float coord_source0 = coord_source - e_x;

  // fetch three linearly interpolated inputs
  float4 tex_source0 = tex1D( tex_source, coord_source0 );
  float4 tex_sourcex = tex1D( tex_source, coord_source );
  float4 tex_source1 = tex1D( tex_source, coord_source1 );

  // weight linear samples
  tex_source0 = tex_source0 - 2 * tex_sourcex + tex_source1;

  return tex_source0;
}
```

A very useful application of high-quality first and second derivative information is computing implicit surface curvature from volume data stored in a 3D texture. Implicit surface curvature in this case is the curvature of isosurfaces, which can easily be rendered on graphics hardware (Westermann and Ertl 1998).

Implicit curvature information can be computed directly from the gradient **g** and the Hessian matrix **H** (Kindlmann et al. 2003), for which tricubic B-spline filters yield high-quality results. Each of the required nine components (three for **g** and six for **H**, due to symmetry), requires the evaluation of a separate tricubic convolution filter, which has traditionally been extremely expensive. However, using the fast filtering scheme described in this chapter, it can actually be done in real time on current GPUs. Figure 20-5 shows images that have been generated in real time with the isosurface volume rendering demo applications that are included on the book's CD.

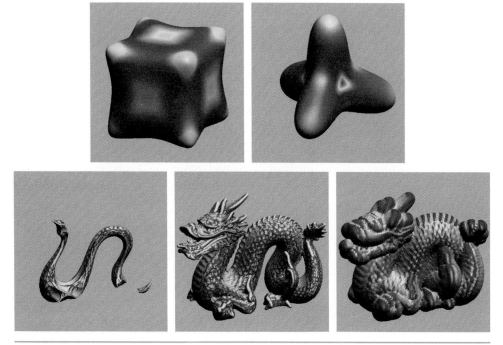

Figure 20-5. Nonphotorealistic Isosurface Rendering Using On-the-Fly Maximum Curvature Evaluation
Top: Two synthetic data sets generated using a regular sampling of blob models. Bottom: Different isolevels of a distance field generated offline from a dragon triangle mesh. All data sets have 128^3 samples and run at interactive speed (approximately 20 frames per second on a GeForce 6800).

20.5 Conclusion

This chapter has presented an efficient method for third-order texture filtering with a considerably reduced number of input texture fetches. Building on the assumption that a linear texture fetch is as fast as or not much slower than a nearest-neighbor texture fetch, we have optimized filtering with a third-order filter kernel such as a cubic B-spline to build on a small number of linear texture fetches. A cubic output sample requires 2 instead of 4 input samples, a bicubic output sample can be computed from 4 instead of 16 input samples, and tricubic filtering is possible with 8 instead of 64 fetches from the input texture. In fact, the corresponding fragment programs are more similar to "hand-coded" linear interpolation than to cubic filtering.

Another advantage of this method is that all computations that depend on the filter kernel are precomputed and stored in small 1D lookup textures. This way, the actual fragment shader can be kept independent from the filter kernel in use (Hadwiger et al. 2001). The fragment shaders for value and first-derivative reconstruction that we have shown can be used without change with a Gaussian filter of appropriate width, for example.

A disadvantage of building on linear input samples is that it may require higher precision of the input texture for high-quality results. On current GPUs, linear interpolation of 8-bit textures is also performed at a similar precision, which is not sufficient for tricubic filtering, where a single trilinearly interpolated sample contains the contribution of 8 input samples. We have used 16-bit textures in our implementation, which provides sufficient precision of the underlying linear interpolation. Many current-generation GPUs also support filtering of floating-point textures, which would provide even higher precision.

In another vein, we have used our filters for function (or derivative) reconstruction, which in OpenGL terminology is called *magnification filtering*. For higher-order filters to also work with texture *minification*, we have shown how to extend their use to mipmapped textures. An important component of this introduced here is the reduction of the memory footprint of the required additional texture information (which we call a meta-mipmap).

Finally, we have shown how our method can be used for high-quality reconstruction of first and second partial derivatives, which is especially useful for volume rendering or rendering implicit surfaces represented by a signed distance field, for example. With this method, differential surface properties such as curvature can also be computed with high quality in real time.

20.6 References

Bjorke, Kevin. 2004. "High-Quality Filtering." In *GPU Gems*, edited by Randima Fernando, pp. 391–415. Addison-Wesley. *Gives a very nice overview of different applications for high-quality filtering with filter kernels evaluated procedurally in the fragment shader.*

Hadwiger, Markus, Thomas Theußl, Helwig Hauser, and Eduard Gröller. 2001. "Hardware-Accelerated High-Quality Filtering on PC Hardware." In *Proceedings of Vision, Modeling, and Visualization 2001*, pp. 105–112. *Stores all filter kernel information in textures and evaluates arbitrary convolution sums in multiple rendering passes without procedural computations or dependent texture lookups. Can be implemented in a single pass on today's GPUs.*

Kindlmann, Gordon, Ross Whitaker, Tolga Tasdizen, and Torsten Möller. 2003. "Curvature-Based Transfer Functions for Direct Volume Rendering: Methods and Applications." In *Proceedings of IEEE Visualization 2003*, pp. 513–520. *Shows how implicit surface curvature can be computed directly from first and second partial derivatives obtained via tricubic B-spline filtering, along with very nice applications, including nonphotorealistic rendering.*

Pharr, Matt. 2004. "Fast Filter-Width Estimates with Texture Maps." In *GPU Gems*, edited by Randima Fernando, pp. 417–424. Addison-Wesley. *Uses the concept of mipmaps that store information about the mipmap level itself in all pixels of a given mipmap level for approximating the* ddx() *and* ddy() *fragment shader instructions.*

Westermann, Rüdiger, and Thomas Ertl. 1998. "Efficiently Using Graphics Hardware in Volume Rendering Applications." In *Proceedings of SIGGRAPH 98*, pp. 169–177. *Shows how to render isosurfaces of volume data by using the hardware alpha test and back-to-front rendering. On current GPUs, using the* discard() *instruction and front-to-back rendering provides better performance in combination with early-z testing.*

The authors would like to thank Markus Gross and Katja Bühler for their valuable contributions and Henning Scharsach for his implementation of a GPU ray caster. The first author has been supported by Schlumberger Cambridge Research, and the second author has been supported by the Kplus program of the Austrian government.

Chapter 21

High-Quality Antialiased Rasterization

Dan Wexler
NVIDIA Corporation

Eric Enderton
NVIDIA Corporation

Finely detailed 3D geometry can show significant aliasing artifacts if rendered using native hardware multisampling, because multisampling is currently limited to one-pixel box filtering and low sampling rates. This chapter describes a tiled supersampling technique for rendering images of arbitrary resolution with arbitrarily wide user-defined filters and high sampling rates. The code presented here is used in the Gelato film renderer to produce images of uncompromising quality using the GPU. Figure 21-1 shows an example.

We describe how to break the image into tiles, render each tile at high resolution, then *downsample* (that is, shrink) each tile to its final resolution, using two-pass separable downsampling with fragment programs constructed on the fly. We present the details involved in proper overlap and padding of the tiles and filters, and we provide code on this book's CD that can be easily incorporated into existing rendering systems without significant modification. The code also includes a number of useful utility libraries for working with the GPU and separable filters.

21.1 Overview

To support large supersampling rates and large final images, we start by breaking the final image into constant-size rectangular *tiles* (sometimes called *buckets*), as shown in Figure 21-2. The frame-buffer memory available on the GPU is often insufficient to

Figure 21-1. An Image Rendered with Gelato
Image courtesy of Frantic Films.

hold a single frame buffer large enough to render a highly supersampled image prior to downsampling. In addition, you may want to use this limited resource to hold other data required for rendering: textures, vertex buffer objects, and so on. Breaking the image into tiles is also handy if you're rendering a poster-sized image too big to fit in a window. This same technique can be used to "bucket" the geometry (Apodaca and Gritz 1999) by tile to reduce the working set during rendering, although this topic is not directly addressed in this chapter. Because our technique does not restrict the algorithm used to render the tiles, it can easily be combined with multipass algorithms for motion blur, depth of field, transparency, or other effects.

We downsample each high-resolution tile on the GPU. This is done using the usual separable convolution (James and O'Rorke 2004), where the first pass filters the rows and the second pass filters the columns, with the added complexity that the output image is smaller than the input image. The fragment program for each pass has the filter values built in as constants (Bjorke 2004). We generate these fragment programs on the fly, based on the selected filter shape, filter width, and supersampling rate.

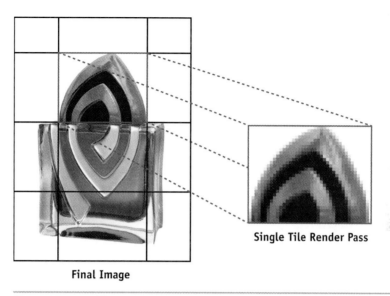

Single Tile Render Pass

Final Image

Figure 21-2. Breaking Up an Image into Tiles
Image courtesy of Tweak Films.

So the overall algorithm is the following. For each tile of the final image:

Step 1. Render the tile into a large off-screen buffer, adjusting the projection matrix to render the 3D geometry at the supersampled resolution using your existing rendering code.

Step 2. Downsample the high-resolution tile to a final-resolution tile using a separable filter kernel, by rendering two full-screen quads with custom fragment programs generated on the fly.

Step 3. Accumulate the low-resolution tile into the final image, either by reading back the tile data onto the CPU or by using another fragment program to add the tile's contribution into a buffer that accumulates the final result.

We now describe the algorithm from the inside out, beginning with the core downsample-filtering algorithm and then expanding to the enclosing scaffolding. The algorithm will be illustrated using a sample program that renders geometry files (.obj) into an off-screen buffer and saves the result to an image file (.ppm). See Listing 21-1 for a summary of algorithm parameters used in the following discussion.

Listing 21-1. Algorithm Parameters Used in Later Listings

```
int resx = 640;    // final image resolution
int resy = 480;
int ssx = 4;       // supersampling rate
int ssy = 4;
int tx = 32;       // tile size
int ty = 32;
int filterx = 3;   // filter diameter
int filtery = 3;
```

21.2 Downsampling

Consider one scanline of one tile. The supersampled tile contains (ssx * tx) input pixels (or "samples"), to be downsampled into tx output pixels. Each output pixel is a weighted average of several nearby input samples. The weights are determined by the chosen filter shape, and the number of samples is determined by the chosen filter width and the supersampling rate. (Again, this is just convolution, but with differing input and output resolutions.) Figure 21-3 shows how the filter sits over the input samples for a given output pixel. Note where the center of the filter lies, on both the source and the destination pixels.

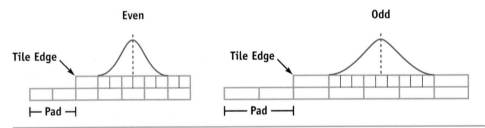

Figure 21-3. Radius 1.5 Gaussian Filter for Even and Odd Supersample Rates

21.2.1 Comparison to Existing Hardware and Software

In current hardware multisampling, each final pixel is a straight average of the samples it covers. This is equivalent to a box (that is, constant) filter of width 1. This works well for many applications, but better antialiasing results from smoother and wider filters. Such filters do a better job of removing spatial frequencies too high to be represented at the final resolution. A 2×2 Gaussian filter is a good default choice, but an examination of current film renderers shows a wide variety of supported filters (sinc, Gaussian, Catmull-Rom, Lanczos, Mitchell, and more) and default filter radii of 2 to 5 pixels. Experiment to see what you like.

Higher supersampling rates also improve antialiasing, especially for small, subpixel 3D geometry, or shaders with subpixel variation. Our algorithm does not entirely escape hardware limitations. The full, supersampled tile resolution (`tx * ssx`) must be smaller than the largest possible rendering surface supported by the hardware.

In addition, better quality images can be obtained with fewer samples if the samples have well-stratified stochastic locations (Dippé and Wold 1985), as shown in Figure 21-4. Our algorithm uses regular samples and often requires higher sample rates than similar stochastic techniques. This issue is somewhat ameliorated because the hardware tends to perform better when rendering larger objects, which happens when the supersampling rate is increased. Nothing prevents the combination of our technique with hardware multisampling. In fact, the newer generations of hardware support rotated sample grids, which provide better results than standard regular multisampling.

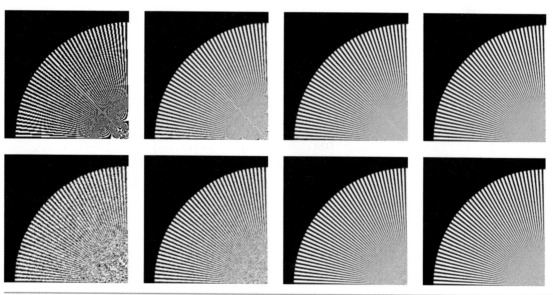

Figure 21-4. Regular vs. Stochastic Sampling
Regular (top) and stochastic (bottom) sampling at 1, 4, 16, and 32 samples per pixel.

21.2.2 Downsampling on the GPU

To downsample on the GPU, we place the input samples in a row of a texture and render the output pixels as a row of an off-screen buffer. Recall that drawing a rectangle that covers the output pixels will cause the current fragment program to be run for each output pixel (rectangles are like `for` loops in x and y). We supply a fragment program that computes a weighted sum of some texels, where the weights are based on the filter, and the texel indices depend on the x position of the current output pixel.

Our approach is to automatically generate the fragment program from the filter parameters. The fragment program is straight-line code that includes all filter weights and pixel offsets as numerical constants. This avoids per-pixel evaluation, or even per-pixel texture lookup, of the filter values, and it avoids loop overhead. Although the current generation of fragment program languages supports looping, we have found that unrolling the loop and inlining the constants results in better performance for this case.

Before diving into the detailed formulas, we need to discuss padding.

21.3 Padding

Consider an output pixel within one filter radius of the edge of a tile. Some of the contributing samples for this pixel are in the neighboring tile. To be correct, the final pixel must combine samples from both tiles (four tiles, in the corner regions). To handle this, we pad the size of the downsampling output buffer: the output tile covers not just the pixels covering the input samples, but all pixels to which the input samples contribute. This expands the tile by one filter radius in each direction. (Note: It can be helpful to think of the filter radius as the maximum distance that a sample can "travel" to participate in an output pixel.) The `accumulate_tile()` function is responsible for summing pixels in the overlap regions to produce the final image.

Considering fractional filter radii, and the fact that some samples fall near the edge of a pixel, the actual padding amount is the following (note the *addition* of 0.5 to account for the maximal distance that the filter may cover from the edge of a pixel):

```
int txpad = ceil(filterx / 2.0 + 0.5);
int typad = ceil(filtery / 2.0 + 0.5);
```

The total size of a downsampled tile is `(tx + 2 * txpad)` by `(ty + 2 * typad)`.

While downsampling any one tile, "missing" input samples (that is, input samples from outside the tile) are treated as black, because those samples will be accounted for by the neighboring tile. Texture lookup modes are set so that out-of-bounds texture lookups return black. The fragment program can then do the same computation at every pixel, including pixels near the edges.

There is one more padding issue. Pixels near the edges of the final image require input samples from outside the final image. Therefore, we pad the final image size as well, before splitting the image into tiles. Considering fractional radii again, and the fact that the corner pixel already covers 0.5 worth of filter radius, the padding here is the following (note the *subtraction* of 0.5 to account for the fact that the filter is centered on each pixel):

```
int resxpad = ceil(filterx / 2.0 - 0.5);
int resypad = ceil(filtery / 2.0 - 0.5);
```

For example, a 200×200 final image, rendered with a filter width of 2 (radius 1), will require rendering `(ssx * 202)` by `(ssy * 202)` samples. See Figure 21-5.

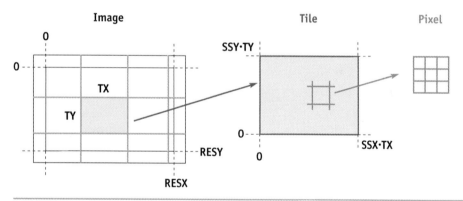

Figure 21-5. Tiling the Image

21.4 Filter Details

There are many details to get right in generating the filter fragment program. The most important detail is that even and odd supersampling rates are subtly different. With even sampling rates, the center of the destination pixel lies on a pixel border in the supersampled image, while odd rates put the pixel center in the center of a source pixel. This is shown in Figure 21-3, which also shows the output tile's padding (on the left side, at least). Samples must be included if the filter overlaps any part of the interval they represent (the `ceil()` function is useful here). Listing 21-2 shows the pseudocode for runtime generation of the ARBFP1 fragment program. Both Cg and HLSL provide program literalization features that obviate the need for the type of direct assembly-language generation shown here.

Listing 21-2. Generating a Downsampling Shader

```
ssx = supersampling rate in x
r = ceil(ssx * filterradius)
evenoffset = ssx is even ? 0.5 : 0
pad = ceil(filterradius + 0.5)
for each pixel x in range (-r, r):
  weight = normalizedfilter((x + evenoffset) / ssx)
  offset = x + evenoffset - pad * ssx
  print "MAD coord.xy fragment.position, {$ssx, 1}, {$offset, 1};"
  print "TEX sample, coord, texture[0], RECT;"
  print "MAD accum, sample, {$weight}, accum;"
```

Here's a piece of the resulting fragment program.

```
TEMP coord, sample, accum;
. . .
MAD coord.xy, fragment.position, {4, 1}, {-6.5, 1};
TEX sample, coord, texture[0], RECT;
MAD accum, sample, {0.04509}, accum;
. . .
```

This fragment program, run for each pixel in a row of a final-resolution tile, samples pixels from the original image stored as a texture to produce a filtered and shrunken version of the row. Note that the number of samples is the product of the supersampling rate and the filter diameter (which is measured in final image pixels).

21.5 Two-Pass Separable Filtering

With a few x's and y's swapped, the same algorithm produces a fragment program for downsampling columns. We use these two fragment programs to do the usual two-pass separable convolution method: first filter the rows, then take the result as a new input and filter the columns. (*Separable* filters are a special case of general convolution filters that can be expressed as the product of one-dimensional filters in *x* and *y*.)

We start with a supersampled tile of dimensions (ssx * tx) by (ssy * ty). We run the row-downsampling fragment program to produce an intermediate texture that is resolution `(tx + 2 * pad)` by `(ssy * ty)`. We then run the column-downsampling fragment program on that texture to produce the output tile at the final resolution, `(tx + 2 * pad)` by `(ty + 2 * pad)`.

21.6 Tiling and Accumulation

Figure 21-5 shows the tiles relative to the final image. Recall that the tiles extend one filter radius beyond the final image. (The tiles, as rendered, do not overlap—never render the same pixel twice. Overlap occurs only after they are downsampled.) Tiles in the last row or column may be mostly empty.

Each tile is rendered in turn at the supersampled resolution. If the projection matrix is set to draw the entire scene at the final resolution `resx` by `resy`, we can append some scales and translates to draw a particular tile. For the tile whose origin is (x, y), the final image region $[x, x+tx] \times [y, y+ty]$ is mapped to the window $[0, ssx*tx] \times [0, ssy*ty]$:

```
// Assume cam2ras = the projection matrix for ordinary rendering,
// that is, the transform from camera space to the final image raster.
Matrix4 ras2tile = Matrix4::TranslationMatrix (Vector3 (-x, -y, 0))
                 * Matrix4::ScaleMatrix (ssx, ssy, 1);
Matrix4 cam2tile = cam2ras * ras2tile;
```

We update the projection matrix using this 2D tile transform and then render the scene once for each tile.

After rendering a supersampled tile, we downsample it to the final resolution using the two-pass filtering method described before. The downsampled tile is then merged (accumulated) into the final image, at its proper position; overlap regions with earlier tiles are summed. The final image may be another OpenGL window or off-screen buffer, in which case accumulation takes place on the GPU, or it may be in main memory, in which case accumulation takes place on the CPU (for example, when the buffer is too large for the GPU).

21.7 The Code

As shown in Listing 21-3, the program begins by creating an off-screen buffer for drawing. Then, using the input parameters, it constructs viewing matrices, image buffers, and filter functions.

Listing 21-3. Setting Up for Supersampled Rendering

```
// Create a drawing surface to render a single supersampled tile
GpuPBuffer pbuffer (resx * ssx, resy * ssy);
GpuCanvas canvas (pbuffer);        // GpuCanvas == OpenGL context

// Create a drawing mode to hold the GPU state vector
GpuDrawmode drawmode;

float fov = 90;
float hither = 0.1;
float yon = 10000;
Matrix4 cam2ras = compute_cam2ras (fov, hither, yon, resx, resy);

// Allocate a 4-channel, fp32, RGBA final output image buffer
size_t nbytes = 4 * resx * resy * sizeof (float);
float *image = (float *) malloc (nbytes);
memset(image, 0, nbytes);

// Create the filter we'll need
Filter2D *filter = Filter2D::MakeFilter ("gaussian", filterx, filtery);

// Allocate a 4-channel, fp32, RGBA tile readback buffer
int tilew = downsample.padded_tile_width (tx, *filter);
int tileh = downsample.padded_tile_height (ty, *filter);
float *tile = (float *) malloc (4 * sizeof (float) * tilew * tileh);
```

The main loop of the program iterates over the output image one tile at a time in row-major order, updating the viewing matrix and calling the render function to render a high-resolution tile. The tile is then downsampled, read back from the GPU, and passed to the accumulate function. Alternatively, the tile could be moved into a texture and the accumulation could happen on the GPU.

21.7.1 The Rendering Loop

Our code uses fp32 precision throughout for the highest possible image quality. It does not use render-to-texture, only because this was not available under Linux at the time it was originally developed. Listing 21-4 shows the rendering loop.

Listing 21-4. Rendering All the Tiles

```
// Pad the final resolution by the filter radius to generate the
// pixels we need to properly filter the edges of the final image
int fx = int (ceil (filter.width() / 2.0 - 0.5));
int fy = int (ceil (filter.height() / 2.0 - 0.5));

// Render all tiles
for (int y = -fy; y < resy + fy; y += ty) {
  for (int x = fx; x < resx + fx; x += tx) {
    // Compute the matrix to render this tile fullscreen
    Matrix4 cam2tile = compute_cam2tile (cam2ras, resx, resy,
                                         false, x, y, tx, ty);
    drawmode.view (cam2tile, tx * ssx, ty * ssy);

    // Draw the entire scene
    render (drawmode, canvas);

    // Create a texture from the current frame buffer
    GpuTexture fbtex ("downsamplefb");
    fbtex.load (canvas, 0,0, tx * ssx, ty * ssy, GL_FLOAT_RGBA_NV,
                true, 0, true);

    // Downsample the rendered texture and store in a new texture
    downsample.run (fbtex, tx, ty, ssx, ssy, *filter);
    downsample.readback_padded_tile (tx, ty, *filter, tile);

    // Accumulate the resulting texture into the final image
    accumulate_tile (tile,
                     downsample.padded_tile_xorigin (x, *filter),
                     downsample.padded_tile_yorigin (y, *filter),
                     resx, resy, tilew, tileh, image);
  }
}
```

21.7.2 The Downsample Class

The GpuDownsample class implements the two-pass separable downsample by creating an off-screen drawing surface and generating the custom fragment programs based on the supersample rate and the filter size and type. The class provides functions to enforce the padding required for the tile buffers. The resulting downsampled tile is left on the GPU, and two functions are provided to read back the data to a CPU buffer or convert the drawing surface into a texture (another place where we could be using render-to-texture).

The main downsample function appears in Listing 21-5.

Listing 21-5. Main Function for Two-Pass Downsampling

```
void
GpuDownsample::run (GpuTexture &fbtex, int tx, int ty,
                    int ssx, int ssy, Filter2D& filter)
{
  // compute the padded resolution for the intermediary passes
  int dstw = tx + 2 * filter.width();
  int dsth = ty + 2 * filter.height();

  // compute the resolution of the source texture
  int srcw = tx * ssx;
  int srch = ty * ssy;

  // create a new pbuffer and canvas if needed
  if (pbuffer == NULL || pbuffer->w() < dstw ||
      pbuffer->h() < max(srch, dsth)) {
    delete canvas;
    delete pbuffer;
    pbuffer = new GpuPBuffer (dstw, max(srch, dsth));
    canvas = new GpuCanvas (*pbuffer);
  }

  canvas->clear (0.2, 0, 0.2);  // for debugging only

  // only create a new program if we need to
  if (xpass == NULL || ssx != last_ssx || ssy != last_ssy) {
    last_ssx = ssx;
    last_ssy = ssy;
    delete ypass;
    delete xpass;

    // generate fragment programs for each pass
    const char *code;
    code = generate_xory_pass_fp10 (filter, ssx, ssy, true);
    xpass = new GpuFragmentProgram ("xpass", code);
    free ((char *)code);
    code = generate_xory_pass_fp10 (filter, ssx, ssy, false);
```

Listing 21-5 *(continued)*. Main Function for Two-Pass Downsampling

```
     ypass = new GpuFragmentProgram ("ypass", code);
     free ((char *)code);
  }

  // dimensions of destination image in each pass
  int pw = dstw;
  int ph = srch;

  GpuDrawmode drawmode;
  drawmode.texture (0, fbtex);              // set src in tex0
  drawmode.fragment_program (xpass);       // set fragment prog
  drawmode.view (pw, ph);                   // set 2D pixel view

  GpuPrimitive rect0 (0, pw, 0, ph);        // fullscreen rect
  rect0.render (drawmode, *canvas);         // compute first pass

  fbtex.load (*canvas, 0,0, pw,ph, GL_FLOAT_RGBA_NV, true,0,true);

  ph = dsth;                                // second pass height

  drawmode.view (pw, ph);                   // dest 2D view
  drawmode.fragment_program (ypass);       // set fragment prog

  GpuPrimitive rect1 (0, pw, 0, ph);        // fullscreen rect
  rect1.render (drawmode, *canvas);         // second pass
}
```

21.7.3 Implementation Details

Our code uses a number of utilities libraries that are included in the sample code on this book's CD. The GPU library is a high-level interface to OpenGL that provides routines for constructing windows, off-screen buffers, textures, and vertex and fragment programs. It also provides optimized vertex buffer object (VBO) primitive drawing routines that work under both Windows and Linux. Its drawmode objects encapsulate OpenGL states, minimizing state changes and making debugging much easier. The library is fully thread-safe and supports drawing to multiple buffers.

The code included on the CD also contains low-level vector and matrix functions (on the CPU), along with a platform-independent thread-management library. The Filter library provides a set of commonly used sampling filters.

21.8 Conclusion

Film, video, and print often require better antialiasing than what current hardware natively provides. The GPU-based technique described here achieves the same image quality as software renderers, while placing almost no limitations on the basic scene rendering method used. The sample code provided is easy to graft onto your existing rendering program (we hope), letting you render beautifully antialiased frames.

This technique works around filter-quality limitations by using fragment programs, and it works around buffer-size limitations by using tiling. The filtering step makes quite effective use of the GPU's parallel floating-point power.

21.9 References

Apodaca, Anthony A., and Larry Gritz, eds. 1999. *Advanced RenderMan: Creating CGI for Motion Pictures.* Morgan Kaufmann.

Bjorke, Kevin. 2004. "High-Quality Filtering." In *GPU Gems*, edited by Randima Fernando, pp. 391–415. Addison-Wesley.

Dippé, Mark A. Z., and Erling H. Wold. 1985. "Antialiasing through Stochastic Sampling." In *Computer Graphics (Proceedings of SIGGRAPH 85)* 19(3), pp. 69–78.

James, Greg, and John O'Rorke. 2004. "Real-Time Glow." In *GPU Gems*, edited by Randima Fernando, pp. 343–362. Addison-Wesley.

Chapter 22

Fast Prefiltered Lines

Eric Chan
Massachusetts Institute of Technology

Frédo Durand
Massachusetts Institute of Technology

This chapter presents an antialiasing technique for lines. Aliased lines appear to have jagged edges, and these "jaggies" are especially noticeable when the lines are animated. Although line antialiasing is supported in graphics hardware, its quality is limited by many factors, including a small number of samples per pixel, a narrow filter support, and the use of a simple box filter. Furthermore, different hardware vendors use different algorithms, so antialiasing results can vary from GPU to GPU.

The prefiltering method proposed in this chapter was originally developed by McNamara, McCormack, and Jouppi (2000) and offers several advantages. First, it supports arbitrary symmetric filters at a fixed runtime cost. Second, unlike common hardware antialiasing schemes that consider only those samples that lie within a pixel, the proposed method supports larger filters. Results are hardware-independent, which ensures consistent line antialiasing across different GPUs. Finally, the algorithm is fast and easy to implement.

22.1 Why Sharp Lines Look Bad

Mathematically speaking, a line segment is defined by its two end points, but it has no thickness or area. In order to see a line on the display, however, we need to give it some thickness. So, a line in our case is defined by two end points plus a width parameter. For computer graphics, we usually specify this width in screen pixels. A thin line might be one pixel wide, and a thick line might be three pixels wide.

Before we try to antialias lines, we must understand why we see nasty aliasing artifacts in the first place. Let's say we draw a black line that is one pixel wide on a white background. From the point of view of signal processing, we can think of the line as a signal with a value of 1 corresponding to maximum intensity and 0 corresponding to minimum intensity. Because our frame buffer and display have only a finite number of pixels, we need to sample the signal. The Sampling Theorem tells us that to reconstruct the signal without aliasing, we must sample the input signal at a rate no less than twice the maximum frequency of the signal.

And that's where the problem lies. A line with perfectly sharp edges corresponds to a signal with infinitely high frequencies! We can think of an edge of a 1D line as a step function, as shown in Figure 22-1a; discrete samples are shown as vertical blue lines in Figure 22-1b. Intuitively, we can see that no matter how finely we sample this step function, we cannot represent the step discontinuity accurately enough. The three images in Figure 22-2 show what happens to the appearance of a line as we increase the pixel resolution. The results are as we expect: aliasing decreases as resolution increases, but it never goes away entirely.

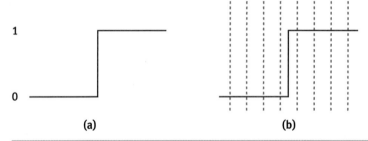

Figure 22-1. Trying to Sample a Line
(a) The sharp edge of a line corresponds to a step function. (b) Unfortunately, discrete samples (vertical blue bars) do not adequately represent this function.

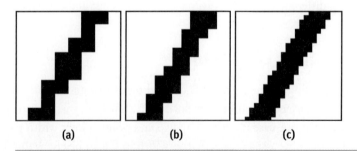

Figure 22-2. Decreasing Aliasing by Increasing Resolution

What have we learned? The only way to reconstruct a line with perfectly sharp edges is to use a frame buffer with infinite resolution—which means it would take an infinite amount of time, memory, and money. Obviously this is not a very practical solution!

22.2 Bandlimiting the Signal

A more practical solution, and the one that we describe in this chapter, is to *bandlimit* the signal. In other words, because we cannot represent the original signal by increasing the screen resolution, we can instead remove the irreproducible high frequencies. The visual result of this operation is that our lines will no longer appear to have sharp edges. Instead, the line's edges will appear blurry. This is what we normally think of when we hear the term "antialiased": a polygon or line with soft, smooth edges and no visible jaggies.

We can remove high frequencies from the original signal by convolving the signal with a low-pass filter. Figure 22-3 illustrates this process with a two-dimensional signal. Figure 22-3a shows the sharp edge of a line. The x and y axes represent the 2D image coordinates, and the vertical z axis represents intensity values. The left half ($z = 1$) corresponds to the interior of the line, and the right half ($z = 0$) lies outside of the line. Notice the sharp discontinuity at the boundary between $z = 0$ and $z = 1$. Figure 22-3b shows a low-pass filter, centered at a pixel; the filter is normalized to have unit volume. To evaluate the convolution of the signal in Figure 22-3a with the filter shown in Figure 22-3b at a pixel, we place the filter at that pixel and compute the volume of intersection between the filter and the signal. An example of such a volume is shown in Figure 22-3c. Repeating this process at every image pixel yields the smooth edge shown in Figure 22-3d.

Although the idea of convolving the signal with a low-pass filter is straightforward, the calculations need to be performed at every image pixel. This makes the overall approach quite expensive! Fortunately, as we see in the next section, all of the expensive calculations can be done in a preprocess.

22.2.1 Prefiltering

McNamara et al. (2000) developed an efficient prefiltering method originally designed for the Neon graphics accelerator. We describe their method here and show how it can be implemented using a pixel shader on modern programmable GPUs.

The key observation is that if we assume that our two-dimensional low-pass filter is symmetric, then the convolution depends only on the distance from the filter to the line.

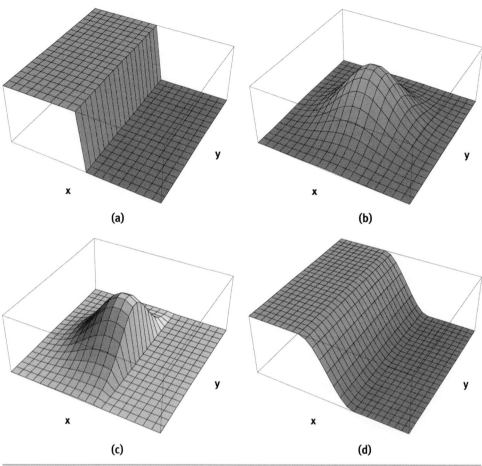

Figure 22-3. Convolution of a Sharp Line with a Low-Pass Filter
The x and y axes represent image coordinates, and the vertical axis represents intensities. (a) The signal of a sharp line. (b) A Gaussian low-pass filter. (c) Convolution of the signal with the filter, evaluated at one pixel; this is equivalent to finding the volume of intersection between the two functions. (d) The resulting signal of the filtered line; high frequencies have been removed.

This means that in a preprocess, we can compute the convolution with the filter placed at several distances from the line and store the results in a lookup table. Then at runtime, we evaluate the distance from each pixel to the line and perform a table lookup to obtain the correct intensity value. This strategy has been used in many other line antialiasing techniques, including those of Gupta and Sproull (1981) and Turkowski (1982).

This approach has several nice properties:

- We can use any symmetric filters that we like, such as box, Gaussian, or cubic filters.
- It doesn't matter if the filters are expensive to evaluate or complicated, because all convolutions are performed offline.
- The filter diameter can be larger than a pixel. In fact, according to the Sampling Theorem, it should be greater than a pixel to perform proper antialiasing. On the other hand, if we make the filter size too large, then the lines will become excessively blurry.

To summarize, this approach supports prefiltered line antialiasing with arbitrary symmetric filters at a fixed runtime cost. Now that we have seen an overview of the prefiltering method, let's dig into some of the details, starting with the preprocess.

22.3 The Preprocess

There are many questions that need to be addressed about this stage, such as how many entries in the table we need, which filter to use, and the size of the filter. We look at answers to these questions as we proceed.

Let's start by studying how to compute the table for a generic set of filter and line parameters. Figure 22-4 shows a line of width w and a filter of radius R. We distinguish between the mathematical line L, which is infinitely thin and has zero thickness, and the wide line whose edges are a distance $w/2$ from L. Let's ignore the line's end points for now and assume the line is infinitely long.

When we convolve the filter with the wide line, we obtain an intensity value. Let's see what values we get by placing the filter at various distances from L. We get a maximum intensity when the filter lies directly on L, as shown in Figure 22-5a, because this is where the overlap between the filter and the wide line is maximized. Similarly, we get a minimum intensity when the filter is placed a distance of $w/2 + R$ from the line, as shown in Figure 22-5b; this is the smallest distance for which there is no overlap between the filter and the wide line. Thus, intensity should drop off smoothly as the filter moves from a distance of 0 from L to a distance of $w/2 + R$.

This observation turns out to be a convenient way to index the table. Instead of using the actual distance measured in pixels to index the table, we use a normalized parameter d that has a value of 1 when the filter is placed directly on L and a value of 0 when the filter is placed a distance of $w/2 + R$ away. The reason for using this parameterization is that it allows us to handle different values for R and w in a single, consistent way.

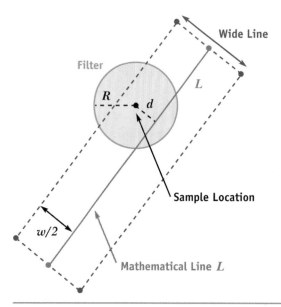

Figure 22-4. Line Configuration and Notation

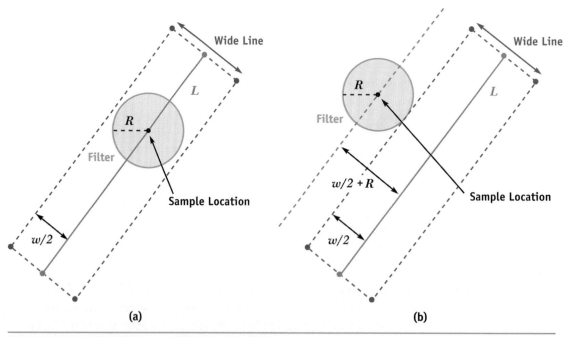

(a)   (b)

Figure 22-5. How Filter Placement Affects the Convolution
(a) The value of the convolution is maximized when the filter is directly on L. (b) The value of the convolution is minimized when the filter is at a distance of w/2 + R from L.

Let's get back to some of the questions we raised earlier about prefiltering the lines. For instance, which filter should we use, and how big should it be? Signal processing theory tells us that to eliminate aliasing in the reconstructed signal, we should use the sinc filter. Unfortunately, this filter is not practical, because it has an infinite support, meaning that R would be unbounded. The good news is that we can achieve good results using simpler filters with a compact support. In practice, for thick lines (that is, with higher values of w), we prefer to use a Gaussian with a two-pixel radius and a variance of $\sigma^2 = 1.0$. For thinner lines, however, the results can be a bit soft and blurry, so in those cases, we use a box filter with a one-pixel radius. Blinn 1998 examines these issues in more detail. Remember, everything computed in this stage is part of a preprocess, and runtime performance is independent of our choice of filter. Therefore, feel free to precompute tables for different filters and pick one that gives results that you like.

Here's another question about our precomputation: How big do our tables need to be? Or in other words, at how many distances from L should we perform the convolution? We have found that a 32-entry table is more than enough. The natural way to feed this table to the GPU at runtime is as a one-dimensional luminance texture. A one-dimensional, 32-entry luminance texture is tiny, so if for some reason you find that 32 entries is insufficient, you can step up to a 64-entry texture and the memory consumption will still be very reasonable.

One more question before we move on to the runtime part of the algorithm: What about the line's end points? We've completely ignored them in the preceding discussion and in Figure 22-4, pretending that the line L is infinitely long. The answer is that for convenience's sake, we can ignore the end points during the preprocess and instead handle them entirely at runtime.

22.4 Runtime

The previous section covered the preprocess, which can be completed entirely on the host processor once and for all. Now let's talk about the other half of the algorithm. At runtime, we perform two types of computations. First, we compute line-specific parameters and feed them to the GPU. Second, we draw each line on the GPU conservatively as a "wide" line, and for each fragment generated by the hardware rasterizer, we use the GPU's pixel shader to perform antialiasing via table lookups. Let's dig into the details.

Each fragment produced by the rasterizer for a given line corresponds to a sample position. We need to figure out how to use this sample position to index into our precomputed lookup table so that we can obtain the correct intensity value for this fragment. Remember that our table is indexed by a parameter d that has a value of 1 when the sample lies directly on the line and a value of 0 when the sample is $w/2 + R$ pixels away. Put another way, we need to map sample positions to the appropriate value of d. This can be done efficiently using the following line-setup algorithm.

22.4.1 Line Setup (CPU)

Let's say we want to draw the line L shown in Figure 22-6. This line is defined by its two end points (x_0, y_0) and (x_1, y_1). The actual wide line that we want to draw has width w, and its four edges surround L as shown. For a sample located at (x, y) in pixel coordinates, we can compute the parameter d efficiently by expressing d as a linear edge function of the form $ax + by + c$, where (a, b, c) are edge coefficients. Figure 22-6 shows four edges E_0, E_1, E_2, and E_3 surrounding L. We will compute the value of d for each edge separately and then see how to combine the results to obtain an intensity value.

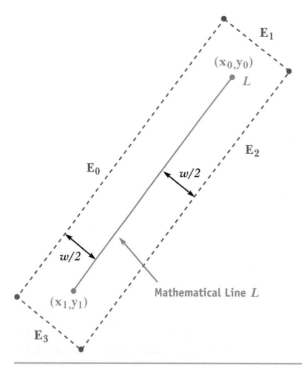

Figure 22-6. Edge Functions for a Line
The mathematical line L is surrounded by four edge functions, E_0, E_1, E_2, and E_3. E_0 and E_2 are the two side edges, whereas E_1 and E_3 are the two end point edges.

First, we transform the line's end points from object space to window space (that is, pixel coordinates). This means we transform the object-space vertices by the modelview projection matrix to obtain clip-space coordinates, apply perspective division to project the coordinates to the screen, and then remap these normalized device coordinates to window space. Let (x_0, y_0) and (x_1, y_1) be the coordinates of the line's end points in window space.

Next, we compute the coefficients of the four linear edge functions. Each set of coefficients is expressed as a three-vector:

$$\vec{e}_0 = \left(k\left(y_0 - y_1\right), k\left(x_1 - x_0\right), 1 + k\left(x_0 y_1 - x_1 y_0\right) \right)$$
$$\vec{e}_1 = \left(k\left(x_1 - x_0\right), k\left(y_1 - y_0\right), 1 + k\left(x_0^2 + y_0^2 - x_0 x_1 - y_0 y_1\right) \right)$$
$$\vec{e}_2 = \left(k\left(y_1 - y_0\right), k\left(x_0 - x_1\right), 1 + k\left(x_1 y_0 - x_0 y_1\right) \right)$$
$$\vec{e}_3 = \left(k\left(x_0 - x_1\right), k\left(y_0 - y_1\right), 1 + k\left(x_1^2 + y_1^2 - x_0 x_1 - y_0 y_1\right) \right)$$

where

$$k = \frac{2}{(2r + w)\sqrt{\left(x_0 - x_1\right)^2 - \left(y_0 - y_1\right)^2}}.$$

These calculations are performed once per line on the CPU.

22.4.2 Table Lookups (GPU)

The four sets of coefficients are passed to a pixel shader as uniform (that is, constant) parameters. The shader itself is responsible for performing the following calculations. If (x, y) are the pixel coordinates (in window space) of the incoming fragment, then we evaluate the four linear edge functions using simple dot products:

$$d_0 = \left(x, y, 1\right) \cdot \vec{e}_0$$
$$d_1 = \left(x, y, 1\right) \cdot \vec{e}_1$$
$$d_2 = \left(x, y, 1\right) \cdot \vec{e}_2$$
$$d_3 = \left(x, y, 1\right) \cdot \vec{e}_3$$

If any of the four results is less than zero, it means that (x, y) is more than $w/2 + R$ pixels away from the line and therefore this fragment should be discarded.

How do we use the results of the four edge functions? We need a method that antialiases both the sides of the wide line and the end points. McNamara et al. (2000) propose the following algorithm:

```
intensity = lookup(min(d0, d2)) * lookup(min(d1, d3))
```

Let's see how this method works. It finds the minimum of d_0 and d_2, the two functions corresponding to the two side edges E_0 and E_2. Similarly, it finds the minimum of d_1 and d_3, the two functions corresponding to the two end point edges E_1 and E_3 (see Figure 22-6). Two table lookups using these minimum values are performed. The lookup associated with $\min(d_0, d_2)$ returns an intensity value that varies in the direction perpendicular to L; as expected, pixels near L will have high intensity, and those near edges E_0 or E_2 will have near-zero intensity. If L was infinitely long, this would be the only lookup required.

Because we need to handle L's end points, however, the method performs a second lookup (with $\min(d_1, d_3)$) that returns an intensity value that varies in the direction parallel to L; pixels near the end points of L will have maximum intensity, whereas those near edges E_1 and E_3 will have near-zero intensity. Multiplying the results of the two lookups yields a very close approximation to the true convolution between a filter and a finite wide line segment. The resulting line has both smooth edges and smooth end points.

Notice that only a few inexpensive operations need to be performed per pixel. This makes line antialiasing very efficient.

Cg pixel shader source code is shown in Listing 22-1. A hand-optimized assembly version requires only about ten instructions.

Listing 22-1. Cg Pixel Shader Source Code for Antialiasing Lines

```
void main (out float4 color : COLOR,
    float4 position : WPOS,
    uniform float3 edge0,
    uniform float3 edge1,
    uniform float3 edge2,
    uniform float3 edge3,
    uniform sampler1D table)
{
    float3 pos = float3(position.x, position.y, 1);
    float4 d = float4(dot(edge0, pos), dot(edge1, pos),
                      dot(edge2, pos), dot(edge3, pos));
```

```
if (any(d < 0)) discard;

// . . . compute color . . .

color.w = tex1D(table, min(d.x, d.z)).x *
          tex1D(table, min(d.y, d.w)).x;
}
```

22.5 Implementation Issues

22.5.1 Drawing Fat Lines

For the pixel shader in Listing 22-1 to work, we have to make sure the hardware rasterizer generates all the fragments associated with a wide line. After all, our pixel shader won't do anything useful without any fragments! Therefore, we must perform conservative rasterization and make sure that all the fragments that lie within a distance of $w/2 + R$ are generated. In OpenGL, this can be accomplished by calling glLineWidth with a sufficiently large value:

```
glLineWidth(ceil((2.0f * R + w) * sqrt(2.0f)));
```

For example, if $R = 1$ and $w = 2$, then we should call glLineWidth with a parameter of 6. We also have to extend the line by $w/2 + R$ in each direction to make it sufficiently long.

22.5.2 Compositing Multiple Lines

Up until now, we have only considered drawing a single line. What happens when we have multiple (possibly overlapping) lines? We need to composite these lines properly.

One way to accomplish this task is to use frame-buffer blending, such as alpha blending. In the pixel shader, we write the resulting intensity value into the alpha component of the RGBA output, as shown in Listing 22-1. In the special case where the lines are all the same color, alpha blending is a commutative operation, so the order in which we draw the lines does not matter. For the more general case of using lines with different colors, however, alpha blending is noncommutative. This means that lines must be sorted and drawn from back to front on a per-pixel basis. This cannot always be done correctly using a standard z-buffer, so instead we can use a heuristic to approximate a back-to-front sort in object space. One heuristic is to sort lines by their midpoints. Although this heuristic can occasionally cause artifacts due to incorrect sorting, the artifacts affect only a limited number of pixels and aren't particularly noticeable in practice.

22.6 Examples

Now that we've seen how to implement prefiltered lines on the GPU, let's take a look at some examples. Figure 22-7 compares hardware rendering with and without the GPU's antialiasing with the method presented in this chapter. In the first row, we draw a single black line of width 1 on an empty, white background; the second row is a close-up view of this line. In the third row, we draw a thicker black line of width 3; the fourth row provides a close-up view of the thick line. The third and fourth columns show the results of prefiltering the line using a box filter with $R = 1$ and a Gaussian filter with $R = 2$ and $\sigma^2 = 1.0$, respectively. The advantages in image quality of the prefiltered approach over hardware antialiasing are especially noticeable with nearly horizontal and nearly vertical lines.

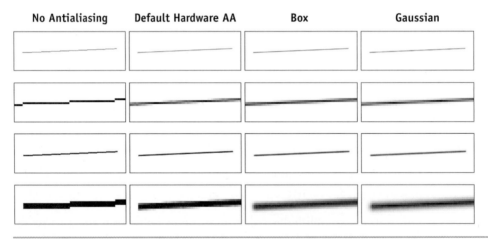

Figure 22-7. Comparing Line Antialiasing Methods for Thin and Thick Lines
The second and fourth rows show zoomed-in images of the first and third rows, respectively. Images in the second column were generated using hardware line antialiasing. Images in the third and fourth columns were generated using the prefiltering method presented in this chapter. A box filter (third column) and a Gaussian filter (fourth column) were used.

An interesting application of line antialiasing is the smoothing of polygon edges. Although graphics hardware offers built-in support for polygon antialiasing, we can achieve better quality by using a simple but effective method proposed by Sander et al. (2001). The idea is first to draw the polygons in the usual way. Then we redraw discontinuity edges (such as silhouettes and material boundaries) as antialiased lines. For example, Figure 22-8a shows a single triangle drawn without antialiasing. Figure 22-8b shows its edges drawn as prefiltered antialiased lines. By drawing these lines on top of the original geometry, we obtain the result in Figure 22-8c.

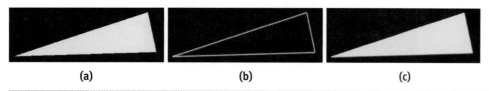

(a) (b) (c)

Figure 22-8. Overview of the Discontinuity Edge Overdraw Method
(a) First, draw polygons normally. (b) Next, draw discontinuity edges (such as silhouettes) as prefiltered lines. (c) Resulting polygon with antialiased edges. (Sander et al. 2001)

Comparisons showing close-ups of the triangle's nearly horizontal edge are shown in Figure 22-9. Close-ups of the triangle's nearly vertical edge are shown in Figure 22-10.

There are some limitations to this polygon antialiasing approach, however. One drawback is that we must explicitly identify the discontinuity edges for a polygonal model, which can be expensive for large models. Another drawback is the back-to-front compositing issue described earlier. Standard hardware polygon antialiasing avoids these issues at the expense of image quality.

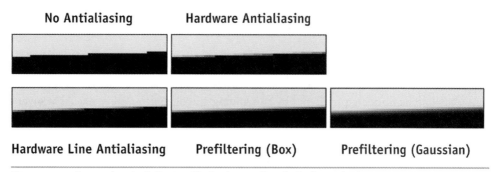

No Antialiasing   **Hardware Antialiasing**

Hardware Line Antialiasing   **Prefiltering (Box)**   **Prefiltering (Gaussian)**

Figure 22-9. Comparing Antialiasing Methods on a Nearly Horizontal Edge

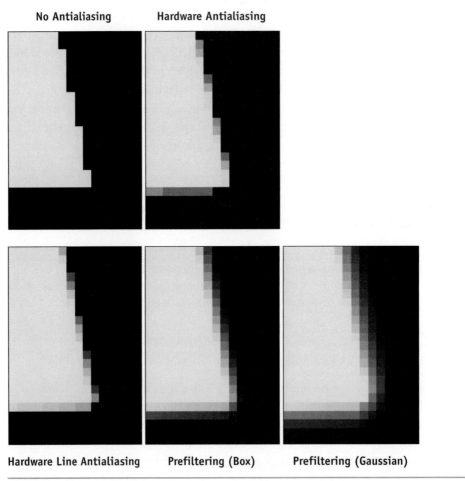

No Antialiasing   **Hardware Antialiasing**

Hardware Line Antialiasing   **Prefiltering (Box)**   **Prefiltering (Gaussian)**

Figure 22-10. Comparing Antialiasing Methods on a Nearly Vertical Edge

22.7 Conclusion

In this chapter we have described a simple and efficient method for antialiasing lines. The lines are prefiltered by convolving an edge with a filter placed at several distances from the edge and storing the results in a small table. This approach allows the use of arbitrary symmetric filters at a fixed runtime cost. Furthermore, the algorithm requires only small amounts of CPU and GPU arithmetic, bandwidth, and storage. These features make the algorithm practical for many real-time rendering applications, such as rendering fences, power lines, and other thin structures in games.

22.8 References

Blinn, Jim. 1998. "Return of the Jaggy." In *Jim Blinn's Corner: Dirty Pixels*, pp. 23–34. Morgan Kaufmann.

Gupta, Satish, and Robert F. Sproull. 1981. "Filtering Edges for Gray-Scale Devices." In *Proceedings of ACM SIGGRAPH 81*, pp. 1–5.

McNamara, Robert, Joel McCormack, and Norman P. Jouppi. 2000. "Prefiltered Anti-aliased Lines Using Half-Plane Distance Functions." In *Proceedings of the ACM SIGGRAPH/Eurographics Workshop on Graphics Hardware*, pp. 77–85.

Sander, Pedro V., Hugues Hoppe, John Snyder, and Steven J. Gortler. 2001. "Discontinuity Edge Overdraw." In *Proceedings of the 2001 Symposium on Interactive 3D Graphics*, pp. 167–174.

Turkowski, Kenneth. 1982. "Anti-Aliasing Through the Use of Coordinate Transformations." *ACM Transactions on Graphics* 1(3), pp. 215–234.

Chapter 23

Hair Animation and Rendering in the Nalu Demo

Hubert Nguyen
NVIDIA Corporation

William Donnelly
NVIDIA Corporation

The single largest technical challenge we faced in developing the Nalu demo for the GeForce 6800 launch was the rendering of realistic hair in real time. Previous NVIDIA demo characters Dawn and Dusk had hair, but it was short, dark, and static. For Nalu, we set out to achieve the goal of rendering long, blonde, flowing hair underwater. In this chapter we describe the techniques we used to achieve this goal in real time. They include a system for simulating the hair's movement, a shadowing algorithm to compute hair self-shadowing, and a reflectance model to simulate light scattering through individual strands of hair. When combined, these elements produce the extremely realistic images of hair in real time. Figure 23-1 shows an example.

In the backstage of Nalu's hair shading, there is a system that generates the hair geometry and controls the dynamics and collisions at every frame. It is basically split in two parts: the geometry generation and the dynamics/collision computations.

The hair is made of 4,095 individual hairs that are rendered using line primitives. We used 123,000 vertices just for the hair rendering. Sending all those vertices through the dynamics and collision detection would be prohibitively slow, so we use *control hairs*: Nalu's haircut can be described and controlled by a smaller set of hundreds of hairs, even though the rendering requires thousands. All the expensive dynamics computations are applied only to these control hairs.

We had no time and no tools to animate the control hair structure by hand. Even if we had had the tools, hand animating so many control hairs is very difficult. A lot of subtle

Figure 23-1. The Nalu Character

secondary motion is needed to make the hair look believable. See Figure 23-2. Physically based animation helped a lot.

Of course, when procedural animation is introduced, some control over the hair motion is lost (in our case, that meant losing 90 percent of the control). Collision detection and response can introduce undesired hair behavior that gets in the way of a creative animation. Our animators did a great job of understanding the inner workings of the dynamics and created some workarounds. A few additional tools were added on the engineering side to get that remaining 10 percent of human control over the dynamics.

23.1 Hair Geometry

23.1.1 Layout and Growth

The control hair structure is used to roughly describe the haircut. We "grow" the control hairs from a dedicated geometry built in Maya that represents the "scalp" (which is invisible at render time). A control hair grows from each vertex of the scalp, along the normal, as shown in Figure 23-3. The growth is 100 percent procedural.

23.1.2 Controlling the Hair

Once we have a set of control hairs, we subject them to physics, dynamics, and collision computations, in order to procedurally animate the hair. In this demo, the motion relies almost entirely on the dynamics. Though such a system may seem attractive, it is much more desirable to have a human-controllable system. When we want to dramatize the

Figure 23-2. Nalu's Hair

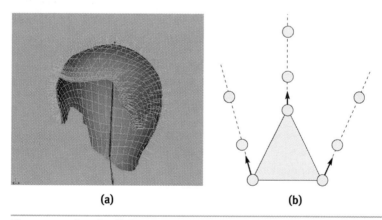

(a)   (b)

Figure 23-3. Growing Hair
(a) Control hairs. (b) Growth along the normals.

animation, we need to be able to "fake" or "fix" the hair behaviors. Additionally, our hair dynamics are not realistic enough to move like real hair in some situations. Having better manual control would allow us to make the motion even more convincing.

23.1.3 Data Flow

Because the hair is totally dynamic and changes every frame, we need to rebuild the final rendering hair set every frame. Figure 23-4 shows how the data moves through the process. The animated control hairs are converted to Bezier curves and tessellated to get smooth lines. The smoothed lines are then interpolated to increase the hair density. The set of interpolated hair is sent to the engine for final frame rendering. We use a dynamic vertex buffer to hold the vertex data.

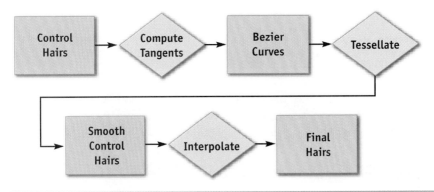

Figure 23-4. How Data Flows When Constructing the Hair

23.1.4 Tessellation

The hair tessellation process consists of smoothing each control hair by adding vertices. We increase more than fivefold, from 7 to 36 vertices. See Figures 23-5 and 23-6.

To compute the new vertices' positions, we convert the control hairs to Bezier curves by calculating their tangents (for every frame) and using them to compute the Bezier control points. From the Bezier curves, we compute the positions of extra vertices introduced to smooth the control hairs.

The smoothed control hairs will be replicated by interpolation to create a dense set of hair, ready for final rendering.

23.1.5 Interpolation

The interpolated hair is created using the scalp mesh topology. See Figure 23-7. The extremities of each triangle have three smoothed control hairs (shown in green). We want to fill up the inside of the triangle surface with hairs, so we interpolate the coordinates of the control hair triplet to create new smoothed hair (shown in gray). The smooth control hairs and the smooth interpolated hairs have the same number of vertices.

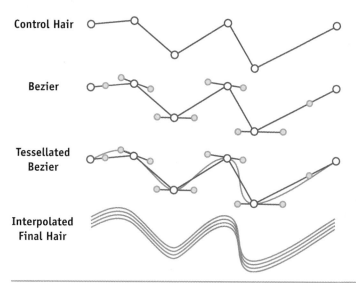

Control Hair

Bezier

Tessellated
Bezier

Interpolated
Final Hair

Figure 23-5. Visualizing the Steps in Creating Nalu's Hair

(a) **(b)**

Figure 23-6. The Effect of Tessellation and Interpolation
(a) Before tessellation and interpolation. (b) After tessellation and interpolation.

To fill up each triangle with hairs, we use barycentric coordinates to create new, inter-polated, hairs. For example, the interpolated hair Y (in Figure 23-7) is computed based on three barycentric coefficients (b_A, b_B, b_C), where $b_A + b_B + b_C = 1$:

$$Y = A \times b_A + B \times b_B + C \times b_C.$$

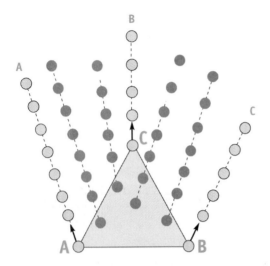

Figure 23-7. Creating the Interpolated Hair

By generating two random values in [0..1], computing 1 minus the larger of them if their sum is greater than 1, and setting the third as 1 minus the other two so that they sum to 1, we can determine positions at which to grow the desired density of hair.

23.2 Dynamics and Collisions

Nalu's hair dynamics are based on a particle system, as shown in Figure 23-3b. Each uninterpolated control hair vertex is animated as a particle. The particles are not evenly spaced along a hair. The segments in a control hair are grown larger as we get away from the skull. This allows having longer hair, without adding too many vertices.

For this project, we chose to use Verlet integration to compute the particles' motion, because it tends to be more stable than Euler integration and is much simpler than Runge-Kutta integration. The explanation is beyond the scope of this chapter, but if you want to learn more about ways to use Verlet integration in games, see Jakobsen 2003.

23.2.1 Constraints

While the particles are moving around, the length of the control hairs must stay constant to avoid stretching. To make this happen, we used constraints between particles within a control hair. The constraints make the particles repel if they are too close to each other, or they contract the segment if the particles are too far apart. Of course, when we pull one particle, the length of the neighboring segment becomes invalid, so the modifications need to be applied iteratively. After several iterations, the system converges toward the desired result. See Figure 23-8.

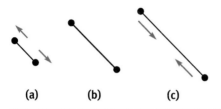

Figure 23-8. How Constraints Work to Make the Length of Hairs Stay Constant
(a) Too close. (b) Ideal length. (c) Too far apart.

23.2.2 Collisions

We tried many collision-detection techniques. We needed to keep the process simple and fast. For this demo, a rig of spheres turned out to work well, and it was the easiest to implement. See Figure 23-9.

At first, the solution did not work as planned, because some hair segments were larger than the collision spheres. Because we are colliding "a point against spheres," nothing prevents the two extremities of a hair from intersecting a sphere.

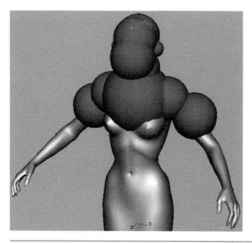

Figure 23-9. Collision Detection with Spheres

To prevent this from happening, we introduced a "pearl configuration" in the control hair collision data, as shown in Figure 23-10. Instead of colliding with a point, each sphere would collide with another sphere localized on a particle.

We also tried to detect collisions between the segments and the spheres. It's not very difficult, but it's not as fast as using the "pearls." Our edge-collision detection worked reasonably well, but it had stability issues, probably due to our collision-reaction code. Regardless, we had something that worked well enough for our purposes.

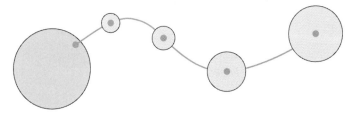

Figure 23-10. Using Pearls to Detect Collisions More Efficiently

23.2.3 Fins

The original conception of the mermaid included fins that were long and soft, and we considered this feature a critical part of the character. Solid fins were built and skinned to the skeleton. However, during the animation process, in Maya, the fins just followed the body, looking quite stiff. You can see what we mean in Figure 23-11.

Fortunately, our hair dynamics code can also be used to perform cloth simulation. So in the real-time engine, we compute a cloth simulation and blend the results of the cloth

Figure 23-11. Rigid Fins on Nalu

to the skinned geometry. A weight map was painted to define how much physics to blend in. The more we applied the physics, the softer the fins looked. On the contrary, blending more skinning resulted in a more rigid motion. We wanted the base of the fins to be more rigid than the tip, and the weight map allowed us to do exactly that, because we could paint exactly the ratio of physics versus skinning we wanted for each cloth vertex. See Figure 23-12. In the end, this combination allowed us to produce soft and realistic fins, as shown in Figure 23-13.

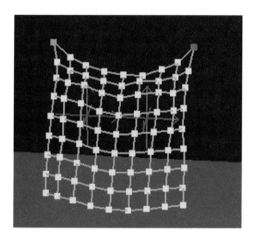

Figure 23-12. A Simple Cloth Simulation

23.3 Hair Shading

The problem of shading hair can be divided into two parts: a local reflectance model for hair and a method for computing self-shadowing between hairs.

23.3.1 A Real-Time Reflectance Model for Hair

For our local reflectance model, we chose the model presented in Marschner et al. 2003. We chose this model because it is a comprehensive, physically based representation of hair reflectance.

The Marschner reflectance model can be formulated as a four-dimensional bidirectional scattering function:

$$S\left(\phi_i, \theta_i; \phi_o, \theta_o\right),$$

Figure 23-13. Fins in the Final Demo

where $\theta_i \in [-\pi/2, \pi/2]$ and $\phi_i \in [0, 2\pi]$ are the input direction in polar coordinates, and $\theta_o \in [-\pi/2, \pi/2]$ and $\phi_o \in [0, 2\pi]$ are the polar coordinates of the light direction.[1] The function S is a complete description of how a hair fiber scatters and reflects light; if we can evaluate this function, then we can compute the shading of the surface for any light position.

Because S is expensive to evaluate, we want to avoid computing it at each pixel. One possible solution is to store S in a lookup table and to read from it at runtime. This lookup table can then be encoded in a texture, allowing us to access it from a pixel shader.

Unfortunately, the function S has four parameters, and GPUs do not have native support for four-dimensional textures. This means that we would require some kind of scheme to encode a four-dimensional function in two-dimensional textures. Fortunately, if we perform our table lookups carefully, we can use only a small number of two-dimensional maps to encode the full four-dimensional function.

The Marschner Reflectance Model

The Marschner model treats each individual hair fiber as a translucent cylinder and considers the possible paths that light may take through the hair. Three types of paths are considered, each labeled differently in path notation. Path notation represents each path of light as a string of characters, each one representing a type of interaction between the light ray and a surface. R paths represent light that bounces off of the surface of the hair fiber toward the viewer. TT paths represent light that refracts into the hair and refracts out again toward the viewer. TRT paths represent light that refracts into the hair fiber, reflects off of the inside surface, and refracts out again toward the viewer. In each case, "R" represents the light reflecting, and "T" represents a ray being transmitted (or refracting) through a surface.

Marschner et al. (2003) showed that each of these paths contributes to a distinct and visually significant aspect of hair reflectance, allowing a degree of realism not possible with previous hair reflectance models. Figure 23-14 shows the three reflectance paths that contribute the most to the appearance of hair.

We can thus write the reflectance model as follows:

$$S = S_R + S_{TT} + S_{TRT}.$$

---

1. This definition is similar to the definition of a bidirectional reflectance distribution function (BRDF) for surfaces. It differs in that it is defined for lines instead of surfaces, and that it allows for the possibility of scattering effects that are neglected by a BRDF.

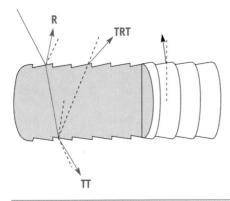

Figure 23-14. Reflectance Paths

Each term S_P can be further factored as the product of two functions. The function M_P describes the effect of the θ angles on the reflectance. The other function, N_P, captures the reflection in the ϕ direction. If we assume a perfectly circular hair fiber, then we can write both M and N in terms of a smaller set of angles. By defining secondary angles $\theta_d = \frac{1}{2}(\theta_i - \theta_o)$ and $\phi_d = \phi_i - \phi_o$, each term of the preceding equation can be written as:

$$S_P = M_P\left(\theta_i, \theta_o\right) \times N_P\left(\theta_d, \phi_d\right) \text{ for } P = R, TT, TRT.$$

In this form, we can see that both M and N are functions of only two parameters. This means that we can compute a lookup table for each of these functions and encode them in two-dimensional textures. Two-dimensional textures are ideal, because the GPU is optimized for two-dimensional texturing. We can also use the GPU's interpolation and mipmapping functionality to eliminate shader aliasing.[2]

Although we are storing six functions, many of them are only single channel and can be stored in the same texture. M_R, M_{TT}, and M_{TRT} are each only a single channel, and so they are packed together into the first lookup texture. N_R is a single channel, but N_{TT} and N_{TRT} are each three channels. We store N_{TT} and N_R together in the second lookup texture. To improve performance and reduce texture usage in the demo, we made a simplifying assumption that $M_{TT}(\theta_i, \theta_o) = M_{TRT}(\theta_i, \theta_o)$. This allowed us to store N_{TT} and N_{TRT} in the same texture, and to cut the number of textures from three down to two. See Figures 23-15 and 23-16.

---

2. In much the same way that textures can exhibit aliasing if they are not sampled at a high enough frequency, so can mathematical functions. This phenomenon is often called shader aliasing. Fortunately, when we encode our functions in textures, mipmapping eliminates the appearance of shader aliasing.

Chapter 23 Hair Animation and Rendering in the Nalu Demo

Figure 23-15. Reflectance
Top: The TT term produces a bright halo when the hair is backlit. Bottom: The R and TRT terms produce two overlapping specular highlights.

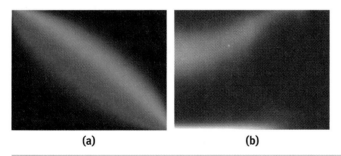

(a) (b)

Figure 23-16. Lookup Textures for the Marschner Hair Reflectance Model
(a) The table that stores the M terms: M_R in red, M_{TT} in green, and M_{TRT} in blue. (b) The table that stores N_{TT} in the red, green, and blue channels, and N_R in the alpha channel.

Although the model is expressed in terms of angles, computing these angles from vectors would require inverse trigonometric functions. These are expensive, and we would like to avoid them if possible. Instead of passing down θ_i and θ_o into the first lookup, we compute the sines:

$$\sin \theta_i = \left(light \cdot tangent \right),$$
$$\sin \theta_o = \left(eye \cdot tangent \right).$$

We can then express M as a function of $\sin \theta_i$ and $\sin \theta_o$, saving some math in the shader.

With a little more work, we can also compute $\cos \phi_d$. We first project the eye and light vectors perpendicular to the hair as follows:

$$lightPerp = light - \left(light \cdot tangent \right) \times tangent,$$
$$eyePerp = eye - \left(eye \cdot tangent \right) \times tangent.$$

Then from the formula

$$\left(lightPerp \cdot eyePerp \right) = \left\| lightPerp \right\| \times \left\| eyePerp \right\| \times \cos \phi_d,$$

we can compute $\cos \phi_d$ as follows:

$$\cos \phi_d = \left(eyePerp \cdot lightPerp \right) \times$$
$$\left(\left(eyePerp \cdot eyePerp \right) \times \left(lightPerp \cdot lightPerp \right) \right)^{-0.5}.$$

The only angle left to calculate is θ_d. To do so, we note that θ_d is a function of θ_i and θ_o. Because we are already using a lookup table indexed by θ_i and θ_o, we can add an extra channel to the lookup table that stores θ_d.

Listing 23-1 is a brief summary of our shader in pseudocode.

In our implementation, the lookup tables were computed on the CPU. We used 128×128 textures with an 8-bit-per-component format. The 8-bit format required us to scale the values to be in the range [0..1]. As a result, we had to add an extra scale factor in the shader to balance out the relative intensities of the terms. If more accuracy were desired, we could skip this step and use 16-bit floating-point textures to store the lookup tables. We found this unnecessary for our purposes.

To actually compute one of these lookup tables, we had to write a program to evaluate the functions M and N. These functions are too complicated to present here; Marschner et al. 2003 provides a complete description as well as a derivation.

Listing 23-1. Pseudocode Summarizing the Shaders

```
// In the Vertex Shader:

SinThetaI = dot(light, tangent)
SinThetaO = dot(eye, tangent)

LightPerp = light - SinThetaI * tangent
eyePerp = eye - SinThetaO * tangent;
CosPhiD = dot(eyePerp, lightPerp) * (dot(eyePerp, eyePerp) *
           dot(lightPerp, lightPerp))^-0.5

// In the Fragment Shader:

(MR, MTT, MTRT, cosThetaD) = lookup1(cosThetaI, cosThetaO)
(NTT, NR) = lookup2(CosPhiD, cosThetaD)
NTRT = lookup3(CosPhiD, cosThetaD)

S = MR * NR + MTT * NTT + MTRT * NTRT
```

Note that there are many other parameters to the reflectance model that are encoded in the lookup tables. These include the width and strength of highlights and the color and index of refraction of the hair, among others. In our implementation, we allowed these parameters to be altered at runtime, and we recomputed the lookup tables on the fly.

Solid Geometry

Though we used this hair reflectance model for rendering hair represented as line strips, it is possible to extend it to hair that is represented as solid geometry. Instead of using the tangent of a line strip, we could use one of the primary tangents of the surface. Finally, we must take into account self-occlusion by the surface. This is done by multiplying by an extra term `(wrap + dot(N, L)) / (1 + wrap)` where `dot(N, L)` is the dot product between the normal light vector and `wrap` is a value between zero and one that controls how far the lighting is allowed to wrap around the model. This is a simple approximation used to simulate light bleeding through the hair (Green 2004).

23.3.2 Real-Time Volumetric Shadows in Hair

Shadows in real-time applications are usually computed with one of two methods: stencil shadow volumes or shadow maps. Unfortunately, neither of these techniques works well for computing shadows on hair. The sheer amount of geometry used in the hair would make stencil shadow volumes intractable, and shadow maps exhibit severe aliasing on highly detailed geometry such as hair.

Instead, we used an approach to shadow rendering specifically designed for rendering shadows in hair. Opacity shadow maps extend shadow mapping to handle volumetric objects and antialiasing (Kim and Neumann 2001). Opacity shadow maps were originally implemented on GeForce 2-class hardware, where the flexibility in terms of programmability was much more limited than what is available on current GPUs. The original implementation did not achieve real-time performance on large data sets, and it required a large portion of the algorithm to be run on the CPU. GeForce 6 Series hardware has sufficient programmability that we can execute the majority of the algorithm on the GPU. In doing so, we achieve real-time performance even for a large hair data set.

Opacity Shadow Maps

Rather than use a discrete test such as traditional shadow maps, we use opacity shadow maps, which allow fractional shadow values. This means that rather than a simple binary test for occlusion, we need a measure of the percentage of light that penetrates to depth z (in light space) over a given pixel. This is given by the following formula:

$$T\left(x, y, z\right) = e^{-k\sigma\left(x, y, z\right)},$$

$$\sigma\left(x, y, z\right) = \int_0^z r\left(x, y, z'\right) dz'.$$

$T(x, y, z)$ is the fraction of light penetrating to depth z at pixel location (x, y), σ is called the opacity thickness, and $r(x, y, z)$ is the extinction coefficient, which describes the percentage of light that is absorbed per unit distance at the point (x, y, z). The value k is a constant chosen such that when $\sigma = 1$, T is approximately 0 (within numerical precision). This allows us to ignore σ values outside of the range $[0..1]$.

The idea of opacity shadow maps is to compute σ at a discrete set of z values $z_0 \ldots z_{n-1}$. Then we determine in-between values for σ by interpolation between the two nearest values as follows:

$$\sigma\left(z\right) = \frac{\sigma\left(z_i\right)\left(z - z_i\right) + \sigma\left(z_{i+1}\right)\left(z_{i+1} - z\right)}{\left(z_{i+1} - z_i\right)},$$

where $z_i < z < z_{i+1}$.

This is a reasonable approximation, because sigma is a strictly increasing function of z. We take n to be 16, with z_0 being the near plane of the hair in light space, and z_{15} being the far plane of the hair in light space. The other planes were distributed uniformly apart, so that $z_i = z_0 + i\, dz$, where $dz = (z_{15} - z_0)/16$. Note that because r is 0 outside of the hair volume, $\sigma(x, y, z_0) = 0$ for all x and y, and so we only have to store σ at $z = z_1 \dots z_{15}$.

Kim and Neumann (2001) noted that the integral sigma could be computed using additive blending on graphics hardware. Our implementation also uses hardware blending, but it also uses shaders to reduce the amount of work done by the CPU.

An Updated Implementation

The naive approach would be to store $\sigma(x, y, z_i)$ in 16 textures. This would require that we render 16 times to generate the full opacity shadow map. Our first observation is that storing σ requires only 1 channel, so we can pack up to 4 sigma values into a single 4-channel texture and render to all of them simultaneously. Using this scheme, we can reduce the number of render passes from 16 to 4.

We can do better than 4 render passes, however, if we use multiple render targets (MRT). MRT is a feature that allows us to render to up to 4 different textures simultaneously. If we use MRT, we can render to 4 separate 4-channel textures simultaneously, allowing us to render to all 16 channels in just a single render pass.

Now if we simply blend additively to every channel, then we will get every strand of hair contributing to every layer. What we really want is for each layer i to be affected by only those parts of the hair with $z_{hair} < z_i$. With a shader, we can simply output 0 if $z_{hair} > z_i$.

Performing a Lookup

Given an opacity shadow map, we must evaluate T at the point (x, y, z), given the slices of the opacity shadow map. We do this by linearly interpolating the values of sigma from the two nearest slices. The value at $\sigma(x, y, z)$ is a linear combination of $\sigma(x, y, z_0) \dots \sigma(x, y, z_n)$. In particular,

$$\sigma(x, y, z) = \sum_{i=0}^{n-1} \left(\sigma(x, y, z_i) \times \max\left(0, 1 - |z - z_i|/dz\right) \right).$$

We can compute $w_i = |z - z_i|/dz$ in the vertex shader for all 16 values.

```
// depth1 contains z0..z3, inverseDeltaD = 1/dz.
v2f.OSM1weight = max(0.0.xxxx, 1 - abs(dist - depth1) * inverseDeltaD);
v2f.OSM2weight = max(0.0.xxxx, 1 - abs(dist - depth2) * inverseDeltaD);
```

```
v2f.OSM3weight = max(0.0.xxxx, 1 - abs(dist - depth3) * inverseDeltaD);
v2f.OSM4weight = max(0.0.xxxx, 1 - abs(dist - depth4) * inverseDeltaD);
```

To improve performance, we compute these weights in the vertex shader and pass them directly to the fragment shader. Although the results are not mathematically equivalent to computing the weights in the fragment shader, they are close enough for our purposes.

Once these weights have been computed, it is simply a matter of computing the sum

$$\sum_{i=0}^{15} w_i \sigma \left(x, \, y, \, z_i \right).$$

Because of the way the data is aligned, we can compute

$$\sum_{i=0}^{3} w_i \sigma \left(x, \, y, \, z_i \right)$$

in a single dot product, and we can compute the sums for $i = 4..7$, $i = 8..11$, and $i = 12..15$ with dot products similarly.

```
/* Compute the total density */
half density = 0;
density  = dot(h4tex2D(OSM1, v2f.shadowCoord.xy), v2f.OSM1weight);
density += dot(h4tex2D(OSM2, v2f.shadowCoord.xy), v2f.OSM2weight);
density += dot(h4tex2D(OSM3, v2f.shadowCoord.xy), v2f.OSM3weight);
density += dot(h4tex2D(OSM4, v2f.shadowCoord.xy), v2f.OSM4weight);
```

Finally, we compute transmittance from optical density to get a value between 0 and 1 that represents the fraction of light that reaches the point (x, y, z) from the light source. We multiply this value by the shading value to get the final color of the hair.

```
half shadow = exp(-5.5 * density);
```

Figure 23-17 shows the dramatic difference between shadowed and unshadowed hair.

23.4 Conclusion and Future Work

We have shown that it is now possible to simulate all aspects of hair rendering in real time: from animation and dynamics to rendering and shading. We hope that our system will provide a basis for real-time rendering of hair in interactive applications such as games.

Figure 23-17. Comparing Shadowed and Unshadowed Hair
Left: Without shadows, the hair has an overly bright appearance, and it looks flat. Right: Shadows give the appearance of depth and significantly increase realism.

Although the ideas here have been applied to the animation and rendering of hair, this is not their only application. The Marschner reflectance model has a natural factorization that we used to decompose it into texture lookups. This approach can be extended to any reflectance model by using approximate factorizations (McCool et al. 2001). These numerical factorizations have all the advantages of analytical factorizations, with the exception of a small amount of error.

Opacity shadow maps, in addition to being extremely useful for rendering hair, can also be used for cases where depth maps fail. For example, they could be applied to volumetric representations such as clouds and smoke, or to highly detailed objects such as dense foliage.

As GPUs become more flexible, it is worthwhile to look for ways to transfer more work to them. This includes not only obviously parallel tasks such as tessellation and interpolation, but also domains more traditionally given to CPUs, such as collision detection and physics.

Performance is not our only focus; we are also looking at making the hair more controllable by the developers, so that it becomes easy to style and animate. Many challenges are ahead, but we hope to see more realistic hair in next-generation applications.

23.5 References

Green, Simon. 2004. "Real-Time Approximations to Subsurface Scattering." In *GPU Gems*, edited by Randima Fernando, pp. 263–278. Addison-Wesley.

Jakobsen, Thomas. 2003. "Advanced Character Physics." *IO Interactive*.

Kim, T.-Y., and U. Neumann. 2001. "Opacity Shadow Maps." In *Proceedings of SIGGRAPH 2001*, pp. 177–182.

Marschner, S. R., H. W. Jensen, M. Cammarano, S. Worley, and P. Hanrahan. 2003. "Light Scattering from Human Hair Fibers." *ACM Transactions on Graphics (Proceedings of SIGGRAPH 2003)* 22(3), pp. 780–791.

McCool, Michael D., Jason Ang, and Anis Ahmad. 2001. "Homomorphic Factorizations of BRDFs for High-Performance Rendering." In *Proceedings of SIGGRAPH 2001*, pp. 171–178.

Chapter 24

Using Lookup Tables to Accelerate Color Transformations

Jeremy Selan
Sony Pictures Imageworks

In feature-film visual-effects production, maintaining interactive feedback of high-quality color operations is extraordinarily beneficial to an artist. On the consumer side, enabling the real-time color correction of video and rendered image streams is becoming an increasingly useful tool to shape media's thematic "look." However, directly applying multiple sophisticated color transforms to high-resolution imagery is beyond the real-time capability of modern graphics hardware.

In this chapter, we present an algorithm that leverages three-dimensional lookup tables to enable the real-time color processing of high-resolution imagery. Our approach offers excellent performance characteristics, being independent of both the number of color operators applied as well as the underlying color transform complexity. The techniques presented in this chapter, and variations thereof, have been successfully utilized in the production of numerous motion pictures and should be regarded as "production ready."

24.1 Lookup Table Basics

Lookup tables (LUTs) are an excellent technique for optimizing the evaluation of functions that are expensive to compute and inexpensive to cache. By precomputing the evaluation of a function over a domain of common inputs, expensive runtime operations can be replaced with inexpensive table lookups. If the table lookups can be performed faster than computing the results from scratch (or if the function is repeatedly

queried at the same input), then the use of a lookup table will yield significant performance gains.[1] For data requests that fall between the table's samples, an interpolation
algorithm can generate reasonable approximations by averaging nearby samples.

24.1.1 One-Dimensional LUTs

A lookup table is characterized by its *dimensionality*, that is, the number of indices necessary to index an output value. The simplest LUTs are indexed by a single variable and
thus referred to as *one-dimensional* (or 1D) LUTs.

The identity lookup table is defined as the transform that maps the input index back to
itself over a given domain, as shown in Figure 24-1.

(a)   (b)

Figure 24-1. How One-Dimensional Lookup Tables Work
*The 1D LUT maps each input scalar to an arbitrary output (a) and is visualized as the intensity
along a 1D ramp (b).*

One-dimensional LUTs have long been utilized in image processing, most commonly
in the form of the monitor *gamma table*. Typically leveraging three LUTs—one for each
color channel—these tables enable the computationally efficient modification of pixel
intensity just before an image reaches the monitor.

Consider an analytical color operator, $f(x)$, applied to an 8-bit grayscale image. The
naive implementation would be to step through the image and for each pixel to evaluate the function. However, one may observe that no matter how complex the function,
it can evaluate to only one of 255 output values (corresponding to each unique input).
Thus, an alternate implementation would be to tabulate the function's result for each
possible input value, then to transform each pixel at runtime by looking up the stored
solution. Assuming that integer table lookups are efficient (they are), and that the rasterized image has more than 255 total pixels (it likely does), using a LUT will lead to a
significant speedup.

---

1. Lookup tables have been utilized to aid numerical computations since long before the invention of
modern computers. In the second century B.C., the Greek astronomer Hipparchus created a lookup table
that—albeit indirectly—provides a solution to the trigonometric sine operator (Toomer 1996).

All color operators that can be parameterized on a single input variable can be accelerated using 1D LUTs, including the brightness, gamma, and contrast operators. See Figure 24-2. By assigning a 1D LUT to each color channel individually, we can implement more sophisticated operations, such as color balancing. For those familiar with the Photoshop image-processing software, all "Curves" and "Levels" operations can be accelerated with 1D LUTs.

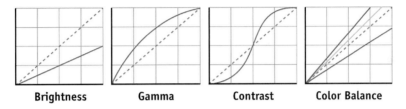

| Brightness | Gamma | Contrast | Color Balance |

Figure 24-2. A Variety of Simple Color Operators

Limitations of 1D LUTs

Unfortunately, many useful color operators cannot be parameterized on a single variable, and are thus impossible to implement using a single-dimensional LUT. For example, consider the "luminance operator" that converts colored pixels into their grayscale equivalent. Because each output value is derived as a weighted average of three input channels, one would be hard-pressed to express such an operator using a 1D LUT. All other operators that rely on such channel "cross talk" are equally inexpressible.

24.1.2 Three-Dimensional LUTs

Three-dimensional lookup tables offer the obvious solution to the inherent limitation of single-dimensional LUTs, allowing tabular data indexed on three independent parameters, as shown in Figure 24-3.

Whereas a 1D LUT requires only 4 elements to sample 4 locations per axis, the corresponding 3D LUT requires $4^3 = 64$ elements. Beware of this added dimensionality; 3D LUTs grow very quickly as a function of their linear sampling rate.[2] As a direct implication of smaller LUT sizes, high-quality interpolation takes on a greater significance for 3D LUTs, as opposed to the 1D realm, where simple interpolators are often practical.

---

2. To put the storage requirements into perspective, a $32 \times 32 \times 32$ LUT (a moderate size) necessitates 393 kB. A $256 \times 256 \times 256$ LUT requires 200 MB. Even if the GPU has such memory available, large 3D LUTs may quickly swamp the texturing cache, which will degrade performance. For real-time applications, think small!

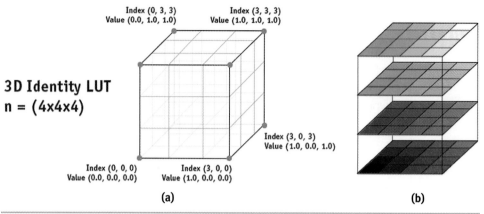

Index (0, 3, 3)
Value (0.0, 1.0, 1.0)

Index (3, 3, 3)
Value (1.0, 1.0, 1.0)

3D Identity LUT
n = (4x4x4)

Index (3, 0, 3)
Value (1.0, 0.0, 1.0)

Index (0, 0, 0)
Value (0.0, 0.0, 0.0)

Index (3, 0, 0)
Value (1.0, 0.0, 0.0)

(a)

(b)

Figure 24-3. A Three-Dimensional Lookup Table
The 3D LUT freely maps each input three-vector to an arbitrary output (a) and for our application is visualized as (b) the unique color for each lattice point over the unit cube. For those readers more familiar with the world of geometric processing, the 3D LUT can be conceptualized as the free-form lattice deformation (FFD) of the color space.

Complex color operators can be expressed using 3D LUTs, as completely arbitrary input-output mappings are allowed. For this reason, 3D LUTs have long been embraced by the colorimetry community and are one of the preferred tools in gamut mapping (Kang 1997). In fact, 3D LUTs are used within ICC profiles to model the complex device behaviors necessary for accurate color image reproduction (ICC 2004).

The majority of color operators are expressible using 3D LUTs. Simple operators (such as gamma, brightness, and contrast) are trivial to encode. More complex transforms, such as hue and saturation modifications, are also possible. Most important, the color operations typical of professional color-grading systems are expressible (such as the independent warping of user-specified sections of the color gamut). See Figure 24-4.

Limitations of 3D LUTs

Unfortunately, in real-world scenarios, not all color transforms are definable as direct input-output mappings. In the general case, 3D LUTs can express only those transforms that obey the following characteristics:

- A pixel's computation must be independent of the spatial image position. Color operators that are influenced by neighboring values, such as Bayesian-matting (Chuang et al. 2001) or garbage masks (Brinkman 1999), are not expressible in lookup-table form.

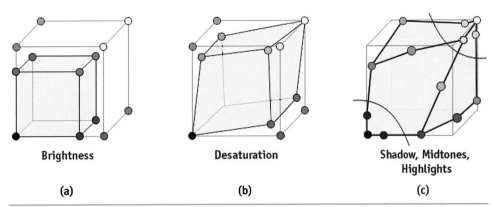

Figure 24-4. Simulating Color Transforms with Three-Dimensional Lookup Tables
Three-dimensional LUTs can simulate a variety of color transforms. Shown here are simple lattice visualizations corresponding to (a) a simple brightness operator; (b) a decrease in color saturation; and (c) the "arbitrary" manipulation of the shadows, midtones, and highlights color balance.

- The color transform must be reasonably continuous, as sparsely sampled data sets are ill suited to represent discontinuous transformations. If smoothly interpolating over the sampled transform grid yields unacceptable results, lookup tables are not the appropriate acceleration technique.

- The input color space must lie within a well-defined domain. An "analytically" defined brightness operator can generate valid results over the entire domain of real numbers. However, that same operator baked into a lookup table will be valid over only a limited domain (for example, perhaps only in the range [0,1]). Section 24.2.4 addresses ways to mitigate this issue.

24.1.3 Interpolation

Interpolation algorithms allow lookup tables to generate results when queried for values between sample points. The simplest method, *nearest-neighbor interpolation*, is to find and return the nearest table entry. Although this method is fast (requiring only a single lookup), it typically yields discontinuous results and is thus rarely utilized in image processing.

A more advanced interpolation algorithm is to compute the weighted average between the two bounding samples (in the case of 1D LUTs), based on the relative distance of the sample to its neighbors. Known as *linear interpolation*, this approach provides significantly smoother results than the nearest-neighbor scheme.

Linear interpolation is adapted to 3D data sets by successively applying 1D linear interpolation along each of the three axes (hence the designation *trilinear interpolation*). By generating intermediate results based on a weighted average of the eight corners of the bounding cube, this algorithm is typically sufficient for color processing, and it is commonly implemented in graphics hardware. Higher-order interpolation functions use progressively more samples in the reconstruction function, though at significantly higher computation costs. (Straightforward cubic interpolation requires $3^3 = 27$ texture lookups, but see Chapter 20 of this book, "Fast Third-Order Texture Filtering," for a technique that reduces this to 8 lookups.)

24.2 Implementation

Our approach is based on the assumption that it is cheap to trilinearly interpolate 3D textures. Whereas this is decidedly not true for software implementations, we can leverage the 3D texturing capabilities of modern GPUs to function as our color-correction engine.

24.2.1 Strategy for Mapping LUTs to the GPU

Most modern GPUs offer hardware-accelerated trilinear, 3D texture lookups (the interpolation unit was originally necessary for mipmapped, 2D texture lookups); thus, our algorithm becomes fairly trivial to implement.

First, we load our high-resolution image into a standard 2D texture. Next, we load our 3D color correction mapping as a 3D texture, being careful to enable trilinear filtering (in OpenGL this requires the texture magnification filter set to GL_LINEAR).

At runtime, we transform our input image by sampling the color in the normal fashion and then by performing a *dependent texture lookup* into the 3D texture (using the result of the 2D texture lookup as the 3D texture's input indices). The output of the 3D texture is our final, color-transformed result.

24.2.2 Cg Shader

The fragment shader code, shown in Listing 24-1, is almost as simple as you would expect. The efficiency of this approach is readily apparent, as the entire color-correction process is reduced to a single (3D) texture lookup.

Listing 24-1. Fragment Shader to Perform the 3D Texture Lookup

```
void main(in float2 sUV : TEXCOORD0,
    out half4 cOut : COLOR0,
    const uniform samplerRECT imagePlane,
    const uniform sampler3D lut,
    const uniform float3 lutSize)
{
    // Get the image color
    half3 rawColor = texRECT(imagePlane, sUV).rgb;

    // Compute the 3D LUT lookup scale/offset factor
    half3 scale = (lutSize - 1.0) / lutSize;
    half3 offset = 1.0 / (2.0 * lutSize);

    // ****** Apply 3D LUT color transform! **************
    // This is our dependent texture read; The 3D texture's
    // lookup coordinates are dependent on the
    // previous texture read's result
    cOut.rgb = tex3D(lut, scale * rawColor + offset);
}
```

Shader Analysis

The most common question is probably "Why are the scale and offset factors necessary?" The answer relates to the coordinate system that the texture-mapping hardware uses to sample from our LUT. Specifically, the hardware texture-sampling algorithms sample (by default) from one extreme of the data set to the other. Though this is entirely reasonable when texturing image data, it is not appropriate for sampling numerical data sets, because it introduces nonlinearities near the texture's edges, as shown in Figure 24-5. Thus, to properly interpolate our "data" image, we must query only the region between the outer sample's *centers*, according to the following equation:

$$\text{Adjusted sample coordinate} = (lutSize - 1.0)/lutSize \times oldCoord + 1.0/(2.0 \times lutSize)$$

Observe that as the size of the LUT grows large, the correction factor becomes negligible. For example, with a 4,096-entry lookup table (a common 1D LUT size), the scaling factor can be safely ignored, as the error is smaller than the precision of the half pixel format. However, for the small lattice sizes common to 3D LUTs, the effect is visually significant and cannot be ignored; uncorrected 8-bit scaling errors on a $32 \times 32 \times 32$ LUT are equivalent to clamping all data outside of [4..251]!

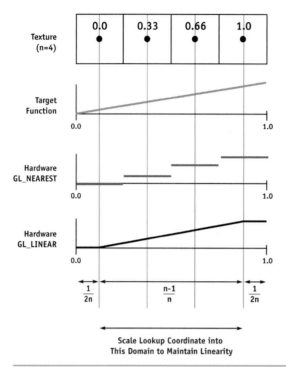

Figure 24-5. Problems Caused by Uncorrected Linear Interpolation

Left uncorrected, linear interpolation will sample between texels' outer edges, resulting in an unintended contrast boost. To maintain the linearity of the 3D texture lookup, it is necessary to modify the lookup coordinates to sample only the range subtended by the texels' centers.

Shader Optimization

This code has obvious acceleration opportunities. First, as the scale and offset factors are constant across the image, they can be computed once and passed in as constants. (Or even better, they can be directly compiled into the fragment shader.) Second, it is good practice to use the smallest LUT that meets your needs (but no smaller). For "primary grading" color corrections, where one only modifies the color of the primaries (RGB) and secondaries (CMY), a $2 \times 2 \times 2$ table will suffice! Finally, for consumer-grade applications, an integer texture format may suffice (of course, still with trilinear interpolation enabled). But be aware that 8 bits is not sufficient to prevent banding in LUT color transforms (Blinn 1998).

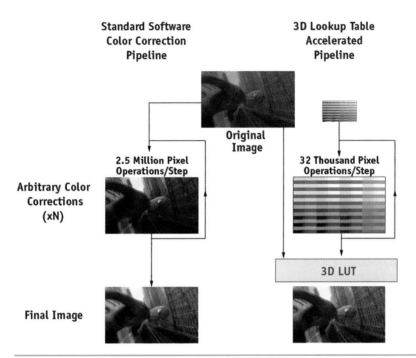

Standard Software Color Correction Pipeline

3D Lookup Table Accelerated Pipeline

Original Image

2.5 Million Pixel Operations/Step

Arbitrary Color Corrections (xN)

32 Thousand Pixel Operations/Step

3D LUT

Final Image

Figure 24-6. Comparing Color-Correction Pipelines

A traditional software color-correction pipeline can be used as the basis for hardware acceleration by sending the low-resolution, 3D LUT "image" down the processing chain. As a final step, the concatenated 3D color transform is applied on the GPU to the high-resolution imagery. ("SPIDER-MAN 2," Motion Picture © 2004 Columbia Pictures Industries, Inc. All Rights Reserved. Spider-Man Character ® & © 2004 Marvel Characters, Inc. All Rights Reserved. Courtesy of Columbia Pictures.)

24.2.3 System Integration

We have thus far not addressed *how* one goes about generating the 3D LUTs—and for good reason. By treating our 3D identity lookup table as a 2D proxy image for the final correction, no special software is required! Simply pass the 3D LUT "image" through an arbitrary color-correction process, then as a final step use the resulting LUT data set to warp the higher-resolution imagery on the GPU. See Figure 24-6. In fact, an unlimited number of color operators can be applied in a row (provided that they obey the requirements listed in Section 24.1.2). It is also useful to observe that as our 3D LUT "image" is typically very small (a $32 \times 32 \times 32$ LUT is equivalent to 256×128 pixels), you can evaluate sophisticated color transforms and still expect interactive performance.

We summarize our 3D LUT acceleration framework as follows:

1. Generate (and cache) the 3D lattice as a 2D image, preferably in the same byte order as the GPU will expect in step 3.

2. Apply arbitrary color correction to this lattice image (using a standard color-correction pipeline), treating the 3D lattice image as a proxy for the final color correction you wish to apply.

3. Load both the high-resolution image and the 3D texture to the GPU.

4. Draw source imagery using the fragment shader in Listing 24-1.

The potential speedups of this optimization are enormous. In our experience, we can often substitute the full image processing (2048×1556 pixels) with a lattice of only $32 \times 32 \times 32$ (256×128 pixels). Assuming the application of the LUT has low overhead (which is definitely the case on modern hardware), this corresponds to a speedup of approximately 100 times! Furthermore, in video playback applications, the LUT transform does not need to be recomputed, and can be applied to each subsequent frame at essentially no cost.

24.2.4 Extending 3D LUTs for Use with High-Dynamic-Range Imagery

High-dynamic-range (HDR) data breaks one of our primary assumptions in the use of lookup tables, that of the limited input domain.

Clamping

We cannot create a tabular form of a color transform if we do not first define the bounds of the table. We thus must choose minimum and maximum values to represent in the lookup table. The subtlety is that if we define a maximum that is too low, then we will unnecessarily clamp our data. However, if we define a maximum that is too high, then we will needlessly throw away table precision. (Which means our LUT sampling will be insufficient to re-create all but the smoothest of color transforms.)

Defining color-space minimums of less than zero is occasionally useful, particularly when color renderings can result in out-of-gamut colors, or when filters with negative lobes have been applied. However, for the majority of users, the transform floor can be safely pinned to zero.

Choosing a color-space ceiling is not too difficult, as HDR spaces are *rarely* completely unconstrained.[3] More often than not, even color spaces defined as "high-dynamic"

---

3. One notable exception is color spaces used to encode physically derived luminance values, such as those used by the Radiance rendering package (Larson and Shakespeare 1998).

(having pixel values greater than one) often have enforceable ceilings dictated for other reasons. For example, in linear color spaces directly derived from the Cineon (log) negative specification (Kennel and Snider 1993), the maximum defined value is approximately 13.5.[4] Even in color space not tied directly to film densities, allowing for completely unconstrained highlights wreaks havoc with filter kernel sizes. In the majority of practical compositing situations, a reasonable maximum does exist—just know your data sets and use your best judgment.

Nonuniformly Sampled Lattices

Once we have picked a ceiling and a floor for the range we wish to sample, we still have the issue of sample distribution. Say we have set our ceiling at a pixel value of 100.0. Dividing this into equally sampled regions for a $32 \times 32 \times 32$ LUT yields a cell size of about 3. Assuming a reasonable exposure transform, almost all perceptually significant results are going to be compressed into the few lowest cells, wasting the majority of our data set.

We thus want to place our samples in the most visually significant locations, which typically occur closer to the dark end of the gamut. We achieve this effect by wrapping our 3D lookup-table transform with a matched pair of 1D "shaper" LUTs, as shown in Figure 24-7. The ideal shaper LUT maps the input HDR color space to a normalized, perceptually uniform color space.[5] The 3D LUT is then applied normally (though during its computation, this 1D transform must be accounted for). Finally, the image is mapped through the inverse of the original 1D LUT, "unwrapping" the pixel data back into their original dynamic range.

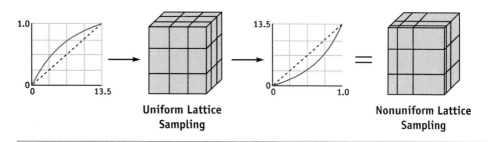

Uniform Lattice Sampling

Nonuniform Lattice Sampling

Figure 24-7. Creating a Nonuniform Lattice Sampling
A nonuniform sampling lattice is often desirable when working with high-dynamic-range color spaces, providing more samples in perceptually relevant regions of the gamut.

---

4. When one assumes a linear light response across the entire negative's dynamic range, the maximum linear value is $2^{(1023-685)/90}$.

5. In a perceptually uniform color space, code values are directly proportional to the perceived color. In our experience, it is often sufficient to independently map each channel of the HDR color space to values approximating the L* component of the CIE 1976 L*a*b* color space (Wyszecki and Stiles 1982).

24.3 Conclusion

We have presented a production-ready algorithm that allows the real-time color processing of high-resolution imagery, offering speedup of greater than 100 times on common applications. This technique is independent of both the number of color operators applied and the underlying color transform complexity. It is our hope that these ideas will enable real-time, sophisticated color corrections to become more commonplace, both in the visual effects industry as well as in consumer applications.

24.4 References

Bjorke, Kevin. 2004. "Color Controls." In *GPU Gems*, edited by Randima Fernando, pp. 363–373. Addison-Wesley. *This chapter presents a general overview of color correction on the GPU. Also outlines the use of 1D LUTs in color correction.*

Blinn, Jim. 1998. *Jim Blinn's Corner: Dirty Pixels*. Morgan Kaufmann. *Contains an excellent discussion of quantization errors inherent in integer color spaces.*

Brinkman, Ron. 1999. *The Art and Science of Digital Compositing*. Morgan Kaufmann. *A primer on basic compositing and image processing.*

Chuang, Yung-Yu, Brian Curless, David H. Salesin, and Richard Szeliski. 2001. "A Bayesian Approach to Digital Matting." In *Proceedings of IEEE Computer Vision and Pattern Recognition (CVPR 2001)* 2, pp. 264–271.

ICC. 2004. International Color Consortium Specification ICC.1:2004-04. Available online at **http://www.color.org**. *ICC profiles leverage 3D LUTs to encode acquisition and display device performance characteristics.*

Kang, Henry. 1997. *Color Technology for Electronic Imaging Devices*. SPIE. *Chapter 4 contains information on 3D LUTs in color applications, including additional interpolation types.*

Kennel, Glenn, and David Snider. 1993. "Gray-Scale Transformations of Digital Film Data for Display, Conversion, and Film Recording." *SMPTE Journal* 103, pp. 1109–1119.

Larson, Greg W., and Rob A. Shakespeare. 1998. *Rendering with Radiance: The Art and Science of Lighting Visualization*. Morgan Kaufmann.

Toomer, G. J. 1996. "Trigonometry." In *Oxford Classical Dictionary*, 3rd ed. Oxford.

Wyszecki, G., and W. S. Stiles. 1982. *Color Science: Concepts and Methods, Quantitative Data and Formulae*, 2nd ed. Wiley.

Chapter 25

GPU Image Processing in Apple's Motion

Pete Warden
Apple Computer

In this chapter I cover some of the challenges we faced, the solutions we found, and the lessons we learned while writing Motion. In here is everything we wish we had known when we started! The speed improvement over CPU-based rendering provided by pixel shaders was amazing, often ten to twenty times faster, but being on the frontier meant facing a steep hill to climb.

We needed to implement complex image-processing operations, so we needed GPUs that were able to run flexible and general-purpose pixel shaders. At the time we wrote Motion, in 2003 and early 2004, there were two families of graphics cards able to do this on the Mac: the ATI R3xx series and the NVIDIA NV34. Today newer GPUs like the NVIDIA GeForce 6 Series are available for the Apple platform. I concentrate on the R3xx and NV34 when I'm discussing implementation details, but most points may still apply to more recent hardware. The biggest differences in new hardware are much-increased resource limits, the advent of floating-point pixel support, and higher performance.

25.1 Design

GPUs are able to solve some problems much faster than CPUs can because they're highly specialized, can do many operations in parallel, and have very high speed parallel memory access. These capabilities come at a cost: GPUs trade off flexibility for speed.

There are lots of problems that they just can't tackle, and it's vital to plan your application knowing their strengths and weaknesses.

25.1.1 Loves and Loathings

Some kinds of image-processing operations map well onto GPUs, and some are awkward or impossible to write in a shader. Here I describe some of these types, and how easy (or difficult) we found them to port to the GPU.

Image In, Image Out

Algorithms that take in one or more input images and output a single output image map to the GPU's capabilities in a very direct manner, giving a good chance of getting peak performance. Of course, these algorithms are very common in image processing, especially the kind needed by graphic design applications.

Image In, Statistics Out

Algorithms that take an input image and output some kind of measurement are more difficult to implement on the GPU. A good example is trying to count how many pixels in an image have different color values, creating a histogram. On the CPU this is simple: we just loop through all the image's pixels and increment an entry in an array, choosing the entry based on the color value of each pixel. In pseudocode:

```
for <all pixels>
    arrayIndex = currentPixel.luminance;
    histogram[ arrayIndex ] += 1;
```

The problem with doing this in a pixel shader is that your result has to be written to a fixed location; you can't do the step where you choose which histogram entry to increment based on the pixel's luminance.

GPUs can flexibly *gather* inputs from many locations, based on runtime choices, but cannot as easily *scatter* their output to different places, based on the input data.

Almost all algorithms that output statistics or measurements need a scattering step, which makes it hard to write a good GPU implementation of them. See Chapter 32 of this book, "GPU Computation Strategies and Tips," for more information about implementing scatter algorithms on the GPU.

Color Transformations

Operations that take in a single pixel's color, apply some function to it, and output the result as a new color are great candidates for a GPU implementation. Often, simple transformations such as gamma correction or brightness adjustments can be calculated directly using a few arithmetic instructions in a pixel shader. More-involved transformations can be precalculated on the CPU and passed in as lookup tables. (See also Chapter 24, "Using Lookup Tables to Accelerate Color Transformations.")

Independent Neighborhood Operations

GPUs are well suited to reading in multiple pixels around a base position and combining them to get an output value. There may be limits on how many pixels can be combined in a single shader, but we can work around this by splitting the operation into several shaders and running multiple passes, with the intermediate results written out to OpenGL pixel buffers (pbuffers) and passed in as textures to following passes. We've had a lot of success implementing convolution filters such as edge detection and Gaussian blurring using this approach.

Sequential Neighborhood Operations

Any algorithm that needs to visit the pixels in an image in a particular order, using results from previous pixels in the same pass, won't work on a GPU. The results must be written to a texture. There's no way to tell in what order the pixels will be processed, and no way to access the result from any other pixel within the same pass. GPUs get some of their speed from doing many operations in parallel; to be able to do this, the programming model doesn't allow shaders that depend on this sort of ordering.

One example of an algorithm that doesn't translate well to the GPU is the sliding boxcar method for doing a box filter. It relies on traveling across rows and down columns, adding or subtracting from a running total to get its result at each pixel. There's no way to keep such a total in a shader, nor to ensure the rows and columns are visited in the right order.

Less obviously, per-pixel random-number generators can be tricky to implement, because they usually rely on storing a seed value that is updated every time a random value is fetched, and that seed value cannot be stored between pixels in a shader.

Conditional Execution

Any operation that contained more than a few branches had trouble fitting on a lot of the hardware we were developing on.[1] Shader support did not include any branch or jump instructions, and the only support at all for anything conditional was instructions that allowed a comparison value to decide which of two inputs gets placed into a result. This means calculating both possible results before doing the comparison, which soon requires a very long program for even a mildly complex decision tree.

---

1. Hardware introduced since the original *GPU Gems*, such as GeForce 6 Series/NV4X-class GPUs, now permits far more flexible branching in the pixel and vertex shading units.

25.1.2 Pick a Language

After evaluating a number of high-level GPU programming languages—including Cg, GLSL, HLSL, Direct3D's pixel shaders, and vendor-specific assembly languages—we chose to use OpenGL's low-level `ARB_fragment_program` extension for Motion.

The advantages of a C-like high-level language are clear: the learning curve is less steep, programs are easier to maintain, the compiler is able to apply high-level optimizations, and programs can be ported easily to different hardware.

It was still early in the evolution of the technology, however, and early versions of high-level compilers were not as mature as modern CPU compilers. Some were available on only a limited range of platforms at the time. These issues are easing as the language technology matures, but at the time of writing Motion, they were still unresolved.

The flaws of writing in an assembler-like language are equally well known: they're tough to learn, fiddly to build programs in, and tricky to debug and maintain. They do have some hidden strengths, though. Importantly for us, it was a lot easier to understand and work around the limits of specific GPUs when dealing with our shaders' low-level instructions than it would have been in a high-level language hiding those sorts of implementation details. Understanding the strengths and weaknesses of the GPUs through the instruction set also helped us to change our algorithms to improve performance.

ARB_fragment_program

We were happy with our choice of `ARB_fragment_program` for our shaders. We had solid support from both ATI and NVIDIA, we didn't suffer any big delays due to implementation bugs, and we learned a lot about how the GPUs worked. As expected, debugging was painful, but there were some other pleasant surprises.

The instruction set is quite elegant and orthogonal, and it mapped very well to many of the image-processing operations we were tackling. In quite a few cases, the GPU version was even easier to write than the C version! The functional style forced on us by the lack of conditional execution instructions in `ARB_fragment_program` also led to some unusual and fruitful approaches to porting over our CPU algorithms. Of course, more recent GPUs such as the GeForce 6 Series do support conditional execution.

25.1.3 CPU Fallback

There are going to be systems around for some time that lack GPUs capable of running the kind of shaders you need to do image processing. If you're adding GPU processing to an existing CPU-based program, then you can just disable the shaders and use the existing code on those systems. For an application built primarily for shader-capable hardware that chooses to support computers without GPUs, you need to decide how to handle running on these legacy systems.

There are two approaches to building a CPU fallback: you can write separate CPU versions of all your algorithms, or you can write a GPU emulator that will run shaders on the CPU.

Having independent CPU versions of your algorithms is extremely useful when implementing and debugging the GPU versions. We strongly recommend that you start off with this sort of reference implementation as a development aid; it's invaluable when you need to tell if a bug is a flaw in the basic algorithm or a problem in the shader implementation. The biggest drawback with this approach is the time needed to implement and maintain parallel versions of all your operations.

Writing a GPU emulator is beyond the scope of this chapter, but it's worth noting that image processing generally needs only a small subset of a GPU's features emulated, and that low-level shader languages use vector instructions that map well to the AltiVec and SSE instruction sets.

For Motion, we chose to support only GPU-capable hardware, because that included the majority of our target market of video professionals, and doing so let us concentrate our development time on expanding the application's capabilities.

25.2 Implementation

As we built Motion, we ran into a number of practical issues implementing our image-processing algorithms as shaders.

25.2.1 GPU Resource Limits

On ATI R3xx cards, the biggest difficulties were caused by the restrictions under which `ARB_fragment_program` shaders could actually be run. The GPU programs could have no more than 64 arithmetic and 32 texture-access instructions. The NVIDIA NV34 had a much higher limit of 1,024 total instructions. In practice, we found that ATI's instruction limits were not much of a problem for most of the operations we needed, though we had to spend time reducing the instruction count on a few of our more complex shaders.

Things were slightly complicated by instructions that mapped to multiple native assembly instructions on the GPU. For example, the SIN instruction on ATI cards executed a multiple-instruction Taylor series, rather than a single-instruction operation, as the NV34 does (which actually produces a higher-precision result than the Taylor series).

Far more serious for us was the limit of four levels of texture indirection on ATI GPUs. The ARB_fragment_program specification explains in detail what defines a level of texture indirection, but for practical purposes it limits you to a chain four-deep of dependent texture reads. A dependent texture read uses the results of a previous texture read or arithmetic instruction for its coordinates. Here's a simple example:

```
!!ARBfp1.0
TEMP inputColor, tableResult;

# Read the input pixel; first level of indirection
TEX inputColor, fragment.texcoord[0], texture[0], 2D;

# Look up a result from a table; second level of indirection
TEX tableResult, inputColor, texture[1], 3D;

# Look up the output in a palette texture; third level of indirection
TEX result.color, tableResult, texture[2], 1D;

END
```

This is an example of a typical operation we'd want to do, and it's already just one level away from the limit.

Avoiding texture indirections became a major headache as we wrote our shaders. One useful approach was moving as many calculations as possible to the vertex level, because reads using interpolated vertex components or program constants do not trigger an indirection. Because we hit the indirection limit more often than we ran out of instructions, we got into the habit of burning up arithmetic instructions to do calculations on the fly rather than reading them from precalculated tables stored in textures. As a last resort, we also broke up algorithms into multiple passes, passing intermediate results between the shader stages in pbuffers. We preferred to avoid this, though, as the pbuffers available on our platform were normally 8-bit-per-channel rather than the internal shader precision of an IEEE 32-bit float on NVIDIA GPUs, or 24-bit floating point on ATI GPUs. Running multiple passes also meant a performance loss.

25.2.2 Division by Zero

The NV34 has generous instruction limits, and no cap on levels of texture indirection, but its handling of divisions by zero forced us to rewrite some of our shaders.

When an R3xx hits an RCP or RSQ instruction with an input of zero, it sets the result to be a very large number. The NV34 correctly follows the IEEE floating-point standard in these situations and outputs a "not a number" (NaN) value, representing either positive or negative infinity, depending on the sign of the numerator. The big difference between this NaN and ATI's big number is that the NaN causes the result of any math instruction it's used in to also become a NaN.

In our specific shaders, we could actually capitalize on the non-IEEE-compliant behavior, because where we had divisions by zero, they were followed by later multiplications by zero. A common example was taking a premultiplied color input, dividing the color channels by alpha to do some calculations in straight color space, and then multiplying by that same input alpha to put the result back in premultiplied space. On an R3xx, when the alpha value was zero, the output red, green, and blue channels would also be zero, which is what we desired. A NaN, however, would propagate to the output, where it would be stored as pure white in the frame buffer, which was undesirable to say the least.

Our solution was to ensure that those instructions never get passed a denominator of zero, at the cost of a few extra instructions. The general idea was to nudge the denominator a very small amount away from zero, by adding a small epsilon value if it was positive:

```
CMP epsilonFudge, denominator.x, 0, 0.00001;
ADD denominator.x, denominator.x, epsilonFudge;
RCP reciprocal.x, denominator.x;
```

This adds two extra instructions per division, but if you know the denominator will never be negative—for example, when it's been read from an 8-bit texture—you can skip the comparison like this:

```
ADD denominator.x, denominator.x, 0.00001;
RCP reciprocal.x, denominator.x;
```

Though this may look as if it sacrifices precision, the epsilon value is so small that in practice it gets lost in the underflow when added to anything but numbers very close to zero.

25.2.3 Loss of Vertex Components

As we mentioned earlier, it can be very useful to pass in vertex components interpolated across a quad into a fragment program. There are eight sets of texture coordinates available to shaders in OpenGL, but we found we could access only the first four of these on some GPUs when using OpenGL's "old-style" fixed-function vertex pipeline. Inserting a simple vertex program that simply passed through all eight coordinates solved the problem.

25.2.4 Bilinear Filtering

The basic way to do image processing using a graphics card is to draw a screen-aligned quad with the image texture mapped onto it, into a frame buffer that will hold the output image. For our compositing package, we often wanted to apply simple geometric transformations to our images, moving, scaling, or rotating them. This is easy to do on a GPU: you just need to transform a quad's vertices and pass them on to the rasterizer. These transforms can be combined with other operations implemented in fragment programs, for no extra cost. To get decent output quality, we used bilinear filtering on the input image, which also comes for free. Because bilinear filtering was so useful and had no performance cost, we used it everywhere by default. This led to two of our trickiest problems: softening and alpha fringes.

Softening

We noticed a subtle blurring or softening of images that we were drawing with no transformations—a problem that got worse as an image went through more stages of the render pipeline. We spent some time making sure that we were setting up our vertex positions and texture coordinates correctly, but it turned out to be caused by a precision problem in the way that graphics hardware rasterizes primitives. Figure 25-1 illustrates the situation.

The texture coordinates for each pixel inside a quad are calculated based on that pixel's distance from each vertex and the texture coordinates that have been set at each vertex. Because this calculation is done for each pixel drawn, everything possible is done to speed it up. Unfortunately for us, some of the optimizations used in graphics hardware trade accuracy for speed in ways that affect us a lot more than they do 3D scene rendering. When rendering scenes, all primitives will be transformed and distorted anyway, so precision errors in texture mapping that are much less than a pixel in size will not be noticeable, as long as the errors are consistent.

But we were trying to draw quads where all the pixels in the input texture were drawn into exactly the same position in the output buffer. Errors of even a fraction of a pixel away from a texel center made the bilinear filtering bleed parts of neighboring pixels

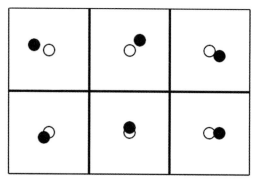

○ Correct Texture Sample Position

● Actual Texture Sample Position

Figure 25-1. Texture Sample Position
There are small discrepancies between the expected texture sample position and the texture sample position generated by the graphics hardware.

into the result, causing the softening we were seeing. The amount of error depended on the way that a specific GPU implemented its texture coordinate calculations (for example, we saw much smaller errors on the NV34 than on ATI GPUs, because the NV34 has many more bits of subpixel precision). See Figure 25-2.

We solved this problem in most cases by switching to nearest-neighborhood filtering where we knew we wanted one-to-one mapping. Because the errors were much less than 1 pixel wide, this produced the result we were after. The errors seemed to grow with the size of the quad, so one method we worked on was splitting a large quad into a grid of much smaller quads, doing the texture coordinate interpolation precisely on the CPU, and then storing the values into the vertices of this grid. This approach greatly reduced the error.

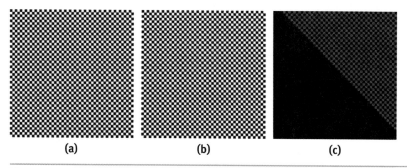

(a)   (b)   (c)

Figure 25-2. A 2×2-Pixel Checkerboard Pattern
(a) Base pattern. (b) Part of the same pattern as shown on the R300. (c) Amplified difference image showing subpixel filtering error.

Alpha Fringes

The other bilinear filtering problem we hit was the dark fringes we were seeing around the alpha edges of our rendered objects, wherever any transformation caused the filtering to kick in. See Figure 25-3 for an example.

Our pipeline was based on rendering to and from pbuffer textures stored in the non-premultiplied alpha format, and this turned out to be the root of our problem. To see what was happening, look at the white, fully opaque pixel surrounded by a sea of completely transparent pixels in Figure 25-4. (Because the transparent pixels have zero alpha values and this is a straight alpha texture, it shouldn't matter what we put in their color channels, so I've set them up as black.)

Bilinear filtering works by taking the four closest pixels and calculating a result by mixing them together in different proportions. Figure 25-5 shows the values you get when you draw this texture scaled up by a factor of three using bilinear filtering, and Figure 25-6 shows what happens when you composite Figure 25-5 on top of another image using the Over operator.

Bilinear interpolation deals with all channels separately and mixes in the color of a fully transparent pixel anywhere there's a fully or partially opaque pixel with a zero-alpha neighbor. In our case, this resulted in a gray fringe when it was blended, because the black was mixed in from the fully transparent pixels.

Dark Fringe from Alpha ⎯⎯⎯⎯⎯⎯➤

Figure 25-3. Fringing Using Bilinear Filtering
A scaled-up straight alpha image.

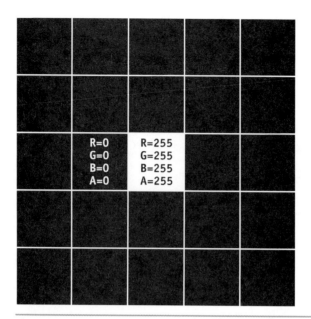

Figure 25-4. A White, Fully Opaque Pixel Surrounded by Transparent Pixels

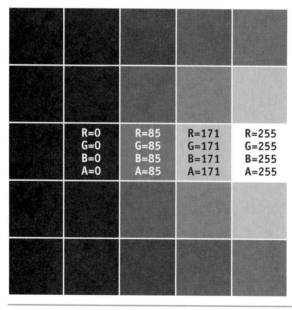

Figure 25-5. A Portion of the Result After Scaling Up the Texture Three Times with Bilinear Filtering

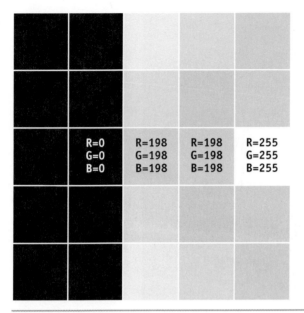

R=0	R=198	R=198	R=255
G=0	G=198	G=198	G=255
B=0	B=198	B=198	B=255

Figure 25-6. Compositing Figure 25-5 with the Over Operator

The usual solution to this is to ensure that zero-alpha pixels with opaque neighbors have sensible values in their color channels. This works well in a 3D-modeling context: content creators can manually fix their textures to fit within this constraint, or the textures can be run through an automated process to set sensible values, as part of the normal texture-loading pipeline.

When we're doing image processing for compositing, though, texture creation is a much more dynamic process; there's no way to intervene manually, and running a fix-up pass on each intermediate texture would be a big hit on performance. One alternative we considered was hand-rolling our own bilinear filtering in a pixel shader and discarding the influence of any fully transparent pixels. This would mean replacing every texture read with four reads wherever we wanted to use bilinear filtering, and extra arithmetic instructions to do the filtering. We ruled out this approach as impractical.

Our eventual solution was to switch our pipeline over to using textures stored in the premultiplied alpha, or associated alpha, format. Bilinear filtering using premultiplied colors doesn't suffer from the fringing problem. See Figure 25-7.

This is also the format that colors need to be in when calculating blurs, though most color-correction operations need to happen in straight-alpha color space. This pipeline

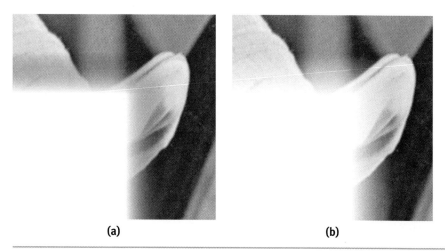

(a)   (b)

Figure 25-7. Using Premultiplied Format to Eliminate Dark Fringing
(a) Dark fringing around a composited object using bilinear filtering. (b) Dark fringing eliminated by using a premultiplied image representation.

change was disruptive because it happened late in development, but once everything had settled down, it worked well for us. Converting between the two color spaces in our shaders when we needed to wasn't difficult, though the division-by-zero differences discussed earlier did complicate things.

25.2.5 High-Precision Storage

Motion uses mostly 8-bit-per-channel images in its pipeline, but there were some places where more precision was needed. We implemented motion blur using an accumulation buffer algorithm, and the banding was unacceptable when using an 8-bit buffer.

At the time of writing, R3xx GPUs supported 16- and 32-bit-per-channel floating-point formats, so all we needed to do was request and create a 16-bit pbuffer. It was surprisingly easy to switch over our render pipeline to run at higher precisions; doing the same in a CPU image-processing pipeline is a lot more work. There are some restrictions on blending and filtering with high-precision pbuffers, but we were able to double-buffer two pbuffers to emulate the additive blending needed for motion blur.[2]

---

2. Newer GPUs such as GeForce 6 Series GPUs now support blending and filtering directly on 16-bit floating-point buffers.

At the time we wrote Motion, the NV34 Mac drivers exposed support for only 8-bit-per-channel textures, so we needed an alternative implementation of motion blur that didn't use the floating-point formats. The flexibility of pixel shaders came in handy, as it enabled us to emulate a 16-bit-per-channel fixed-point pbuffer using two 8-bit textures. The accumulation buffer needed to sum up to 256 8-bit samples, so we chose to use an 8.8 fixed-point format, packing the whole number and fractional parts of each color channel into an 8-bit channel in the pbuffer, so that each color channel needed two channels in the stored texture.

Packing the value into two channels meant dividing the original value by 256, to get the whole-number part into a range where it wouldn't get clipped, and taking the modulo of the value with 1, to get the fractional part to store:

```
MUL output.x, value.x, reciprocalOf256;
FRC output.y, value.x;
```

Reconstructing the packed value meant multiplying the whole-number part stored in one channel by 256 and adding it to the fractional part to get the original value.

```
MAD value.x, input.x, 256, input.y;
```

Implementing the accumulation buffer algorithm took two shader passes: one dealing with the red and green channels, the other with the blue and alpha, because a shader then could output its results to only one buffer at a time, and each buffer could hold only two channels.

25.3 Debugging

We spent a lot of time trying to figure out why our shaders weren't working. There are some debugging tools that work with `ARB_fragment_program` shaders—notably Apple's Shader Builder and the open source ShaderSmith project—but there was nothing available that would let us debug our GPU programs as they ran within our application. We had to fall back to some old-fashioned techniques to pry open the black box of the GPU.

Syntax errors were easiest to track down: invalid programs give a white output when they're used, just like using invalid textures. When you first load a program, calling `glGetString(GL_PROGRAM_ERROR_STRING)` will return a message describing any syntax error that was found.

In theory, detecting when a program has too many instructions or levels of texture indirection should just need the following call:

```
glGetProgramivARB(GL_fragment_program_ARB,
                  GL_PROGRAM_UNDER_NATIVE_LIMITS_ARB,
                  &isUnderNativeLimits)
```

In practice, this didn't always detect when such a limit was hit, and we learned to recognize the completely black output we'd get when we went over limits on ATI GPUs. We found that the best way to confirm we had a limit problem and not a calculation error was to put a `MOV result.color, { 1, 1, 0, 1 }` instruction at the end of the shader. If the output became yellow, then the shader was actually executing, but if it remained black, then the program was not executing because it was over the GPU's limits.

To understand what limit we were hitting, we could comment out instructions and run the program again. Eventually, after we cut enough instructions, we'd see yellow. The type of instructions that were cut last would tell us which limit we had hit.

The nastiest errors to track down were mistakes in our logic or math, because we really needed to see the inner workings of the shader while it was running to understand what was going wrong. We found that the best way to start debugging this sort of problem was to have a simple CPU version of the algorithm that we knew was working; then we would step through the shader instruction by instruction, comparing by eye each instruction with that of the equivalent stage in the CPU implementation.

When this sort of inspection doesn't work, there's only one way to get information out of a shader: by writing it to the frame buffer. First you need to comment out the final output instruction and, instead, store some intermediate value you're interested in. You may need to scale this value so that it's in the 0–1 range storable in a normal buffer. You can then use `glReadPixels()` to retrieve the exact values, but often the rough color shown on screen is enough to help figure out what's happening.

If something's really baffling, try it on different GPUs, to make sure that the problem isn't caused by differences in the vendors' implementations.

25.4 Conclusion

Trying to use hardware designed for games to do high-quality image processing was both frustrating and rewarding for us. The speed of the GPU didn't just help us to convert existing algorithms; it also inspired us to experiment with new ideas. The ability to see our results instantly, combined with the convenience of reloading shaders while the application was running, gave us a fantastic laboratory in which to play with images.

25.5 References

ARB_fragment_program Specification. *Not light reading, but Table X.5 has a good summary of all instructions, and Section 3.11.5 has full explanations of how each one works.* **http://oss.sgi.com/projects/ogl-sample/registry/ARB/fragment_program.txt**

Apple's OpenGL Web Site. *Lots of developer information and some great tools.* **http://developer.apple.com/graphicsimaging/opengl/**

GPGPU Web Site. *News and links to current research and tools.* **http://www.gpgpu.org/**

My thanks to the Apple OpenGL and Core Imaging teams; to ATI and NVIDIA for making all this possible; to all the Motion team; and in particular to Tim Connolly and Richard Salvador, who generously shared their expertise.

Chapter 26

Implementing Improved Perlin Noise

Simon Green
NVIDIA Corporation

This chapter follows up on Ken Perlin's chapter in *GPU Gems*, "Implementing Improved Perlin Noise" (Perlin 2004). Whereas Ken's chapter discussed how to implement fast approximations to procedural noise using 3D textures, here we describe a working GPU implementation of the improved noise algorithm in both Microsoft Direct 3D Effects (FX) and CgFX syntax that exactly matches the reference CPU implementation.

26.1 Random but Smooth

Noise is an important building block for adding natural-looking variety to procedural textures. In the real world, nothing is perfectly uniform, and noise provides a controlled way of adding this randomness to your shaders.

The noise function has several important characteristics:

- It produces a repeatable pseudorandom value for each input position.
- It has a known range (usually $[-1, 1]$).
- It has band-limited spatial frequency (that is, it is smooth).
- It doesn't show obvious repeating patterns.
- Its spatial frequency is invariant under translation.

Perlin's improved noise algorithm meets all these requirements (Perlin 2002). We now go on to explain how it can be implemented on the GPU.

26.2 Storage vs. Computation

Procedural noise is typically implemented in today's shaders using precomputed 3D textures. Implementing noise directly in the pixel shader has several advantages over this approach:

- It requires less texture memory.
- The period is large (that is, the pattern doesn't repeat as often).
- The results match existing CPU implementations exactly.
- It allows four-dimensional noise, which is useful for 3D effects with animation. (Current hardware doesn't support 4D textures.)
- The interpolation used is higher quality than what is available with hardware texture filtering, which results in smoother-looking noise.

Figure 26-1a shows the result of using a 3D texture to render an object with noise. Note the artifacts due to linear interpolation being used for texture map filtering. In contrast, the image in Figure 26-1b, which shows the result of using the procedural approach described in this chapter, is substantially better.

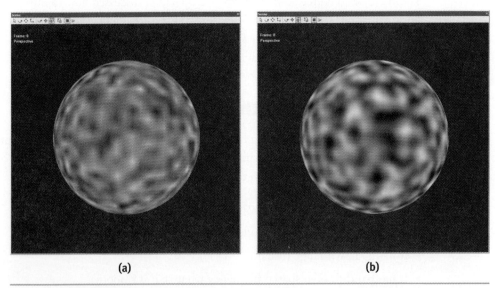

(a)   (b)

Figure 26-1. 3D Noise
(a) Generated using a small precomputed 3D texture. Note the linear filtering artifacts.
(b) Generated using the improved pixel shader noise algorithm.

The obvious disadvantage of this approach is that it is more computationally expensive. This is largely because we have to perform the interpolation in the shader, and are not taking advantage of the texture-filtering hardware present in the GPU. The optimized implementation of 3D noise compiles to around 50 Pixel Shader 2.0 instructions using the latest compilers; fortunately, this doesn't pose a challenge for current high-end GPUs.

26.3 Implementation Details

Perlin's noise algorithm consists of two main stages.

The first stage generates a repeatable pseudorandom value for every integer (x, y, z) position in 3D space. This can be achieved in several ways, but Perlin's algorithm uses a hash function. The hash function is based on a permutation table that contains the integers from 0 to 255 in random order. (This table can be standardized between implementations so that they produce the same results.) First the table is indexed based on the x coordinate of the position. Then the y coordinate is added to the value at this position in the table, and the result is used to look up in the table again. After this process is repeated for the z coordinate, the result is a pseudorandom integer for every possible (x, y, z) position.

In the second stage of the algorithm, this pseudorandom integer is used to index into a table of 3D gradient vectors. In the "improved" algorithm, only eight different gradients are used. A scalar value is calculated by taking the dot product between the gradient and the fractional position within the noise space. The final value is obtained by interpolating between the noise values for each of the neighboring eight points in space.

The CPU implementation of Perlin's improved noise algorithm stores the permutation and gradient tables in arrays. Pixel shaders do not currently support indexing into constant memory, so instead we store these tables in textures and use texture lookups to access them. The texture addressing is set to wrap (or repeat) mode, so we don't have to worry about extending the tables to avoid indexing past the end of the array, as is done in the CPU implementation. Listing 26-1 shows how these textures can be initialized in an FX file.

One of the most useful features of the Microsoft Direct 3D Effects and CgFX runtimes is a virtual machine that can be used to procedurally generate textures from functions. We use this feature to build the permutation and gradient textures from the same data given in the reference implementation. If you are using another shading language, such as the OpenGL Shading Language, it should be trivial to include this code in your application instead.

Listing 26-1. Source Code for Initializing the Permutation Texture for Noise

```
// permutation table
static int permutation[] = {
  151, /* 254 values elided . . . */, 180
};

// Generate permutation and gradient textures using CPU runtime
texture permTexture
<
  string texturetype = "2D";
  string format = "l8";
  string function = "GeneratePermTexture";
  int width = 256, height = 1;
>;

float4 GeneratePermTexture(float p : POSITION) : COLOR
{
  return permutation[p * 256] / 255.0;
}

sampler permSampler = sampler_state
{
  texture = <permTexture>;
  AddressU  = Wrap;
  AddressV  = Clamp;
  MAGFILTER = POINT;
  MINFILTER = POINT;
  MIPFILTER = NONE;
};
```

The reference implementation uses bit-manipulation code to generate the gradient vectors directly from the hash values. Because current pixel shader hardware does not include integer operations, this method is not feasible, so instead we precalculate a small 1D texture containing the 16 gradient vectors. The code to generate this texture is shown in Listing 26-2.

The final code that uses these two textures to compute noise values is given in Listing 26-3. It includes Perlin's new interpolation function, which is a Hermite polynomial of degree five and results in a C^2 continuous noise function. Alternatively, you can also use the original interpolation function, which is less expensive to evaluate but results in discontinuous second derivatives.

Listing 26-2. Source Code to Compute Gradient Texture for Noise

```
// gradients for 3D noise
static float3 g[] = {
  1,1,0,    -1,1,0,    1,-1,0,   -1,-1,0,
  1,0,1,    -1,0,1,    1,0,-1,   -1,0,-1,
  0,1,1,     0,-1,1,    0,1,-1,   0,-1,-1,
  1,1,0,     0,-1,1,   -1,1,0,    0,-1,-1,
};


texture gradTexture
<
  string texturetype = "2D";
  string format = "q8w8v8u8";
  string function = "GenerateGradTexture";
  int width = 16, height = 1;
>;

float3 GenerateGradTexture(float p : POSITION) : COLOR
{
  return g[p * 16];
}


sampler gradSampler = sampler_state
{
  texture = <gradTexture>;
  AddressU  = Wrap;
  AddressV  = Clamp;
  MAGFILTER = POINT;
  MINFILTER = POINT;
  MIPFILTER = NONE;
};
```

Listing 26-3. Source Code for Computing 3D Perlin Noise Function

```
float3 fade(float3 t)
{
  return t * t * t * (t * (t * 6 - 15) + 10); // new curve
//   return t * t * (3 - 2 * t); // old curve
}


float perm(float x)
{
  return tex1D(permSampler, x / 256.0) * 256;
}
```

```
float grad(float x, float3 p)
{
  return dot(tex1D(gradSampler, x), p);
}

// 3D version
float inoise(float3 p)
{
  float3 P = fmod(floor(p), 256.0);
  p -= floor(p);
  float3 f = fade(p);

  // HASH COORDINATES FOR 6 OF THE 8 CUBE CORNERS
  float A = perm(P.x) + P.y;
  float AA = perm(A) + P.z;
  float AB = perm(A + 1) + P.z;
  float B =  perm(P.x + 1) + P.y;
  float BA = perm(B) + P.z;
  float BB = perm(B + 1) + P.z;

  // AND ADD BLENDED RESULTS FROM 8 CORNERS OF CUBE
  return lerp(
    lerp(lerp(grad(perm(AA), p),
              grad(perm(BA), p + float3(-1, 0, 0)), f.x),
         lerp(grad(perm(AB), p + float3(0, -1, 0)),
              grad(perm(BB), p + float3(-1, -1, 0)), f.x), f.y),
    lerp(lerp(grad(perm(AA + 1), p + float3(0, 0, -1)),
              grad(perm(BA + 1), p + float3(-1, 0, -1)), f.x),
         lerp(grad(perm(AB + 1), p + float3(0, -1, -1)),
              grad(perm(BB + 1), p + float3(-1, -1, -1)), f.x), f.y),
    f.z);
}
```

This same code could be also be compiled for the vertex shader with some modifications. Vertex shaders support variable indexing into constant memory, so it is not necessary to use texture lookups.

For brevity, the code in Listing 26-3 provides the implementation for only 3D noise. The version of the code on this book's CD includes the 4D version.

26.3.1 Optimization

The code in Listing 26-3 is a straightforward port of the reference CPU implementation. There are several ways this code can be optimized to take better advantage of the graphics hardware. (The optimized code is included on the accompanying CD, along with the implementation for 4D noise.)

The reference implementation uses six recursive lookups into the permutation table to generate the initial four hash values. The obvious way to implement this on the GPU is as six texture lookups into a 1D texture, but instead we can precalculate a 256×256-pixel RGBA 2D texture that contains four values in each texel, and use a single 2D lookup.

We can also remove the final lookup into the permutation table by expanding the gradient table and permuting the gradients. So instead of using a 16-pixel gradient texture, we create a 256-pixel texture with the gradients rearranged based on the permutation table. This eliminates eight 1D texture lookups.

The unoptimized implementation compiles to 81 Pixel Shader 2.0 instructions, including 22 texture lookups. After optimization, it is 53 instructions, only nine of which are texture lookups.

Because much of the code is scalar, there may also be potential for taking more advantage of vector operations.

26.4 Conclusion

We have described an implementation of procedural noise for pixel shaders. Procedural noise is an important building block for visually rich rendering, and it can be used for bump mapping and other effects, as shown in Figure 26-2. Although developers of most real-time applications running on today's GPUs will not want to dedicate 50 pixel shader instructions to a single noise lookup, this technique is useful for high-quality, offline-rendering applications, where matching existing CPU noise implementations is important. As the computational capabilities of GPUs increase and memory access becomes relatively more expensive due to continued hardware trends, procedural techniques such as this will become increasingly attractive.

Figure 26-2. Pixel Shader Noise Used for Procedural Bump Mapping

26.5 References

Ebert, David S., F. Kenton Musgrave, Darwyn Peachey, Ken Perlin, and Steven Worley. 2003. *Texturing and Modeling: A Procedural Approach*, 3rd ed. Morgan Kaufmann.

Perlin, Ken. 2004. "Implementing Improved Perlin Noise." In *GPU Gems*, edited by Randima Fernando, pp. 73–85. Addison-Wesley.

Perlin, Ken. 2002. "Improving Noise." *ACM Transactions on Graphics (Proceedings of SIGGRAPH 2002)* 21(3), pp. 681–682. Updated version available online at **http://mrl.nyu.edu/~perlin/noise/**

Perlin, Ken. 1985. "An Image Synthesizer." In *Computer Graphics (Proceedings of ACM SIGGRAPH 85)* 19(3), pp. 287–296.

Chapter 27

Advanced High-Quality Filtering

Justin Novosad
discreet

Advanced filtering methods have been around for a long time. They were developed primarily for scientific applications such as analyzing MRIs and satellite images. Thanks to recent advances in GPU technology, these methods can be made available to PC users who simply want their computer graphics to look as nice as possible.

This chapter provides a general overview of GPU-based texture-filter implementation issues and solutions, with an emphasis on texture interpolation and antialiasing problems. We explore a series of high-quality texture-filtering methods for rendering textured surfaces. These techniques can be used to perform several common imaging tasks such as resizing, warping, and deblurring, or for simply rendering textured 3D scenes better than with the standard filters available from graphics hardware.

Readers should be familiar with the following topics: fundamental computer graphics techniques such as mipmapping, antialiasing, and texture filtering; basic frequency-domain image analysis and image processing; and calculus.

27.1 Implementing Filters on GPUs

The most practical and straightforward way to implement digital image filters on GPUs is to use pixel shaders on textured polygons. For an introduction to this approach, see Bjorke 2004. For most image-filtering applications, in which image dimensions need to be preserved, one should simply use a screen-aligned textured quad of the same dimensions as the input image.

27.1.1 Accessing Image Samples

Common digital-image-filtering methods require access to multiple arbitrary pixels from the input image. Typically, texture filters need to sample data at discrete texel locations corresponding to samples of the input image. Unfortunately, current pixel shader languages do not natively provide direct integer-addressed access to texels (except for `samplerRECT` in Cg). Instead, texture lookups use real coordinates in the interval 0 to 1, making lookups independent of texture resolution, which is optimal for most texture-mapping operations but not for filters. So the first step in writing a filter shader is to understand how to compute the integer sample coordinate corresponding to the current texture coordinate and how to convert sample coordinates back into conventional texture coordinates. The following equations comply with Direct3D's texture-mapping specifications:

```
sampleCoord = floor(textureCoord * texSize);
textureCoord = (sampleCoord + 0.5) / texSize;
```

We add 0.5 to the sample coordinates to get the coordinate of the center of the corresponding texel. Although the coordinates of texel corners could be used, it is always safer to use centers to guard against round-off errors. Variable `texSize` is a uniform value containing the dimensions of the texture excluding border texels.

In many situations, filters need to access only those pixels in their immediate neighborhood, in which case coordinate conversions may not be necessary. The following macros can be used to compute the texture coordinates of adjacent pixels in a single arithmetic operation:

```
#define TC_XMINUS_YMINUS(coord)  (coord - texIncrement.xy)
#define TC_XPLUS_YPLUS(coord)    (coord + texIncrement.xy)
#define TC_XCENTER_YMINUS(coord) (coord - texIncrement.zy)
#define TC_XCENTER_YPLUS(coord)  (coord + texIncrement.zy)
#define TC_XMINUS_YCENTER(coord) (coord - texIncrement.xz)
#define TC_XPLUS_YCENTER(coord)  (coord + texIncrement.xz)
#define TC_XMINUS_YPLUS(coord)   (coord - texIncrement.xw)
#define TC_XPLUS_YMINUS(coord)   (coord + texIncrement.xw)
```

Here, `texIncrement` is a uniform variable whose components are initialized as follows:

$$x = \frac{1}{texture\ width},$$

$$y = \frac{1}{texture\ height},$$

$$z = 0,$$

$$w = -\frac{1}{texture\ height}.$$

One additional tip is that it is not necessary to snap texture coordinates to the center of the nearest texel as long as texture lookups do not perform any type of filtering. This means setting filtering to GL_NEAREST in OpenGL or D3DTEXF_POINT in Direct3D. This way, coordinate snapping is performed automatically during texture lookups.

27.1.2 Convolution Filters

In Bjorke 2004, as well as in Rost 2004, there are some interesting techniques for implementing convolution filters in shaders. In most situations, storing the convolution coefficients in constants or uniforms works well and is very efficient for conventional discrete convolution. However, we would like to promote the usage of textures for representing continuous convolution kernels that are required for subpixel filtering.

Subpixel filtering is an important tool for achieving high-quality filtered texture magnification. The idea is simple: we want to apply the convolution kernel centered precisely at the current texture coordinates, which is not necessarily at the center of a texel. In this case, the kernel must be viewed as a continuous function $k(\Delta s, \Delta t)$. Hence, the convolution can be represented as follows:

$$Filtered\ color = \sum k\left(s - s_0, t - t_0\right) tex\left(s, t\right),$$

where the summation is over the neighborhood of the current texel coordinate (s_0, t_0), and *tex* is the texture lookup function. In this chapter, we use (i, j) to designate screen coordinates and (s, t) to designate image and texture coordinates.

In image processing, it is often desirable to work with filters that have a steady-state response of 1, to preserve the image's mean intensity. Therefore, we want the sum of kernel coefficients to be 1, as shown in Figure 27-1.

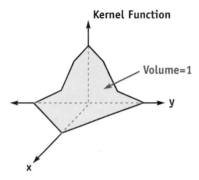

Figure 27-1. A Kernel with Unit Volume

In continuous convolution, we want to ensure that the integral of the kernel over its domain is 1. In the case of subpixel filtering, it is not that simple, because we are using a continuous kernel on a discrete image. So the kernel will have to be sampled. As a consequence, the summation of kernel samples may not be constant. The solution is to divide the resulting color by the sum of kernel samples, which gives us the following equation:

$$\textit{Filtered color} = \frac{\sum k\left(s - s_0, t - t_0\right) \textit{tex}\left(s, t\right)}{\sum k\left(s - s_0, t - t_0\right)}.$$

Listing 27-1 is an example of an HLSL pixel shader that performs subpixel filtering. In Listing 27-1, the convolution summation is performed in the RGB channels, while the kernel sample summation is done in the alpha channel. This little trick saves a lot of GPU instructions and helps accelerate the process. If the alpha channel needs to be processed, the kernel sample summation will have to be done separately. The variable `fact` is a scale factor that will convert texture coordinate offsets from the image frame of reference to kernel texture coordinates. The value of `fact` should be computed as image size divided by filter domain. We add 0.5 to the filter lookup coordinates because we assume that the origin of the kernel is at the center of the `Filter` texture.

Notice in Figure 27-2 how the subpixel Gaussian yields a nice and smooth interpolation. Unfortunately, this quality comes at a high computational cost, which is likely to make fragment processing the bottleneck in the rendering pipeline.

Listing 27-1. Discrete Convolution with a Continuous Kernel

```
int2 texSize;
half2 fact;
sampler2D Filter;
sampler2D Image;
const half pi = 3.141592654;

half4 ps_main( half4 inTex: TEXCOORD0 ) : COLOR0
{
  half4 color = half4(0, 0, 0, 0);
  half2 base = floor(inTex * texSize);
  half2 pos;
  half2 curCoord;
  for (pos.x = -3; pos.x <= 3; pos.x++)
  for (pos.y = -3; pos.y <= 3; pos.y++)
  {
    curCoord = (base + pos + 0.5) / texSize;
    color += half4(tex2D(Image, curCoord).rgb, 1)*
                  tex2D(Filter, (inTex - curCoord) * fact + 0.5).r;
  }
  return color / color.a;
}
```

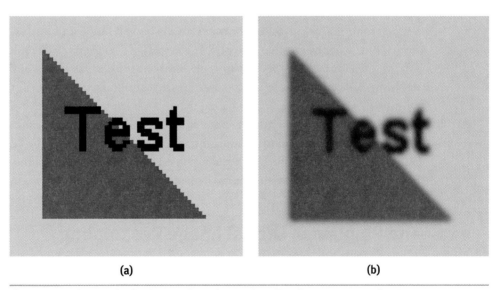

(a)   (b)

Figure 27-2. The Result of Using a Subpixel Gaussian Filter for Image Magnification
(a) Original image at 64×64. (b) Blown up to 512×512 using a subpixel Gaussian filter.

Using 1D Textures for Rotationally Invariant Kernels

Representing in 2D a kernel that is invariant to rotation is highly redundant. All the necessary information could be encoded into a 1D texture by simply storing a cross section of the kernel. To apply this technique, replace the color summation line in Listing 27-1 with the following:

```
color += half4(tex2D(Image, curCoord).rgb,1) *
              tex1D(Filter, length(inTex - curCoord) * fact).r;
```

This method requires us to add an expensive `length()` function call to the inner loop, which will likely hinder the performance of the shader, although it saves texture memory. Trading performance for texture memory is not so relevant with recent GPUs—which are typically equipped with 128 MB or more memory—unless we are dealing with very large kernels. We discuss that situation briefly in the next section.

Another, more efficient method is to take advantage of the separability of convolution kernels. A 2D convolution filter is said to be separable when it is equivalent to applying a 1D filter on the rows of the image, followed by a 1D filter on the columns of the image. The Gaussian blur and the box filter are examples of separable kernels. The downside is that the filter has to be applied in two passes, which may be slower than regular 2D convolution when the kernel is small.

Applying Very Large Kernels

Because some GPUs can execute only a relatively limited number of instructions in a shader, it may not be possible to apply large kernels in a single pass. The solution is to subdivide the kernel into tiles and to apply one tile per pass. The ranges of the two loops in Listing 27-1 must be adjusted to cover the current tile. The results of all the passes must be added together by accumulating them in the render target, which should be a floating-point renderable texture (a pbuffer in OpenGL), or an accumulation buffer. The convolution shader must no longer perform the final division by the kernel sample sum (the alpha channel), because the division can only be done once all the samples have been accumulated. The division has to be performed in a final post-processing step.

27.2 The Problem of Digital Image Resampling

In this section we look at methods for improving the visual quality of rendered textures using interpolation filters and antialiasing. We also present a method for restoring sharp edges in interpolated textures.

27.2.1 Background

A digital image is a two-dimensional array of color samples. To display a digital image on a computer screen, often the image must be resampled to match the resolution of the screen. Image resampling is expressed by the following equation:

$$P(i, j) = I(f(i, j)),$$

where $P(i, j)$ is the color of the physical pixel at viewport coordinates (i, j); $I(u, v)$ is the image color at coordinates (u, v); and function f maps screen coordinates to image coordinates (or texture coordinates) such that $(u, v) = f(i, j)$. The topic we want to address is how to evaluate $I(u, v)$ using pixel shaders to obtain high-quality visual results.

The function $f(i, j)$ is an abstraction of the operations that go on in the software, the operating system, the graphics driver, and the graphics hardware that result in texture coordinates (u, v) being assigned to a fragment at screen coordinates (i, j). These computations are performed upstream of the fragment-processing stage, which is where $I(u, v)$ is typically evaluated by performing a texture lookup.

OpenGL and Direct3D have several built-in features for reducing the artifacts caused by undersampling and oversampling. Undersampling occurs when the image is reduced by f, which may cause aliasing artifacts. Oversampling occurs when the image is enlarged by f, which requires sample values to be interpolated. Texture-aliasing artifacts can be eliminated through texture mipmapping, and sample interpolation can be performed using hardware bilinear filtering. Most GPUs also provide more advanced techniques, such as trilinear filtering and anisotropic filtering, which efficiently combine sample interpolation with mipmapping.

27.2.2 Antialiasing

Aliasing is a phenomenon that occurs when the Sampling Theorem, also known as Nyquist's rule, is not respected. The Sampling Theorem states that a continuous signal must be sampled at a frequency greater than twice the upper bound of the signal spectrum, or else the signal cannot be fully reconstructed from the samples (that is, information is lost). When aliasing occurs, the part of the signal spectrum that is beyond the sampling bandwidth gets reflected, which causes undesirable artifacts in the reconstructed signal (by *bandwidth*, we mean the frequency range allowed by Nyquist's rule). The theory behind the phenomenon of spectral aliasing is beyond the scope of this chapter; more on the topic can be found in any good signal-processing textbook.

The classic approach to antialiasing is to filter the signal to be sampled to eliminate frequency components that are beyond the sampling bandwidth. That way, the high-frequency components of the signal remain unrecoverable, but at least the low-frequency components aren't corrupted by spectral reflection. One of the best-known ways of doing this is mipmapping, which provides prefiltered undersampled representations of the texture. Mipmapping is great for interactive applications such as games, but it is not ideal, because it does not achieve optimal signal preservation, even with tri-linear or anisotropic filtering.

Quasi-Optimal Antialiasing

Ideal antialiasing consists in computing sample values as the average of the sampled signal over the sampling area, which is given by the integral of the sampled signal over the sampling area divided by the sampling area. In the case of texture mapping, the sampled signal is discrete, meaning that the integral can be computed as a summation. To compute the summation, we must devise a method to determine which texels belong to the sampling area of a given pixel.

Assuming that pixels are spaced by 1 unit in both x and y directions, the screen-space corners of the sampling area of the pixel at (i, j) are $(i - 0.5, j - 0.5)$, $(i + 0.5, j - 0.5)$, $(i + 0.5, j + 0.5)$, and $(i - 0.5, j + 0.5)$. We want to compute the mapping of the sampling area in texture space. This is difficult to solve in the general case, so we propose a solution that is valid under the assumption that $f(i, j)$ is a linear 2D vector function—hence, *quasi-optimal antialiasing*. Because we know that in the general case, $f(i, j)$ is not linear,[1] we approximate the function locally for each pixel using the two first terms of its Taylor series expansion:

$$f(i, j) \approx [s_0, t_0]^T + J_0 [i - i_0, j - j_0]^T,$$

where (i_0, j_0) are the coordinates of the center of the current pixel; (s_0, t_0) is the value of $f(i_0, j_0)$; J is the texture-coordinate Jacobian matrix; and J_0 is the Jacobian matrix evaluated at the center of the current pixel.

$$J = \begin{pmatrix} \dfrac{\partial s}{\partial i} & \dfrac{\partial s}{\partial j} \\ \dfrac{\partial t}{\partial i} & \dfrac{\partial t}{\partial j} \end{pmatrix}$$

---

1. In fact, $f(i, j)$ is a rational function in the case of a perspective projection of a 3D textured polygon.

It is a known property of linear transformations that linearity is preserved; therefore, the square sampling area is guaranteed to map to a quadrilateral in texture space. To implement texture antialiasing as a pixel shader, we will scan through each texel in the bounding box of the mapped quadrilateral and test it to determine whether it is within the quadrilateral. Another approach would be to use an edge-walking rasterization-style algorithm to select pixels. This would be more efficient for covering very large quadrilaterals, but it is too complex for GPUs that do not have advanced flow control (GPUs prior to the GeForce 6 Series).

There are several ways to test whether a pixel belongs to a quadrilateral. The one we propose here is to use the reciprocal of f to convert texture coordinates back to screen coordinates, where the test is much easier to perform. See Figure 27-3. The reciprocal function is this:

$$\left[i, j\right]^{T} = \left[i_0, j_0\right]^{T} + J_0^{-1}\left[s - s_0, t - t_0\right]^{T}.$$

In pixel coordinates, all we have to verify is that $|i - i_0|$ and $|j - j_0|$ are smaller than 0.5.

Listing 27-2 is a basic pixel shader that performs antialiased texture mapping that can be run on a Pixel Shader 2.0a target.

In this example, we use intrinsic function `fwidth` to quickly compute a conservative bounding box without having to transform the corners of the sampling area. The drawback of this approach is that it will generate bounding boxes slightly larger than necessary, resulting in more samples being thrown out by the quadrilateral test. Another particularity of this shader is that it divides the bounding box into a fixed number of

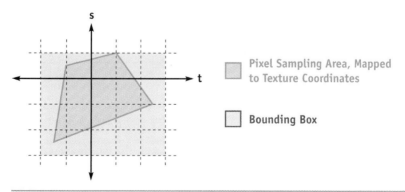

Figure 27-3. Testing Whether a Pixel Belongs to a Quadrilateral

Listing 27-2. A Quasi-Optimal Antialiasing Pixel Shader

```
bool doTest;
int2 texSize;
sampler2D Image;
const int SAMPLES = 5;  // should be an odd number
const int START_SAMPLE = -2;  // = -(SAMPLES-1)/2

// Compute the inverse of a 2-by-2 matrix
float2x2 inverse (float2x2 M)
{
  return float2x2(M[1][1], -M[0][1], -M[1][0], M[0][0]) / determinant(M);
}

float4 ps_main( float2 inTex: TEXCOORD0 ) : COLOR0
{
  float2 texWidth = fwidth(inTex);
  float4 color = float4(0, 0, 0, 0);
  float2 texStep = texWidth / SAMPLES;
  float2 pos = START_SAMPLE * texStep;
  float2x2 J = transpose(float2x2(ddx(inTex), ddy(inTex)));
  float2x2 Jinv = inverse(J);
  for (int i = 0; i < SAMPLES; i++, pos.x += texStep.x)
  {
    pos.y = START_SAMPLE * texStep.y;
    for (int j = 0; j < SAMPLES; j++, pos.y += texStep.y)
    {
      float2 test = abs(mul(Jinv, pos));
      if (test.x < 0.5h && test.y < 0.5h)
        color += float4(tex2D(Image, inTex + pos).rgb, 1);
    }
  }
  return color / (color.a);
}
```

rectangular subdivisions, which are not likely to have one-to-one correspondence with texels. Using advanced flow control, it is possible to improve the shader by making it use a variable-size texel-aligned sampling grid. See Figures 27-4 and 27-5.

Figure 27-5 is the result of sampling the texture over the window given by fwidth, which is a primitive form of anisotropic filtering. The difference is subtle, but by looking at the images closely, we see that the benefit of the quasi-optimal antialiasing

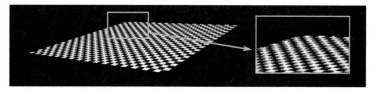

Figure 27-4. Checkerboard Texture Using Quasi-Optimal Antialiasing

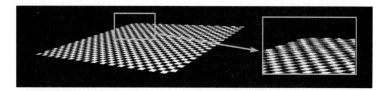

Figure 27-5. Antialiased Checkerboard Texture Without Quadrilateral Test

method is a sharper perspective texture mapping. Also note that antialiasing is applied only to the texture, not to the polygon, which explains why the outer edges of the textured quad are still jaggy. To smooth polygon edges, hardware multisampling (that is, full-scene antialiasing) should be used.

27.2.3 Image Reconstruction

When oversampling (enlarging) an image, the strategy is to reconstruct the original continuous signal and to resample it in a new, higher resolution. Bilinear texture filtering is a very quick way to do this, but it results in poor-quality, fuzzy images. In this subsection, we see how to implement some more-advanced image-reconstruction methods based on information theory.

First let's look at the Shannon-Nyquist signal reconstruction method, which can yield a theoretically perfect reconstruction of any signal that respects the Nyquist limit. The theoretical foundation of the method can be found in Jähne 2002. To apply the method in a shader, simply use the following equation to generate a subpixel convolution kernel and apply it to the texture using the shader presented in Listing 27-1.

$$k(\Delta s, \Delta t) = \frac{\sin(\pi r)}{\pi r}, \quad \text{where } r = \sqrt{\Delta s^2 + \Delta t^2}$$

This kernel is in fact an ideal low-pass filter, also known as the *sine cardinal*, or *sinc* for short. The simplest way to explain Shannon-Nyquist reconstruction is that it limits the spectrum of the reconstructed signal to the bandwidth of the original sampling while preserving all frequency components present in the sampled signal.

Implementation

The kernel used in Shannon-Nyquist reconstruction is invariant to rotation, so we have the option of storing it as a 1D texture. However, the impulse response is infinite and dampens very slowly, as can be seen in Figure 27-6.

To achieve acceptable performance, it is important to restrict the domain of the impulse response. A common practice is to dampen the function by multiplying it with a windowing function, for example a Gaussian. The resulting filter has a compact kernel, but it is no longer an ideal low-pass filter; the frequency-response step is somewhat smoother. When multiplying with a Gaussian, the impulse response will no longer have an integral of 1; but there is no reason to bother with finding a scale factor to normalize the impulse response, because the shader takes care of all this.

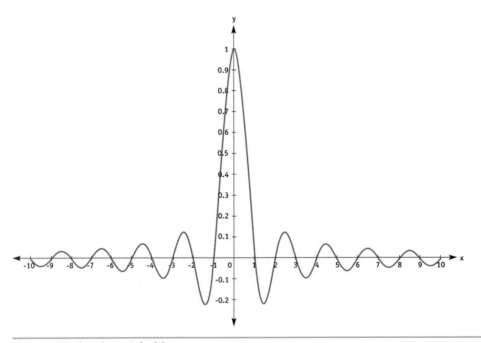

Figure 27-6. Plot of $y = \sin(\pi x)/\pi x$

Chapter 27 Advanced High-Quality Filtering

Let's use the following function as our kernel:

$$k\left(\Delta s,\, \Delta t\right) = \frac{\sin\left(\pi r\right)e^{-r^2/\alpha^2}}{\pi r},$$

where α is a domain scale factor that must be proportional to the size of the kernel. As a rule of thumb, α should be around 75 percent of the range of the kernel. Figure 27-7 shows a cross section of k with $\alpha = 6$, which would be appropriate for a kernel with a domain of $[-8, 8]$.

Figure 27-8 shows that Shannon-Nyquist reconstruction performs very nicely on natural images but produces resonation artifacts along very sharp edges, which are more likely to occur in synthetic images. The resonation is a result of the lack of high-frequency information that is necessary to accurately define an image-intensity step in the resampled image. For processing synthetic images, it is usually preferable to simply use a Gaussian kernel. The Gaussian filter will not produce any resonating artifacts, but it will degrade fine details in the image because of its very smooth frequency cutoff, which attenuates the high-frequency components in the image. (See the results in Section 27.1.2.)

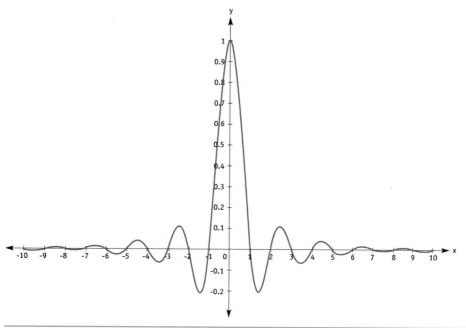

Figure 27-7. Plot of $y = \sin(\pi x)e^{(-x^2/36)}/\pi x$

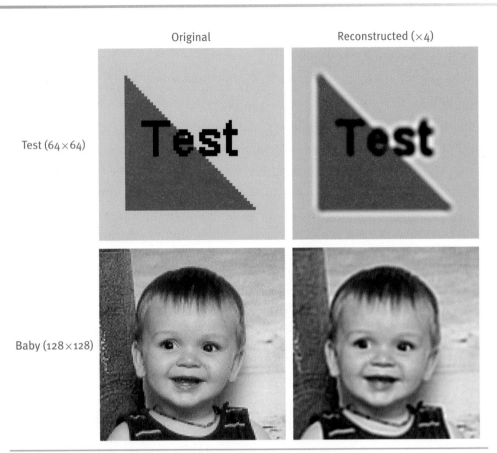

Original   Reconstructed (×4)

Test (64×64)

Baby (128×128)

Figure 27-8. Examples of Shannon-Nyquist Image Reconstruction

27.3 Shock Filtering: A Method for Deblurring Images

The absence of high-frequency components in an image makes it harder for observers to discern objects, because the ganglion cells, which link the retina to the optic nerve, respond acutely to high-frequency image components (see the Nobel-prize-winning work of Hubel and Wiesel [1979]). Because of this, the brain's visual cortex will lack the information it requires to discern objects in a blurry image. Sharpening a blurred image (thereby recovering those high-frequency components) can greatly enhance its visual quality.

Many traditional digital-image-sharpening filters amplify the high-frequency components in an image, which may enhance visual quality. In this section, we look at a different type of sharpening filter that is more appropriate for enhancing reconstructed images: the shock filter, which transforms the smooth transitions resulting from texture interpolation into abrupt transitions. The mathematical theory behind shock filtering is clearly presented in Osher and Rudin 1990. The underlying principle is based on diffusing energy between neighboring pixels. In areas of the image where the second derivative is positive, pixel colors are diffused in the reverse gradient direction, and vice versa. To sharpen an image properly, many passes are usually required.

This method is difficult to apply to images of textured 3D scenes because blurriness may be anisotropic and uneven due to varying depth and perspective texture mapping. This is a problem because the shock-filtering algorithm has no knowledge of the distribution of blurriness in the image. Shock filtering is nonetheless of considerable interest for many types of 2D applications, where blur is often uniform. Listing 27-3 is a simple pixel shader that uses centered differences to estimate the image gradient and a five-sample method to determine convexity (the sign of the second derivative).

Listing 27-3. Shock Filter Pixel Shader

```
uniform float shockMagnitude;
uniform int2 destSize;
sampler2D Image;
const float4 ones = float4(1.0, 1.0, 1.0, 1.0);

float4 ps_main( float4 inTex : TEXCOORD0 ) : COLOR0
{
  float3 inc = float3(1.0/destSize, 0.0);  // could be a uniform
  float4 curCol = tex2D(Image, inTex);
  float4 upCol = tex2D(Image, inTex + inc.zy);
  float4 downCol = tex2D(Image, inTex - inc.zy);
  float4 rightCol = tex2D(Image, inTex + inc.xz);
  float4 leftCol = tex2D(Image, inTex - inc.xz);
  float4 Convexity = 4.0 * curCol - rightCol - leftCol - upCol - downCol;
  float2 diffusion = float2(dot((rightCol - leftCol) * Convexity, ones),
                      dot((upCol - downCol) * Convexity, ones));
  diffusion *= shockMagnitude/(length(diffusion) + 0.00001);
  curCol += (diffusion.x > 0 ? diffusion.x * rightCol :
            -diffusion.x*leftCol) +
            (diffusion.y > 0 ? diffusion.y * upCol :
            -diffusion.y * downCol);
  return curCol/(1 + dot(abs(diffusion), ones.xy));
}
```

The images in the right column in Figure 27-9 were generated with eight passes of shock filtering with the magnitude parameter set to 0.05.

Notice that the edges of the images are generally sharper after shock filtering. Grainy textures and fine details are better preserved with Shannon-Nyquist reconstruction thanks to the sharp spectrum cutoff. However, there are shadowy artifacts around object silhouettes. The Gaussian reconstruction produces no artifacts, and a more aesthetically pleasing result, but the fine details in the image are attenuated.

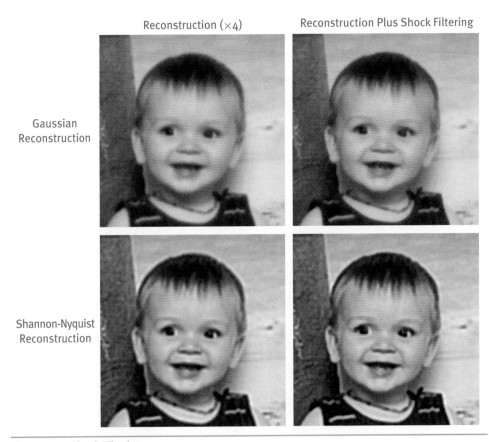

Figure 27-9. Shock Filtering

27.4 Filter Implementation Tips

In many situations, shaders need to evaluate complex functions. Performance of a shader is generally closely related to the number of operations that are performed, so it is important to precompute everything that can be precomputed. Shader developers often encounter this limitation and try to use uniform variables and constants wherever possible to pass precomputed data. One particular strategy that is often overlooked is to use textures as lookup tables in order to evaluate functions quickly by performing a simple texture read instead of evaluating a complicated expression.

Here is a list of tips to consider when designing a shader that uses textures as function lookup tables:

- Choose your texture format carefully, according to the desired precision and range of your function.
- Scale your function properly, so that useful parts fit into the bounds of the texture. For periodic functions, use texture-coordinate wrapping. For functions with horizontal asymptotes, use texture-coordinate clamping.
- Use linear texture filtering to get better precision through interpolation.
- Set the resolution of your texture carefully, to make a reasonable compromise between precision and texture-memory consumption.
- Not all GPUs allow linear texture filtering with floating-point textures. When filtering is not available, a higher-resolution texture may be necessary to achieve the required precision.
- Whenever possible, use the different color components of the texture to evaluate several functions simultaneously.

27.5 Advanced Applications

In this section, we expose some ideas on how to use the techniques presented earlier in the chapter. These suggestions are intended for readers who wish to extend the functionality of the presented shaders to perform advanced image-processing tasks.

27.5.1 Time Warping

We have seen how subpixel convolution filtering can be used for image reconstruction, but it is also possible to generalize the method to higher-dimensional signals. By representing a sequence of images as a 3D array, the third dimension being time, it is possible to interpolate frames to yield fluid slow-motion effects. The frames of the original image sequence can be passed to the shader either as a 3D texture or as multiple 2D textures. For superior interpolation of sequences with fast-moving objects, be sure to use Shannon-Nyquist reconstruction with a very large kernel.

This technique may be considered an interesting compromise between the simple but low-quality frame-blending method and the high-quality but complex motion-estimation approach.

27.5.2 Motion Blur Removal

A slow-motion time warp by means of signal reconstruction may yield motion blur that corresponds to shutter speeds slower than the interpolated frame intervals. In such cases, one may use an adapted shock filter that diffuses only along the time dimension to attenuate motion blur.

27.5.3 Adaptive Texture Filtering

A smart and versatile shader for high-quality rendering of textured 3D scenes would combine the antialiasing and reconstruction filters presented in this chapter into one shader, which would choose between the two using a minification/magnification test. A good example of how to perform this test is given in the OpenGL specifications at http://www.opengl.org.

27.6 Conclusion

The techniques presented in this chapter are designed to produce optimal-quality renderings of 2D textures. Despite the simplicity of these techniques, their computational cost is generally too high to use them at render time in full-screen computer games and interactive applications that require high frame rates. They are more likely to be useful for applications that prioritize render quality over speed, such as medical and scientific imaging, photo and film editing, image compositing, video format conversions, professional 3D rendering, and so on. They could also be used for resolution-dependent texture preparation (preprocessing) in games.

These techniques are feasible in multimedia applications today thanks to the recent availability of highly programmable GPUs. Before, most image-processing tasks had to be performed by the CPU or by highly specialized hardware, which made advanced image-filtering methods prohibitively slow or expensive.

27.7 References

Aubert, Gilles, and Pierre Kornprobst. 2002. *Mathematical Problems in Image Processing.* Springer.

Bjorke, Kevin. 2004. "High-Quality Filtering." In *GPU Gems*, edited by Randima Fernando, pp. 391–415. Addison-Wesley.

Hubel, D. H., and T. N. Wiesel. 1979. "Brain Mechanisms of Vision." *Scientific American* 241(3), pp. 150–162.

Jähne, Bernd. 2002. *Digital Image Processing.* Springer.

Osher, S., and L. Rudin. 1990. "Feature-Oriented Image Enhancement Using Shock Filters." *SIAM Journal on Numerical Analysis* 27(4), pp. 919–940.

Rost, R. 2004. *OpenGL Shading Language.* Chapter 16. Addison-Wesley.

Chapter 28

Mipmap-Level Measurement

Iain Cantlay
Climax Entertainment

In the original *GPU Gems*, Cem Cebenoyan asks the question, "Do your users ever get to see your highest mip level?" (Cebenoyan 2004). If the answer is no, performance can be enhanced and memory can be saved by swapping those unused mipmap levels out of video memory.

One approach to answering this question is to substitute a "false-colored" mipmap and then render the scene. Such a mipmap is one in which each mip level has a different, contrasting color. Figure 28-1a shows a view of some textured terrain; Figure 28-1b shows the same view substituting a false-colored mipmap. Although the viewpoint is that of a character standing on the terrain, it is easy to see that the highest-detail yellow mip level is hardly visible.

The false-coloring technique is useful for authoring art assets, but it requires a person in the loop. This chapter shows how we can use the GPU to automate the process. The technique can then be extended to the more general question: Which mip levels are visible?

Our GPU-based approach is efficient enough to be used in a game engine. Thus, the visible mip level can be dynamically fed back into the engine's texture management routines to reduce memory consumption. The memory that is saved can be used to increase texture resolution elsewhere, improving the richness of the scene. We recently applied the technique to terrain in Climax's Leviathan engine, producing texture-memory savings of 80 percent, with no detectable loss of visual quality.

(a)   (b)

Figure 28-1. Applying a False-Colored Mipmap to a Terrain
(a) Terrain rendered using Climax's Leviathan engine. (b) The effect of substituting the false-colored mipmap from Figure 28-3. Note that the highest level (yellow) is barely visible.

28.1 Which Mipmap Level Is Visible?

The GPU's choice of mipmap level depends on many factors: screen resolution, antialiasing settings, texture-filtering options, anisotropy, clever driver optimizations, the distance to the textured polygons, and the orientations of the polygons. These factors are mostly under the user's control, especially in highly unpredictable situations such as online multiplayer games.

In theory, all the factors can be analyzed on the CPU, allowing us to predict the GPU's choice of mip levels. See, for example, Williams 1983 for information about the theory of mipmapping. However, there are several practical difficulties if we wish to apply the mathematics in an application such as a game.

First, it is not always possible to know all the variables. Antialiasing and texture filtering options can often be overridden from the control panel. It is difficult or impossible for the application to determine these settings.

Second, although the theory of mipmapping is widely understood, GPUs are much more complex than the theory. They contain optimizations and enhancements that are usually complex and proprietary.

Finally, modern scene complexity defies efficient real-time analysis on a CPU. Computer graphics texts describe the mathematics of mipmapping for a *single* polygon. Current 3D applications display objects that use tens or hundreds of thousands of polygons. Although we could analyze the orientation and screen-space size of the polygons in a 100,000-triangle character mesh, doing so would unnecessarily consume lots of CPU power.

28.2 GPU to the Rescue

Fortunately, the GPU excels at analyzing a 100,000-triangle mesh. It does not have an explicit function that reports which mip levels will be used to draw a mesh, but it does implicitly perform this analysis every time that it draws an object.[1] The result is not explicitly available in the form that we need, but it is implicitly there in the pixels that appear in the frame buffer. The trick is to somehow analyze those pixels and convert them into a result of the form "mipmap levels 0 and 1 are not required."

28.2.1 Counting Pixels

Consider the false-coloring example cited in the introduction. Our approach is loosely based on automating this process.

We could false-color a texture, render the object, and copy the frame buffer to system memory. The various colored pixels could then be counted to give an analysis of the visible mip levels. Though this *is* possible, it is not fast. Copying from video memory to system memory is currently prohibitively slow. Note the "currently": PCI Express changes the speed of video-to-system memory transfers. Even so, using the CPU to count frame-buffer pixels is likely to be inefficient.

The GPU, however, can efficiently count pixels using occlusion queries. (Strictly speaking, it counts visible fragments, but the distinction makes no difference to our approach.) An occlusion query indicates how many pixels of a draw call passed the z-buffer test. That test cannot be used to directly analyze our color frame buffer, but it can be made to work if we rephrase the problem.

Is the First Mip Level Visible?

First, return to the simpler initial question: Is the highest mip level visible? How can we answer this with an occlusion query?

Fortunately, occlusion queries take into account all of the render state in the pipeline; that includes the alpha test. Our approach exploits this: we create a special calibration texture with opaque alpha (1) in the highest level and translucent alpha (0) in the other levels; we enable alpha testing with a reference value of 0; we render the target object, substituting the calibration texture; and we create an occlusion query for the draw call. The alpha test rejects any entirely transparent pixels and passes any with alpha greater than 0. So only those pixels that have sampled the highest mipmap level are counted by the occlusion query.

---

1. We can, however, *wish* for an explicit function that would determine the mipmap levels used as a by-product of rendering a mesh.

Figure 28-2 illustrates the result on a piece of terrain. Figure 28-2a shows the original terrain; Figure 28-2b shows a version rendered with false coloring and opaque alpha in all mipmap levels; Figure 28-2c shows the same object with opaque alpha in only the top, yellow mipmap level. The more distant parts of the terrain (and the flatter parts) do not sample the highest mipmap level; therefore, the output alpha values are entirely transparent (0) and the pixels are not rendered.

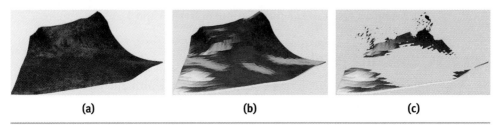

(a) (b) (c)

Figure 28-2. Applying the Test to a Piece of Terrain

Extending to Multiple Mipmap Levels

We can use an occlusion query to determine if any given level of a mipmap is visible. To determine which level is visible, we simply repeat the process for each mipmap level that we care to measure. Our goal is to save texture memory, so it is not necessary to measure all the levels in a mipmap. Significant savings will result if we can avoid the highest few mipmap levels. For example, in an uncompressed $512 \times 512 \times 4$-byte texture, the highest four levels consume 1 MB, 256 kB, 64 kB, and 16 kB of memory (or 100 percent, 25 percent, 6.3 percent, and 1.6 percent). The third and subsequent levels are insignificant.

Rather than create a calibration texture corresponding to each measured level, we use a single texture and fill successive levels with decreasing alpha values. Figure 28-3 shows a sample calibration texture. Linear mipmap filtering will thus produce a continuous gradient of alpha values through the top four levels, as shown in Figure 28-4.

Only the alpha values are important to the algorithm; the different RGB colors in each level are useful for illustration and debugging.

We could test each mip level against a different alpha reference value. However, we instead choose to keep the alpha test constant and use a pixel shader to offset and scale the alpha value differently for each level:

```
ps.1.1

tex t0
mov r0.rgb, t0
  +sub_x4 r0.a, t0, c0
```

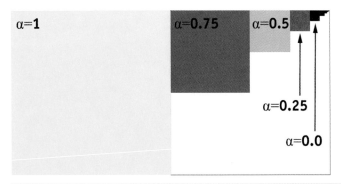

Figure 28-3. The Calibration Texture

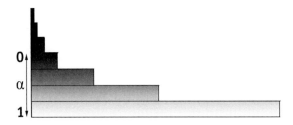

Figure 28-4. The Alpha Gradient

We set $c0$ to 0.75, 0.5, 0.25, and 0.0, respectively, for each of the four levels that we measure. The alpha values of the level that we are measuring are thus remapped to the [0,1] range. Scaling the values in the pixel shader means that each level uses the full range of values possible in the alpha test.

We also create a baseline reference query that is used to count all of the test object's pixels without any alpha test. This value is required for interpreting the results.

Interpreting the Results

Visually, the results of the draw calls might look like Figure 28-5. The occlusion queries return a set of pixel counts for each level and the reference. They are typically something like the following:

```
reference: 13000
level 0:        0
level 1:      650       5%
level 2:    10530      81%
level 3:    13000     100%
```

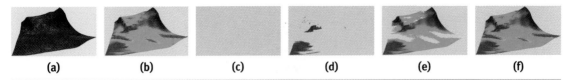

| (a) | (b) | (c) | (d) | (e) | (f) |

Figure 28-5. Draw Calls Used to Measure the Visible Mip Level
(a) A terrain tile textured normally. (b) – (f) The draw calls used to measure the visible mipmap level. The reference draw call is shown in (b); mipmap level 0 is yellow and invisible in (c); (d), (e), and (f) show levels 1 through 3.

We run through the levels searching for the highest one that exceeds a significance threshold; this is deemed the first visible level. The threshold corresponds to the visual significance of the mip level in the output. By default, we use a threshold that is 15 percent of the reference value. Figure 28-6 shows how little visual fidelity is lost for low thresholds, while the image becomes progressively blurrier as the threshold increases.

Using the Results

Having measured the mip level that is displayed on an object, how can we use the result? In Climax's Leviathan engine (Climax 2004), we use the results in two ways.

First, we use Direct3D's managed resources. Therefore, we can pass the mip level to the resource manager using `IDirect3DBaseTexture9::SetLOD`. Simply making that function call will cause Direct3D to save video memory. (We highly recommend using managed resources.)

Second, our Leviathan engine supports a massively multiplayer online game. Contrary to recommended practice, we have to generate most textures on the fly while the game's rendering loop is running. For example, player characters have to be loaded on demand at arbitrary times. Thus, we use texture mip-level measurement to drive some on-the-fly texture generation. In addition to saving video memory, this also saves the system memory copy that Direct3D keeps, and it saves the cost of generating unused levels.

28.2.2 Practical Considerations in an Engine

The concepts behind measuring mipmap levels are simple, but applying the idea in practice, in a real-time engine, is not so straightforward. The implementation in Climax's Leviathan engine has required several revisions over a period of more than a year.

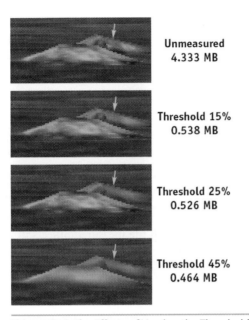

Unmentioned
4.333 MB

Threshold 15%
0.538 MB

Threshold 25%
0.526 MB

Threshold 45%
0.464 MB

Figure 28-6. The Effects of Varying the Threshold
As the threshold increases, less texture memory is needed, as fewer mipmap levels are stored on the GPU. However, the result becomes progressively blurrier. The arrows indicate a part of the image where the differences are particularly evident.

Emitting Modified Draw Calls

To measure the mip level of an object, we must redraw it with altered render states. We must override the following:

1. The pixel shader

2. The alpha-test render states (D3DRS_ALPHATESTENABLE, D3DRS_ALPHAFUNC, and D3DRS_ALPHAREF)

3. The texture

Additionally, D3DRS_COLORWRITEENABLE is used to ensure that the calibration objects do not appear in the frame buffer. Fortunately, disabling color writes does not affect the results of the occlusion queries.

The design of the Leviathan engine naturally supports overriding states in this manner. Each draw call is buffered and stored as a vector of abstract state. Thus, any draw call can be re-emitted with a slightly altered list of render states.

We might also wish to modify one other render state: the view transform. As it stands, objects will not be measured if they are outside the view frustum. It would be possible to center the view transform on each object, measuring them even if they are outside the view frustum.

Amortizing the Overheads

Measuring the mip level of an object is not a cheap operation: you must redraw the target object several times. It is highly unlikely that we can afford to multiply a game's draw call count by four or five times.

Fortunately, it is not necessary to measure every object in every frame; texture mip levels tend to vary slowly and predictably as the relative positions of objects change. For our game, we have found that it suffices to put all the measured objects in a round-robin queue and measure one per frame. We measure four mip levels, so our overhead is only five draw calls per frame. We have been unable to measure a performance impact in typical game conditions.

The round-robin queue can result in some latency: moving objects sometimes visibly pop texture resolution. A more sophisticated management algorithm would probably solve this; for example, we could use a priority queue and measure objects that were moving quickly more often. However, we have not done this in our game, as we find that the latency is seldom visible.

RGB Calibration Data

Only the alpha channel of the calibration texture is used by our algorithm. That does not mean, however, that we leave the RGB values blank. They can serve two purposes.

First, RGB data is useful for visual debugging; we have illustrated many figures with colored mipmap levels, and in practice, false color is equally useful when developing an application.

Second, it has been known for drivers to analyze textures in order to adapt their filtering to the characteristics of a particular texture. If that occurs, it would be best for the calibration texture to be representative of the actual textures that we wish to measure. In practice, we fill it with the RGB values of a representative image, rather than leave it blank.

28.2.3 Extensions

Magnification and Juggling Powers of Two

As it is, our calibration texture must match the size of the one being measured. Doubling the dimensions of the calibration texture relative to the one being measured would permit us to detect a degree of texture magnification. The extra level of the calibration texture would be displayed when our target texture requires a magnification filter.

Decreasing the size of the viewport would give a similar result. In general, we can trade off viewport size, calibration texture size, and the number of levels being measured. In practice, it might make sense to decrease both the viewport size and the calibration texture size by equal amounts, as this would reduce the overheads of the test.

Mip-Level Velocity

Imagine that you are driving in a racing game, approaching a wall at speed. The wall's surface is perpendicular to the view direction. Figure 28-7 shows the mip level as a function of distance. The hardware's linear mipmap filtering gradually varies the proportion of the visible levels, whereas our measurement produces a stair-step result because it is a simple threshold.

We can extract more information by changing the calibration texture. As shown in Figure 28-8, we randomize the texel values within a level. In each level, the values are uniformly distributed within one quarter of the texture's total range.

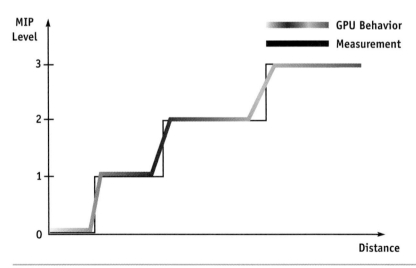

Figure 28-7. Mipmap Level vs. Distance

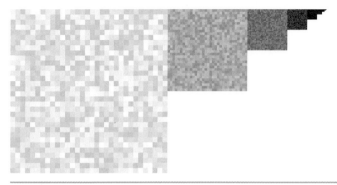

Figure 28-8. Calibration Alpha Values for Velocity

So:

```
level0.a ∈ (0.75, 1.00]
level1.a ∈ (0.50, 0.75]
level2.a ∈ (0.25, 0.50]
level3.a ∈ [0.00, 0.25]
```

Figure 28-9 shows the second level in histogram form.

Each level is not a different random pattern: they are all magnified, biased versions of the level 3 pattern. The result is that the gradient of values in Figure 28-4 is randomly offset at each texel. Hence, some part of the texture is always straddling our threshold test.

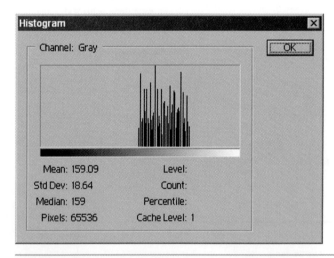

Figure 28-9. The Second Mipmap Level in Histogram Form

Now as we vary the distance to the measured object, any small change moves some of the measured texels through the threshold tests. The stair-step behavior of Figure 28-7 is smoothed out.

Initially, we thought that the modified calibration texture might permit us to measure the degree to which each mipmap level contributes to the output image. Though this is possible for simple geometry—such as a flat polygon perpendicular to the view direction—the behavior of useful objects is more complex, and we believe that the pixel counts defy analysis. However, this modified calibration texture can provide a measure of how the mipmap levels are changing; information that the mipmap level is increasing, decreasing, or static could be useful.

Derivative Instructions

Using Shader Model ps_2_x or above, the `dsx` and `dsy` instructions can be used to directly compute the mip level in the pixel shader (or the HLSL `ddx()` and `ddy()` calls could be used). We could dispense with the calibration texture and thus reduce texture bandwidth at the expense of a more complex shader. Retrieving the result from the GPU is still a problem that requires several occlusion queries.

We have not investigated this approach in Leviathan because we support lower pixel shader models with a unified algorithm.

28.3 Sample Results

Useful terrain tends to be flat, and in typical viewpoints, standing on the terrain, polygons will often be seen edge-on. Thus, the required mipmap levels tend to be low. However, any nonflat surfaces will require higher mipmap levels. Figure 28-10 shows a typical example: the same piece of terrain is viewed from two different positions. At viewpoint A, the cliff is visible and requires a higher mipmap level than at viewpoint B, even though both viewpoints are equidistant.

This orientation dependence is exactly the problem that we set out to solve. So it's not a surprise that mipmap-level measurement can be extremely useful for terrain. We applied the technique to our terrain engine in Leviathan; the results are shown in Table 28-1.

Figure 28-6 shows the visual impact of different threshold values on a piece of terrain. (The view is highly magnified.) The most difference can be seen on the side of a small hill: the hillside is closer to being perpendicular to the view direction, so it displays a

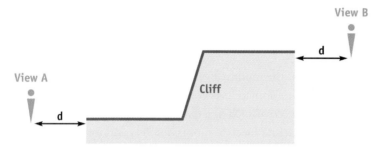

Figure 28-10. Two Views of a Cliff

higher mipmap level than the surrounding plain. Thus, it "breaks through" the significance threshold first. Increasing the significance threshold produces a gradual degradation in image quality; this is a useful property, and we make our threshold user-configurable, providing a quality-space trade-off.

Table 28-1. Memory Savings Measured from the Leviathan Terrain Engine

	Memory Used (MB)	Percentage Savings
Without Measurement	4.333	0%
0% Threshold	0.864	80%
15% Threshold	0.538	88%
30% Threshold	0.464	89%

28.4 Conclusion

The GPU can be used to determine which texture mipmap levels are being used. Our approach relies on the GPU's own texture-mapping hardware to produce this information. This technique has two advantages: First, we do not need to know exactly how the GPU chooses visible mip levels. We have quite deliberately avoided any mathematical discussion of mipmap filtering in this chapter, because it is unnecessary with our approach. The second advantage of using the GPU is that it produces a definitive, accurate answer, taking into account all the complex factors that determine which mip levels get used.

The technique may not be useful in every type of application. For example, in a racing game, the players often proceed linearly around a fixed track; they have limited ability to move in a way that will affect the mipmap levels needed. In that case, the required mipmap levels could be determined statically with less efficient methods.

However, as a developer of massively multiplayer online games, we face novel challenges. Our players have much more control than in many other games, and the result is an environment where texture sizes cannot be predicted in advance. We have successfully applied the technique described in this chapter to produce significant reductions in memory consumption without detectable degradation of the resulting images.

28.5 References

Cebenoyan, Cem. 2004. "Graphics Pipeline Performance." In *GPU Gems*, edited by Randima Fernando, pp. 473–486. Addison-Wesley.

Climax. 2004. Climax Entertainment Web site.
  http://www.climaxgroup.com/technology/technology.aspx?ArticleID=152

Williams, Lance. 1983. "Pyramidal Parametrics." *Computer Graphics (Proceedings of SIGGRAPH 83)* 17(3), pp. 1–11.

GENERAL-PURPOSE COMPUTATION ON GPUS: A PRIMER

This part of the book aims to provide a gentle introduction to the world of general-purpose computation on graphics processing units, or "GPGPU," as it has come to be known. The text is intended to be understandable to programmers with no graphics experience, as well as to those who have been programming graphics for years but have little knowledge of parallel computing for other applications.

Since the publication of *GPU Gems*, GPGPU has grown from something of a curiosity to a well-respected active new area of graphics and systems research.

Why would you want to go to the trouble of converting your computational problems to run on the GPU? There are two reasons: price and performance. Economics and the rise of video games as mass-market entertainment have driven down prices to the point where you can now buy a graphics processor capable of several hundred billion floating-point operations per second for just a few hundred dollars.

The GPU is not well suited to all types of problems, but there are many examples of applications that have achieved significant speedups from using graphics hardware. The applications that achieve the best performance are typically those with high "arithmetic intensity"; that is, those with a large ratio of mathematical operations to memory accesses. These applications range all the way from audio processing and physics simulation to bioinformatics and computational finance.

Anybody with any exposure to modern computing cannot fail to notice the rapid pace of technological change in our industry. The first chapter in this part, **Chapter 29, "Streaming Architectures and Technology Trends," by John Owens** of the University of California, Davis, sets the stage for the chapters to come by describing the trends in semiconductor design and manufacturing that are driving the evolution of both the CPU and the GPU. One of the important factors driving these changes is the memory "gap"—the fact that computation speeds are increasing at a much faster rate than memory access speeds. This chapter also introduces the "streaming" computational model, which is a reasonably close match to the characteristics of modern GPU hardware. By using this style of programming, application programmers can take advantage of the GPU's massive computation and memory bandwidth resources, and the resulting programs can achieve large performance gains over equivalent CPU implementations.

Chapter 30, "The GeForce 6 Series GPU Architecture," by **Emmett Kilgariff** and **Randima Fernando** of NVIDIA, describes in detail the design of a current state-of-the-art graphics processor, the GeForce 6800. Cowritten by one of the lead architects of the chip, this chapter includes many low-level details of the hardware that are not available anywhere else. This information is invaluable for anyone writing high-performance GPU applications.

The remainder of this part of the book then moves on to several tutorial-style chapters that explain the details of how to solve general-purpose problems using the GPU.

Chapter 31, "Mapping Computational Concepts to GPUs," by **Mark Harris** of NVIDIA, discusses the issues involved with converting computational problems to run efficiently on the parallel hardware of the GPU. The GPU is actually made up of several programmable processors plus a selection of fixed-function hardware, and this chapter describes how to make the best use of these resources.

Chapter 32, "Taking the Plunge into GPU Computing," by **Ian Buck** of Stanford University, provides more details on the differences between the CPU and the GPU in terms of memory bandwidth, floating-point number representation, and memory access models. As Ian mentions in his introduction, the GPU was not really designed for general-purpose computation, and getting it to operate efficiently requires some care.

One of the most difficult areas of GPU programming is general-purpose data structures. Data structures such as lists and trees that are routinely used by CPU programmers are not trivial to implement on the GPU. The GPU doesn't allow arbitrary memory access and mainly operates on four-vectors designed to represent positions and colors. Particularly difficult are sparse data structures that do not have a regular layout in memory and where the size of the structure may vary from element to element.

Chapter 33, "Implementing Efficient Parallel Data Structures on GPUs," by **Aaron Lefohn** of the University of California, Davis; **Joe Kniss** of the University of Utah; and **John Owens** gives an overview of the stream programming model and goes on to explain the details of implementing data structures such as multidimensional arrays and sparse data structures on the GPU.

Traditionally, GPUs have not been very good at executing code with branches. Because they are parallel machines, they achieve best performance when the the same operation can be applied to every data element. **Chapter 34, "GPU Flow-Control Idioms,"** by **Mark Harris** and **Ian Buck**, explains different ways in which flow-control structures such as loops and if statements can be efficiently implemented on the GPU. This includes using the depth-test and z-culling capabilities of modern GPUs, as well as the branching instructions available in the latest versions of the pixel shader hardware.

Cliff Woolley of the University of Virginia has spent many hours writing GPGPU applications, and (like many of our other authors) he has published several papers based on his research. In **Chapter 35, "GPU Program Optimization,"** he passes on his experience on the best ways to optimize GPU code, and how to avoid the common mistakes made by novice GPU programmers. It is often said that premature optimization is the root of all evil, but it has to be done at some point.

On the CPU, it is easy to write programs that have variable amounts of output per input data element. Unfortunately, this is much more difficult on a parallel machine like the GPU. **Chapter 36, "Stream Reduction Operations for GPGPU Applications,"** by **Daniel Horn** of Stanford University, illustrates several ways in which the GPU can be programmed to perform filtering operations that remove elements from a data stream in order to generate variable amounts of output. He demonstrates how this technique can be used to efficiently implement collision detection and subdivision surfaces.

Only time will tell what the final division of labor between the CPU, the GPU, and other processors in the PC ecosystem will be. One thing is sure: the realities of semiconductor design and the memory gap mean that data-parallel programming is here to stay. By learning how to express your problems in this style today, you can ensure that your code will continue to execute at the maximum possible speed on all future hardware.

Simon Green, NVIDIA Corporation

Chapter 29

Streaming Architectures and Technology Trends

John Owens
University of California, Davis

Modern technology allows the designers of today's processors to incorporate enormous computation resources into their latest chips. The challenge for these architects is to translate the increase in capability to an increase in performance. The last decade of graphics processor development shows that GPU designers have succeeded spectacularly at this task. In this chapter, we analyze the technology and architectural trends that motivate the way GPUs are built today and what we might expect in the future.

29.1 Technology Trends

As computer users, we have become accustomed to each new generation of computer hardware running faster, with more capabilities—and often a lower price—than the last. This remarkable pace of development is made possible by continued advances in the underlying technologies, allowing more processing power to be placed on each chip. Each year in the *International Technology Roadmap for Semiconductors* (ITRS), the semiconductor industry forecasts how a number of chip metrics of interest, such as the size of transistors, the number of transistors per chip, and overall power consumption, will change in the coming years (ITRS 2003). These projections have an enormous impact on the companies that make chips and chip-making equipment, as well as the designers of next-generation chips. In this section we explain some of the trends we can expect in the future, as well as what they will mean for the development of next-generation graphics processors.

29.1.1 Core Technology Trends

Today's processors are constructed from millions of connected switching devices called transistors. As process technologies advance, these transistors, and the connections between them, can be fabricated in a smaller area. In 1965, Gordon Moore noted that the number of transistors that could be economically fabricated on a single processor die was doubling every year (Moore 1965). Moore projected that such an increase was likely to continue in the future. This oft-quoted prediction, termed "Moore's Law," today means that each year, approximately 50 percent more components can be placed on a single die.[1] In the forty years since Moore made his prediction, the number of transistors per die has gone from fifty (in 1965) to hundreds of millions (in 2005), and we can expect this rate of growth to continue for at least the next decade.

New chip generations not only increase the number of transistors, they also decrease transistor size. Because of their smaller size, these transistors can operate faster than their predecessors, allowing the chip to run faster overall. Historically, transistor speeds have increased by 15 percent per year (Dally and Poulton 1998). In modern processors, a global signal called a *clock* synchronizes computation that occurs throughout the processor, and so processor users see the increase in transistor speed reflected in a faster clock. Together, the increase in transistor count and clock speed combine to increase the *capability* of a processor at 71 percent per year. This yearly increase in capability means that each year, we can expect 71 percent more computation on a chip compared to the year before.

Semiconductor computer memory, which uses slightly different fabrication methods than processor logic, also benefits from similar advances in fabrication technology. The ITRS forecasts that commodity dynamic random-access memory (DRAM) will continue to double in capacity every three years. DRAM performance can be measured in two ways: by *bandwidth*, which measures the amount of data it can transfer each second, and by *latency*, which measures the length of time between the time data is requested and the time it is returned. DRAM performance does not increase as quickly as processor capability. DRAM bandwidth increases by 25 percent each year (ITRS 2003, Tables 4c, 4d), and DRAM latency improves by only 5 percent per year.

29.1.2 Consequences

In general, most of the trends just described are positive ones: with each new generation of fabrication technology, processor capability, memory bandwidth, and memory latency

---

1. Though references to "Moore's Law" in the popular press often refer to *performance* increases, Moore's actual prediction referred only to the number of devices that could fit on a single die.

all improve. For example, the yearly capability increase has led to an enormous degree of integration on a single die. Fifteen years ago, designers were only just beginning to integrate floating-point arithmetic units onto a processor die; today, such a unit occupies less than a square millimeter of die area, and hundreds can be placed onto the same die.

However, the most important consequences of these technology trends are the *differences* between them. When one metric changes at a different rate than another, it requires rethinking the assumptions behind processor and system design. We can identify three major issues that will help drive GPU architectures of the future: compute versus communicate, latency versus bandwidth, and power.

Compute vs. Communicate

As both clock speeds and chip sizes increase, the amount of time it takes for a signal to travel across an entire chip, measured in clock cycles, is also increasing. On today's fastest processors, sending a signal from one side of a chip to another typically requires multiple clock cycles, and this amount of time increases with each new process generation. We can characterize this trend as an increase in the cost of communication when compared to the cost of computation. As a consequence, designers of the future will increasingly use computation via cheap transistors to replace the need for expensive communication. Another likely impact will be an increase in the amount of computation available per word of memory bandwidth. As an example, let us compare NVIDIA's last three flagship GPUs (2002's GeForce FX 5800, 2003's GeForce FX 5950, and 2004's GeForce 6800) in measured peak programmable floating-point performance against peak off-chip bandwidth to memory. The GeForce FX 5800 could sustain 2 floating-point operations for every word of off-chip bandwidth, while the GeForce FX 5950 could sustain 2.66 operations, and the GeForce 6800 could sustain nearly 6. We expect this trend to continue in future chip generations. Figure 29-1 shows historical data for observed floating-point operations per second and available memory bandwidth for a series of GPU architectures.

Latency vs. Bandwidth

The gap between the trends of bandwidth and latency will also be an important driver of future architectures. Because latency will continue to improve more slowly than bandwidth (Patterson 2004), designers must implement solutions that can tolerate larger and larger amounts of latency by continuing to do useful work while waiting for data to return from operations that take a long time.

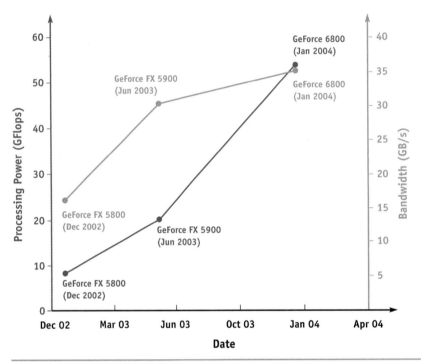

Figure 29-1. Rapidly Changing GPU Capabilities
The number of observed floating-point operations per second on the GeForce FX 5800, 5950, and the GeForce 6800 has been growing at a rapid pace, while off-chip memory bandwidth has been increasing much more slowly. (Data courtesy of Ian Buck, Stanford University)

Power

Although smaller transistors require less power than larger ones, the number of transistors on a single processor die is rising faster than the amount at which power per transistor is falling. Consequently, each generation of processors requires more power: the ITRS estimates that the maximum power allowed for 2004 chips with a heat sink is 158 watts and will gradually rise to a ceiling of 198 watts by 2008. This power constraint will be one of the primary limitations of future processors; the future figure of merit may no longer be the number of operations per second but instead the number of operations per second per watt.

Figure 29-2 summarizes the forecasted change in capability, DRAM bandwidth, DRAM latency, and power over the next decade.

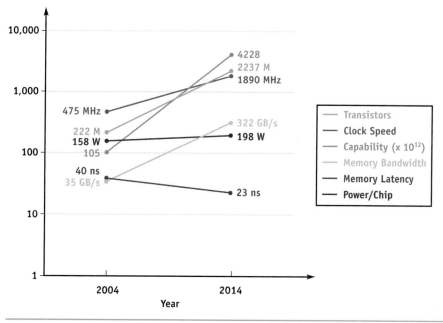

Figure 29-2. Changes in Key GPU Properties over Time

29.2 Keys to High-Performance Computing

In the previous section, we have seen that modern technology allows each new generation of hardware a substantial increase in capability. Effectively utilizing this wealth of computational resources requires addressing two important goals. First, we must organize our computational resources to allow high performance on our applications of interest. Simply providing large amounts of computation is not sufficient, however; efficient management of communication is necessary to feed the computation resources on the chip. In this section we describe techniques that allow us to achieve efficient computation and efficient communication, and we discuss why modern microprocessors (CPUs) are a poor match for these goals.

29.2.1 Methods for Efficient Computation

In Section 29.1 we saw that it is now possible to place hundreds to thousands of computation units on a single die. The keys to making the best use of transistors for computation are to maximize the hardware devoted to computation, to allow multiple computation units to operate at the same time through parallelism, and to ensure that each computation unit operates at maximum efficiency.

Though modern technologies allow us a large number of transistors on each die, our resources are not infinite. Our use of transistors can be broadly divided into three categories: *control*, the hardware used to direct the computation; *datapath*, the hardware used to perform the computation; and *storage*, the hardware used to store data. If our goal is to maximize performance, we must make hardware and software decisions that allow us to maximize the transistors in the datapath that are devoted to performing computation.

Within the datapath, we can allow simultaneous operations at the same time. This technique is termed *parallelism*. We can envision several ways to exploit parallelism and permit simultaneous execution. Complex tasks such as graphics processing are typically composed of several sequential tasks. When running these applications, we may be able to run several of these tasks on different data at the same time (*task parallelism*). Within a stage, if we are running a task on several data elements, we may be able to exploit *data parallelism* in evaluating them at the same time. And within the complex evaluation of a single data element, we may be able to evaluate several simple operations at the same time (*instruction parallelism*). To effectively use hundreds of computation units, we may take advantage of any or all of these types of parallelism.

Within each of the tasks, we could make each of our arithmetic units fully programmable and thus able to perform any task. However, we can gain more efficiency from our transistors by taking advantage of *specialization*. If a specific arithmetic unit performs only one kind of computation, that unit can be specialized to that computation with a considerable gain in efficiency. For example, triangle rasterization, in which a screen-space triangle is transformed into the fragments that cover that triangle, realizes an enormous efficiency benefit when the rasterization task is implemented in special-purpose hardware instead of programmable hardware.

29.2.2 Methods for Efficient Communication

As we saw in Section 29.1.2, off-chip bandwidth is growing more slowly than on-chip arithmetic capability, so high-performance processors must minimize off-chip communication. The easiest way to reduce this cost is to eliminate it: modern processors attempt to keep as much required data communication on-chip as possible, requiring off-chip communication only to fetch or store truly global data.

Another common way to mitigate the increasing cost of communication is through caching: a copy of recently used data memory is stored on-chip, removing the need for a fetch from off-chip if that data is needed again. Such data caching will be more common in future architectures, extending to local caches or user-controlled memories that relieve the need for on-chip communication. These caches effectively trade transistors in the form of cache memory for bandwidth. Another powerful technique is compression; only the compressed form of data is transmitted and stored off-chip. Compression also trades transistors (compression and decompression hardware) and computation (the compression/decompression operation) for off-chip bandwidth.

29.2.3 Contrast to CPUs

Today's high-performance microprocessors target general-purpose applications with different goals from a computer graphics pipeline. In general, these general-purpose programs have less parallelism, more complex control requirements, and lower performance goals than the rendering pipeline. Consequently, the design goals we enumerated previously are not those addressed by CPUs, and CPUs have made different design choices that result in a poor mapping to the graphics pipeline and many other applications with similar attributes.

CPU programming models are generally serial ones that do not adequately expose data parallelism in their applications. CPU hardware reflects this programming model: in the common case, CPUs process one piece of data at a time and do not exploit data parallelism. They do an admirable job of taking advantage of instruction parallelism, and recent CPU additions to the instruction set such as Intel's SSE and the PowerPC's AltiVec allow some data parallel execution, but the degree of parallelism exploited by a CPU is much less than that of a GPU.

One reason parallel hardware is less prevalent in CPU datapaths is the designers' decision to devote more transistors to control hardware. CPU programs have more complex control requirements than GPU programs, so a large fraction of a CPU's transistors and wires implements complex control functionality such as branch prediction and out-of-order execution. Consequently, only a modest fraction of a CPU's die is devoted to computation.

Because CPUs target general-purpose programs, they do not contain specialized hardware for particular functions. GPUs, however, can implement special-purpose hardware for particular tasks, which is far more efficient than a general-purpose programmable solution could ever provide.

Finally, CPU memory systems are optimized for minimum latency rather than the maximum throughput targeted by GPU memory systems. Lacking parallelism, CPU programs must return memory references as quickly as possible to continue to make progress. Consequently, CPU memory systems contain several levels of cache memory (making up a substantial fraction of the chip's transistors) to minimize this latency. However, caches are ineffective for many types of data, including graphics inputs and data that is accessed only once. For the graphics pipeline, maximizing throughput for all elements rather than minimizing latency for each element results in better utilization of the memory system and a higher-performance implementation overall.

29.3 Stream Computation

In the previous section, we have seen that building high-performance processors today requires both efficient computation and efficient communication. Part of the reason that CPUs are poorly suited to many of these high-performance applications is their serial programming model, which does not expose the parallelism and communication patterns in the application. In this section, we describe the *stream* programming model, which structures programs in a way that allows high efficiency in computation and communication (Kapasi et al. 2003). This programming model is the basis for programming GPUs today.

29.3.1 The Stream Programming Model

In the stream programming model, all data is represented as a *stream*, which we define as an ordered set of data of the same data type. That data type can be simple (a stream of integers or floating-point numbers) or complex (a stream of points or triangles or transformation matrices). While a stream can be any length, we will see that operations on streams are most efficient if streams are long (hundreds or more elements in a stream). Allowed operations on streams include copying them, deriving substreams from them, indexing into them with a separate index stream, and performing computation on them with *kernels*.

A kernel operates on entire streams, taking one or more streams as inputs and producing one or more streams as outputs. The defining characteristic of a kernel is that it operates on entire *streams* of elements as opposed to individual elements. The most typical use of a kernel is to evaluate a function on each element of an input stream (a "map" operation); for example, a transformation kernel may project each element of a stream of points into a different coordinate system. Other desirable kernel operations include expansions (in which more than one output element is produced for each input element), reductions (in which more than one element is combined into a single output element), or filters (in which a subset of input elements are output).

Kernel outputs are functions only of their kernel inputs, and within a kernel, computations on one stream element are never dependent on computations on another element. These restrictions have two major advantages. First, the data required for kernel execution is completely known when the kernel is written (or compiled). Kernels can thus be highly efficient when their input elements and their intermediate computed data are stored locally or are carefully controlled global references. Second, requiring independence of computation on separate stream elements within a single kernel allows mapping what appears to be a serial kernel calculation onto data-parallel hardware.

In the stream programming model, applications are constructed by chaining multiple kernels together. For instance, implementing the graphics pipeline in the stream programming model involves writing a vertex program kernel, a triangle assembly kernel, a clipping kernel, and so on, and then connecting the output from one kernel into the input of the next kernel. Figure 29-3 shows how the entire graphics pipeline maps onto the stream model. This model makes the communication between kernels explicit, taking advantage of the data locality between kernels inherent in the graphics pipeline.

The graphics pipeline is a good match for the stream model for several reasons. The graphics pipeline is traditionally structured as stages of computation connected by data flow between the stages. This structure is analogous to the stream and kernel abstractions of the stream programming model. Data flow between stages in the graphics pipeline is highly localized, with data produced by a stage immediately consumed by the next stage; in the stream programming model, streams passed between kernels exhibit similar behavior. And the computation involved in each stage of the pipeline is typically uniform across different primitives, allowing these stages to be easily mapped to kernels.

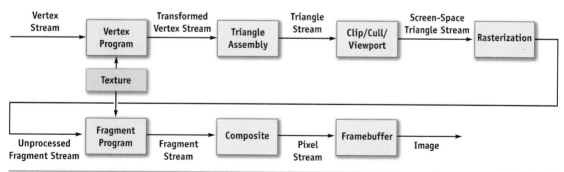

Figure 29-3. Mapping the Graphics Pipeline to the Stream Model
The stream formulation of the graphics pipeline expresses all data as streams (indicated by arrows) and all computation as kernels (indicated by blue boxes). Both user-programmable and nonprogrammable stages in the graphics pipeline can be expressed as kernels.

Efficient Computation

The stream model enables efficient computation in several ways. Most important, streams expose parallelism in the application. Because kernels operate on entire streams, stream elements can be processed in parallel using data-parallel hardware. Long streams with many elements allow this data-level parallelism to be highly efficient. Within the processing of a single element, we can exploit instruction-level parallelism. And because applications are constructed from multiple kernels, multiple kernels can be deeply pipelined and processed in parallel, using task-level parallelism.

Dividing the application of interest into kernels allows a hardware implementation to specialize hardware for one or more kernels' execution. Special-purpose hardware, with its superior efficiency over programmable hardware, can thus be used appropriately in this programming model.

Finally, allowing only simple control flow in kernel execution (such as the data-parallel evaluation of a function on each input element) permits hardware implementations to devote most of their transistors to datapath hardware rather than control hardware.

Efficient Communication

Efficient communication is also one of the primary goals of the stream programming model. First, off-chip (global) communication is more efficient when entire streams, rather than individual elements, are transferred to or from memory, because the fixed cost of initiating a transfer can be amortized over an entire stream rather than a single element. Next, structuring applications as chains of kernels allows the intermediate results between kernels to be kept on-chip and not transferred to and from memory. Efficient kernels attempt to keep their inputs and their intermediate computed data local within kernel execution units; therefore, data references within kernel execution do not go off-chip or across a chip to a data cache, as would typically happen in a CPU. And finally, deep pipelining of execution allows hardware implementations to continue to do useful work while waiting for data to return from global memories. This high degree of latency tolerance allows hardware implementations to optimize for through-put rather than latency.

29.3.2 Building a Stream Processor

The stream programming model structures programs in a way that both exposes parallelism and permits efficient communication. Expressing programs in the stream model is only half the solution, however. High-performance graphics hardware must effectively exploit the high arithmetic performance and the efficient computation exposed by the stream model. How do we structure a hardware implementation of a GPU to ensure the highest overall performance?

The first step to building a high-performance GPU is to map kernels in the graphics pipeline to independent functional units on a single chip. Each kernel is thus implemented on a separate area of the chip in an organization known as *task parallel*, which permits not only task-level parallelism (because all kernels can be run simultaneously) but also hardware specialization of each functional unit to the given kernel. The task-parallel organization also allows efficient communication between kernels: because the functional units implementing neighboring kernels in the graphics pipeline are adjacent on the chip, they can communicate effectively without requiring global memory access.

Within each stage of the graphics pipeline that maps to a processing unit on the chip, GPUs exploit the independence of each stream element by processing multiple data elements in parallel. The combination of task-level and data-level parallelism allows GPUs to profitably use dozens of functional units simultaneously.

Inputs to the graphics pipeline must be processed by each kernel in sequence. Consequently, it may take thousands of cycles to complete the processing of a single element. If a high-latency memory reference is required in processing any given element, the processing unit can simply work on other elements while the data is being fetched. The deep pipelines of modern GPUs, then, effectively tolerate high-latency operations.

For many years, the kernels that make up the graphics pipeline were implemented in graphics hardware as fixed-function units that offered little to no user programmability. In 2000, for the first time, GPUs allowed users the opportunity to program individual kernels in the graphics pipeline. Today's GPUs feature high-performance data-parallel processors that implement two kernels in the graphics pipeline: a *vertex program* that allows users to run a program on each vertex that passes through the pipeline, and a *fragment program* that allows users to run a program on each fragment. Both of these stages permit single-precision floating-point computation. Although these additions were primarily intended to provide users with more flexible shading and lighting calculations, their ability to sustain high computation rates on user-specified programs with sufficient precision to address general-purpose computing problems has effectively made them *programmable stream processors*—that is, processors that are attractive for a much wider variety of applications than simply the graphics pipeline.

29.4 The Future and Challenges

The migration of GPUs into programmable stream processors reflects the culmination of several historical trends. The first trend is the ability to concentrate large amounts of computation on a single processor die. Equally important has been the ability and talent of GPU designers in effectively using these computation resources. The economies of scale that are associated with building tens of millions of processors per year have allowed the cost of a GPU to fall enough to make a GPU a standard part of today's desktop computer. And the addition of reasonably high-precision programmability to the pipeline has completed the transition from a hard-wired, special-purpose processor to a powerful programmable processor that can address a wide variety of tasks.

What, then, can we expect from future GPU development?

29.4.1 Challenge: Technology Trends

Each new generation of hardware will present a challenge to GPU vendors: How can they effectively use additional hardware resources to increase performance and functionality? New transistors will be devoted to increased performance, in large part through greater amounts of parallelism, and to new functionality in the pipeline. We will also see these architectures evolve with changes in technology.

As we described in Section 29.1.2, future architectures will increasingly use transistors to replace the need for communication. We can expect more aggressive caching techniques that not only alleviate off-chip communication but also mitigate the need for some on-chip communication. We will also see computation increasingly replace communication when appropriate. For example, the use of texture memory as a lookup table may be replaced by calculating the values in that lookup table dynamically. And instead of sending data to a distant on-chip computation resource and then sending the result back, we may simply replicate the resource and compute our result locally. In the trade-off between *communicate* and *recompute/cache*, we will increasingly choose the latter.

The increasing cost of communication will also influence the microarchitecture of future chips. Designers must now explicitly plan for the time required to send data across a chip; even local communication times are becoming significant in a timing budget.

29.4.2 Challenge: Power Management

Ideas for how to use future GPU transistors must be tempered by the realities of their costs. Power management has become a critical piece of today's GPU designs as each generation of hardware has increased its power demand. The future may hold more aggressive dynamic power management targeted at individual stages; increasing amounts of custom or power-aware design for power-hungry parts of the GPU; and more sophisticated cooling management for high-end GPUs. Technology trends indicate that the power demand will only continue to rise with future chip generations, so continued work in this area will remain an important challenge.

29.4.3 Challenge: Supporting More Programmability and Functionality

While the current generation of graphics hardware features substantially more programmability than previous generations, the general programmability of GPUs is still far from ideal. One step toward addressing this trend is to improve the functionality and flexibility within the two current programmable units (vertex and fragment). It is likely that we will see their instruction sets converge and add functionality, and that their control flow capabilities will become more general as well. We may even see programmable hardware shared between these two stages in an effort to better utilize these resources. GPU architects will have to be mindful, however, that such improvements not affect the GPU's performance on its core tasks. Another option will be expanding programmability to different units. Geometric primitives particularly benefit from programmability, so we may soon see programmable processing on surfaces, triangles, and pixels.

As GPU vendors support more general pipelines and more complex and varied shader computation, many researchers have used the GPU to address tasks outside the bounds of the graphics pipeline. This book contains examples of many of these efforts; the general-purpose computation on GPUs (GPGPU) community has successfully addressed problems in visual simulation, image processing, numerical methods, and databases with graphics hardware. We can expect that these efforts will grow in the future as GPUs continue to increase in performance and functionality.

Historically, we have seen GPUs subsume functionality previously belonging to the CPU. Early consumer-level graphics hardware could not perform geometry processing on the graphics processor; it was only five years ago that the entire graphics pipeline could be fabricated on a single chip. Though since that time the primary increase in GPU functionality has been directed toward programmability within the graphics pipeline, we should not expect that GPU vendors have halted their efforts to identify more functions to integrate onto the GPU. In particular, today's games often require large amounts of computation in physics and artificial intelligence computations. Such computation may be attractive for future GPUs.

29.4.4 Challenge: GPU Functionality Subsumed by CPU (or Vice Versa)?

We can be confident that CPU vendors will not stand still as GPUs incorporate more processing power and more capability onto their future chips. The ever-increasing number of transistors with each process generation may eventually lead to conflict between CPU and GPU manufacturers. Is the core of future computer systems the CPU, one that may eventually incorporate GPU or stream functionality on the CPU itself? Or will future systems contain a GPU at their heart with CPU functionality incorporated into the GPU? Such weighty questions will challenge the next generation of processor architects as we look toward an exciting future.

29.5 References

Dally, William J., and John W. Poulton. 1998. *Digital Systems Engineering.* Cambridge University Press.

ITRS. 2003. *International Technology Roadmap for Semiconductors.* http://public.itrs.net

Kapasi, Ujval J., Scott Rixner, William J. Dally, Brucek Khailany, Jung Ho Ahn, Peter Mattson, and John D. Owens. 2003. "Programmable Stream Processors." *IEEE Computer*, pp. 54–62.

Moore, Gordon. 1965. "Cramming More Components onto Integrated Circuits." *Electronics* 38(8). More information is available at http://www.intel.com/research/silicon/mooreslaw.htm

Owens, John D. 2002. "Computer Graphics on a Stream Architecture." Ph.D. Thesis, Stanford University, November 2002.

Patterson, David A. 2004. "Latency Lags Bandwidth." *Communications of the ACM* 47(10), pp. 71–75.

Chapter 30

The GeForce 6 Series GPU Architecture

Emmett Kilgariff
NVIDIA Corporation

Randima Fernando
NVIDIA Corporation

The previous chapter described how GPU architecture has changed as a result of computational and communications trends in microprocessing. This chapter describes the architecture of the GeForce 6 Series GPUs from NVIDIA, which owe their formidable computational power to their ability to take advantage of these trends. Most notably, we focus on the GeForce 6800 (NVIDIA's flagship GPU at the time of writing, shown in Figure 30-1), which delivers hundreds of gigaflops of single-precision floating-point computation, as compared to approximately 12 gigaflops for current high-end CPUs. In this chapter—and throughout the book—references to GeForce 6 Series GPUs should be read to include the latest Quadro FX GPUs supporting Shader Model 3.0, which provide a superset of the functionality offered by the GeForce 6 Series. We start with a general overview of where the GPU fits into the overall computer system, and then we describe the architecture along with details of specific features and performance characteristics.

30.1 How the GPU Fits into the Overall Computer System

The CPU in a modern computer system communicates with the GPU through a graphics connector such as a PCI Express or AGP slot on the motherboard. Because the graphics connector is responsible for transferring all command, texture, and vertex data from the CPU to the GPU, the bus technology has evolved alongside GPUs over the past few years. The original AGP slot ran at 66 MHz and was 32 bits wide, giving a transfer rate of 264 MB/sec. AGP 2×, 4×, and 8× followed, each doubling the available

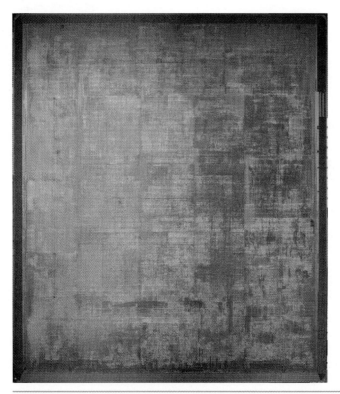

Figure 30-1. The GeForce 6800 Microprocessor

bandwidth, until finally the PCI Express standard was introduced in 2004, with a maximum theoretical bandwidth of 4 GB/sec simultaneously available to and from the GPU. (Your mileage may vary; currently available motherboard chipsets fall somewhat below this limit—around 3.2 GB/sec or less.)

It is important to note the vast differences between the GPU's memory interface bandwidth and bandwidth in other parts of the system, as shown in Table 30-1.

Table 30-1. Available Memory Bandwidth in Different Parts of the Computer System

Component	Bandwidth
GPU Memory Interface	35 GB/sec
PCI Express Bus (×16)	8 GB/sec
CPU Memory Interface (800 MHz Front-Side Bus)	6.4 GB/sec

Table 30-1 reiterates some of the points made in the preceding chapter: there is a vast amount of bandwidth available internally on the GPU. Algorithms that run on the GPU can therefore take advantage of this bandwidth to achieve dramatic performance improvements.

30.2 Overall System Architecture

The next two subsections go into detail about the architecture of the GeForce 6 Series GPUs. Section 30.2.1 describes the architecture in terms of its graphics capabilities. Section 30.2.2 describes the architecture with respect to the general computational capabilities that it provides. See Figure 30-2 for an illustration of the system architecture.

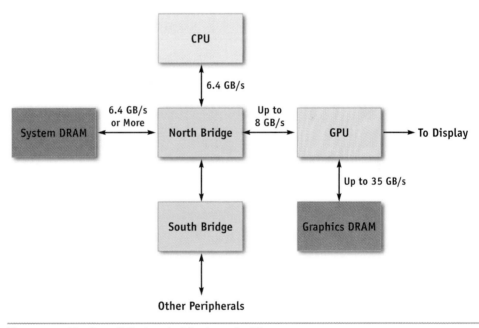

Figure 30-2. The Overall System Architecture of a PC

30.2.1 Functional Block Diagram for Graphics Operations

Figure 30-3 illustrates the major blocks in the GeForce 6 Series architecture. In this section, we take a trip through the graphics pipeline, starting with input arriving from the CPU and finishing with pixels being drawn to the frame buffer.

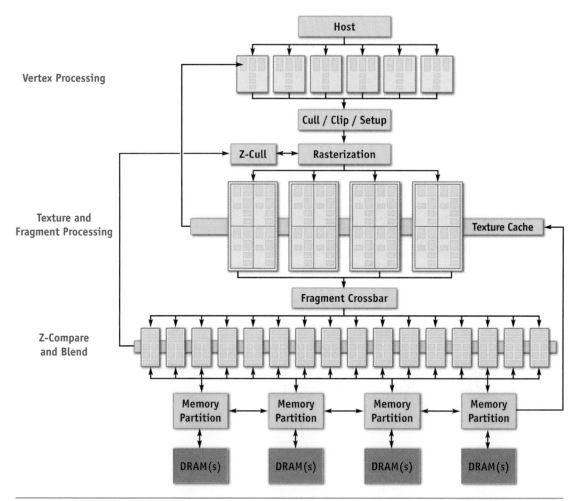

Figure 30-3. A Block Diagram of the GeForce 6 Series Architecture

First, commands, textures, and vertex data are received from the host CPU through shared buffers in system memory or local frame-buffer memory. A command stream is written by the CPU, which initializes and modifies state, sends rendering commands, and references the texture and vertex data. Commands are parsed, and a vertex fetch unit is used to read the vertices referenced by the rendering commands. The commands, vertices, and state changes flow downstream, where they are used by subsequent pipeline stages.

The vertex processors (sometimes called "vertex shaders"), shown in Figure 30-4, allow for a program to be applied to each vertex in the object, performing transformations, skinning, and any other per-vertex operation the user specifies. For the first time, a

GPU—the GeForce 6 Series—allows vertex programs to fetch texture data. All operations are done in 32-bit floating-point (fp32) precision per component. The GeForce 6 Series architecture supports scalable vertex-processing horsepower, allowing the same architecture to service multiple price/performance points. In other words, high-end models may have six vertex units, while low-end models may have two.

Because vertex processors can perform texture accesses, the vertex engines are connected to the texture cache, which is shared with the fragment processors. In addition, there is a vertex cache that stores vertex data both before and after the vertex processor, reducing fetch and computation requirements. This means that if a vertex index occurs twice in a draw call (for example, in a triangle strip), the entire vertex program doesn't have to be rerun for the second instance of the vertex—the cached result is used instead.

Vertices are then grouped into primitives, which are points, lines, or triangles. The Cull/Clip/Setup blocks perform per-primitive operations, removing primitives that aren't visible at all, clipping primitives that intersect the view frustum, and performing edge and plane equation setup on the data in preparation for rasterization.

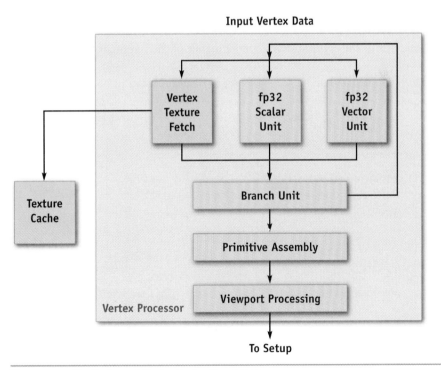

Figure 30-4. The GeForce 6 Series Vertex Processor

The rasterization block calculates which pixels (or samples, if multisampling is enabled) are covered by each primitive, and it uses the z-cull block to quickly discard pixels (or samples) that are occluded by objects with a nearer depth value. Think of a fragment as a "candidate pixel": that is, it will pass through the fragment processor and several tests, and if it gets through all of them, it will end up carrying depth and color information to a pixel on the frame buffer (or render target).

Figure 30-5 illustrates the fragment processor (sometimes called a "pixel shader") and texel pipeline. The texture and fragment-processing units operate in concert to apply a shader program to each fragment independently. The GeForce 6 Series architecture supports a scalable amount of fragment-processing horsepower. Another popular way to say this is that GPUs in the GeForce 6 Series can have a varying number of *fragment pipelines* (or "pixel pipelines"). Similar to the vertex processor, texture data is cached on-chip to reduce bandwidth requirements and improve performance.

The texture and fragment-processing unit operates on squares of four pixels (called *quads*) at a time, allowing for direct computation of derivatives for calculating texture level of detail. Furthermore, the fragment processor works on groups of hundreds of pixels at a time in single-instruction, multiple-data (SIMD) fashion (with each fragment processor engine working on one fragment concurrently), hiding the latency of texture fetch from the computational performance of the fragment processor.

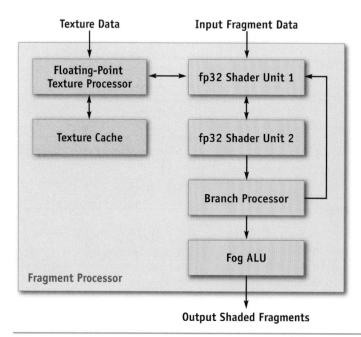

Figure 30-5. The GeForce 6 Series Fragment Processor and Texel Pipeline

The fragment processor uses the texture unit to fetch data from memory, optionally filtering the data before returning it to the fragment processor. The texture unit supports many source data formats (see Section 30.3.3, "Supported Data Storage Formats"). Data can be filtered using bilinear, trilinear, or anisotropic filtering. All data is returned to the fragment processor in fp32 or fp16 format. A texture can be viewed as a 2D or 3D array of data that can be read by the texture unit at arbitrary locations and filtered to reconstruct a continuous function. The GeForce 6 Series supports filtering of fp16 textures in hardware.

The fragment processor has two fp32 shader units per pipeline, and fragments are routed through both shader units and the branch processor before recirculating through the entire pipeline to execute the next series of instructions. This rerouting happens once for each core clock cycle. Furthermore, the first fp32 shader can be used for perspective correction of texture coordinates when needed (by dividing by w), or for general-purpose multiply operations. In general, it is possible to perform eight or more math operations in the pixel shader during each clock cycle, or four math operations if a texture fetch occurs in the first shader unit.

On the final pass through the pixel shader pipeline, the fog unit can be used to blend fog in fixed-point precision with no performance penalty. Fog blending happens often in conventional graphics applications and uses the following function:

```
out = FogColor * fogFraction + SrcColor * (1 - fogFraction)
```

This function can be made fast and small using fixed-precision math, but in general IEEE floating point, it requires two full multiply-adds to do effectively. Because fixed point is efficient and sufficient for fog, it exists in a separate small unit at the end of the shader. This is a good example of the trade-offs in providing flexible programmable hardware while still offering maximum performance for legacy applications.

Fragments leave the fragment-processing unit in the order that they are rasterized and are sent to the z-compare and blend units, which perform depth testing (z comparison and update), stencil operations, alpha blending, and the final color write to the target surface (an off-screen render target or the frame buffer).

The memory system is partitioned into up to four independent memory partitions, each with its own dynamic random-access memories (DRAMs). GPUs use standard DRAM modules rather than custom RAM technologies to take advantage of market economies and thereby reduce cost. Having smaller, independent memory partitions allows the memory subsystem to operate efficiently regardless of whether large or small blocks of data are transferred. All rendered surfaces are stored in the DRAMs, while textures and input data can be stored in the DRAMs or in system memory. The four independent memory partitions give the GPU a wide (256 bits), flexible memory subsystem, allowing for streaming of relatively small (32-byte) memory accesses at near the 35 GB/sec physical limit.

30.2.2 Functional Block Diagram for Non-Graphics Operations

As graphics hardware becomes more and more programmable, applications unrelated to the standard polygon pipeline (as described in the preceding section) are starting to present themselves as candidates for execution on GPUs.

Figure 30-6 shows a simplified view of the GeForce 6 Series architecture, when used as a graphics pipeline. It contains a programmable vertex engine, a programmable fragment engine, a texture load/filter engine, and a depth-compare/blending data write engine.

In this alternative view, a GPU can be seen as a large amount of programmable floating-point horsepower and memory bandwidth that can be exploited for compute-intensive applications completely unrelated to computer graphics.

Figure 30-7 shows another way to view the GeForce 6 Series architecture. When used for non-graphics applications, it can be viewed as two programmable blocks that run serially: the vertex processor and the fragment processor, both with support for fp32 operands and intermediate values. Both use the texture unit as a random-access data fetch unit and access data at a phenomenal 35 GB/sec (550 MHz DDR memory clock × 256 bits per clock cycle × 2 transfers per clock cycle). In addition, both the vertex and the fragment processor are highly computationally capable. (Performance details follow in Section 30.4.)

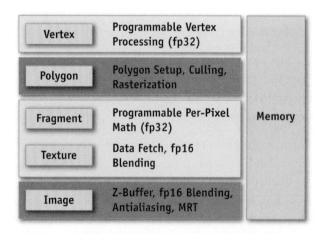

Figure 30-6. The GeForce 6 Series Architecture Viewed as a Graphics Pipeline

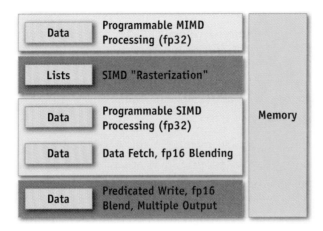

Figure 30-7. The GeForce 6 Series Architecture for Non-Graphics Applications

The vertex processor operates on data, passing it directly to the fragment processor, or by using the rasterizer to expand the data into interpolated values. At this point, each triangle (or point) from the vertex processor has become one or more *fragments*.

Before a fragment reaches the fragment processor, the z-cull unit compares the pixel's depth with the values that already exist in the depth buffer. If the pixel's depth is greater, the pixel will not be visible, and there is no point shading that fragment, so the fragment processor isn't even executed. (This optimization happens only if it's clear that the fragment processor isn't going to modify the fragment's depth.) Thinking in a general-purpose sense, this *early culling* feature makes it possible to quickly decide to skip work on specific fragments based on a scalar test. Chapter 34 of this book, "GPU Flow-Control Idioms," explains how to take advantage of this feature to efficiently predicate work for general-purpose computations.

After the fragment processor runs on a potential pixel (still a "fragment" because it has not yet reached the frame buffer), the fragment must pass a number of tests in order to move farther down the pipeline. (There may also be more than one fragment that comes out of the fragment processor if multiple render targets [MRTs] are being used. Up to four MRTs can be used to write out large amounts of data—up to 16 scalar floating-point values at a time, for example—plus depth.)

First, the scissor test rejects the fragment if it lies outside a specified subrectangle of the frame buffer. Although the popular graphics APIs define scissoring at this location in the pipeline, it is more efficient to perform the scissor test in the rasterizer. Scissoring in x and y actually happens in the rasterizer, before fragment processing, and z scissoring happens during z-cull. This avoids all fragment processor work on scissored (rejected) pixels. Scissoring is rarely useful for general-purpose computation because general-purpose programmers typically draw rectangles to perform computations in the first place.

Next, the fragment's depth is compared with the depth in the frame buffer. If the depth test passes, the fragment moves on in the pipeline. Optionally, the depth value in the frame buffer can be replaced at this stage.

After this, the fragment can optionally test and modify what is known as the stencil buffer, which stores an integer value per pixel. The stencil buffer was originally intended to allow programmers to mask off certain pixels (for example, to restrict drawing to a cockpit's windshield), but it has found other uses as a way to count values by incrementing or decrementing the existing value. This feature is used for stencil shadow volumes, for example.

If the fragment passes the depth and stencil tests, it can then optionally modify the contents of the frame buffer using the blend function. A blend function can be described as

```
out = src * srcOp + dst * dstOp
```

where `source` is the fragment color flowing down the pipeline; `dst` is the color value in the frame buffer; and `srcOp` and `dstOp` can be specified to be constants, source color components, or destination color components. Full blend functionality is supported for all pixel formats up to fp16×4. However, fp32 frame buffers don't support blending—only updating the buffer is allowed.

Finally, a feature called *occlusion query* makes it possible to quickly determine if any of the fragments that would be rendered in a particular computation would cause results to be written to the frame buffer. (Recall that fragments that do not pass the z-test don't have any effect on the values in the frame buffer.) Traditionally, the occlusion query test is used to allow graphics applications to avoid making draw calls for occluded objects, but it is useful for GPGPU applications as well. For instance, if the depth test is used to determine which outputs need to be updated in a sparse array, updating depth can be used to indicate when a given output has converged and no further work is needed. In this case, occlusion query can be used to tell when all output calculations are done. See Chapter 34 of this book, "GPU Flow-Control Idioms," for further information about this idea.

30.3 GPU Features

This section covers both fixed-function features and Shader Model 3.0 support (described in detail later) in GeForce 6 Series GPUs. As we describe the various pieces, we focus on the many new features that are meant to make applications shine (in terms of both visual quality and performance) on GeForce 6 Series GPUs.

30.3.1 Fixed-Function Features

Geometry Instancing

With Shader Model 3.0, the capability for sending multiple batches of geometry with one Direct3D call has been added, greatly reducing driver overhead in these cases. The hardware feature that enables instancing is *vertex stream frequency*—the ability to read vertex attributes at a frequency less than once every output vertex, or to loop over a subset of vertices multiple times. Instancing is most useful when the same object is drawn multiple times with different positions, for example, when rendering an army of soldiers or a field of grass.

Early Culling/Clipping

GeForce 6 Series GPUs are able to cull nonvisible primitives before shading at a high rate and clip partially visible primitives at full speed. Previous NVIDIA products would cull nonvisible primitives at primitive-setup rates, and clip all partially visible primitives at full speed.

Rasterization

Like previous NVIDIA products, GeForce 6 Series GPUs are capable of rendering the following objects:

- Point sprites
- Aliased and antialiased lines
- Aliased and antialiased triangles

Multisample antialiasing is also supported, allowing accurate antialiased polygon rendering. Multisample antialiasing supports all rasterization primitives. Multisampling is supported in previous NVIDIA products, though the $4\times$ multisample pattern was improved for GeForce 6 Series GPUs.

Z-Cull

NVIDIA GPUs since GeForce3 have technology, called *z-cull*, that allows hidden surface removal at speeds much faster than conventional rendering. The GeForce 6 Series z-cull unit is the third generation of this technology, which has increased efficiency for a wider range of cases. Also, in cases where stencil is not being updated, early stencil reject can be employed to remove rendering early when stencil test (based on equals comparison) fails.

Occlusion Query

Occlusion query is the ability to collect statistics on how many fragments passed or failed the depth test and to report the result back to the host CPU. Occlusion query can be used either while rendering objects or with color and z-write masks turned off, returning depth test status for the objects that would have been rendered, without modifying the contents of the frame buffer. This feature has been available since the GeForce3 was introduced.

Texturing

Like previous GPUs, GeForce 6 Series GPUs support bilinear, trilinear, and anisotropic filtering on 2D and cube-map textures of various formats. Three-dimensional textures support bilinear, trilinear, and quad-linear filtering, with and without mipmapping. Here are the new texturing features on GeForce 6 Series GPUs:

- Support for all texture types (2D, cube map, 3D) with fp16×2, fp16×4, fp32×1, fp32×2, and fp32×4 formats
- Support for all filtering modes on fp16×2 and fp16×4 texture formats
- Extended support for non-power-of-two textures to match support for power-of-two textures, specifically:
  - Mipmapping
  - Wrapping and clamping
  - Cube map and 3D textures

Shadow Buffer Support

NVIDIA GPUs support shadow buffering directly. The application first renders the scene from the light source into a separate z-buffer. Then during the lighting phase, it fetches the shadow buffer as a projective texture and performs z-compares of the shadow buffer data against a value corresponding to the distance from the light. If the distance passes the test, it's in light; if not, it's in shadow. NVIDIA GPUs have dedicated transistors to perform four z-compares per pixel (on four neighboring z-values) per clock, and to perform bilinear filtering of the pass/fail data. This more advanced variation of percentage-closer filtering saves many shader instructions compared to GPUs that don't have direct shadow buffer support.

High-Dynamic-Range Blending Using fp16 Surfaces, Texture Filtering, and Blending

GeForce 6 Series GPUs allow for fp16×4 (four components, each represented by a 16-bit float) filtered textures in the pixel shaders; they also allow performing all alpha-blending operations on fp16×4 filtered surfaces. This permits intermediate rendered buffers at a much higher precision and range, enabling high-dynamic-range rendering, motion blur, and many other effects. In addition, it is possible to specify a separate blending function for color and alpha values. (The lowest-end member of the GeForce 6 Series family, the GeForce 6200 TC, does not support floating-point blending or floating-point texture filtering because of its lower memory bandwidth, as well as to save area on the chip.)

30.3.2 Shader Model 3.0 Programming Model

Along with the fixed-function features listed previously, the capabilities of the vertex and the fragment processors have been enhanced in GeForce 6 Series GPUs. With Shader Model 3.0, the programming models for vertex and fragment processors are converging: both support fp32 precision, texture lookups, and the same instruction set. Specifically, here are the new features that have been added.

Vertex Processor

- **Increased instruction count.** The total instruction count is now 512 static instructions and 65,536 dynamic instructions. The static instruction count represents the number of instructions in a program as it is compiled. The dynamic instruction count represents the number of instructions actually executed. In practice, the dynamic count can be much higher than the static count due to looping and subroutine calls.

- **More temporary registers.** Up to 32 four-wide temporary registers can be used in a vertex program.

- **Support for instancing.** This enhancement was described earlier.

- **Dynamic flow control.** Branching and looping are now part of the shader model. On the GeForce 6 Series vertex engine, branching and looping have minimal overhead of just two cycles. Also, each vertex can take its own branches without being grouped in the way pixel shader branches are. So as branches diverge, the GeForce 6 Series vertex processor still operates efficiently.

- **Vertex texturing.** Textures can now be fetched in a vertex program, although only nearest-neighbor filtering is supported in hardware. More advanced filters can of course be implemented in the vertex program. Up to four unique textures can be accessed in a vertex program, although each texture can be accessed multiple times. Vertex textures generate latency for fetching data, unlike true constant reads. Therefore, the best way to use vertex textures is to do a texture fetch and follow it with arithmetic operations to hide the latency before using the result of the texture fetch.

Each vertex engine is capable of simultaneously performing a four-wide SIMD MAD (multiply-add) instruction and a scalar special function per clock cycle. Special function instructions include:

- Exponential functions: EXP, EXPP, LIT, LOG, LOGP
- Reciprocal instructions: RCP, RSQ
- Trigonometric functions: SIN, COS

Fragment Processor

- **Increased instruction count.** The total instruction count is now 65,535 static instructions and 65,535 dynamic instructions. There are limitations on how long the operating system will wait while the shader finishes working, so a long shader program working on a full screen of pixels may time-out. This makes it important to carefully consider the shader length and number of fragments rendered in one draw call. In practice, the number of instructions exposed by the driver tends to be smaller, because the number of instructions can expand as code is translated from Direct3D pixel shaders or OpenGL fragment programs to native hardware instructions.

- **Multiple render targets.** The fragment processor can output to up to four separate color buffers, along with a depth value. All four separate color buffers must be the same format and size. MRTs can be particularly useful when operating on scalar data, because up to 16 scalar values can be written out in a single pass by the fragment processor. Sample uses of MRTs include particle physics, where positions and velocities are computed simultaneously, and similar GPGPU algorithms. Deferred shading is another technique that computes and stores multiple four-component floating-point values simultaneously: it computes all material properties and stores them in separate textures. So, for example, the surface normal and the diffuse and specular material properties could be written to textures, and the textures could all be used in subsequent passes when lighting the scene with multiple lights. This is illustrated in Figure 30-8.

- **Dynamic flow control (branching).** Shader Model 3.0 supports conditional branching and looping, allowing for more flexible shader programs.

- **Indexing of attributes.** With Shader Model 3.0, an index register can be used to select which attributes to process, allowing for loops to perform the same operation on many different inputs.

- **Up to ten full-function attributes.** Shader Model 3.0 supports ten full-function attributes/texture coordinates, instead of Shader Model 2.0's eight full-function attributes plus specular color and diffuse color. All ten Shader Model 3.0 attributes are interpolated at full fp32 precision, whereas Shader Model 2.0's diffuse and specular color were interpolated at only 8-bit integer precision.

- **Centroid sampling.** Shader Model 3.0 allows a per-attribute selection of center sampling, or *centroid sampling*. Centroid sampling returns a value inside the covered portion of the fragment, instead of at the center, and when used with multisampling, it can remove some artifacts associated with sampling outside the polygon (for example, when calculating diffuse or specular color using texture coordinates, or when using texture atlases).

- **Support for fp32 and fp16 internal precision.** Fragment programs can support full fp32-precision computations and intermediate storage or partial-precision fp16 computations and intermediate storage.

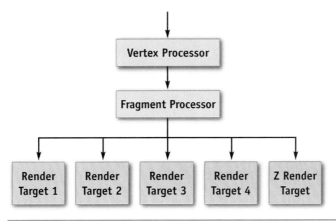

Figure 30-8. How MRTs Work
MRTs make it possible for a fragment program to return four four-wide color values plus a depth value.

- **3:1 and 2:2 coissue.** Each four-component-wide vector unit is capable of executing two independent instructions in parallel, as shown in Figure 30-9: either one three-wide operation on RGB and a separate operation on alpha, or one two-wide operation on red-green and a separate two-wide operation on blue-alpha. This gives the compiler more opportunity to pack scalar computations into vectors, thereby doing more work in a shorter time.

- **Dual issue.** Dual issue is similar to coissue, except that the two independent instructions can be executed on different parts of the shader pipeline. This makes the pipeline easier to schedule and, therefore, more efficient. See Figure 30-10.

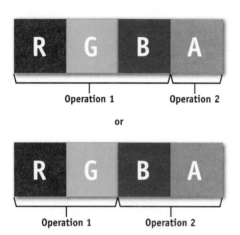

Figure 30-9. How Coissue Works
Two separate operations can concurrently execute on different parts of a four-wide register.

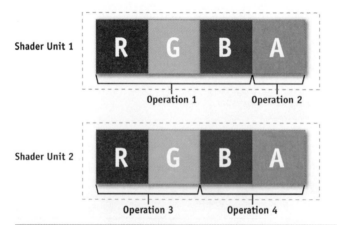

Figure 30-10. How Dual Issue Works
Independent instructions can be executed on independent units in the computational pipeline.

Fragment Processor Performance

The GeForce 6 Series fragment processor architecture has the following performance characteristics:

- Each pipeline is capable of performing a four-wide, coissue-able multiply-add (MAD) or four-term dot product (DP4), plus a four-wide, coissue-able and dual-issuable multiply instruction per clock in series, as shown in Figure 30-11. In addition, a multifunction unit that performs complex operations can replace the alpha channel MAD operation. Operations are performed at full speed on both fp32 and fp16 data, although storage and bandwidth limitations can favor fp16 performance sometimes. In practice, it is sometimes possible to execute eight math operations and a texture lookup in a single cycle.

- Dedicated fp16 normalization hardware exists, making it possible to normalize a vector at fp16 precision in parallel with the multiplies and MADs just described.

- An independent reciprocal operation can be performed in parallel with the multiply, MAD, and fp16 normalization described previously.

- Because the GeForce 6800 has 16 fragment-processing pipelines, the overall available performance of the system is given by these values multiplied by 16 and then by the clock rate.

- There is some overhead to flow-control operations, as defined in Table 30-2.

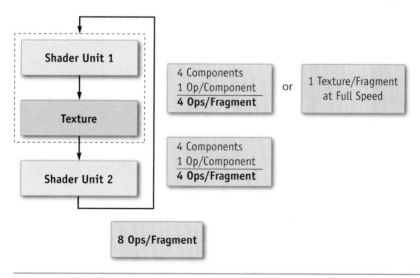

Figure 30-11. Shader Units and Capabilities in the Fragment Processor

Table 30-2. Overhead Incurred When Executing Flow-Control Operations in Fragment Programs

Instruction	Cost (Cycles)
If / endif	4
If / else / endif	6
Call	2
Ret	2
Loop / endloop	4

Furthermore, branching in the fragment processor is affected by the level of divergence of the branches. Because the fragment processor operates on hundreds of pixels per instruction, if a branch is taken by some fragments and not others, all fragments execute both branches, but only writing to the registers on the branches each fragment is supposed to take. For low-frequency and mid-frequency branch changes, this effect is hidden, although it can become a limiter as the branch frequency increases.

30.3.3 Supported Data Storage Formats

Table 30-3 summarizes the data formats supported by the graphics pipeline.

30.4 Performance

The GeForce 6800 Ultra is the flagship product of the GeForce 6 Series family at the time of writing. Its performance is summarized as follows:

- 425 MHz internal graphics clock
- 550 MHz memory clock
- 600 million vertices/second
- 6.4 billion texels/second
- 12.8 billion pixels/second, rendering z/stencil-only (useful for shadow volumes and shadow buffers)
- 6 four-wide fp32 vector MADs per clock cycle in the vertex shader, plus one scalar multi-function operation (a complex math operation, such as a sine or reciprocal square root)
- 16 four-wide fp32 vector MADs per clock cycle in the fragment processor, plus 16 four-wide fp32 multiplies per clock cycle
- 64 pixels per clock cycle early z-cull (reject rate)

As you can see, there's plenty of programmable floating-point horsepower in the vertex and fragment processors that can be exploited for computationally demanding problems.

Table 30-3. Data Storage Formats Supported by GeForce 6 Series GPUs   ✓ = Yes   ✗ = No

Format	Description of Data in Memory	Vertex Texture Support	Fragment Texture Support	Render Target Support
B8	One 8-bit fixed-point number	✗	✓	✓
A1R5G5B5	A 1-bit value and three 5-bit unsigned fixed-point numbers	✗	✓	✓
A4R4G4B4	Four 4-bit unsigned fixed-point numbers	✗	✓	✗
R5G6B5	5-bit, 6-bit, and 5-bit fixed-point numbers	✗	✓	✓
A8R8G8B8	Four 8-bit fixed-point numbers	✗	✓	✓
DXT1	Compressed 4×4 pixels into 8 bytes	✗	✓	✗
DXT2,3,4,5	Compressed 4×4 pixels into 16 bytes	✗	✓	✗
G8B8	Two 8-bit fixed-point numbers	✗	✓	✓
B8R8_G8R8	Compressed as YVYU; two pixels in 32 bits	✗	✓	✗
R8B8_R8G8	Compressed as VYUY; two pixels in 32 bits	✗	✓	✗
R6G5B5	6-bit, 5-bit, and 5-bit unsigned fixed-point numbers	✗	✓	✗
DEPTH24_D8	A 24-bit unsigned fixed-point number and 8 bits of garbage	✗	✓	✓
DEPTH24_D8_FLOAT	A 24-bit unsigned float and 8 bits of garbage	✗	✓	✓
DEPTH16	A 16-bit unsigned fixed-point number	✗	✓	✓
DEPTH16_FLOAT	A 16-bit unsigned float	✗	✓	✓
X16	A 16-bit fixed-point number	✗	✓	✗
Y16_X16	Two 16-bit fixed-point numbers	✗	✓	✗
R5G5B5A1	Three unsigned 5-bit fixed-point numbers and a 1-bit value	✗	✓	✓
HILO8	Two unsigned 16-bit values compressed into two 8-bit values	✗	✓	✗
HILO_S8	Two signed 16-bit values compressed into two 8-bit values	✗	✓	✗
W16_Z16_Y16_X16 FLOAT	Four fp16 values	✗	✓	✓
W32_Z32_Y32_X32 FLOAT	Four fp32 values	✓ (unfiltered)	✓ (unfiltered)	✓
X32_FLOAT	One 32-bit floating-point number	✓ (unfiltered)	✓ (unfiltered)	✓
D1R5G5B5	1 bit of garbage and three unsigned 5-bit fixed-point numbers	✗	✓	✓
D8R8G8B8	8 bits of garbage and three unsigned 8-bit fixed-point numbers	✗	✓	✓
Y16_X16 FLOAT	Two 16-bit floating-point numbers	✗	✓	✗

30.5 Achieving Optimal Performance

While graphics hardware is becoming more and more programmable, there are still some tricks to ensuring that you exploit the hardware fully to get the most performance. This section lists some common techniques that you may find helpful. A more detailed discussion of performance advice is available in the *NVIDIA GPU Programming Guide*, which is freely available in several languages from the NVIDIA Developer Web site (http://developer.nvidia.com/object/gpu_programming_guide.html).

30.5.1 Use Z-Culling Aggressively

Z-cull avoids work that won't contribute to the final result. It's better to determine early on that a computation doesn't matter and save doing the work. In graphics, this can be done by rendering the z-values for all objects first, before shading. For general-purpose computation, the z-cull unit can be used to select which parts of the computation are still active, culling computational threads that have already resolved. See Section 34.2.3 of Chapter 34, "GPU Flow-Control Idioms," for more details on this idea.

30.5.2 Exploit Texture Math When Loading Data

The texture unit filters data before returning it to the fragment processor, thus reducing the total data needed by the shader. The texture unit's bilinear filtering can frequently be used to reduce the total work done by the shader if it's performing more sophisticated shading.

Often, large filter kernels can be dissected into groups of bilinear footprints, which are scaled and accumulated to build the large kernel. A few caveats apply here, most notably that all filter coefficients must be positive for bilinear footprint assembly to work properly. (See Chapter 20, "Fast Third-Order Texture Filtering," for more information about this technique.)

Similarly, the filtering support given by shadow buffering can be used to offload the work from the processor when performing compares, then filtering the results.

30.5.3 Use Branching in Fragment Programs Judiciously

Because the fragment processor is a SIMD machine operating on many fragments at a time, if some fragments in a given group take one branch and other fragments in that group take another branch, the fragment processor needs to take both branches. Also, there is a six-cycle overhead for if-else-endif control structures. These two effects can reduce the performance of branching programs if not considered carefully. Branching can be very beneficial, as long as the work avoided outweighs the cost of branching.

Alternatively, conditional writes (that is, write if a condition code is set) can be used when branching is not performance-effective. In practice, the compiler will use the method that delivers higher performance when possible.

30.5.4 Use fp16 Intermediate Values Wherever Possible

Because GeForce 6 Series GPUs support a full-speed fp16 normalize instruction in parallel with the multiplies and adds, and because fp16 intermediate values reduce internal storage and datapath requirements, using fp16 intermediate values wherever possible can be a performance win, saving fp32 intermediate values for cases where the precision is needed.

Excessive internal storage requirements can adversely affect performance in the following way: The shader pipeline is optimized to keep hundreds of fragments in flight given a fixed amount of register space per fragment (four $fp32 \times 4$ registers or eight $fp16 \times 4$ registers). If the register space is exceeded, then fewer fragments can remain in flight, reducing the latency tolerance for texture fetches, and adversely affecting performance. The GeForce 6 Series fragment processor will have the maximum number of fragments in flight when shader programs use up to four $fp32 \times 4$ temporary registers (or eight $fp16 \times 4$ registers). That is, at any one time, a maximum of four temporary $fp32 \times 4$ (or eight $fp16 \times 4$) registers are in use. This decision was based on the fact that for the overwhelming majority of analyzed shaders, four or fewer simultaneously active $fp32 \times 4$ registers proved to be the sweet spot during the shaders' execution. In addition, the architecture is designed so that performance degrades slowly if more registers are used.

Similarly, the register file has enough read and write bandwidth to keep all the units busy if reading $fp16 \times 4$ values, but it may run out of bandwidth to feed all units if using $fp32 \times 4$ values exclusively. NVIDIA's compiler technology is smart enough to reduce this effect's impact substantially, but fp16 intermediate values are never slower than fp32 values; because of the resource restrictions and the fp16 normalize hardware, they can often be much faster.

30.6 Conclusion

GeForce 6 Series GPUs provide the GPU programmer with unparalleled flexibility and performance in a product line that spans the entire PC market. After reading this chapter, you should have a better understanding of what GeForce 6 Series GPUs are capable of, and you should be able to use this knowledge to develop applications—either graphical or general purpose—in a more efficient way.

Chapter 31

Mapping Computational Concepts to GPUs

Mark Harris
NVIDIA Corporation

Recently, graphics processors have emerged as a powerful computational platform. A variety of encouraging results, mostly from researchers using GPUs to accelerate scientific computing and visualization applications, have shown that significant speedups can be achieved by applying GPUs to data-parallel computational problems. However, attaining these speedups requires knowledge of GPU programming and architecture.

The preceding chapters have described the architecture of modern GPUs and the trends that govern their performance and design. Continuing from the concepts introduced in those chapters, in this chapter we present intuitive mappings of standard computational concepts onto the special-purpose features of GPUs. After presenting the basics, we introduce a simple GPU programming framework and demonstrate the use of the framework in a short sample program.

31.1 The Importance of Data Parallelism

As with any computer, attaining maximum performance from a GPU requires some understanding of its architecture. The previous two chapters provide a good overview of GPU architecture and the trends that govern its evolution. As those chapters showed, GPUs are designed for computer graphics, which has a highly parallel style of computation that computes output streams of colored pixels from input streams of independent data elements in the form of vertices and texels. To do this, modern GPUs have many programmable processors that apply kernel computations to stream elements in parallel.

The design of GPUs is essential to keep in mind when programming them—whether for graphics or for general-purpose computation. In this chapter, we apply the stream processing concepts introduced in Chapter 29, "Streaming Architectures and Technology Trends," to general-purpose computation on GPUs (GPGPU). The biggest difficulty in applying GPUs to general computational problems is that they have a very specialized design. As a result, GPU programming is entrenched in computer graphics APIs and programming languages. Our goal is to abstract from those APIs by drawing analogies between computer graphics concepts and general computational concepts. In so doing, we hope to get you into the data-parallel frame of mind that is necessary to make the most of the parallel architecture of GPUs.

31.1.1   What Kinds of Computation Map Well to GPUs?

Before we get started, let's get an idea of what GPUs are really good at. Clearly they are good at computer graphics. Two key attributes of computer graphics computation are data parallelism and independence: not only is the same or similar computation applied to streams of many vertices and fragments, but also the computation on each element has little or no dependence on other elements.

Arithmetic Intensity

These two attributes can be combined into a single concept known as *arithmetic intensity*, which is the ratio of computation to bandwidth, or more formally:

$$arithmetic\ intensity = operations\ /\ words\ transferred.$$

As discussed in Chapter 29, the cost of computation on microprocessors is decreasing at a faster rate than the cost of communication. This is especially true of parallel processors such as GPUs, because as technology improvements make more transistors available, more of these transistors are applied to functional units (such as arithmetic logic units) that increase computational throughput, than are applied to memory hierarchy (caches) that decrease memory latency. Therefore, GPUs demand high arithmetic intensity for peak performance.

As such, the computations that benefit most from GPU processing have high arithmetic intensity. A good example of this is the solution of systems of linear equations.

Chapter 44, "A GPU Framework for Solving Systems of Linear Equations," discusses the efficient representation of vectors and matrices and how to use this representation to rapidly solve linear partial differential equations. These computations perform well on GPUs because they are highly data-parallel: they consist of large streams of data elements (in the form of matrices and vectors), to which identical computational kernels are applied. The data communication required to compute each element of the output is small and coherent. As a result, the number of data words transferred from main memory is kept low and the arithmetic intensity is high.

Other examples of computation that works well on GPUs include physically based simulation on lattices, as discussed in Chapter 47, "Flow Simulation with Complex Boundaries," and all-pairs shortest-path algorithms, as described in Chapter 43, "GPU Computing for Protein Structure Prediction."

31.1.2 Example: Simulation on a Grid

For the rest of this chapter, we employ a simple but effective example: simulating natural phenomena on a grid. The Cartesian grid shown in Figure 31-1 is a discrete representation of the 2D spatial domain on which our phenomenon evolves. The example in this case is a physically based cloud simulation. We won't go into the physical and mathematical detail of this simulation, except to illustrate some basic GPGPU concepts. For more information on cloud simulation, see Harris et al. 2003.

Computation on a grid is common in GPGPU, because grids have a natural representation on GPUs: textures. Also, GPUs contain small texture caches that are optimized for 2D data locality, unlike the 1D data caches employed in CPUs. Many computations map naturally to grids, including matrix algebra; image and volume processing; physically based simulation; and global illumination algorithms such as ray tracing, photon mapping, and radiosity (see Chapter 39, "Global Illumination Using Progressive Refinement Radiosity"). Computations that aren't naturally performed on grids can also be mapped to grid computation by converting 1D addresses into 2D addresses.

The cloud simulation algorithm consists of a number of steps, as shown in Figure 31-1. The important detail about the algorithm steps is that each step updates the entire grid, and each step must complete before the next proceeds. In stream processing terms, the data stored in the grid cells make up our streams, and the algorithm steps are our computational kernels. Each kernel is applied to each stream element, generating a new stream that becomes the input to the next step.

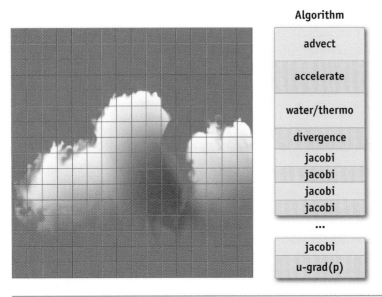

Algorithm

advect
accelerate
water/thermo
divergence
jacobi
jacobi
jacobi
jacobi

...

jacobi
u-grad(p)

Figure 31-1. Simulation on a Grid

This cloud simulation executes on the GPU. The data streams used in the simulation are represented on the grid (shown with exaggerated coarseness) and stored in textures. The algorithm is shown at right; each step in the algorithm is a kernel, implemented using a fragment program on the GPU.

31.1.3   Stream Communication: Gather vs. Scatter

High arithmetic intensity requires that communication between stream elements be minimized, but for many computations, communication is a necessary evil. In the cloud simulation, for example, some of the kernels must obtain information from cells other than the one currently being processed by the kernel. When discussing data communication on GPUs, it is helpful to consider two main types of communication: *gather* and *scatter*. Gather occurs when the kernel processing a stream element requests information from other elements in the stream: it "gathers" information from other parts of memory. Scatter, on the other hand, occurs when the kernel processing a stream element distributes information to other stream elements: it "scatters" information to other parts of memory. In terms of traditional memory concepts, gather requires only random-access load capability, while scatter requires only random-access store capability. Later we show why gather is typically preferable to scatter.

31.2 An Inventory of GPU Computational Resources

To start mapping general computation onto the specialized hardware of a GPU, we should first survey the computational resources that GPUs provide. We start with the computational workhorses: the processors.

31.2.1 Programmable Parallel Processors

GPUs have two types of programmable processors: *vertex processors* and *fragment processors*. Vertex processors process streams of vertices (made up of positions, colors, normal vectors, and other attributes), which are the elements that compose polygonal geometric models. Computer graphics typically represents 3D objects with triangular meshes. The vertex processors apply a *vertex program* (sometimes called a *vertex shader*) to transform each vertex based on its position relative to the camera, and then each set of three vertices is used to compute a triangle, from which streams of *fragments* are generated. A fragment can be considered a "proto-pixel." It contains all information needed to generate a shaded pixel in the final image, including color, depth, and destination in the frame buffer. The fragment processors apply a *fragment program* (sometimes called a *pixel shader*) to each fragment in the stream to compute the final color of each pixel.

Vertex Processors

Modern GPUs have multiple vertex processors (the NVIDIA GeForce 6800 Ultra and the ATI Radeon X800 XT both have six). These processors are fully programmable and operate in either SIMD- or MIMD-parallel fashion on the input vertices (see Chapter 34 for more information on these terms). The basic primitives of 3D computer graphics are 3D vertices in projected space, represented by an (x, y, z, w) vector, and four-component colors stored as (red, green, blue, alpha) vectors (often abbreviated RGBA), where alpha typically represents an opacity percentage. Because of this, vertex processors have hardware to process four-component vectors. This allows them to produce transformed vertex positions in fewer cycles.

Vertex processors are capable of changing the position of input vertices. If you think about this, the position of these vertices ultimately affects where in the image pixels will be drawn. An image is nothing but an array of memory; thus, because vertex processors can control where in memory data will be written, they are thus capable of scatter. However, most current vertex processors cannot directly read information from vertex elements in the input stream other than the one currently being processed. Therefore, they are incapable of gather. The NVIDIA GeForce 6 Series GPUs have a new feature called *vertex texture fetch* (VTF). This means that GeForce 6 vertex processors are capable of random-access memory reads. So, we can store part or all of our input stream data in a vertex texture and use VTF to implement a gather operation.

Fragment Processors

Modern GPUs also have multiple fragment processors (the NVIDIA GeForce 6800 Ultra and the ATI X800 XT both have 16). Like vertex processors, these are fully programmable. Fragment processors operate in SIMD-parallel fashion on input elements, processing four-element vectors in parallel. Fragment processors have the ability to fetch data from textures, so they are capable of gather. However, the output address of a fragment is always determined before the fragment is processed: the processor cannot change the output location of a pixel. Fragment processors are thus not natively capable of scatter. However, see Section 31.3 for further discussion and techniques for working around this limitation.

For GPGPU applications, the fragment processors are typically used more heavily than the vertex processors. There are two main reasons for this. First, there are more fragment processors than vertex processors on a typical programmable GPU. Second, the output of the fragment processors goes more or less directly into memory, which can be fed straight back in as a new stream of texture data. Vertex processor output, on the other hand, must pass through the rasterizer and fragment processors before reaching memory. This makes direct output from vertex processors less straightforward.

Rasterizer

As mentioned earlier, after the vertex processors transform vertices, each group of three vertices is used to compute a triangle (in the form of edge equations), and from this triangle a stream of fragments is generated. This work of generating fragments is done by the *rasterizer*. We can think of the rasterizer as an address interpolator. Later we show how memory addresses are represented as texture coordinates. The rasterizer interpolates these addresses and other per-vertex values based on the fragment position. Because it generates many data elements from only a few input elements, we can also think of the rasterizer as a data amplifier. These functions of the rasterizer are very specialized to rendering triangles and are not user-programmable.

Texture Unit

Fragment processors (and vertex processors on the latest GPUs) can access memory in the form of textures. We can think of the texture unit as a read-only memory interface.

Render-to-Texture

When an image is generated by the GPU, it can be written to frame-buffer memory that can be displayed, or it can be written to texture memory. This *render-to-texture* functionality is essential for GPGPU, because it is the only current mechanism with which to implement direct feedback of GPU output to input without going back to the host processor. (Indirect feedback is also available via *copy-to-texture*, which requires a copy from one location in the GPU's memory to another.) We can think of render-to-texture as a write-only memory interface.

You may be wondering why we don't consider the texture unit and render-to-texture together as a read-write memory interface. The reason is that the fragment processor can read memory as many times as it wants inside a kernel, but it can write data only at the *end* of the kernel program (this is *stream out*). Thus, memory reads and writes are fundamentally separate on GPUs, so it helps to think about them that way.

Data Types

When programming CPUs, we are used to dealing with multiple data types, such as integers, floats, and Booleans. Current GPUs are more limited in this regard. Although some of the high-level shading languages used by GPUs expose integer and Boolean data types, current GPUs process only real numbers in the form of fixed- or floating-point values. Also, there are multiple floating-point formats supported by current GPUs. For example, NVIDIA GeForce FX and GeForce 6 Series GPUs support both 16-bit (a sign bit, 10 mantissa bits, and 5 exponent bits) and 32-bit (a sign bit, 23 mantissa bits, and 8 exponent bits: identical to the IEEE-754 standard) floating-point formats. All current ATI products, including the Radeon 9800 and X800, support a 24-bit floating-point format, with a sign bit, 16 mantissa bits, and 7 exponent bits. The lack of integer data types on GPUs is a current limitation. This can typically be worked around using floating-point numbers, but, for example, not all 32-bit integers can be represented in 32-bit floating-point format (because there are only 23 bits in the mantissa). One must be careful because floating-point numbers cannot exactly represent the same range of whole numbers that their same-size integer counterparts can represent. Table 31-1 shows the bit fields of each floating-point format and a description of the values they can represent.

Table 31-1. Floating-Point Formats Currently Supported by NVIDIA and ATI GPUs

Name	Sign	Exponent	Mantissa	Largest Values	Smallest Values	Whole Number Range[1]	Supports Specials (NaN, Inf, etc.)
NVIDIA 16-bit	15 (1)	14:10 (5)	9:0 (10)	$\pm 65{,}504$	$\pm 2^{-14} \cong 10^{-5}$ ($\pm 2^{-24}$ with denorms)	± 2048	Yes
ATI 16-bit	15 (1)	14:10 (5)	9:0 (10)	$\pm 131{,}008$	$\pm 2^{-15} \cong 10^{-5}$	± 2048	No
ATI 24-bit	23 (1)	22:16 (7)	15:0 (16)	$\pm \sim 2^{64} \cong 10^{19}$	$\pm \sim 2^{-62} \cong 10^{-19}$	$\pm 131{,}072$	No
NVIDIA 32-bit (IEEE 754)	31 (1)	30:23 (8)	22:0 (23)	$\pm \sim 2^{128} \cong 10^{38}$	$\pm \sim 2^{-126} \cong 10^{-38}$	$\pm 16{,}777{,}216$	Yes

1. This is the contiguous zero-centered range of exactly representable whole numbers.

31.3 CPU-GPU Analogies

Even for expert CPU programmers, getting started in GPU programming can be tricky without some knowledge of graphics programming. In this section, we try to aid your understanding by drawing some very simple analogies between traditional CPU computational concepts and their GPU counterparts. We start with the concept of streams and kernels.

31.3.1 Streams: GPU Textures = CPU Arrays

This one is easy. The fundamental array data structures on GPUs are textures and vertex arrays. As we observed before, fragment processors tend to be more useful for GPGPU than vertex processors. Therefore, anywhere we would use an array of data on the CPU, we can use a texture on the GPU.

31.3.2 Kernels: GPU Fragment Programs = CPU "Inner Loops"

The many parallel processors of a GPU are its computational workhorses—they perform the kernel computation on data streams. On the CPU, we would use a loop to iterate over the elements of a stream (stored in an array), processing them sequentially. In the CPU case, the instructions inside the loop are the kernel. On the GPU, we write similar instructions inside a fragment program, which are applied to all elements of the stream. The amount of parallelism in this computation depends on the number of processors on the GPU we use, but also on how well we exploit the instruction-level parallelism enabled by the four-vector structure of GPU arithmetic. Note that vertex programs can also be thought of as kernels operating on a stream of vertices.

31.3.3 Render-to-Texture = Feedback

As mentioned before, most computations are broken into steps. Each step depends on the output of previous steps. In terms of streams, typically a kernel must process an entire stream before the next kernel can proceed, due to dependencies between stream elements. Also, in the case of physically based simulation, each time step of the simulation depends on the results of the previous time step.

All of this feedback is trivial to implement on the CPU because of its unified memory model, in which memory can be read or written anywhere in a program. Things aren't so easy on the GPU, as we discussed before. To achieve feedback, we must use render-to-texture to write the results of a fragment program to memory so they can then be used as input to future programs.

31.3.4 Geometry Rasterization = Computation Invocation

Now we have analogies for data representation, computation, and feedback. To run a program, though, we need to know how to invoke computation. Our kernels are fragment programs, so all we need to know is how to generate streams of fragments. This should be clear from the previous section; to invoke computation, we just draw geometry. The vertex processors will transform the geometry, and the rasterizer will determine which pixels in the output buffer it covers and generate a fragment for each one.

In GPGPU, we are typically processing every element of a rectangular stream of fragments representing a grid. Therefore, the most common invocation in GPGPU programming is a single quadrilateral.

31.3.5 Texture Coordinates = Computational Domain

Each kernel (fragment program) that executes on the GPU takes a number of streams as input and typically generates one stream of output. Newer GPUs that support multiple render targets can generate multiple output streams (currently limited to four RGBA streams). Any computation has an input domain and an output range. In many cases, the domain of a computation on the GPU may have different dimensions than the input streams.

GPUs provide a simple way to deal with this, in the form of texture coordinates. These coordinates are stored at vertices, and the rasterizer linearly interpolates the coordinates at each vertex to generate a set of coordinates for each fragment. The interpolated coordinates are passed as input to the fragment processor. In computer graphics, these coordinates are used as indices for texture fetches. For GPGPU, we can think of them as array indices, and we can use them to control the domain of the computation. The domain and range may be the same size, or the domain can be smaller than the range (data amplification/magnification), or the domain can be larger than the range (data minification). The rasterizer makes it easy to correctly sample the input stream at the correct intervals for each of these cases.

31.3.6 Vertex Coordinates = Computational Range

As discussed before, fragments are generated from input geometry by the rasterizer, and these fragments become output pixels after fragment processing. Because the fragment processors are not directly capable of scatter, the input vertices and the vertex program determine which pixels are generated. Typically, we specify four vertices of a quad in output pixel coordinates and apply a vertex program that simply passes the vertices through untransformed. Thus, vertex coordinates directly control the output range of the computation.

31.3.7 Reductions

Everything we've discussed up to this point has assumed purely parallel computation: each element is computed largely independently of the rest of the stream. However, there are times when we need to *reduce* a large vector of values to a smaller vector, or even to a single value. For example, we might need to compute the sum or the maximum of all values in an array. This sort of computation is called a *parallel reduction*.

On GPUs, reductions can be performed by alternately rendering to and reading from a pair of buffers. On each pass, the size of the output (the computational range) is reduced by some fraction. To produce each element of the output, a fragment program reads two or more values and computes a new one using the reduction operator, such as addition or maximum. These passes continue until the output is a single-element buffer, at which point we have our reduced result. In general, this process takes $O(\log n)$ passes, where n is the number of elements to reduce. For example, for a 2D reduction, the fragment program might read four elements from four quadrants of the input buffer, such that the output size is halved in both dimensions at each step. Figure 31-2 demonstrates a max reduction on a 2D buffer.

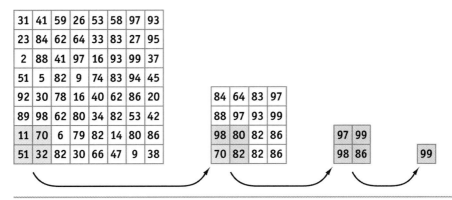

Figure 31-2. Max Reduction Performed with Multiple Passes

31.4 From Analogies to Implementation

By now you have a high-level understanding of how most GPGPU programs operate on current GPUs. The analogies from the previous section provide us a general implementation plan. Now, so that you can start putting the GPU to work, we dig into the nitty-gritty implementation details that you will need in practice.

31.4.1 Putting It All Together: A Basic GPGPU Framework

To make this easy, we've put together a very basic framework in C++ that you can use to write GPGPU programs. You'll find the framework on the CD included with this book. The framework, called *pug*, incorporates all of the analogies from the previous section in order to abstract GPGPU programming in a manner more accessible to experienced CPU programmers.

Initializing and Finalizing a GPGPU Application

The first step in a GPGPU application is to initialize the GPU. This is very easy in the framework: just call `pugInit()`. When the application is finished with the GPU, it can clean up the memory used by the graphics API by calling `pugCleanup()`.

Specifying Kernels

Kernels in our framework are written in the Cg language. Although Cg is designed for graphics, it is based on the C language and therefore is very easy to learn. For more information, we recommend *The Cg Tutorial* (Fernando and Kilgard 2003) and the documentation included with the Cg distribution (NVIDIA 2004). There are very few graphics-specific keywords in Cg. We provide a Cg file, pug.cg, that you can include in your kernel files. This file defines a structure called `Stream` that abstracts the most graphics-centric concept: texture fetching. `Stream` is a wrapper for the texture sampler Cg type. Calling one of the `value()` functions of the `Stream` structure gives the value of a stream element.

To load and initialize a kernel program from a file, use the `pugLoadProgram()` function. The function returns a pointer to a `PUGProgram` structure, which you will need to store and pass to the other framework functions to bind constants and streams to the kernel and to run it.

Stream Management

Arrays of data in the framework are called *buffers*. The `pugAllocateBuffer()` function creates a new buffer. Buffers can be read-only, write-only, or read-write, and this can be specified using the `mode` parameter of this function. This function returns a pointer to a `PUGBuffer` structure, which can be passed to a number of functions in the framework, including the following two.

To load initial data into a buffer, pass the data to the `pugInitBuffer()` function.

To bind an input stream for a kernel to a buffer, call `pugBindStream()`, which takes as arguments a pointer to the `PUGProgram` to bind to, the `PUGBuffer` pointer, and a string containing the name of the `Stream` parameter in the Cg kernel program to which this `PUGBuffer` should be bound.

Specifying Computational Domain and Range

To specify the domain and range of a computation, define a `PUGRect` structure with the coordinates of the corners of the rectangle that should be used as either the domain or range. Multiple domains can be specified. These will generate additional texture coordinates that the kernel program can use as needed.

To bind a domain, call `pugBindDomain()`, passing it the `PUGProgram`, a string parameter name for this domain defined in the kernel Cg program, and the `PUGRect` for the domain.

There can be only one range for a kernel, due to the inability of fragment programs to scatter. To specify the range, simply pass a `PUGRect` to the range parameter of the `pugRunProgram()` function.

Specifying Constant Parameters

Constant one-, two-, three-, or four-component floating-point parameters can be specified using `pugBindFloat()`, which takes as arguments a pointer to the `PUGProgram`, a string parameter name, and up to four floating-point values.

Invoking a Kernel

Once the preceding steps have been done, executing the computation is simple: just call the function `pugRunProgram()`. Pass it a pointer to the `PUGProgram`, the output `PUGBuffer` (which must be writable), and an optional `PUGRect` to specify the range. The entire buffer will be written if the range is not specified.

Note that a stream cannot be bound to a buffer if that buffer is currently being used for the output of a kernel. The framework will automatically release all streams bound to any buffer that is specified as the output buffer in `pugRunProgram()`.

Getting Data Back to the CPU

To bring results on the GPU back to the CPU, call the `pugGetBufferData()` function, passing it a pointer to the `PUGBuffer`. This function returns a pointer to a C array of type `float`. Reading data back from the GPU can cause the GPU pipeline to flush, so use this function sparingly to avoid hurting application performance.

Parallel Reductions

The framework provides support for three types of simple parallel reduction. Buffers can be reduced along rows (to a single column vector), along columns (to a single row vector), or both (to a single value). The framework functions for these operations are `pugReduce1D()` and `pugReduce2D()`.

31.5 A Simple Example

As a basic but nontrivial GPGPU example, we use a simulation of a phenomenon known as chemical reaction-diffusion. Reaction-diffusion is a model of how the concentrations of two or more reactants in a solution evolve in space and time as they undergo the processes of chemical reaction and diffusion. The reaction-diffusion model we use is called the Grey-Scott model (Pearson 1993) and involves just two chemical reactants. This phenomenological model does not represent a particular real chemical reaction; it serves as a simple model for studying the general reaction-diffusion phenomenon. Figure 31-3 shows the results of many iterations of the Grey-Scott model.

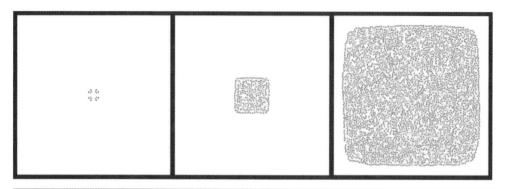

Figure 31-3. Visualizing the Grey-Scott Model

Grey-Scott consists of two simple partial differential equations that govern the evolution of the concentrations of two chemical reactants, U and V:

$$\frac{\partial U}{\partial t} = \boxed{D_u \nabla^2 U} - \boxed{UV^2 + F(1 - U)},$$

$$\frac{\partial V}{\partial t} = \boxed{D_v \nabla^2 V} + \boxed{UV^2 - (F + k)V}.$$

Diffusion   Reaction

Here k and F are constants; D_u and D_v are the diffusion rates of the reactants; and ∇^2 is the Laplacian operator, which represents diffusion. The Laplacian operator appears commonly in physics, most notably in the form of diffusion equations, such as the heat equation. A finite difference form of the Laplacian operator applied to a scalar field p on a two-dimensional Cartesian grid (with indices i, j, and cell size Δx) is

$$\nabla^2 p = \frac{p_{i+1,j} + p_{i-1,j} + p_{i,j+1} + p_{i,j-1} - 4p_{i,j}}{(\Delta x)^2}.$$

The implementation of the Grey-Scott model is fairly simple. There is a single data stream: the U and V chemical concentrations are stored in two channels of a single texture that represents a discrete spatial grid. This stream serves as input to a simple kernel, which implements the preceding equations in discrete form. The kernel is shown in Listing 31-1. C code that uses the framework to implement the simulation is shown in Listing 31-2.

Listing 31-1. The Reaction-Diffusion Kernel Program

```
float4 rd(float2 coords : DOMAIN,
  uniform stream concentration,
  uniform float2 DuDv, uniform float F, uniform float k) : RANGE
{
  float2 center = concentration.value2(coords).xy;

  float2 diffusion = concentration.value2(coords + half2(1, 0));
  diffusion += concentration.value2(coords + half2(-1, 0));
  diffusion += concentration.value2(coords + half2(0, 1));
  diffusion += concentration.value2(coords + half2(0, -1));

  // Average and scale by diffusion coeffs
  diffusion *= 0.25f * DuDv;

  float2 reaction = center.xx * center.yy * center.yy;
  reaction.x = -1;
  reaction.x += (1 - DuDv.x) * center.x + F * (1 - center.x);
  reaction.y += (-F - k + (1 - DuDv.y)) * center.y;

  // Now add the diffusion to the reaction to get the result.
  return float4(diffusion + reaction, 0, 0);
}
```

Listing 31-2. C++ Code to Set Up and Run a Reaction-Diffusion Simulation on the GPU
See the source code on the accompanying CD for more details.

```
PUGBuffer *rdBuffer; PUGProgram *rdProgram;

void init_rd(){ // Call this once.
  pugInit();   // Start up the GPU framework

  // Create a "double-buffered" PUGBuffer. Two buffers allow the
  // simulation to alternate using one as input, one as output
  PUGBuffer *rdBuffer = pugAllocateBuffer(width, height,
                                PUG_READWRITE, 4, true);

  PUGProgram *rdProgram = pugLoadProgram("rd.cg", "rd");

  pugBindFloat(rdProgram, "DuDv", du, dv); // bind parameters
  pugBindFloat(rdProgram, "F", F);
  pugBindFloat(rdProgram, "k", k);
```

```cpp
    // Initialize the state of the simulation with values in array
    pugInitBuffer(rdBuffer, array);
}

void update_rd(){ // Call this every iteration
    pugBindStream(rdProgram, "concentration", rdBuffer, currentSource);
    PUGRect range(0, width, 0, height);
    pugRunProgram(rdProgram, rdBuffer, range, currentTarget);

    std::swap(currentSource, currentTarget);
}
```

31.6 Conclusion

You should now have a good understanding of how to map general-purpose computations onto GPUs. With this basic knowledge, you can begin writing your own GPGPU applications and learn more advanced concepts. The simple GPU framework introduced in the previous section is included on this book's CD. We hope that it provides a useful starting point for your own programs.

31.7 References

Fernando, Randima, and Mark J. Kilgard. 2003. *The Cg Tutorial: The Definitive Guide to Programmable Real-Time Graphics*. Addison-Wesley.

Harris, Mark J., William V. Baxter III, Thorsten Scheuermann, and Anselmo Lastra. 2003. "Simulation of Cloud Dynamics on Graphics Hardware." In *Proceedings of the SIGGRAPH/Eurographics Workshop on Graphics Hardware 2003*, pp. 92–101.

NVIDIA Corporation. 2004. *The Cg Toolkit*. Available online at **http://developer.nvidia.com/object/cg_toolkit.html**

Pearson, John E. 1993. "Complex Patterns in a Simple System." *Science* 261, p. 189.

Chapter 32

Taking the Plunge into GPU Computing

Ian Buck
Stanford University

This and many other chapters in this book demonstrate how we can use GPUs as general computing engines, but it is important to remember that GPUs are primarily designed for interactive rendering, not computation. As a result, you can run into some stumbling blocks when trying to use the GPU as a computing engine. There are significant differences between the GPU and the CPU regarding both capabilities and performance, ranging from memory bandwidth and floating-point number representation to indirect memory access. Because our goal in porting applications to the GPU is to outperform the CPU implementations, it is important to understand these differences and structure our computation optimally for the GPU. In this chapter, we cover some of these differences and show how to write fast and efficient GPU-based applications.

32.1 Choosing a Fast Algorithm

Given that the GPU is primarily designed for rendering, the memory and compute units are optimized for shading rather than general-purpose computing such as signal processing, complex linear algebra, ray tracing, or whatever we might want to cram into the shader pipeline. In this section, we examine some of the performance characteristics of GPUs, contrasting them with CPUs. Understanding these characteristics can help us decide whether a given algorithm can capitalize on the capabilities of the GPU and, if so, how best to structure the computation for the GPU.

32.1.1 Locality, Locality, Locality

Getting good memory performance on CPUs is always about the locality of the references. The same is true for GPUs, but with several important variances. Figure 32-1 shows the performance of reading single-component floating-point texture data on the GeForce 6800 Ultra memory system compared to a 3.0 GHz Pentium 4 with three different access patterns: cached (reading the same memory location repeatedly), sequential, and random. It is clear that the GPU has much higher sequential memory access performance than the CPU. This is not surprising, considering that one of the key tasks of GPUs is filling regions of memory with contiguous texture data. From a computation standpoint, however, to get peak memory performance, computation must be structured around sequential memory accesses or else suffer a huge performance penalty with random memory reads. This is good news for accelerating linear algebra operations such as adding two large vectors, where data is naturally accessed sequentially. However, algorithms that do a lot of pointer chasing are going to suffer from poor random-access performance.

Another important distinction in memory performance between the GPU and the CPU is the role of the cache. Unlike the cache on the CPU, the GPU texture cache exists primarily to accelerate texture filtering. As a result, GPU caches need to be only as large as the size of the filter kernel for the texture sampler (typically only a few texels), which is too small to be useful for general-purpose computation. GPU cache formats are also optimized for locality in two dimensions, which is not always desirable. This is in contrast to the Pentium 4 cache, which operates at a much higher clock rate

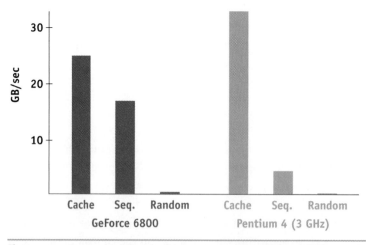

Figure 32-1. Comparing Memory Performance of the GPU and CPU

and contains megabytes of data. In addition, the Pentium 4 is able to cache both read and write memory operations, while the GPU cache is designed for read-only texture data. Any data written to memory (that is, the frame buffer) is not cached but written out to memory.

What does this mean for general-purpose computation on GPUs? The read-write CPU cache permits programmers to optimize algorithms to operate primarily out of the cache. For example, if your application data set is relatively small, it may fit entirely inside the Pentium 4 cache. Even with larger data sets, an application writer can "block" the computation to ensure that most reads and writes occur in the cache. In contrast, the limited size and read-only nature of the GPU cache puts it at a significant disadvantage. Therefore, an application that is more limited by sequential or random read bandwidth, such as adding two large vectors, will see much more significant performance improvements when ported to the GPU. The vector addition example sequentially reads and writes large vectors with no reuse of the data—an optimal access pattern on the GPU.

32.1.2 Letting Computation Rule

Memory access patterns are not the only determining characteristic in establishing whether an algorithm will run faster on a GPU versus a CPU. Certainly, if an application is dominated by computation, it does not matter much how we access memory. The rate of computation is where GPUs clearly outperform CPUs. Today's GPUs offer more than 60 gigaflops (billions of floating-point operations per second, or Gflops) of computing power in the fragment program hardware alone. Compare this to the Pentium 4 processor, which is limited to only 12 Gflops.[1] Therefore, with enough computation in GPU programs, any differences in memory performance should be unnoticeable.

But how much computation is necessary to avoid becoming limited by memory performance? To answer that question, we need to first review how memory accesses behave on the GPU. When we issue a texture fetch instruction, the memory read is serviced by the texture subsystem, which will likely have to fetch the texel from off-chip memory. To hide the time, or *latency*, of the texture fetch, the GPU begins work on the next fragment to be shaded after issuing the texel read request. When the texture data returns, the GPU suspends work on the next fragment and returns to continue shading the original fragment. Therefore, if we want to be limited by the computing performance of the GPU and not by the memory, our programs need to contain enough arithmetic instructions to cover the latency of any texture fetches we perform.

---

1. Comparing the observed performance of a fragment program's MAD instruction with the theoretical SSE MAD instruction rate on a 3.0 GHz Pentium 4.

As explained in Section 29.1.2 of Chapter 29, "Streaming Architectures and Technology Trends," the number of floating-point operations that GPUs can perform per value read from memory has increased over the past few years and is currently at a factor of seven to ten. From this discrepancy, we can make some conclusions regarding the kinds of GPU-based applications that are likely to outperform their CPU counterparts. To avoid being limited by the memory system, we must examine the ratio of arithmetic and memory operations for a given algorithm. This ratio is called the *arithmetic intensity* of the algorithm. If an algorithm has high arithmetic intensity, it performs many more arithmetic operations than memory operations. Because today's GPUs have five or more times more computing performance than CPUs, applications with high arithmetic intensity are likely to perform well on GPUs. Furthermore, we are more likely to be able to hide the costs of any memory fetch operations with arithmetic instructions.

32.1.3 Considering Download and Readback

One final performance consideration when using the GPU as a computing platform is the issue of download and readback. Before we even start computing on the GPU, we need to transfer our initial data down to the graphics card. Likewise, if the results of the computation are needed by the CPU, we need to read the data back from the GPU. Performing the computation on the CPU does not require these extra operations. When comparing against the CPU, we must consider the performance impact of downloading and reading back data.

Consider the example of adding two large vectors on the GPU. Executing a fragment program that simply fetches two floating-point values, adds them, and writes the result will certainly run faster than a CPU implementation, for reasons explained earlier. However, if we add the cost of downloading the vector data and reading back the results to the CPU, we are much better off simply performing the vector add on the CPU. Peak texture download and readback rates for today's PCI Express graphics cards max out around 3.2 GB/sec. A 3.0 GHz Pentium 4 can add two large vectors at a rate of approximately 700 megaflops (millions of floating-point operations per second, or Mflops).[2] So before we could even download both of the vectors to the GPU, the CPU could have completed the vector addition.

To avoid this penalty, we need to amortize the cost of the download and readback of our data. For simulation applications, this is less of a problem, because most such algorithms iterate over the data many times before returning. However, if you plan to use the GPU

---

2. Based on observed results running SSE-optimized code.

to speed up linear algebra operators (such as vector add), make sure you are doing enough operations on the data to cover the additional cost of download and readback.

One further consideration is the different pixel formats. Not all texture and framebuffer formats operate at the same speed. In some cases, the graphics driver may have to use the CPU to convert from user data provided as RGBA to the native GPU format, which might be BGRA. This can significantly affect download and readback performance. Native formats vary between vendors and different GPUs. It is best to experiment with a variety of formats to find the one that is fastest.

32.2 Understanding Floating Point

Today's GPUs perform all their computation using floating-point arithmetic. While desktop CPUs generally support a single floating-point standard, GPU vendors have implemented a variety of floating-point formats. Understanding the differences between these formats can help you both understand whether your application can produce accurate results and avoid some of the more common floating-point arithmetic mistakes, which can be more treacherous when using GPUs compared to CPUs.

First, let's review floating-point representation. A floating-point number is represented by the following expression:

$$sign \times 1.matissa \times 2^{\left(exponent - bias\right)}.$$

Consider representing the number 143.5, which corresponds to 1.435×10^2 in scientific notation. The scientific binary representation is $1.00011111 \times 2^{111}$. Thus the mantissa is set to 00011111 (the leading 1 is implied), and the exponent is stored biased by 127 (set by the particular floating-point format standard), which corresponds to 10000110. Different floating-point formats have differing numbers of bits dedicated to the mantissa and the exponent. For example, in the IEEE 754 standard used by most CPUs, a 32-bit float value consists of 1 sign bit, an 8-bit exponent, and a 23-bit mantissa. The number of bits available in the mantissa and exponent determines how accurately we can represent numbers. For IEEE 754, 143.5 is represented exactly; however 143.98375329 is rounded to 143.98375, because there are only 23 bits available for the mantissa. The GPU floating-point formats available today are the following:

- NVIDIA fp32: 23-bit mantissa, 8-bit exponent
- ATI fp24: 16-bit mantissa, 7-bit exponent
- NVIDIA fp16: 10-bit mantissa, 5-bit exponent

What does this mean for GPU-based applications? First, the NVIDIA fp32 format mimics the CPU, so calculations performed in that format should be accurate to approximately the seventh significant digit, which is the limit of the 23-bit mantissa. In contrast, ATI fp24 should be accurate to the fifth significant digit, while the NVIDIA fp16 format is accurate to the third digit. Although such lower precisions are perfectly reasonable for shading computations where the exact color value is not critical, the errors introduced from these formats can grossly affect numerical applications. Table 32-1 illustrates how accurately we can represent the number 143.98375329 with the different formats.

Table 32-1. Comparing the Accuracy of Floating-Point Formats
Number to represent: 143.98375329

Format	Result	Error
NVIDIA fp32	143.98375	0.00000329 (2×10^{-6}%)
ATI fp24	143.98242	0.00133329 (9×10^{-4}%)
NVIDIA fp16	143.875	0.10875329 (7×10^{-2}%)

32.2.1 Address Calculation

One particularly nasty consequence of this limited floating-point precision occurs when dealing with address calculations. Consider the case where we are computing addresses into a large 1D array that we'll store in a 2D texture. When computing a 1D address, it may be possible to end up with unaddressable elements of the array, due to the limited precision of the floating-point arithmetic. For example, if we are using an NVIDIA fp16 float, we cannot address element 3079, because the closest representable numbers with a 10-bit mantissa are 3078 and 3080. These off-by-one addressing bugs can be difficult to track down, because not all calculations will generate them. Even with 24-bit floats, it is not possible to address all of the pixels in a large 2D texture with a 1D address. Table 32-2 specifies the largest possible counting number that can be represented in each of the different formats before integer values start to be skipped.

Table 32-2. Comparing the Last Representable Integer Before Values Start to Be Skipped

Format	Largest Number
NVIDIA fp32	16,777,216
ATI fp24	131,072
NVIDIA fp16	2,048

As future GPUs begin to provide integer arithmetic, address calculation should become less of a problem. Until then, be aware of the floating-point precision you are using in your application, particularly when relying on floating-point values for memory addressing.

32.3 Implementing Scatter

One of the first things GPU programmers discover when using the GPU for general-purpose computation is the GPU's inability to perform a scatter operation in the fragment program. A *scatter* operation, also called an *indirect write*, is any memory write operation from a computed address. For example, the C code `a[i] = x` is a scatter operation in which we are "scattering" the value `x` into the array `a` from a computed address `i`. Scatter operations are extremely common in even the most basic algorithms. Examples include quicksort, hashing, histograms, or any algorithm that must write to memory from a computed address.

To see why scatters are hard to implement in a fragment program, let's look at the opposite of a scatter operation: *gather*. A gather is an indirect read operation, such as `x = a[i]`. Implementing gather inside a fragment program is straightforward, because it corresponds to a dependent texture read. For example, `a` is a texture, `i` is any computed value, and `a[i]` is a simple texture fetch instruction. Implementing scatter (`a[i] = x`) in a fragment program is not so simple, because there is no texture *write* instruction. In fact, the only memory writes we can perform in the GPU are at the precomputed fragment address, which cannot be changed by a fragment program. Each fragment writes to a fixed position in the frame buffer. In this section, we discuss some ways to get around this limitation of GPUs for applications that need to scatter data.

32.3.1 Converting to Gather

In some cases, it is possible to convert a scatter operation into a gather operation. To illustrate this, let's consider the example of simulating a spring-mass system on the GPU.

Figure 32-2 illustrates a simple mass-spring system in which we loop over each spring, compute the force exerted by the spring, and add the force contribution to the masses connected to the spring. The problem with implementing this algorithm on the GPU is that the spring force is scattered to the `mass_force` array. This scatter cannot be performed inside the fragment program.

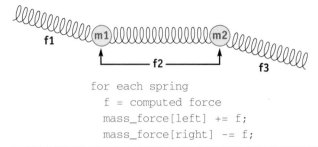

```
for each spring
    f = computed force
    mass_force[left] += f;
    mass_force[right] -= f;
```

Figure 32-2. A Simple Spring-Mass System, Updated with a Scatter

We can convert the scatter into a gather by performing another pass over the array into which we were previously scattering. As shown in Figure 32-3, instead of scattering the forces, we first output the spring forces to memory. With a second pass, we loop over all of the masses and gather the force values that affect that mass.[3] In general, this technique works wherever the connectivity is static. Because the spring connectivity is not changing during our simulation, we know exactly which element in the forces array we need to gather for each mass.

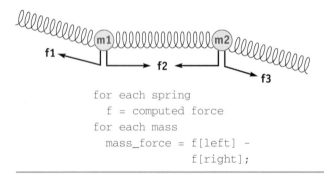

```
for each spring
    f = computed force
for each mass
    mass_force = f[left] -
                 f[right];
```

Figure 32-3. New Mass-Spring System with Only Gather Operations

32.3.2 Address Sorting

But what if our scatter address is not fixed? For example, let's assume we are implementing a particle simulation in which we have divided space into a grid of rectangular voxels. We wish to compute the net particle velocity for each voxel of the space. This type of operation is common when working with level sets. Figure 32-4 shows a typical implementation.

---

3. We could further combine these operations by recomputing the spring force inside the mass loop; however, this would cause each spring force to be computed twice. Although the actual computation of a spring force is quite simple, the additional bandwidth required to fetch the spring parameters can make this an ineffective optimization.

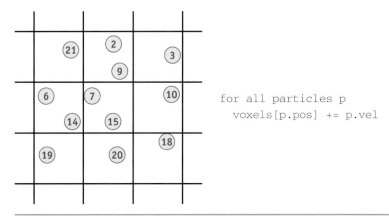

```
for all particles p
    voxels[p.pos] += p.vel
```

Figure 32-4. Computing the Net Particle Velocity in a Voxel

Here the address we are using for the scatter is not fixed, because the particles are moving from voxel to voxel in each time step of our simulation. We cannot convert this scatter into a gather directly because we don't know where to fetch our scatter data until runtime.

We can still convert these scatter operations into gathers using a technique called *address sorting*. The algorithm is similar to the earlier example except instead of simply outputting the data to scatter, we also output the scatter address with the data. We can then sort the data address pairs based on the address. This places all of the data to be scattered in contiguous array locations. Finally, we loop over each element of the array into which we want to scatter, using a binary search to fetch the data to scatter. See Figure 32-5.

Scatter Data with Write Addresses

Data	a	b	c	d	e	f	g	h
Address	5	2	1	5	2	3	6	0

Sorted Scatter Data

Data	h	c	b	e	f	a	d	g
Address	0	1	2	2	3	5	5	6

array[i] = binarysearch(data, i)

Array	h	c	b+e	f	f	a+d	g

Figure 32-5. Converting Scatters to Gathers with Address Sorting

Using address sorting to convert scatters to gathers is a fairly extensive multipass solution, but it may be the only option if your scatter addresses are not fixed in advance. Exactly how to implement sorting and searching on the GPU is explained in Buck and Purcell 2004, as well as in Chapter 46 of this book, "Improved GPU Sorting."

32.3.3 Rendering Points

Although fragment programs cannot change the address to which they are writing, vertex programs can by their very nature specify where to render in the output image. We can therefore use a vertex program to perform our scatter operation. This technique is fairly straightforward. The application simply issues points to render and the vertex program fetches from texture the scatter address and assigns it to the point's destination address with the appropriate scatter data. If the GPU does not support vertex textures, we can use the vertex and pixel buffer object extensions to remap texture data into a vertex array. The downside to this approach is that rendering points does not make very efficient use of the rasterization hardware. Also, you will have to be conscious of collisions in the scatter addresses (that is, when two points end up in the same position). Some simple ways to resolve collisions are either to use the z-buffer to prioritize them or to use blending operations to combine the values.

In summary, if you need to perform a scatter operation, you should convert the scatter into gather operations wherever you have fixed scatter addresses. If your scatter addresses are not fixed, you can use either address sorting or point rendering. Deciding which will be faster may differ from GPU to GPU; however, in general, if you are going to do very few scatters into a large region of memory, consider rendering points. The time it takes to scatter data with point rendering is a function of only the number of values to scatter. If you are scattering lots of data, it may be better to use the address sorting method to avoid reading data back to the CPU or being limited by the rate at which the GPU can render points.

32.4 Conclusion

In this chapter, we have touched on some of the challenges programmers discover when transitioning from CPU-based to GPU-based computing. To outperform the CPU, we need to understand GPU performance strengths, specifically favoring algorithms with sequential memory access and a good ratio of computation to memory operations. In addition, we have discussed some of the different types of floating-point formats available on GPUs and how they can affect the correctness of a program. Finally, we've shown how to work around the GPU's limited support for scatter operations. As you discover how the GPU can be used to accelerate your own algorithms, we hope the strategies described in this chapter will help you improve your application through efficient GPU-based computing.

32.5 References

Buck, Ian, and Purcell, Tim. 2004. "A Toolkit for Computation on GPUs." In *GPU Gems*, edited by Randima Fernando, pp. 621–636. Addison-Wesley.

Fatahalian, Kayvon, Jeremy Sugerman, and Pat Hanrahan. 2004. "Understanding the Efficiency of GPU Algorithms for Matrix-Matrix Multiplication." *Proceedings of Graphics Hardware*.

Goldberg, David. 1991. "What Every Computer Scientist Should Know About Floating Point Arithmetic. *ACM Computing Surveys* 23(1), pp. 5–48.

IEEE Standards Committee 754. 1987. "IEEE Standard for Binary Floating-Point Arithmetic, ANSI/IEEE Standard 754-1985." Reprinted in *SIGPLAN Notices* 22(2), pp. 9–25.

NVIDIA fp16 specification. Available online at
http://www.nvidia.com/dev_content/nvopenglspecs/GL_NV_half_float.txt

Chapter 33

Implementing Efficient Parallel Data Structures on GPUs

Aaron Lefohn
University of California, Davis

Joe Kniss
University of Utah

John Owens
University of California, Davis

Modern GPUs, for the first time in computing history, put a data-parallel, streaming computing platform in nearly every desktop and notebook computer. A number of recent academic research papers—as well as other chapters in this book—demonstrate that these streaming processors are capable of accelerating a much broader scope of applications than the real-time rendering applications for which they were originally designed. Leveraging this computational power, however, requires using a fundamentally different programming model that is foreign to many programmers. This chapter seeks to demystify one of the most fundamental differences between CPU and GPU programming: the memory model. Unlike traditional CPU-based programs, GPU-based programs have a number of limitations on when, where, and how memory can be accessed. This chapter gives an overview of the GPU memory model and explains how fundamental data structures such as multidimensional arrays, structures, lists, and sparse arrays are expressed in this data-parallel programming model.

33.1 Programming with Streams

Modern graphics processors are now capable of accelerating much more than real-time computer graphics. Recent work in the emerging field of general-purpose computation on graphics processing units (GPGPU) has shown that GPUs are capable of accelerating applications as varied as fluid dynamics, advanced image processing, photorealistic rendering, and even computational chemistry and biology (Buck et al. 2004, Harris et al. 2004). The key to using the GPU for purposes other than real-time rendering is to view it as a *streaming, data-parallel* computer (see Chapter 29 in this book, "Streaming Architectures and Technology Trends," as well as Dally et al. 2004). The way in which we structure computation and access memory in GPU programs is greatly influenced by this stream computation model. As such, we first give a brief overview of this model before discussing GPU-based data structures.

Streaming processors such as GPUs are programmed in a fundamentally different way than serial processors like today's CPUs. Most programmers are familiar with a programming model in which they can write to any location in memory at any point in their program. When programming a streaming processor, in contrast, we access memory in a much more structured manner. In the stream model, programs are expressed as series of operations on data streams, as shown in Figure 33-1. The elements in a *stream* (that is, an ordered array of data) are processed by the instructions in a *kernel* (that is, a small program). A kernel operates on each element of a stream and writes the results to an output stream.

The stream programming model restrictions allow GPUs to execute kernels in parallel and therefore process many data elements simultaneously. This *data parallelism* is made possible by ensuring that the computation on one stream element cannot affect the computation on another element in the same stream. Consequently, the only values that can be used in the computation of a kernel are the inputs to that kernel and global memory reads. In addition, GPUs require that the outputs of kernels be independent: kernels cannot perform random writes into global memory (in other words, they may write only to a single stream element position of the output stream). The data parallelism afforded by this model is fundamental to the speedup offered by GPUs over serial processors.

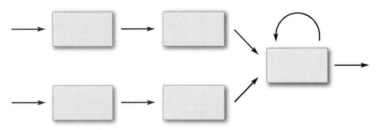

Figure 33-1. Stream Program as Data-Dependency Graph
The nodes are kernels and the edges are data streams. Kernels process all stream elements in parallel and write their results to output streams.

Following are two sample snippets of code showing how to transform a serial program into a data-parallel stream program. The first sample shows a loop over an array (for example, the pixels in an image) for a serial processor. Note that the instructions in the loop body are specified for only a single data element at a time:

```
for (i = 0; i < data.size(); i++)
  loopBody(data[i])
```

The next sample shows the same section of code written in pseudocode for a streaming processor:

```
inDataStream  = specifyInputData()
kernel        = loopBody()
outDataStream = apply(kernel, inDataStream)
```

The first line specifies the data stream. In the case of our image example, the stream is all of the pixels in the image. The second line specifies the computational kernel, which is simply the body of the loop from the first sample. Lastly, the third line applies the kernel to all elements in the input stream and stores the results in an output stream. In the image example, this operation would process the entire image and produce a new, transformed image.

Current GPU fragment processors have an additional programming restriction beyond the streaming model described earlier. Current GPU fragment processors are single-instruction, multiple-data (SIMD) parallel processors. This has traditionally meant that all stream elements (that is, fragments) must be processed by the same sequence of instructions. Recent GPUs (those supporting Pixel Shader 3.0 [Microsoft 2004a]) relax this strict SIMD model slightly by allowing variable-length loops and limited fragment-level branching. The hardware remains fundamentally SIMD, however, and thus branching must be spatially coherent between fragments for efficient execution (see Chapter 34 in this book, "GPU Flow-Control Idioms," for more information). Current vertex processors (Vertex Shader 3.0 [Microsoft 2004b]) are multiple-instruction, multiple-data (MIMD) machines, and can therefore execute kernel branches more efficiently than fragment processors. Although less flexible, the fragment processor's SIMD architecture is highly efficient and cost-effective.

Because nearly all GPGPU computations are currently performed with the more powerful fragment processor, GPU-based data structures must fit into the fragment processor's streaming, SIMD programming model. Therefore, all data structures in this chapter are expressed as streams, and the computations on these data structures are in the form of SIMD, data-parallel kernels.

33.2 The GPU Memory Model

Graphics processors have their own memory hierarchy analogous to the one used by serial microprocessors, including main memory, caches, and registers. This memory hierarchy, however, is designed for accelerating graphics operations that fit into the streaming programming model rather than general, serial computation. Moreover, graphics APIs such as OpenGL and Direct3D further limit the use of this memory to graphics-specific primitives such as vertices, textures, and frame buffers. This section gives an overview of the current memory model on GPUs and how stream-based computation fits into it.

33.2.1 Memory Hierarchy

Figure 33-2 shows the combined CPU and GPU memory hierarchy. The GPU's memory system creates a branch in a modern computer's memory hierarchy. The GPU, just like a CPU, has its own caches and registers to accelerate data access during computation. GPUs, however, also have their own main memory with its own address space—meaning that programmers must explicitly copy data into GPU memory before beginning program execution. This transfer has traditionally been a bottleneck for many applications, but the advent of the new PCI Express bus standard may make sharing memory between the CPU and GPU a more viable possibility in the near future.

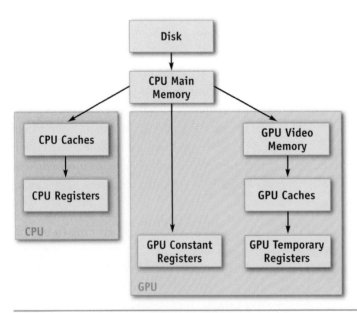

Figure 33-2. The CPU and GPU Memory Hierarchies

33.2.2 GPU Stream Types

Unlike CPU memory, GPU memory has a number of usage restrictions and is accessible only via the abstractions of a graphics programming interface. Each of these abstractions can be thought of as a different stream type with its own set of access rules. The three types of streams visible to the GPU programmer are vertex streams, frame-buffer streams, and texture streams. A fourth stream type, fragment streams, is produced and consumed entirely within the GPU. Figure 33-3 shows the pipeline for a modern GPU, the three user-accessible streams, and the points in the pipeline where each can be used.

Vertex Streams

Vertex streams are specified as vertex buffers via the graphics API. These streams hold vertex positions and a variety of per-vertex attributes. These attributes have traditionally been used for texture coordinates, colors, normals, and so on, but they can be used for arbitrary input stream data for vertex programs.

Vertex programs are not allowed to randomly index into their input vertices. Until recently, vertex streams could be updated only by transferring data from the CPU to the GPU. The GPU was not allowed to write to vertex streams. Recent API enhancements, however, have made it possible for the GPU to write to vertex streams. This is accomplished by either "copy-to-vertex-buffer" or "render-to-vertex-buffer." In the former technique, rendering results are copied from a frame buffer to a vertex buffer; in the latter technique, the rendering results are written directly to a vertex buffer. The recent addition of GPU-writable vertex streams enables GPUs, for the first time, to loop stream results from the end to the beginning of the pipeline.

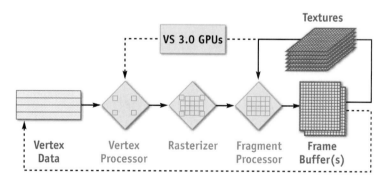

Figure 33-3. Streams in Modern GPUs
The GPU programmer can directly access vertices, frame buffers, and textures. Fragment streams are generated by the rasterizer and consumed by the fragment processor. They are the input streams to fragment programs but are created and consumed entirely within the GPU and so are not directly accessible to the programmer.

Fragment Streams

Fragment streams are generated by the rasterizer and consumed by the fragment processor. They are the stream inputs to fragment programs, but they are not directly accessible to programmers because they are created and consumed entirely within the graphics processor. Fragment stream values include all of the interpolated outputs from the vertex processor: position, color, texture coordinates, and so on. As with per-vertex stream attributes, the per-fragment values that have traditionally been used for texture coordinates may now be used for any stream value required by the fragment program.

Fragment streams cannot be randomly accessed by fragment programs. Permitting random access to the fragment stream would create a dependency between fragment stream elements, thus breaking the data-parallel guarantee of the programming model. If random access to fragment streams is needed by algorithms, the stream must first be saved to memory and converted to a texture stream.

Frame-Buffer Streams

Frame-buffer streams are written by the fragment processor. They have traditionally been used to hold pixels for display to the screen. Streaming GPU computation, however, uses frame buffers to hold the results of intermediate computation stages. In addition, modern GPUs are able to write to multiple frame-buffer surfaces (that is, multiple RGBA buffers) simultaneously. Current GPUs can write up to 16 floating-point scalar values per render pass (this value is expected to increase in future hardware).

Frame-buffer streams cannot be randomly accessed by either fragment or vertex programs. They can, however, be directly read from or written to by the CPU via the graphics API. Lastly, recent API enhancements have begun to blur the distinction between frame buffers, vertex buffers, and textures by allowing a render pass to be directly written to any of these stream types.

Texture Streams

Textures are the only GPU memory that is randomly accessible by fragment programs and, for Vertex Shader 3.0 GPUs, vertex programs. If programmers need to randomly index into a vertex, fragment, or frame-buffer stream, they must first convert it to a texture. Textures can be read from and written to by either the CPU or the GPU. The GPU writes to textures either by rendering directly to them instead of to a frame buffer or by copying data from a frame buffer to texture memory.

Textures are declared as 1D, 2D, or 3D streams and addressed with a 1D, 2D, or 3D address, respectively. A texture can also be declared as a cube map, which can be treated as an array of six 2D textures.

33.2.3 GPU Kernel Memory Access

Vertex and fragment programs (kernels) are the workhorses of modern GPUs. Vertex programs operate on vertex stream elements and send output to the rasterizer. Fragment programs operate on fragment streams and write output to frame buffers. The capabilities of these programs are defined by the arithmetic operations they can perform and the memory they are permitted to access. The variety of available arithmetic operations permitted in GPU kernels is approaching those available on CPUs, yet there are numerous memory access restrictions. As described previously, many of these restrictions are in place to preserve the parallelism required for GPUs to maintain their speed advantage. Other restrictions, however, are artifacts of the evolving GPU architecture and will almost certainly be relaxed in future generations.

The following is a list of memory access rules for vertex and fragment kernels on GPUs that support Pixel Shader 3.0 and Vertex Shader 3.0 functionality (Microsoft 2004a, b):

- No CPU main memory access; no disk access.
- No GPU stack or heap.
- Random reads from global texture memory.
- Reads from constant registers.
    - Vertex programs can use relative indexing of constant registers.
- Reads/writes to temporary registers.
    - Registers are local to the stream element being processed.
    - No relative indexing of registers.
- Streaming reads from stream input registers.
    - Vertex kernels read from vertex streams.
    - Fragment kernels read from fragment streams (rasterizer results).
- Streaming writes (at end of kernel only).
    - Write location is fixed by the position of the element in the stream.
      Cannot write to computed address (that is, no scatter).
    - Vertex kernels write to vertex output streams.
      Can write up to 12 four-component floating-point values.
    - Fragment kernels write to frame-buffer streams.
      Can write up to 4 four-component floating-point values.

An additional access pattern emerges from the preceding set of rules and the stream types described in Section 33.2.2: pointer streams (Purcell et al. 2002). Pointer streams arise out of the ability to use any input stream as the address for a texture read. Figure 33-4 shows that pointer streams are simply streams whose values are memory addresses. If the pointer stream is read from a texture, this capability is called *dependent texturing*.

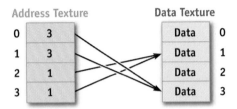

Figure 33-4. Implementing Pointer Streams with Textures

33.3 GPU-Based Data Structures

While the previous sections have described the GPU and its programming model with elegant abstractions, we now delve into the details of real-world data structures on current GPUs. The abstractions from Sections 33.1 and 33.2 continue to apply to the data structures herein, but the architectural restrictions of current GPUs make the real-world implementations slightly more complicated.

We first describe implementations of basic structures: multidimensional arrays and structures. We then move on to more advanced structures in Sections 33.3.3 and 33.3.4: static and dynamic sparse structures.

33.3.1 Multidimensional Arrays

Why include a section about multidimensional arrays if the GPU already provides 1D, 2D, and 3D textures? There are two reasons. First, current GPUs provide only 2D rasterization and 2D frame buffers. This means the only kind of texture that can be easily updated is a 2D texture, because it is a natural replacement for a 2D frame buffer.[1] Second, textures currently have restrictions on their size in each dimension. For example, current GPUs do not support 1D textures with more than 4,096 elements. If GPUs could write to an N-D frame buffer (where $N = 1, 2, 3, \ldots$) with no size restrictions, this section would be trivial.

---

1. Upcoming extensions to OpenGL allow rendering to a slice of a 3D texture.

Given these restrictions, 2D textures with nearest-neighbor filtering are the substrate on which nearly all GPGPU-based data structures are built.[2] Note that until recently, the size of each texture dimension was required to be a power of two, but this restriction is thankfully no longer in place.

All of the following examples use address translation to convert an N-D array address into a 2D texture address. Although it is important to minimize the cost of this address translation, remember that CPU-based multidimensional arrays must also perform address translation to look up values in the underlying 1D array. In fact, the GPU's texture-addressing hardware actually helps make these translations very efficient. Current GPUs do, however, suffer from one problem related to these address translations: the limitations of floating-point addressing. Chapter 32 of this book discusses important limitations and errors associated with using floating-point rather than integer addresses, and those problems apply to the techniques presented in this section.

1D Arrays

One-dimensional arrays are represented by packing the data into a 2D texture, as shown in Figure 33-5. Current GPUs can therefore represent 1D arrays containing up to 16,777,216 ($4,096 \times 4,096$) elements.[3] Each time this packed array is accessed from a fragment or vertex program, the 1D address must be converted to a 2D texture coordinate.

Two versions of this address translation are shown in Cg syntax in Listings 33-1 and 33-2. Listing 33-1 (Buck et al. 2004) shows code for using *rectangle* textures, which use integer

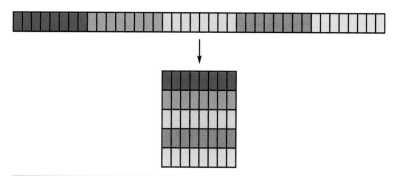

Figure 33-5. 1D Arrays Packed into 2D Arrays
Doing so avoids the size restrictions that current GPUs place on 1D textures.

2. If a data structure will remain static throughout an entire computation (for example, traditional texture uses), then 1D and 3D textures can and should be used.

3. Note that a 4096×4096 texture containing floating-point RGBA texels consumes 256 MB of RAM—as of January 2005, only the NVIDIA Quadro FX 4400 with unified frame buffer provides adequate contiguous memory.

addresses and do not support repeat-tiling address modes. Note that CONV_CONST is a constant based on the texture size and should be precomputed rather than recomputed for each stream element. Section 33.4 describes an elegant technique for computing values such as CONV_CONST with a feature of the Cg compiler called *program specialization*. With this optimization, Listing 33-1 compiles to three assembly instructions.

Listing 33-1. 1D to 2D Address Translation for Integer-Addressed Textures

```
float2 addrTranslation_1DtoRECT( float address1D, float2 texSize )
{
  // Parameter explanation:
  // - "address1D" is a 1D array index into an array of size N
  // - "texSize" is size of RECT texture that stores the 1D array

  // Step 1) Convert 1D address from [0,N] to [0,texSize.y]
  float CONV_CONST = 1.0 / texSize.x;
  float normAddr1D = address1D * CONV_CONST;

  // Step 2) Convert the [0,texSize.y] 1D address to 2D.
  // Performing Step 1 first allows us to efficiently compute the
  // 2D address with "frac" and "floor" instead of modulus
  // and divide. Note that the "floor" of the y-component is
  // performed by the texture system.
  float2 address2D = float2( frac(normAddr1D) * texSize.x, normAddr1D );
  return address2D;
}
```

Listing 33-2 shows an address translation routine that can be used with traditional 2D textures, which use normalized [0,1] addressing. If CONV_CONST is precomputed, this address translation takes two fragment assembly instructions. It may also be possible to eliminate the frac instruction from Listing 33-2 by using the repeating-tiled addressing mode (such as GL_REPEAT). This reduces the conversion to a single assembly instruction. This optimization may be problematic on some hardware and texture configurations, however, so it should be carefully tested on your target architecture.

2D Arrays

Two-dimensional arrays are represented simply as 2D textures. Their maximum size is limited by the GPU driver. That limit for current GPUs ranges from 2048×2048 to 4096×4096 depending on the display driver and the GPU. These limits can be queried via the graphics API.

Listing 33-2. 1D to 2D Address Translation for Normalized-Addressed Textures

```
float2 addrTranslation_1Dto2D( float address1D, float2 texSize )
{
  // Parameter explanation:
  // - "address1D" is a 1D array index into an array of size N
  // - "texSize" is size of 2D texture that stores the 1D array

  // NOTE: Precompute CONV_CONST before running the kernel.
  float2 CONV_CONST = float2( 1.0 / texSize.x,
                              1.0 / (texSize.x * texSize.y );

  // Return a normalized 2D address (with values in [0,1])
  float2 normAddr2D = address1D * CONV_CONST;
  float2 address2D = float2( frac(normAddr2D.x), normAddr2D.y );
  return address2D;
}
```

3D Arrays

Three-dimensional arrays may be stored in one of three ways: in a 3D texture, with each slice stored in a separate 2D texture, or packed into a single 2D texture (Harris et al. 2003, Lefohn et al. 2003, Goodnight et al. 2003). Each of these techniques has pros and cons that affect the best representation for an application.

The simplest approach, using a 3D texture, has two distinct advantages. The first is that no address translation computation is required to access the memory. The second advantage is that the GPU's native trilinear filtering may be used to easily create high-quality volume renderings of the data. A disadvantage is that GPUs can update at most only four slices of the volume per render pass—thus requiring many passes to write to the entire array.

The second solution is to store each slice of the 3D texture in a separate 2D texture, as shown in Figure 33-6. The advantages are that, like a native 3D representation, no address translation is required for data access, and yet each slice can be easily updated without requiring render-to-slice-of-3D-texture API support. The disadvantage is that the volume can no longer be truly randomly accessed, because each slice is a separate texture. The programmer must know which slice numbers will be accessed before the kernel executes, because fragment and vertex programs cannot dynamically compute which texture to access at runtime.

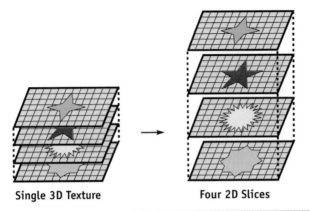

Single 3D Texture   **Four 2D Slices**

Figure 33-6. Storing a 3D Texture with Separate 2D Slices
Three-dimensional textures can be stored with each slice in a separate 2D texture. The advantage is that no address translation is required to access the data and 2D slices are easily updated in separate render passes. The disadvantages are that each slice must be updated in separate render passes and the slice number to be accessed must be known before a kernel may access the data.

The third option is to pack the 3D array into a single 2D texture, as shown in Figure 33-7. This solution requires an address translation for each data access, but the entire 3D array can be updated in a single render pass and no render-to-slice-of-3D-texture functionality is required. The ability to update the entire volume in a single render pass may have significant performance benefits, because the GPU's parallelism is better utilized when processing large streams. Additionally, unlike the 2D slice layout, the entire 3D array can be randomly accessed from within a kernel.

A disadvantage of both the second and third schemes is that the GPU's native trilinear filtering cannot be used for high-quality volume rendering of the data. Fortunately,

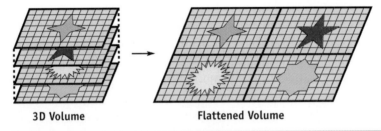

3D Volume   **Flattened Volume**

Figure 33-7. 3D Arrays Flattened into a Single 2D Texture
Three-dimensional arrays can be flattened into a single 2D texture (or pbuffer) so that the entire volume can be updated in a single render pass and the entire 3D array may be randomly accessed. The data may be laid out in slices (as shown here) or in a linear packing, as described in Listing 33-3.

alternate volume rendering algorithms can efficiently render high-quality, filtered images from these complex 3D texture formats (see Chapter 41 of this book, "Deferred Filtering: Rendering from Difficult Data Formats").

The Cg code in Listing 33-3 shows one form of address translation to convert a 3D address into a 2D address for a packed representation. This packing is identical to the one used for the 1D arrays in Listings 33-1 and 33-2. It simply converts the 3D address to a large 1D address space before packing the 1D space into a 2D texture. This packing scheme was presented in Buck et al. 2004. Note that this scheme can use either of the conversions shown in Listing 33-1 and 33-2, depending on the type of the data texture (2D or rectangle).

Listing 33-3. Converting a 3D Address into a 2D Address

```
float2 addrTranslation_3Dto2D(float3 address3D,
                              float3 sizeTex3D,
                              float2 sizeTex2D)
{
  // Parameter explanation:
  // - "address3D" is 3D array index into a 3D array of "sizeTex3D"
  // - "sizeTex2D" is size of 2D texture that stores the 3D array

  // Step 1) Texture size constant (This should be precomputed!)
  float3 SIZE_CONST = float3(1.0, sizeTex3D.x,
                             sizeTex3D.y * sizeTex3D.x);

  // Step 2) Convert 3D address to 1D address in [0, sizeTex2D.y]
  float address1D = dot( address3D, SIZE_CONST );

  // Step 3) Convert [0, texSize.y] 1D address to 2D using the
  // 1D-to-2D translation function defined in Listing 33-1.
  return addrTranslation_1Dto2D( address1D, sizeTex2D );
}
```

The Cg code for a slice-based, alternate packing scheme is shown in Listing 33-4. This scheme packs slices of the 3D texture into the 2D texture. One difficulty in this scheme is that the width of the 2D texture must be evenly divisible by the width of a slice of the 3D array. The advantage is that native bilinear filtering may be used within each slice. Note that the entire address translation reduces to two instructions (a 1D texture lookup and a multiply-add) if the sliceAddr computation is stored in a 1D lookup table texture indexed by address3D.z and nSlicesPerRow is precomputed.

Listing 33-4. Source Code for Packing Slices of 3D Texture in a 2D Texture

```
float2 addrTranslation_slice_3Dto2D( float3 address3D,
                                     float3 sizeTex3D,
                                     float2 sizeTex2D)
{
  // NOTE: This should be precomputed
  float nSlicesPerRow = sizeTex2D.x / sizeTex3D.x;

  // Compute (x,y) for slice in address space of the slices
  float2 sliceAddr = float2( fmod(address3D.z, nSlicesPerRow),
                             floor(address3D.z / nSlicesPerRow) );

  // Convert sliceSpace address to 2D texture address
  float2 sliceSize = float2(address3D.x, address3D.y );
  float2 offset = sliceSize * sliceAddr;

  return addr3D.xy + offset;
}
```

Note that there would be no reason to store 3D arrays in 2D textures if GPUs supported either 3D rasterization with 3D frame buffers or the ability to "cast" textures from 2D to 3D. In the latter case, the GPU would rasterize the 2D, flattened form of the array but allow the programmer to read from it using 3D addresses.

Higher-Dimensional Arrays

Higher-dimensional arrays can be packed into 2D textures using a generalized form of the packing scheme shown in Listing 33-3 (Buck et al. 2004).

33.3.2 Structures

A "stream of structures" such as the one shown in Listing 33-5 must be defined instead as a "structure of streams," as shown in Listing 33-6. In this construct, a separate stream is created for each structure member. In addition, the structures may not contain more data than can be output per fragment by the GPU.[4] These restrictions are due to the inability of fragment programs to specify the address to which their frame-buffer result is written (that is, they cannot perform a *scatter* operation). By specifying structures as a "structure of streams," each structure member has the same stream index, and all members can therefore be updated by a single fragment program.

---

4. Current GPUs as of January 2005 (NVIDIA GeForce 6 Series and ATI Radeon 9800 and X800) can output up to 16 floating-point values per fragment.

Listing 33-5. Stream of Structures

```
// WARNING: "Streams of structures" like the one shown
// in this example cannot be easily updated on current GPUs.
struct Foo {
  float4 a;
  float4 b;
};


// This "stream of structures" is problematic
Foo foo[N];
```

Listing 33-6. Structure of Streams

```
// This "structure of streams" can be easily updated on
// current GPUs if the number of data members in each structure
// is <= the number of fragment outputs supported by the GPU.
struct Foo {
  float4 a[N];
  float4 b[N];
};


// Define a separate stream for each member
float4 Foo_a[N];
float4 Foo_b[N];
```

33.3.3 Sparse Data Structures

The arrays and structures we've discussed thus far are *dense* structures. In other words, all elements in the address space of the arrays contain valid data. There are many problems, however, whose efficient solution requires sparse data structures (such as lists, trees, or sparse matrices). Sparse data structures are an important part of many optimized CPU-based algorithms; brute-force GPU-based implementations that use dense data structures in their place are often slower than their optimized CPU counterparts. In addition, sparse data structures can reduce an algorithm's memory requirement—an important consideration given the limited amount of available GPU memory.

Despite their importance, GPU implementations of sparse data structures are problematic. The first reason is that updating sparse structures usually involves writing to a computed memory address (that is, scattering). The second difficulty is that traversing a sparse structure often involves a nonuniform number of pointer dereferences to access the data. This is problematic because, as discussed in Section 33.1, current fragment processors are SIMD machines that must process coarse batches of stream elements with exactly the same instructions. Researchers have nonetheless recently shown that a number of sparse structures can be implemented with current GPUs.

Static Sparse Structures

We begin by describing static GPU-based sparse data structures whose structure does not change during GPU computation. Examples of such data structures include the list of triangles in Purcell's ray acceleration grid (Purcell et al. 2002) and the sparse matrices in Bolz et al. 2003 and Krüger and Westermann 2003. In these structures, the location and number of sparse elements are fixed throughout the GPU computation. For example, the location and number of triangles in the ray-traced scene do not change. Because the structures are static, they do not have to write to computed memory addresses.

All of these structures use one or more levels of indirection to represent the sparse structures in memory. Purcell's ray acceleration structure, for example, begins with a regular 3D grid of triangle list pointers, as shown in Figure 33-8. The 3D grid texture contains a pointer to the start of the triangle list (stored in a second texture) for that grid cell. Each entry in the triangle list, in turn, contains a pointer to vertex data stored in a third texture. Similarly, the sparse matrix structures use a fixed number of levels of indirection to find nonzero matrix elements.

These structures solve the problem of irregular access patterns with one of two different methods. The first method is to break the structure into blocks, where all elements in the block have an identical access pattern and can therefore be processed together. The second method is to have each stream element process one item from its list per render

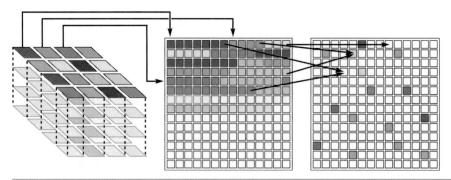

Figure 33-8. Purcell's Sparse Ray-Tracing Data Structure
Rays traverse a 3D grid, accessing the 3D texture to get the location of the start of the triangle list for that cell in the triangle list texture. The triangle list entries index into a third texture that stores vertex positions and texture coordinates for all triangles in the scene.

pass. Those elements with more items to process will continue to compute results, while those that have reached the end of their list will be disabled.[5]

An example of the blocking strategy is found in Bolz et al. 2003. They split sparse matrices into blocks that have the same number of nonzero elements and pad similar rows so that they have identical layouts. The algorithm for traversing the triangle lists found in Purcell et al. 2002 is an example of nonuniform traversal via conditional execution. All active rays (stream elements) process one element from their respective lists in each render pass. Rays become inactive when they reach the end of their triangle list, while rays that have more triangles to process continue to execute.

Note that the constraint of uniform access patterns for all stream elements is a restriction of the SIMD execution model of current GPUs. If future GPUs support MIMD stream processing, accessing irregular sparse data structures may become much easier. For example, the limited branching offered in Pixel Shader 3.0 GPUs already offers more options for data structure traversal than previous GPU generations.

Dynamic Sparse Structures

GPU-based sparse data structures that are updated during a GPU computation are an active area of research. Two noteworthy examples are the photon map in Purcell et al. 2003 and the deformable implicit surface representation in Lefohn et al. 2003, 2004. This section gives a brief overview of these data structures and the techniques used to update them.

A photon map is a sparse, adaptive data structure used to estimate the irradiance (that is, the light reaching a surface) in a scene. Purcell et al. (2003) describe an entirely GPU-based photon map renderer. To create the photon map on the GPU, they devise two schemes for writing data to computed memory addresses (that is, *scatter*) on current GPUs. The first technique computes the memory addresses and the data to be stored at those addresses. It then performs the scatter by performing a data-parallel sort operation on these buffers. The second technique, *stencil routing*, uses the vertex processor to draw large points at positions defined by the computed memory addresses. It resolves conflicts (when two data elements are written to the same address) via an ingenious stencil-buffer trick that routes data values to unique bins (pixel locations) even when they are drawn at the same fragment position. The nonuniform data are accessed in a manner similar to the triangle list traversal described in the previous subsection.

---

5. Disabling computation on a sparse subset of stream elements is itself a difficult problem. Researchers have used the depth buffer, stencil buffer, substreams (drawing smaller sets of geometry), and other tricks to prevent stream elements from being processed. NVIDIA GeForce 6 Series GPUs have full support for branching in the vertex processor and a limited form of branching in the fragment processor. Combining conditional execution with data-parallel computation is an active area of research.

Another GPU-based dynamic sparse data structure is the sparse volume structure used for implicit surface deformation by Lefohn et al. (2003, 2004). An *implicit surface* defines a 3D surface as an *isosurface* (or level set) of a volume. A common example of 2D isosurfaces is the contour lines drawn on topographic maps. A contour line comprises points on the map that have the same elevation. Similarly, an implicit 3D surface is an isosurface of the scalar values stored in a volume's voxels. Representing surfaces in this way is very convenient from a mathematical standpoint, allowing the surface to freely distort and change topology.

Efficient representations of implicit surfaces use a sparse data structure that stores only the voxels near the surface rather than the entire volume, as shown in Figure 33-9.

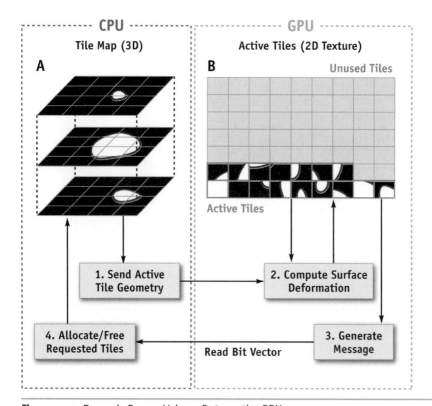

Figure 33-9. Dynamic Sparse Volume Data on the GPU
The tile-based sparse data structure and algorithm used in Lefohn et al. 2003, 2004 to represent a deforming implicit surface. The implicit surface deformation computation is performed only on the sparse set of tiles that contain the surface. As the surface moves, new tiles must be allocated and others must be freed. The algorithm uses the GPU to compute the surface deformation and uses the CPU as a memory (tile) manager. The GPU requests tile allocations by sending a bit vector message to the CPU.

Lefohn et al. (2003, 2004) describe a GPU-based technique for deforming implicit surfaces from one shape into another. As the surface evolves, the sparse data structure representing it must also evolve (because the size of the data structure is proportional to the surface area of the implicit surface). For example, if the initial surface is a small sphere and the final form is a large square, the final form will require significantly more memory than was required for the initial sphere. The remainder of this section describes this sparse volume structure and how it evolves with the moving surface.

The sparse structure is created by subdividing the 3D volume into small 2D tiles (see the section marked "A" in Figure 33-9). The CPU stores tiles that contain the surface (that is, *active* tiles) in GPU texture memory (see the section marked "B" in Figure 33-9). The GPU performs the surface deformation computation on only the active tiles (see step 2 in Figure 33-9). The CPU keeps a map of the active tiles and allocates/frees tiles as necessary for the GPU computation. This scheme solves the dynamic update problem by employing the CPU as a memory management coprocessor for the GPU.

A key component of the system is the way in which the GPU requests that the CPU allocate or free tiles. The CPU receives the communication by reading a small encoded message (image) from the GPU (see steps 3 and 4 in Figure 33-9). This image contains one pixel per active tile, and the value of each pixel is a bit code. The 7-bit code has 1 bit for the active tile and 6 bits for each of the tiles neighboring it in the 3D volume. The value of each bit instructs the CPU to allocate or free the associated tile. The CPU, in fact, interprets the entire image as a single bit vector. The GPU creates the bit vector image by computing a memory request at each active pixel, then reducing the requests to one per tile by using either automatic mipmap generation or the reduction techniques described in Buck et al. 2004. Once the CPU decodes the memory request message, it allocates/frees the requested tiles and sends a new set of vertices and texture coordinates to the GPU (see step 1 in Figure 33-9). These vertex data represent the new active set of tiles on which the GPU computes the surface deformation.

In summary, this dynamic sparse data structure solves the problem of requiring scatter functionality by sending small messages to the CPU when the GPU data structure needs to be updated. The structure uses the blocking strategy, discussed at the beginning of this section, to unify computation on a sparse domain. The scheme is effective for several reasons. First, the amount of GPU-CPU communication is minimized by using the compressed bit vector message format. Second, the CPU serves only as a memory manager and lets the GPU perform all of the "heavy" computation. Note that the implicit surface data resides only on the GPU throughout the deformation. Lastly, the dynamic sparse representation enables the computation and memory requirements to scale with the surface area of the implicit surface rather than the volume of its bounding box. This is an important optimization, which if ignored would allow CPU-based implementations to easily outpace the GPU version.

The two dynamic sparse data structures described in this section both adhere to the rules of data-parallel data structures in that their data elements can be accessed independently in parallel. Purcell et al.'s structure is updated in a data-parallel fashion, whereas Lefohn et al.'s structure is updated partially in parallel (the GPU generates a memory allocation request using data-parallel computation) and partially with a serial program (the CPU services the array of memory requests one at a time using stacks and queues). Complex GPU-compatible data structures will remain an active area of research due to their importance in creating scalable, optimized algorithms. Whether or not these data structures are contained entirely within the GPU or use a hybrid CPU/GPU model will depend largely on how the GPU evolves and at what speed/latency the CPU and GPU can communicate.

33.4 Performance Considerations

This last section describes low-level details that can have a large impact on the overall performance of GPU-based data structures.

33.4.1 Dependent Texture Reads

One of the GPU's advantages over a CPU is its ability to hide the cost of reading out-of-cache values from memory. It accomplishes this by issuing asynchronous memory read requests and performing other, nondependent operations to fill the time taken by the memory request. Performing multiple dependent memory accesses (that is, using the result of a memory access as the address for the next) reduces the amount of available nondependent work and thus gives the GPU less opportunity to hide memory access latency. As such, certain types of dependent texture reads can cause severe slowdowns in your program if not used with discretion.

Not all dependent texture reads will slow down your program. The publicly available benchmarking tool GPUBench (Fatahalian et al. 2004) reports that the cost of dependent texture reads is entirely based on the cache coherency of the memory accesses. The danger, then, with dependent texture reads is their ability to easily create cache-incoherent memory accesses. Strive to make dependent texture reads in your data structures as cache-coherent as possible. Techniques for maintaining cache coherency include grouping similar computations into coherent blocks, using the smallest possible lookup tables, and minimizing the number of levels of texture dependencies (thereby reducing the risk of incoherent accesses).

33.4.2 Computational Frequency and Program Specialization

The data streams described in Section 33.2.2 are computed at different computational frequencies. Vertex streams, for example, are a lower-frequency stream than fragment streams. This means that vertex streams contain fewer elements than fragment streams. The available computational frequencies for GPU computation are these: constant, uniform, vertex, and fragment. Constant values are known at compile time, and uniform arguments are runtime values computed only once per kernel execution. We can take advantage of the different computational frequencies in GPUs by computing values at the lowest possible frequency. For example, if a fragment program accesses multiple neighboring texels, it is generally more efficient to compute the memory addresses for those texels in a vertex program rather than a fragment program if there are fewer vertices than fragments.

Another example of computational frequency optimizations is kernel code that computes the same value at each data element. This computation should be precomputed on the CPU at uniform frequency before the GPU kernel executes. Such code is common in the address translation code shown earlier (Listings 33-1, 33-2, and 33-3). One way to avoid such redundant computation is to precompute the uniform results by hand and change the kernel code accordingly (including the kernel's parameters). Another, more elegant, option is to use the Cg compiler's *program specialization* functionality to perform the computation automatically. Program specialization (Jones et al. 1993) recompiles a program at runtime after "runtime constant" uniform parameters have been set. All code paths that depend only on these known values are executed, and the constant-folded values are stored in the compiled code. Program specialization is available in Cg via the `cgSetParameterVariability` API call (NVIDIA 2004). Note that this technique requires recompiling the kernel and is thus applicable only when the specialized kernel is used many times between changes to the uniform parameters. The technique often applies to only a subset of uniform parameters that are set only once (that is, "runtime constants").

33.4.3 Pbuffer Survival Guide

Pbuffers, or pixel buffers, are off-screen frame buffers in OpenGL. In addition to providing floating-point frame buffers, these special frame buffers offer the only render-to-texture functionality available to OpenGL programmers until very recently. Unfortunately, pbuffers were not designed for the heavy render-to-texture usage that many GPGPU applications demand (sometimes having hundreds of pbuffers), and many performance pitfalls exist when trying to use pbuffers in this way.

The OpenGL Architecture Review Board (ARB) is currently working on a new mechanism for rendering to targets other than a displayable frame buffer (that is, textures, vertex arrays, and so on). This extension, in combination with the vertex and pixel buffer object extensions, will obviate the use of pbuffers for render-to-texture. We have nonetheless included the following set of pbuffer tips because a large number of current applications use them extensively.

The fundamental problem with pbuffers is that each pbuffer contains its own OpenGL render and device context. Changing between these contexts is a very expensive operation. The traditional use of pbuffers for render-to-texture has been to use one pbuffer with each renderable texture. The result is that switching from one renderable texture to the next requires a GPU context switch—leading to abysmal application performance. This section presents two techniques that greatly reduce the cost of changing render targets by avoiding switching contexts.

The first of these optimizations is to use *multisurface* pbuffers. A pbuffer *surface* is one of the pbuffer's color buffers (such as front, back, aux0, and so on). Each pbuffer surface can serve as its own renderable texture, and switching between surfaces is very fast. It is important to ensure that you do not bind the same surface as both a texture and a render target. This is an illegal configuration and will most likely lead to incorrect results because it breaks the stream programming model guarantee that kernels cannot write to their input streams. Listing 33-7 shows pseudocode for creating and using a multisurface pbuffer for multiple render-to-texture passes.

Listing 33-7. Efficient Render-to-Texture Using Multisurface Pbuffers in OpenGL

```
void draw( GLenum readSurface, GLenum writeSurface )
{
  // 1) Bind readSurface as texture
  wglBindTexImageARB(pbuffer, readSurface);

  // 2) Set render target to the writeSurface
  glDrawBuffer(writeSurface);

  // 3) Render
  doRenderPass(. . .);
```

```
  // 4) Unbind readSurface texture
  wglReleaseTexImageARB(pbuffer, readSurface);
}

// 1) Allocate and enable multisurface pbuffer (Front, Back, AUX buffers)
Pbuffer pbuff = allocateMultiPbuffer( GL_FRONT, GL_BACK, GL_AUX0, . . .);
EnableRenderContext( pbuff );

// 2) Read from FRONT and write to BACK
draw( WGL_FRONT_ARB, GL_BACK );

// 3) Read from BACK and write to FRONT
draw( WGL_BACK_ARB, GL_FRONT );
```

The second pbuffer optimization is to use the packing techniques described in Section 33.3.1 for flattening a 3D texture into a 2D texture. Storing your data in multiple "viewports" of the same, large pbuffer will further avoid the need to switch OpenGL contexts. Goodnight et al. (2003) use this technique extensively in their multigrid solver. Just as in the basic multisurface pbuffer case, however, you must avoid simultaneously reading from and writing to the same surface.

33.5 Conclusion

The GPU memory model is based on a streaming, data-parallel computation model that supports a high degree of parallelism and memory locality. The model has a number of restrictions on when, how, and where memory can be used. Many of these restrictions exist to guarantee parallelism, but some exist because GPUs are designed and optimized for real-time rendering rather than general high-performance computing. As the application domains that drive GPU sales include more than real-time graphics, it is likely that GPUs will become more general and these artificial restrictions will be relaxed.

Techniques for managing basic GPU-based data structures such as multidimensional arrays and structures are well established. The creation, efficient use, and updating of complex GPU data structures such as lists, trees, and sparse arrays is an active area of research.

33.6 References

Bolz, J., I. Farmer, E. Grinspun, and P. Schröder. 2003. "Spare Matrix Solvers on the GPU: Conjugate Gradients and Multigrid." *ACM Transactions on Graphics (Proceedings of SIGGRAPH 2003)* 22(3), pp. 917–924.

Buck, I., T. Foley, D. Horn, J. Sugerman, and P. Hanrahan. 2004. "Brook for GPUs: Stream Computing on Graphics Hardware." *ACM Transactions on Graphics (Proceedings of SIGGRAPH 2004)* 23(3), pp. 777–786.

Dally, W. J., U. J. Kapasi, B. Khailany, J. Ahn, and A. Das. 2004. "Stream Processors: Programmability with Efficiency." *ACM Queue* 2(1), pp. 52–62.

Fatahalian, K., I. Buck, and P. Hanrahan. 2004. "GPUBench: Evaluating GPU Performance for Numerical and Scientific Applications." GP^2 Workshop. Available online at **http://graphics.stanford.edu/projects/gpubench/**

Goodnight, N., C. Woolley, G. Lewin, D. Luebke, and G. Humphreys. 2003. "A Multigrid Solver for Boundary Value Problems Using Programmable Graphics Hardware." In *Proceedings of the SIGGRAPH/Eurographics Workshop on Graphics Hardware 2003*, pp. 102–111.

Harris, M. J. 2004. "GPGPU: General Purpose Computing on Graphics Processing Units." Available online at **http://www.gpgpu.org**

Harris, M. J., W. V. Baxter, T. Scheuermann, and A. Lastra. 2003. "Simulation of Cloud Dynamics on Graphics Hardware." In *Proceedings of the SIGGRAPH/Eurographics Workshop on Graphics Hardware 2003*, pp. 92–101.

Jones, N. D., C. K. Gomard, and P. Sestoft. 1993. *Partial Evaluation and Automatic Program Generation*. Prentice Hall.

Krüger, J., and R. Westermann. 2003. "Linear Algebra Operators for GPU Implementation of Numerical Algorithms." *ACM Transactions on Graphics (Proceedings of SIGGRAPH 2003)* 22(3), pp. 908–916.

Lefohn, A. E., J. M. Kniss, C. D. Hansen, and R. T. Whitaker. 2003. "Interactive Deformation and Visualization of Level Set Surfaces Using Graphics Hardware." *IEEE Visualization*, pp. 75–82.

Lefohn, A. E., J. M. Kniss, C. D. Hansen, and R. T. Whitaker. 2004. "A Streaming Narrow-Band Algorithm: Interactive Deformation and Visualization of Level Sets." *IEEE Transactions on Visualization and Computer Graphics* 10(2), pp. 422–433.

Microsoft Corporation. 2004a. "Pixel Shader 3.0 Spec."
Available online at **http://msdn.microsoft.com/library/default.asp?
url=/library/en-us/directx9_c/directx/graphics/reference/assemblylanguageshaders/
pixelshaders/ps_3_0.asp**

Microsoft Corporation. 2004b. "Vertex Shader 3.0 Spec."
Available online at **http://msdn.microsoft.com/library/default.asp?
url=/library/en-us/directx9_c/directx/graphics/reference/assemblylanguageshaders/
vertexshaders/vs_3_0.asp**

NVIDIA Corporation. 2004. "Cg Language Reference." Available online at
http://developer.nvidia.com/

OpenGL Extension Registry. 2004. Available online at
http://oss.sgi.com/projects/ogl-sample/registry/

Purcell, T. J., I. Buck, W. R. Mark, and P. Hanrahan. 2002. "Ray Tracing on Programmable Graphics Hardware." *ACM Transactions on Graphics (Proceedings of
SIGGRAPH 2002)* 21(3), pp. 703–712.

Purcell, T. J., C. Donner, M. Cammarano, H. W. Jensen, and P. Hanrahan. 2003.
"Photon Mapping on Programmable Graphics Hardware." In *Proceedings of the
SIGGRAPH/Eurographics Workshop on Graphics Hardware 2003*, pp. 41–50.

Chapter 34

GPU Flow-Control Idioms

Mark Harris
NVIDIA Corporation

Ian Buck
Stanford University

Flow control is one of the most fundamental concepts taught to beginning programmers. Branching and looping are such basic concepts that it can be daunting to write software for a platform that supports them in a limited manner. The latest GPUs support vertex and fragment program branching in multiple forms, but their highly parallel nature requires care in how they are used. This chapter surveys some of the limitations of branching on current GPUs and describes a variety of techniques for iteration and decision making in GPGPU programs.

34.1 Flow-Control Challenges

Let's start by discussing the most obvious form of flow control on GPUs. All current high-level shading languages for GPUs support traditional C-style explicit flow-control constructs, such as if-then-else, for, and while. The underlying implementations of these, however, are much different from their implementations on CPUs.

For example, consider the following code:

```
if (a)
  b = f();
else
  b = g();
```

CPUs can easily branch based on the Boolean `a` and evaluate either the `f()` or `g()` functions. The performance characteristics of this branch are relatively easily understood: CPUs generally have long instruction pipelines, so it is important that the CPU be able to accurately predict whether a particular branch will be taken. If this prediction is done successfully, branching generally incurs a small penalty. If the branch is not correctly predicted, the CPU may stall for a number of cycles as the pipeline is flushed and must be refilled from the correct target address. As long as the functions `f()` and `g()` have a reasonable number of instructions, these costs aren't too high.

The latest GPUs, such as the NVIDIA GeForce 6 Series, have similar branch instructions, though their performance characteristics are slightly different. Older GPUs do not have native branching of this form, so other strategies are necessary to emulate these operations.

The two most common control mechanisms in parallel architectures are single instruction, multiple data (SIMD) and multiple instruction, multiple data (MIMD). All processors in a SIMD-parallel architecture execute the same instruction at the same time; in a MIMD-parallel architecture, different processors may simultaneously execute different instructions. There are three current methods used by GPUs to implement branching: MIMD branching, SIMD branching, and condition codes.

MIMD branching is the ideal case, in which different processors can take different data-dependent branches without penalty, much like a CPU. The NVIDIA GeForce 6 Series supports MIMD branching in its vertex processors.

SIMD branching allows branching and looping inside a program, but because all processors must execute identical instructions, divergent branching can result in reduced performance. For example, imagine a fragment program that decides the output value of each fragment by branching using conditions based on random input numbers. The fragments will randomly take different branches, which can cause processors that are running threads for fragments that do not take the branch to stall until other processors are finished running threads for fragments that do take the branch. The end result is that many fragments will take as long as both branches together, plus the overhead of the branch instruction. SIMD branching is very useful in cases where the branch conditions are fairly "spatially" coherent, but lots of incoherent branching can be expensive. NVIDIA GeForce FX GPUs support SIMD branching in their vertex processors, and NVIDIA GeForce 6 Series GPUs support it in their fragment processors.

Condition codes (predication) are used in older architectures to emulate true branching. If-then statements compiled to these architectures must evaluate both taken and not taken branch instructions on all fragments. The branch condition is evaluated and a condition code is set. The instructions in each part of the branch must check the value of the condition code before writing their results to registers. As a result, only instructions in taken branches write their output. Thus, in these architectures all branches cost as much as both parts of the branch, plus the cost of evaluating the branch condition. Branching should be used sparingly on such architectures. NVIDIA GeForce FX Series GPUs use condition-code branch emulation in their fragment processors.

34.2 Basic Flow-Control Strategies

34.2.1 Predication

The simplest approach to implementing branching on the GPU is predication, as discussed earlier. With predication, the GPU effectively evaluates both sides of the branch and then discards one of the results, based on the value of the Boolean branch condition. The disadvantage of this approach is that evaluating both sides of the branch can be costly if f() and g() are large functions. While predication may be effective for small branches, alternative strategies are necessary for more complex branching.

34.2.2 Moving Branching up the Pipeline

Because explicit branching can be tricky on GPUs, it's handy to have a number of techniques in your repertoire. A useful strategy is to move flow-control decisions up the pipeline to an earlier stage, where they can be more efficiently evaluated.

Static Branch Resolution

When performing computations on streams or arrays of data on the CPU, most programmers know that they should strive to avoid branching inside the inner loops of the computation. Doing so can cause the pipeline to stall due to incorrect branch prediction. For example, consider evaluating a partial differential equation (PDE) on a discrete spatial grid. Correct evaluation of the PDE on a finite domain requires boundary conditions. A naive CPU implementation might iterate over the entire grid, deciding at each cell if it is a boundary cell and applying the appropriate computation based on the result of the decision. A better implementation divides the processing into multiple loops: one over the interior of the grid, excluding boundary cells, and one or more over the boundary edges. This *static branch resolution* results in loops that contain efficient code without branches.

The same optimization is even more important on most GPUs. In this case, the computation is divided into two fragment programs: one for interior cells and one for boundary cells. The interior program is applied to the fragments of a quad drawn over all but the outer single-cell-wide edge of the output buffer. The boundary program is applied to fragments of lines drawn over the edge pixels.

Precomputation

In the preceding example, the result of a branch was constant over a large domain of input (or range of output) values. Similarly, sometimes the result of a branch is constant for a period of time or a number of iterations of a computation. In this case, we can evaluate the branches only when the results change, and store the results for use over many subsequent iterations. This can result in a large performance boost.

The "gpgpu_fluid" example in the NVIDIA SDK uses this technique to avoid branching when computing boundary conditions at the edges of arbitrary obstacles in the flow field. In this case, fluid cells with no neighboring obstacles can be processed normally, but cells with neighboring obstacles require more work. These cells must check their neighbors to figure out in which direction the obstacle lies, and they use this direction to look up more data to be used in the computation. In the example, the obstacles change only when the user "paints" them. Therefore, we can precompute the offset direction and store it in an offset texture to be reused until the user changes the obstacles again.

34.2.3 Z-Cull

We can take precomputed branch results a step further and use another GPU feature to entirely skip unnecessary work. Modern GPUs have a number of features designed to avoid shading pixels that will not be seen. One of these is z-cull. Z-cull is a technique for comparing the depth (z) of incoming fragments with the depth of the corresponding fragments in the z-buffer such that if the incoming fragments fail the depth test, they are discarded before their pixel colors are calculated in the fragment processor. Thus, only fragments that pass the depth test are processed, work is saved, and the application runs faster.

We can use this technique for general-purpose computation, too. In the example of obstacles in fluid flow given earlier, there are some cells that are completely "landlocked": all of their neighbors are obstacle cells. We don't need to do *any* computation on these cells. To skip these cells, we do a bit of setup work whenever the user paints new obstacles. We run a fragment program that examines the neighbors of each fragment. The program draws only fragments that are landlocked and discards all others using the discard keyword. (The discard keyword is available in Cg and GLSL. The HLSL equivalent is clip()). The Cg code for this program is shown in Listing 34-1. The pseudocode that follows in Listing 34-2 demonstrates how z-cull is set up and then used to skip processing of landlocked cells.

What happens in the code in these two listings is that the preprocessing pass sets up a "mask" in the z-buffer where landlocked cells have a depth of 0.0 and all other cells have a depth of 1.0. Therefore, when we draw a quad at $z = 0.5$, the landlocked cells will be "blocked" by the values of 0.0 in the z-buffer and will be automatically culled by the GPU. If the obstacles are fairly large, then we will save a lot of work by not processing these cells.

Listing 34-1. Cg Code to Set Z-Depth Values for Z-Culling in Subsequent Passes

```
half obstacles(half2 coords : WPOS,
  uniform samplerRECT obstacleGrid) : COLOR
{
  // get neighboring boundary values (on or off)
  half4 bounds;
  bounds.x = texRECT(obstacleGrid, coords - half2(1, 0)).x;
  bounds.y = texRECT(obstacleGrid, coords + half2(1, 0)).x;
  bounds.z = texRECT(obstacleGrid, coords - half2(0, 1)).x;
  bounds.w = texRECT(obstacleGrid, coords + half2(0, 1)).x;

  bounds.x = dot(bounds, (1).xxxx); // add them up

  // discard cells that are not landlocked
  if (bounds.x < 4)
    discard;

  return 0;
}
```

Listing 34-2. Application Pseudocode
We set z values in the first pass. In the second pass, we execute a fragment program at pixels where the z test passes.

```
// Application Code--Preprocess pass
ClearZBuffer(1.0);
Enable(DEPTH_TEST);
DepthFunc(LESS);
BindFragmentProgram("obstacles");
DrawQuad(Z=0.0);
```

Listing 34-2 *(continued)*. Application Pseudocode

```
// Application code--Passes in which landlocked cells are to be skipped
Enable(DEPTH_TEST);
Disable(DEPTH_WRITE); // want to read depth, but not modify it
DepthFunc(LESS);
// bind normal fragment program for each pass
DrawQuad(Z=0.5);
```

One caveat with this technique is that z-culling is often performed by the GPU at a coarser resolution than a per-fragment basis. The GPU will skip shading operations only if all the fragments in a small contiguous region of the frame buffer fail the depth test. The exact size of this region varies from GPU to GPU, but in general, z-cull will provide a performance improvement only if your branches have some locality.

To illustrate this, we can compare the performance of z-cull with a random Boolean condition versus a Boolean condition with high spatial locality. For the random Boolean case, we fill a texture with random values. For the Boolean with high spatial locality, we simply set a rectangular region to a constant Boolean value.

As you can see from Figure 34-1, z-cull is most effective if there is plenty of locality in the branch. The good news is that this locality is naturally present if the probability of taking the branch is either very low (that is, if very few fragments pass the depth test) or very high. If locality is not present, z-cull is not much better than predication.

Note, however, that z-cull is very different from branching inside a fragment program. Z-cull prevents the fragment program from ever executing. Therefore, z-cull is a powerful method for skipping lots of unnecessary work based on a static, preevaluated condi-

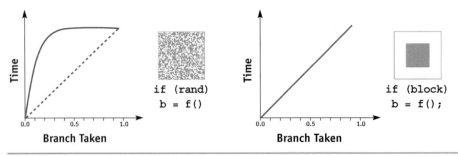

Figure 34-1. The Costs of Different Types of Branches When Using Z-Cull
The time of executing a program versus the probability of taking a branch with a random or a block Boolean condition. The diagonal line indicates the ideal execution time, assuming the Boolean always prevents f() *from executing.*

tion. To do the same with fragment program branching would require the program to be executed, the condition to be evaluated, and the program to exit early. All of this requires more processor cycles than skipping the fragment program altogether.

34.2.4 Branching Instructions

The first GPUs to support fragment branching instructions are the NVIDIA GeForce 6 Series. These instructions are available with both the Microsoft DirectX Pixel Shader 3.0 instruction set and the OpenGL `NV_fragment_program2` extension. As more GPUs support branch instructions, using predication for branching should no longer be necessary. Note, however, that the locality issues that affect early z-cull also apply to these branch instructions. GPUs execute fragment programs on groups of fragments in parallel, where each group can execute only one branch. Where this is not possible, the GPU will effectively fall back to predication. Figure 34-2 shows the time versus probability test implemented using branch instructions.

As you can see, the same spatial locality caveat applies to branching efficiency. However, as with z-cull, if the branch has either a very low or a very high probability, branching instructions are quite effective.

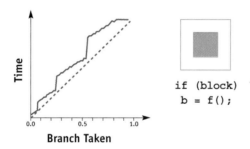

```
if (block)
    b = f();
```

Figure 34-2. The Costs of Different Types of Branches with Pixel Shader 3.0
The time to execute a program using the branch instructions with a high-locality Boolean branch condition.

34.2.5 Choosing a Branching Mechanism

Choosing an effective branching mechanism for your program depends primarily on the amount of code inside a branch and the amount of state present. For short branches—two to four operations—predication is preferred, because the overhead for either z-cull or the branching instructions can negate any benefits. For branches that are embedded in larger programs, consider using the branching instructions rather than z-cull. Even though the branching instructions are more sensitive to locality issues, using z-cull requires you to save all program state, execute the branch in a separate pass, and restore the state of the program to continue. For large programs, these saves and restores can make z-culling inefficient. However, if we can effectively isolate the branch component of our program, z-cull can provide the best performance.

34.3 Data-Dependent Looping with Occlusion Queries

Another GPU feature designed to avoid drawing what is not visible is the hardware *occlusion query*. This feature enables you to query the number of pixels updated by a rendering call. Such queries are pipelined, which means that they provide a way to get a limited amount of data (an integer count) back from the GPU without stalling the pipeline, as occurs when we read back actual pixels. Because in GPGPU we are almost always drawing quads with known pixel coverage, we can use occlusion query with the `discard` keyword discussed in Section 34.2.3 to get a count of fragments updated and discarded. This allows us to implement global decisions controlled by the CPU based on GPU processing.

Suppose we have a computation that needs to proceed iteratively on elements of a stream until all elements satisfy a termination criterion. To implement this on the GPU, we write a fragment program that implements the computation and one that tests the termination criterion. The latter program `discards` fragments that satisfy the termination criterion. We then write a loop on the CPU like the following pseudocode, which will execute until all stream elements satisfy the termination criteria.

```
int numberNotTerminated = streamSize;
while ( numberNotTerminated > 0 ) {
  gpuRunProgram(computationProgram);

  gpuBeginQuery(myQuery);
  gpuRunProgram(terminationProgram);
  gpuEndQuery(myQuery);

  numberNotTerminated = gpuGetQueryResults(myQuery);
}
```

This technique can also be used for subdivision algorithms, such as the adaptive radiosity solution in Chapter 39 of this book, "Global Illumination Using Progressive Refinement Radiosity."

34.4 Conclusion

With their support for branching at the fragment processor level, the latest generation of GPUs makes branching much easier to use in GPGPU programs. Higher-level language constructs such as `if`, `for`, and `while` compile directly to GPU assembly instructions, freeing the developer from having to use more complex strategies such as z-cull and occlusion queries, as is necessary on earlier GPUs.

Nevertheless, there is still a penalty for incoherent branching on GPUs. Employing techniques based on precomputation and moving computation higher up the pipeline— either to the vertex processing unit or to the CPU, as described in Section 34.2.2—will continue to be a useful GPGPU strategy.

Chapter 35

GPU Program Optimization

Cliff Woolley
University of Virginia

As GPU programmability has become more pervasive and GPU performance has become almost irresistibly appealing, increasing numbers of programmers have begun to recast applications of all sorts to make use of GPUs. But an interesting trend has appeared along the way: it seems that many programmers make the same performance mistakes in their GPU programs regardless of how much experience they have programming CPUs. The goal of this chapter is to help CPU programmers who are new to GPU programming avoid some of these common mistakes so that they gain the benefits of GPU performance without all the headaches of the GPU programmer's learning curve.

35.1 Data-Parallel Computing

One of the biggest hurdles you'll face when first programming a GPU is learning how to get the most out of a data-parallel computing environment. This parallelism exists at several levels on the GPU, as described in Chapter 29 of this book, "Streaming Architectures and Technology Trends." First, parallel execution on multiple data elements is a key design feature of modern GPUs. Vertex and fragment processors operate on four-vectors, performing four-component instructions such as additions, multiplications, multiply-accumulates, or dot products in a single cycle. They can schedule more than one of these instructions per cycle per pipeline. This provides ample opportunities for the extraction of instruction-level parallelism within a GPU program. For example, a series of sequential but independent scalar multiplications might be combined into a single four-component vector multiplication. Furthermore, parallelism can often be extracted by rearranging the data itself. For example, operations on a large array of scalar data will be inherently scalar. Packing the data in such a way that multiple identical scalar operations can occur simultaneously provides another means of exploiting the inherent parallelism of the GPU. (See Chapter 44 of this book, "A GPU Framework for Solving Systems of Linear Equations," for examples of this idea in practice.)

35.1.1 Instruction-Level Parallelism

While modern CPUs do have SIMD processing extensions such as MMX or SSE, most CPU programmers never attempt to use these capabilities themselves. Some count on the compiler to make use of SIMD extensions when possible; some ignore the extensions entirely. As a result, it's not uncommon to see new GPU programmers writing code that ineffectively utilizes vector arithmetic.

Let's take an example from a real-world application written by a first-time GPU programmer. In the following code snippet, we have a texture coordinate `center` and a uniform value called `params`. From them, a new coordinate `offset` is computed that will be used to look up values from the texture `Operator`:

```
float2 offset = float2(params.x * center.x - 0.5f * (params.x - 1.0f),
                       params.x * center.y - 0.5f * (params.x - 1.0f));

float4 O = f4texRECT(Operator, offset);
```

While the second line of this snippet (the actual texture lookup) is already as concise as possible, the first line leaves a lot to be desired. Each multiplication, addition, or subtraction is operating on a scalar value instead of a four-vector, wasting computational resources. Compilers for GPU programs are constantly getting better at detecting situations like this, but it's best to express arithmetic operations in vector form up front whenever possible. This helps the compiler do its job, and more important, it helps the programmer get into the habit of *thinking* in terms of vector arithmetic.

The importance of that habit becomes clearer when we look at the next snippet of code from that same fragment program. Here we take the `center` texture coordinate and use it to compute the coordinates of the four texels adjacent to `center`.

```
float4 neighbor = float4(center.x - 1.0f, center.x + 1.0f,
                         center.y - 1.0f, center.y + 1.0f);
```

```
float output =
    (-O.x * f1texRECT(Source, float2(neighbor.x, center.y)) +
     -O.x * f1texRECT(Source, float2(neighbor.y, center.y)) +
     -O.y * f1texRECT(Source, float2(center.x, neighbor.z)) +
     -O.z * f1texRECT(Source, float2(center.x, neighbor.w))) / O.w;
```

Now not only have we made the mistake of expressing our additions and subtractions in scalar form, but we've also constructed from the four separate scalar results a four-vector `neighbor` that isn't even exactly what we need. To get the four texture coordinates we *actually* want, we have to assemble them one by one. That requires a number of move instructions. It would have been better to let the four-vector addition operation assemble the texture coordinates for us. The *swizzle* operator, discussed later in Section 35.2.4, helps here by letting us creatively rearrange the four-vector produced by the addition into multiple two-vector texture coordinates.

Performing the necessary manipulations to improve vectorization, here is an improved version of the preceding program:

```
float2 offset = center.xy - 0.5f;
offset = offset * params.xx + 0.5f; // multiply-and-accumulate

float4 x_neighbor = center.xyxy + float4(-1.0f, 0.0f, 1.0f, 0.0f);
float4 y_neighbor = center.xyxy + float4(0.0f, -1.0f, 0.0f, 1.0f);

float4 O = f4texRECT(Operator, offset);

float output = (-O.x * f1texRECT(Source, x_neighbor.xy) +
                -O.x * f1texRECT(Source, x_neighbor.zw) +
                -O.y * f1texRECT(Source, y_neighbor.xy) +
                -O.z * f1texRECT(Source, y_neighbor.zw)) / O.w;
```

An additional point of interest here is that the expression `offset * params.xx + 0.5f`, a multiply-and-accumulate operation, can be expressed as a single GPU assembly instruction and thus can execute in a single cycle. This allows us to achieve twice as many floating-point operations in the same amount of time.

Finally, notice that the `output` value could have been computed using a four-vector dot product. Unfortunately, while one of the two input vectors, `O`, is already on hand, the second one must be assembled from the results of four separate scalar texture lookups. Fortunately, the multiply-and-accumulate operation comes to the rescue once again in this instance. But in general, it seems wasteful to assemble four-vectors from scalar values just to get the benefit of a single vector operation. That's where data-level parallelism comes into play.

35.1.2 Data-Level Parallelism

Some problems are inherently scalar in nature and can be more effectively parallelized by operating on multiple data elements simultaneously. This data-level parallelism is particularly common in GPGPU applications, where textures and render targets are used to store large 2D arrays of scalar source data and output values. Packing the data more efficiently in such instances exposes the data-level parallelism. Of course, determining which packing of the data will be the most efficient requires a bit of creativity and is application-specific. Two common approaches are as follows:

- Split the data grid up into quadrants and stack the quadrants on top of each other by packing corresponding scalar values into a single RGBA texel, as shown in Figure 35-1.
- Take each group of four adjacent texels and pack them down into a single RGBA texel, as shown in Figure 35-2.

There are ups and downs to each of these approaches, of course. While in theory there is a 4× speedup to be had by quartering the total number of fragments processed, the additional overhead of packing the data is significant in some cases, especially if the application requires the data to be unpacked again at the end of processing.

In some cases, application-specific data arrangements can be used to provide the speed of vector processing without the packing or unpacking overhead. For example, Goodnight et al. (2003a) use a data layout tailored to their application, which accelerates

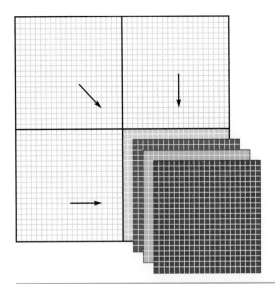

Figure 35-1. Packing Data by Stacking Grid Quadrants

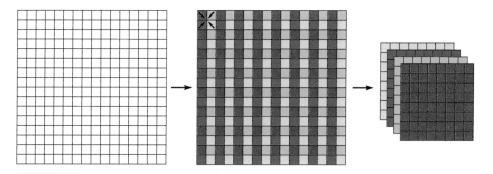

Figure 35-2. Packing Data by Stacking Adjacent Texels

arbitrary-size separable convolutions on the GPU. Their approach trades off space for computation time by replicating the scalar data four times into the four channels for an RGBA texture, shifting the data by one texel in a given dimension per channel, as shown in Figure 35-3. Although this does not have the advantage of decreasing the number of fragments processed, it still leverages data-level parallelism by arranging data that will be used together in such a way that it can be accessed more efficiently, providing an overall speedup.

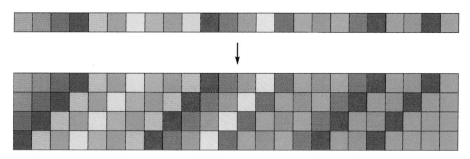

Figure 35-3. Custom Data Packing for Separable Convolutions

35.2 Computational Frequency

The next step in learning how to program GPUs effectively is learning to exploit the fact that the GPU comprises several different processors. Consider the typical rasterization pipeline. As implemented in hardware, the pipeline consists of a sequence of processors that operate in parallel and have different capabilities, degrees of programmability, strengths, and weaknesses. Between each stage of the pipeline is a work queue.

Unless a pipeline stage's output work queue is full, that stage can work in parallel with other stages. While the CPU is busy handing off geometry and state information to the GPU, the GPU's vertex processor can process each vertex that arrives, transforming it and so forth. Simultaneously, the rasterizer can convert groups of transformed vertices into fragments (potentially many fragments), queuing them up for processing by the fragment processor.

Notice that the relative amount of work at each stage of the pipeline is typically increasing: a few vertices can result in the generation of many fragments, each of which can be expensive to process. Given this relative increase in the amount of work done at each stage, it is helpful to view the stages conceptually as a series of nested loops (even though each loop operates in parallel with the others, as just described). These conceptual nested loops work as shown in pseudocode in Listing 35-1.

Listing 35-1. The Standard Rasterization Pipeline as a Series of Nested Loops

```
foreach tri in triangles {
    // run the vertex program on each vertex
    v1 = process_vertex(tri.vertex1);
    v2 = process_vertex(tri.vertex2);
    v3 = process_vertex(tri.vertex2);

    // assemble the vertices into a triangle
    assembledtriangle = setup_tri(v1, v2, v3);

    // rasterize the assembled triangle into [0..many] fragments
    fragments = rasterize(assembledtriangle);

    // run the fragment program on each fragment
    foreach frag in fragments {
        outbuffer[frag.position] = process_fragment(frag);
    }
}
```

For each operation we perform, we must be mindful of how computationally expensive that operation is and how frequently it is performed. In a normal CPU program, this is fairly straightforward. With an actual series of nested loops (as opposed to the merely conceptual nested loops seen here), it's easy to see that a given expression inside an inner loop is loop-invariant and can be hoisted out to an outer loop and computed less frequently. Inner-loop branching in CPU programs is often avoided for similar reasons; the branch is expensive, and if it occurs in the inner loop, then it occurs frequently.

When writing GPU programs, it is particularly crucial to minimize the amount of redundant work. Naturally, all of the same techniques discussed previously for reducing computational frequency in CPU programs apply to GPU programs as well. But given the nature of GPU programming, each of the conceptual nested loops in Listing 35-1 is actually a *separate* program running on different hardware and possibly even written in different programming languages. That separation makes it easy to overlook some of these sorts of optimizations.

35.2.1 Precomputation of Loop Invariants

The first mistake a new GPU programmer is likely to make is to needlessly recompute values that vary linearly or are uniform across the geometric primitives inside a fragment program. Texture coordinates are a prime example. They vary linearly across the primitive being drawn, and the rasterizer interpolates them automatically. But when multiple related texture coordinates are used (such as the `offset` and `neighbor` coordinates in the example in Section 35.1.1), a common mistake is to compute the related values in the fragment program. This results in a possibly expensive computation being performed very frequently.

It would be much better to move the computation of the related texture coordinates into the vertex program. Though this effectively just shifts load around and interpolation in the rasterizer is still a per-fragment operation, the question is how *much* work is being done at each stage of the pipeline and how *often* that work must be done. Either way we do it, the result will be a set of texture coordinates that vary linearly across the primitive being drawn. But interpolation is often a lot less computationally expensive than recomputation of a given value on a per-fragment basis. As long as there are many more fragments than vertices, shifting the bulk of the computation so that it occurs on a per-vertex rather than a per-fragment basis makes sense.

It is worth reemphasizing, however, that *any* value that varies linearly across the domain can be computed in this way, regardless of whether it will eventually be used to index into a texture. Herein lies one of the keys to understanding GPU programming: the names that "special-purpose" GPU features go by are mostly irrelevant as long as you understand how they correspond to general-purpose concepts. Take a look at Chapter 31 of this book, "Mapping Computational Concepts to GPUs," for an in-depth look at those correspondences.

To take the concept of hoisting loop-invariant code a step further, some values are best precomputed on the CPU rather than on the GPU. Any value that is constant across the geometry being drawn can be factored all the way out to the CPU and passed to the GPU program as a uniform parameter. This sometimes results in parameters that are less than semantically elegant; for example, suppose we pass a uniform parameter `size` to a vertex or fragment program, but the program only uses the value `size * size * 100`. Although *size* and even *size squared* have semantic meaning, *size squared times 100* has little. But again, if the GPU programs are equated to a series of nested loops and the goal is to remove redundant loop-invariant computations, it is likely still preferable to compute `size * size * 100` on the CPU and pass that as the uniform parameter value to the GPU.

35.2.2 Precomputation Using Lookup Tables

In the more classic sense, "precomputation" means computation that is done offline in advance—the classic storage versus computation trade-off. This concept also maps readily onto GPUs: functions with a constant-size domain and range that are constant across runs of an algorithm—even if they vary in complex ways based on their input—can be precomputed and stored in texture maps.

Texture maps can be used for storing functions of one, two, or three variables over a finite domain as 1D, 2D, or 3D textures. Textures are usually indexed by floating-point texture coordinates between 0 and 1. The range is determined by the texture format used; 8-bit texture formats can only store values in the range [0, 1], but floating-point textures provide a much larger range of possible values. Textures can store up to four channels, so you can encode as many as four separate functions in the same texture. Texture lookups also provide filtering (interpolation), which you can use to get piecewise linear approximations to values in between the table entries.

As an example, suppose we had a fragment program that we wanted to apply to a checkerboard: half of the fragments of a big quad, the "red" ones, would be processed in one pass, while the other half, the "black" fragments, would be processed in a second pass. But how would the fragment program determine whether the fragment it was currently processing was red or black? One way would be to use modulo arithmetic on the fragment's position:

```
// Calculate red-black (odd-even) masks
float2 intpart;
float2 place = floor(1.0f - modf(round(position + 0.5f) / 2.0f,
                                  intpart));
```

```
float2 mask = float2((1.0f - place.x) * (1.0f - place.y),
                     place.x * place.y);

if (((mask.x + mask.y) && do_red) ||
    (!(mask.x + mask.y) && !do_red))
{
    . . .
}
```

Here, roughly speaking, `place` is the location of the fragment modulo 2 and `mask.x` and `mask.y` are Boolean values that together tell us whether the fragment is red or black. The uniform parameter `do_red` is set to 0 if we want to process the black fragments and 1 if we want the red fragments.

But clearly this is all a ridiculous amount of work for a seemingly simple task. It's much easier to precompute a checkerboard texture that stores a 0 in black texels and a 1 in red texels. Then we can skip all of the preceding arithmetic, replacing it with a single texture lookup, providing a substantial speedup. What we're left with is the following:

```
half4 mask = f4texRECT(RedBlack, IN.redblack);
/*
 *  mask.x and mask.w tell whether IN.position.x and IN.position.y
 *  are both odd or both even, respectively. Either of these two
 *  conditions indicates that the fragment is red. params.x==1
 *  selects red; params.y==1 selects black.
 */
if (dot(mask, params.xyyx)) {
    . . .
}
```

However, although table lookups in this case were a win in terms of performance, that's not always going to be the case. Many GPU applications—particularly those that use a large number of four-component floating-point texture lookups—are memory-bandwidth-limited, so the introduction of an additional texture read in order to save a small amount of computation might in fact be a loss rather than a win. Furthermore, texture cache coherence is critical; a lookup table that is accessed incoherently will thrash the cache and hurt performance rather than help it. But if enough computation can be "pre-baked" or if the GPU programs in question are compute-limited already, and if the baked results are read from the texture in a spatially coherent way, table lookups can improve performance substantially. See Section 35.3 later in this chapter for more on benchmarking and GPU application profiling.

35.2.3 Avoid Inner-Loop Branching

In CPU programming, it is often desirable to avoid branching inside inner loops. This usually involves making several copies of the loop, with each copy acting on a subset of the data and following the execution path specific to that subset. This technique is sometimes called *static branch resolution* or *substreaming*.

The same concept applies to GPUs. Because a fragment program conceptually represents an inner loop, applying this technique requires a fragment program containing a branch to be divided into multiple fragment programs without the branch. The resulting programs each account for one code execution path through the original, monolithic program. This technique also requires the application to subdivide the data, which for the GPU means rasterization of multiple primitives instead of one. See Chapter 34 of this book, "GPU Flow-Control Idioms," for details.

A typical example is a 2D grid where data elements on the boundary of the grid require special handling that does not apply to interior elements. In this case, it is preferable to create two separate fragment programs—a short one that does not account for boundary conditions and a longer one that does—and draw a filled-in quad over the interior elements and an outline quad over the boundary elements.

35.2.4 The Swizzle Operator

An easily overlooked or underutilized feature of GPU programming is the *swizzle* operator. Because all registers on the GPU are four-vectors but not all instructions take four-vectors as arguments, some mechanism for creating other-sized vectors out of these four-vector registers is necessary. The swizzle operator provides this functionality. It is syntactically similar to the C concept of a structure member access but has the additional interesting property that data members can be rearranged, duplicated, or omitted in arbitrary combinations, as shown in the following example:

```
float4 f = float4(1.0f, 2.0f, 3.0f, 4.0f);
float4 g = float4(5.0f, 6.0f, 7.0f, 8.0f);
float4 h = float4(0.1f, 0.2f, 0.3f, 0.4f);

// note that h.w is syntactically equivalent to h.wwww
float4 out = f.xyyz * g.wyxz + h.w; // this is one instruction!
                                    // multiply-and-accumulate again.

// result: out is (8.4f, 12.4f, 10.4f, 21.4f)
```

The swizzle operator has applications in the computational frequency realm. For example, consider the common case of a fragment program that reads from three adjacent texels: (x, y), $(x - 1, y)$, and $(x + 1, y)$. Computing the second and third texture coordinates from the first is a job best left to the vertex program and rasterizer, as has already been discussed. But the rasterizer can interpolate four-vectors as easily as it can two-vectors, so there is no reason that these three texture coordinates should have to occupy three separate interpolants. In fact, there are only four distinct values being used: x, $x - 1$, $x + 1$, and y. So all three texture coordinates can actually be packed into and interpolated as a single four-vector. The three distinct two-vector texture coordinates are simply extracted (for free) from the single four-vector interpolant in the fragment program by using swizzle operators, as shown here:

```
struct vertdata {
    float4 position : POSITION;
    float4 texcoord : TEXCOORD0;
}
vertdata vertexprog(vertdata IN)
{
    vertdata OUT;
    OUT.position = IN.position;
    OUT.texcoord = float4(IN.texcoord.x, IN.texcoord.y,
                          IN.texcoord.x - 1, IN.texcoord.x + 1);
    return vertdata;
}
frag2frame fragmentprog(vertdata IN, uniform samplerRECT texmap)
{
    . . .
    float4 center = f4texRECT(texmap, IN.texcoord.xy);
    float4 left   = f4texRECT(texmap, IN.texcoord.zy);
    float4 right  = f4texRECT(texmap, IN.texcoord.wy);
    . . .
}
```

Not only does this save on arithmetic in the vertex processor, but it saves interpolants as well. Further, it avoids the construction of vectors in the fragment program: swizzles are free (on NVIDIA GeForce FX and GeForce 6 Series GPUs), but the move instructions required to construct vectors one channel at a time are not. We saw this same issue in Section 35.1.1.

Also worth mentioning is a syntactic cousin of the swizzle operator: the *write mask* operator. The write mask specifies a subset of the destination variable's components that should be modified by the current instruction. This can be used as a hint to the compiler that unnecessary work can be avoided. For example, if a write mask is applied to a texture lookup, memory bandwidth could be saved because texture data in channels that will never be used need not be read from texture memory. Note that although the syntax of a write mask is similar to that of a swizzle, the concepts of rearranging or duplicating channels do not apply to a write mask.

```
float4 out;

out = float4(1.0f, 2.0f, 3.0f, 4.0f);
out.xz = float4(5.0f, 6.0f, 7.0f, 8.0f);

// result: out is (5.0f, 2.0f, 7.0f, 4.0f)
```

35.3 Profiling and Load Balancing

As with CPU programming, the best way to write efficient GPU code is to write something straightforward that works and then optimize it iteratively as necessary. Unfortunately, this process currently isn't quite as easy with GPU code, because fewer tools exist to help with it. But a bit of extra diligence on the part of the programmer allows optimization to be done effectively even in the absence of special tools.

Frequent timing measurements are the key. In fact, *every* optimization that gets applied should be independently verified by timing it. Even optimizations that seem obvious and *certain* to result in a speedup can in fact provide no gain at all or, worse, cause a slowdown. When this happens, it might indicate a load imbalance in the graphics pipeline, but such problems can also arise because the final optimization step occurs inside the graphics driver, making it difficult for the programmer to know exactly what code is really being executed. A transformation made on the source code that seems beneficial might in fact disable some other optimization being done by the driver, causing a net loss in performance. These sorts of problems are much more easily detected by benchmarking after each optimization; backtracking to isolate problematic optimizations after the fact is a waste of time and energy.

Once the obvious optimizations have been applied, a low-level understanding of the capabilities of the hardware, particularly in terms of superscalar instruction issues, becomes useful. The more detailed your knowledge of what kinds of instructions can be executed simultaneously, the more likely you will be to recognize additional opportunities for code transformation and improvement. The NVShaderPerf tool helps with this by showing you exactly how your fragment programs schedule onto the arithmetic units of the GPU, taking much of the guesswork out of fragment program optimization. (For more information on NVShaderPerf, see "References" at the end of the chapter.)

Even with the most highly tuned fragment programs imaginable, there's *still* a chance that a GPU application can be made to run faster. At this point it becomes a matter of finding the main bottleneck in the application and shifting load away from it as much as possible. The first step is to use a CPU-application profiling tool, such as Rational Quantify, Intel VTune, or AMD CodeAnalyst. This can help pinpoint problems like driver overhead (such as in context switching). Not *all* of the information that such a profiler provides will be reliable; many graphics API calls are nonblocking so that the CPU and GPU can operate in parallel. At some point, the GPU's work queue will fill up and an arbitrary API call on the CPU side will block to wait for the GPU to catch up. The blocked call will be counted by the CPU profiler as having taken a long time to execute, even if the work done during that time would be more fairly attributed to an earlier API call that did not block. As long as this caveat is kept in mind, however, CPU profilers can still provide valuable insights.

Once CPU overhead is minimized, the only remaining issue is determining where the GPU bottlenecks lie. Specialized tools for monitoring GPU performance are beginning to appear on the market for this purpose; NVPerfHUD is a good example (see "References" for more on NVPerfHUD). To the extent that these tools do not yet provide detailed information or are inapplicable to a particular application (NVPerfHUD, for example, is currently Direct3D-only and is not well suited to GPGPU applications), other techniques can be utilized to fill in the gaps. Each involves a series of experiments. One approach is to test whether the addition of work to a given part of the GPU pipeline increases the total execution time or the reduction of work decreases execution time. If so, it's likely that that is where the main bottleneck lies. For example, if a fragment program is compute-limited, then inserting additional computation instructions will increase the time it takes the program to execute; but if the program is memory-bandwidth-limited, the extra computation can probably be done for free. An alternate approach is to underclock either the compute core or the memory system of the graphics card. If the memory system can be underclocked without decreasing performance, then memory bandwidth is not the limiting factor. These techniques and many more are detailed in the *NVIDIA GPU Programming Guide* (NVIDIA 2004).

Ultimately, *understanding* the bottlenecks is the key to knowing how to get them to go away. A combination of the preceding techniques and a bit of experience will aid in that understanding.

35.4 Conclusion

As we've seen, GPU program optimization shares many common themes with CPU program optimization. High-level languages for GPGPU that provide a unified stream programming model (and thus, hopefully, more opportunities for global GPU application optimization) are emerging (McCool et al. 2002, Buck et al. 2004), and automatic optimization of GPU code is constantly improving. But until those technologies have matured, GPU programmers will continue to have to take responsibility for high-level optimizations and understand the details of the hardware they're working with to get the most out of low-level optimizations. Hopefully this chapter has given you the tools you need to learn how best to extract from your GPU application all of the performance that the GPU has to offer.

35.5 References

Buck, Ian, Tim Foley, Daniel Horn, Jeremy Sugerman, Kayvon Fatahalian, Mike Houston, and Pat Hanrahan. 2004. "Brook for GPUs: Stream Computing on Graphics Hardware." *ACM Transactions on Graphics (Proceedings of SIGGRAPH 2004)* 23(3), pp. 777–786. Available online at **http://graphics.stanford.edu/projects/brookgpu/**

Goodnight, Nolan, Rui Wang, Cliff Woolley, and Greg Humphreys. 2003a. "Interactive Time-Dependent Tone Mapping Using Programmable Graphics Hardware." In *Eurographics Symposium on Rendering: 14th Eurographics Workshop on Rendering*, pp. 26–37.

Goodnight, Nolan, Cliff Woolley, Gregory Lewin, David Luebke, and Greg Humphreys. 2003b. "A Multigrid Solver for Boundary Value Problems Using Programmable Graphics Hardware." In *Proceedings of the SIGGRAPH/Eurographics Workshop on Graphics Hardware 2003*, pp. 102–111.

McCool, Michael D., Zheng Qin, and Tiberiu S. Popa. 2002. "Shader Metaprogramming." In *Proceedings of the SIGGRAPH/Eurographics Workshop on Graphics Hardware 2002*, pp. 57–68. Revised article available online at **http://www.cgl.uwaterloo.ca/Projects/rendering/Papers/index.html#metaprog**

NVIDIA. 2004. *NVIDIA GPU Programming Guide.* Available online at
http://developer.nvidia.com/object/gpu_programming_guide.html

NVPerfHUD. Available online at
http://developer.nvidia.com/object/nvperfhud_home.html

NVShaderPerf. Available online at
http://developer.nvidia.com/object/nvshaderperf_home.html

Chapter 36

Stream Reduction Operations for GPGPU Applications

Daniel Horn
Stanford University

Many GPGPU-based applications rely on the fragment processor, which operates across a large set of output memory locations, consuming a fixed number of input elements per location and operating a small program on those elements to produce a single output element in that location. Because the fragment program must write its results to a preordained memory location, it is not able to vary the amount of data that it outputs according to the input data it processes. (See Chapter 30 in this book, "The GeForce 6 Series GPU Architecture," for more details on the capabilities and limits of the fragment processor.)

Many algorithms are difficult to implement under these limitations—specifically, algorithms that reduce many data elements to few data elements. The reduction of data by a fixed factor has been carefully studied on GPUs (Buck et al. 2004); such operations require an amount of time linear in the size of the data to be reduced. However, nonuniform reductions—that is, reductions that filter out data based on its content on a per-element basis—have been less thoroughly studied, yet they are required for a number of interesting applications. We refer to such a technique of nonuniform reduction as a method of *data filtering*.

This chapter presents a data filtering algorithm that makes it possible to write GPU programs that efficiently generate varying amounts of output data.

36.1 Filtering Through Compaction

Assume we have a data set with arbitrary values and we wish to extract all positive values. On current GPUs, a fragment program that filters streams must produce null records for each output that should not be retained in the final output stream. Null records are represented with some value that the program will never generate when it does want to output a value. (In the examples that follow, we use floating-point infinity for this purpose. Floating-point infinity can be generated by computing 1.0/0.0, and it can be detected with the isinf() standard library function.) The following example uses the Brook programming language:

```
kernel void positive(float input<>, out float output<>, float inf<>){
  if (input > 0)
    output = input;
  else
    output = inf; //inf 1./0 must be passed in as a stream on ATI GPUs
}
```

The output must then be compacted, moving null records to the end. The most obvious method for compaction utilizes a stable sort to eliminate the null records; however, using bitonic sort to do this will result in a running time of $O(n (\log n)^2)$ (Buck and Purcell 2004). Instead, we present a technique here that uses a scan (Hillis and Steele 1986) to obtain a running count of the number of null records, and then a search and gather to compact them, for a final running time of $O(n \log n)$.

36.1.1 Running Sum Scan

Given a list of data peppered with null records, to decide where a particular non-null record should redirect itself, it is sufficient to count the number of null records to the left of the non-null record, then move the record that many records to the left. On a parallel system, the cost of finding a running count of null records is actually $O(n \log n)$. The multipass technique to perform a running sum is called a scan. It starts by counting the number of nulls in the current record and the adjacent record exactly one index to the left, resulting in a number between 0 and 2 per record. This number is saved to a stream for further processing.

```
kernel void StartScan(float4 value[],
  out float count<>,
  iter float here<>,
  iter float left_1<>)
```

```
   {
     count = isinf(value[here].x) ? 1 : 0;
     if (here >= 1)
       count += isinf(value[left_1].x) ? 1 : 0;
   }
```

Now each record in the stream holds the number of null records at its location and to the left of its location. This can be used to the algorithm's advantage in another pass, where the stream sums itself with records indexed two values to the left and saves the result to a new stream. Now each record in the new stream effectively has added the number of null records at zero, one, two, and three records to its left, because the record two items to the left in the previous stream already added the third item in the first pass. The subsequent steps add their values to values indexed at records of increasing powers of two to their left, until the power of two exceeds the length of the input array. This process is illustrated in Figure 36-1.

```
kernel void Scan (float input[],
   out float count<>,
   iter float here<>,
   iter float left_2toi<>,
   float twotoi)
{
   count = input[here];
   if (here > twotoi)
     count += input[left_2toi];
}
```

After performing this multipass counting kernel log n times, each record knows how many nodes to the left to send its item. The value at the very right of the stream indicates how many null records there are in the entire stream, and hence the length of the compacted output, which is the total length minus the last value in the running sum stream. However, current fragment processors provide no way to send records, or scatter them, only to receive them with a texture fetch, or gather operation. Although vertex processors can scatter by rendering a stream of input points to various locations on the frame buffer, this does not make efficient use of the rasterizer.

36.1.2 Scatter Through Search/Gather

To overcome the lack of scatter on the fragment processor, we can use a parallel search algorithm to complete the filtering process. Luckily, a running sum is always monotonically increasing, so the result of the running sum scan step is a sorted, increasing set of numbers, which we can search to find the correct place from which to gather data.

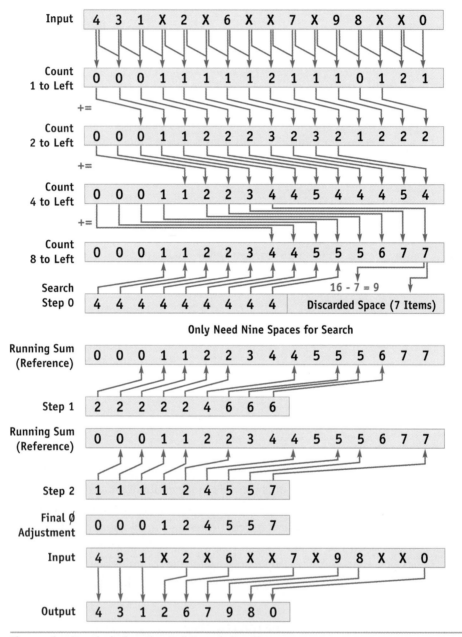

Figure 36-1. Iteratively Counting Null Records in a Stream

At each iteration, each stream element sums the number of null elements at its position and progressive powers-of-two positions to the left. The end result lets a subsequent pass quickly determine how to compact the stream so that there are no null elements remaining.

Each record can do a parallel binary search, again in a total of $O(\log n)$ time to find the appropriate record from which to gather, using the running sum as a guide. This results in a total time of $O(n \log n)$ for n searches in parallel. If the running sum is equal to the distance from the current record to the record under consideration, then that record under consideration clearly wishes to displace its data to the current record; thus, the current record may just gather from it for the same effect. If the running sum is less, then the candidate record is too far to the right and must move left later in the algorithm. If the running sum is more than the distance, then the candidate must move to the right in the next iteration. Each iteration moves the candidate half as far away as the previous round until the current record narrows down the search to the actual answer. This search replaces the necessity of redirecting records (a scatter) and does not increase the asymptotic running time of $O(n \log n)$. See Listing 36-1.

Listing 36-1. Search for Displaced Values Implemented in a Brook Kernel

```
kernel void GatherSearch(float scatterValues[],
  out float outGuess<>,
  float4 value[],
  float twotoi,
  float lastguess<>,
  iter float here<>)
{
  float guess = scatterValues[here + lastguess];
  float4 finalValue = value[here + lastguess];
  if (guess > lastguess)
    outGuess = lastguess + twotoi; //too low
  else if (guess == lastguess && !isinf(finalValue.x))
    outGuess = lastguess; // correct
  else
    outGuess = lastguess - twotoi; //too high
}
kernel void RelGather(out float4 outp<>,
  float gatherindex<>,
  float4 value[],
  iter float here<>)
{
  outp = value[here + gatherindex];
}
```

The final result is obtained by gathering from the indices that the search located. Because the stream is already the correct size, the gathered values represent the filtered stream.

Optimization

On GPUs that support data-dependent looping or large numbers of instructions, there is an optimization that can make the parallel search cost negligible in comparison with the scan. The scan requires each subsequent pass to finish before using the results garnered from the pass; however, a search has no data dependency between passes and therefore may be completed in a single pass using dependent texture reads. See Listing 36-2.

Listing 36-2. Using Looping to Search for Displaced Values

```
kernel void GatherSearch(float scatterValues[],
  out float4 output<>,
  float4 value[],
  float halfN, /* ceil(numNullElements/2+.5) */
  float logN,  /* ceil(log(numNullElements)/log(2)) */
  iter float here<>)
{
  float lastguess = halfN;
  float twotoi = halfN;
  float i;
  for (i = 0; i < logN; ++i) {
    float4 finalValue = value[here + lastguess];
    float guess = scatterValues[here + lastguess];
    twotoi /= 2;
    if (guess > lastguess)
      lastguess = lastguess + twotoi; // too low
    else if (guess == lastguess && !isinf(finalValue.x))
      lastguess = lastguess; // correct
    else
      lastguess = lastguess - twotoi; // too high
  }
  if (scatterValues[here] == 0)
    output = value[here];
  else
    output = value[here + lastguess];
}
```

On GPUs that do not support data-dependent loop limits, the kernel in Listing 36-2 may be compiled for each possible value of $\log_2 n$ for the given application.

36.1.3 Filtering Performance

To measure whether the scan/search algorithm is faster than the bitonic sort, we implemented both algorithms in Brook using 1D-to-2D address translation and the same programming style. Scan is almost exactly $0.5 \times \log_2 n$ times faster than a bitonic sort, because bitonic sort requires a factor of $0.5 \times (\log_2 n - 1)$ extra passes and has a similar number of instructions and pattern of memory access. In Table 36-1, we see how many microseconds it takes to filter each element on various hardware.

Clearly the scan/search filtering method illustrated here is more efficient than sorting. Although the cost per element is not constant in data size, as is the same operation on the CPU, the cost does not increase much as the data size increases exponentially. Note that the looping construct is used to perform the parallel search on the NVIDIA GeForce 6800 Ultra, which gives it an added advantage over the bitonic sort on that hardware.

Table 36-1. Timing of Compaction Methods on Modern Hardware
In µs per record (lower is better).

		Number of Records						
		64k	128k	256k	512k	1024k	2048k	4096k
6800 Ultra	Scan/Search	0.138	0.131	0.158	0.151	0.143	0.167	0.161
6800 Ultra	Bitonic Sort	1.029	0.991	1.219	1.190	1.455	1.593	1.740
X800	Scan/Search	0.428	0.267	0.288	0.355	0.182	0.169	0.168
X800	Bitonic Sort	0.762	0.912	0.968	1.051	1.175	1.269	1.383

36.2 Motivation: Collision Detection

To see the utility of this filtering idiom, consider search algorithms based on tree traversal, for example, the University of North Carolina's RAPID hierarchical bounding volume collision-detection scheme (Gottschalk et al. 1996). The basic idea is that two trees of bounding volumes for two models may be traversed in unison to find overlapping volumes and eventually overlapping leaf nodes, which contain potentially touching triangles. Fast collision detection among rigid meshes is important for many graphics applications. For instance, haptic rendering, path planning, and scene interaction all require this form of collision detection.

We begin by porting an algorithm to perform collision detection to the streaming language Brook (Buck et al. 2004). The inputs to the collision-detection scheme are two triangulated 3D models, and a rigid transformation between the two; the output is a list of pairs of triangles that overlap. An offline computation creates a tree of bounding boxes for each 3D model, starting from a top-level bounding box containing that whole model. The tree is created such that each bounding box node either has two smaller bounding boxes within it, or else is a leaf node containing a pointer to a single triangle from the input model. This tree may be downloaded to the GPU for online collision-detection processing. Each bounding box contains a rigid transformation, a size, and a pointer to its children. In Brook, for each model, we may make two streams of structures that contain this static information: one for the list of triangles and the other for the hierarchy of bounding boxes that encloses them. See Listing 36-3.

Listing 36-3. Data Structures for Collision Detection

```
typedef struct Tri_t {
  float3 A, B, C;
} Tri;

typedef struct bbox_t {
  float4 Rotationx; // The x axis of the bounding box coordinate system
                    // Rotationx.w -1 for left-handed coordinate system
  float3 Rotationy; // The y axis of the bounding box coordinate system
  // float3 Rotationz; // since Rotationx and Rotationy are orthogonal
                    // use cross(Rotationx,Rotationy)*Rotationx.w;
  float3 Translation;  // the bottom corner of the bounding box
  float4 Radius; // The dimensions of the bounding box
                // Radius.w holds bool whether this node is a leaf
  float2 Children;
  // if leaf, Children.xy is an index to the Triangle in the model
  // if node, Children.xy is an index to left child,
  //          Children.xy+float2(1,0) is right child
} BBox;
```

To determine which triangles overlap in the two models, we process the trees of bounding boxes breadth-first. A stream of candidate pairs is processed, and pairs that can be trivially rejected because their bounding boxes do not intersect are dropped from the stream. Pairs that cannot be rejected are divided into a set of pairs of child nodes. The process is repeated until only leaf nodes remain. This process requires removing some pairs from the stream and inserting others. It would be impractical to start with a stream of maximum necessary length and ignore elements that do not collide, because doing so loses the advantages of the tree traversal and pruning process.

For example, to determine which triangles overlap in the two models A and B, we begin with the largest bounding boxes that form the root of each of the two trees in the input models. Suppose model A is a small model that has bounding box root R_a and model B is a larger model with bounding box root R_b. We will first check if R_a overlaps with R_b, and if not, then there must be no collision, because the entire models are contained in R_a and R_b, respectively. Assuming that R_a and R_b overlap, we take the two children of the larger bounding box C_b and D_b and compare each in turn with R_a to check for overlap. We can repeat this procedure, checking R_a's children C_a and D_a with the potential colliders from C_b and D_b, splitting each bounding box into its two components at each phase until we reach leaf nodes that point to actual triangles. Finally, we compare the pairs of triangles contained in each overlapping leaf node with each other, checking for collisions. See Figure 36-2. On average, far fewer leaf nodes are processed with this approach than there are pairs of triangles, but it is easily conceivable that a pair of degenerate models could be designed such that each triangle must be checked with each other triangle in the two models.

A data structure to contain the dynamic state needed for the traversal of the node hierarchies could thus be contained in the following:

```
typedef struct traverser_t {
   float4 index; // index.xy is index into the first model
                 // index.zw is index into the second model
   float3 Translation;
   float3 Rotationx;
   float3 Rotationy;
   float3 Rotationz;
} Traverser;
```

In Listing 36-4, we examine some CPU pseudocode to check collisions on two given models, with the preceding data structures.

Porting Collision Detection to the GPU

Now that we have established a systematic method for searching the pair of trees for triangle intersections, the question remains how to best implement this algorithm as a fragment program on the graphics hardware. To do so, a breadth-first search on a tree may be represented as follows: At any given stage of the algorithm, a stream of candidate pairs of bounding box nodes for a collision may be checked in parallel. Pairs of candidates that clearly do not collide must be filtered, and overlapping pairs of bounding boxes must be split, one for each child node of the larger bounding box. Another pass may be made on the filtered and split candidate pairs until only leaf nodes remain. Those leaf nodes may be checked for actual geometry collisions.

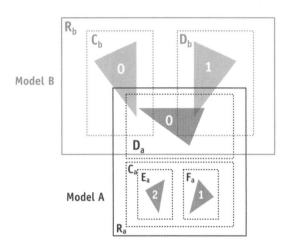

Model B

Model A

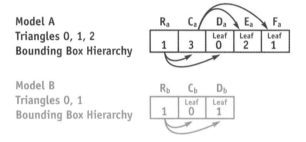

Model A
Triangles 0, 1, 2
Bounding Box Hierarchy

R_a	C_a	D_a	E_a	F_a
		Leaf	Leaf	Leaf
1	3	0	2	1

Model B
Triangles 0, 1
Bounding Box Hierarchy

R_b	C_b	D_b
	Leaf	Leaf
1	0	1

Algorithm

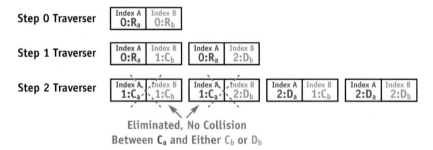

Step 0 Traverser

Index A	Index B
$0:R_a$	$0:R_b$

Step 1 Traverser

Index A	Index B	Index A	Index B
$0:R_a$	$1:C_b$	$0:R_a$	$2:D_b$

Step 2 Traverser

Index A	Index B	Index A	Index B	Index A	Index B	Index A	Index B
$1:C_a$	$1:C_b$	$1:C_a$	$2:D_b$	$2:D_a$	$1:C_b$	$2:D_a$	$2:D_b$

Eliminated, No Collision
Between C_a and Either C_b or D_b

Step 3: Test Blue Triangle 0 in Model A with Green Triangles 0 and 1 in Model B

Figure 36-2. Collision Detection with Two Bounding Box Trees
Given two bounding box trees, it is possible to efficiently detect collisions by traversing both trees simultaneously, quickly culling geometry that is certain to be not colliding.

Listing 36-4. Collision Pseudocode

```
bool collide (BBox mA[], BBox mB[], Triangle tri[], Traverser state){
  BBox A = mA[state.index.xy]
  BBox B = mB[state.index.zw]
  if (bb_overlap(state, A.Radius, B.Radius)){
    if (isLeaf(A) && isLeaf(B)){
      return tri_overlap(tri[A.Children], tri[B.Children])
    } else {
      if (AisBigger(A, B)) { // bigger or nonleaf
        state = Compose(state, A.Translation, A.Rotationx, A.Rotationy);
        state.index.xy = LeftChild(A);
        bool ret = collide(mA, mB, tri, state);
        state.index.xy = RightChild(A);
        return ret || collide(mA, mB, tri, state);
      } else { // B is bigger than A or A is a leaf node
        state = invCompose(state, B.Translation, B.Rotationx, B.Rotationy);
        state.index.zw = LeftChild(B);
        bool ret = collide(mA, mB, tri, state);
        state.index.zw = RightChild(B);
        return ret || collide(mA, mB, tri, state);
      }
    }
  }
  return false;
}
```

Thus, given a filtering operator primitive, the overall collision-detection algorithm itself runs as follows, depicted in Figure 36-2. Starting from a single pair of top-level bounding boxes for the models in question, each active bounding box pair is checked for collision. Next, bounding box pairs that do not collide are filtered out using the filtering primitive described in Section 36.1. The short list of remaining pairs of leaf bounding boxes that point to triangles in the respective models are checked for physical collision. The remaining list of nonleaf pairs is doubled in length, one for each child of the larger of the two bounding boxes. The algorithm is then repeated for this doubled list, until it has been filtered to length zero.

36.3 Filtering for Subdivision Surfaces

The filtering idiom we presented is useful not only in tree searches such as collision detection, but also in conjunction with imbalanced trees, graphs, and other sparse data sets such as meshes. A hardware-accelerated adaptive subdivision surface tessellation algorithm offers an interesting possibility as the computational capabilities of fragment programs continue to improve. Subdivision surfaces operate as follows: Given an input mesh with connectivity information, an output mesh of four times the number of triangles is produced. Each triangle is then split into four smaller triangles, and those triangles' vertex positions are updated based on neighboring vertex positions. The result is a smoother mesh. Repetition of this algorithm causes the mesh to converge to a smooth limit surface.

Adaptive subdivision surfaces operate similarly, but with the caveat that some triangles may be frozen based on image-space size, curvature, or any per-edge constraint, and hence not divided. In this case, we examine Loop's subdivision scheme (Loop 1987), which uses neighbor information from the adjacent polygons to compute a smoothed vertex position. This process may be repeated until the desired polygon count is reached. In the limiting case, Loop subdivision guarantees C^2 continuity at vertices that have six neighbors and hence a valence of six; it guarantees C^1 continuity at the vertices that have a valence other than six. A surface with C^1 continuity has no sharp corners, and a surface with C^2 continuity has no drastic changes in curvature along that surface. Loop subdivision never creates new vertices with higher valence than the original model, so the original model dictates the highest possible valence.

36.3.1 Subdivision on Streaming Architectures

We implement adaptive subdivision surfaces in Brook using the filtering process presented in Section 36.1. An adaptive subdivision scheme requires filtering completed triangles at each stage of the algorithm, and it requires communication to determine which neighbors are filtered.

In a streaming application that operates on a stream of triangles of increasing sparseness, it is prudent to have each triangle be self-contained, tracking the coordinates of its neighboring vertices, instead of saving and updating indices to neighbors. The texture indirection from its neighbor list, and the as-yet-unsolved problem of tracking updates to the neighbor list as subdivision continues, make tracking pointers to neighbors a difficult proposition. However, tracking the coordinates of neighbors directly uses only a quarter more storage and results in far fewer dependent texture lookups and thus faster performance.

The algorithm operates on a stream of triangles, consisting of three coordinates per vertex, and a Boolean value indicating if any edge that the vertex touches has completed its subdivision. Alongside this stream of triangles is a stream of neighboring vertices, consisting of nine vertices arranged in a clockwise ordering, as illustrated in Figure 36-3. Thus, we assert a maximum valence of six for code brevity, though no such limit is imposed by the algorithm in general. After a triangle is split, the floats in the neighbor list refer to differing items based on the extra three neighboring vertices that are created during the split. A separate split-triangle structure is used to contain the six split and perturbed vertices within the original triangle. See Listing 36-5.

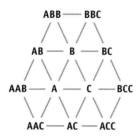

Figure 36-3. Triangle ABC and Its Neighbors

Listing 36-5. Data Structures for Subdivision

```
typedef struct STri_t{
    float4 A; // A.w indicates whether edge AB may stop subdivision
    float4 B; // B.w also indicates if BC may stop subdivision
    float4 C; // C.w tells if AC is small enough to stop subdividing
} STri;

// Stores the neighbors of a given triangle.
// The extra w component holds:
// a) whether respective edge may stop subdividing of triangle.
//    This could be altered to any per-edge qualifier.
// b) or for the intermediate triangle split, the recomputed
//    averaged neighbor list when a triangle is split
typedef struct Neighbor_t {
    float4 AB;   // AB.w = avg(AB,B).x
    float4 BBC;  // BBC.w = avg(AB,B).y
    float4 ABB;  // ABB.w = avg(AB,B).z
    float4 BC;   // BC.w = avg(BC,C).x
    float4 ACC;  // ACC.w = avg(BC,C).y
    float4 BCC;  // BCC.w = avg(BC,C).z
    float4 AC;   // AC.w = avg(AC,A).x
    float4 AAB;  // AAB.w = avg(AC,A).y
    float4 AAC;  // AAC.w = avg(AC,A).z
} Neighbor;
```

The initial data is given as two streams: a stream of triangles forming a closed mesh and a stream of neighbors to the triangles that make up the first stream. Triangle edges are each checked in turn for completion, and the stream is filtered for completed triangles. These triangles are saved for rendering, and the inverse filter is applied to the list to determine which triangles are in need of further subdivision. For nonadaptive subdivision, the filter stage can be replaced with a polygon count check to terminate subdivision altogether.

When a triangle is completed but its neighbors are not, a T-junction can appear where the edge of one triangle abuts a vertex of another. These need to be patched so as to preserve the mesh's state of being closed. At each stage, T-junctions can be detected by measuring whether two edges of a vertex have reached the exit condition, even if the triangle in question is still subdividing. When a T-junction is detected, our implementation has opted to place a sliver triangle there, filling in the potential rasterization gap between the polygons that have a T-junction. Other techniques, such as Red-Green triangulation (Seeger et al. 2001), may make more pleasing transitions, but this choice was made for its simplicity.

Finally, the subdivision calculation stage occurs. Each vertex in the triangle stream is weighted by its neighbors and split according to Loop's subdivision rule, resulting in six vertices per triangle: three near the original triangle corners and three new ones near the midpoints of the original triangle edges. The neighbors are likewise split, and the resulting 12 vertices are spread over the nine `float4` values. To recurse on this data, new streams are made that are four times as long as the split triangle and split neighbor streams. The new values are ordered into the appropriate original `Neighbor` and `Triangle` structures, depending on the arithmetic remainder of the output index divided by four. At this point, Boolean values declaring whether the edges of the triangle in question meet the per-edge constraint are computed, giving a hint to the filtering stage in the next round. The algorithm is repeated until a maximum depth is reached, or until all triangles have been filtered out as complete.

Details Specific to Streaming on the GPU

There are a few caveats that should be noted: Each of the triangles surrounding a given vertex must make the same decision about where the vertex ends up. This requires a few cautionary practices. First, vertices that are currently in the mesh must be weighted independently by all neighbors. Because floating-point addition is not associative, the surrounding values must be sorted from smallest to largest before being added together. This results in each of the triangles containing a vertex making the same decision about the final location of that vertex. Second, some optimizing compilers do not always respect IEEE floating-point standards in their optimizations and may reorder floating-point operations in ways that break the commutativity of floating-point addition. Others, like the Cg compiler, provide a command-line switch to control this behavior.

36.4 Conclusion

In this chapter we have demonstrated the utility of a filtering idiom for graphics hardware. The filtering paradigm enables a number of new applications that operate by filtering a data set at the price of a scan and search. Searching is becoming faster due to the recent addition of branching and looping to vertex programs, yet improvement of the scanning phase of the algorithm is largely predicated on having new hardware. Specifically, a central running sum register that can quickly produce unique, increasing values for fragments to use, and the ability to send fragments to other locations in the frame buffer would allow for a linear-time scan phase, and then would result in a direct output of the appropriate values. However, using a running sum register would destroy any order of the filtered fragments. The order has, however, been largely unnecessary in the algorithms presented here.

Future hardware has the distinct possibility of supporting order-preserving filtering natively and offers an exciting possibility for improving performance of general-purpose programmability.

There are plenty of other applications that can benefit from this idiom. For example, Monte Carlo ray tracing produces zero, one, or more rays per intersection with a surface. The scene may be traversed using the filtering idiom described in this chapter to propagate rays, terminating them when necessary, and producing more after an intersection. Marching Cubes takes a large 3D data set and culls it down into a 2D surface of interest, weighting the triangle vertices by the measured density values. An example of the Marching Cubes algorithm utilizing filtering is included with the Brook implementation available online at the Brook Web site (Buck et al. 2004). Furthermore, as shown by our collision-detection application, filtering permits GPUs to traverse tree data structures. This same approach could be used with other applications that operate on trees.

36.5 References

To learn more about collisions on the GPU, see the published papers on how to do collision detection on GPUs. A majority of the algorithms operate in image space, selecting views from which to render two objects such that colliding objects overlap. These algorithms, although fast in practice, often rely heavily on fine sampling to cull enough work away initially. They require $O(n)$ time, where n is the sum total of polygons in their objects (Govindaraju et al. 2003).

Hierarchical schemes are on average asymptotically faster. Gress and Zachmann (2003) also devised an object-space scheme for hierarchical collision detection, instead of a balanced tree of axis-aligned bounding boxes. They perform a breadth-first search into the respective collision trees, but at each level they use occlusion query to count the number of overlapping bounding boxes at that level. They allocate a texture of the appropriate size and search for the sequential filtered list of bounding boxes using a progressively built balanced tree structure. This technique, requiring $O(\log n)$ extra passes over the data to perform filtering effectively, emulates the technique presented in this chapter, but it is limited in scope to collision detection on balanced trees, instead of a more generic filtering technique.

Likewise, for more information on tessellation of subdivision surfaces, Owens et al. (2002) presented adaptive Catmull-Clark quadrilateral subdivision on the Imagine processor using a technique similar to the one presented in this chapter, but that algorithm utilized the conditional move operation present in the Imagine processor architecture (Khailany et al. 2001), which provides data filtering in hardware.

Buck, I., T. Foley, D. Horn, J. Sugarman, and P. Hanrahan. 2004. "Brook for GPUs: Stream Computing on Graphics Hardware." *ACM Transactions on Graphics (Proceedings of SIGGRAPH 2004)* 23(3). Available online at **http://graphics.stanford.edu/projects/brookgpu/**

Buck, I., and T. Purcell. 2004. "A Toolkit for Computation on GPUs." In *GPU Gems*, edited by Randima Fernando, pp. 621–636.

Gottschalk, S., M. C. Lin, and D. Manocha. 1996. "OBB-Tree: A Hierarchical Structure for Rapid Interference Detection." In *Proceedings of SIGGRAPH 96*, pp. 171–180.

Govindaraju, N. K., S. Redon, M. C. Lin, and D. Manocha. 2003. "CULLIDE: Interactive Collision Detection Between Complex Models in Large Environments Using Graphics Hardware." In *Proceedings of the SIGGRAPH/Eurographics Workshop on Graphics Hardware 2003*, pp. 25–32.

Gress, A., and G. Zachmann. 2003. "Object-Space Interference Detection on Programmable Graphics Hardware." In *Proceedings of the SIAM Conference on Geometric Design and Computing*, pp. 13–17.

Hillis, W. D., and G. L. Steele, Jr. 1986. "Data Parallel Algorithms." *Communications of the ACM* 29(12), p. 139.

Khailany, B., W. J. Dally, et al. 2001. "Imagine: Media Processing with Streams." *IEEE Micro*, March/April 2001.

Loop, C. 1987. "Smooth Subdivision Surfaces Based on Triangles." Master's thesis, Department of Mathematics, University of Utah.

Owens, J. D., B. Khailany, B. Towles, and W. J. Dally. 2002. "Comparing Reyes and OpenGL on a Stream Architecture." In *Proceedings of the SIGGRAPH/Eurographics Workshop on Graphics Hardware*, pp. 47–56.

Seeger, S., K. Hormann, G. Hausler, and G. Greiner. 2001. "A Sub-Atomic Subdivision Approach." In *Proceedings of the Vision, Modeling, and Visualization Conference*.

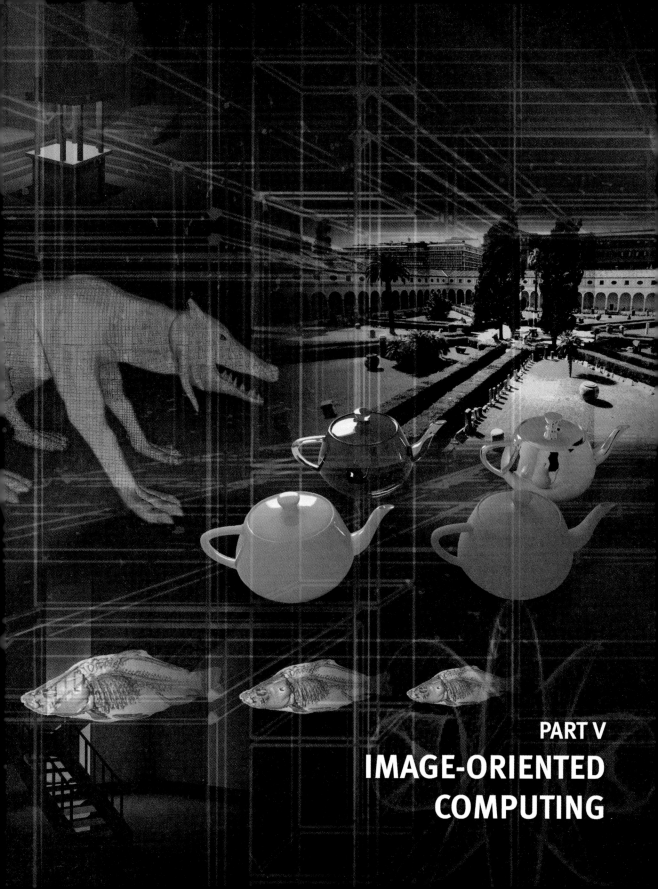

PART V
IMAGE-ORIENTED COMPUTING

Programmable vertex and fragment shaders have proven to be powerful additions to the OpenGL and Direct3D rendering pipelines. Beyond its expected uses in traditional graphics applications, this programmability has also enabled entirely new classes of GPU-based algorithms for image creation and analysis. This part of the book focuses on these kinds of image-oriented GPGPU techniques.

Hardware-assisted texture mapping is a key part of the modern graphics pipeline. Texture mapping on the GPU normally requires that objects be parameterized with texture coordinates, which can be difficult with certain types of models. Octree textures provide the usual benefits of texture mapping but do not require the use of texture coordinates. In **Chapter 37, "Octree Textures on the GPU,"** Sylvain **Lefebvre, Samuel Hornus,** and **Fabrice Neyret** of GRAVIR/IMAG–INRIA show how octree textures can be implemented on GPUs and demonstrate their use in two interactive applications.

Images produced by GPUs typically only account for direct illumination from light sources and ignore diffuse and glossy reflection between objects. **Toshiya Hachisuka** of the University of Tokyo describes how the GPU's high-performance rasterization capabilities can be leveraged to implement a global illumination rendering system in **Chapter 38, "High-Quality Global Illumination Rendering Using Rasterization."** By using rasterization to effectively cast many rays in the same direction at once, it is possible to efficiently include a wide variety of non-local illumination effects.

Next, in **Chapter 39, "Global Illumination Using Progressive Refinement Radiosity,"** **Greg Coombe** of the University of North Carolina at Chapel Hill and **Mark Harris** of NVIDIA describe a different kind of GPU-based global illumination renderer. By inverting the usual roles of "shooters" and "receivers" in progressive refinement radiosity, they are able to use the GPU to efficiently produce images that account for diffuse interreflection between large numbers of scene elements.

Computer vision is often referred to as the inverse of computer graphics: graphics generates images from models; vision does the opposite. **James Fung** of the University of Toronto turns the traditional graphics pipeline on its head in **Chapter 40, "Computer Vision on the GPU."** James shows how a GPU—or multiple GPUs—can be leveraged to form the backbone of a low-cost, high-performance computer vision system capable of running sophisticated vision algorithms at interactive rates.

Rendering images of data that is in a format not directly supported by graphics hardware is a common problem in GPGPU applications. In **Chapter 41, "Deferred Filtering: Rendering from Difficult Data Formats," Joe Kniss** of the University of Utah, **Aaron Lefohn,** and **Nathaniel Fout,** both of the University of California, Davis, demonstrate how these "difficult" data formats can be tamed through a two-pass rendering approach that takes advantage of the GPU's native texturing capabilities.

In the final chapter of this part, **Chapter 42, "Conservative Rasterization," Jon Hasselgren, Tomas Akenine-Möller**, and **Lennart Ohlsson** of Lund University make a valuable contribution to the GPGPU toolbox. They show how an application can control when and how fragments for partially covered pixels are generated, which is extremely useful when running a GPGPU calculation over a discretized domain. This capability allows applications to make conservative assumptions about which pixels are rasterized, resulting in more accurate GPU-based algorithms for applications ranging from collision detection to occlusion culling.

By their very nature, GPUs will continue to excel at image-oriented computation as their capabilities evolve. The techniques presented in this part offer a broad look at what is possible today, and they provide foundations upon which tomorrow's cutting-edge applications can be built. I trust you will find them to be as useful and thought provoking as I have.

Craig Kolb, NVIDIA

Chapter 37

Octree Textures on the GPU

Sylvain Lefebvre
GRAVIR/IMAG – INRIA

Samuel Hornus
GRAVIR/IMAG – INRIA

Fabrice Neyret
GRAVIR/IMAG – INRIA

Texture mapping is a very effective and efficient technique for enriching the appearance of polygonal models with details. Textures store not only color information, but also normals for bump mapping and various shading attributes to create appealing surface effects. However, texture mapping usually requires parameterizing a mesh by associating a 2D texture coordinate with every mesh vertex. Distortions and seams are often introduced by this difficult process, especially on complex meshes.

The 2D parameterization can be avoided by defining the texture inside a volume enclosing the object. Debry et al. (2002) and Benson and Davis (2002) have shown how 3D hierarchical data structures, named *octree textures*, can be used to efficiently store color information along a mesh surface *without* texture coordinates. This approach has two advantages. First, color is stored only where the surface intersects the volume, thus reducing memory requirements. Figures 37-1 and 37-2 illustrate this idea. Second, the surface is regularly sampled, and the resulting texture does not suffer from any distortions. In addition to mesh painting, any application that requires storing information on a complex surface can benefit from this approach.

This chapter details how to implement octree textures on today's GPUs. The octree is directly stored in texture memory and accessed from a fragment program. We discuss the trade-offs between performance, storage efficiency, and rendering quality. After explaining our implementation in Section 37.1, we demonstrate it on two different interactive applications:

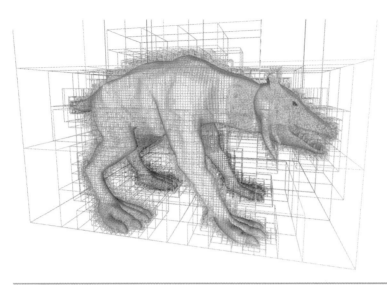

Figure 37-1. An Octree Texture Surrounding a 3D Model
Data is stored only on the mesh surface. (3D model courtesy of Mr. CAD, www.mr-cad.com)

Figure 37-2. Unparameterized Mesh Textures with an Octree Texture
Only 6 MB are required to store the octree texture in GPU memory. The octree is directly accessed from the fragment program.

- A surface-painting application (Section 37.2). In particular, we discuss the different possibilities for filtering the resulting texture (Section 37.2.3). We also show how a texture defined in an octree can be converted into a standard texture, possibly at runtime (Section 37.2.4).

- A nonphysical simulation of liquid flowing along a surface (Section 37.3). The simulation runs entirely on the GPU.

37.1 A GPU-Accelerated Hierarchical Structure: The N³-Tree

37.1.1 Definition

An octree is a regular hierarchical data structure. The first node of the tree, the *root*, is a cube. Each node has either eight children or no children. The eight children form a $2 \times 2 \times 2$ regular subdivision of the parent node. A node with children is called an *internal node*. A node without children is called *a leaf*. Figure 37-3 shows an octree surrounding a 3D model where the nodes that have the bunny's surface inside them have been refined and empty nodes have been left as leaves.

In an octree, the resolution in each dimension increases by two at each subdivision level. Thus, to reach a resolution of $256 \times 256 \times 256$, eight levels are required ($2^8 = 256$). Depending on the application, one might prefer to divide each edge by an arbitrary number N rather than 2. We therefore define a more generic structure called an N^3-*tree*. In an N³-tree, each node has N^3 children. The octree is an N³-tree with $N = 2$. A larger value of N reduces the tree depth required to reach a given resolution, but it tends to waste memory because the surface is less closely matched by the tree.

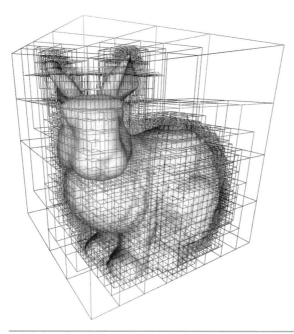

Figure 37-3. An Octree Surrounding a 3D Model

37.1.2 Implementation

To implement a hierarchical tree on a GPU, we need to define how to store the structure in texture memory and how to access the structure from a fragment program.

A simple approach to implement an octree on a CPU is to use pointers to link the tree nodes together. Each internal node contains an array of pointers to its children. A child can be another internal node or a leaf. A leaf contains only a data field.

Our implementation on the GPU follows a similar approach. Pointers simply become indices within a texture. They are encoded as RGB values. The content of the leaves is directly stored as an RGB value within the parent node's array of pointers. We use the alpha channel to distinguish between a pointer to a child and the content of a leaf. Our approach relies on dependent texture lookups (or *texture indirections*). This requires the hardware to support an arbitrary number of dependent texture lookups, which is the case for GeForce FX and GeForce 6 Series GPUs.

The following sections detail our GPU implementation of the N^3-tree. For clarity, the figures illustrate the 2D equivalent of an octree (a *quadtree*).

Storage

We store the tree in an 8-bit RGBA 3D texture called the *indirection pool*. Each "pixel" of the indirection pool is called a *cell*.

The indirection pool is subdivided into *indirection grids*. An indirection grid is a cube of $N \times N \times N$ cells (a $2 \times 2 \times 2$ grid for an octree). Each node of the tree is represented by an indirection grid. It corresponds to the array of pointers in the CPU implementation described earlier.

A cell of an indirection grid can be empty or can contain one of the following:

- Data, if the corresponding child is a leaf
- The index of an indirection grid, if the corresponding child is another internal node

Figure 37-4 illustrates our tree storage representation.

We note $S = S_u \times S_v \times S_w$ as the number of indirection grids stored in the indirection pool and $R = (N \times S_u) \times (N \times S_v) \times (N \times S_w)$ as the resolution in cells of the indirection pool.

Data values and indices of children are both stored as RGB triples. The alpha channel is used as a flag to determine the cell content (alpha = 1 indicates data; alpha = 0.5 indicates index; alpha = 0 indicates empty cell). The root of the tree is always stored at $(0, 0, 0)$ within the indirection pool.

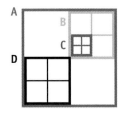

A Quadtree

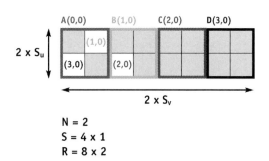

Corresponding Indirection Pool

A(0,0) B(1,0) C(2,0) D(3,0)

2 x S_u

2 x S_v

N = 2
S = 4 x 1
R = 8 x 2

Figure 37-4. Storage in Texture Memory (2D Case)
The indirection pool encodes the tree. Indirection grids are drawn with different colors. The gray cells contain data.

Accessing the Structure: Tree Lookup

Once the tree is stored in texture memory, we need to access it from a fragment program. As with standard 3D textures, the tree defines a texture within the unit cube. We want to retrieve the value stored in the tree at a point $M \in [0, 1]^3$. The tree lookup starts from the root and successively visits the nodes containing the point M until a leaf is reached.

Let I_D be the index of the indirection grid of the node visited at depth D. The tree lookup is initialized with $I_0 = (0, 0, 0)$, which corresponds to the tree root. When we are at depth D, we know the index I_D of the current node's indirection grid. We now explain how we retrieve I_{D+1} from I_D.

The lookup point M is inside the node visited at depth D. To decide what to do next, we need to read from the indirection grid I_D the value stored at the location corresponding to M. To do so, we need to compute the coordinates of M *within* the node.

At depth D, a complete tree produces a regular grid of resolution $N^D \times N^D \times N^D$ within the unit cube. We call this grid the *depth-D grid*. Each node of the tree at depth D corresponds to a cell of this grid. In particular, M is within the cell corresponding to the node visited at depth D. The coordinates of M *within* this cell are given by $frac(M \times N^D)$. We use these coordinates to read the value from the indirection grid I_D. The lookup coordinates within the indirection pool are thus computed as:

$$P = \frac{I_D + frac\left(M \times N^D\right)}{S}.$$

We then retrieve the RGBA value stored at P in the indirection pool. Depending on the alpha value, either we will return the RGB color if the child is a leaf, or we will interpret the RGB values as the index of the child's indirection grid (I_{D+1}) and continue to the next tree depth. Figure 37-5 summarizes this entire process for the 2D case (quadtree).

The lookup ends when a leaf is reached. In practice, our fragment program also stops after a fixed number of texture lookups: on most hardware, it is only possible to implement loop statements with a fixed number of iterations (however, early exit is possible on GeForce 6 Series GPUs). The application is in charge of limiting the tree depth with respect to the maximum number of texture lookups done within the fragment program. The complete tree lookup code is shown in Listing 37-1.

Listing 37-1. The Tree Lookup Cg Code

```
float4 tree_lookup(uniform sampler3D IndirPool, // Indirection Pool
  uniform float3 invS, // 1 / S
  uniform float N,
  float3 M) // Lookup coordinates
{
  float4 I = float4(0.0, 0.0, 0.0, 0.0);
  float3 MND = M;

  for (float i=0; i<HRDWTREE_MAX_DEPTH; i++) { // fixed # of iterations
    float3 P;
    // compute lookup coords. within current node
    P = (MND + floor(0.5 + I.xyz * 255.0)) * invS;
    // access indirection pool
    if (I.w < 0.9)                      // already in a leaf?
      I =(float4)tex3D(IndirPool,P); // no, continue to next depth

#ifdef DYN_BRANCHING // early exit if hardware supports dynamic branching
    if (I.w > 0.9)    // a leaf has been reached
      break;
#endif

    if (I.w < 0.1)    // empty cell
      discard;
    // compute pos within next depth grid
    MND = MND * N;
  }
  return (I);
}
```

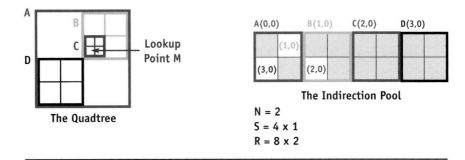

A

B

C

Lookup Point M

D

The Quadtree

A(0,0)   B(1,0)   C(2,0)   D(3,0)

(1,0)

(3,0)   (2,0)

The Indirection Pool

N = 2
S = 4 x 1
R = 8 x 2

Lookup at Point M:

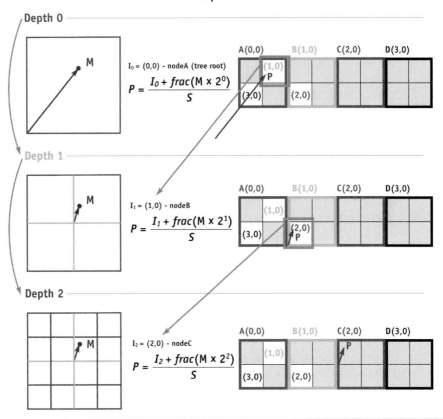

Depth 0

M

$I_0 = (0,0)$ - nodeA (tree root)

$$P = \frac{I_0 + frac(M \times 2^0)}{S}$$

A(0,0)   B(1,0)   C(2,0)   D(3,0)

(1,0)
P

(3,0)   (2,0)

Depth 1

M

$I_1 = (1,0)$ - nodeB

$$P = \frac{I_1 + frac(M \times 2^1)}{S}$$

A(0,0)   B(1,0)   C(2,0)   D(3,0)

(1,0)

(3,0)   (2,0)
P

Depth 2

M

$I_2 = (2,0)$ - nodeC

$$P = \frac{I_2 + frac(M \times 2^2)}{S}$$

A(0,0)   B(1,0)   C(2,0)   D(3,0)

(1,0)

(3,0)   (2,0)

P

Figure 37-5. Example of a Tree Lookup
At each step, the value stored within the current node's indirection grid is retrieved. If this value encodes an index, the lookup continues to the next level. Otherwise, the value is returned.

Further Optimizations

In our tree lookup algorithm, as we explained earlier, the computation of P requires a `frac` instruction. In our implementation, however, as shown Listing 37-1, we actually avoid computing the `frac` by relying on the cyclic behavior of the texture units (repeat mode). We leave the detailed explanations as an appendix, located on the book's CD.

We compute P as

$$P = \frac{M \times N^D + \Delta_D}{S},$$

where Δ_D is an integer within the range $[0, S[$.

We store Δ_D instead of directly storing the I_D values. Please refer to the appendix on the CD for the code to compute Δ_D.

Encoding Indices

The indirection pool is an 8-bit 3D RGBA texture. This means that we can encode only 256 different values per channel. This gives us an addressing space of 24 bits (3 indices of 8 bits), which makes it possible to encode octrees large enough for most applications.

Within a fragment program, a texture lookup into an 8-bit texture returns a value mapped between [0,1]. However, we need to encode integers. Using a floating-point texture to do so would require more memory and would reduce performance. Instead, we map values between [0,1] with a fixed precision of 1/255 and simply multiply the floating-point value by 255 to obtain an integer. Note that on hardware without fixed-precision registers, we need to compute `floor(0.5 + 255 * v)` to avoid rounding errors.

37.2 Application 1: Painting on Meshes

In this section we use the GPU-accelerated octree structure presented in the previous section to create a surface-painting application. Thanks to the octree, the mesh does not need to be parameterized. This is especially useful with complex meshes such as trees, hairy monsters, or characters.

The user will be able to paint on the mesh using a 3D brush, similar to the brush used in 2D painting applications. In this example, the painting resolution is homogeneous along the surface, although multiresolution painting would be an easy extension if desired.

37.2.1 Creating the Octree

We start by computing the bounding box of the object to be painted. The object is then rescaled such that its largest dimension is mapped between [0,1[. The same scaling is applied to the three dimensions because we want the painting resolution to be the same in every dimension. After this process, the mesh fits entirely within the unit box.

The user specifies the desired resolution of the painting. This determines the depth of the leaves of the octree that contain colors. For instance, if the user selects a resolution of 512^3, the leaves containing colors will be at depth 9.

The tree is created by subdividing the nodes intersecting the surface until all the leaves either are empty or are at the selected depth (color leaves). To check whether a tree node intersects the geometry, we rely on the box defining the boundary of the node. This process is depicted in Figure 37-6. We use the algorithm shown in Listing 37-2.

This algorithm uses our GPU octree texture API. The links between nodes (indices in the indirection grids) are set up by the createChild() call. The values stored in tree leaves are set up by calling setChildAsEmpty() and setChildColor(), which also set the appropriate alpha value.

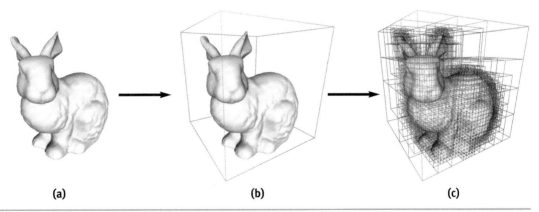

(a) **(b)** **(c)**

Figure 37-6. Building an Octree Around a Mesh Surface
(a) Input mesh. (b) Unit box. (c) Final octree.

Listing 37-2. Recursive Algorithm for Octree Creation

```
void createNode(depth, polygons, box)
  for all children (i, j, k) within (N, N, N)
    if (depth + 1 == painting depth)   // painting depth reached?
      setChildColor(i, j, k, white)    // child is at depth+1
    else
      childbox = computeSubBox(i, j, k, box)
      if (childbox intersect polygons)
        child = createChild(i, j, k)
        // recurse
        createNode(depth + 1, polygons, childbox)
      else
        setChildAsEmpty(i, j, k)
```

37.2.2 Painting

In our application, the painting tool is drawn as a small sphere moving along the surface of the mesh. This sphere is defined by a painting center P_{center} and a painting radius P_{radius}. The behavior of the brush is similar to that of brushes in 2D painting tools.

When the user paints, the leaf nodes intersecting the painting tool are updated. The new color is computed as a weighted sum of the previous color and the painting color. The weight is such that the painting opacity decreases as the distance from P_{center} increases.

To minimize the amount of data to be sent to the GPU as painting occurs, only the modified leaves are updated in texture memory. This corresponds to a partial update of the indirection pool texture (under OpenGL, we use glTexSubImage3D). The modifications are tracked on a copy of the tree stored in CPU memory.

37.2.3 Rendering

To render the textured mesh, we need to access the octree from the fragment program, using the tree lookup defined in Section 37.1.2.

The untransformed coordinates of the vertices are stored as 3D texture coordinates. These 3D texture coordinates are interpolated during the rasterization of the triangles. Therefore, within the fragment program, we know the 3D point of the mesh surface being projected in the fragment. By using these coordinates as texture coordinates for the tree lookup, we retrieve the color stored in the octree texture.

However, this produces the equivalent of a standard texture lookup in "nearest" mode. Linear interpolation and mipmapping are often mandatory for high-quality results. In the following section, we discuss how to implement these techniques for octree textures.

Linear Interpolation

Linear interpolation of the texture can be obtained by extending the standard 2D linear interpolation. Because the octree texture is a volume texture, eight samples are required for linear interpolation, as shown in Figure 37-7.

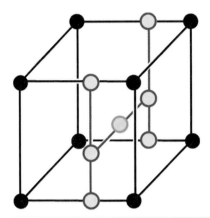

Figure 37-7. Linear Interpolation Using Eight Samples

However, we store information only where the surface intersects the volume. Some of the samples involved in the 3D linear interpolation are not on the surface and have no associated color information. Consider a sample at coordinates (i, j, k) within the maximum depth grid (recall that the depth D grid is the regular grid produced by a complete octree at depth D). The seven other samples involved in the 3D linear interpolation are at coordinates $(i+1, j, k)$, $(i, j+1, k)$, $(i, j, k+1)$, $(i, j+1, k+1)$, $(i+1, j, k+1)$, $(i+1, j+1, k)$, and $(i+1, j+1, k+1)$. However, some of these samples may not be included in the tree, because they are too far from the surface. This leads to rendering artifacts, as shown in Figure 37-8.

We remove these artifacts by modifying the tree creation process. We make sure that all of the samples necessary for linear interpolation are included in the tree. This can be done easily by enlarging the box used to check whether a tree node intersects the geometry. The box is built in such a way that it includes the *previous* samples in each dimension. Indeed, the sample at (i, j, k) must be added if one of the previous samples (for example, the one at $(i-1, j-1, k-1)$) is in the tree. This is illustrated in Figure 37-9.

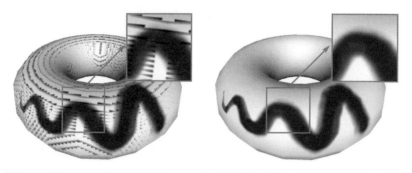

Figure 37-8. Fixing Artifacts Caused by Straightforward Linear Interpolation

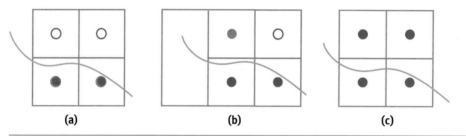

| (a) | (b) | (c) |

Figure 37-9. Modifying the Tree Creation to Remove Linear Interpolation Artifacts
(a) Top samples are not stored in the tree, which leads to false interpolation. (b) The enlarged box shown for the upper-left sample (orange) now intersects with the surface. The sample will be included in the octree. (c) All the samples required for correct linear interpolation are now stored in the octree.

In our demo, we use the same depth for all color leaves. Of course, the octree structure makes it possible to store color information at different depths. However, doing so complicates linear interpolation. For more details, refer to Benson and Davis 2002.

Mipmapping

When a textured mesh becomes small on the screen, multiple samples of the texture fall into the same pixel. Without a proper filtering algorithm, this leads to aliasing. Most GPUs implement the mipmapping algorithm on standard 2D textures. We extend this algorithm to our GPU octree textures.

We define the mipmap levels as follows. The finest level (level 0) corresponds to the leaves of the initial octree. A coarser level is built from the previous one by merging the leaves in their parent node. The node color is set to the average color of its leaves, and the leaves are suppressed, as shown in Figure 37-10. The octree depth is therefore reduced by one at each mipmapping level. The coarsest level has only one root node, containing the average color of all the leaves of the initial tree.

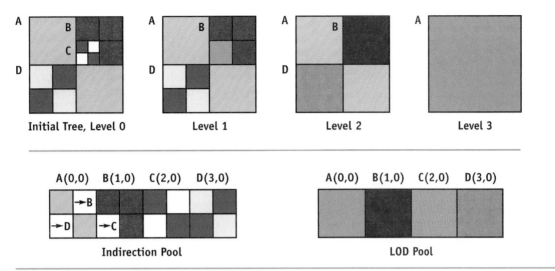

Figure 37-10. An Example of a Tree with Mipmapping

Storing one tree per mipmapping level would be expensive. Instead, we create a second 3D texture, called the *LOD pool*. The LOD pool has one cell per indirection grid of the indirection pool (see Figure 37-10, bottom row). Its resolution is thus $S_u \times S_v \times S_w$ (see "Storage" in Section 37.1.2). Each node of the initial tree becomes a leaf at a given mipmapping level. The LOD pool stores the color taken by the nodes when they are used as leaves in a mipmapping level.

To texture the mesh at a specific mipmapping level, we stop the tree lookup at the corresponding depth and look up the node's average color in the LOD pool. The appropriate mipmapping level can be computed within the fragment program using partial-derivative instructions.

37.2.4 Converting the Octree Texture to a Standard 2D Texture

Our ultimate goal is to use octree textures as a replacement for 2D textures, thus completely removing the need for a 2D parameterization. However, the octree texture requires explicit programming of the texture filtering. This leads to long fragment programs. On recent GPUs, performance is still high enough for texture-authoring applications, where a single object is displayed. But for applications displaying complex scenes, such as games or simulators, rendering performance may be too low. Moreover, GPUs are extremely efficient at displaying filtered standard 2D texture maps.

Being able to convert an octree texture into a standard 2D texture is therefore important. We would like to perform this conversion dynamically: this makes it possible to select the best representation at runtime. For example, an object near the viewpoint would use the linearly interpolated octree texture and switch to the corresponding filtered standard 2D texture when it moves farther away. The advantage is that filtering of the 2D texture is natively handled by the GPU. Thus, the extra cost of the octree texture is incurred only when details are visible.

In the following discussion, we assume that the mesh is already parameterized. We describe how we create a 2D texture map from an octree texture.

To produce the 2D texture map, we render the triangles using their 2D (u, v) coordinates instead of their 3D (x, y, z) coordinates. The triangles are textured with the octree texture, using the 3D coordinates of the mesh vertices as texture coordinates for the tree lookup. The result is shown in Figure 37-11.

However, this approach produces artifacts. When the 2D texture is applied to the mesh with filtering, the background color bleeds inside the texture. This happens because samples outside of the 2D triangles are used by the linear interpolation for texture filtering. It is not sufficient to add only a few border pixels: more and more pixels outside of the triangles are used by coarser mipmapping levels. These artifacts are shown in Figure 37-12.

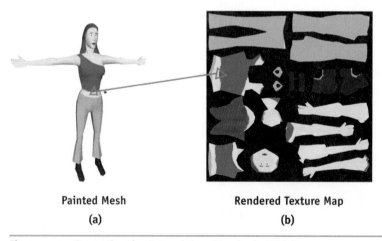

Painted Mesh   Rendered Texture Map
(a)   (b)

Figure 37-11. Converting the Octree into a Standard 2D Texture
3D model courtesy of Philippe Chaubaroux

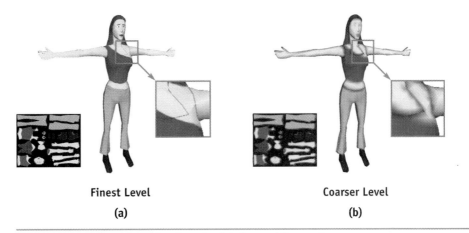

Finest Level

(a)

Coarser Level

(b)

Figure 37-12. Artifacts Resulting from Straightforward Conversion

To suppress these artifacts, we compute a new texture in which the colors are extrapo-
lated outside of the 2D triangles. To do so, we use a simplified GPU variant of the
extrapolation method known as *push-pull*. This method has been used for the same
purpose in Sander et al. 2001.

We first render the 2D texture map as described previously. The background is set with
an alpha value of 0. The triangles are rendered using an alpha value of 1. We then ask
the GPU to automatically generate the mipmapping levels of the texture. Then we
collapse all the mipmapping levels into one texture, interpreting the alpha value as a
transparency coefficient. This is done with the Cg code shown in Listing 37-3.

Finally, new mipmapping levels are generated by the GPU from this new texture.
Figures 37-13 and 37-14 show the result of this process.

Listing 37-3. Color Extrapolation Cg Code

```
PixelOut main(V2FI IN,
  uniform sampler2D Tex) // texture with mipmapping levels
{
  PixelOut OUT;

  float4 res = float4(0.0, 0.0, 0.0, 0.0);
  float alpha = 0.0;
  // start with coarsest level
  float sz = TEX_SIZE;
```

Listing 37-3 *(continued)*. Color Extrapolation Cg Code

```
// for all mipmapping levels
for (float i=0.0; i<=TEX_SIZE_LOG2; i+=1.0)
{
   // texture lookup at this level
   float2 MIP = float2(sz/TEX_SIZE, 0.0);
   float4 c = (float4)tex2D(Tex, IN.TCoord0, MIP.xy, MIP.yx);
   // blend with previous
   res = c + res * (1.0 - c.w);
   // go to finer level
   sz /= 2.0;
}
// done - return normalized color (alpha == 1)
OUT.COL = float4(res.xyz/res.w,1);
return OUT;
}
```

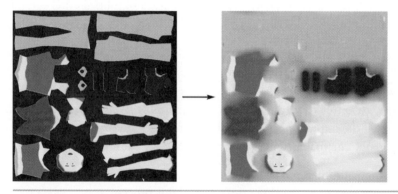

Figure 37-13. Color Extrapolation

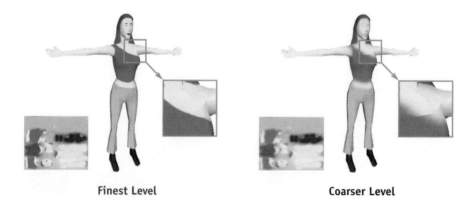

Finest Level   **Coarser Level**

Figure 37-14. Artifacts Removed Due to Color Extrapolation

37.3 Application 2: Surface Simulation

We have seen with the previous application that octree structures are useful for storing color information along a mesh surface. But octree structures on GPUs are also useful for simulation purposes. In this section, we present how we use an octree structure on the GPU to simulate liquid flowing along a mesh.

We do not go through the details of the simulation itself, because that is beyond the scope of this chapter. We concentrate instead on how we use the octree to make available all the information required by the simulation.

The simulation is done by a cellular automaton residing on the surface of the object. To perform the simulation, we need to attach a 2D density map to the mesh surface. The next simulation step is computed by updating the value of each pixel with respect to the density of its neighbors. This is done by rendering into the next density map using the previous density map and neighboring information as input.

Because physical simulation is very sensitive to distortions, using a standard 2D parameterization to associate the mesh surface to the density map would not produce good results in general. Moreover, computation power could be wasted if some parts of the 2D density map were not used. Therefore, we use an octree to avoid the parameterization.

The first step is to create an octree around the mesh surface (see Section 37.2.1). We do not directly store density within the octree: the density needs to be updated using a render-to-texture operation during the simulation and should therefore be stored in a 2D texture map. Instead of density, each leaf of the octree contains the index of a pixel within the 2D density map. Recall that the leaves of the octree store three 8-bit values (in RGB channels). To be able to use a density map larger than 256×256, we combine the values of the blue and green channels to form a 16-bit index.

During simulation, we also need to access the density of the neighbors. A set of 2D RGB textures, called *neighbor textures*, is used to encode neighboring information. Let I be an index stored within a leaf L of the octree. Let D_{map} be the density map and N a neighbor texture. The Cg call `tex2D(Dmap,I)` returns the density associated with leaf L. The call `tex2D(N,I)` gives the index within the density map corresponding to a neighbor (in 3D space) of the leaf L. Therefore, `tex2D(Dmap, tex2D(N,I))` gives us the density of the neighbor of L.

To encode the full 3D neighborhood information, 26 textures would be required (a leaf of the tree can have up to 26 neighbors in 3D). However, fewer neighbors are required in practice. Because the octree is built around a 2D surface, the average number of neighbors is likely to be closer to 9.

Once these textures have been created, the simulation can run on the density map. Rendering is done by texturing the mesh with the density map. The octree is used to retrieve the density stored in a given location of the mesh surface. Results of the simulation are shown in Figure 37-15. The user can interactively add liquid on the surface. Videos are available on the book's CD.

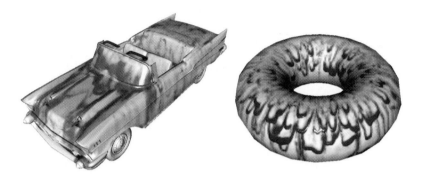

Figure 37-15. Liquid Flowing Along Mesh Surfaces

37.4 Conclusion

We have presented a complete GPU implementation of octree textures. These structures offer an efficient and convenient way of storing undistorted data along a mesh surface. This can be color data, as in the mesh-painting application, or data for dynamic texture simulation, as in the flowing liquid simulation. Rendering can be done efficiently on modern hardware, and we have provided solutions for filtering to avoid texture aliasing. Nevertheless, because 2D texture maps are preferable in some situations, we have shown how an octree texture can be dynamically converted into a 2D texture without artifacts.

Octrees are very generic data structures, widely used in computer science. They are a convenient way of storing information on unparameterized meshes, and more generally in space. Many other applications, such as volume rendering, can benefit from their hardware implementation.

We hope that you will discover many further uses for and improvements to the techniques presented in this chapter! Please see http://www.aracknea.net/octreetextures for updates of the source code and additional information.

37.5 References

Benson, D., and J. Davis. 2002. "Octree Textures." *ACM Transactions on Graphics (Proceedings of SIGGRAPH 2002)* 21(3), pp. 785–790.

Debry, D., J. Gibbs, D. Petty, and N. Robins. 2002. "Painting and Rendering Textures on Unparameterized Models." *ACM Transactions on Graphics (Proceedings of SIGGRAPH 2002)* 21(3), pp. 763–768.

Sander, P., J. Snyder, S. Gortler, and H. Hoppe. 2001. "Texture Mapping Progressive Meshes." In *Proceedings of SIGGRAPH 2001*, pp. 409–416.

Chapter 38

High-Quality Global Illumination Rendering Using Rasterization

Toshiya Hachisuka
The University of Tokyo

While the visual richness of images that current GPUs can render interactively continues to increase quickly, there are many important lighting effects that are not easily handled with current techniques. One important lighting effect that is difficult for GPUs is high-quality global illumination, where light that reflects off of objects in the scene that are not themselves light emitters is included in the final image. Incorporating this indirect illumination in rendered images greatly improves their visual quality; Figure 38-1 shows an indoor scene with indirect lighting and large area light sources. Like all images in this chapter, it was rendered with a GPU-based global illumination algorithm that uses rasterization hardware for efficient ray casting.

Techniques for including these effects usually require ray tracing for high-quality results. At each pixel, a "final gather" computation is done, in which a large number of rays are cast over the hemisphere around the point, in order to sample the light arriving from many different directions. This chapter describes an approach for using the GPU's rasterization hardware to do fast ray casting for final gathering for high-quality offline rendering. In contrast to previous techniques for GPU ray tracing (for example, Purcell et al. 2002 and Carr et al. 2002), this approach is based on using the rasterization hardware in an innovative way to perform ray-object intersections, rather than on mapping classic ray-tracing algorithms to the GPU's programmable fragment processing unit. Even though our target is images of the highest quality, rather than images rendered at interactive frame rates, the enormous amounts of computational capability and bandwidth available on the GPU make it worthwhile to use for offline rendering.

Figure 38-1. An Image Rendered with Global Illumination Accelerated by the GPU

38.1 Global Illumination via Rasterization

Rather than adapt various CPU-based global illumination methods to the GPU, we argue that it is more natural and efficient to derive a new global illumination algorithm that employs rasterization, because graphics hardware is based on rasterization rendering. Although many previous techniques use the GPU to perform real-time rendering with some features of global illumination—such as precomputed radiance transfer (Sloan et al. 2002)—it is also attractive to use the GPU for accelerating high-quality offline rendering. One important advantage of using rasterization in this way is that we do not need to maintain ray-tracing acceleration structures (such as uniform grids) on the GPU. This is a significant advantage, because previous GPU-based ray tracers have depended on the CPU for building these structures and were thus limited both by the CPU's processing speed as well as by the amount of memory available on the GPU for storing the complete scene description. Our technique suffers essentially from neither of these problems.

We have posted our global illumination renderer, named "Parthenon," which uses the techniques presented here, at http://www.bee-www.com/parthenon/. This application can also be found on the book's CD. Figure 38-2 shows additional images rendered by Parthenon.

Figure 38-2. Images Rendered Using Parthenon, a GPU-Accelerated Renderer

38.2 Overview of Final Gathering

38.2.1 Two-Pass Methods

Conceptually, the easiest way to solve global illumination is to use path tracing, but this approach requires a great number of rays to obtain an image without noise. As a result, most global illumination renderers today implement a more efficient two-pass method. Two-pass methods compute a rough approximation to the global illumination in the scene as a first pass, and then in a second pass, they render the final image efficiently using the results of the first pass. Many renderers use radiosity or photon mapping for the first pass. Although the result of the first pass can be used directly in the final image, achieving sufficient quality to do so often requires more computation time than using a two-pass method (that is, we need a large number of photons to obtain a sufficiently accurate image if we use photon mapping). Figure 38-3 shows global illumination renderings of a Cornell Box using direct visualization of photon mapping and using the two-pass method. These images take nearly the same amount of computation time.

Figure 38-3. Comparing Results from Direct Use of the Photon Map and from the Two-Pass Method
Left: Photon map directly visualized. Right: Photon map indirectly used by final gathering.

Although it sounds redundant to process the same scene twice, the computational cost of a first pass is usually not very large, because it computes an approximate result. Thus, the first pass accounts for only a small part of the total rendering time. This method is the de facto standard of recent global illumination renderers because it can produce a final image with sufficient quality faster than path tracing usually can.

38.2.2 Final Gathering

There is a wide variety of ways in which the first-pass solution can be used, but the most popular method is to use it as a source of indirect illumination when evaluating a hemi-spherical integral via ray casting in the second pass. At each visible point, we would like to determine how much light is arriving at the point from other objects in the scene. To do so, we cast a large number of rays over the hemisphere at that point to determine which object in the scene is visible along each direction and how much light is arriving from it, as shown in Figure 38-4. This process is called *final gathering*. The resulting radiance (brightness) of each visible point can be computed by the following integral:

$$L\left(x, \vec{\omega}'\right) = \int_{\Omega} BRDF\left(x, \vec{\omega}, \vec{\omega}'\right) L_{in}\left(x, \vec{\omega}\right)\left(\vec{\omega} \cdot \vec{n}\right) d\vec{\omega}.$$

This equation shows that the outgoing radiance of the specified point is the integral of the cosine-weighted reflected incident radiance according to the BRDF. We need ray casting to compute the incident radiance L_{in} in this integral.

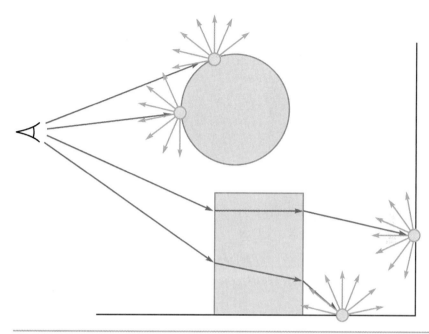

Figure 38-4. The Basic Idea of Final Gathering
The sphere is the diffuse object, the box is the refractive object, and the green arrows are the final gathering rays. At first we trace the eye ray. If this ray intersects a diffuse object, the intersection point is passed to the final gathering process. In the final gathering process, many rays are cast over the hemisphere from the point being shaded. The intersection points with other diffuse objects are used for radiance calculation.

38.2.3 Problems with Two-Pass Methods

In practice, the final gathering step is usually the bottleneck of the whole rendering process, because it requires a great number of ray-casting operations to achieve sufficiently accurate results for a final image. Table 38-1 shows the number of rays of each process in a typical scene.

If we assume that CPU ray tracing has a performance of 250,000 rays per second to render the Cornell Box scene in Table 38-1, the final gathering process takes about 20 minutes, whereas ray tracing from the camera takes about 1 second. For this reason, many renderers use an interpolation approach that performs final gathering on only a sparse sampling point set and interpolates the result on the rest of the points (Ward 1994). Although this approach can reduce the duration of the final gathering process, it cannot

Table 38-1. The Number of Rays for a Typical Scene

	Photon Tracing	Ray Tracing from Camera	1024 Samples Final Gathering
Cornell Box 512×512; 500,000 photons	607,002	262,144	268,435,456
Buddha 512×512; 400,000 photons	15,886,408	323,212	101,261,312
Teapot 512×512; 300,000 photons	368,793	379,452	253,227,008

be greatly reduced if the scene generates many sampling points due to geometric complexity. Moreover, as a practical problem, it is necessary to adjust many nonintuitive parameters for the interpolation not to introduce obvious artifacts. Because we need to render the scene several times to find optimal values of the parameter, this approach may not reduce "total" rendering time so much if such trial-and-error time is included.

38.3 Final Gathering via Rasterization

Our GPU-based final gathering method calculates the hemispherical integral at all visible points, so interpolation is no longer necessary—all you need to adjust is the total number of samples! Moreover, because this method processes all visible points at the same time, we can see this rendering process progressively and terminate the computation when the resulting image achieves sufficient quality. Our method leverages the capabilities of the GPU's rasterization hardware, such that this approach is usually faster than those based on final gathering on the CPU at a sparse set of points and using interpolation.

38.3.1 Clustering of Final Gathering Rays

For each visible point, the final gathering step generates N uniformly distributed rays over the hemisphere centered around the visible point's normal vector, as shown in Figure 38-5a. Rather than choose these directions differently at every point, as most CPU-based implementations do (we call it *hemispherical clustering*), our method chooses the direction of each generated ray from a predetermined set of N fixed directions (we call it *parallel clustering*). This set of directions can be thought of as a discretization of all the directions over the unit sphere. Consider now all of the rays generated for all of the visible points. If you group the rays that have the same predetermined direction into N subsets, each subset will consist of rays with different origins but the same direction (Figure 38-5b).

Our method makes direct use of parallel clustering of rays: instead of tracing the rays associated with each visible point separately, we choose one of the N predetermined directions at a time, and we effectively trace all of the rays with this direction simultaneously using rasterization. This rasterization is performed via a parallel projection of the scene along the current direction. The currently selected direction is called the *global ray direction*. The concept of the global ray direction itself has been previously proposed by Szirmay-Kalos and Purgathofer (1998). Although we can use the hemicube method

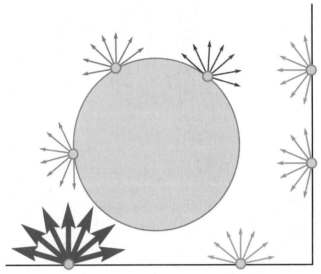

Set of Rays in Conventional Final Gathering

(a)

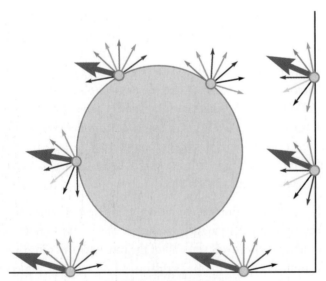

Set of Rays in Our Method

(b)

Figure 38-5. Two Different Clusterings of Final Gathering Rays
With conventional final gathering, a different set of directions is used at each gather point. With our approach, the same direction is used at many different points.

(Cohen et al. 1993) with hemispherical clustering of rays, this is a very time-consuming approach, because we need to rasterize the scene on the order of the number of pixels. Note that our method only requires rasterization on the order of the number of global ray directions (that is, the number of final gathering samples). Usually, the number of pixels is orders of magnitude larger than the number of final gathering samples, so the proposed method is very efficient.

38.3.2 Ray Casting as Multiple Parallel Projection

The key to considering final gathering as multiple parallel projections is the concept of a depth layer. Depth layers are subsets of the geometry in a scene, based on the number of intersections along a certain direction, starting from outside the scene, as shown in Figure 38-6. For example, a ray arrives at the second depth layer for rays shot in the opposite of the global ray direction after intersecting the first depth layer. Thus, after choosing a particular global ray direction, all we have to do is obtain the nearest point

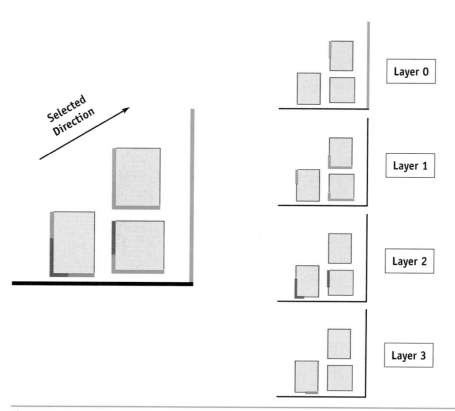

Figure 38-6. Depth Layers of a Simple Scene Along a Particular Direction

along the global ray direction starting from a particular position by using depth layers. Because the nearest point exists on the nearest depth layer starting from a visible point, if we can fetch the nearest depth layer based on the position of the parallel projection of the visible point (see Figure 38-7), this process is equivalent to ray casting.

To obtain each depth layer by using the GPU, we use the multipass rendering method called *depth peeling* (Everitt 2001). Although this method was invented to sort geometry for correct alpha blending, it is essentially based on the concept of depth layers. With depth peeling, the rendering of the scene is first performed as usual. The next rendering pass ignores fragments with the same depth as those rendered in the first pass, so that the fragments that have the next larger depth value than those in the first depth layer are stored in the frame buffer. As a result, we can extract all depth layers in order by repeating this process.

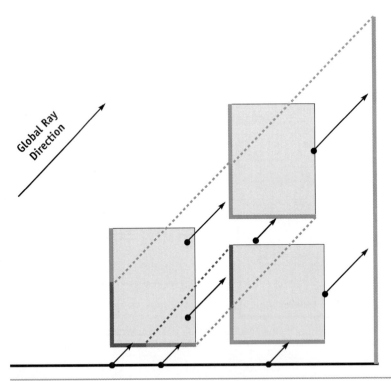

Figure 38-7. Parallel Multiple Ray Casts as a Parallel Projection

38.4 Implementation Details

Now that we have the tools for performing final gathering on the GPU by rasterization, we explain the details of the implementation of our algorithm. The following steps summarize the method.

1. Store the position and normal at each visible point to visible point buffer A.

2. Initialize "depth" buffer B and buffer C to maximum distance.

3. Clear sampled depth layer buffer D to zero.

4. Sample one global ray direction by uniform sampling.

5. Read buffer D at the position of parallel projection of the visible point in buffer A, and store the result into buffer E if this point is in front of the visible point along the selected global ray direction.

6. Render the scene geometry, including the data from the first pass, into buffer B (for depth value) and buffer D (for color) using parallel projection by selected global ray direction, with reversed depth test (that is, render the farthest point of the mesh). If the fragment of the point has larger depth value than buffer C, then it is culled.

7. Copy buffer B into buffer C.

8. Return to step 5 until the number of the rendered fragments becomes 0 at step 6.

9. Accumulate buffer E into indirect illumination buffer.

10. Return to step 2 until the number of samplings becomes sufficient.

38.4.1 Initialization

At first, we need to store the data of visible points to the floating-point texture, to start the final gathering process. The simplest way to do this is to render the position and the normal of vertices by storing this data as texture coordinates. We describe later the details of generating this data for global illumination rendering. Note that these visible points are arbitrary (that is, each visible point's data is independent of the others). Therefore, we can process not only points visible from the camera, but also any set of data such as texels of light maps, the baked colors of vertices, and so on. In addition to the data of visible points, we also need to sample global ray direction and store this vector into a pixel shader constant. For the successive depth peeling process, we fill the two "depth" buffers B and C (these buffers are not depth stencil buffers!) to maximum distance.

38.4.2 Depth Peeling

Because depth peeling needs two depth buffers, we use two textures as depth buffers. We extract depth layers from farthest to nearest along the global ray direction. Therefore, at first, each visible point samples the farthest intersection point, whereas we need the nearest intersection point. We extract depth layers in turn and sample the depth layer if the sampled point is in front of the visible point along the selected direction. By iterating this process, each visible point finally gets its nearest intersection point, as shown in Figure 38-8.

To extract each depth layer, we render the scene depth value with the reversed depth test (that is, the farthest fragment is rendered) to "depth" buffer B and cull the resulting fragment if its distance is farther than the corresponding value in "depth" buffer C. The data of this fragment is stored into buffer D for sampling of the depth layer. Then buffer B is copied to buffer C for the next iteration. This iteration extracts each depth layer to buffer D.

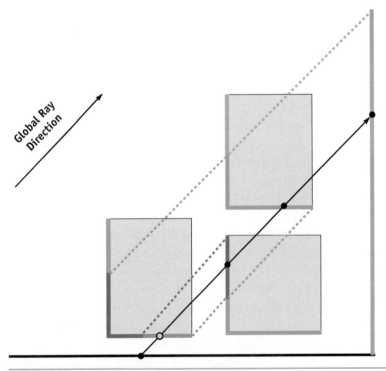

Figure 38-8. Obtaining the Nearest Intersection Point
The nearest intersection point is found by sampling the nearest depth layer.

38.4.3 Sampling

We can sample the nearest intersection points by depth peeling, as just described. For each iteration, we project visible points by parallel projection and read the buffer D if the point is in front of the projected visible point. The resulting sampled point is stored into buffer E. Note that buffer E will be overwritten if the sampled point is nearer than the stored point in buffer E. Finally, buffer E stores the nearest intersection point from the visible point position with the global ray direction.

If we clear buffer D to the corresponding color from the environment map at step 3, we can simultaneously sample direct illumination by image-based lighting. (However, this sampling method is limited to uniform sampling because the distribution of indirect illumination for each point is different. Therefore, we usually use a separate direct illumination step with a more elaborate sampling method, as described later.) Note that the number of fragments does not need to be completely zero at the conditional branch of step 8 of our algorithm. If you are willing to allow some rendering errors, the number of fragments used as the ending condition can be some value (such as 2 percent of the total number of fragments) rather than zero; setting this value larger than zero can reduce the number of iterations and improve performance.

38.4.4 Performance

Because the presented algorithm is completely different from ray-traced final gathering on the CPU, comparing the two is difficult. However, current performance is nearly the same as an interpolation method (such as irradiance gradients) on the CPU. Note that our method does final gathering on *all* pixels. Compared to doing final gathering on all pixels using the CPU, our GPU-rasterization-based method is much faster. Its performance typically approaches several million rays cast per second. That matches or beats the best performance of highly optimized CPU ray tracing (Wald et al. 2003). Note that this high CPU performance depends on all rays being coherent, which is not the case when final gathering is used.

38.5 A Global Illumination Renderer on the GPU

Given the ability to do final gathering quickly with the GPU, we now discuss the practical implementation of a global illumination renderer on the GPU using our technique. The actual implementation of any global illumination renderer is quite complex, so to simplify the explanation here, we limit the discussion to Lambertian materials, and to such renderer features as soft shadows, interreflection, antialiasing, depth-of-field effects, and image-based lighting.

38.5.1 The First Pass

As already explained, a rough global illumination calculation is performed in the first pass. Here we use grid photon mapping on the CPU because this method is somewhat faster than ordinary photon mapping. Grid photon mapping accumulates photons into a grid data structure and uses a constant-time, nearest-neighbor query (that is, a query of the grid) at the cost of precision. After constructing this grid representation of the photon map, we compute the irradiance values as vertex colors in a finely tessellated mesh. Note that you can also use any data structure to store irradiance, such as light maps or volume textures (for example, Greger et al. 1998). We don't explain the implementation details here because you can use any kind of global illumination technique on the CPU or the GPU. The important thing is to generate the irradiance distribution quickly, and the resulting data should be accessed easily and instantly by the GPU's rasterization in the successive GPU final gathering step. Therefore, for example, it may not be efficient to use photon mapping on the GPU (Purcell et al. 2003), because implementations of this approach so far have all estimated the irradiance on the fly. Note that, as mentioned in Section 38.2, we can get a rough global illumination result by rendering this mesh with irradiance data.

38.5.2 Generating Visible Points Data

Before beginning the illumination process, we have to prepare the position, normal vector, and color of visible points. To do so, we simply render the scene from the camera and write out this data to floating-point buffers using a fragment shader. Using multiple render target functionality for this process is useful, if it is available.

These buffers can be used directly during the illumination process, or you can use accumulation buffer techniques to increase the quality of the final image. For example, antialiasing can be performed by jittering the near plane of the view frustum on a sub-pixel basis when generating the visible point set (Haeberli and Akeley 1990). It is better to use quasi-Monte Carlo methods or stratified sampling for jittering. In rasterization rendering, we can use a great number of samples to perform antialiasing, because it is done simply by changing the perspective projection matrix.

Similarly, to achieve depth-of-field effects, the position of the camera can also be jittered. The amount of jittering in this case is varied with the aperture/form of the lens or the position of the focal plane. Because the image resulting from this technique is equivalent to a ray-traced depth-of-field effect, we don't have any of the problems that are associated with image-based depth of field, such as edge bleeding. If you would like to combine this effect with antialiasing, all you have to do is jitter both the camera position and the near plane.

38.5.3 The Second Pass

Because the proposed final gathering computes indirect illumination only, we have to compute direct illumination independently and sum these results later. When computing direct illumination, we use typical real-time shadowing techniques, such as shadow mapping and stencil shadows. In our system, area lights are simulated by using many point light source samples and taking the average of these contributions.

To perform image-based lighting, we consider each environment light as a collection of parallel light sources. Note that uniform sampling is not helpful in almost all image-based lighting, because the use of high dynamic range usually produces very large variation in illumination. Therefore, one should use an importance-based sampling method, such as the one presented in Agarwal et al. 2003.

In both cases, note that the calculation of direct illumination using graphics hardware is very fast compared to CPU-based ray tracing. As a result, we can very quickly obtain an image with a much larger number of samples compared to using ray-traced shadows.

For indirect illumination, we perform the final gathering method on the GPU, as described earlier, by using the result of the first pass as vertex colors. We use the position, normal vector, and color buffers as a visible points set, and we use mesh data with irradiance values at the vertices as a mesh for rendering. To obtain a final image, we add the indirect illumination to the direct illumination.

38.5.4 Additional Solutions

We now discuss some additional implementation problems, along with examples of how they can be solved.

Aliasing

Because the final gathering method is based on rasterization using parallel projection to a limited resolution buffer, there is an aliasing problem similar to that of shadow mapping. This aliasing often results in leaks of indirect illumination. An example of this aliasing is shown in Figure 38-9. This problem is exactly the same as that of shadow

Figure 38-9. Close-up of an Aliasing Artifact
Note that indirect illumination is leaking slightly under the box.

mapping; therefore, as in shadow mapping, we can address aliasing to some degree by using perspective shadow mapping (Stamminger and Dretakkis 2002) or some other elaborate method. We don't go into the implementation details here because they exceed the range of this chapter.

Flickering and Popping

Although using photon mapping for the first pass is an efficient global illumination method, in a scene with a moving object, flickering may occur due to the randomness of photon shooting. To solve this problem, we can also use the final gathering method described in this chapter. Note that the final gathering method generates the radiance distribution reflected N times, given the radiance distribution reflected $N-1$ times. This observation implies that you can solve the global illumination problem itself using the following algorithm, which is illustrated in Figure 38-10.

First, a light source is sampled using a quasi-Monte Carlo sampling, and the resulting illumination data (irradiance distribution reflected zero times), consisting of direct illumination only, is recorded into a buffer of vertex data using the direct illumination technique. Next, we perform final gathering with global ray direction at the triangle vertices

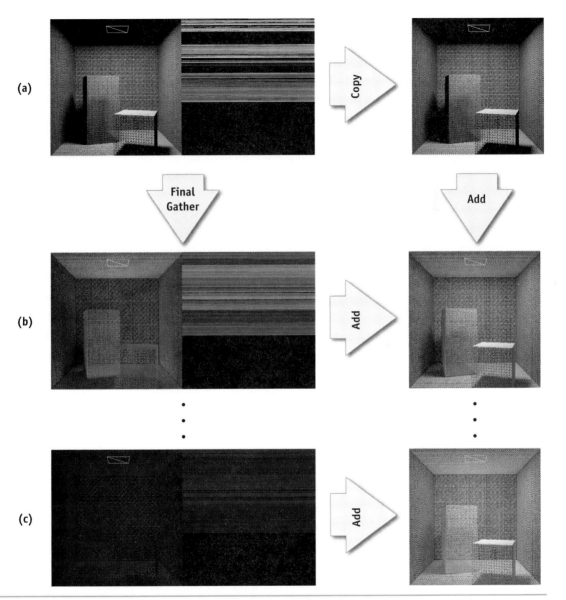

Figure 38-10. Computing Global Illumination Using Final Gathering
(a) Direct illumination is computed at the triangle vertices by quasi-Monte Carlo sampling of lights, and the resulting data is copied to another buffer. (b) One-time reflected illumination is computed at the vertices by final gathering using direct illumination, and the resulting data is accumulated to another buffer. (c) Global illumination is computed by iterating the process.

using the quasi-Monte Carlo method and this illumination data, and we accumulate the results into another buffer of vertex data. As a result, we get reflected "0 + 1" time global illumination data (that is, direct illumination and indirect illumination data after reflecting one time) using the GPU-based final gathering method. To compute all of the indirect illumination, we simply iterate this process, generating illumination data reflected $n + 1$ times, one after another, and then accumulate this data into a buffer. Note that each step doesn't need a large number of samples, as final rendering does. By using this precomputation method, flickering and popping are suppressed, because the sampling direction (that is, the global ray direction) does not change in time when we use a quasi-Monte Carlo method.

38.6 Conclusion

In this chapter we have demonstrated how to perform global illumination rendering using rasterization on the GPU. The resulting algorithm can render high-quality images efficiently. Moreover, because the proposed final gathering method is performed on all points, any set of points (such as texels of light maps or baked colors of vertices) can be easily processed. The final gather step itself is simply a hemispherical integral calculation by ray casting, so you can also use the proposed method to perform any calculation that needs this integral value (such as form factor calculation or precomputation of radiance transfer). Our method does not currently run at interactive rates on modern GPUs, but it greatly accelerates offline rendering compared to a CPU implementation of equivalent algorithms.

38.7 References

Agarwal, S., R. Ramamoorthi, S. Belongie, and H. W. Jensen. 2003. "Structured Importance Sampling of Environment Maps." *ACM Transactions on Graphics* 22(3), pp. 605–612.

Carr, N. A., J. D. Hall, and J. C. Hart. 2002. "The Ray Engine." In *Proceedings of the SIGGRAPH/Eurographics Workshop on Graphics Hardware 2002*, pp. 37–46.

Cohen, M., and J. Wallace. 1993. *Radiosity and Realistic Image Synthesis*. Morgan Kaufmann.

Everitt, C. 2001. "Interactive Order-Independent Transparency." NVIDIA technical report. Available online at **http://developer.nvidia.com/object/Interactive_Order_Transparency.html**

Greger, G., P. Shirley, P. M. Hubbard, and D. P. Greenberg. 1998. "The Irradiance Volume." *IEEE Computer Graphics and Applications* (18)2, pp. 32–43.

Haeberli, P., and K. Akeley. 1990. "The Accumulation Buffer: Hardware Support for High-Quality Rendering." In *Computer Graphics (Proceedings of SIGGRAPH 90)* 24(4), pp. 309–318.

Purcell, T. J., I. Buck, W. R. Mark, and P. Hanrahan. 2002. "Ray Tracing on Programmable Graphics Hardware." *ACM Transactions on Graphics (Proceedings of SIGGRAPH 2002)* 21(3), pp. 703–712.

Purcell, T. J., C. Donner, M. Cammarano, H.-W. Jensen, and P. Hanrahan. 2003. "Photon Mapping on Programmable Graphics Hardware." In *Proceedings of the SIGGRAPH/Eurographics Workshop on Graphics Hardware 2003*, pp. 41–50.

Sloan, P-P., J. Kautz, and J. Snyder. 2002. "Precomputed Radiance Transfer for Real-Time Rendering in Dynamic, Low-Frequency Lighting Environments." *ACM Transactions on Graphics (Proceedings of SIGGRAPH 2002)* 21(3), pp. 527–536.

Stamminger, M., and G. Drettakis. 2002. "Perspective Shadow Maps." *ACM Transactions on Graphics (Proceedings of SIGGRAPH 2002)* 21(3), pp. 557–562.

Szirmay-Kalos, L., and W. Purgathofer. 1998. "Global Ray-Bundle Tracing with Hardware Acceleration." In *Proceedings of the 9th Eurographics Workshop on Rendering*, Vienna.

Wald, I., T. J. Purcell, J. Schmittler, C. Benthin, and P. Slusallek. 2003. "Realtime Ray Tracing and Its Use for Interactive Global Illumination." In *Eurographics State of the Art Reports 2003*.

Ward, G. 1994. "The RADIANCE Lighting Simulation and Rendering System." *Computer Graphics*, pp. 459–472.

Chapter 39

Global Illumination Using Progressive Refinement Radiosity

Greg Coombe
University of North Carolina at Chapel Hill

Mark Harris
NVIDIA Corporation

With the advent of powerful graphics hardware, people have begun to look beyond local illumination models toward more complicated global illumination models, such as those made possible by ray tracing and radiosity. Global illumination, which incorporates interobject effects such as shadows and interreflections, attains a compelling level of visual realism that is difficult to achieve with local illumination models.

In this chapter we describe a method for computing radiosity that performs all of the computation on the GPU. The radiosity energy is stored in texels, and fragment programs are used to compute the form factors and interobject visibility. We avoid the problem of writing to arbitrary locations in memory by casting progressive refinement radiosity as a "gather" operation, which has a regular memory access pattern that is amenable to running on current GPUs.

Figure 39-1 shows an image rendered in our system that demonstrates the compelling effects that can be obtained with global illumination, such as soft shadows and indirect lighting.

Figure 39-1. A Scene with a GPU-Accelerated Radiosity Solution
An image rendered in our system that demonstrates global illumination effects such as soft shadows and indirect lighting.

39.1 Radiosity Foundations

Radiosity is a finite-element approach to the problem of global illumination (Cohen and Wallace 1993). It breaks the scene into many small elements and calculates how much energy is transferred between the elements. The fraction of energy transferred between each pair of elements is described by an equation called the *form factor*. Here is a simple version of a form factor equation (Cohen and Wallace 1993), giving the form factor between two differential areas on surfaces in the scene:

$$F_{i \to j} = \frac{\cos \theta_i \cos \theta_j}{\pi r^2} V(i, j).$$

The equation is composed of two parts: a visibility term and a geometric term. The geometric term states that the fraction of energy transferred between the elements i and j is a function of the distance and relative orientation of the elements. The visibility term $V(i, j)$ is 0 for elements that are occluded and 1 for elements that are fully visible from each other.

This formula is accurate only if i and j are infinitesimal areas (or are far enough apart to be treated as such). However, to increase the speed of the computation, we would like to use large-area elements, which break this assumption. One way to deal with large-area elements is to explicitly integrate over the area of the element. Because this is computationally expensive, we can approximate these large elements with oriented discs (Wallace et al. 1989). This approach is shown in Figure 39-2, and the form factor for this situation is:

$$F_{i \to \Delta j} = \Delta j \frac{\cos \theta_i \cos \theta_j}{\pi r^2 + \Delta j} V(i, \Delta j).$$

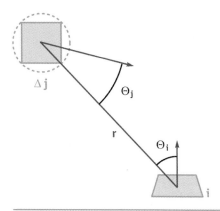

Figure 39-2. The Oriented-Disc Form Factor
The form factor from elements i to j is a function of θ_i and θ_j, the orientation angles; r, the distance between the elements; and Δj, the area of element j.

39.1.1 Progressive Refinement

The classical radiosity algorithm (Goral et al. 1984) constructs and solves a large system of linear equations composed of the pairwise form factors. These equations describe the radiosity of an element as a function of the energy from every other element, weighted by their form factors and the element's reflectance, ρ. Thus the classical linear system requires $O(N^2)$ storage, which is prohibitive for large scenes. The progressive refinement algorithm (Cohen et al. 1988) calculates these form factors on the fly, avoiding these storage requirements. It does this by repeatedly "shooting" out the energy from one element to all other elements in the scene.

Here's how progressive refinement works (Figure 39-3 illustrates two iterations of the algorithm). Each element in the scene maintains two energy values: an *accumulated* energy value and *residual* (or "unshot") energy. We choose one of the elements in the

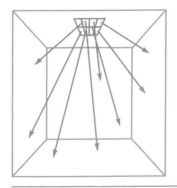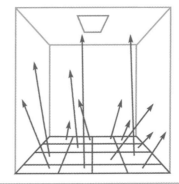

Figure 39-3. Two Iterations of the Progressive Refinement Solution

scene as the "shooter" and test the visibility of every other element from this shooter. If a receiving element is visible, then we calculate the amount of energy transferred from the shooter to the receiving element, as described by the corresponding form factor and the shooter's residual energy. This energy is multiplied by the receiver's reflectance, which is the fraction of incoming energy that is reflected back out again, and is usually represented by an RGB color. The resulting value is added to both the accumulated and the residual values of the receiving elements. Now that the shooter has cast out all of its energy, its residual energy is set to zero and the next shooter is selected. This process repeats until the residual energy of all of the elements has dropped below a threshold.

Initially, the residual energy of each light source element is set to a specified value and all other energy values are set to zero. After the first iteration, the scene polygon that has received the largest residual power ($power = energy \times area$) is the next shooter. Selecting the largest residual power guarantees that the solution will converge rapidly (Cohen et al. 1988).

39.2 GPU Implementation

To implement this algorithm on the GPU, we use texels as radiosity elements (Heckbert 1990). There are two textures per scene polygon: a radiosity texture and a residual texture. Using textures as radiosity elements is similar to uniformly subdividing the scene, where the texture resolution determines the granularity of the radiosity solution.

If you sat down to implement progressive refinement radiosity, you might first try rendering the scene from the point of view of the shooter, and then "splatting" the energy into the textures of all of the visible polygons. This was our initial approach, and it had poor performance. The problem with this approach is that it requires the GPU to write to arbitrary locations in multiple textures. This type of "scatter" operation is difficult to implement on current graphics hardware.

Instead, we invert the computation by iterating over the receiving polygons and testing each element for visibility. This exploits the data-parallel nature of GPUs by executing the same small kernel program over many texels. This approach combines the high-quality reconstruction of gathering radiosity with the fast convergence and low storage requirements of shooting radiosity.

Each "shot" of the radiosity solution involves two passes: a visibility pass and a reconstruction pass. The visibility pass renders the scene from the point of view of the shooter and stores the scene in an item buffer. The reconstruction pass draws every potential receiving polygon orthographically into a frame buffer at the same resolution as the texture. This establishes a one-to-one correspondence between texels of the radiosity texture and fragments in the frame buffer. A fragment program tests the visibility and computes the analytic form factor. Pseudocode for our algorithm is shown in Listing 39-1. The next two sections describe the visibility and form factor computation in more detail.

Listing 39-1. Pseudocode for Our Algorithm

```
initialize shooter residual E
while not converged {
  render scene from POV of shooter
  for each receiving element {
    if element is visible {
      compute form factor FF
      ΔE = ρ * FF * E
      add ΔE to residual texture
      add ΔE to radiosity texture
    }
  }
  shooter's residual E = 0
  compute next shooter
}
```

39.2.1 Visibility Using Hemispherical Projection

The visibility term of the form factor equation is usually computed using a hemicube (Cohen and Greenberg 1985), as shown in Figure 39-4. The scene is rendered onto the five faces of a cube map, which is then used to test visibility. Instead, we can avoid

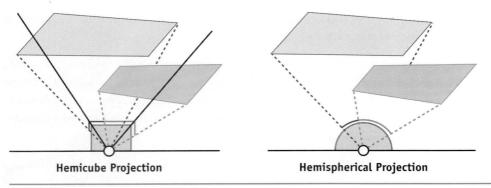

Hemicube Projection **Hemispherical Projection**

Figure 39-4. Hemicube and Hemispherical Projection

rendering the scene five times by using a vertex program to project the vertices onto a hemisphere. The *hemispherical projection*, also known as a *stereographic projection*, allows us to compute the visibility in only one rendering pass. The Cg code for this technique, which is similar to parabolic projection (Heidrich and Seidel 1998), is shown in Listing 39-2. Note that the z value is projected separately from the (x, y) position, which maintains the correct depth ordering and avoids precision issues.

Listing 39-2. Cg Code for Hemispherical Projection

```
void hemiwarp(float4 Position: POSITION,    // pos in world space
  uniform half4x4 ModelView,                // modelview matrix
  uniform half2 NearFar,                    // near and far planes
  out float4 ProjPos: POSITION)             // projected position
{
  // transform the geometry to camera space
  half4 mpos = mul(ModelView, Position);

  // project to a point on a unit hemisphere
  half3 hemi_pt = normalize( mpos.xyz );

  // Compute (f-n), but let the hardware divide z by this
  // in the w component (so premultiply x and y)
  half f_minus_n = NearFar.y - NearFar.x;
  ProjPos.xy = hemi_pt.xy * f_minus_n;

  // compute depth proj. independently, using OpenGL orthographic
  ProjPos.z  = (-2.0 * mpos.z - NearFar.y - NearFar.x);
  ProjPos.w  = f_minus_n;
}
```

The hemispherical projection vertex program calculates the positions of the projected elements, and the fragment program renders the unique ID of each element as color. Later, when we need to determine visibility, we use a fragment program to compare the ID of the receiver with the ID at the projected location in the item buffer. The Cg code for this lookup is shown in Listing 39-3.

Listing 39-3. Cg Code for the Visibility Test

```
bool Visible(half3 ProjPos,   // camera-space pos of element
  uniform fixed3 RecvID,       // ID of receiver, for item buffer
  sampler2D HemiItemBuffer )
{
  // Project the texel element onto the hemisphere
  half3 proj = normalize(ProjPos);

  // Vector is in [-1,1], scale to [0..1] for texture lookup
  proj.xy = proj.xy * 0.5 + 0.5;

  // Look up projected point in hemisphere item buffer
  fixed3 xtex = tex2D(HemiItemBuffer, proj.xy);

  // Compare the value in item buffer to the ID of the fragment
  return all(xtex == RecvID);
}
```

This process is a lot like shadow mapping, except using polygon IDs rather than depth. Using the IDs avoids problems with depth precision, but it loses the advantages of the built-in shadow mapping hardware (such as percentage-closer filtering).

One drawback of hemispherical projection is that although polygon edges project to curves on a hemisphere, rasterization produces only straight edges. This is shown in Figure 39-5. To deal with this limitation, the scene polygons must be tessellated at a higher level of subdivision so that they can more closely approximate a curved edge.

39.2.2 Form Factor Computation

Once the visibility has been determined, we compute the energy transferred from the shooter to the receiver using the shooter-receiver form factor. This form factor computation is typically the most time-consuming part of the radiosity computation. We've implemented this in a fragment program in order to exploit the computational power of the fragment processor.

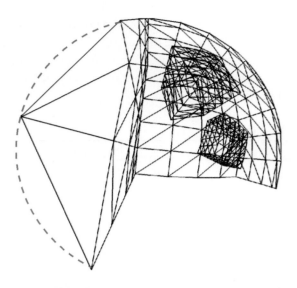

Figure 39-5. Rasterization Artifacts Caused by Insufficient Tessellation During Hemispherical Projection

Listing 39-4 shows the code for the form factor computation, implemented in Cg.

Listing 39-4. Cg Code for Form Factor Computation

```
half3 FormFactorEnergy(
  half3 RecvPos,              // world-space position of this element
  uniform half3 ShootPos,     // world-space position of shooter
  half3 RecvNormal,           // world-space normal of this element
  uniform half3 ShootNormal,  // world-space normal of shooter
  uniform half3 ShootEnergy,  // energy from shooter residual texture
  uniform half ShootDArea,    // the delta area of the shooter
  uniform fixed3 RecvColor )  // the reflectivity of this element
{
  // a normalized vector from shooter to receiver
  half3 r = ShootPos - RecvPos;
  half distance2 = dot(r, r);
  r = normalize(r);

  // the angles of the receiver and the shooter from r
  half cosi = dot(RecvNormal, r);
  half cosj = -dot(ShootNormal, r);
```

Listing 39-4 (continued). Cg Code for Form Factor Computation

```
    // compute the disc approximation form factor
    const half pi = 3.1415926535;
    half Fij = max(cosi * cosj, 0) / (pi * distance2 + ShootDArea);
    Fij *= Visible();    // returns visibility as 0 or 1

    // Modulate shooter's energy by the receiver's reflectivity
    // and the area of the shooter.
    half3 delta = ShooterEnergy * RecvColor * ShootDArea * Fij;
    return delta;
}
```

39.2.3 Choosing the Next Shooter

Progressive refinement techniques achieve fast convergence by shooting from the scene element with the highest residual power. To find the next shooter, we use a simple z-buffer sort. A mipmap pyramid is created from the residual texture of each element. The top level of this mipmap pyramid, which represents the average energy of the entire texture, is multiplied by the texture resolution to get the sum of the energy in the texture. Reductions of this sort are described in more detail in Buck and Purcell 2004 and Chapter 31 of this book, "Mapping Computational Concepts to GPUs."

This scalar value is multiplied by the area of the polygon, which gives us the total power of the polygon. We then draw a screen-aligned quadrilateral into a 1×1 frame buffer with the reciprocal of power as the depth and the unique polygon ID as the color. Each residual texture is rendered in this way, and z-buffering automatically selects the polygon with the highest power. We read back the 1-pixel frame buffer to get the ID of the next shooter. This technique also allows us to test convergence by setting the far clipping plane to the reciprocal of the convergence threshold. If no fragments are written, then the solution has converged.

39.3 Adaptive Subdivision

Until this point, we have been assuming that the radiosity textures are mapped one-to-one onto the scene geometry. This means that the scene is uniformly and statically tessellated (based on the texture resolution). However, uniform tessellation cannot adapt to the variable spatial frequency of the lighting. We would like to have more elements in areas of high-frequency lighting, such as shadow boundaries, and fewer elements in areas of low frequency, such as flat walls.

39.3.1 Texture Quadtree

A common technique for addressing these problems is to use an adaptive meshing solution (Heckbert 1990). Using this technique, we see that scene geometry is adaptively subdivided, with areas of higher lighting variation receiving a larger number of elements. In our system, each scene polygon acts as the root of a quadtree, and the radiosity data is stored in small (16×16) textures at the leaf nodes of the tree. This hierarchy can be thought of as a coarse adaptive geometric subdivision followed by a fine uniform texture subdivision. Figure 39-6 illustrates how a scene polygon can be subdivided into smaller quads based on the light variation.

Using this approach, we can reuse much of the code that we developed for the uniform case. The visibility and shooting are computed at each leaf node (instead of at each scene polygon), and the radiosity is reconstructed in a similar manner. The only difference is that as we compute the radiosity, we also must determine when to subdivide the quadtree.

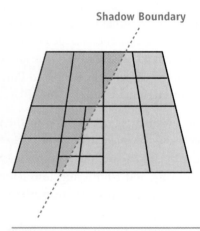

Figure 39-6. Quadtree Subdivision Adapts to the Frequency of the Lighting

39.3.2 Quadtree Subdivision

After every reconstruction pass, the leaf textures are evaluated for subdivision using a fragment program. There are several different techniques for determining when a quadtree node should be split. We use a technique that splits a node when the gradient of the radiosity exceeds a certain threshold (Vedel and Puech 1991). Using the gradient instead of the value avoids oversubdividing in areas where linear interpolation will adequately represent the function.

The gradient of the radiosity is evaluated in a fragment program, and fragments with gradient discontinuities are discarded. A hardware occlusion query is used to count these discarded fragments. If the number of discarded fragments exceeds our threshold, the current node is subdivided, and the process is repeated recursively. The recursion terminates when the radiosity is found to be smooth, or when a maximum depth is reached.

39.4 Performance

There are several optimization techniques for achieving interactive rates on small models. We use occlusion queries in the visibility pass to avoid reconstructing radiosity on surfaces that are not visible. We also shoot at a lower resolution than the texture resolution, which is called *substructuring* (Cohen et al. 1986). This can be done using the mipmaps that were created for the next-shooter selection.

If a polygon is selected as the next shooter, then all of the polygon's elements shoot their radiosity in turn. This amortizes the cost of mipmapping and sorting over multiple shots. We also batch together multiple shooters to reduce context switching.

Using these techniques, we've been able to compute a radiosity solution of a 10,000-element version of the Cornell Box scene to 90 percent convergence at about 2 frames per second.

For real-time applications, this technique can be combined with standard rendering techniques for higher performance. We can split the lighting into indirect and direct illumination by assuming that the indirect lighting is low frequency. This allows us to drastically reduce the texture resolution, which speeds up the calculation. The radiosity is calculated using the low-resolution textures, and the direct illumination is removed by setting the accumulated radiosity to zero after first iteration. The direct illumination is computed separately using lighting techniques such as per-pixel lighting and shadow volumes. The indirect illumination is added to this direct illumination to get the final image.

39.5 Conclusion

We've presented a method for implementing global illumination on graphics hardware by using progressive refinement radiosity. By exploiting the computational power of the fragment processor and rasterization hardware to compute the form factors, we can achieve interactive rates for scenes with a small number of elements (approximately

10,000). A scene with a large number of elements, such as that shown in Figure 39-7, can currently be rendered at noninteractive rates. As graphics hardware continues to increase in computational speed, we envision that global illumination will become a common part of lighting calculations.

We use several GPU tricks to accelerate this algorithm, including the hemispherical projection and the z-buffer sort. These may have interesting applications beyond our implementation, such as environment mapping or penetration-depth estimation.

One of the limitations of radiosity is that it represents only diffuse surfaces. It would be interesting to try to extend this approach to nondiffuse surfaces. One approach could be to convolve the incoming lighting with an arbitrary BRDF and approximate the result with a low-coefficient polynomial or spherical harmonics (Sillion et al. 1991).

Figure 39-7. A Scene with One Million Elements Rendered with Our System

39.6 References

Buck, I., and T. Purcell. 2004. "A Toolkit for Computation on GPUs." In *GPU Gems*, edited by Randima Fernando, pp. 621–636. Addison-Wesley.

Cohen, M., S. E. Chen, J. R. Wallace, and D. P. Greenberg. 1988. "A Progressive Refinement Approach to Fast Radiosity Image Generation." In *Computer Graphics (Proceedings of SIGGRAPH 88)* 22(4), pp. 75–84.

Cohen, M., and D. P. Greenberg. 1985. "The Hemi-Cube: A Radiosity Solution for Complex Environments." In *Computer Graphics (Proceedings of SIGGRAPH 85)* 19(3), pp. 31–40.

Cohen, M., D. P. Greenberg, D. S. Immel, and P. J. Brock. 1986. "An Efficient Radiosity Approach for Realistic Image Synthesis." *IEEE Computer Graphics and Applications* 6(3), pp. 26–35.

Cohen, M., and J. Wallace. 1993. *Radiosity and Realistic Image Synthesis*. Morgan Kaufmann.

Goral, C. M., K. E. Torrance, D. P. Greenberg, and B. Battaile. 1984. "Modelling the Interaction of Light Between Diffuse Surfaces." In *Computer Graphics (Proceedings of SIGGRAPH 84)* 18(3), pp. 213–222.

Heckbert, P. 1990. "Adaptive Radiosity Textures for Bidirectional Ray Tracing." In *Computer Graphics (Proceedings of SIGGRAPH 90)* 24(4), pp. 145–154.

Heidrich, W., and H.-P. Seidel. 1998. "View-Independent Environment Maps." In *Eurographics Workshop on Graphics Hardware 1998*, pp. 39–45.

Sillion, F. X., J. R. Arvo, S. H. Westin, and D. P. Greenberg. 1991. "A Global Illumination Solution for General Reflectance Distributions." In *Computer Graphics (Proceedings of SIGGRAPH 91)* 25(4), pp. 187–196.

Vedel, C., and C. Puech. 1991. "A Testbed for Adaptive Subdivision in Progressive Radiosity." In *Second Eurographics Workshop on Rendering*.

Wallace, J. R., K. A. Elmquist, and E. A. Haines. 1989. "A Ray Tracing Algorithm for Progressive Radiosity." In *Computer Graphics (Proceedings of SIGGRAPH 89)* 23(4), pp. 315–324.

Chapter 40

Computer Vision on the GPU

James Fung
University of Toronto

Computer vision tasks are computationally intensive and repetitive, and they often exceed the real-time capabilities of the CPU, leaving little time for higher-level tasks. However, many computer vision operations map efficiently onto the modern GPU, whose programmability allows a wide variety of computer vision algorithms to be implemented. This chapter presents methods of efficiently mapping common mathematical operations of computer vision onto modern computer graphics architecture.

40.1 Introduction

In some sense, computer graphics and computer vision are the opposites of one another. Computer graphics takes a numerical description of a scene and renders an image, whereas computer vision analyzes images to create numerical representations of the scene. Thus, carrying out computer vision tasks in graphics hardware uses the graphics hardware in an "inverse" fashion.

The GPU provides a streaming, data-parallel arithmetic architecture. This type of architecture carries out a similar set of calculations on an array of image data. The single-instruction, multiple-data (SIMD) capability of the GPU makes it suitable for running computer vision tasks, which often involve similar calculations operating on an entire image.

Special-purpose computer vision hardware is rarely found in typical mass-produced personal computers. Instead, the CPU is usually used for computer vision tasks. Optimized computer vision libraries for the CPU often consume many of the CPU cycles to achieve real-time performance, leaving little time for other, nonvision tasks.

GPUs, on the other hand, are found on most personal computers and often exceed the capabilities of the CPU. Thus, we can use the GPU to accelerate computer vision computation and free up the CPU for other tasks. Furthermore, multiple GPUs can be used on the same machine, creating an architecture capable of running multiple computer vision algorithms in parallel.

40.2 Implementation Framework

Many computer vision operations can be considered sequences of filtering operations, with each sequential filtering stage acting upon the output of the previous filtering stage. On the GPU, these filtering operations are carried out by fragment programs. To apply these fragment programs to input images, the input images are initialized as textures and then mapped onto quadrilaterals. By displaying these quadrilaterals in appropriately sized windows, we can ensure that there is a one-to-one correspondence of image pixels to output fragments.

When the textured quadrilateral is displayed, the fragment program then runs, operating identically on each pixel of the image. The fragment program is analogous to the body of a common for-loop program statement, but each iteration of the body can be thought of as executing in parallel. The resulting output is not the original image, but rather the filtered image. Modern GPUs allow input and results in full 32-bit IEEE floating-point precision, providing sufficient accuracy for many algorithms.

A complete computer vision algorithm can be created by implementing sequences of these filtering operations. After the texture has been filtered by the fragment program, the resulting image is placed into texture memory, either by using render-to-texture extensions or by copying the frame buffer into texture memory. In this way, the output image becomes the input texture to the next fragment program. This creates a pipeline that runs the entire computer vision algorithm.

However, often a complete vision algorithm will require operations beyond filtering. For example, summations are common operations; we present examples of how they can be implemented and used. Furthermore, more-generalized calculations, such as feature tracking, can also be mapped effectively onto graphics hardware.

These methods are implemented in the OpenVIDIA GPU computer vision library, which can be used to create real-time computer vision programs (http://openvidia.sourceforge.net).

40.3 Application Examples

This chapter presents examples that implement common computer vision techniques on the GPU. The common thread between each of these algorithms is that they are all used in our system to create a fully interactive, real-time *computer-mediated reality*, in which the environment of a user appears to be augmented, diminished, or otherwise altered. Some examples are shown in Figure 40-1.

Figure 40-1. Using Computer Vision to Mediate Reality
Computer vision techniques can analyze video to augment, diminish, or otherwise alter a user's perception of the environment. On the left, detected ceiling planes become terminal windows. On the right, a terminal window is mapped to the plane of the floppy disk.

40.3.1 Using Sequences of Fragment Programs for Computer Vision

In this section, we demonstrate how a sequence of fragment programs can work together to perform more-complex computer vision operations.

Correcting Radial Distortion
Many camera lenses cause some sort of radial distortion (also known as *barrel distortion*) of the image, most commonly in wide-field-of-view or low-cost lenses. There are several ways of correcting for radial distortion on the graphics hardware; we present an example of how a fragment program can be used to do so.

We begin by assuming that the displacement of a pixel due to radial distortion is Δx, Δy and is commonly modeled by:

$$\Delta x = x\left(\kappa_1 r^2 + \kappa_2 r^4 + \ldots\right),$$

$$\Delta y = y\left(\kappa_1 r^2 + \kappa_2 r^4 + \ldots\right),$$

where x, y are the image coordinates, r is the distance of the pixel from the principal point of the camera, and the coefficients $\kappa_{1,2,3\ldots}$ are camera parameters determined by some known calibration method. Given a particular camera, the required calibration parameters can be found using the tools provided at Bouguet 2004.

The fragment program shown in Listing 40-1 applies this correction by using the current texture coordinates to calculate an offset. The program then adds this offset to the current pixel's coordinates and uses the result to look up the texture value at the corrected coordinate. This texture value is then output, and the image's radial distortion is thereby corrected.

Listing 40-1. Radial Undistortion

```
float4 CorrectBarrelDistortion(
  float2 fptexCoord : TEXCOORD0,
  float4 wpos : WPOS,
  uniform samplerRECT FPE1 ) : COLOR
{
  // known constants for the particular lens and sensor
  float f = 368.28488;  // focal length
  float ox = 147.54834; // principal point, x axis
  float oy = 126.01673; // principal point, y axis
  float k1 = 0.4142;    // constant for radial distortion correction
  float k2 = 0.40348;

  float2 xy = (fptexCoord - float2(ox, oy))/float2(f,f);

  r = sqrt( dot(xy, xy) );
  float r2 = r * r;
  float r4 = r2 * r2;
  float coeff = (k1 * r2 + k2 * r4);
```

Listing 40-1 (continued). Radial Undistortion

```
    // add the calculated offsets to the current texture coordinates
    xy = ((xy + xy * coeff.xx) * f.xx) + float2(ox, oy);
    // look up the texture at the corrected coordinates
    // and output the color
    return texRECT(FPE1, xy);
}
```

A Canny Edge Detector

Edge detection is a key algorithm used in many vision applications. Here we present an implementation of the commonly used "Canny" edge-detection algorithm that runs entirely on the GPU. See Figure 40-2 for an example. We implement the Canny edge detector as a series of fragment programs, each performing a step of the algorithm:

- **Step 1.** Filter the image using a separable Gaussian edge filter (Jargstorff 2004). The filter footprint is typically around 15×15 elements wide, and separable. A separable filter is one whose 2D mask can be calculated by applying two 1D filters in the x and y directions. The separability saves us a large number of texture lookups, at the cost of an additional pass.

- **Step 2.** Determine the magnitude, l, of the derivatives at each pixel computed in step 1, and quantize the direction d. The values of d and l are given by:

$$d = \arctan 2\left(d_y, d_x\right),$$

$$l = \sqrt{d_x^2 + d_y^2},$$

where d is the direction of the gradient vector, quantized to one of the eight possible directions one may traverse a 3×3 region of pixels. The length l is the magnitude of the vector.

- **Step 3.** Perform a nonmaximal suppression, as shown in Listing 40-2. The nonmaximal suppression uses the direction of the local gradient to determine which pixels are in the forward and backward direction of the gradient. This direction is used to calculate the x and y offset of the texture coordinates to look up the forward and backward neighbors. An edge is considered found only if the gradient is at a maximum as compared to its neighbors, ensuring a thin line along the detected edge.

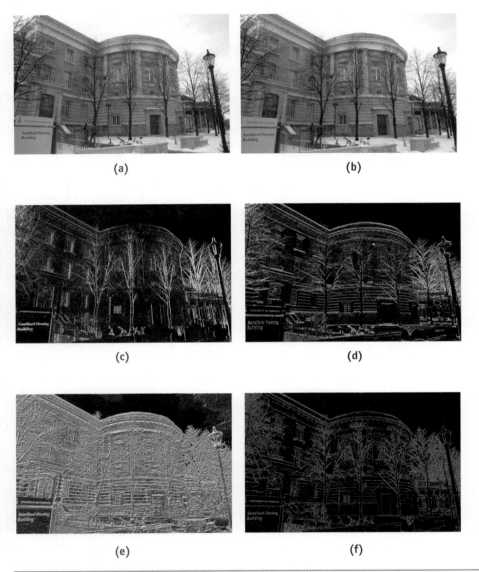

Figure 40-2. Canny Edge Detection

Each image shows the result of a fragment program operating on the previous image.
(a) Original input. (b) Radial undistorted image. (c) Horizontal derivative. (d) Vertical derivative.
(e) Gradient quantization. (f) Canny edges.

Listing 40-2. A Canny Edge Detector Using Nonmaximal Suppression

This program looks up the direction of the gradient at the current pixel and then retrieves the pixels in the forward and backward directions along the gradient. The program returns 1 if the current pixel value is greater than the two values along the gradient; otherwise, it suppresses (or zeroes) the output. A thresholding value allows the sensitivity of the edge detector to be varied in real time to suit the vision apparatus and environment.

```
float4 CannySearch(
  uniform float4 thresh,
  float2 fptexCoord : TEXCOORD0,
  uniform samplerRECT FPE1 ) : COLOR
{
  // magdir holds { dx, dy, mag, direct }
  float4 magdir = texRECT(FPE1, fptexCoord);
  float alpha = 0.5/sin(3.14159/8); // eight directions on grid

  float2 offset = round( alpha.xx * magdir.xy/magdir.zz );

  float4 fwdneighbour, backneighbour;
  fwdneighbour = texRECT(FPE1, fptexCoord + offset );
  backneighbour = texRECT(FPE1, fptexCoord + offset );

  float4 colorO;
  if ( fwdneighbour.z > magdir.z || backneighbour.z > magdir.z )
    colorO = float4(0.0, 0.0, 0.0, 0.0); // not an edgel
  else
    colorO = float4(1.0, 1.0, 1.0, 1.0); // is an edgel
  if ( magdir.z < thresh.x )
    colorO = float4(0.0, 0.0, 0.0, 0.0); // thresholding

  return colorO;
}
```

40.3.2 Summation Operations

Many common vision operations involve the summation of an image buffer. Some methods that require the summation are moment calculations and the solutions to linear systems of equations.

Buck and Purcell (2004) discuss a general method of efficiently summing buffers by using local neighborhoods. On systems that do not support render-to-texture, however, the number of passes required by this technique can be limiting, due to the number of graphics context switches involved. We have found performing the computation in two passes to be more efficient on such systems. In our approach, we create a fragment program that sums each row of pixels, resulting in a single column holding the sums of each row. Then, in a second pass, we draw a single pixel and execute a program that sums down the column. The result is a single pixel that has as its "color" the sum of the entire buffer. The Cg code for computing the sum in this way is given in this chapter's appendix on the book's CD.

We use the summation operation within the context of two different, but commonly used, algorithms that require summation over a buffer: a hand-tracking algorithm and an algorithm for creating panoramas from images by determining how to stitch them together.

Tracking Hands

Tracking a user's hands or face is a useful vision tool for creating interactive systems, and it can be achieved on the GPU by using a combination of image filtering and moment calculations. A common way to track a user's hand is to use color segmentation to find areas that are skin-colored, and then continually track the location of those areas through the image. Additionally, it is useful to track the average color of the skin tone, because it changes from frame to frame, typically due to changes in lighting.

It is common to carry out the segmentation in an HSV color space, because skin tone of all hues tends to cluster in HSV color space. The HSV color space describes colors in terms of their *hue* (the type of color, such as red, green, or blue); *saturation* (the vibrancy of that color); and *value* (the brightness of the color). Cameras typically produce an RGB image, so a fragment program can be used to perform a fast color space conversion as a filtering operation.

Assuming that we have some sort of initial guess for the HSV color of the skin, we can also use a fragment program to threshold pixels. Given a particular pixel's HSV value, we can determine its difference from the mean HSV skin color and either output to 0 if the difference is too great or output the HSV value otherwise. For instance, the comparison might be easily done as:

```
if ( distance( hsv, meanhsv ) < thresh ) {
  colorO = hsv;
}
else
  colorO = float4(0.0, 0.0, 0.0, 0.0);
```

Finally, we determine the centroid of the skin-colored region and update the mean skin value based on what is currently being seen. For both of these steps, we need to calculate sums over the image.

To compute centroids, we can first compute the first three moments of the image:

$$M_{00} = \sum_{x=0}^{x=W} \sum_{y=0}^{y=H} E(x, y),$$

$$M_{10} = \sum_{x=0}^{x=W} \sum_{y=0}^{y=H} xE(x, y),$$

$$M_{01} = \sum_{x=0}^{x=W} \sum_{y=0}^{y=H} yE(x, y),$$

where W and H are the sizes of the image in each axis, and $E(x, y)$ is the pixel value at location (x, y). The x coordinate of the centroid is then computed as M_{10}/M_{00}, and M_{01}/M_{00} is the centroid's y coordinate.

These summations can be done by first running a fragment program that fills a buffer with:

$$E(x, y), \quad xE(x, y), \quad yE(x, y)$$

and then using a GPU summation method to sum the entire buffer. The result will be a single pixel whose value can then be read back to the CPU to update the location of the centroid.

In our case—tracking the centroid of a thresholded skin-tone blob—we might simply let the fragment program output 1.0 in skin-colored areas and 0 elsewhere. Listing 40-3 shows a Cg program that produces four output components that, after summation, will provide the sums needed to calculate the zeroth and first-order moments. Figure 40-3 depicts this process.

Should we require more statistics like the preceding, we could either reduce the precision and output eight 16-bit floating-point results to a 128-bit floating-point texture or use the multiple render targets (MRTs) OpenGL extension.

Listing 40-3. Creating Output Statistics for Moment Calculations

```
float4 ComputeMoments(
  float2 texCoord : TEXCOORD0,
  uniform samplerRECT FPE1: TEXUNIT0 ) : COLOR
{
  float4 samp = texRECT(FPE1, fptexCoord);
  float4 color0 = float4(0, 0, 0, 0);
  if ( samp.x != 0.0 )
    color0 = float4( 1.0, fptexCoord.x, fptexCoord.y, samp.y);
}
```

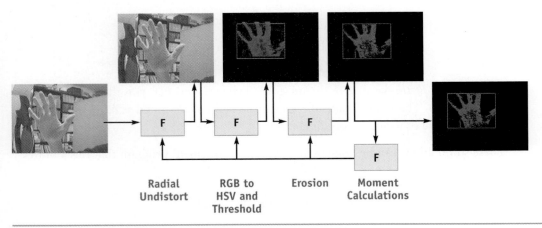

Radial   RGB to   Erosion   Moment
Undistort   HSV and   Calculations
             Threshold

Figure 40-3. Tracking a User's Hand

40.3.3 Systems of Equations for Creating Image Panoramas

We also encounter this compute-and-sum type of calculation when we form systems of equations of the familiar form $\mathbf{Ax} = \mathbf{b}$.

VideoOrbits

VideoOrbits is an image-registration algorithm that calculates a coordinate transformation between pairs of images taken with a camera that is free to pan, tilt, rotate about its optical axis, and zoom. The technique solves the problem for two cases: (1) images taken from the same location of an arbitrary 3D scene or (2) images taken from arbitrary locations of a flat scene. Figure 40-4 shows an image panorama composed from several frames of video. Equivalently, Mann and Fung (2002) show how the same algorithm can be used to replace planes in the scene with computer-generated content, such as in Figure 40-1.

Figure 40-4. A VideoOrbits Panorama
This panorama shows how the images have been projected to fit together properly.

VideoOrbits solves for a projection of an image in order to register it with another image. Consider a pair of images of the same scene, with the camera having moved between images. A given point in the scene appearing at coordinates $[x, y]$ in the first image now appears at coordinates $[x', y']$ in the second image. Under the constraints mentioned earlier, all the points in the image can be considered to move according to eight parameters, given by the following equation:

$$\begin{bmatrix} x' \\ y' \end{bmatrix} = \frac{\begin{bmatrix} a_{11} & a_{12} \\ a_{21} & a_{22} \end{bmatrix}\begin{bmatrix} x \\ y \end{bmatrix} + \begin{bmatrix} b_1 \\ b_2 \end{bmatrix}}{\begin{bmatrix} c_1 c_2 \end{bmatrix}\begin{bmatrix} x \\ y \end{bmatrix} + 1}. \tag{1}$$

The eight scalar parameters describing the projection are denoted by:

$$\mathbf{p} = \begin{bmatrix} a_{11}, a_{12}, b_1, a_{21}, a_{22}, b_2, c_1, c_2 \end{bmatrix}$$

and are calculated by VideoOrbits. Once the parameters $\mathbf{p}$ have been determined for each image, the images can then be transformed into the same coordinate system to create the image panoramas of Figure 40-4. (For a more in-depth treatment of projective flow and the VideoOrbits algorithm, see Mann 1998.)

VideoOrbits calculates the parameters **p** by solving a linear system of equations. The bulk of the computation is in the initialization of this system of equations, which is of the form $\mathbf{Ax} = \mathbf{b}$. Here, **A** is an 8×8 matrix whose values we must initialize, **x** is an 8×1 column vector that corresponds to **p**, and **b** is an 8×1 column vector we must also initialize.

Solving this system is computationally expensive because each element of **A** and **b** is actually a summation of a series of multiplications and additions at each point in the image. Initializing each of the 64 entries of the matrix **A** involves many multiplications and additions over all the pixels. **A** is of the form:

$$
\mathbf{A} = \begin{bmatrix}
\sum a_{11} & \sum a_{12} & \sum a_{13} & \cdots & & \sum a_{18} \\
\sum a_{21} & \sum a_{22} & \sum a_{23} & \cdots & & \sum a_{28} \\
\vdots & & & & & \vdots \\
\sum a_{81} & \sum a_{82} & \sum a_{83} & \cdots & & \sum a_{88}
\end{bmatrix}_{8 \times 8} ,
\tag{2}
$$

where each of the elements is a summation. (Note that the elements a_{11}, a_{12}, a_{21}, a_{22} are not those of Equation 1.) The arguments of these summations involve many arithmetic operations. For instance, element a_{21} is:

$$
a_{21} = \left(x^2 \mathbf{E}_x + xy \mathbf{E}_y \right) \left(xy \mathbf{E}_x + y^2 \mathbf{E}_y \right).
\tag{3}
$$

This operation must be carried out at every pixel and then summed to obtain each entry in matrix **A**.

This compute-and-sum operation is similar to moment calculations discussed previously. Not surprisingly, we can calculate this on the GPU in a similar fashion, filling a buffer with the argument of the summation and then summing the buffer. Typically, to calculate all the matrix entries, multiple passes will be required.

As each summation is completed, the results are copied to a texture that stores the results. After all the entries for the matrix **A** and vector **b** are computed, the values are read back to the CPU. This keeps the operations on the GPU, deferring the readback until all matrix entries have been calculated. This allows the GPU to operate with greater independence from the CPU. The system can then be solved on the CPU, with the majority of the per-pixel calculations already solved by the GPU.

40.3.4 Feature Vector Computations

Calculating *feature vectors* at detected feature points is a common operation in computer vision. A *feature* in an image is a local area around a point with some higher-than-average amount of "uniqueness." This makes the point easier to recognize in subsequent frames of video. The uniqueness of the point is characterized by computing a feature vector for each feature point. Feature vectors can be used to recognize the same point in different images and can be extended to more generalized object recognition techniques. Figure 40-5 shows the motion of the features between frames as the camera moves.

Figure 40-5. Detecting Distinctive Points as the Camera Pans
The GPU is used to detect and track distinctive points (features) in real time as the camera pans. The green lines connect the same point in the previous image to its new location in the current image.

Computing feature vectors on the GPU requires handling the image data in a different manner than the operations we have thus far presented. Because only a few points in the image are feature points, this calculation does not need to be done at every point in the image. Additionally, for a single feature point, a large feature vector (100 elements or more) is typically calculated. Thus, each single point produces a larger number of results, rather than the one-to-one or many-to-one mappings we have discussed so far.

These types of computations can still be carried out on the GPU. We take as an example a feature vector that is composed of the filtered gradient magnitudes in a local region around a located feature point.

Feature detection can be achieved using methods similar to the Canny edge detector that instead search for corners rather than lines. If the feature points are being detected using sequences of filtering, as is common, we can perform the filtering on the GPU and read back to the CPU a buffer that flags which pixels are feature points. The CPU can then quickly scan the buffer to locate each of the feature points, creating a list of image locations at which we will calculate feature vectors on the GPU.

There are many approaches to generating feature vectors in order to track feature points. We show one approach as an example. For each detected feature point, we examine a 16×16 neighborhood of gradient magnitudes and directions (as computed in the Canny edge example). This neighborhood is divided up into 4×4-pixel regions, giving 16 different regions of 16 pixels. In each region, we create an 8-element histogram of gradient magnitudes. Each pixel's gradient magnitude is added to the bin of the histogram corresponding to its quantized gradient direction. For each region, the result is then an 8-element histogram. The feature vector is the concatenation of all 16 of these 8-element histograms, giving a feature vector length of $16 \times 8 = 128$ elements. Features in different images can be matched to each other by computing the Euclidean distance between pairs of feature vectors, with the minimum distance providing a best match.

To produce the 128-element feature vector result, we draw rows of vertices, with one row for each feature, such that each drawn point in the row corresponds to an element of the feature vector for that feature. Associating texture values pointwise allows for the most flexibility in mapping texture coordinates for use in computing the feature vector. Figure 40-6 shows how the vertices are laid out, and the binding of the image texture coordinates. Each point has different texture coordinates mapped to it to allow a single fragment program to access the appropriate gradients of the local region used to calculate the histogram.

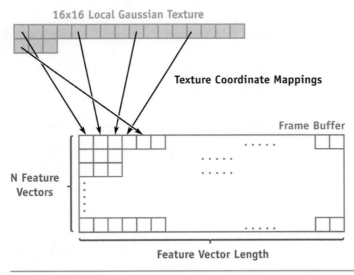

Figure 40-6. OpenGL Vertex Layout and Texture Bindings for Feature Vertices

By associating the correct texture coordinates for each point vertex, the single fragment program shown in Listing 40-4 calculates the feature vectors. To produce 8 elements per region, we have packed the results into 16-bit half-precision floating-point values; alternatively, we could use MRTs to output multiple 32-bit values. After completion, we read back the frame buffer, containing one feature vector per row, to the CPU.

Listing 40-4. Fragment Program for Calculating Feature Vectors

```
float4 FeatureVector(
  float2 fptexCoord : TEXCOORD0,
  float2 tapsCoord : TEXCOORD1,
  float4 colorZero : COLOR0,
  float4 wpos : WPOS,
  uniform samplerRECT FPE1,
  uniform samplerRECT FPE2 ) : COLOR
{
  const float4x4 lclGauss = { 0.3536, 0.3536, 0.3536, 0.3536,
                              0.3536, 0.7071, 0.7071, 0.3536,
                              0.3536, 0.7071, 0.7071, 0.3536,
                              0.3536, 0.3536, 0.3536, 0.3536 };
  const float eps = 0.001;
  float4 input;
  int xoffset = 1, yoffset = 1;
  float4 bins_0 = float4( 0.0, 0.0, 0.0, 0.0 );
  float4 bins_1 = float4( 0.0, 0.0, 0.0, 0.0 );

  for ( xoffset = 0 ; xoffset < 4 ; xoffset++ ) {
    for ( yoffset = 0 ; yoffset < 4 ; yoffset++ ) {
      input = texRECT( FPE1, fptexCoord + float2(xoffset, yoffset));
      float dir = input.y;
      input *= lclGauss[xoffset,yoffset].xxxx *
              texRECT( FPE2, tapsCoord + float2(xoffset, yoffset)).xxxx;
      if ( dir <= (1.0 + eps)/8.0 )
        bins_0.x += input.z;

      /* . . . for each bin . . . */
      else if ( dir <= (7.0 + eps)/8.0 )
        bins_1.z += input.z;
      else bins_1.w += input.z;
    }
  }
  return float4( pack_2half(bins_0.xy), pack_2half(bins_0.zw),
                pack_2half(bins_1.xy), pack_2half(bins_1.zw) )
}
```

40.4 Parallel Computer Vision Processing

When multiple computer vision algorithms are needed for an application, parallel GPU processing can be achieved by placing multiple graphics cards in the PCI bus slots of a motherboard. Figure 40-7 shows a machine built to explore the benefits of parallel computations by using multiple graphics cards. Running each computer vision program on a different GPU allows the cards to process in parallel; conventional shared memory can be used to allow the programs to interact.

Although creating multi-GPU systems using PCI cards will soon no longer be possible due to the obsolescence of the PCI bus, the advent of PCI Express has made new multi-GPU approaches possible. One such approach is NVIDIA's SLI, which makes the presence of multiple GPUs transparent to the developer by automatically distributing work between them.

Figure 40-7. Multiple GPUs Used for a Computer Vision Application
Left: A computer vision application (Fung and Mann 2002) using graphics hardware to display six video streams in a hexagonal form. Right: A computer vision machine that runs computer vision tasks in parallel using six PCI graphics cards and one AGP graphics card. Each PCI card is a GeForce FX 5200 GPU, resulting in an inexpensive, powerful, and easily constructible parallel architecture well suited for pattern recognition and computer vision.

40.5 Conclusion

This chapter has presented techniques for mapping computer vision algorithms onto modern GPUs. We hope that this chapter has provided an understanding of how to write computer vision algorithms for fast processing on the GPU. Although other special-purpose hardware systems could be used to provide hardware acceleration of computer vision algorithms, the low cost and widespread availability of GPUs will make hardware-accelerated computer vision algorithms more accessible.

40.6 References

The methods presented here are implemented in the OpenVIDIA project. OpenVIDIA is an open-source project that includes library functions and sample programs that run computer vision applications on the GPU. For more information, visit OpenVidia's Web site: http://openvidia.sourceforge.net.

Bouguet, J.-Y. 2004. Camera Calibration Toolbox for Matlab. Available online at **http://www.vision.caltech.edu/bouguetj/calib_doc/index.html**

Bradski, G. 1998. "Computer Vision Face Tracking for Use in a Perceptual User Interface." *Intel Technology Journal.*

Buck, I., and T. Purcell. 2004. "A Toolkit for Computation on GPUs." In *GPU Gems,* edited by Randima Fernando, pp. 621–636. Addison-Wesley.

Canny, J. F. 1986. "A Computational Approach to Edge Detection." *IEEE PAMI* 8(6), pp. 679–698.

Fung, J., and S. Mann. 2004a. "Computer Vision Signal Processing on Graphics Processing Units." In *Proceedings of the IEEE International Conference on Acoustics, Speech, and Signal Processing (ICASSP 2004),* Montreal, Quebec, Canada, pp. 83–89.

Fung, J., and S. Mann. 2004b. "Using Multiple Graphics Cards as a General Purpose Parallel Computer: Applications to Computer Vision." In *Proceedings of the 17th International Conference on Pattern Recognition (ICPR2004),* Cambridge, United Kingdom, pp. 805–808.

Fung, J., F. Tang, and S. Mann. 2002. "Mediated Reality Using Computer Graphics Hardware for Computer Vision." In *Proceedings of the International Symposium on Wearable Computing 2002 (ISWC2002),* Seattle, Washington, pp. 83–89.

Horn, B., and B. Schunk. 1981. "Determining Optical Flow." *Artificial Intelligence* 17, pp. 185–203.

Jargstorff, F. 2004. "A Framework for Image Processing." In *GPU Gems,* edited by Randima Fernando, pp. 445–467. Addison-Wesley.

Lowe, D. 2004. "Distinctive Image Features from Scale-Invariant Keypoints." *International Journal of Computer Vision* 60(2), pp. 91–110.

Mann, S. 1998. "Humanistic Intelligence/Humanistic Computing: 'Wearcomp' as a New Framework for Intelligent Signal Processing." *Proceedings of the IEEE* 86(11), pp. 2123–2151. Available online at **http://wearcam.org/procieee.htm**

Mann, S., and J. Fung. 2002. "Eye Tap Devices for Augmented, Deliberately Diminished or Otherwise Altered Visual Perception of Rigid Planar Patches of Real World Scenes." *Presence* 11(2), pp. 158–175.

Tsai, R. 1986. "An Efficient and Accurate Camera Calibration Technique for 3D Machine Vision." In *Proceedings of IEEE Conference on Computer Vision and Pattern Recognition*, Miami Beach, Florida, pp. 364–374.

Chapter 41

Deferred Filtering: Rendering from Difficult Data Formats

Joe Kniss
University of Utah

Aaron Lefohn
University of California, Davis

Nathaniel Fout
University of California, Davis

In this chapter, we describe a toolkit of tricks for interactively rendering 2D and 3D data sets that are stored in *difficult* formats. These data formats are common in GPGPU computations and when volume rendering from compressed data. GPGPU examples include the "flat 3D textures" used for cloud and fire simulations and the sparse formats used for implicit surface deformations. These applications use complex data formats to optimize for efficient GPU computation rather than for efficient rendering. However, such nonstandard and difficult data formats do not easily fit into standard rendering pipelines, especially those that require texture filtering. This chapter introduces deferred filtering and other tips and tricks required to efficiently render high-quality images from these complex custom data formats.

41.1 Introduction

The key concept for achieving filtered, interactive rendering from difficult data formats is *deferred filtering*. Deferred filtering is a two-pass rendering approach that first reconstructs a subset of the data into conventional 2D textures. A second pass uses the hardware's native interpolation to create high-quality, filtered renderings of 2D or 3D data.

The algorithm is incremental, such that rendering 3D data sets requires approximately the same amount of memory as rendering 2D data.

The deferred filtering approach is relevant to GPGPU computations that simulate or compress 2D and 3D effects using a difficult or nonstandard memory layout, as well as volume renderers that use compressed data formats. Relevant GPGPU applications include sparse computations and flat 3D textures (see Chapter 33, "Implementing Efficient Parallel Data Structures on GPUs"). Traditionally, high-quality rendering of these data sets requires that interpolation be done "by hand" in a fragment program, which in turn requires the reconstruction of multiple neighboring data samples. This approach leads to an enormous amount of redundant work.

Deferred filtering was first described in Lefohn et al. 2004. The paper presents algorithms for interactively computing and rendering deformable implicit surfaces. The data are represented in a sparse tiled format, and deferred filtering is a key component of the interactive volume rendering pipeline described in the paper. In this chapter we expand and generalize their description of the technique.

41.2 Why Defer?

Let's examine a simple scenario: imagine that you are rendering a volumetric effect such as a cloud or an explosion, and the 3D data have been compressed using vector quantization (see Schneider and Westermann 2003). This scheme compresses blocks of data by using a single value, called the *key*. The key value is used as an index into a *code book*, which allows blocks of data with similar characteristics to share the same memory. Reconstructing these data requires you first to read from the key texture, and then to read from the corresponding texel in the code book texture. Let's imagine that it takes four fragment program instructions to reconstruct a single texel.

One problem with this approach is that you cannot simply enable linear texture interpolation on the GPU and expect a smoothly filtered texture. Instead, linear interpolation must be implemented "by hand" as part of your fragment program. In practice, this is so expensive that renderers often resort to nearest-neighbor sampling only and forgo filtering completely. See Figure 41-1, top right. To perform "by-hand" filtering means we must reconstruct the 8 nearest texels and then perform 7 linear interpolations (LERPs) to get just a single trilinearly filtered value for each rendered fragment. Let's say that the original data size is 128^3 voxels, the rendering fills a viewport of size 256^2 (that is, the rendering magnifies the data by $2\times$), and we are sampling the data twice

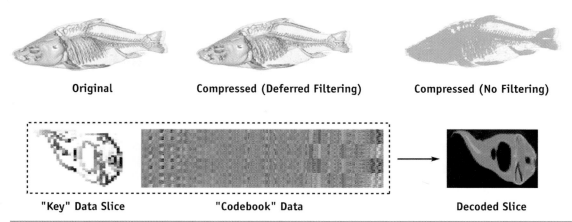

Figure 41-1. Vector Quantization Compressed 3D Data
Top left: The original (uncompressed) data. Top center: The compressed data rendered using deferred filtering.
Top right: The compressed data rendered without filtering (nearest neighbor). Bottom left: A slice of the "key"
value data volume. Bottom center: The entire 256×64 code book. Bottom right: The decoded slice of data.

per voxel. The number of fragments rendered would be $256 \times 256 \times 128 \times 2$, which totals approximately 16 million fragments. Now let's look at the number of fragment program instructions per fragment: 8×4 (8 texels times 4 instructions for each reconstruction) + 8 (texture reads) + 14 (for trilinear interpolation; LERP and ADD), which equals 54 instructions per filtered texture read. This brings us to a grand total of one billion fragment instructions for this simple rendering. As you can imagine, this might put a damper on your application's interactivity.

41.3 Deferred Filtering Algorithm

To combat the explosion of fragment instructions required for texture filtering in the previous example, we advocate a two-pass rendering approach. This two-pass approach avoids redundant work (texture reads and math) and leverages the hardware's native filtering capabilities. The first pass reconstructs a local subset of the data at its native resolution, and the second pass renders the reconstructed data using the GPU's hardware filtering capabilities.

In the previous example, we described naive slice-based volume rendering (see Ikits et al. 2004) of 3D data stored in a custom, compressed memory format. Deferring the filtering to another pass has huge advantages, but it requires us to solve the problem slightly differently. Instead of rendering the volume by using arbitrary slice planes, we use axis-aligned slicing (utilizing 2D textures). This method renders the volume slices along the major volume axis that most closely aligns with the view direction. Just like Rezk et al. (2000), we generate trilinearly filtered samples between volume slices by reading from two adjacent 2D slices and computing the final LERP in a fragment program.

Figure 41-2 depicts the process. The algorithm proceeds as follows (note that steps A and B in the algorithm correspond to steps A and B in Figure 41-2):

1. Reconstruct first volume data slice, `i = 1`.

2. For each slice, `i = 1` to `number of data slices - 1`:

   A. Reconstruct slice `i + 1`.

   B. For each sample slice between data slices `i` and `i + 1`:

       I. Read reconstructed values from slice `i` and `i + 1`.

       II. Perform the final LERP (for trilinear filtering).

       III. Shade and light the fragment.

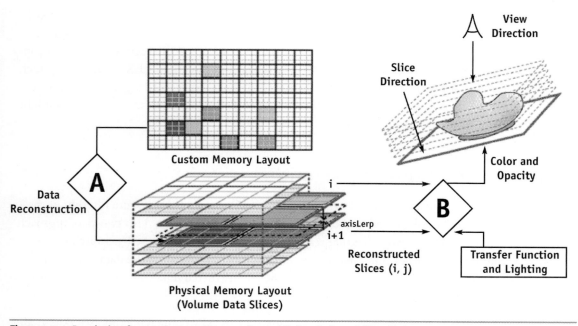

Figure 41-2. Rendering from a Custom Memory Format Using Deferred Filtering
Step A shows reconstruction of a physical volume slice `i+1`. *Step B renders trilinearly interpolated slices between* `i` *and* `i+1`.

Now, instead of reconstructing and filtering the data for each fragment rendered, we reconstruct the data at its native resolution and let the GPU's texture engine do the bulk of the filtering. The savings are dramatic: 3 fragment instructions (2 texture reads and 1 LERP) compared to 54 fragment instructions for single-pass reconstruction and rendering. Naturally, there is some overhead for the additional pass, which must include the reconstruction cost (but only once per texel). Be sure to avoid unnecessary texture copies by using *render-to-texture* (such as pbuffers) for slice textures i and i + 1.

The function in Listing 41-1 shows the three instructions needed to read a trilinearly filtered 3D texture by using deferred filtering. Notice that the axisLerp variable is a constant. Because we are using axis-aligned slicing, we know that every fragment rendered for the current slice will have the exact same texture coordinate along the slice axis; that is, the axisLerp represents the slice's position within the current voxel and is constant across the entire slice (see Figure 41-2).

Listing 41-1. A Cg Function for a Trilinearly Filtered 3D Texture Read Using Deferred Filtering
This code would be used in step B of Figure 41-2.

```
float4 deferredTex3D(float2 texCoord2D,     // slice texcoord
    const uniform float axisLerp,           // major axis pos
    uniform sampler2D textureI,             // tex slice "i"
    uniform sampler2D textureJ)             // tex slice "j"
{
    float4 texValI = tex2D(textureI, texCoord);
    float4 texValJ = tex2D(textureJ, texCoord);
    return lerp(texValI, texValJ, axisLerp);
}
```

When the data set is stored as 2D slices of a 3D domain, we can easily volume-render it if the preferred slice axis corresponds to the axis along which the data was sliced for storage, as shown in part A of Figure 41-3. When the slice axis is perpendicular to the storage slice axis, the data are reconstructed from lines of the 2D storage layout, as shown in part B of Figure 41-3.

Although there is some overhead for the separate reconstruction and filtering passes, in general we observed speedups from 2× to 10× in practice. In Figure 41-4, we show the timings for an implementation using deferred filtering to render from a compressed volume format. We can see that in some cases, deferred filtering is even faster than nearest-neighbor filtering. This is because when sampling more than once per voxel, nearest-neighbor filtering will perform redundant reconstruction.

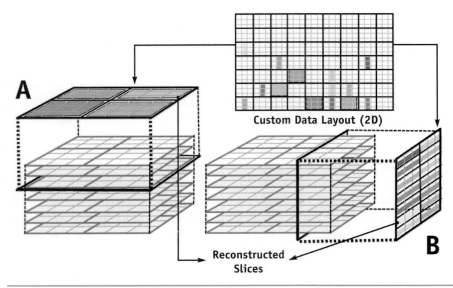

Figure 41-3. Reconstructing 3D Data from a Custom 2D Memory Layout
A: A data slice reconstructed when the preferred rendering axis is the same as the memory layout.
B: A slice reconstructed perpendicular to the memory layout using lines.

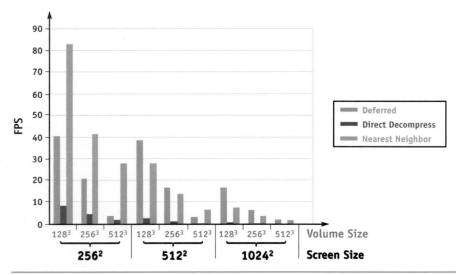

Figure 41-4. A Comparison of Various Filtering Methods
Comparing deferred filtering (DF), direct decompression (DD, which is reconstruction and filtering in a fragment program), and nearest-neighbor filtering (NN, or no filtering). Colored bars represent different data set sizes. Notice that deferred filtering is at worst half as fast as nearest-neighbor and at least twice as fast as nearest-neighbor when the volume size is large. Tested on an NVIDIA GeForce 6800 Series GPU.

41.4 Why It Works

The major problem with reconstructing and filtering custom data formats without deferred filtering is that, for a given rendered fragment, there are often many neighboring fragments that reconstruct identical values. The burden of this obvious inefficiency increases greatly as the cost of reconstruction goes up.

For the foreseeable future, the hard-wired efficiency of the GPU texturing and filtering engine will greatly exceed that of "hand-coded" fragment program trilinear filtering. Lifting computation from the fragment program to the appropriate built-in functional units will nearly always be a performance win. In the examples and algorithm, we assume the use of trilinear interpolation. However, even when we implement a higher-order filtering scheme, deferred filtering is still a big win (see Hadwiger et al. 2001). As the filter support grows (that is, as the number of data samples required for filtering increases), so does the redundancy (and therefore cost) of reconstruction. *Deferred filtering guarantees that the cost of reconstruction is incurred only once per texel.*

Depending on your memory layout, other, more subtle issues come into play. Multi-dimensional cache coherence is an important mechanism that GPUs utilize to achieve their stellar performance. Reading multiple texels from disparate memory locations can cause significant cache-miss latency, thus increasing render times. Deferred filtering may not be able to entirely prevent this effect, but it ensures that such problems happen only once per texel rather than eight times per fragment.

41.5 Conclusions: When to Defer

The need to represent volume data in difficult formats arises in two scenarios. The first case is when the data are stored on the GPU in a compressed format, as in our example earlier. The second case arises when the 3D data are generated by the GPU (that is, dynamic volumes). Dynamic volumes arise when performing GPGPU techniques for simulation, image processing, or segmentation/morphing. Current GPU memory models require us to store dynamic volume data either in a collection of 2D textures or as a "flat 3D texture" (see Chapter 33 of this book, "Implementing Efficient Parallel Data Structures on GPUs," for more details). Rendering the collection of 2D textures requires a new variant of 2D-texture-based volume rendering that uses only a *single* set of 2D slices described earlier. Deferred filtering frees you from worrying about whether or not your GPGPU computational data structure is suitable for interactive rendering. Deferred filtering makes it possible to interactively render images from any of these data formats.

Deferred filtering is efficient in both time and space because it nearly eliminates reconstruction costs (because they are incurred only once per texel) and is incremental (requiring only two slices at a time). Even if the reconstruction cost is negligible, it is still more efficient to add the deferred reconstruction pass than to filter the data in a fragment program for each fragment.

One disadvantage of deferred filtering is the fact that it requires us to "split" our fragment programs. In general, this isn't a problem, because texture reads often occur up front before other computation. When the texture read is dependent on other computation, however, using deferred filtering may require sophisticated multipass partitioning schemes (Chan et al. 2002, Foley et al. 2004, Riffel et al. 2004).

41.6 References

Chan, Eric, Ren Ng, Pradeep Sen, Kekoa Proudfoot, and Pat Hanrahan. 2002. "Efficient Partitioning of Fragment Shaders for Multipass Rendering on Programmable Graphics Hardware." In *Proceedings of Graphics Hardware 2002*, pp. 69–78. *This paper, along with Foley et al. 2004 and Riffel et al. 2004, demonstrates automatic methods for multipass partitioning of fragment programs.*

Foley, Tim, Mike Houston, and Pat Hanrahan. 2004. "Efficient Partitioning of Fragment Shaders for Multiple-Output Hardware." In *Proceedings of Graphics Hardware 2004*.

Hadwiger, Markus, Thomas Theußl, Helwig Hauser, and Eduard Gröller. 2001. "Hardware-Accelerated High-Quality Filtering on PC Hardware." In *Proceedings of Vision, Modeling, and Visualization 2001*, pp. 105–112.

Harris, Mark J. 2004. "Fast Fluid Dynamics Simulation on the GPU." In *GPU Gems*, edited by Randima Fernando, pp. 637–665. Addison-Wesley.

Ikits, Milan, Joe Kniss, Aaron Lefohn, and Charles Hansen. 2004. "Volume Rendering Techniques." In *GPU Gems*, edited by Randima Fernando, pp. 667–692. Addison-Wesley.

Lefohn, A. E., J. M. Kniss, C. D. Hansen, and R. T. Whitaker. 2004. "A Streaming Narrow-Band Algorithm: Interactive Deformation and Visualization of Level Sets." *IEEE Transactions on Visualization and Computer Graphics* 10(2).
Available online at **http://graphics.idav.ucdavis.edu/~lefohn/work/pubs/**
This paper describes an efficient GPGPU algorithm for sparse, nonlinear partial differential equations that permit real-time morphing and animation. This algorithm dynamically remaps data blocks to ensure that only the necessary, active data blocks receive computation. The authors describe how deferred filtering works in their rendering pipeline.

Rezk-Salama, C., K. Engel, M. Bauer, G. Greiner, and T. Ertl. 2000. "Interactive Volume Rendering on Standard PC Graphics Hardware Using Multi-Textures and Multi-Stage Rasterization." In *Proceedings of the SIGGRAPH/Eurographics Workshop on Graphics Hardware 2000*, pp. 109–118. *These authors were among the first to leverage the capabilities of programmable graphics hardware for volume rendering. They were also the first to demonstrate trilinear interpolation of 3D textures stored as 2D slices.*

Riffel, Andrew T., Aaron E. Lefohn, Kiril Vidimce, Mark Leone, and John D. Owens. 2004. "Mio: Fast Multipass Partitioning via Priority-Based Instruction Scheduling." In *Proceedings of Graphics Hardware 2004*.

Schneider, J., and R. Westermann. 2003. "Compression Domain Volume Rendering." In *Proceedings of IEEE Visualization 2003*, pp. 293–300. *This article presents an approach for volume data (3D) compression using vector quantization that allows decompression during rendering using programmable graphics hardware.*

Chapter 42

Conservative Rasterization

Jon Hasselgren
Lund University

Tomas Akenine-Möller
Lund University

Lennart Ohlsson
Lund University

Over the past few years, general-purpose computation using GPUs has received much attention in the research community. The stream-based rasterization architecture provides for much faster performance growth than that of CPUs, and therein lies the attraction in implementing an algorithm on the GPU: if not now, then at some point in time, your algorithm is likely to run faster on the GPU than on a CPU.

However, some algorithms that discretize their continuous problem domain do not return exact results when the GPU's standard rasterization is used. Examples include algorithms for collision detection (Myzskowski et al. 1995, Govindaraju et al. 2003), occlusion culling (Koltun et al. 2001), and visibility testing for shadow acceleration (Lloyd et al. 2004). The accuracy of these algorithms can be improved by increasing rendering resolution. However, one can never guarantee a fully correct result. This is similar to the antialiasing problem: you can never avoid sampling artifacts by just increasing the number of samples; you can only reduce the problems at the cost of performance.

A simple example of when *standard rasterization* does not compute the desired result is shown in Figure 42-1a, where one green and one blue triangle have been rasterized. These triangles overlap geometrically, but the standard rasterization process does not detect this fact. With *conservative rasterization*, the overlap is always properly detected, no matter what resolution is used. This property can enable load balancing between the CPU and the GPU. For example, for collision detection, a lower resolution would result in less work for the GPU and more work for the CPU, which performs exact intersection tests. See Figure 42-1b for the results of using conservative rasterization.

There already exists a simple algorithm for conservative rasterization (Akenine-Möller and Aila, forthcoming). However, that algorithm is designed for hardware implementation. In this chapter we present an alternative that is adapted for implementation using vertex and fragment programs on the GPU.

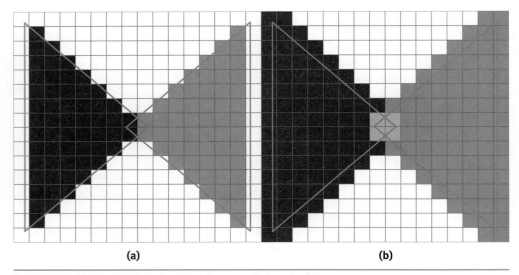

(a)   (b)

Figure 42-1. Comparing Standard and Conservative Rasterization
A blue and a green triangle rasterized at 16×16 pixels resolution using additive blending. (a) Standard rasterization. (b) Overestimating conservative rasterization. Note that the small overlap of the triangles is missed with standard rasterization and correctly detected using conservative rasterization.

42.1 Problem Definition

In this section, we define what we mean by *conservative rasterization* of a polygon. First, we define a *pixel cell* as the rectangular region around a pixel in a pixel grid. There are two variants of conservative rasterization, namely, *overestimated* and *underestimated* (Akenine-Möller and Aila, forthcoming):

- An overestimated conservative rasterization of a polygon includes all pixels for which the intersection between the pixel cell and the polygon is nonempty.

- An underestimated conservative rasterization of a polygon includes only the pixels whose pixel cell lies completely inside the polygon.

Here, we are mainly concerned with the overestimated variant, because that one is usually the most useful. If not specified further, we mean the overestimated variant when writing "conservative rasterization."

As can be seen, the definitions are based only on the pixel cell and are therefore independent of the number of sample points for a pixel. To that end, we choose not to consider render targets that use multisampling, because this would be just a waste of resources. It would also further complicate our implementation.

The solution to both of these problems can be seen as a modification of the polygon before the rasterization process. Overestimated conservative rasterization can be seen as the image-processing operation *dilation* of the polygon by the pixel cell. Similarly, underestimated conservative rasterization is the *erosion* of the polygon by the pixel cell. Therefore, we transform the rectangle-polygon overlap test of conservative rasterization into a point-in-region test.

The dilation is obtained by locking the center of a pixel-cell-size rectangle to the polygon edges and sweeping it along them while adding all the pixel cells it touches to the dilated triangle. Alternatively, for a convex polygon, the dilation can be computed as the convex hull of a set of pixel cells positioned at each of the vertices of the polygon. This is the equivalent of moving the vertices of the polygon in each of the four possible directions from the center of a pixel cell to its corners and then computing the convex hull. Because the four vectors from the center of a pixel cell to each corner are important in any algorithm for conservative rasterization, we call them the *semidiagonals*. This type of vertex movement is shown by the green lines in Figure 42-2a, which also shows the *bounding polygon* for a triangle.

The erosion is obtained by sweeping the pixel-cell-size rectangle in the same manner as for dilation, but instead we erase all the pixel cells it touches. We note that for a general convex polygon, the number of vertices may be decreased due to this operation. In the case of a triangle, the result will always be a smaller triangle or an "empty" polygon. The erosion of a triangle is illustrated in Figure 42-2b.

42.2 Two Conservative Algorithms

We present two algorithms for conservative rasterization that have different performance characteristics. The first algorithm computes the optimal bounding polygon in a vertex program. It is therefore optimal in terms of fill rate, but it is also costly in terms of geometry processing and data setup, because every vertex must be replicated. The

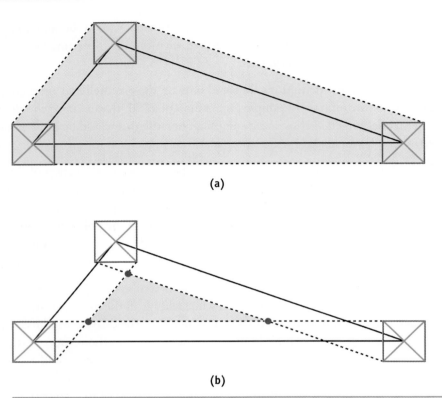

(a)

(b)

Figure 42-2. Overestimated and Underestimated Rasterization
(a) Overestimated rasterization. (b) Underestimated rasterization. Solid lines show the input triangle. The dashed lines, dots, and shaded area indicate the bounding polygon's edges, vertices, and area.

second algorithm computes a bounding triangle—a bounding polygon explicitly limited to only three vertices—in a vertex program and then trims it in a fragment program. This makes it less expensive in terms of geometry processing, because constructing the bounding triangle can be seen as repositioning each of the vertices of the input triangle. However, the bounding triangle is a poor fit for triangles with acute angles; therefore, the algorithm is more costly in terms of fill rate.

To simplify the implementation of both algorithms, we assume that no edges resulting from clipping by the near or far clip planes lie inside the view frustum. Edges resulting from such clipping operations are troublesome to detect, and they are very rarely used for any important purpose in this context.

42.2.1 Clip Space

We describe both algorithms in *window space*, for clarity, but in practice it is impossible to work in window space, because the vertex program is executed before the clipping and perspective projection. Fortunately, our reasoning maps very simply to *clip space*. For the moment, let us ignore the z component of the vertices (which is used only to interpolate a depth-buffer value). Doing so allows us to describe a line through each edge of the input triangle as a plane in homogeneous (x_c, y_c, w_c)-space. The plane is defined by the two vertices on the edge of the input triangle, as well as the position of the viewer, which is the origin, $(0, 0, 0)$. Because all of the planes pass through the origin, we get plane equations of the form

$$ax_c + by_c + cw_c = 0 \Leftrightarrow a\left(xw_c\right) + b\left(yw_c\right) + cw_c = 0 \Rightarrow ax + by + c = 0.$$

The planes are equivalent to lines in two dimensions. In many of our computations, we use the normal of an edge, which is defined by (a, b) from the plane equation.

42.2.2 The First Algorithm

In this algorithm we compute the optimal bounding polygon for conservative rasterization, shown in Figure 42-2a. Computing the convex hull, from the problem definition section, sounds like a complex task to perform in a vertex program. However, it comes down to three simple cases, as illustrated in Figure 42-3. Given two edges e_1 and e_2 connected in a vertex v, the three cases are the following:

- If the normals of e_1 and e_2 lie in the same quadrant, the convex hull is defined by the point found by moving the vertex v by the semidiagonal in that quadrant (Figure 42-3a).
- If the normals of e_1 and e_2 lie in neighboring quadrants, the convex hull is defined by two points. The points are found by moving v by the semidiagonals in those quadrants (Figure 42-3b).
- If the normals of e_1 and e_2 lie in opposite quadrants, the convex hull is defined by three points. Two points are found as in the previous case, and the last point is found by moving v by the semidiagonal of the quadrant between the opposite quadrants (in the winding order) (Figure 42-3c).

Implementation

We implement the algorithm as a vertex program that creates output vertices according to the three cases. Because we cannot create vertices in the vertex program, we must assume the worst-case scenario from Figure 42-3c. To create a polygon from a triangle,

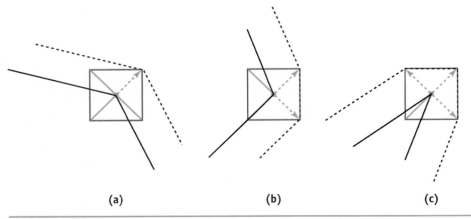

| (a) | (b) | (c) |

Figure 42-3. Computing an Optimal Bounding Polygon

we must send three instances of each vertex of the input triangle to the hardware and then draw the bounding polygon as a triangle fan with a total of nine vertices. The simpler cases from Figure 42-3, resulting in only one or two vertices, are handled by collapsing two or three instances of a vertex to the same position and thereby generating degenerate triangles. For each instance of every vertex, we must also send the positions of the previous and next vertices in the input triangle, as well as a local index in the range [0,2]. The positions and indices are needed to compute which case and which semidiagonal to use when computing the new vertex position.

The core of the vertex program consists of code that selects one of the three cases and creates an appropriate output vertex, as shown in Listing 42-1.

Listing 42-1. Vertex Program Implementing the First Algorithm

```
// semiDiagonal[0,1] = Normalized semidiagonals in the same
// quadrants as the edge's normals.
// vtxPos = The position of the current vertex.
// hPixel = dimensions of half a pixel cell

float dp = dot(semiDiagonal[0], semiDiagonal[1]);
float2 diag;

if (dp > 0) {
  // The normals are in the same quadrant -> One vertex
  diag = semiDiagonal[0];
}
```

```
else if (dp < 0) {
  // The normals are in neighboring quadrants -> Two vertices
  diag = (In.index == 0 ? semiDiagonal[0] : semiDiagonal[1]);
}
else {
  // The normals are in opposite quadrants -> Three vertices
  if (In.index == 1) {
    // Special "quadrant between two quadrants case"
    diag = float2(semiDiagonal[0].x * semiDiagonal[0].y *
                  semiDiagonal[1].x,
                  semiDiagonal[0].y * semiDiagonal[1].x *
                  semiDiagonal[1].y);
  }
  else
    diag = (In.index == 0 ? semiDiagonal[0] : semiDiagonal[1]);
}

vtxPos.xy += hPixel.xy * diag * vtxPos.w;
```

In cases with input triangles that have vertices behind the eye, we can get projection problems that force tessellation edges out of the bounding polygon in its visible regions. To solve this problem, we perform basic near-plane clipping of the current edge. If orthographic projection is used, or if no polygon will intersect the near clip plane, we skip this operation.

42.2.3 The Second Algorithm

The weakness of the first algorithm is that it requires multiple output vertices for each input vertex. An approach that avoids this problem is to compute a bounding triangle for every input triangle, instead of computing the optimal bounding polygon, which may have as many as nine vertices. However, the bounding triangle is a bad approximation for triangles with acute angles. As a result, we get an overly conservative rasterization, as shown in Figure 42-4. The poor fit makes the bounding triangles practically useless. To work around this problem, we use an alternative interpretation of a simple test for conservative rasterization (Akenine-Möller and Aila, forthcoming). The bounding polygon (as used in Section 42.2.2) can be computed as the intersection of the bounding triangle and the axis-aligned bounding box (AABB) of itself. The AABB of the bounding polygon can easily be computed from the input triangle. Figure 42-5 illustrates this process.

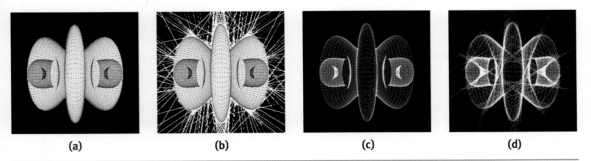

Figure 42-4. Objects Rasterized in Different Ways
(a) An object rasterized with the first algorithm. (b) The object rasterized using bounding triangles only.
(c) Overdraw for the first algorithm. (d) Overdraw for the second algorithm.

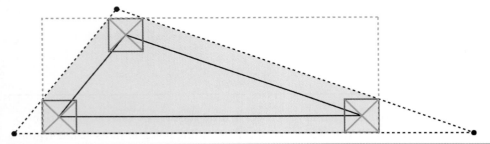

Figure 42-5. An Input Triangle and Its Optimal Bounding Polygon
The bounding triangle is shown by the black dashed line. Its axis-aligned bounding box is shown by the orange dashed line. The blue area is the optimal bounding polygon.

In our second algorithm, we compute the bounding triangle in a vertex program and then use a fragment program to discard all fragments that do not overlap the AABB.

We can find the three edges of the bounding triangle by computing the normal of the line through each edge of the input triangle and then moving that line by the worst-case semidiagonal. The worst-case semidiagonal is always the one found in the same quadrant as the line normal.

After computing the translated lines, we compute the intersection points of adjacent edges to get the vertices of the bounding triangle. At this point, we can make good use of the clip-space representation. Because each line is represented as a plane through the origin, we can compute the intersection of two planes with normals $\mathbf{n}_1 = (x_1, y_1, w_1)$ and $\mathbf{n}_2 = (x_2, y_2, w_2)$ as the cross product $\mathbf{n}_1 \times \mathbf{n}_2$.

Note that the result is a direction rather than a point, but all points in the given direction will project to the same point in window space. This also ensures that the w component of the computed vertex receives the correct sign.

Implementation

Because the bounding triangle moves every vertex of the input triangle to a new position, we need to send only three vertices for every input triangle. However, along with each vertex, we also send the positions of the previous and next vertices, as texture coordinates, so we can compute the edges. For the edges, we use planes rather than lines. A parametric representation of the lines, in the form of a point and a direction, would simplify the operation of moving the line at the cost of more problems when computing intersection. Because we represent our lines as equations of the form:

$$(a, b) \cdot \mathbf{x} + c = 0,$$

we must derive how to modify the line equation to represent a movement by a vector $\mathbf{v}$. It can be done by modifying the c component of the line equation as:

$$c_{moved} = c - \mathbf{v} \cdot (a, b).$$

If we further note that the problem of finding a semidiagonal is symmetric with respect to 90-degree rotations, we can use a fixed semidiagonal in the first quadrant along with the component-wise absolute values of the line normal to move the line. The code in Listing 42-2 shows the core of the bounding triangle computation.

Listing 42-2. Cg Code for Computing the Bounding Triangle

```
// hPixel = dimensions of half a pixel cell

// Compute equations of the planes through the two edges
float3 plane[2];
plane[0] = cross(currentPos.xyw - prevPos.xyw, prevPos.xyw);
plane[1] = cross(nextPos.xyw - currentPos.xyw, currentPos.xyw);

// Move the planes by the appropriate semidiagonal
plane[0].z -= dot(hPixel.xy, abs(plane[0].xy));
plane[1].z -= dot(hPixel.xy, abs(plane[1].xy));

// Compute the intersection point of the planes.
float4 finalPos;
finalPos.xyw = cross(plane[0], plane[1]);
```

We compute the screen-space AABB for the optimal bounding polygon in our vertex program. We iterate over the edges of the input triangle and modify the current AABB candidate to include that edge. The result is an AABB for the input triangle. Extending its size by a pixel cell gives us the AABB for the optimal bounding polygon. To guarantee the correct result, we must clip the input triangle by the near clip plane to avoid back projection. The clipping can be removed under the same circumstances as for the previous algorithm.

We send the AABB of the bounding polygon and the clip-space position to a fragment program, where we perform perspective division on the clip-space position and discard the fragment if it lies outside the AABB. The fragment program is implemented by the following code snippet:

```
// Compute the device coordinates of the current pixel
float2 pos = In.clipSpace.xy / In.clipSpace.w;

// Discard fragment if outside the AABB. In.AABB contains min values
// in the xy components and max values in the zw components
discard(pos.xy < In.AABB.xy || pos.xy > In.AABB.zw);
```

Underestimated Conservative Rasterization

So far, we have covered algorithms only for overestimated conservative rasterization. However, we have briefly implied that the optimal bounding polygon for underestimated rasterization is a triangle or an "empty" polygon. The bounding triangle for underestimated rasterization can be computed just like the bounding triangle for overestimated rasterization: simply swap the minus for a plus when computing a new c component for the lines. The case of the empty polygon is automatically addressed because the bounding triangle will change winding order and be culled by the graphics hardware.

42.3 Robustness Issues

Both our algorithms have issues that, although not equivalent, suggest the same type of solution. The first algorithm is robust in terms of floating-point errors but may generate front-facing triangles when the bounding polygon is tessellated, even though the input primitive was back-facing. The second algorithm generates bounding triangles with the correct orientation, but it suffers from precision issues in the intersection computations when near-degenerate input triangles are used. Note that degenerate triangles may be the result of projection (with a very large angle between view direction and polygon), rather than a bad input.

To solve these problems, we first assume that the input data contains no degenerate triangles. We introduce a value, ε, small enough that we consider all errors caused by ε to fall in the same category as other floating-point precision errors. If the signed distance from the plane of the triangle to the viewpoint is less than ε, we consider the input triangle to be back-facing and output the vertices expected for standard rasterization. This hides the problems because it allows the GPU's culling unit to remove the back-facing polygons.

42.4 Conservative Depth

When performing conservative rasterization, you often want to compute conservative depth values as well. By *conservative depth*, we mean either the maximum or the minimum depth values, z_{max} and z_{min}, in each pixel cell. For example, consider a simple collision-detection scenario (Govindaraju et al. 2003) with two objects A and B. If any part of object A is occluded by object B and any part of object B is occluded by object A, we say that the objects potentially collide. To perform the first half of this test using our overestimating conservative rasterizer, we would first render object B to the depth buffer using a computed z_{min} as the depth. We would then render object A with depth writes disabled and occlusion queries enabled, and using a computed z_{max} as depth. If any fragments of object A were discarded during rasterization, the objects potentially collide. This result could be used to initiate an exact intersection point computation on the CPU.

When an attribute is interpolated over a plane covering an entire pixel cell, the extreme values will always be in one of the corners of the cell. We therefore compute z_{max} and z_{min} based on the plane of the triangle, rather than the exact triangle representation. Although this is just an approximation, it is conservatively correct. It will always compute a z_{max} greater than or equal to the exact solution and a z_{min} less than or equal to it. This is illustrated in Figure 42-6.

The depth computation is implemented in our fragment program. A ray is sent from the eye through one of the corners of the current pixel cell. If z_{max} is desired, we send the ray through the corner found in the direction of the triangle normal; the z_{min} depth value can be found in the opposite corner. We compute the intersection point between the ray and the plane of the triangle and use its coordinates to get the depth value. In some cases, the ray may not intersect the plane (or have an intersection point behind the viewer). When this happens, we simply return the maximum depth value.

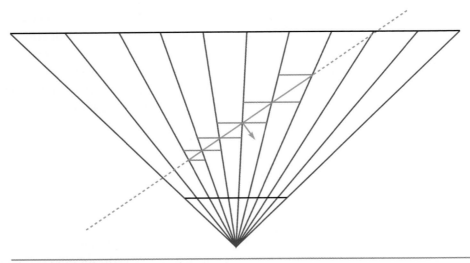

Figure 42-6. Finding the Farthest Depth Value
A view frustum (in black), with pixel cells (blue lines) and a triangle (orange), as seen from above. The dashed line is the plane of the triangle, and the orange arrow indicates its normal. The range of possible depth values is also shown for the rasterized pixels. The direction of the normal can be used to find the position in a pixel cell that has the farthest depth value. In this case, the normal is pointing to the right, and so the farthest depth value is at the right side of the pixel cell.

We can compute the depth value from an intersection point in two ways. We can compute interpolation parameters for the input triangle in the vertex program and then use the intersection point coordinates to interpolate the z (depth) component. This works, but it is computationally expensive and requires many interpolation attributes to transfer the (constant) interpolation base from the vertex program to the fragment program. If the projection matrix is simple, as produced by `glFrustum`, for instance, it will be of the form:

$$
\begin{pmatrix}
\cdots & \cdots & \cdots & \cdots \\
\cdots & \cdots & \cdots & \cdots \\
0 & 0 & -\dfrac{far + near}{far - near} & -\dfrac{2\,far \times near}{far - near} \\
0 & 0 & -1 & 0
\end{pmatrix}.
$$

In this case we can use a second, simpler way of computing the depth value. Under the assumption that the input is a normal point with $w_e = 1$ (the eye-space w component), we can compute the z_w (window-depth) component of an intersection point from the w_c (clip-space w) component. For a depth range $[n, f]$, we compute z_w as:

$$z_w = \left(\frac{f + n}{2} \right) + \left(\frac{f - n}{2} \right) \left[\left(\frac{far + near}{far - near} \right) - \frac{2\,far \times near}{\left(far - near \right) w_c} \right].$$

42.5 Results and Conclusions

We have implemented two GPU-accelerated algorithms for conservative rasterization. Both algorithms have strong and weak points, and it is therefore hard to pick a clear winner. As previously stated, the first algorithm is costly in terms of geometry processing, while the second algorithm requires more fill rate. However, the distinction is not that simple. The overdraw complexity of the second algorithm depends both on the acuity of the triangles in a mesh and on the rendering resolution, which controls how far an edge is moved. The extra overdraw caused by the second algorithm therefore depends on the mesh tessellation in proportion to the rendering resolution. Our initial benchmarks in Figure 42-7 show that the first algorithm seems to be more efficient on high-end hardware (such as GeForce 6800 Series GPUs). Older GPUs (such as the GeForce FX 5600) quickly become vertex limited; therefore, the second algorithm may be more suitable in such cases.

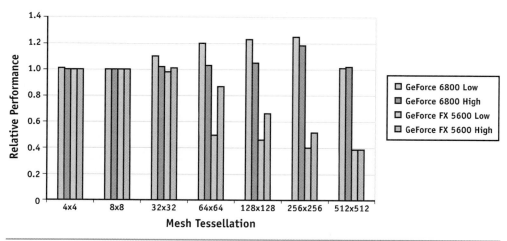

Figure 42-7. Relative Performance of the Two Algorithms
Benchmarks on a GeForce 6800 Series GPU and a GeForce FX 5600. Tests were performed at low (128×128 pixels) and high (1024×1024 pixels) resolution. The graph shows the relative performance of the first algorithm compared to the second.

It is likely that the first algorithm will be the better choice in the future. The vertex-processing power of graphics hardware is currently growing faster than the fragment processing power. And with potential future features such as "geometry shaders," we could make a better implementation of the first algorithm.

We can probably enhance the performance of both of our algorithms by doing silhouette edge detection on the CPU and computing bounding polygons only for silhouette edges, or for triangles with at least one silhouette edge. This would benefit the GPU load of both of our algorithms, at the expense of more CPU work.

Our algorithms will always come with a performance penalty when compared to standard rasterization. However, because we can always guarantee that the result is conservatively correct, it is possible that the working resolution can be significantly lowered. In contrast, standard rasterization will sometimes generate incorrect results, which for many applications is completely undesirable.

42.6 References

Akenine-Möller, Tomas, and Timo Aila. Forthcoming. "Conservative and Tiled Rasterization Using a Modified Triangle Setup." *Journal of Graphics Tools*.

Govindaraju, Naga K., Stephane Redon, Ming C. Lin, and Dinesh Manocha. 2003. "CULLIDE: Interactive Collision Detection Between Complex Models in Large Environments Using Graphics Hardware." In *Proceedings of the SIGGRAPH/Eurographics Workshop on Graphics Hardware 2003*, pp. 25–32.

Koltun, Vladlen, Daniel Cohen-Or, and Yiorgos Chrysanthou. 2001. "Hardware-Accelerated From-Region Visibility Using a Dual Ray Space." In *12th Eurographics Workshop on Rendering*, pp. 204–214.

Lloyd, Brandon, Jeremy Wendt, Naga Govindaraju, and Dinesh Manocha. 2004. "CC Shadow Volumes." In *Eurographics Symposium on Rendering 2004*, pp. 197–205.

McCormack, Joel, and Robert McNamara. 2000. "Tiled Polygon Traversal Using Half-Plane Edge Functions." In *Proceedings of the SIGGRAPH/Eurographics Workshop on Graphics Hardware 2000*, pp. 15–21.

Myzskowski, Karol, Oleg G. Okunev, and Tosiyasu L. Kunii. 1995. "Fast Collision Detection Between Complex Solids Using Rasterizing Graphics Hardware." *The Visual Computer* 11(9), pp. 497–512.

Seitz, Chris. 2004. "Evolution of NV40." Presentation at NVIDIA GPU BBQ 2004. Available online at
http://developer.nvidia.com/object/gpu_bbq_2004_presentations.html

PART VI
SIMULATION AND NUMERICAL ALGORITHMS

Real-world computational problems have a variety of needs. Some computations, such as everyday office tasks like word processing, are inherently sequential in nature; others, such as computer graphics, physics simulation, and image processing, exhibit a large amount of data parallelism. Most applications require a mix of sequential and data-parallel computation, and modern computer systems are evolving to support these needs. The wide availability and relatively low cost of GPUs make them uniquely suited to serving the data-parallel needs of modern computing. This part of the book focuses on several examples of data-parallel computations that perform well on GPUs.

Bioinformatics and computational biology and chemistry are fast-growing areas in scientific computing. **Chapter 43, "GPU Computing for Protein Structure Prediction,"** by **Paulius Micikevicius** of Armstrong Atlantic State University, presents a GPU implementation of a simple but important problem in the study of protein structure. The algorithm is highly data-parallel and is based on the well-known Floyd-Warshall all-pairs shortest-paths algorithm.

Systems of linear equations are very common in many types of problems. **Chapter 44, "A GPU Framework for Solving Systems of Linear Equations,"** by **Jens Krüger** and **Rüdiger Westermann** of Technische Universität München, shows how to efficiently represent a variety of matrix and vector types on the GPU. Their framework provides basic operations that can be used to build up more complicated linear system solvers. As an example, they use the framework to build a conjugate gradient solver used in the simulation of the 2D wave equation.

Another growing area in parallel computing is computational finance. Investment firms currently use large clusters of processors to crunch huge amounts of data for purposes such as pricing stock options and credit derivatives. In **Chapter 45, "Options Pricing on the GPU,"** **Craig Kolb** and **Matt Pharr** of NVIDIA describe an efficient GPU implementation of two widely used algorithms for options pricing.

Sorting is a fundamental algorithm in computer science. GPU implementation of sorting is important because when using the GPU for other parts of a computational system, even in cases where the CPU outperforms GPU-based sorting, it is more efficient to keep the data on the GPU and avoid unnecessary transfers back and forth to the CPU. In **Chapter 46, "Improved GPU Sorting," Peter Kipfer** and **Rüdiger Westermann** of Technische Universität München improve on the current state of the art in GPU-based sorting, showing how to bring as many GPU resources to bear on the problem as possible. The result is a useful and essential component for many applications.

Simulating fluid flow is important in many industries, from automotive and aerospace engineering to medicine. GPU simulation of fluids has been a popular topic for the past couple of years, because physically based simulation is a naturally data-parallel problem that maps well to the GPU architecture. **Chapter 47, "Flow Simulation with Complex Boundaries,"** by **Wei Li** of Siemens Corporate Research and **Zhe Fan, Xiaoming Wei**, and **Arie Kaufman** of Stony Brook University, describes fluid simulation on the GPU using the Lattice-Boltzman technique, which models the transfer of "packets" of fluid between cells in a lattice. They also describe a novel technique for simulating the flow around arbitrary dynamic obstacles.

Electronic imaging has revolutionized how physicians diagnose and treat patients. Medical image processing is a growing field that involves large amounts of parallel computation. An essential algorithmic tool used in medical imaging (and any other type of signal processing) is the Fast Fourier Transform (FFT). **Chapter 48, "Medical Image Reconstruction with the FFT,"** by **Thilaka Sumanaweera** and **Donald Liu** of Siemens Medical Solutions USA, presents an efficient implementation of the FFT on the GPU, including a number of insightful optimizations. Sumanaweera and Liu also describe how the FFT is used to reconstruct MRI and ultrasonic images on the GPU.

This part of the book demonstrates that GPUs are a powerful computational platform for solving a variety of data-parallel problems. The chapters included here are just a sample: many other types of computation have been implemented on GPUs, and I expect to see a wider variety, with even better performance, in the future. To keep up to date with developments in this exciting field, visit www.GPGPU.org.

Mark Harris, NVIDIA Corporation

Chapter 43

GPU Computing for Protein Structure Prediction

Paulius Micikevicius
Armstrong Atlantic State University

43.1 Introduction

Determining protein 3D structure is one of the greatest challenges in computational biology. Nuclear magnetic resonance (NMR) spectroscopy is the second most popular method (after X-ray crystallography) for structure prediction. Given a molecule, NMR experiments provide upper and lower bounds on the interatomic distances. If all distances are known exactly, Cartesian coordinates for each atom can be easily computed. However, only a fraction (often fewer than 10 percent) of all distance bounds are obtained by NMR experiments (unknown upper and lower bounds are set to the molecule's diameter and the diameter of a hydrogen atom, respectively). Thus, a number of heuristics are used in practice to generate 3D structures from NMR data. Because the quality of the computed structures and the time required to obtain them depend on the bound tightness, it is necessary to use efficient procedures for bound smoothing (that is, increasing lower bounds or decreasing upper bounds). The most widely used procedure is based on the triangle inequality and is included in popular molecular dynamics software packages, such as X-PLOR and DYANA. In this chapter we describe a GPU implementation of the triangle inequality distance-bound smoothing procedure. Figure 43-1 shows one example of results obtained.

An n-atom molecule is modeled with a complete graph on n nodes, K_n, where nodes represent atoms. Each edge (i, j) is assigned two labels—upper and lower bounds, denoted by u_{ij} and l_{ij}, on the distance between the ith and jth atoms. Let i, j, and k be

Figure 43-1. 3D Structure of IgG2a Monoclonal Antibody (Mouse Immunoglobulin)

arbitrary points in three-dimensional Euclidean space. The distances between points, d_{ij}, d_{ik}, and d_{kj} must satisfy the triangle inequality; for example, $d_{ij} \leq d_{ik} + d_{kj}$. The triangle inequality can also be stated in terms of the upper and lower bounds on the distances. The upper bound on d_{ij} must satisfy the inequality $u_{ij} \leq u_{ik} + u_{kj}$, while the lower bound must satisfy $l_{ij} \geq \max \{l_{ik} - u_{kj}, l_{kj} - u_{ik}\}$. Upper bounds must be tightened first, because lower values for upper bounds will lead to larger lower bounds. Dress and Havel (1988) have shown that violation of the triangle inequality can be eliminated in $O(n^3)$ time by means of a Floyd-Warshall-type algorithm for the all-pairs shortest-paths problem.

43.2 The Floyd-Warshall Algorithm and Distance-Bound Smoothing

Given a weighted graph on n nodes, the all-pairs shortest-paths problem asks to find the shortest distances between each pair of nodes. The problem is fundamental to computer science and graph theory. In addition to bound smoothing, it has other practical applications, such as network analysis and solving a system of difference constraints (Cormen et al. 2001). A number of sequential approaches exist for solving the all-pairs shortest-paths problem (for a brief discussion, see Bertsekas 1993), but the Floyd-Warshall algorithm is generally favored for dense graphs due to its simplicity and an efficient memory-access pattern. The sequential Floyd-Warshall algorithm is shown in Algorithm 43-1 (we assume that the nodes are labeled with integers $1, 2, \ldots, n$). We assume that a graph is stored as a 2D distance matrix $\mathbf{D}$, where $\mathbf{D}[i, j]$ contains the distance between nodes i and j. The Floyd-Warshall algorithm requires $O(n^3)$ time and $O(n^2)$ storage. The upper-bound smoothing algorithm is obtained by replacing line 4 of Algorithm 43-1 with $u_{ij} \leftarrow \min \{u_{ij}, u_{ik} + u_{kj}\}$. Similarly, the algorithm for tightening lower bounds is obtained by replacing line 4 with $l_{ij} \leftarrow \max \{l_{ij}, l_{ik} - u_{kj}, l_{kj} - u_{ik}\}$.

Algorithm 43-1. The Sequential Floyd-Warshall Algorithm

1. **for** $k \leftarrow 1$ **to** n **do**
2.   **for** $i \leftarrow 1$ **to** $(n - 1)$ **do**
3.   **for** $j \leftarrow (i + 1)$ **to** n **do**
4. $d_{ij} \leftarrow \min \{d_{ij}, d_{ik} + d_{kj}\}$

A classic parallelization for $O(n^2)$ processors is shown in Algorithm 43-2, where P_{ij} refers to the processor responsible for updating the distance d_{ij}.

Algorithm 43-2. Parallelization of the Floyd-Warshall Algorithm for n^2 Processors

1. **for** $k \leftarrow 1$ **to** n **do**
2.   **for** each P_{ij}, where $1 \leq i, j \leq n$ **do in parallel**
3. $d_{ij} \leftarrow \min \{d_{ij}, d_{ik} + d_{kj}\}$

The parallelization in Algorithm 43-2 is amenable to a GPU implementation because each processor reads from multiple locations but writes to one predetermined location.

43.3 GPU Implementation

To be solved on the GPU, the distance-bound smoothing problem is formulated as a rendering task for the programmable fragment unit. Both the lower and the upper bounds are stored as separate 2D textures. Although such a storage choice wastes memory (texels (i, j) and (j, i) contain the same value), it leads to fewer texture fetches in vectorized implementations, and thus to higher performance, as described later in Section 43.3.4. For simplicity of presentation, we first describe the scalar version of the algorithm, leaving the vectorization for the end of the section.

43.3.1 Dynamic Updates

Because of the dynamic nature of the Floyd-Warshall algorithm, the output of iteration k is the input for iteration $(k + 1)$. Although this requires no special considerations when programming for a CPU, current GPU architectures do not allow the same memory block to be a render target and a texture at the same time. We overcome this constraint with *ping-pong buffering*: rendering alternates between the front and back buffers. For example, we render to the front buffer when the back buffer is bound as a texture. The functions of the buffers are flipped in the next iteration, and the process is repeated. Because there is no memory copy, we have experimentally confirmed that ping-pong buffering is twice as fast as a copy-to-texture approach.

43.3.2 Indexing Data Textures

An all-pairs shortest-paths solution for a graph with n nodes is computed by rendering an $n \times n$ pixel square in n passes, each corresponding to a single iteration of the for loop on line 1 in Algorithm 43-2. The pixel in position (i, j) corresponds to distance d_{ij}. Thus, a fragment shader performs the computation corresponding to line 3 in Algorithm 43-2. In the naive implementation, given distance d_{ij}, the shader generates two sets of texture coordinates to index the storage for distances d_{ik} and d_{kj}, and then performs algebraic operations. Performance is improved by moving the texture coordinate generation from the shader to the rasterizer: during the kth iteration, the four vertices of the rectangle are each assigned three texture coordinates, as shown in Figure 43-2a. Thus, after interpolation, every fragment (i, j) receives the necessary three texture coordinates. Moving texture coordinate generation from the shader to the rasterizer increased the performance by approximately 10 percent.

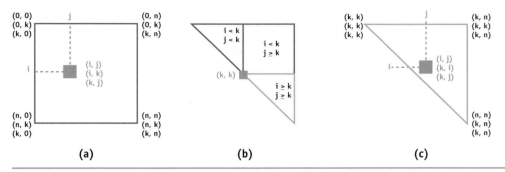

Figure 43-2. Texture Coordinates for the *k*th Iteration

43.3.3 The Triangle Approach

The upper and lower distance bounds can be stored respectively in the upper and lower triangles of a texture. Under this assumption, it is necessary to ensure that the shader for smoothing the upper bounds fetches only the upper-triangle texels. This is achieved when texture coordinate (u, v) satisfies $u < v$: during the *k*th iteration, the upper triangle is partitioned into three regions determined by the relation between i, j, and k, as shown in Figure 43-2b. Thus, three geometric primitives are rendered with texture coordinates adjusted according to the region. For example, texture coordinates for the bottom triangle are shown in Figure 43-2c. If a single primitive is rendered instead of three as described, the GPU has to execute additional instructions for each fragment to determine to which region the fragment belongs. A similar approach can be used to smooth the lower bounds.

43.3.4 Vectorization

We can improve performance by vectorizing the algorithm, because each of the GPU pipelines operates on four-component vectors. We can do so by packing the distances of four consecutive edges into RGBA components of a single texel. As shown in Figure 43-3, texel $\mathbf{T}[i, j]$ contains the following entries of the distance matrix: $\mathbf{D}[i, 4j]$, $\mathbf{D}[i, 4j + 1]$, $\mathbf{D}[i, 4j + 2]$, $\mathbf{D}[i, 4j + 3]$. Thus, only an $n \times n/4$ rectangle needs to be rendered. Note that rendering pixels in the *i*th row during the *k*th iteration requires fetching the distance value $\mathbf{D}[i, k]$, so we need to modify the computation for the upper-bound smoothing,

$$\mathbf{D}[i, j] \leftarrow \min\left\{\mathbf{D}[i, j], \mathbf{D}[i, k] + \mathbf{D}[k, j]\right\},$$

for vector operations:

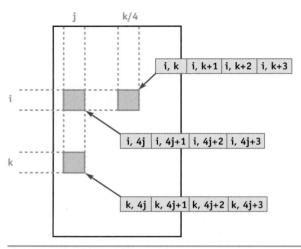

Figure 43-3. Data Packing for Vectorization

$$\mathbf{T}[i,\,j] \leftarrow \min\big\{\mathbf{T}[i,\,j],\ \Psi + \mathbf{T}[k,\,j]\big\},$$

where Ψ is a vector created by replicating the R, G, B, or A component value of $\mathbf{T}[i,\,\lfloor k/4 \rfloor]$, depending on whether $k \equiv 0$, 1, 2, or 3 (mod 4), respectively. The code for smoothing the lower bounds is modified similarly. Generating the Ψ vector on the GPU can be expensive because under certain circumstances, branching or integer operations are inefficient in current fragment units. We can overcome this limitation by running four separate shader programs, each hard-coded for a different value of k mod 4, thus avoiding branching and integer operations (replicating a scalar value across the Ψ does not impose any additional cost [Mark et al. 2003]). The OpenGL application must explicitly bind the appropriate shader program for each of the n iterations, with a negligible overhead.

Although the upper and lower distance bounds could be stored in the upper and lower triangles, respectively, of the same 2D texture, this would lead to more texture fetches. For example, to update the upper bounds in texel $\mathbf{T}[i,\,j]$, we need to ensure that fetching $\mathbf{T}[k,\,j]$ returns the upper bounds on distances $\mathbf{D}[k,\,4j]$, $\mathbf{D}[k,\,4j+1]$, $\mathbf{D}[k,\,4j+2]$, and $\mathbf{D}[k,\,4j+3]$. However, if $k > j$, the texel $\mathbf{T}[k,\,j]$ is in the lower triangle and contains the lower bounds. As a result, we would need to fetch 4 texels ($\mathbf{T}[4j,\,k]$, $\mathbf{T}[4j+1,\,k]$, $\mathbf{T}[4j+2,\,k]$, $\mathbf{T}[4j+3,\,k]$) instead of 1. This approach would require 11 texture fetches for each lower bound and either 3 (when $i,\,j < k$) or 6 (when $i,\,j$, or both are greater than k) texture fetches for each upper bound. Thus, we achieve better performance by storing 2 textures and rendering twice as many fragments as theoretically necessary, because 3 and 5 texture fetches are required when smoothing the upper and lower bounds, respectively.

43.4 Experimental Results

We conducted the experiments on a 2.4 GHz Intel Xeon-based PC with 512 MB RAM and an NVIDIA GeForce 6800 Ultra GPU. The GeForce 6800 Ultra has 16 fragment pipelines, each operating on four-element vectors at 425 MHz. The applications were written in ANSI C++ using OpenGL, GLUT, and Cg (Mark et al. 2003) for graphics operations. The pbuffers, textures, and shader programs all used 32-bit IEEE-standard floating-point types, because precision is critical to distance-bound smoothing. The executables were compiled using the Intel C++ 8.1 compiler with SSE2 optimizations enabled. Furthermore, the CPU implementation was hand-optimized to minimize cache misses.

The timing results for problem sizes 128 to 4096 are shown in Table 43-1. We show the overall times as well as separate times for smoothing the lower and upper bounds. The maximum size was dictated by the graphics system, because no pbuffer larger than 4096×4096 could be allocated. All results are in milliseconds and were computed by averaging 1000 (for $n = 128, 256$), 100 (for $n = 512$), 10 (for $n = 1024, 2048$), or 1 (for $n = 4096$) consecutive executions. The compiled shaders for smoothing the lower and upper bounds consisted of nine and five assembly instructions, respectively.

Table 43-1. Times for the Optimized GPU Implementation

	Time (ms)						Speedup		
	CPU			GPU			GPU		
Size	Lower	Upper	Overall	Lower	Upper	Overall	Lower	Upper	Overall
128	4.8	5.5	10.3	2.1	2.0	4.1	2.3	2.7	2.5
256	36.4	40.0	76.4	9.7	5.4	15.1	3.8	7.4	5.1
512	517.2	393.3	910.5	69.7	35.3	105.0	7.4	11.1	8.7
1024	3,828.0	2,937.5	6,765.5	531.7	266.6	798.3	7.2	11.0	8.5
2048	29,687.0	22,560.9	52,247.9	4,156.2	2,084.3	6,240.5	7.1	10.8	8.4
4096	233,969.0	183,281.0	417,250.0	32,969.0	16,610.0	49,579.0	7.1	11.0	8.4

43.5 Conclusion and Further Work

The GPU implementation of the distance-bound smoothing procedure achieves a speedup of more than eight when compared to a CPU-only implementation. This is due to the parallel nature as well as high memory bandwidth of graphics hardware. Further work can proceed in two directions: (1) designing algorithms to accommodate

GPU memory limitations in order to increase the solvable problem size (4096 atoms is a modest size for a protein molecule) and (2) overlapping the computation between the CPU and the GPU.

To overcome the 4096×4096 pbuffer size restriction, the algorithm should be designed so that segments (stripes or blocks) of the adjacency matrix can be updated one at a time. Thus, the adjacency matrix would be distributed among several pixel buffers. An application-specific method for explicitly caching data in the GPU memory should also be developed to overcome the physical restriction on GPU memory. Alternatively, a recursive approach similar to the one in Park et al. 2002 could be adopted, with the GPU executing the base cases.

Sharing the computation load between the CPU and the GPU will require data transfer between the GPU and CPU memories n times for a graph on n nodes. However, the overhead may be acceptable because for each of n iterations, only one row and one column need to be communicated. Thus, communication cost is $O(n^2)$ while computation complexity is $O(n^3)$.

43.6 References

Bertsekas, D. P. 1993. "A Simple and Fast Label Correcting Algorithm for Shortest Paths." *Networks* 23, pp. 703–709.

Cormen, T. H., C. E. Leiserson, R. L. Rivest, and C. Stein. 2001. *Introduction to Algorithms*. MIT Press.

Dress, W. M., and T. F. Havel. 1988. "Shortest-Path Problems and Molecular Conformation." *Discrete Applied Mathematics* 19, pp. 129–144.

Mark, W. R., R. S. Glanville, K. Akeley, and M. J. Kilgard. 2003. "Cg: A System for Programming Graphics Hardware in a C-like Language." *ACM Transactions on Graphics (Proceedings of SIGGRAPH 2003)* 22(3), pp. 896–907.

Park, J.-S., M. Penner, and V. K. Prasanna. 2002. "Optimizing Graph Algorithms for Improved Cache Performance." *IEEE Transactions on Parallel and Distributed Systems* 15(9), pp. 769–782.

The author would like to thank Mark Harris and Rayann Kovacik for helpful suggestions.

Chapter 44

A GPU Framework for Solving Systems of Linear Equations

Jens Krüger
Technische Universität München

Rüdiger Westermann
Technische Universität München

44.1 Overview

The development of numerical techniques for solving partial differential equations (PDEs) is a traditional subject in applied mathematics. These techniques have a variety of applications in physics-based simulation and modeling, geometry processing, and image filtering, and they have been frequently employed in computer graphics to provide realistic simulation of real-world phenomena.

One of the basic methods to solve a PDE is to transform it into a large linear system of equations via discretization. This system can then be solved using linear algebra operations.

In this chapter, we present a general framework for the computation of linear algebra operations on programmable graphics hardware. Built upon efficient representations of vectors and matrices on the GPU, vector-vector and matrix-vector operations are implemented using fragment programs on DirectX 9-class hardware. By means of these operations, implicit solvers for systems of algebraic equations can be implemented, thus enabling stable numerical simulation on programmable graphics hardware.

We describe a C++ class hierarchy that allows easy and efficient use of the proposed operations. The library provides routines for solving systems of linear equations, least-squares solutions of linear systems of equations, and standard operations on vector and matrix elements. Our system handles dense, banded, and general sparse matrices. The complete library, together with the "implicit water surface" demo (see Figure 44-9, later in the chapter), can be found on this book's CD.

We demonstrate the efficiency of our GPU solver using a particular PDE: the Poisson equation. Poisson's equation is of particular importance in physics, and its solution is frequently employed in computer graphics for the simulation of fluids and flow (as shown in Figure 44-10, later in the chapter). Throughout this chapter, we show a variety of graphics effects that involve the solution of this PDE.

44.2 Representation

To solve linear PDEs on the GPU, we need a linear algebra package. Built upon efficient GPU representations of scalar values, vectors, and matrices, such a package can implement high-performance linear algebra operations such as vector-vector and matrix-vector operations. In this section, we describe in more detail the internal representation of linear algebra operators in our GPU linear algebra library.

44.2.1 The "Single Float" Representation

In addition to representing vectors and matrices, the library needs to represent individual scalar floating-point values. At first glance, a representation of single floating-point values on the GPU might seem needless; the values could just be given via uniform program parameters. However, because many operations generate and work with single scalar values, we need to carefully choose how to represent such values on the GPU. A reasonable representation (and one that fits well with the representations of other types) is to use single-element textures. Because GPUs provide an efficient memory interface to texture data, in our system, single floating-point values are stored in textures of size 1×1. No matter the actual size of the GPU texture cache, we can safely assume that one float value will fit into it.

44.2.2 Vectors

Because a vector is a 1D data structure, we could simply represent a vector as a 1D texture on the GPU. The drawbacks of such a representation quickly become apparent after investigating the constraints that are imposed on textures by the GPU. All textures on current generations of GPUs are limited in size; this limit is currently 4096 for 1D textures. Thus we can represent only vectors of length 4096 using 1D textures, which is not sufficient for the simulation of reasonable problem sizes. In addition, we often will compute a vector as the result of a computation by rendering a primitive that covers the area of the vector being computed. On recent GPUs, rendering 2D textured primitives is far faster than rendering 1D primitives that generate the same number of fragments. Therefore, we reorder 1D vectors to be laid out as 2D textures on the GPU, as illustrated in Figure 44-1. To further reduce the size of the internal representation, we pack contiguous blocks of 2×2 entries into one RGBA texel. On some GPUs, this layout also improves texture access performance.

Now that we have an efficient vector representation, we can advance to a more complex linear algebra entity: the matrix.

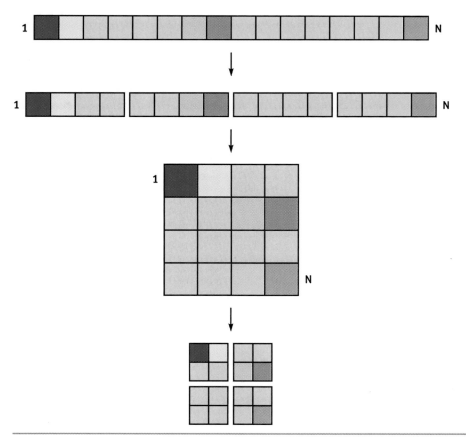

Figure 44-1. Representing a 1D Vector on the GPU
Our system represents 1D vectors in 2D textures, leading to greater efficiency and the ability to support much larger vectors than 1D textures allow.

44.2.3 Matrices

While vectors are usually treated as *full vectors*—vectors in which practically all elements are nonzero—matrices often have only a few nonzero entries, especially those matrices derived from PDE discretizations. Therefore, we describe different representations for different types of matrices. We start with the representation for *full matrices*, also called *dense matrices*, in which almost every value is nonzero. Later we take a look at alternative *sparse matrix* types.

Full Matrices

To represent a dense matrix, we split up the matrix into a set of column vectors and store each vector in the format described earlier. Figure 44-2 illustrates the procedure. As we show later, matrix-vector operations can be performed very efficiently on this representation.

Banded Sparse Matrices

In real-world applications, sparse matrices exhibiting a regular pattern of nonzero elements often arise from domain discretizations. Banded matrices occur if computations on grid points in a regular grid involve a fixed stencil of adjacent grid points. Then, nonzero elements are arranged in a diagonal pattern. See Equation 44-1 for an example of such a matrix.

$$
\begin{bmatrix}
4\alpha+1 & -\alpha & & -\alpha & & & & & \\
-\alpha & 4\alpha+1 & -\alpha & & -\alpha & & & & \\
& -\alpha & 4\alpha+1 & & & -\alpha & & & \\
-\alpha & \cdot & & 4\alpha+1 & -\alpha & & -\alpha & & \\
& -\alpha & & -\alpha & 4\alpha+1 & -\alpha & & -\alpha & \\
& & -\alpha & & -\alpha & 4\alpha+1 & & & -\alpha \\
& & & -\alpha & & & 4\alpha+1 & -\alpha & \\
& & & & -\alpha & & -\alpha & 4\alpha+1 & -\alpha \\
& & & & & -\alpha & & -\alpha & 4\alpha+1
\end{bmatrix}
\begin{bmatrix}
y_1^{t+1} \\ y_2^{t+1} \\ y_3^{t+1} \\ y_4^{t+1} \\ y_5^{t+1} \\ y_6^{t+1} \\ y_7^{t+1} \\ y_8^{t+1} \\ y_9^{t+1}
\end{bmatrix}
=
\begin{bmatrix}
c_1^t \\ c_2^t \\ c_3^t \\ c_4^t \\ c_5^t \\ c_6^t \\ c_7^t \\ c_8^t \\ c_9^t
\end{bmatrix},
$$

where $c_i^t = \alpha \times \left(y_{i-1,j}^t + y_{i,j-1}^t + y_{i+1,j}^t + y_{i,j+1}^t \right) + (2 - 4\alpha) \times y_{i,j}^t - y_{i,j}^{t-1}$

Equation 44-1. A Banded Sparse Matrix After Discretization of the 2D Wave Equation

Representing such matrices as full matrices wastes a lot of space and leads to unnecessary numerical computations, because zero elements cannot easily be discarded during computations on the GPU. Therefore, we need a special representation for this type of

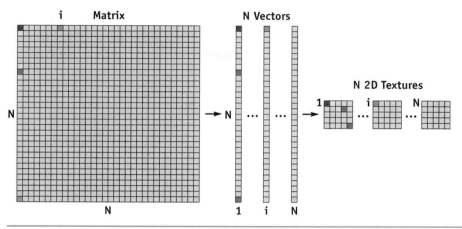

Figure 44-2. Representing a Dense Matrix on the GPU

matrix. Due to the diagonal structure, this becomes straightforward: instead of storing the columns of the matrix, we store its diagonals in the proposed vector format. Note that in this representation, some space for the *off-middle* diagonals is wasted and padded with zeroes. If the matrix has many nonzero diagonals and a significant amount of memory is wasted this way, we can combine two opposing diagonals into one vector. See Figure 44-3 for an example. By doing so, we can store even a full matrix in the diagonal format without wasting a single byte of texture space.

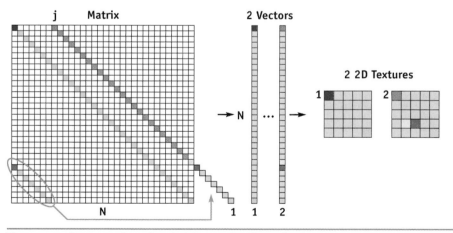

Figure 44-3. Representing a Banded Sparse Matrix on the GPU
Two diagonals can be combined into one texture vector.

Random Sparse Matrices

Now let's have a closer look at how to represent matrices in which nonzero elements are scattered randomly. In this case, a texture-based representation either leads to highly fragmented textures that waste a lot of space or else requires a complex indexing scheme that significantly reduces the performance of matrix access operations. For this particular kind of matrix, we prefer a vertex-based representation: We generate one vertex for sets of four nonzero entries in a matrix row. We choose the position of this vertex in such a way that it encodes the row index as a 2D coordinate; the vertex renders at exactly the same position where the respective vector element was rendered via the corresponding 2D texture. Similarly, we encode columns as 2D indices in texture coordinates 1 through 4. Matrix entries are stored in the XYZW components of the first texture coordinate of each vertex. Then we store the entire set of vertices in a vertex buffer on the GPU. As long as the matrix is not going to be modified, the internal representation does not have to be changed. The left part of Figure 44-4 shows the encoding scheme (we explain the matrix-vector product on the right side in Section 44.3.3).

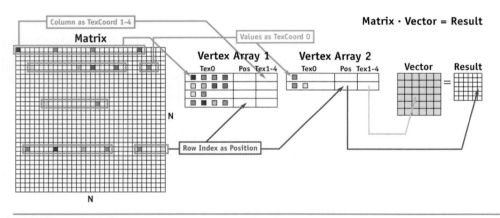

Figure 44-4. Representing a Random Sparse Matrix
The matrix-vector product is explained in Section 44.3.3.

44.3 Operations

Now that we have representations for scalars, vectors, and matrices, let's describe some basic operations on these representations. Again, we begin with the simplest case: a component-wise vector-vector operation.

44.3.1 Vector Arithmetic

Using the vector representation as proposed, a vector-vector operation reduces to rendering a dual-textured quad. To explain our approach, we describe the implementation of a vector-vector sum, as shown in Figure 44-5.

First we set up the viewport to cover exactly as many pixels as there are elements in the 2D target vector, and we make the target vector texture the current render target. We then render a quad that covers the entire viewport. Vertices pass through the vertex stage to the rasterizer, which generates one fragment for every vector element. For every fragment, a fragment program is executed. The program fetches respective elements from both operand vectors, adds these values together, and writes the result into the render target. Note that the result is already in the appropriate format and is ready to be used in upcoming operations. In particular, elements don't need to be rearranged, and the processing of RGBA encoded data is done simultaneously.

While the vector-vector sum operates component-wise on its input operands and outputs a vector of equal length, other operations reduce the contents of a vector to a single scalar value—for instance, computing the sum of all vector elements.

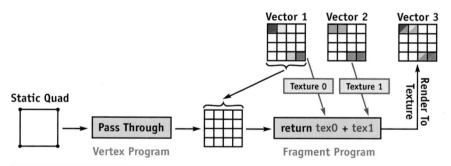

Figure 44-5. An Example of a Vector-Vector Add Operation

44.3.2 Vector Reduce

A vector that is represented by a texture of size $n \times n$ can be reduced to the sum of the values of its elements in $\log(n)$ passes. Starting with the original 2D texture, we set up a viewport of half the size of this texture in both directions. A full-screen quad is rendered into this viewport, and a fragment program fetches four adjacent values from the current source texture. These values are added, and they are written into the render texture target, which becomes the source texture in the next pass. We repeat this process $\log(n)$ times to produce the sum of all elements, which is written into the single float texture described earlier. Figure 44-6 gives an overview of this process.

Now that we have found a way to handle component-wise operations and reduce operations, we have all we need to operate on vectors. We now advance to the matrix operations.

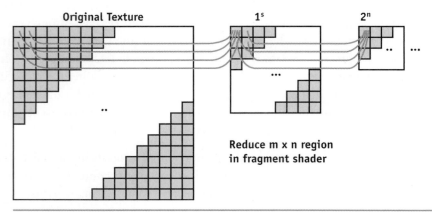

Figure 44-6. A Vector Reduction Operation

44.3.3 Matrix-Vector Product

The way we compute a matrix-vector product depends on whether our matrix is stored in the vector stack format (for banded and full matrices) or in the vertex format (for random sparse matrices).

Full and Banded Sparse Matrix-Vector Product

To compute a matrix-vector product, we split up the computation into a series of vector-vector products. Again, we show the process by means of an example. The banded sparse matrix-vector product and full matrix-vector product algorithms are the same. For this example, we use a matrix with two nonzero diagonals, as shown in Figure 44-7.

As we described in the previous section, the matrix **A** is encoded as two vectors stored in two 2D textures, and the upper diagonal is padded with zeroes. The vector is stored as a single 2D texture. We compute the final result in two passes. First we write a vector-vector product of the left diagonal and **b** into **x**. Then **b** is shifted by two elements and another vector-vector product of this shifted **b** and the second diagonal of **A** is added to the intermediate result of the first pass, stored in **x**. We perform the shift

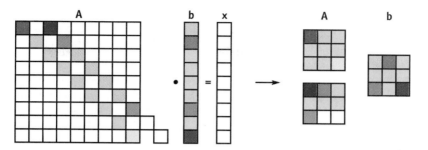

Figure 44-7. Setup for the Matrix-Vector Product **A · b = x**

with a texture coordinate transformation, so that we don't need any expensive element moves. After these two vector-vector products, we are already done! The vector **x** now stores the final result of the matrix-vector product, and once again no further processing or rearranging is needed.

The only change needed to compute a full matrix-vector product is to skip the coordinate shift of **b**. The random sparse matrix representation, however, requires slightly different handling.

Random Sparse Matrix-Vector Product

The general approach to computing this matrix-vector product has already been encoded into the production scheme of the vertices. Let's take a look at how a result vector **x** is computed from a matrix **A** and vector **b**.

$$
\begin{bmatrix}
a_{1,1} & a_{1,2} & \cdots & a_{1,n} \\
a_{2,1} & & & \vdots \\
\vdots & & \ddots & \\
a_{2,n} & \cdots & & a_{n,n}
\end{bmatrix}
\begin{bmatrix}
b_1 \\ b_2 \\ \vdots \\ b_n
\end{bmatrix}
=
\begin{bmatrix}
x_1 \\ x_2 \\ \vdots \\ x_n
\end{bmatrix}
\quad \Rightarrow \quad
x_i = \sum_{j=1}^{n} a_{i,j} \times b_j
$$

Equation 44-2. Matrix-Vector Product

You can see that the row index i influences the final position of the value $a_{i,j}$, while the column index j specifies what values of the vector **b** are to be combined with $a_{i,j}$. Taking a second look at Figure 44-4 reveals that for a given matrix entry, the column is encoded in the vertex position while the row is encoded as a texture coordinate. To compute the result vector **x**, all we have to do is render the vertices as points into the texture of **x** while multiplying the color values with values fetched from **b** using the given texture coordinates. This automatically places the values at the correct positions within the target vector and fetches the correct combination from the vector **b**. As always, after all points are rendered, the vector-matrix product is stored in the texture of vector **x** in the correct format.

Note that even though this product is computed in a completely different way compared to the full or banded sparse matrix-vector product, the input and output vector types are identical to the ones used before. This means that we can use both matrix types simultaneously in one algorithm.

44.3.4 Putting It All Together

Now that we know how to implement the very basic linear algebra operations, we can put them together into a C++ framework. Figure 44-8 shows a simplified UML diagram of how our library is organized.

The classes marked in green are the interface classes; the others provide internal structure. One can see that in addition to the operations described earlier, we have implemented other methods such as data setting and getting functions—implemented as texture uploads and downloads—and packing and unpacking routines to convert from RGBA-encoded to nonencoded vectors and back. The clMemMan class is a virtual

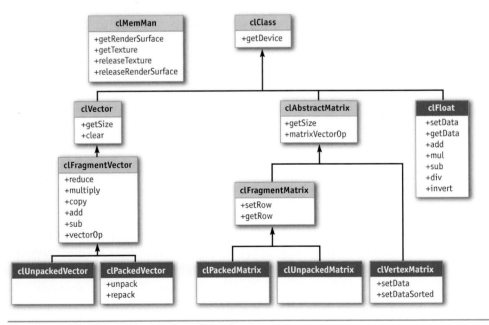

Figure 44-8. The Linear Algebra Class Collection

memory manager that is useful because some computations, such as reduce, need intermediate textures. Because the memory space on the GPU is limited, these textures should be shared among vectors. The clMemMan class manages a pool of textures to be used by the vectors and matrices.

44.3.5 Conjugate Gradient Solver

We now possess an easy-to-use class framework that completely abstracts the underlying hardware implementation, so we can easily write more-complex algorithms such as the conjugate gradient linear system solver. Using our implementation, the complete GPU conjugate gradient class appears in Listing 44-1.

Listing 44-1. The Conjugate Gradient Solver

```
void clCGSolver::solveInit() {
  Matrix->matrixVectorOp(CL_SUB, X, B, R);   // R = A * x - b
  R->multiply(-1);   // R = -R
  R->clone(P);   // P =  R
  R->reduceAdd(R, Rho);   // rho = sum(R * R);
}
void clCGSolver::solveIteration() {
  Matrix->matrixVectorOp(CL_NULL, P, NULL,Q);   // Q = Ap;
  P->reduceAdd(Q, Temp);   // temp  = sum(P * Q);
  Rho->div(Temp, Alpha);   // alpha = rho/temp;
  X->addVector(P, X, 1, Alpha);   // X = X + alpha * P
  R->subtractVector(Q, R, 1, Alpha);   // R = R - alpha * Q
  R->reduceAdd(R, NewRho);   // newrho = sum(R * R);
  NewRho->divZ(Rho, Beta);   // beta = newrho/rho
  R->addVector(P, P, 1, Beta);   // P = R + beta * P;
  clFloat *temp; temp=NewRho;
  NewRho=Rho; Rho=temp;   // swap rho and newrho pointers
}
void clCGSolver::solve(int maxI) {
  solveInit();
  for (int i = 0; i < maxI; i++) solveIteration();
}

int clCGSolver::solve(float rhoTresh, int maxI) {
  solveInit(); Rho->clone(NewRho);
  for (int i = 0; i < maxI && NewRho.getData() > rhoTresh; i++)
    solveIteration();
  return i;
}
```

The code demonstrates the goal of our linear algebra framework: to abstract all GPU-specific details of the computation. Now, more complex algorithms can be built on top of this framework. In the following section, we demonstrate its use for numerical simulation.

44.4 A Sample Partial Differential Equation

In this section, we show how to numerically solve a particular linear PDE—the 2D wave equation—on the GPU. The 2D wave equation, shown in Equation 44-3, describes the behavior of an oscillating membrane such as a shallow water surface. The equation describes the dynamic behavior of membrane displacements y depending on wave speed c. Here, t refers to time, and x and z represent the 2D spatial domain.

$$c^2 \left(\frac{\partial^2 y}{\partial x^2} + \frac{\partial^2 y}{\partial z^2} \right) = \frac{\partial^2 y}{\partial t^2}$$

Equation 44-3. 2D Shallow-Water Wave Equation

To numerically solve this PDE, we first discretize it into a set of finite-difference equations by replacing partial derivatives with central differences. A central-difference approximation can be derived from the Taylor expansion, shown in Equation 44-4. The equation shows first-order forward, backward, and central differences, as well as second-order central differences.

$$f(x) = f(x + \Delta h) + f'(x + \Delta h) \times \Delta h + \Omega(\Delta h)$$

$$\Rightarrow \left(\frac{\partial y}{\partial h} \right)_{i,j} = \begin{cases} \dfrac{y_{i+1,j} - y_{i,j}}{\Delta h} + O(\Delta h) \\[2ex] \dfrac{y_{i,j} - y_{i-1,j}}{\Delta h} + O(\Delta h) \\[2ex] \dfrac{y_{i+1,j} - y_{i-1,j}}{2\Delta h} + O(\Delta h)^2 \end{cases}$$

$$\Rightarrow \left(\frac{\partial^2 y}{\partial h^2} \right)_{i,j} = \frac{y_{i+1,j} - 2y_{i,j} + y_{i-1,j}}{(\Delta h)^2} + O(\Delta h)^2$$

Equation 44-4. Taylor Expansion and Central Differences

By applying the central differences of Equation 44-4 to Equation 44-3, we get the system of difference equations shown in Equation 44-5.

$$\frac{y_{i,j}^{t+1} - 2y_{i,j}^{t} + y_{i,j}^{t-1}}{(\Delta t)^2} = c^2 \left(\frac{y_{i+1,j}^{t} - 2y_{i,j}^{t} + y_{i-1,j}^{t}}{(\Delta x)^2} + \frac{y_{i,j+1}^{t} - 2y_{i,j}^{t} + y_{i,j-1}^{t}}{(\Delta z)^2} \right) \quad \Bigg| \quad x = z = h$$

$$\Leftrightarrow \frac{y_{i,j}^{t+1} - 2y_{i,j}^{t} + y_{i,j}^{t-1}}{(\Delta t)^2} = c^2 \left(\frac{y_{i+1,j}^{t} - 2y_{i,j}^{t} + y_{i-1,j}^{t}}{(\Delta h)^2} + \frac{y_{i,j+1}^{t} - 2y_{i,j}^{t} + y_{i,j-1}^{t}}{(\Delta h)^2} \right)$$

$$\Leftrightarrow y_{i,j}^{t+1} = \beta \cdot \left(y_{i+1,j}^{t} + y_{i-1,j}^{t} + y_{i,j+1}^{t} + y_{i,j-1}^{t} \right) + (2 - 4\beta) y_{i,j}^{t} - y_{i,j}^{t-1},$$

where $\beta = \dfrac{c^2 (\Delta t)^2}{(\Delta h)^2}$

Equation 44-5. The Explicit Discrete 2D Wave Equation

Equation 44-5 can now be rewritten as a matrix-vector operation, using the operands in Equation 44-6.

$$
\begin{bmatrix}
2-4\beta & \beta & & \beta & & & & & \\
\beta & 2-4\beta & \beta & & \beta & & & & \\
& \beta & 2-4\beta & & & \beta & & & \\
\beta & & & 2-4\beta & \beta & & \beta & & \\
& \beta & & \beta & 2-4\beta & \beta & & \beta & \\
& & \beta & & \beta & 2-4\beta & & & \beta \\
& & & \beta & & & 2-4\beta & \beta & \\
& & & & \beta & & \beta & 2-4\beta & \beta \\
& & & & & \beta & & \beta & 2-4\beta
\end{bmatrix}
\begin{bmatrix}
y_1^t \\ y_2^t \\ y_3^t \\ y_4^t \\ y_5^t \\ y_6^t \\ y_7^t \\ y_8^t \\ y_9^t
\end{bmatrix}
-
\begin{bmatrix}
y_1^{t-1} \\ y_2^{t-1} \\ y_3^{t-1} \\ y_4^{t-1} \\ y_5^{t-1} \\ y_6^{t-1} \\ y_7^{t-1} \\ y_8^{t-1} \\ y_9^{t-1}
\end{bmatrix}
=
\begin{bmatrix}
y_1^{t+1} \\ y_2^{t+1} \\ y_3^{t+1} \\ y_4^{t+1} \\ y_5^{t+1} \\ y_6^{t+1} \\ y_7^{t+1} \\ y_8^{t+1} \\ y_9^{t+1}
\end{bmatrix}
$$

Equation 44-6. Explicit Discrete 2D Wave Equation Written as a Matrix-Vector Operation

The new values for $y_{i,j}^{t+1}$ can be computed easily with our framework by applying one matrix-vector operation:

```
clMatrix->matrixVectorOp(CL_SUB, clCurrent, clLast, clNext);

clLast->copyVector(clCurrent);        // save for next iteration
clCurrent->copyVector(clNext);        // save for next iteration
cluNext->unpack(clNext);              // unpack for rendering

renderHF(cluNext->m_pVectorTexture);  // render as height field
```

Although this method is very fast, it is only conditionally stable. If the integration time step becomes too large, the system will become unstable—a well-known drawback of explicit approaches. Therefore, we will employ an implicit scheme to numerically solve the wave equation.

44.4.1 The Crank-Nicholson Scheme

To turn this unstable discretization of the wave equation into an unconditionally stable version, we use the Crank-Nicholson scheme. In this scheme, the average of the current and the next time steps is used for the special discretization. This yields the formula shown in Equation 44-7.

$$\frac{y_{i,j}^{t+1} - 2y_{i,j}^{t} + y_{i,j}^{t-1}}{(\Delta t)^2} = \frac{1}{2}c^2\left(\frac{y_{i+1,j}^{t} - 2y_{i,j}^{t} + y_{i-1,j}^{t}}{(\Delta h)^2} + \frac{y_{i,j+1}^{t} - 2y_{i,j}^{t} + y_{i,j-1}^{t}}{(\Delta h)^2}\right)$$

$$+ \frac{1}{2}c^2\left(\frac{y_{i+1,j}^{t+1} - 2y_{i,j}^{t+1} + y_{i-1,j}^{t+1}}{(\Delta h)^2} + \frac{y_{i,j+1}^{t+1} - 2y_{i,j}^{t+1} + y_{i,j-1}^{t+1}}{(\Delta h)^2}\right)$$

$$\Leftrightarrow (1 + 4\alpha)\,y_{i,j}^{t+1} - \alpha \times \left(y_{i+1,j}^{t+1} + y_{i-1,j}^{t+1} + y_{i,j+1}^{t+1} + y_{i,j-1}^{t+1}\right)$$

$$= \alpha \times \left(y_{i+1,j}^{t} + y_{i-1,j}^{t} + y_{i,j+1}^{t} + y_{i,j-1}^{t}\right) + (2 - 4\alpha)\,y_{i,j}^{t} - y_{i,j}^{t-1},$$

where $\alpha = \dfrac{c^2(\Delta t)^2}{2(\Delta h)^2}$

Equation 44-7. Implicit Discrete 2D Wave Equation

If we write this as a matrix-vector product, we get the matrix from the beginning of this chapter in Equation 44-1. However, finding a solution for $y_{i,j}^{t+1}$ now requires a solver for a system of linear equations. Fortunately, we have developed a solver for such matrices already: the conjugate gradient solver. The program to implicitly solve the wave equation now looks like this:

```
cluRHS->computeRHS(cluLast, cluCurrent);  // generate c(i, j, t)
clRHS->repack(cluRHS);                     // encode into RGBA

iSteps = pCGSolver->solve(iMaxSteps);      // solve using CG

cluLast->copyVector(cluCurrent);           // save for next iteration
clNext->unpack(cluCurrent);                // unpack for rendering
renderHF(cluCurrent->m_pVectorTexture);
```

As you can see, with only a few more lines of code—and with the help of the linear algebra framework—we can turn an unstable solution into an unconditionally stable version that allows us to increase the simulation step size and improve performance. Moreover, for some problems, explicit solutions do not work at all; without an implicit solver, some simulations cannot be implemented. An example is the Poisson-pressure equation that arises in the solution of the Navier-Stokes equations for fluid flow. See Figures 44-9 and 44-10.

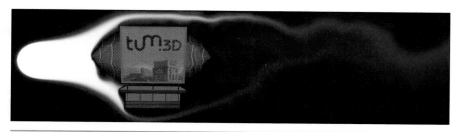

Figure 44-9. A Navier-Stokes Fluid Dynamics Simulation
On a 512 x 128 grid running at 110 frames/sec, including rendering time.

Figure 44-10. Simulation of the 2D Wave Equation on a 1024 × 1024 Grid

44.5 Conclusion

In this chapter, we have described a general framework for the implementation of numerical simulation techniques on graphics hardware; our emphasis has been on providing building blocks for the design of general numerical computing techniques. The framework includes our efficient internal layouts for vectors and matrices. By considering matrices as a set of diagonal or column vectors and by representing vectors as 2D texture maps, matrix-vector and vector-vector operations can be accelerated considerably compared to software-based approaches. Table 44-1 shows the performance of our framework on the NVIDIA GeForce 6800 GT, including basic framework operations and the complete sample application using the conjugate gradient solver. We achieve about the same performance on other vendors' GPUs, with some vendor-specific optimizations during initialization, such as texture allocation order.

Table 44-1. Timings for the Framework and Sample Application
As measured on an NVIDIA GeForce 6800 GT

	Resolution					
	2048×1024	1024×1024	1024×512	512×512	512×256	256×256
Vector Reduce	1.11 ms	0.49 ms	0.28 ms	0.17 ms	0.16 ms	0.14 ms
Vector-Vector Operation	0.89 ms	0.31 ms	0.15 ms	0.08 ms	0.04 ms	0.02 ms
2D Wave Equation Demo	12 fps	27 fps	52 fps	102 fps	185 fps	335 fps

44.6 References

Bolz, J., I. Farmer, E. Grinspun, and P. Schröder. 2003. "Sparse Matrix Solvers on the GPU: Conjugate Gradients and Multigrid." *ACM Transactions on Graphics (Proceedings of SIGGRAPH 2003)* 22(3), pp. 917–924.

Krüger, Jens, and Rüdiger Westermann. 2003. "Linear Algebra Operators for GPU Implementation of Numerical Algorithms." *ACM Transactions on Graphics (Proceedings of SIGGRAPH 2003)* 22(3), pp. 908–916.

Chapter 45

Options Pricing on the GPU

Craig Kolb
NVIDIA Corporation

Matt Pharr
NVIDIA Corporation

In the past three decades, options and other derivatives have become increasingly important financial tools. Options are commonly used to hedge the risk associated with investing in securities, and to take advantage of pricing anomalies in the market via arbitrage.

A key requirement for utilizing options is calculating their fair value. Finding ways of efficiently solving this pricing problem has been an active field of research for more than thirty years, and it continues to be a focus of modern financial engineering. As more computation has been applied to finance-related problems, finding efficient ways to implement these algorithms on modern architectures has become more important.

This chapter describes how options can be priced efficiently using the GPU. We perform our evaluations using two different pricing models: the Black-Scholes model and lattice models. Both of these approaches map well to the GPU, and both are substantially faster on the GPU than on modern CPUs. Although both also have straightforward mappings to the GPU, implementing lattice models requires additional work because of interdependencies in the calculations.

45.1 What Are Options?

Options belong to the family of investment tools known as *derivatives*. Traditional investment instruments, such as real estate or stocks, have inherent value. Options, on the other hand, *derive* their value from another investment instrument, known as the *underlying asset*. The underlying asset is typically stock or another form of security.

Options come in several varieties. A *call option* contract gives the purchaser (or *holder*) the right, *but not the obligation*, to buy the underlying asset for a particular, predetermined price at some future date. The predetermined price is known as the *strike price*, and the future date is termed the *expiration date*. Similarly, a *put* gives the holder the option of selling the underlying asset for a predetermined price on the expiration date.

For example, consider a call option written on the stock of the XYZ Corporation. Imagine that this contract guaranteed that you could buy 100 shares of XYZ's stock at a price of $100 six months from today. If the stock were trading for less than $100 on the date of expiration, it would make little sense to exercise the option—you could buy the stock for less money on the open market, after all. In this case, you would simply let the option expire, worthless. On the other hand, if XYZ were trading for, say, $120 per share on the expiration date, you would exercise the option to buy the shares at $100 each. If you then sold the shares immediately, you would profit $20 a share, minus whatever you had paid for the option.

As just illustrated, both the strike price, X, and the price of the underlying asset at the expiration date strongly influence the future value of the option, and thus how much you should pay for it today. Under certain simplifying assumptions, we can statistically model the asset's future price fluctuations using its current price, S, and its volatility, v, which describes how widely the price changes over time.

A number of additional factors influence how much you'd likely be willing to pay for an option:

- **The time to the expiration date, T.** Longer terms imply a wider range of possible values for the underlying asset on the expiration date, and thus more uncertainty about the value of the option when it expires.

- **The riskless rate of return, r.** Even if the option made you a profit of P dollars six months from now, the value of those P dollars to you today is less than P. If a bond or other "riskless" investment paid interest at a continually compounded annual rate of r, you could simply invest $P \times e^{-r(6/12)}$ dollars in the bond today, and you would be guaranteed the same P dollars six months from now. As such, the value of an asset at some future time $0 < t \leq T$ must be *discounted* by multiplying it by e^{-rt} in order to determine its effective value today.

- **Exercise restrictions.** So far, we have discussed only so-called *European* options, which may be exercised only on the day the option expires. Other types of options with different exercise restrictions also exist. In particular, *American* options may be exercised at any time up to and including the expiration date. This added flexibility means that an American option will be priced at least as high as the corresponding European option.

Other factors, such as dividend payouts, can also enter into the picture. For this chapter, however, we will limit ourselves to the preceding considerations.

The rest of this chapter describes two standard methods of pricing options and how they are traditionally implemented on the CPU. We show how these methods can be implemented on the GPU with greater throughput, as measured by the number of options priced per second.

We omit the majority of the mathematical details in the discussion that follows. See Hull 2002 for extensive background material, including supporting theory, derivations, and assumptions used in these pricing models.

45.2 The Black-Scholes Model

In 1973, Fischer Black and Myron Scholes famously derived an analytical means of computing the price of European options (Black and Scholes 1973). For this work, Scholes was awarded the Nobel Prize for economics in 1997. (Black had passed away before the prize was awarded.)

The Black-Scholes equation is a differential equation that describes how, under a certain set of assumptions, the value of an option changes as the price of the underlying asset changes. More precisely, it is a *stochastic* differential equation; it includes a random-walk term—which models the random fluctuation of the price of the underlying asset over time—in addition to a deterministic term. This random term necessitates using slightly different mathematical tools than you'd normally use to solve differential equations; see the references for details.

The Black-Scholes equation implies that the value of a European call option, V, may be computed as:

$$V = S \times CND(d_1) - Xe^{-rT} \times CND(d_2),$$

where

$$d_1 = \frac{\log\left(\dfrac{S}{X}\right) + T\left(r + \dfrac{v^2}{2}\right)}{v\sqrt{T}},$$

$$d_2 = d_1 - v\sqrt{T}.$$

(The formula for a put option is similar.) The cumulative normal distribution function, $CND(x)$, gives the probability that a normally distributed random variable will have a value less than x. There is no closed-form expression for this function, and as such it must be evaluated numerically. It is typically approximated using a polynomial function, as we do here.

We use the GPGPU framework described in Chapter 31 of this book, "Mapping Computational Concepts to GPUs," together with the Cg code in Listing 45-1, to price options in parallel on the GPU. We first initialize four 2D arrays of data with the exercise price, asset price, time to expiration, and asset volatility corresponding to each option, with the input data for a particular option residing at the same location in each array. It is then a simple matter to price all of the options in parallel by running the fragment program at every pixel. For our tests, we assumed that the riskless rate of return for all options was constant and thus could be given via a uniform parameter to the Cg program. For some applications, it may also be useful to vary this value, a straightforward change to the program. The implementation of the cumulative normal distribution function, CND(), is shown later in Listing 45-2.

Listing 45-1. Implementing the Black-Scholes Model in Cg

```
float BlackScholesCall(float S, float X, float T, float r, float v) {
  float d1 = (log(S/X) + (r + v * v * .5f) * T) / (v * sqrt(T));
  float d2 = d1 - v * sqrt(T);
  return S * CND(d1) - X * exp(-r * T) * CND(d2);
}
```

Pricing a given option using this method thus depends on five input parameters, requires a relatively large amount of floating-point calculation, and produces a single float-point value. The result is a computation with very high arithmetic intensity, making it extremely well suited for running on the GPU, as can be seen in Figure 45-1.

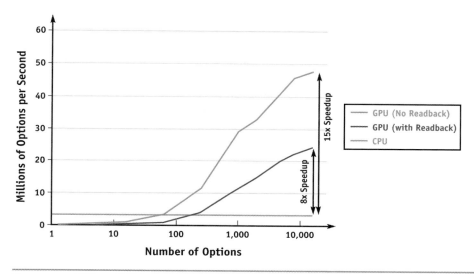

Figure 45-1. GPU vs. CPU Performance of Black-Scholes Option Pricing
The horizontal axis gives the total number of pricing problems to be solved. The GPU substantially outperforms the CPU when enough options are priced to allow for high resource utilization, and to allow the constant costs of GPU buffer management to be amortized. The "GPU, no readback" results exclude the time required to read back results from the GPU. If both data upload and readback time are ignored and pure compute power is measured, GPU performance peaks at 220 million options per second, a factor of 55 times faster than the CPU. We used a GeForce 6800 to generate the GPU results and an AMD Athlon 64 3200+ with 1 GB of memory to generate the CPU results.

Listing 45-2 shows that, rather than directly evaluate the polynomial—for example, using Horner's rule—a more efficient approach for the GPU is to take advantage of its four-way vector hardware, precompute the powers of K, and use the dot() function to quickly compute an inner product with appropriate constants.

Interestingly enough, the PCI Express bus has the potential to be the bottleneck for a GPU implementation of this model: assuming ideal PCI Express performance of 4 GB/sec of bandwidth, it is possible to transfer 1 billion 4-byte floating-point values to and from the GPU each second. For our test program, 4 of the input parameters were varying, which means that it is possible to feed the GPU enough data to do roughly 250 million Black-Scholes computations per second (4 GB/sec divided by 4 values times 4 bytes per float value). The Black-Scholes implementation here compiles to approximately 50 floating-point operations. Therefore, any GPU that is capable of more than 10 Gflops of arithmetic computation will be limited by the rate at which data can be sent to the GPU (recall that current GPUs are capable of hundreds of Gflops of computation).

Listing 45-2. Implementing the Cumulative Normal Distribution Function

```
float CND(float X)
{
    float L = abs(X);
    // Set up float4 so that K.x = K, K.y = K^2, K.z = K^3, K.w = K^4
    float4 K;
    K.x = 1.0 / (1.0 + 0.2316419 * L);
    K.y = K.x * K.x;
    K.zw = K.xy * K.yy;

    // compute K, K^2, K^3, and K^4 terms, reordered for efficient
    // vectorization. Above, we precomputed the K powers; here we'll
    // multiply each one by its corresponding scale and sum up the
    // terms efficiently with the dot() routine.
    //
    // dot(float4(a, b, c, d), float4(e, f, g, h)) efficiently computes
    // the inner product a*e + b*f + c*g + d*h, making much better
    // use of the 4-way vector floating-point hardware than a
    // straightforward implementation would.
    float w = dot(float4(0.31938153f, -0.356563782f,
                        1.781477937f, -1.821255978f), K);
    // and add in the K^5 term on its own
    w += 1.330274429f * K.w * K.x;
    w *= rsqrt(2.f * PI) * exp(-L * L * .5f); // rsqrt() == 1/sqrt()

    if (X > 0)
        w = 1.0 - w;
    return w;
}
```

In spite of this potential bottleneck, the GPU is still substantially faster than the CPU for our implementation: it is effectively able to run at its peak potential computational rate, subject to PCI Express limitations. For complete applications that need to compute option prices, it is likely that additional computation would be done on the GPU with the Black-Scholes results, which also reduces the impact of PCI Express bandwidth. (In general, the GPU works best as more computation is done on it and there is less communication with the CPU. The PCI Express bandwidth limitation is just a manifestation of the fact that the GPU particularly excels as the ratio of computation to bandwidth increases, as discussed in Chapter 29 of this book, "Streaming Architectures and Technology Trends.")

45.3 Lattice Models

The Black-Scholes equation provides a convenient analytical method of computing the price of European options. However, it is not suitable for pricing American options, which can be exercised at any time prior to the date of expiration. In fact, there is no known closed-form expression that gives the fair price of an American option under the same set of assumptions used by the Black-Scholes equation.

Another family of option pricing models is *lattice models*. These models use a dynamic programming approach to derive the value of an option at time 0 (that is, now) by starting at time T (that is, the expiration date) and iteratively stepping "backward" toward $t = 0$ in a discrete number of time steps, N. This approach is versatile and simple to implement, but it can be computationally expensive due to its iterative nature. In this section, we discuss the implementation of the binomial lattice model on the GPU and how it can be used to compute prices of both European and American options.

45.3.1 The Binomial Model

The most commonly used lattice model is the binomial model. The binomial model is so named because it assumes that if the underlying asset has a price S_k at time step k, its price at step $k + 1$ can take on only two possible values, uS_k and dS_k, corresponding to an "up" or "down" movement in the price of the stock. Typically, u is calculated by assuming that during a small time duration dt, the change of the asset value is normally distributed, with a standard deviation equal to $S_k v \sqrt{dt}$.

If d is chosen such that $u \times d = 1$, the possible asset prices during the lifetime of the option form a tree, as shown in Figure 45-2. Each path from the root node of the tree to a leaf corresponds to a "walk" of the underlying asset's price over time. The set of nodes at depth k from the root represent the range of possible asset prices at time $t = k \times dt$, where $dt = T/N$. The leaf nodes, at depth $k = N$, represent the range of prices the asset might have at the time the option expires.

To price the option using the binomial tree, we also compute the *pseudo-probability* P_u that the asset price will move "up" at any given time. The pseudo-probability of a down movement is simply $1 - P_u$. To compute the value of P_u, we assume a risk-neutral world, which implies that the expected return on the underlying asset is equal to r:

$$\left(uP_u + d\left(1 - P_u\right)\right) S_k = e^{r\,dt} S_k \Rightarrow P_u = \frac{e^{r\,dt} - d}{u - d}.$$

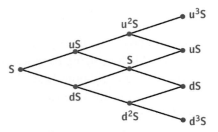

Figure 45-2. Binomial Tree of *N* = 3 Steps, with Associated Asset Prices
The current price of the security, S, is at the root of the tree. Each time step in the future is represented by successive columns of the tree, moving from left to right. The leaves of the tree, in the rightmost column, represent the range of expected possible asset values in the future, based on a set of assumptions about how the price of the asset varies.

Although P_u is not a true probability (that is, it is not the actual probability that the asset price will move up), it is useful to treat it as such, as shown in the following discussion.

45.3.2 Pricing European Options

Given a tree of asset values over time, like the one shown in Figure 45-2, we can calculate an option value at each node of the tree. The value computed for a node at depth k gives the expected value of the option at time $t = k \times dt$, assuming that the underlying asset takes on the range of prices associated with the node's children in the future. Our problem, then, is to compute the value of the option at the root of the tree. We do so by starting at the leaves and working backward toward the root.

Computing the option value at each leaf node i is simple. First we calculate the asset price S_i associated with each leaf node directly by raising u to the appropriate power (recall that $d = u^{-1}$) and multiplying the result by S. Next we compute the corresponding value of the option at each leaf, V_i. On the expiration date, a call option is worthless if $S_i > X$; otherwise, it has a value of $X - S_i$. The computation is similar for put options. Using these initial values, we can then calculate the option value for each node at the previous time step. We do so by computing the expected future value of the option using the "probability" of an upward movement, P_u, and the option values associated with the nodes in the "up" and "down" directions, $V_{i,up}$ and $V_{i,down}$. We then discount this future expected value by $e^{-r\,dt}$ to arrive at the option value corresponding to the node:

$$V_i = \left(\left(1 - P_u\right)V_{i,down} + P_u V_{i,up}\right)e^{-r\,dt}.$$

We perform this computation for all nodes at a given level of the tree, and then iteratively repeat for the next-highest level, and so on until reaching the root of the tree. The value at the root gives us the value of the option at $t = 0$: "now". Pseudocode for this algorithm (assuming a European call option) is shown in Listing 45-3. A 1D array, V, is used to iteratively compute option values. At termination, V[0] holds the value of the option at the present time.

Listing 45-3. Pseudocode for Pricing a European Put Option Using the Binomial Method

```
dt = T/N
u = exp(v * sqrt(dt))
d = 1/u
disc = exp(r * dt)
Pu = (disc - d) / (u - d)

// initialize option value array with values at expiry
for i = 0 to N
  Si = S * pow(u, 2 * i - N)
  V[i] = max(0, X - Si)

// for each time step
for j = N-1 to 0
  // for each node at the current time step
  for i = 0 to j
    // compute the discounted expected value of the option
    V[i] = ((1 - Pu) * V[i] + Pu * V[i + 1])/disc
```

To adapt the binomial model to run on the GPU, we need to deal with the fact that, unlike Black-Scholes, this calculation is iterative and requires the use of intermediate computed values—the various values of V[i]. One way to parallelize this task for the GPU is to work on a single time step (column) of the binomial tree at a time: one thread is launched for each node of a column of the tree, and it computes the option value for that node. Starting with the rightmost column, the option value at expiry is computed. For the column associated with each previous time step, in turn, option values are computed using the previously computed values for the two child nodes in the manner described earlier. This strategy is illustrated in Figure 45-3. After each thread computes its result, those values are used as input to a new set of threads launched to compute values for the next column to the left. (The general ideas behind this process are related to how reductions are computed on the GPU, as described in Chapter 31 of this book.)

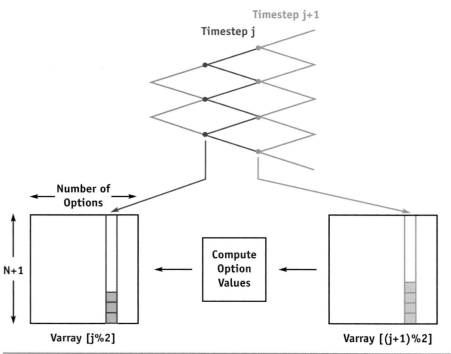

Timestep j+1

Timestep j

Number of Options

N+1

Compute Option Values

Varray [j%2]

Varray [(j+1)%2]

Figure 45-3. Computation Strategy and Data Layout
Each iteration computes the option values for a single time step in parallel. Data is arranged such that each column represents a single pricing problem, with the rows in the column holding the V array for that problem. Multiple pricing problems (that is, multiple columns) are run at the same time, further increasing parallelism and thus overall throughput. The algorithm will use a maximum buffer size of (N + 1) times the number of options priced in parallel.

To increase the parallelism available to the GPU, our implementation simultaneously runs this algorithm for a thousand or so independent options to price at the same time. Thus, the total number of threads running on the GPU at any time is equal to the number of options being priced times the number of tree nodes in the column currently being processed. This additional parallelism is easy to incorporate, and it gives better GPU performance than just parallelizing over a single option-pricing calculation at a time.

We use two fragment programs to price the set of options. The first program computes the initial $N + 1$ leaf option values (V[0] ... V[N]) and corresponds to the first for loop in Listing 45-3. The second program is run multiple times to iteratively compute the V[i]s for the interior nodes. The application invokes this program N times, one for each time step (corresponding to the second for loop in Listing 45-3), with each iteration using the previously computed V[i]s to compute the values for the current time step. Each invocation of the program corresponds to the innermost for loop in Listing 45-3; as shown there, at each iteration, the number of computed nodes is reduced by one, leaving us with a single result value corresponding to V[0].

Running the second program involves using the output of one iteration as the input to the next. To do so efficiently, we use a double-buffered pbuffer, which avoids context switching and texture copying overhead. The Cg code for these programs is shown in Listing 45-4, and the pseudocode for driving them is given in Listing 45-5.

Listing 45-4. Computing Lattice Model Option Pricing

```
void init(Stream stockPrice,
  Stream strikePrice,
  Stream yearsToMaturity,
  Stream volatility,
  uniform float riskFreeRate,
  uniform float numSteps,
  float2 offset : DOMAIN0,
  out float4 result : RANGE0)
{
  float deltaT = yearsToMaturity.value(offset.x)/numSteps;
  float u = exp(volatility.value(offset.x) * sqrt(deltaT));

  float price = stockPrice.value(offset.x) *
                pow(u, 2 * (offset.y - 0.5) - numSteps);
  float value = max(strikePrice.value(offset.x) - price, 0);
  result = value;
}

void iterate(Stream Pu,
  Stream Pd,
  Stream optval,
  float2 offset : DOMAIN0,
  float2 offsetplus1 : DOMAIN1,
  out float4 result : RANGE0)
{
  float val = (Pu.value(offset.x) * optval.value(offsetplus1) +
               Pd.value(offset.x) * optval.value(offset));
  result = val;
}
```

Listing 45-5. Lattice Model Application Pseudocode

```
domain = [0, nproblems, 0, N + 1]
Varray[N % 2] = init(Range, S, X, T, v, r, N, domain)
for j = N - 1 to 0
  offset = [0, nproblems, 0, j + 1]
  offsetplus1 = [0, nproblems, 1, j + 2]
  Varray[(j % 2)] = iterate(Pu, Pd, Varray[((j + 1) % 2)], offset,
                              offsetplus1)
```

As we increase the number of time steps N, the value computed using the binomial method converges to that computed by the Black-Scholes method. The binomial method is far more computationally expensive than the Black-Scholes method; its asymptotic time complexity is $O(N^2)$, for example, versus Black-Scholes's $O(1)$. However, this computational expense does come with an advantage: unlike Black-Scholes, lattice methods can be adapted for use on a wide variety of options-pricing problems.

For example, we can modify the previous algorithm to price American options. When calculating the expected value of holding the option at each node, we can also compute the value of exercising it immediately. If exercising is more valuable than holding, we set the value of the option at that node to the exercise value, rather than the expected value of holding. In the case of a call option, the value of exercising is $X - S_i$, where S_i is the computed price of the asset at node i. A full implementation may be found on the CD that accompanies this book.

As with Black-Scholes, the GPU outperforms the CPU when pricing American options with the binomial approach, as shown in Figure 45-4. As in Figure 45-1, a GeForce 6800 was used for the GPU tests, and an AMD Athlon 64 3200+ was used for the CPU tests.

45.4 Conclusion

Both the Black-Scholes model and the lattice model for option pricing are basic building blocks of computational finance. In this chapter, we have shown how the GPU can be used to price options using these models much more efficiently than the CPU. As GPUs continue to become faster more quickly than CPUs, the gap between the two is likely to grow for this application.

Another widely used approach for pricing options is to implement algorithms based on Monte Carlo or quasi-Monte Carlo simulation. These algorithms are also well suited to the GPU, because they rely on running a large number of independent trials and then

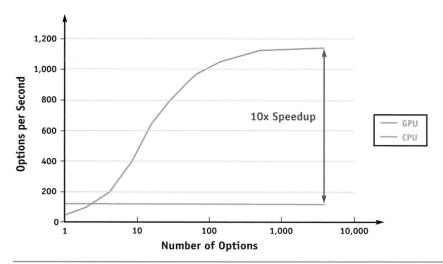

Figure 45-4. GPU vs. CPU Performance of a Binomial Lattice Model with *N* = 1024 Steps
As with the Black-Scholes algorithm, the GPU implementation of the binomial method substantially outperforms the CPU implementation when more than a small number of pricing problems are solved in parallel. Unlike the Black-Scholes GPU implementation, I/O is not a substantial bottleneck in this case due to the large amount of computation performed for each result value.

computing overall estimates based on all of the trials together. The independent trials are trivially parallelizable, and producing the final estimates is a matter of computing reductions. The early-exercise right associated with American options makes it challenging to use Monte Carlo methods to compute their fair value. Finding the means to do so efficiently is an active area of research.

One detail that makes these algorithms slightly more difficult to map to the GPU is the lack of native integer instructions, which are the basis for the pseudorandom number generators needed for Monte Carlo and the low-discrepancy sequences used for quasi-Monte Carlo. This limitation can be sidestepped on current GPUs by generating these numbers on the CPU and downloading them to the GPU. As long as a reasonable amount of computation is done with each random or quasi-random sample, this step isn't a bottleneck.

45.5 References

Black, Fischer, and Myron Scholes. 1973. "The Pricing of Options and Corporate Liabilities." *Journal of Political Economy* 81(3), pp. 637–654.

Hull, John C. 2002. *Options, Futures, and Other Derivatives*, 5th ed. Prentice Hall.

Chapter 46

Improved GPU Sorting

Peter Kipfer
Technische Universität München

Rüdiger Westermann
Technische Universität München

Sorting is one of the most important algorithmic building blocks in computer science. Being able to efficiently sort large amounts of data is a critical operation. Although implementing sorting algorithms on the CPU is relatively straightforward—mostly a matter of choosing a particular sorting algorithm to use—sorting on the GPU is less easily implemented because the GPU is effectively a highly parallel single-instruction, multiple-data (SIMD) architecture. Given that the GPU can outperform the CPU both for memory-bound and compute-bound algorithms, finding ways to sort efficiently on the GPU is important. Furthermore, because reading back data from the GPU to the CPU to perform operations such as sorting is inefficient, sorting the data on the GPU is preferable.

Buck and Purcell 2004 showed how the parallel bitonic merge sort algorithm could be used to sort data on the GPU. In this chapter, we show how to improve the efficiency of sorting on the GPU by making full use of the GPU's computational resources. We also demonstrate a sorting algorithm that does not destroy the ordering of nearly sorted arrays at intermediate steps of the algorithm. This can be useful for effects such as particle systems, where geometric objects need to be sorted according to viewer distance but small sorting errors can be tolerable temporarily in exchange for improved application response.

46.1 Sorting Algorithms

Sorting algorithms are among the most important building blocks of virtually every program. Computer graphics applications require visibility sorting for correctly rendering transparent objects and efficiently exploiting acceleration features such as the early-z test. In physics simulation, sorting is necessary for inserting the participating objects into spatial structures for collision detection.

Sorting algorithms can be divided into two categories: data-driven ones and data-independent ones. In practice, the fastest algorithms are data-driven, which means that the step the algorithm takes depends on the value of the key currently under consideration. This may result in unexpected bad performance if the sequence to sort is already in order. The well-known Quicksort algorithm is one example. When sorting n items, it has $O(n \log(n))$ complexity on average, which is provably optimal. But in the worst case, Quicksort has $O(n^2)$ complexity, which is not acceptable. There are other sorting algorithms such as Heapsort that do not have this problem, but they exhibit more difficult data access patterns or require more comparison operations. Heapsort is most useful when you need only partially ordered lists (such as in a priority queue).

The second category of algorithms, the data-independent ones, does not exhibit this discrepancy. As the algorithms do not change their processing according to the current key value, they always take the same processing path. This makes their operation sequence completely rigid, a fact that we can exploit to implement them on multiple processors, because the points at which communication must occur are known in advance. This feature is key when considering an implementation of sorting on the GPU, because the sorting program will run on the fragment processors, which cannot change their output location in memory based on input data values.

46.2 A Simple First Approach

Data-independent sorting algorithms can be represented as a sorting network, as shown in Figure 46-1. To study the general approach, let's look at a simple example. For simplicity, we assume that we are sorting a 1D array of keys. In the sorting network, each column is a series of compare operations that execute in parallel. We call this *one pass* of the sorting network. The input keys get sorted as they travel from left to right through the network. In this simple example, called *odd-even transition sort*, if the compare operation is *less-than*, as indicated by the direction of the arrows, small keys will move one row upward with each iteration, while large keys move downward. In the worst case, if the smallest key starts in position n, it will take n iterations to bring it all the way up to position 0. This sorting algorithm therefore has a complexity of $O(n^2)$, which is not optimal.

Implementation of this algorithm is easy, and it is easily parallelizable in nature. We render to two texture buffers in double-buffer mode. For each pass, we draw a full-size quad

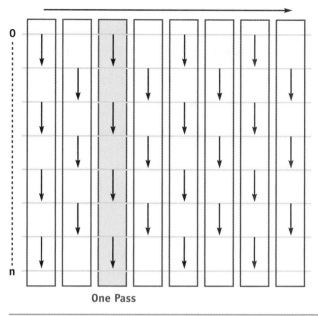

Figure 46-1. The Odd-Even Transition Sorting Network for *n* Keys
Arrows indicate the compare operation "less-than".

and execute a fragment program that fetches the key at its fragment's position, fetches the key at its neighbor's position from the source buffer, compares the two keys, and writes the result to the target buffer. Note that because we can write only one fragment at a time, comparing two keys involves processing two fragments; we perform a *less-than* comparison on the first and a *greater-equal* comparison on the second. The decision of which operation to perform can be computed with a modulo operation on the current row number. This also means that both fragments do two data (texture) fetches. This approach therefore needs twice the bandwidth of a CPU implementation that fetches the data once and then swap-writes the result according to the comparison result.

46.3 Fast Sorting

Although each pass of the simple network is very cheap, the number of passes to perform a complete sort will be too high to be acceptable in most (real-time) situations. Suppose we use the sorter within a particle engine to keep the particles in back-to-front order for correct transparent rendering with depth test turned on. We will run into serious performance problems with such an approach, because we will want to use a large number of particles (up to one million). Even with a faster sort, we might want to distribute the workload over several displayed frames, and we might even accept locally inexact ordering if it converges to the full sort within a short period of time.

For such an application, what we would like to have is a fast yet smooth transition of the input into an ordered sequence. This will allow us to use intermediate results of the algorithm that converge to the correct sequence while we do more passes incrementally (Kolb et al. 2004). Figure 46-2 shows a sorting network that has the desired property: the *odd-even merge sort* (Sedgewick 1998). The idea is to sort all odd and all even keys separately and then merge them. Each step like this is called a *stage* of the sorting algorithm. The stages are then scaled and repeated for all powers of two until the whole field is merged. To sort the m keys of a stage, $\log(m)$ passes are needed. For sorting all n keys, we therefore need $\log(n)$ stages, resulting in an overall $O(n \log^2(n) + \log(n))$ passes. This is more than the $O(n \log(n))$ of Quicksort, but it is still optimal in the limit case, which is why odd-even merge sort is also called an optimal algorithm. Sorting one million keys therefore takes 210 passes, compared to one million passes for the simple first approach.

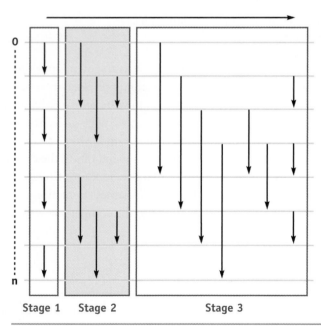

Figure 46-2. The Odd-Even Merge Sorting Network for *n* Keys
Each stage establishes two partial sorts that are merged in the next stage.

46.3.1 Implementing Odd-Even Merge Sort

We take the same approach as in the simple odd-even transition sort example shown earlier. The sorting algorithm is implemented in a fragment program. It is driven by two nested loops on the CPU that just transport stage, pass number, and some derived values via uniform parameters to the shader before drawing the quad. If we want to sort many items, we have to store them in a 2D texture. To sort the entire 2D field, the fragment program must convert the 1D array index into 2D texture coordinates. Listing 46-1 is GLSL code for the odd-even merge sort fragment shader.

Listing 46-1. The GLSL Fragment Program Implementing Odd-Even Merge Sort

```
uniform vec3 Param1;
uniform vec3 Param2;
uniform sampler2D Data;

#define OwnPos gl_TexCoord[0]

// contents of the uniform data fields
#define TwoStage Param1.x
#define Pass_mod_Stage Param1.y
#define TwoStage_PmS_1 Param1.z
#define Width Param2.x
#define Height Param2.y
#define Pass Param2.z

void main(void)
{
  // get self
  vec4 self = texture2D(Data, OwnPos.xy);
  float i = floor(OwnPos.x * Width) + floor(OwnPos.y * Height) * Width;

  // my position within the range to merge
  float j = floor(mod(i, TwoStage));

  float compare;

  if ( (j < Pass_mod_Stage) || (j > TwoStage_PmS_1) )
    // must copy -> compare with self
    compare = 0.0;
```

```
else
  // must sort
  if ( mod((j + Pass_mod_Stage) / Pass, 2.0) < 1.0)
    // we are on the left side -> compare with partner on the right
    compare = 1.0;
  else
    // we are on the right side -> compare with partner on the left
    compare = -1.0;

  // get the partner
  float adr = i + compare * Pass;
  vec4 partner = texture2D(Data, vec2(floor(mod(adr, Width)) / Width,
                                      floor(adr / Width) / Height));

  // on the left it's a < operation; on the right it's a >= operation
  gl_FragColor =
      (self.x * compare < partner.x * compare) ? self : partner;
}
```

We now have an algorithmically efficient sorter. However, when taking a critical look at the code and how it uses the GPU resources, we notice some shortcomings that are typical of attempts to bring algorithms to the GPU. First, we still need twice the number of data fetches as the CPU. Second, the code seems to do many operations on uniform parameters. Can we pull them out of the fragment shader and save unnecessarily repeated computation? Third, the shader uses branching and thus may unnecessarily execute many operations even for values that only need to be copied. Also, what are the vertex unit and the rasterizer doing all the time? Almost nothing. Can we do better?

46.4 Using All GPU Resources

The GPU is optimized for very regular highly parallel access patterns. In the odd-even merge sort, some values get compared, while others just get copied. We would like to avoid this situation, because both cases take the same time to execute. We can do more comparisons per pass without penalty if we get rid of the copies. Overall, this will make the program even faster, because the determination of whether to copy or compare can be dropped. This is due to the network performing alternating odd-even accesses. In summary, we need a different sorting network.

Figure 46-3 shows the sorting network for the *bitonic merge sort* algorithm (Batcher 1968), which builds both an ascending and a descending subsequence of keys (that is, a bitonic sequence) and then merges the two subsequences. Starting with $n/2$ two-item sequences, this continues until one fully sorted ascending sequence is left. This means we have to build $\log(n)$ bitonic sequences and merge them. The sorting network reflects this pattern, showing $\log(n)$ sorting stages, where the ith stage has to perform i passes. This results in a total complexity of $O(n \log^2(n) + \log(n))$, which is the same as the odd-even merge sort. This is still not as fast as Quicksort, but remember that we do not have a bad worst-case complexity here.

The straightforward implementation would be to simply encode the stage and pass numbers in texture coordinates and have the fragment shader execute the "inner loop" of the sorting procedure (that is, one column of the network), as other work has shown (Purcell et al. 2003). However, from Figure 46-3, we note that this incurs only integer operations for computing the compare distance and change of compare operation. Moreover, these changes occur always at positions that are powers of two and do not

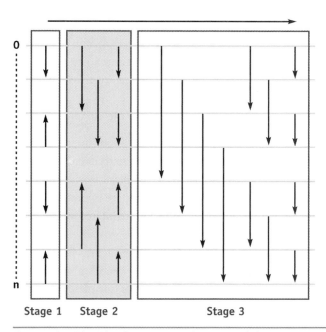

Stage 1   Stage 2   Stage 3

Figure 46-3. The Bitonic Merge Sorting Network for *n* Keys
Each stage merges a bitonic sequence of the previous stage, consisting of one ascending and one descending sorted sequence.

straddle certain power-of-two boundaries. Unfortunately, integer operations that could efficiently detect these cases are not supported on current GPUs. They therefore have to be emulated by appropriate floating-point operations. Specifically, the operations that we need for the sorting procedure, such as modulo and bitwise operations, are possible only with floating-point arithmetic on the GPU. The straightforward implementation of this algorithm in a fragment shader will therefore not be as efficient as possible.

We need a smarter solution, one that reduces the amount of work done in the fragment units and makes use of the vertex processors and the rasterizer (Kipfer et al. 2004). By rotating Figure 46-3 90 degrees to the right, we obtain Figure 46-4, for sorting a 1D array of n keys. Observe that in each pass, there are always groups of items that are treated alike (yellow or green boxes). This means that their sorting parameters are the same. Moreover, there is a strong relationship between neighboring groups: they sometimes have parameters with opposite values. These changes depend on the stage and pass and can be expressed as a simple modulo relationship. In sorting passes where there is more than one group, instead of drawing one single, big quad and computing the appropriate parameters in the fragment shader, we now draw several quads per sorting pass that exactly fit pairs of groups (one yellow and one green box) and together cover the entire buffer. On the right side of each quad, we perform the operation opposite that of the left side. To compute this flip, we observe that texture parameters specified in the vertex program are linearly interpolated by the rasterizer over the fragments. If we simply specify a flag value of $+1$ on the left side of the quad and a flag value of -1 on the right side, the fragment program can determine the current fragment's position within the quad by simply looking at the sign of the flag.

The remaining two actions that have to be computed are to decide which compare operation to use and to locate the partner item to compare. Both can also be expressed using the interpolation technique. We first fix the compare operation to be a *less-than* operation. Multiplying the two key values with the interpolated flag value from the vertex shader now makes the operation implicitly flip to *greater-equal* halfway across the quad, which is exactly what we want. The same is done for the compare distance. Its absolute value is constant for the quad. We extract the sign of another interpolated flag value and multiply it with the absolute value in order to not scale the distance. The numeric precision of the interpolator on all current GPUs is high enough to prevent subpixel rounding problems.

If we want to sort many items, we have to store them in a 2D texture. To sort an entire 2D field, we understand each row of the field to be one bitonic sequence of the whole field. We therefore perform the same sorting operations for every row. The quads we have

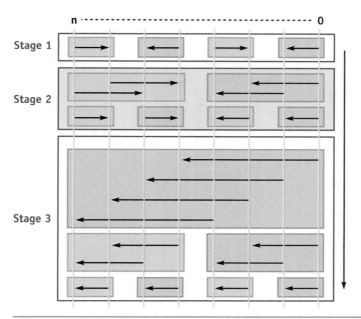

Figure 46-4. Grouping Keys for the Bitonic Merge Sort

introduced previously need simply to be extended vertically to cover all rows. Figure 46-5 shows the compare operation performed and the underlying quads that are rendered. If we now introduce another modulation to the compare operation according to the row number, we easily get rows completely sorted in alternating ascending/descending order. All that's left is to merge them in pairs, groups of 4, groups of 8, groups of 16, until the whole field is processed. Note that this uses the same sorting procedure along the columns that we used along the rows. We take the same approach for the columns as for the rows, using vertical compare distances (instead of horizontal) by simply transposing the quads that form each pass.

The final optimization we make is to generalize the sorter to work on key/index pairs. Because the GPU processes four-vectors, we can pack two key/index pairs into one fragment. Because the last pass of each sorting stage only compares neighboring items (see Figure 46-3), this will happen inside the fragment, saving the second texture fetch. Packing two consecutive items also cuts the row width in half and consequently the overall number of fragments to process. We now do the same number of data fetches as a CPU implementation. Note that the concept of packing can also be used for the odd-even transition sort shader, but there it obviously helps only every other pass avoid the second data fetch.

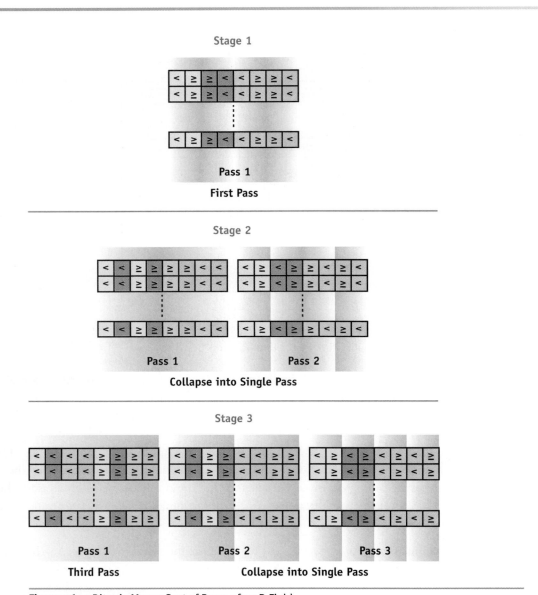

Figure 46-5. Bitonic Merge Sort of Rows of a 2D Field
In one row, equal colors indicate elements to be compared. For each element, the compare operation is also shown. The underlying quad shading represents the interpolated decision value for the compare operation.

46.4.1 Implementing Bitonic Merge Sort

For the sample application of sorting particles according to camera distance, we implement a small fragment program that computes the sorting keys (distance) and indices (particle numbers) and packs two of them into one RGBA texture value. Because we must touch every item to sort anyway, we take the opportunity and also perform the very first sorting pass while writing the packed representation. The first pass simply has to produce alternating ascending/descending pairs of keys—an operation that is internal to each fragment (see Figure 46-3).

All quads for one sorting pass are recorded in a display list. To sort the entire field, we just call the next list and swap the buffers until we're done. The display list records the vertices of the quads and two texture coordinates. The first texture coordinate holds all data that varies per quad (that is, the fragment position, the search direction, and the compare operation flag that is to be interpolated). The second texture coordinate holds data that is constant for the quad. Because we pack two consecutive items into one fragment, in the last pass of each stage, the fragment shader accesses the same items as the previous pass (compare Figure 46-4). We account for this by folding both passes into one, using a special shader for this case. Note that the fragment program does not need to perform a conversion from 1D indices to 2D texture coordinates, because this is done implicitly by the texture coordinates of the quads. Listing 46-2 shows the GLSL code for the special program.

The program for passes greater than 1 along the rows skips the last compare operation in Listing 46-2 and returns the `result` variable. The program for passes along the columns differs just in building the `adr` variable: here x is 0 and y is computed according to the search direction.

In summary, we need four programs to perform the sorting: The first one computes the key/index pairs and does the first sorting pass. The second performs row sorting for passes 0 and 1 of each stage simultaneously. The third does row sorting for all passes greater than 1 of each stage, and the fourth performs the column sort.

When the sort is done, we have a permutation of the key/index pairs. The application can now reorder any data buffer according to the sorting criterion by simple indexed lookup.

Listing 46-2. GLSL Fragment Program Implementing the Combined Passes 1 and 0 for Row-wise Sorting of the Bitonic Merge Sort

```glsl
uniform sampler2D PackedData;

// contents of the texcoord data
#define OwnPos gl_TexCoord[0].xy
#define SearchDir gl_TexCoord[0].z
#define CompOp gl_TexCoord[0].w
#define Distance gl_TexCoord[1].x
#define Stride gl_TexCoord[1].y
#define Height gl_TexCoord[1].z
#define HalfStrideMHalf gl_TexCoord[1].w

void main(void)
{
  // get self
  vec4 self = texture2D(PackedData, OwnPos);

  // restore sign of search direction and assemble vector to partner
  vec2 adr = vec2( (SearchDir < 0.0) ? -Distance : Distance , 0.0);

  // get the partner
  vec4 partner = texture2D(PackedData, OwnPos + adr);

  // switch ascending/descending sort for every other row
  // by modifying comparison flag
  float compare = CompOp * -(mod(floor(gl_TexCoord[0].y * Height),
                             Stride) - HalfStrideMHalf);

  // x and y are the keys of the two items
  // --> multiply with comparison flag
  vec4 keys = compare * vec4( self.x, self.y, partner.x, partner.y);

  // compare the keys and store accordingly
  // z and w are the indices
  // --> just copy them accordingly
  vec4 result;
  result.xz = (keys.x < keys.z) ? self.xz : partner.xz;
  result.yw = (keys.y < keys.w) ? self.yw : partner.yw;

  // do pass 0
  compare *= adr.x;
  gl_FragColor =
      (result.x * compare < result.y * compare) ? result : result.yxwz;
}
```

46.5 Conclusion

We have implemented the bitonic merge sort very efficiently on the GPU. Table 46-1 lists the number of passes required to sort various field sizes and the sorting performance obtained on a 425 MHz NVIDIA GeForce 6800 Ultra GPU. The CPU and the GPU sorted 16-bit key/16-bit index pairs.[1] Additional performance information can be found in Kipfer et al. 2004. Note that the CPU timings do not include the time that would be necessary for upload. A limitation of the bitonic merge sort is that we cannot distribute sorting passes over multiple displayed frames in order to make the system more responsive, because the intermediate stages of the sort do not maintain a globally ordered sequence. Because they always produce a bitonic pair (one ascending and one descending partial sequence), at least half of the field gets completely reordered in each stage.

Table 46-1. Performance of the CPU and GPU Sorting Algorithms

`std::sort`: 16-Bit Data, Pentium 4 3.0 GHz

N	Full Sorts/Sec	Sorted Keys/Sec
256^2	82.5	5.4 M
512^2	20.6	5.4 M
1024^2	4.7	5.0 M

Odd-Even Merge Sort: 16-Bit Data, NVIDIA GeForce 6800 Ultra

N	Passes	Full Sorts/Sec	Sorted Keys/Sec
256^2	136	36.0	2.4 M
512^2	171	7.8	2.0 M
1024^2	210	1.25	1.3 M

Bitonic Merge Sort: 16-Bit Float Data, NVIDIA GeForce 6800 Ultra

N	Passes	Full Sorts/Sec	Sorted Keys/Sec
256^2	120	90.07	6.1 M
512^2	153	18.3	4.8 M
1024^2	190	3.6	3.8 M

The odd-even merge sort maintains the sort-while-drawing property, but the last pass of each stage performs a merge of the odd and the even items. This is not a good access pattern for the packing we have done. For this sorting algorithm, it thus does not make sense to combine the last two passes of each stage into a special program, as we did with the bitonic merge sort. The implementation therefore performs $\log(n)$ more passes than the bitonic merge sort. Although this results in inferior overall performance, the workload can be spread over several displayed frames.

---

1. Note that there is no 16-bit floating-point format on the CPU, so the CPU sorted 16-bit short data. Comparisons of signed floating-point values are slightly more expensive than integer comparisons.

You now have two optimal sorting algorithms, each with its own advantages and drawbacks. Both, however, execute very efficiently on the GPU. So if your shiny new GPU algorithm requires sorting, there is no longer a need to return to the CPU. On the book's CD, you will find a small demo program implemented in C++, OpenGL, and GLSL that performs the GPU sorting techniques discussed in this chapter.

46.6 References

Batcher, Kenneth E. 1968. "Sorting Networks and Their Applications." *Proceedings of AFIPS Spring Joint Computer Conference* 32, pp. 307–314.

Buck, Ian, and Tim Purcell. 2004. "A Toolkit for Computation on GPUs." In *GPU Gems*, edited by Randima Fernando, pp. 621–636. Addison-Wesley.

Kipfer, Peter, Mark Segal, and Rüdiger Westermann. 2004. "UberFlow: A GPU-Based Particle Engine." In *Proceedings of the SIGGRAPH/Eurographics Workshop on Graphics Hardware 2004*, pp. 115–122.

Kolb, A., L. Latta, and C. Rezk-Salama. 2004. "Hardware-Based Simulation and Collision Detection for Large Particle Systems." In *Proceedings of the SIGGRAPH/Eurographics Workshop on Graphics Hardware 2004*, pp. 123–131.

Purcell, Tim, Craig Donner, Mike Cammarano, Henrik Wann Jensen, and Pat Hanrahan. 2003. "Photon Mapping on Programmable Graphics Hardware." In *Proceedings of the SIGGRAPH/Eurographics Workshop on Graphics Hardware 2003*, pp. 41–50.

Sedgewick, Robert. 1998. *Algorithms in C++*, 3rd ed., Parts 1–4. Addison-Wesley.

Chapter 47

Flow Simulation with Complex Boundaries

Wei Li
Siemens Corporate Research

Zhe Fan
Stony Brook University

Xiaoming Wei
Stony Brook University

Arie Kaufman
Stony Brook University

47.1 Introduction

Physically based fluid flow simulation is commonplace in many prediction and scientific computation problems. It also greatly improves the visual fidelity in computer graphics applications. However, an accurate simulation is computationally expensive. In this chapter, we present a physically plausible yet fast fluid flow simulation approach based on the Lattice Boltzmann Method (LBM) (Chen and Doolean 1998). Figure 47-1 shows the results of fluid simulation around different obstacles. In Figure 47-1a, the obstacle is a static vase, while in Figure 47-1b, it is a sphere that moves toward the top right. Figure 47-1c and Figure 47-1d are two snapshots showing a jellyfish swimming from right to left. Note that when the jellyfish deforms its body, the liquid-solid boundary also deforms. To visualize the flow field, we inject a slice of colored particles and advect them according to the velocity field of the flow. All the computations, the simulation, the generation of the boundaries, the advection, and the rendering of the particles are executed on the GPU in real time.

The LBM model is composed of many nodes arranged on Cartesian grids, usually called a *lattice*. Each node is associated with several attributes. At discrete time steps, the attributes are updated to determine the dynamics of a flow field. The basic computation of the LBM

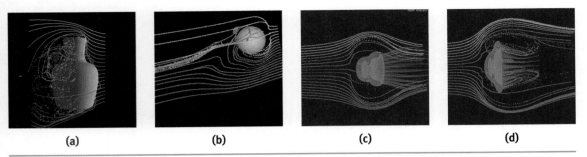

Figure 47-1. Flow Fields Simulated on the GPU Using Different Obstacles

naturally fits the stream-processing framework of the GPU, hence it is not very difficult to express the LBM equations using GPU programs. However, a straightforward translation results in a very slow implementation. In this chapter, we present various algorithm-level and machine-level optimizations. With the proper optimizations, a GPU-based flow simulation can be an order of magnitude faster than its CPU counterpart.

One of the advantages of the LBM is that it is relatively easy to handle complex, moving, and deformable boundaries. However, the boundaries must be voxelized to discrete boundary nodes that are aligned with the LBM lattice. Voxelization of moving and deforming boundaries primarily involves finding intersections of the boundary polygons with the LBM lattice. Voxelization must be repeated whenever the boundaries change. If CPU-based voxelization is used with GPU-based LBM, the transfer of boundary nodes from main memory to graphics memory becomes a bottleneck. To address these problems, we propose a fast voxelization algorithm on the GPU and use it to model the interaction of complex obstacles and even living objects with the flow.

47.2 The Lattice Boltzmann Method

Figure 47-2 shows a 2D model with the nodes represented as green dots. The figure shows only 12 nodes, but in practice, we need thousands or even millions of nodes to generate a delicate flow field. Each node is connected to its direct neighbors with vectors, denoted as $\mathbf{e}_{qi}$ and shown as black arrows in Figure 47-2. There is also an $\mathbf{e}_{qi}$ pointing to the node itself (not shown in the figure). The model in Figure 47-2 is called *D2Q9*, because each node has 9 $\mathbf{e}_{qi}$ vectors. Each node is associated with various attributes, such as packet distribution f_{qi}, density ρ, and velocity $\mathbf{u}$. We don't need to worry about their physical meanings. All we need to know is that densities and velocities are derived from packet distributions, and velocities are the output that we need for our application. Interested

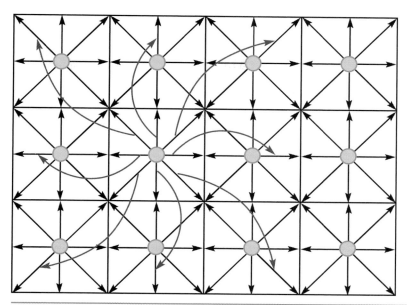

Figure 47-2. A 2D LBM Model

readers may find more details about LBM in the literature, such as Chen and Doolean 1998 and Wei et al. 2004. For each node, there is one packet distribution for every e_{qi} vector. Therefore in this 2D model, each node has 9 packet distributions.

We are most interested in 3D flow. The 3D model that we use in this chapter is called *D3Q19* because it has 19 packet distributions for each node. These packet distributions account for most of the memory requirements of the LBM model. All the attributes are updated at every time step, using the values of the previous step. Every packet distribution moves along its e_{qi} vector to the neighbor node and replaces the packet distribution of the neighbor node, except the one pointing to the node itself, as indicated by the blue arrows in Figure 47-2. This is called *propagation* or *streaming*.

47.3 GPU-Based LBM

47.3.1 Algorithm Overview

To compute the LBM equations on graphics hardware, we divide the LBM lattice and group the packet distributions f_{qi} into arrays according to their velocity vectors e_{qi}. All packet distributions of the same velocity vector are grouped into an array, maintaining the layout of the original lattice. Figure 47-3 shows the division of a 2D model into a collection of arrays (one per velocity vector $\mathbf{e}_{qi}$). The division of a 3D model is similar. We store the arrays as 2D textures. For a 2D model, all such arrays are naturally 2D; for a 3D model, each array forms a volume. The volume is treated as a set of slices and is stored as a stack of 2D textures or a large tiled 2D texture. All the other variables are stored similarly in 2D textures. To update these values at each time step, we render quadrilaterals mapped with those textures, so that a fragment program running at each texel computes the LBM equations.

Figure 47-4 is a diagram of the data flow of the LBM computation on the GPU; green boxes represent the textures storing lattice properties, and blue boxes represent the operations. An LBM update iteration starts with the packet distribution textures as inputs. Density and velocity textures are then dynamically generated from the distribution textures. Next, intermediate distributions, called equilibrium distributions, are obtained from the densities and velocities. New distributions are then computed from the input distributions and the equilibrium distributions according to the collision and the streaming equations. Finally, the boundary and outflow conditions are used to update the distribution textures. The updated distribution textures are then used as inputs for the next simulation step. Readers can find the details of these computations in Wei et al. 2004.

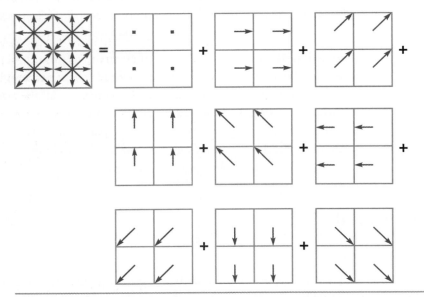

Figure 47-3. Division of a D2Q9 Model According to Its Velocity Directions
A separate array is used for each velocity vector.

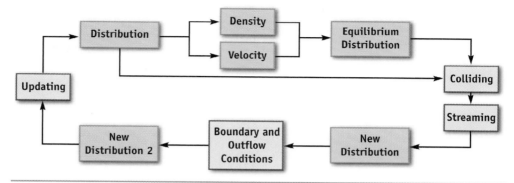

Figure 47-4. Flow Chart of LBM Computation on the GPU
Green boxes are the textures, and blue boxes are operations.

47.3.2 Packing

During the simulation, textures are updated dynamically at every step by copying from or binding to the frame buffer (or an off-screen buffer). In current graphics hardware, it is most efficient to use 8-bit-per-component RGBA (or BGRA) textures. Each RGBA texel has four channels, so it can store up to four scalars or a vector with up to four components.

We pack multiple variables into each texel. For example, four packet distributions, f_{qi}, from different directions are stored in a single RGBA texel. It is important to pack those variables involved in the same LBM equations into the same texture or even the same texel, if possible, in order to reduce the number of texture fetches. This also improves data locality and texture-cache coherence.

Table 47-1 lists the contents of the textures packed with the variables of the D3Q19 model, including densities, velocities, and packet distributions. In texture $\mathbf{u}\rho$, v_x, v_y, and v_z are the three components of the velocity stored in the RGB channels, while the density ρ is stored in the alpha channel. The rows in Table 47-1 for textures f_0 through f_4 show the packing patterns of the packet distributions f_{qi}. The distribution in the direction of (x, y, z) is $f_{(x,y,z)}$. Note that we pack pairs of distributions of opposite directions into the same texture. There are two reasons for this. First, when we handle complex or moving boundaries, neighboring distributions at opposite directions are needed to evaluate the effects on a boundary link. Second, when programming the fragment processor, we typically need to pass the corresponding velocity vector $\mathbf{e}_{qi}$ as an argument of the fragment program. When opposite distributions are packed together, just two $\mathbf{e}_{qi}$'s are needed, instead of four, and the other two are easily inferred.

Table 47-1. Packed LBM Variables of the D3Q19 Model

Texture	R	G	B	A
$\mathbf{u}\rho$	v_x	v_y	v_z	ρ
f_0	$f_{(1, 0, 0)}$	$f_{(-1, 0, 0)}$	$f_{(0, 1, 0)}$	$f_{(0, -1, 0)}$
f_1	$f_{(1, 1, 0)}$	$f_{(-1, -1, 0)}$	$f_{(1, -1, 0)}$	$f_{(-1, 1, 0)}$
f_2	$f_{(1, 0, 1)}$	$f_{(-1, 0, -1)}$	$f_{(1, 0, -1)}$	$f_{(-1, 0, 1)}$
f_3	$f_{(0, 1, 1)}$	$f_{(0, -1, -1)}$	$f_{(0, 1, -1)}$	$f_{(0, -1, 1)}$
f_4	$f_{(0, 0, 1)}$	$f_{(0, 0, -1)}$	$f_{(0, 0, 0)}$	unused

Instead of using a stack of 2D textures to represent a volume, we tile the slices into a large 2D texture that can be considered a "flat" volume. Similar approaches have been reported in the literature, for example, in Harris et al. 2003. One advantage of the flat volume is the reduced amount of texture switching. Using the flat volume is critical in two stages of our algorithms: particle advection and boundary node generation. The conversion from the volume coordinates (x, y, z) to the coordinates (u, v) of the flattened texture is as follows:

$$u = (z \bmod d) \times W + x,$$
$$v = \text{floor}(z/d) \times H + y,$$

(1)

where W and H are dimensions of each slice in the volume, and every set of d slices is tiled in a row along the x direction in the flat volume. The computation of Equation 1 can be done either in the fragment program or via a 1D texture lookup.

47.3.3 Streaming

Recall that each packet distribution with nonzero velocity propagates to a neighbor node at every time step. On modern GPUs, the texture unit can fetch texels at arbitrary positions indicated by texture coordinates computed by the fragment program. If a distribution f_{qi} is propagated along vector $\mathbf{e}_{qi}$, we simply fetch from the distribution texture at the position of current node minus $\mathbf{e}_{qi}$. Because the four channels are packed with four distributions with different velocity vectors, four fetches are needed for each fragment.

Figure 47-5 shows an example of the propagation of distribution texture f_1, which is packed with $f_{(1, 1, 0)}, f_{(-1, -1, 0)}, f_{(1, -1, 0)},$ and $f_{(-1, 1, 0)}$. The fragment program fetches texels by adding the negative values of the velocity directions to the texture coordinates of the current fragment and extracting the proper color component.

To propagate using the flat volume, for each channel we can add the 3D position of the fragment to the negative of the corresponding e_{qi}, then convert it to the texture coordinate of the flat volume according to Equation 1 before fetching. However, this requires execution of Equation 1 four times per fragment. We can push the coordinates' conversion to the vertex level, because for each channel inside a slice, the velocity vectors are the same. We can either assign each vertex of the proxy quad four texture coordinates containing the converted values or generate the texture coordinates with a vertex program.

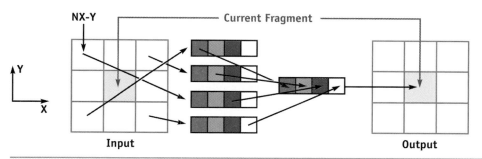

Figure 47-5. Streaming of Packet Distribution
Distribution texels are fetched by adding the negative values of the velocity directions to the texture coordinates of the current fragment.

47.4 GPU-Based Boundary Handling

The previous computations apply only to internal nodes, away from any obstacle boundaries. To make the simulation work properly, and to make the flow interact with obstacles, we need to consider boundary conditions. To handle an obstacle boundary, we need to compute the intersections of the boundary surface with all the LBM lattice links. For static obstacles, the intersections can be precomputed, whereas for moving or deformable boundaries, the intersection positions change dynamically. The boundary description can be either continuous, such as a polygonal mesh or a higher-order surface, or discrete, such as a voxel volume. Regardless, the handling of the boundary conditions requires discrete boundary nodes to be aligned with the LBM lattice. Even if the boundary representation is already volumetric, it has to be revoxelized whenever it moves or deforms. One solution is to compute the intersection and voxelization on the CPU and then transfer the computed volumetric boundary information from the main memory to the graphics memory. Unfortunately, both the computation and the data transfer are too time-consuming for interactive applications.

In the following sections, we first propose a general-purpose GPU-based voxelization algorithm that converts an arbitrary model into a Cartesian grid volume. Then we discuss the handling of three different boundary conditions, while focusing on arbitrary complex boundaries that can move and deform. The generation of the boundary nodes of arbitrary boundaries is performed by extending our general-purpose GPU-based voxelization.

47.4.1 GPU-Based Voxelization

An intuitive voxelization approach is the slicing method, which sets the near and far clip planes so that for each rendering pass, only the geometry falling into the slab between the two clip planes is rendered (Fang and Chen 2000). This creates one slice of the resulting volume. The clip planes are shifted to generate subsequent slices. Obviously, for this slicing method, the number of rendering passes is the same as the number of slices in the volume. In most cases, the boundaries are sparse in a volume. In other words, only a small percentage of voxels are intersected by the boundary surfaces. There is no need to voxelize the "empty" space that corresponds to nonboundary voxels.

Our GPU-based voxelization avoids this slicing. Instead, we adapt the idea of depth peeling (Everitt 2001) used for order-independent transparency, in which the depth layers in the scene are stripped away with successive rendering passes. In the first pass, the scene is rendered normally, and we obtain the layer of nearest fragments—or equivalently, voxels. From the second rendering pass, each fragment is compared with a depth texture obtained from the depth buffer of the previous pass. A fragment reaches the frame buffer only if its depth value is greater than that of the corresponding pixel in the depth texture, while the ordinary depth test is still enabled. Therefore, the second pass generates the second-nearest layer, and so on. The process continues until no fragment is farther away than the corresponding pixel in the depth texture. This condition is best determined by using a hardware occlusion query, which returns the number of pixels written to the frame buffer. The number of rendering passes of the depth-peeling algorithm is the number of layers plus one, which typically is significantly smaller than the number of slices.

When rendering order-independent transparent objects, all the layer images are blended in depth order. In contrast, for voxelization, we want the layers to be separated, which is similar to a layered depth image (Shade et al. 1998). The pixels of the layered images are the attributes of the corresponding voxels. The first attribute is the 3D position, and the other attributes depend on the application. Assume that the maximum size along any of the major axes of the object being voxelized is D. We allocate an off-screen buffer with width and height equal to the maximum number of layers times D and the number of attributes times D, respectively. Then, between rendering passes, we translate the viewport so that the layer images do not overlap but are tiled as tightly as possible. We apply the peeling process three times; each time, the image plane is orthogonal to one of the major axes. That is, we perform the peeling from three orthogonal views to avoid missing voxels. As a result, some of the voxels may be rendered more than once. However, the replication does not affect the accuracy. The images containing the voxel attributes are then copied to a vertex array allocated in video memory (using OpenGL extensions such as `ARB_pixel_buffer_object` and `ARB_vertex_buffer_object` [NVIDIA 2004]). Note that different types of voxel attributes are copied to different locations inside the vertex array. We may avoid the copying if either render-to-vertex-array or vertex texture fetch is available. Figure 47-6 illustrates the process in 2D. The line segments are the boundary lines (surfaces in 3D). The small red, green, and blue boxes represent the voxels generated when the boundary lines are projected onto the layered off-screen buffers. Note that the red boundary will only result in two voxels if it is only rendered into layer X.

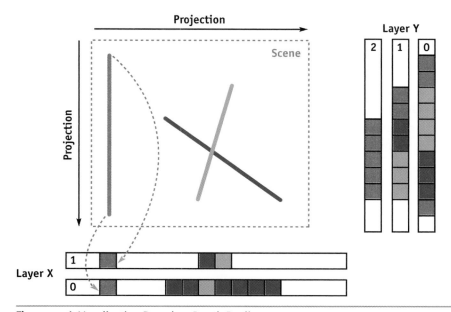

Figure 47-6. Voxelization Based on Depth Peeling

The vertex array is essentially an array of voxel positions and other attributes, which can generate all the boundary voxels for further processing. We use the vertex array because current GPU fragment programs cannot scatter (that is, the output location of a fragment is fixed). Therefore, we must rely on the transformation capability of vertex programs. We convert the vertex array into a flat volume by rendering each vertex as a point of size 1, so that each voxel has a footprint of 1 pixel. All the vertices of the array pass through a vertex program that translates each voxel properly according to its z coordinate, using equations similar to Equation 1. The frame buffers for the depth peeling are initialized with large numbers. If a pixel is not covered by any boundary voxels, then the corresponding vertex created from the pixel falls far away from the view frustum and is clipped.

47.4.2 Periodic Boundaries

For periodic boundaries, outgoing packet distributions wrap around and reenter the lattice from the opposite side. In practice, periodic boundaries are actually computed during the propagation of the packet distributions. If a periodic boundary face is orthogonal to the x or y axis, we call it an *in-slice periodic boundary face*, because a distribution on the face is copied to the opposite side of the lattice but stays inside the same xy slice. For in-slice periodic boundaries, we simply apply a modulo operation to the texture coordinates by the width or the height of each slice. If a periodic boundary face is perpendicular to the z axis, we call it an *out-slice periodic boundary face*, for which we need to copy distribution textures of one slice to another.

A naive implementation of the in-slice periodic boundary condition is to apply the modulo operation to the texture coordinates of all the distribution texels. However, this can be very slow. Therefore, one optimization we use first propagates without the periodic boundary condition. Then we draw strips of single-texel width that only cover the boundary and apply the modulo operation. (See Chapter 34 of this book, "GPU Flow-Control Idioms," for more information on this technique.) In this way, the cost for computing is negligible, because the periodic boundary nodes account for only a small percentage of the lattice.

47.4.3 Outflow Boundaries

For outflow conditions, some packet distributions of the boundary nodes propagate outside of the lattice and can simply be discarded. However, these nodes also expect some packet distributions to propagate inward from fictitious nodes just outside the boundary. One solution is to copy the distribution of the internal nodes to those boundary nodes, according to Equations 2, 3, and 4, in which $f(B)(i, j, k)$ is the distribution of a boundary node in the velocity direction of (i, j, k); $f(I)(i, j, k)$ is the distribution of the corresponding internal node; and $i, j, k \in \{-1, 0, 1\}$. For example, boundary nodes on slice 0 are copied from internal nodes two slices away, which are on slice 2.

For an outflow face orthogonal to the x axis:

$$f(B)_{(i,j,k)} = f(I)_{(-i,j,k)}. \tag{2}$$

For an outflow face orthogonal to the y axis:

$$f(B)_{(i,j,k)} = f(I)_{(i,-j,k)}. \tag{3}$$

For an outflow face orthogonal to the z axis:

$$f(B)_{(i,j,k)} = f(I)_{(i,j,-k)}. \tag{4}$$

Similar to periodic boundaries, an outflow boundary condition is applied by drawing single-texel-wide stripes. Note that when packing the distributions, we guarantee that $f_{(i,j,k)}$ and $f_{(-i,j,k)}$ of the same node are in the same texture, as well as the pairs $f_{(i,j,k)}$ and $f_{(i,-j,k)}$, $f_{(i,j,k)}$ and $f_{(i,j,-k)}$. You can easily verify these with Table 47-1. Therefore, each boundary distribution texture copies from only one distribution texture. To flip the distributions around the major axes, we use the swizzling operator to rearrange the order of the color elements.

47.4.4 Obstacle Boundaries

For obstacle boundaries, we adopt the improved bounce-back rule of Mei et al. 2000, which can handle deformable and moving boundaries. As indicated in Figure 47-7, all packet distributions with corresponding links that are intersected by a boundary are updated using the curved boundary equations rather than the standard LBM equations. For example, the link between the two nodes in Figure 47-7 is intersected by a boundary, hence the boundary rules are applied to the packet distributions marked in blue, f_1 and f_2. Again, we don't need to worry about the details of these equations; interested readers will find these equations in Mei et al. 2000. We just need to know that the boundary equations require two values in addition to the values of f_1 and f_2 at the previous time step. The first value is the exact intersection location, which is described by the ratio Δ, where

$\Delta = t_1/(t_1 + t_2)$ for f_1, and $\Delta = t_2/(t_1 + t_2)$ for f_2. The second value is the moving speed at the intersection, $\mathbf{u}_w$, which is useful for moving and deformable boundaries. Note that for each boundary link, the boundary condition affects two distributions, one on each side of the boundary. The two distributions are in opposite directions, but they are colinear with the link. We refer to them as *boundary distributions*.

To generate the boundary information, we first create a voxelization of the boundaries using the method described in the previous section. Besides the position of the voxels, we also need the wall velocity $\mathbf{u}_w$, as well as the coefficients of polygon plane equations, which will be used to compute Δ. That is, we need three attributes in total. To preserve accuracy, we treat these attributes as texture coordinates when rendering the vertex array in the next step.

In practice, we don't explicitly generate the flat volume of the boundary voxels. Rather, we combine the generation with the computation of the boundary conditions, by rendering the boundary vertex array directly into the off-screen buffer containing the propagated new distributions and then applying the fragment program for complex boundary conditions. Note that in most cases only one node of each boundary link is covered by a voxel from the generated voxel array. However, we need each boundary node to receive a fragment so that the boundary distributions are updated. Therefore, for each packed distribution texture, we render the voxel array three times. In the first pass, they are rendered normally, covering those voxels in the generated voxel array. In the second pass, we first set the color mask so that only the R and G channels can be

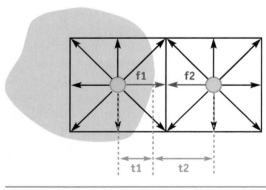

Figure 47-7. Curved-Wall Boundary in LBM Lattice

modified. Then we apply a translation to all the voxels using a vertex program. The translated offset is computed according to the following rule:

$$\cdot\ \mathbf{e}_{qi} \quad : \text{if } flag_1 \times flag_2 > 0;$$

$$\cdot - \mathbf{e}_{qi} \quad : \text{if } flag_1 \times flag_2 < 0;$$

$$\cdot\ 0 \quad\quad : \text{if } flag_1 \times flag_2 = 0;$$

where $flag_1 = (pos_x, pos_y, pos_z, 1) \cdot (A, B, C, D)$, $flag_2 = (A, B, C) \cdot \mathbf{e}_{qi}$, and $\cdot$ represents a dot product. The coordinates (pos_x, pos_y, pos_z) represent the 3D position of the voxel without translation. The boundary surface inside the voxel is defined by $Ax + By + Cz + D = 0$, where (A, B, C) is a normalized plane normal pointing from the solid region to the liquid region. The value $\mathbf{e}_{qi}$ is the velocity vector associated with the distribution in the red channel. The third pass is similar to the second pass, except that this time the blue and alpha channels are modified, and $\mathbf{e}_{qi}$ is the velocity vector corresponding to the blue channel distribution.

In this way, all the boundary nodes are covered by the voxels. We then compute Δ at the beginning of the boundary condition fragment program with the following equations:

$$\Delta' = flag_1 / flag_2,$$

$$\Delta = 1 - \Delta'.$$

The meanings of $flag_1$ and $flag_2$ are the same as before. Note that each channel computes its $flag_1$, $flag_2$, and Δ independently, with its own $\mathbf{e}_{qi}$. A distribution is a boundary distribution only if, for the corresponding color channel, $1 \geq \Delta \geq 0$. If it is not a boundary distribution, the fragment program prevents modifying the corresponding color channel by assigning it the old value.

47.5 Visualization

To visualize the simulation, we inject particles into the flow field. The positions of the particles are stored in a texture and are updated every time step by a fragment program using the current velocity field. Similar to the generation of boundary voxels, the updated particle positions are then copied to a vertex array residing in the graphics memory for rendering. The whole simulation and rendering cycle is inside the GPU, hence there is no need to transfer large chunks of data between the main memory and the graphics memory. To better display the flow field, we arrange particles in a regular grid before injection and color them according to the position where they enter the flow field, as shown in Figure 47-1. Due to the requirements of the vertex array, the total number of particles is constant during the simulation. We use a fragment program to recycle particles that flow out of the border of the field or stay in a zero-velocity region and place them back at the inlet. If two particles coincide at exactly the same location at the same time, they will never separate during the advection. Visually, we will see fewer and fewer particles. To avoid this, we add a random offset to each particle when placing it at the inlet.

In 2D LBM, there is only one velocity slice, while in 3D LBM, the velocities form a volume. The advection fragment program fetches the velocity indicated by the current position of the particles. Therefore, the fragment program needs to access either a 3D texture or a 2D texture storing the flat volume. We chose the flat volume storage, which is much faster. Please note that if we stored the velocity as a stack of separate 2D textures, the advection would be very difficult.

47.6 Experimental Results

We have experimented with our GPU-based LBM implemented using OpenGL and Cg on an NVIDIA GeForce FX 5900 Ultra. This GPU has 256 MB of 425 MHz DDR SDRAM, and its core speed is 400 MHz. The host computer has a Pentium 4 2.53 GHz CPU with 1 GB PC800 RDRAM. All the results related to the GPU are based on 32-bit single-precision computation of the fragment pipeline. For comparison, we have also implemented a software version of the LBM simulation using single-precision floating point, and we measured its performance on the same machine.

Figure 47-8 shows a 2D flow field simulation based on the D2Q9 model with a lattice size of 256^2. We insert two circles (shown in red) into the field as the obstacles' boundary conditions. Vortices are generated because of the obstacles. The figure shows only a snapshot of the flow; the flow is relatively stable, but not constant. Figure 47-1 shows 3D flow simulations using the D3Q19 model with a lattice size of 50^3. Note that our simulation can handle arbitrarily complex and dynamic boundaries, which usually results in a complex flow field. We show only particles injected from a slit, to reduce clutter. The motion of the particles and the ability to change the viewing angle help in understanding the shape of the flow.

Figure 47-9 shows the time in milliseconds per step of the 3D LBM model as a function of the lattice size, running on both the CPU and the GPU. Note that both the x

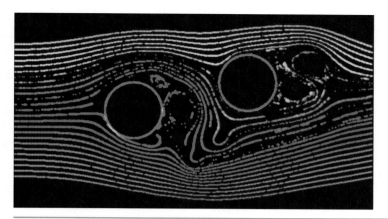

Figure 47-8. Particles Advected in a 2D Flow Field Based on the D2Q9 LBM Model

and y axes are in logarithmic scale. Figure 47-10 compares the two from a different perspective by showing the speedup factor. The time includes both simulation and visualization. Note that there is no need to transfer the velocity field or the particle positions between the main memory and the graphics memory. The time spent on advecting and rendering the particles is negligible with respect to the simulation. The speedup factor varies between 8 and 9 for most of the lattice sizes. When the lattice size approaches 128^3, the speedup is as high as 15. We are sure to get higher speedups with more recent GPUs, such as a GeForce 6800-class GPU. The step in the GPU timing curve—as well as in the GPU versus CPU speedup—is good evidence showing their different cache behavior. When the grid size gets bigger and surpasses a certain threshold, cache misses significantly slow down the CPU version. Due to the mostly sequential access patterns of the LBM algorithm and the GPU's optimization for sequential access, the cache-miss rate on the GPU is relatively independent of the grid size, and we don't see such a performance jump. The performance of the CPU version actually drops dramatically for lattice size of exactly power of two, possibly caused by 64K aliasing (Intel 2004). Therefore, we actually use lattices of size power-of-two-plus-one for the measurement. The CPU-based LBM implementation does not utilize SSE.

47.7 Conclusion

We have presented a fluid flow simulation using the physically based Lattice Boltzmann Method, accelerated by programmable graphics hardware. The LBM simulation and its boundary conditions are of second-order accuracy in both time and space. Our GPU-based simulation using floating-point computation achieves the same accuracy as the

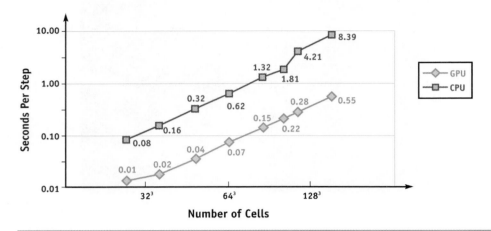

Figure 47-9. Time per Step of a D3Q19 LBM Simulation
The GPU is typically 8 to 9 times faster, though it is 15 times faster for the 128^3 lattice.

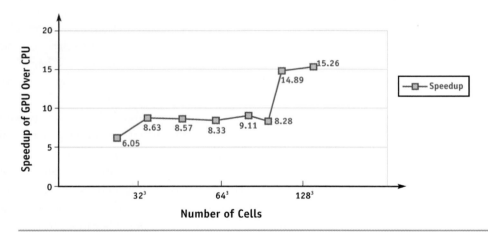

Figure 47-10. Speedup of the LBM on the GPU
The large jump in performance for 128^3 lattices is due to the data set no longer fitting into the CPU cache. The GPU, which is well optimized for the sequential memory accesses that the LBM implementation uses, doesn't suffer from performance degradation for these large data sets.

CPU-based LBM simulation, yet it is much faster. Our experimental results have shown that the GPU version is significantly faster (for example, 8 to 15 times faster, for the D3Q19 model) for most lattice sizes in both 2D and 3D simulations. To attain these speeds, we have incorporated several optimization techniques into the GPU method. We have also proposed a GPU-based general-purpose voxelization algorithm and its extension to handle arbitrarily complex and dynamic boundary conditions in real time.

47.8 References

Other graphics researchers have explored the approach of solving the Navier-Stokes (NS) equations to simulate amorphous phenomena, such as gases and fluid: Foster and Metaxas 1997, Stam 1999, and Fedkiw et al. 2001. Readers may find a comparison of direct NS solvers with the LBM in Wei et al. 2004. Researchers have also developed GPU-accelerated conjugate gradient solvers that can be used for NS equations: Bolz et al. 2003, Krüger and Westermann 2003. There are also other works on using GPUs to compute fluid dynamics: Harris et al. 2003, Goodnight et al. 2003, and Harris 2004. More details of the GPU-accelerated LBM can be found in Li 2004.

Bolz, J., I. Farmer, E. Grinspun, and P. Schröder. 2003. "Sparse Matrix Solvers on the GPU: Conjugate Gradients and Multigrid." *ACM Transactions on Graphics (Proceedings of SIGGRAPH 2003)* 22(3), pp. 917–924.

Chen, S., and G. D. Doolean. 1998. "Lattice Boltzmann Method for Fluid Flows." *Annual Review of Fluid Mechanics* 30, pp. 329–364.

Everitt, C. 2001. "Interactive Order-Independent Transparency." NVIDIA technical report. Available online at
http://developer.nvidia.com/object/Interactive_Order_Transparency.html

Fang, S., and H. Chen. 2000. "Hardware Accelerated Voxelization." *Computers and Graphics* 24(3), pp. 433–442.

Fedkiw, R., J. Stam, and H. W. Jensen. 2001. "Visual Simulation of Smoke." In *Proceedings of SIGGRAPH 2001*, pp. 15–22.

Foster, N., and D. Metaxas. 1997. "Modeling the Motion of a Hot, Turbulent Gas." In *Proceedings of SIGGRAPH 97*, pp. 181–188.

Goodnight, N., C. Woolley, G. Lewin, D. Luebke, and G. Humphreys. 2003. "A Multigrid Solver for Boundary Value Problems Using Programmable Graphics Hardware." In *Proceedings of the SIGGRAPH /Eurographics Workshop on Graphics Hardware 2003*, pp. 102–111.

Harris, M. 2004. "Fast Fluid Dynamics Simulation on the GPU." In *GPU Gems*, edited by Randima Fernando, pp. 637–665. Addison-Wesley.

Harris, M., W. V. Baxter, T. Scheuermann, and A. Lastra. 2003. "Simulation of Cloud Dynamics on Graphics Hardware." In *Proceedings of the SIGGRAPH/Eurographics Workshop on Graphics Hardware 2003*, pp. 92–101.

Intel. 2004. "Capacity Limits and Aliasing in Caches." In Chapter 2 of *IA-32 Intel Architecture Optimization Reference Manual*, pp. 41–43. Available online at **http://www.intel.com/design/pentium4/manuals/index_new.htm**

Krüger, J., and R. Westermann. 2003. "Linear Algebra Operators for GPU Implementation of Numerical Algorithms." *ACM Transactions on Graphics (Proceedings of SIGGRAPH 2003)* 22(3), pp. 908–916.

Li, W. 2004. "Accelerating Simulation and Visualization on Graphics Hardware." Ph.D. dissertation, Computer Science Department, Stony Brook University.

Mei, R., W. Shyy, D. Yu, and L.-S. Luo. 2000. "Lattice Boltzmann Method for 3-D Flows with Curved Boundary." *Journal of Computational Physics* 161, pp. 680–699.

NVIDIA Corporation. 2004. OpenGL Extension Specifications. Available online at **http://developer.nvidia.com/object/nvidia_opengl_specs.html**

Shade, J., S. J. Gortler, L. He, and R. Szelisk. 1998. "Layered Depth Images." In *Proceedings of SIGGRAPH 98*, pp. 231–242.

Stam, J. 1999. "Stable Fluids." In *Proceedings of SIGGRAPH 99*, pp. 121–128.

Wei, X., W. Li, K. Mueller, and A. Kaufman. 2004. "The Lattice-Boltzmann Method for Gaseous Phenomena." *IEEE Transactions on Visualization and Computer Graphics* 10(2), pp. 164–176.

Chapter 48

Medical Image Reconstruction with the FFT

Thilaka Sumanaweera
Siemens Medical Solutions USA

Donald Liu
Siemens Medical Solutions USA

In a number of medical imaging modalities, the Fast Fourier Transform (FFT) is being used for the reconstruction of images from acquired raw data. In this chapter, we present an implementation of the FFT in a GPU performing image reconstruction in magnetic resonance imaging (MRI) and ultrasonic imaging. Our implementation automatically balances the load between the vertex processor, the rasterizer, and the fragment processor; it also uses several other novel techniques to obtain high performance on the NVIDIA Quadro NV4x family of GPUs.

48.1 Background

The FFT has been implemented in GPUs before (Ansari 2003, Spitzer 2003, Moreland and Angel 2003). The improvements presented in this chapter, however, obtain higher performance from GPUs through numerous optimizations. In medical imaging devices used in computed tomography (CT), MRI, and ultrasonic scanning, among others, specialized hardware or CPUs are used to reconstruct images from acquired raw data. GPUs have the potential for providing better performance compared to the CPUs in medical image reconstruction at a cheaper cost, thanks to economic forces resulting from the large consumer PC market.

We review the Fourier transform and the classic Cooley-Tukey algorithm for the FFT and present an implementation of the algorithm for the GPU. We then present several specific approaches that we have employed for obtaining higher performance. We also briefly review the image-formation physics of MRI and ultrasonic imaging and present results obtained by reconstructing sample cine MRI and ultrasonic images on an NVIDIA Quadro FX NV40-based GPU using the FFT.

48.2 The Fourier Transform

The Fourier transform is an important mathematical transformation that is used in many areas of science and engineering, such as telecommunications, signal processing, and digital imaging. We briefly review the Fourier transform in this section. See Bracewell 1999 for a thorough introduction to Fourier transforms.

The Fourier transform of the 1D function $f(x)$ is given by:

$$F(s) = \int_{-\infty}^{+\infty} f(x) e^{-j2\pi sx} \, dx, \tag{1}$$

and the inverse Fourier transform is given by:

$$f(x) = \int_{-\infty}^{+\infty} F(s) e^{j2\pi sx} \, ds. \tag{2}$$

The Fourier transform can also be extended to 2, 3, . . . , N dimensions. For example, the 2D Fourier transform of the function $f(x, y)$ is given by:

$$F(p, q) = \int_{-\infty}^{+\infty} \int_{-\infty}^{+\infty} f(x, y) e^{-j2\pi px} e^{-j2\pi qy} \, dx \, dy. \tag{3}$$

Note that the 2D Fourier transform can be carried out as two 1D Fourier transforms in sequence by first performing a 1D Fourier transform in x and then doing another 1D Fourier transform in y:

$$F(p, q) = \int_{-\infty}^{+\infty} \left[\int_{-\infty}^{+\infty} f(x, y) e^{-j2\pi px} \, dx \right] e^{-j2\pi qy} \, dy. \tag{4}$$

When processing digital signals, it is necessary to convert Equation 1 into a discrete form, turning the Fourier transform into a Discrete Fourier Transform (DFT):

$$F(k) = \sum_{n=0}^{N-1} f(n) W_N^{kn},$$ (5)

where

$$W_N^{kn} = e^{-j\frac{2\pi kn}{N}}; \ f(n), \ n = 0, \ldots, N-1,$$

is a set of discrete samples of a continuous signal and $F(k)$, $k = 0, \ldots, N-1$, are the coefficients of its DFT. The inverse DFT is given by:

$$f(n) = \frac{1}{N} \sum_{k=0}^{N-1} F(k) W_N^{-kn}.$$ (6)

Note that both $f(n)$ and W_N^{kn} are complex numbers. When performing the DFT, $F(k)$ is to be evaluated as shown in Equation 5 for all k, requiring N^2 complex multiplications and additions. However, the most widely used algorithm for computing the DFT is the FFT algorithm, which can perform the DFT using only $N \log_2 N$ complex multiplications and additions, making it substantially faster, although it requires that N be a power of two. This algorithm is known as the Cooley-Tukey algorithm (Cooley and Tukey 1965), although it was also known to Carl Friedrich Gauss in 1805 (Gauss 1805, Heideman et al. 1984). We review this FFT algorithm in the next section.

48.3 The FFT Algorithm

For simplicity, let us consider a discrete digital signal of eight samples: $x(0), \ldots, x(7)$. Figure 48-1 shows a flow chart of the FFT algorithm (the so-called *decimation-in-time butterfly algorithm*) for computing the DFT.

On the left side of the figure, in Stage 1, the input samples are first sent through an *input scrambler* stage. If n is the index of the sample, that sample is sent to the kth output of the input scrambler, where

```
k = BIT_REVERSE(n)
```

For example, sample index 3 (that is, 011 in binary) is sent to the output index (110 binary), which is 6. Every other output of the input scrambler is then multiplied by W_N^0,

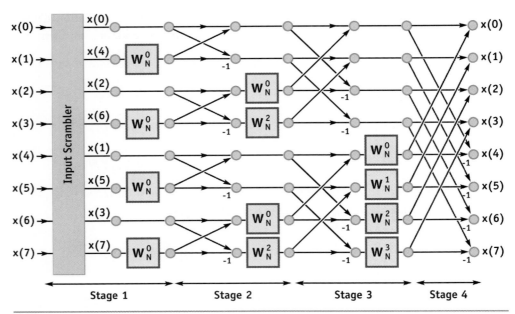

Figure 48-1. The Decimation-in-Time Butterfly Algorithm
Used for computing the DFT of a discrete digital signal of eight samples.

which has the value 1, and all outputs are sent to Stage 2. The input to Stage 2 is then scrambled again, multiplied by weights, and summed to generate the output of Stage 2. Each output of Stage 2 is generated by linearly combining two inputs. This process repeats for Stage 3 and Stage 4. The Fourier transform of the input signal is generated at the output of Stage 4.

In the more general case, if there are N input samples, there will be $\log_2 N + 1$ stages, requiring $N \log_2 N$ complex multiplications and additions. The preceding algorithm can also be applied to do 2D, 3D, and ND FFTs. For example, consider an image, a 2D array of numbers. Using Equation 4, we could do a 1D FFT across all columns first and then do another 1D FFT across all rows to generate the 2D FFT.

48.4 Implementation on the GPU

The FFT can be implemented as a multipass algorithm. Referring to Figure 48-1, we observe that each stage can be implemented as a single pass in a fragment program. Note also that we can combine the input scrambler in Stage 1 and the scrambler in Stage 2 into a single stage (because W_N^0 is 1), an improvement over Ansari 2003 and Spitzer 2003. For our implementation, we make use of the following OpenGL extensions:

- `WGL_ARB_pbuffer`: We use a single pbuffer, with multiple draw buffers, as both the inputs and the outputs to each stage. Alternatively, we could have used one pbuffer as the input and another as the output to each stage. We chose the former method because it is slightly faster: using two pbuffers involves switching the rendering contexts, as in Ansari 2003.

- `WGL_ARB_render_texture`: The output of each stage is written to 2D textures for use as the input for the next stage.

- `NV_float_buffer`, `NV_texture_rectangle`: Used to create floating-point pbuffers and to input and output IEEE 32-bit floating-point numbers to and from each stage. The FFT operates on complex numbers. Furthermore, in applications such as MRI and ultrasonic imaging, it is important to use 32-bit floating-point numbers to obtain good numerical stability. Because of memory bandwidth limitations, looking up 32-bit floating-point scalars four times on a Quadro FX NV40-based GPU is faster than looking up a 32-bit floating-point four-vector once. Thus, it is advantageous to use `GL_FLOAT_R32_NV` texture internal format, instead of `GL_FLOAT_RGBA32_NV` format.

- `ATI_texture_float`: For certain texture lookups that do not require high precision (see the discussion later), two 16-bit floating-point numbers can be packed into a single 32-bit memory location using the `GL_LUMINANCE_ALPHA_FLOAT16_ATI` texture internal format.

- `ATI_draw_buffers`: Many modern GPUs support up to four render targets. Furthermore, on the Quadro FX NV4x family of GPUs, it is possible to create a pbuffer with eight draw buffers: `GL_FRONT_LEFT`, `GL_BACK_LEFT`, `GL_FRONT_RIGHT`, `GL_BACK_RIGHT`, `GL_AUX0`, `GL_AUX1`, `GL_AUX2`, and `GL_AUX3`, using the stereo mode. Using these two aspects, we can compute two FFTs in parallel by outputting two complex numbers to four render targets, and then use those four render targets as input to the next stage—without having to switch contexts, as is the case when using two separate pbuffers.

- `ARB_fragment_program`: The weights, W_N^{kn}, can be computed inside the fragment program using a single `SCS` instruction, as discussed in Section 48.4.2.

The application first creates a single `GL_FLOAT_R32_NV` floating-point stereo pbuffer. Note that the stereo mode must be enabled from the control panel for this to be effective. The pbuffer comes with eight 32-bit scalar draw buffers:

- `GL_FRONT_LEFT`

- `GL_BACK_LEFT`

- `GL_FRONT_RIGHT`

- `GL_BACK_RIGHT`

- `GL_AUX0`

- `GL_AUX1`

- `GL_AUX2`

- `GL_AUX3`

In the first pass, `GL_FRONT_LEFT`, `GL_BACK_LEFT`, `GL_FRONT_RIGHT`, and `GL_BACK_RIGHT` are the source draw buffers, and `GL_AUX0`, `GL_AUX1`, `GL_AUX2`, and `GL_AUX3` are the destination draw buffers. `GL_FRONT_LEFT` and `GL_AUX0` contain the real part of the first FFT, while `GL_BACK_LEFT` and `GL_AUX1` contain the imaginary part of the first FFT. `GL_FRONT_RIGHT` and `GL_AUX2` contain the real part of the second FFT, while `GL_BACK_RIGHT` and `GL_AUX3` contain the imaginary part of the second FFT. In subsequent passes, the source and destination draw buffers are swapped and the process continues. After all the stages are complete, what are remaining in the destination draw buffers are the FFTs of the two input 2D data arrays. The application then displays the magnitude of the FFT for one of the data arrays.

We employ two approaches: (1) mostly loading the fragment processor and (2) loading the vertex processor, the rasterizer, and the fragment processor. We present the advantages and limitations of the two approaches and discuss a way to use a combination of the two to obtain the best performance from a Quadro NV40 GPU.

48.4.1 Approach 1: Mostly Loading the Fragment Processor

In this approach, the application renders a series of quads covering the entire 2D data array, parallel to the pbuffer for each stage of the algorithm. The application also creates a series of 1D textures, called *butterfly lookups*, required for each stage for scrambling the input data and for looking up W_N^{kn}. Naturally, the scrambling indices are integers. The largest possible index when pbuffers are used is 2048, the size of the largest texture that can be created in an NV40-based Quadro FX. This means we can use 16-bit precision to store these indices. Because there are two indices to look up, we can pack two 16-bit indices into a single 32-bit memory location of a texture with the `GL_LUMINANCE_ALPHA_FLOAT16_ATI` internal format. This way, a single texture lookup can generate both scrambling indices. As for the weights, W_N^{kn}, we use two separate `GL_FLOAT_R32_NV` textures to store the real and imaginary parts of them.

A fragment program is executed for each sample of the data array. In this approach, the fragment processor is the bottleneck. The vertex processor and the rasterizer are idling for the most part, because there is just a single quad drawn for each stage. Listing 48-1 shows the Cg fragment program for this case.

Listing 48-1. Cg Fragment Program for a Single Stage of the FFT (Approach 1)

```
void FragmentProgram(in float4 TexCoordRect : TEXCOORD0,
  out float4 sColor0 : COLOR0,
  out float4 sColor1 : COLOR1,
  out float4 sColor2 : COLOR2,
  out float4 sColor3 : COLOR3,
  uniform samplerRECT Real1,
  uniform samplerRECT Imag1,
  uniform samplerRECT Real2,
  uniform samplerRECT Imag2,
  uniform samplerRECT ButterflyLookupI,
  uniform samplerRECT ButterflyLookupWR,
  uniform samplerRECT ButterflyLookupWI)
{
  float4 i = texRECT(ButterflyLookupI,
                     TexCoordRect.xy);   // Read in scrambling
                                         // coordinates
  float4 WR = texRECT(ButterflyLookupWR,
                      TexCoordRect.xy);   // Read in weights
  float4 WI = texRECT(ButterflyLookupWI, //
                      TexCoordRect.xy);

  float2 Res;
  float2 r1 = float2(i.x, TexCoordRect.y);
  float2 r2 = float2(i.w, TexCoordRect.y);

  float4 InputX1 = texRECT(Real1, r1);
  float4 InputY1 = texRECT(Imag1, r1);

  float4 InputX2 = texRECT(Real1, r2);
  float4 InputY2 = texRECT(Imag1, r2);

  Res.x = WR.x * InputX2.x - WI.x * InputY2.x;
  Res.y = WI.x * InputX2.x + WR.x * InputY2.x;

  sColor0.x = InputX1.x + Res.x;   // Output data array 1
  sColor1.x = InputY1.x + Res.y;   //
```

```
    float4 InputX1_ = texRECT(Real2, r1);
    float4 InputY1_ = texRECT(Imag2, r1);

    float4 InputX2_ = texRECT(Real2, r2);
    float4 InputY2_ = texRECT(Imag2, r2);

    Res.x = WR.x * InputX2_.x - WI.x * InputY2_.x;
    Res.y = WI.x * InputX2_.x + WR.x * InputY2_.x;

    sColor2.x = InputX1_.x + Res.x;   // Output data array 2
    sColor3.x = InputY1_.x + Res.y;   //
}
```

The input to this program is the texture coordinates of the data sample, TexCoordRect, and the outputs are the render targets: sColor0 through sColor3. The uniform variables (Real1, Imag1) are the real and imaginary parts of the first 2D data array and (Real2, Imag2) the real and imaginary parts of the second 2D data array. The uniform variable ButterflyLookupI contains the scrambling coordinates. The uniform variables ButterflyLookupWR and ButterflyLookupWI contain the real and imaginary parts of the weights.

Lines 1–3 of Listing 48-1 read in the coordinates, i, for scrambling the input data samples and the real and imaginary parts of the weights (WR and WI) for combining the two inputs. The variables r1 and r2 contain the coordinates for looking up the data values, InputX1, InputY1, InputX2, and InputY2. Lines 13 and 14 compute the output values for the first 2D data array, while lines 21 and 22 compute the output values for the second 2D data array.

As mentioned earlier, the vertex processor and the rasterizer are idling for the most part in this approach. If we moved more computing load to the vertex processor and the rasterizer, we might improve the performance for some cases. We do just that in the second approach.

48.4.2 Approach 2: Loading the Vertex Processor, the Rasterizer, and the Fragment Processor

Figure 48-2 shows an alternate representation of Figure 48-1. Each circle corresponds to a fragment in a given pass. Shown in square brackets are the two scrambling indices used by the fragment program. Also shown is the weight, W_N^{kn}, used by the fragment program.

For each stage, groups of fragments are lumped together to form contiguous blocks, shown in blue and green. It can be observed that for each block, the scrambling indices and the angular argument of the weight, $2\pi k/N$, vary linearly. What this means is that instead of drawing a single quad covering the entire 2D data array, if we draw a series of smaller quads corresponding to each block and let the vertex processor interpolate the scrambling indices and the angular argument, we should be able to move some load off of the fragment processor into the vertex processor and the rasterizer. Listing 48-2 shows the Cg fragment program for Approach 2.

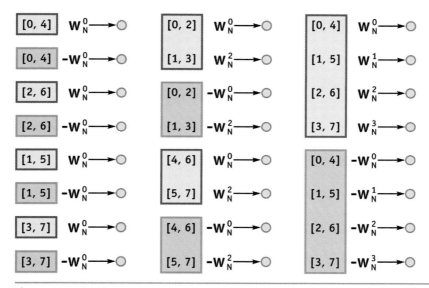

Figure 48-2. Another Way to Represent the Decimation-in-Time Butterfly Algorithm
Showing blocks in which scrambling indices and the angular arguments of the weights can be interpolated in the vertex processor.

Listing 48-2. Cg Fragment Program for a Single Stage of the FFT (Approach 2)

```
void FragmentProgram(in float4 TexCoordRect0 : TEXCOORD0,
    in float4 TexCoordRect1 : TEXCOORD1,
    out float4 sColor0 : COLOR0,
    out float4 sColor1 : COLOR1,
    out float4 sColor2 : COLOR2,
    out float4 sColor3 : COLOR3,
    uniform samplerRECT Real1,
    uniform samplerRECT Imag1,
    uniform samplerRECT Real2,
    uniform samplerRECT Imag2)
```

```cg
{
  float4 WR;
  float4 WI;
  float4 i0 = float4(TexCoordRect0.z, 0.0, 0.0, 0.0); // Scrambling
                                                      // coordinates
  float4 i1 = float4(TexCoordRect0.w, 0.0, 0.0, 0.0); //
  sincos(TexCoordRect1.x, WI.x, WR.x);                // Compute
                                                      // weights

  float2 Res;
  float2 r1     = float2(i0.x, TexCoordRect.y);
  float2 r2     = float2(i1.x, TexCoordRect.y);

  float4 InputX1 = texRECT(Real1, r1);
  float4 InputY1 = texRECT(Imag1, r1);

  float4 InputX2 = texRECT(Real1, r2);
  float4 InputY2 = texRECT(Imag1, r2);

  Res.x = WR.x * InputX2.x - WI.x * InputY2.x;
  Res.y = WI.x * InputX2.x + WR.x * InputY2.x;

  sColor0.x = InputX1.x + Res.x;  // Output data array 1
  sColor1.x = InputY1.x + Res.y;  //

  float4 InputX1_ = texRECT(Real2, r1);
  float4 InputY1_ = texRECT(Imag2, r1);

  float4 InputX2_ = texRECT(Real2, r2);
  float4 InputY2_ = texRECT(Imag2, r2);

  Res.x = WR.x * InputX2_.x - WI.x * InputY2_.x;
  Res.y = WI.x * InputX2_.x + WR.x * InputY2_.x;

  sColor2.x = InputX1_.x + Res.x;  // Output data array 2
  sColor3.x = InputY1_.x + Res.y;  //
}
```

Notice that compared to Listing 48-1, the butterfly lookup texture uniform variables are now missing. The inputs to this program are the texture coordinates of the data sample, `TexCoordRect0` and `TexCoordRect1`. The values of `TexCoordRect0.z` and `TexCoordRect0.w` contain the scrambling coordinates, and the value of `Tex-CoordRect1.x` contains the angular argument, all interpolated by the rasterizer. Note also that in line 5 of the body of the program, the weights `WR` and `WI` are computed by calling the `sincos` instruction.

48.4.3 Load Balancing

Notice also that for later stages of Approach 2, the number of quads we have to draw is only a handful. For the early stages, the number of quads we have to draw is quite large. For example, for Stage 1, we need to draw one quad for each fragment. This means that the vertex processor and the rasterizer can become the bottleneck for early stages, resulting in performance degradation worse than that of Approach 1.

However, it is possible to use Approach 1 for the early stages and Approach 2 for the later stages and reach an overall performance better than using Approaches 1 or 2 alone. The accompanying software automatically chooses the transition point by trying out all possible transition points and picking the one with the best performance.

48.4.4 Benchmarking Results

Table 48-1 compares the performance of our 2D FFT implementation with optimized 2D FFT implementations available in the FFTW library (http://www.fftw.org). For the NV40-based Quadro FX, two 2D images were uploaded once into the GPU's video memory and then Fourier-transformed continuously. All inputs and outputs were 32-bit IEEE numbers. The `FFTW_PATIENT` mode of the FFTW library was used; this mode spends some time when the library is initialized choosing the fastest CPU implementation. The second column lists the frame rates reached using Approach 1 alone, while the third column lists the frame rates reached using load balancing. The fourth column lists the frame rates for using the CPU, and the fifth column shows the frame rate gain of using load balancing on the GPU over using the CPU. All results were acquired on an NVIDIA Quadro FX 4000 using driver 7.0.4.1 (beta), released on October 9, 2004. Notice that in all cases, the GPU outperformed the CPU. We saw the largest gain over the CPU for a 2048×64 2D image, reaching a factor of 1.97.

Table 48-1. Comparing GPU and CPU Performance

Image Size	Fragment Processor Only Quadro NV40 GPU (Hz)	Vertex and Fragment Processors Quadro NV40 GPU (Hz)	FFTW 2.5 GHz P4 (Hz)	Gain over CPU (Column 3/Column 4)
256×256	430	473	355	1.33
512×512	95	104	56	1.86
2048×32	387	426	230	1.85
2048×64	190	207	105	1.97
2048×128	91	100	53	1.89
2048×256	44	48	26	1.85
2048×512	21	23	13	1.77
2048×1024	10	11	6	1.83
1024×256	93	102	54	1.89
1024×512	45	49	27	1.81

48.5 The FFT in Medical Imaging

The FFT is a heavily used mathematical tool in medical imaging. A number of medical imaging modalities, such as CT, MRI, and ultrasonic imaging, rely on the FFT to generate images of the human anatomy from the acquired raw data. We look at MRI and ultrasonic imaging in more detail here. See Bushberg et al. 2001 for an excellent in-depth review of the basics of CT, MRI, and ultrasonic imaging.

48.5.1 Magnetic Resonance Imaging

We review MRI image formation physics very briefly in this section. A more thorough introduction to MRI can be found in Liang and Lauterbur 2000. The density of protons, or hydrogen (^{1}H) atoms, in the human body can be imaged using MRI. The human body contains primarily water, carrying large quantities of protons. The behavior of the protons is governed by the principles of quantum mechanics. However, we can use principles from classical mechanics to explain the process of forming images using MRI more intuitively.

Consider a 1D object, for simplicity. The protons in the object can be thought of as tiny magnets, with magnetism produced by spinning charged particles. In the absence of an external magnetic field, these tiny magnets are randomly oriented, thus displaying no preferred direction of magnetization. If the object is placed in a strong magnetic field, B_0, on the order of 1 Tesla, the majority of these tiny magnets will align along the magnetic field and will spin at a rate given by:

$$\omega_0 = \gamma B_0, \tag{7}$$

where γ is the gyromagnetic ratio for ^{1}H and ω_0 is called the *Larmor frequency*. An MRI scanner contains a strong constant magnetic field, superimposed on linear magnetic gradients. If the magnetic field B varies linearly across the field of view as:

$$B = B_0 + G_x x, \tag{8}$$

then the Larmor frequency varies linearly as:

$$\omega = \omega_0 + \gamma G_x x. \tag{9}$$

Without going into more detail, it is possible to collect a signal from the object sitting in this magnetic field by exciting the tissue with a radio frequency (RF) pulse and listening to the echo, using an antenna or a coil. The received RF signal is given by:

$$s_r(t) = e^{-j\omega_0 t} \int_{-\Delta/2}^{+\Delta/2} \rho(x) e^{-j\gamma G_x xt} \, dx, \tag{10}$$

where, $\rho(x)$ is the proton density, Δ is the extent of our 1D object, $s_r(t)$ is the received signal from the tissue, and t is time, which corresponds to the Fourier spatial-frequency dimension of the object. Equation 10 shows an amplitude-modulated signal on a carrier tone with an angular frequency, ω_0. After amplitude demodulation, the received signal is:

$$s(t) = \int_{-\Delta/2}^{+\Delta/2} \rho(x) e^{-j\gamma G_x xt} \, dx. \tag{11}$$

Equation 11 shows that the collected data is the Fourier transform of the proton density of the object. Hence the proton density, $\rho(x)$, of the object can be reconstructed by performing an inverse Fourier transform on the acquired signal.

Equation 11 can be thought of as "traversing" the Fourier spatial-frequency space as time changes. When time is zero, we are at the origin of the Fourier domain. As time increases, we are at high frequencies. Equation 11 shows only 1D MRI imaging, but it can be extended to do 2D and 3D MRI imaging as well. Briefly, in 2D MRI imaging, a slice through the object is imaged by first selectively exciting the desired slice of tissue and then traversing the Fourier spatial-frequency space in 2D, line by line:

$$s\left(t, t_y\right) = \iint\limits_A \rho\left(x, y\right) e^{-j\gamma G_x\, xt}\, e^{-j\gamma G_y\, y t_y}\; dx\, dy, \tag{12}$$

where the spatial-frequency space is given by (t, t_y), G_y is the y gradient of the magnetic field, and $\rho(x, y)$ is the 2D proton density of the object. Once again, $\rho(x, y)$ can be reconstructed from the acquired data by doing a 2D inverse Fourier transform.

48.5.2 Results in MRI

In this section, we present some examples of MRI images reconstructed using the GPU.

Example 1: Mouse Heart

Figure 48-3a shows the acquired Fourier space data and Figure 48-3b the reconstructed data of a mouse heart.[1] The AVI file named MouseOut.avi on the book's CD shows the beating heart of the mouse, although the playback speed of the movie is slowed to

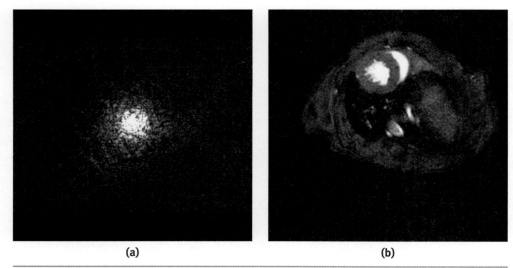

(a)   (b)

Figure 48-3. Images Generated from MRI Data
(a) The magnitude of the acquired Fourier space complex (in-phase and quadrature) MRI data of a mouse heart. There are 256 complex samples horizontally and 192 vertically. The vertical dimension is zero-padded to generate 256 samples. (b) An image is generated by performing the 2D IFFT on a Quadro NV40 GPU using the data in (a).

---

1. The data shows a short-axis view of a mouse heart with normal cardiac function, acquired on a 7 Tesla magnet using $T_E/T_R = 2.8/7.9$ ms, 1 mm slice thickness, 32×32 mm field of view, using an ECG and respiratory-gated FLASH MRI pulse sequence. The time between two successive frames is 7.9 ms. Data courtesy of Dr. Janaka Wansapura, Assistant Professor, Imaging Research Center, Cincinnati Children's Hospital Medical Center.

15 Hz to facilitate viewing, down significantly from the actual data acquisition rate, 127 Hz. This movie contains 13 frames and was acquired using 192 cardiac cycles, with each cycle acquiring 13 Fourier-space raster lines corresponding to different frames. The temporal sampling rate between frames is 7.9 ms (127 Hz). The inputs to the GPU were two floating-point 256×256 arrays containing real and imaginary parts of the data. The GPU reconstructed this data at 172 Hz on a 2.5 GHz Pentium 4, AGP $4\times$ PC. This frame rate includes the time to upload the data over the AGP bus.

The book's CD contains the original raw data in Fourier space and a program demonstrating the use of the GPU for reconstructing the data.

Example 2: Human Head

Figure 48-4a shows the acquired Fourier space data and Figure 48-4b the reconstructed data of a human head.[2] The AVI file named HeadOut.avi on the book's CD shows 16 axial slices through the head, played as a movie. Again, the inputs to the GPU were two floating-point 256×256 arrays containing real and imaginary parts of the data.

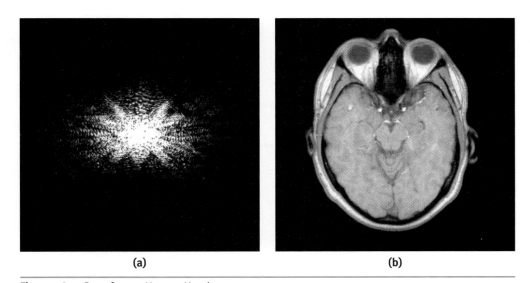

(a) (b)

Figure 48-4. Data from a Human Head
(a) The magnitude of the acquired Fourier space complex (in-phase and quadrature) MRI data of a human head. There are 256 complex samples horizontally and 256 vertically. (b) An image is generated by performing the 2D IFFT on the GPU using the data in (a).

2. The data show an axial section through the head, acquired on a Siemens Quantum whole-body MRI scanner with a 1.5 Tesla magnet, using a standard one-channel circularly polarized head coil and a Gradient Recalled Echo pulse sequence with $T_E/T_R = 4.1/135$ ms, 40-degree flip angle, 133 KHz bandwidth, 5 mm slice thickness, 23×23 mm field of view. Sixteen slices were acquired in 35 seconds. Data courtesy of Drs. Stephan Kannengiesser and Oliver Heid, Siemens Medical Solutions, MR Division, Erlangen, Germany.

The book's CD contains the original raw data in Fourier space and a program demonstrating the use of the GPU for reconstructing the data.

48.5.3 Ultrasonic Imaging

Traditional ultrasonic imaging does not make use of the FFT for image formation, but rather uses a time-domain delay-sum data-processing approach for beam forming. Beam forming is the process of forming an image by firing and receiving ultrasonic pulses into an object. See Wright 1997 for an introduction to traditional ultrasonic beam forming. In this section, we describe a new method called *pulse plane-wave imaging* (PPI) for forming images using the FFT (Liu 2002), which has the advantage of reaching frame rates an order of magnitude higher than those reachable by traditional ultrasonic imaging.

Figure 48-5a shows an ultrasonic transducer, containing an array of N piezoelectric elements. Each piezoelectric element is connected to a channel containing a transmitter and is capable of transmitting an ultrasonic pulse such as the one shown in Figure 48-5b with frequencies on the order of 1 to 20 MHz. The transducer (with a layer of coupling gel) is placed on the body for imaging the human anatomy. In traditional beam forming, ultrasound beams are fired into the body starting from one end of the transducer to the other end, acquiring an image line by line, just as is done in radar imaging.

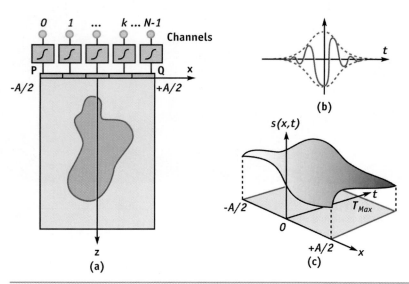

Figure 48-5. Ultrasonic Imaging Using PPI
(a) An array of piezoelectric elements, PQ, transmits an ultrasonic plane-wave pulse into the body. (b) An ultrasonic pulse contains several cycles, shaped inside an envelope. (c) An element at location x then records the returned echo over time, t, acquiring a 2D matrix of data s(x, t).

In the PPI approach, all the elements are pulsed at the same time, producing a single plane-wave front oriented along the z axis, illuminating the entire field of view to be scanned. Immediately after the pulse is sent, the piezoelectric elements are switched to a set of receive circuitry in the channel. The signal received by each element in the array is sent to a receive amplifier and then on to an analog-to-digital converter in the channel. For simplicity, let's assume that the array is a continuous function. Figure 48-5c shows the signal, $s(x, t)$, recorded by all elements within $x \in [-A/2, +A/2]$ for $t \in [0, T_{max}]$. Let the ultrasonic scattering coefficient at a point be $\rho(x, z)$. Our goal is to reconstruct the scattering coefficient using $s(x, t)$. As can be seen from the appendix on the book's CD, the 2D Fourier transform of the scattering coefficient is given by:

$$\Gamma\left(f_x, f_z\right) = -\pi S\left(f_x, f_t\right)\sqrt{\frac{f_t^2}{c^2} - f_x^2},\tag{13}$$

where

$$f_t = \frac{c}{2f_z}\left(f_x^2 + f_z^2\right)\tag{14}$$

and $S(f_x, f_t)$ is the 2D Fourier transform of $s(x, t)$. Equations 13 and 14 show the gist of ultrasonic image formation using pulse plane-wave imaging. The scattering coefficient can be reconstructed by using the following steps:

1. Send a plane wave into the body and record the returned signal, $s(x, t)$.
2. Do a 2D Fourier transform on the returned signal to produce $S(f_x, f_t)$.
3. Remap the values of f_t frequencies in $S(f_x, f_t)$ using Equation 13 to produce $\Gamma(f_x, f_z)$.
4. Perform an inverse 2D Fourier transform on $\Gamma(f_x, f_z)$ to produce $\rho(x, z)$.

Figure 48-6 shows these four steps diagrammatically. The 2D FFT and 2D IFFT can be implemented on the GPU as shown in Section 48.4. The frequency remapping between steps 2 and 3 can also be easily implemented on the GPU. Figure 48-7 shows a block diagram of the pipeline of processing the ultrasound data.

The $[R1, I1]$ channels perform the FFT, while $[R2, I2]$ channels perform the IFFT in each transform step. Note that the algorithm for the IFFT is the same as that for the FFT, except for a change in sign for the angular argument of the weight. At the kth iteration, we are inputting the acquired data (I_k, Q_k) to the $[R1, I1]$ channels for undergoing the FFT. The output of this step is then sent to the frequency-remapping step, which essentially warps the Fourier domain data along f_t. The $[R1, I1]$ output of this

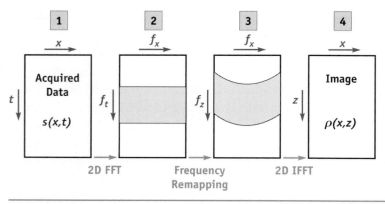

Figure 48-6. The Steps in Forming an Ultrasonic Image Using PPI

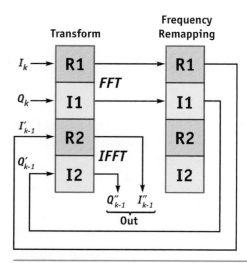

Figure 48-7. The Processing Pipeline for Reconstructing Ultrasound Data

step is then sent to the $[R2, I2]$ input of the transform step, which does the IFFT on $[R2, I2]$ and the FFT on the next input frame of data in $[R1, I1]$. The $[R2, I2]$ output of the transform step then contains the reconstructed image data.

Results in Ultrasonic Imaging

Figure 48-8a shows the acquired data of a simulated phantom containing four point targets, and Figure 48-8b shows the resulting phantom image after processing using steps 1–4. Notice that the point targets can be resolved well in the reconstructed image. The frame rate of the PPI approach is at least an order of magnitude faster than the traditional delay-sum beam-forming approach.

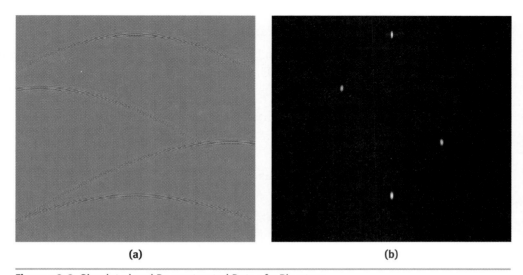

(a)   (b)

Figure 48-8. Simulated and Reconstructed Data of a Phantom
(a) The simulated data of a phantom containing four pin targets. (b) The reconstructed data of the phantom.

48.6 Conclusion

We presented an optimized implementation of the 2D FFT on an NV40-based Quadro FX GPU, as well as its application in MRI and ultrasonic imaging for image reconstruction. We also presented a new method for ultrasonic beam forming, which is more amenable to an implementation in the GPU. The performance of the GPU for the 2D FFT is better than that of a 2.5 GHz Pentium 4 CPU for all cases we tested. For some cases, the performance of the GPU was close to a factor of two better than the CPU's performance.

Besides the performance advantage of using a GPU over a CPU for medical image reconstruction, there are other advantages as well. In a medical imaging device, the CPU can be preoccupied with time-critical tasks such as controlling the data acquisition hardware. In this case, it is advantageous to use the GPU for image reconstruction, leaving the CPU to do data acquisition. Furthermore, unlike the CPU, the GPU is free of interrupts from the operating system, resulting in more predictable behavior. The rate of increase in performance of GPUs is expected to surpass that of CPUs in the next few years, increasing the appeal of the GPU as the processor of choice for medical image reconstruction.

48.7 References

Ansari, Marwan. 2003. "Video Image Processing Using Shaders." Presentation at Game Developers Conference 2003.

Bracewell, Ronald N. 1999. *The Fourier Transform and Its Applications.* McGraw-Hill.

Bushberg, Jerrold T., J. Anthony Seibert, Edwin M. Leidholdt, Jr., and John M. Boone. 2001. *The Essential Physics of Medical Imaging,* 2nd ed. Lippincott Williams & Wilkins.

Cooley, James W., and John Tukey. 1965. "An Algorithm for the Machine Calculation of Complex Fourier Series." *Mathematics of Computation* 19, pp. 297–301.

Gauss, Carl F. 1805. "Nachlass: Theoria Interpolationis Methodo Nova Tractata." *Werke* 3, pp. 265–327, Königliche Gesellschaft der Wissenschaften, Göttingen, 1866.

Heideman, M. T., D. H. Johnson, and C. S. Burrus. 1984. "Gauss and the History of the Fast Fourier Transform." *IEEE ASSP Magazine* 1(4), pp. 14–21.

Liang, Z. P., and P. Lauterbur. 2000. *Principles of Magnetic Resonance Imaging: A Signal Processing Perspective.* IEEE Press.

Liu, Donald. 2002. Pulse Wave Scanning Reception and Receiver. U.S. Patent 6,685,641, filed Feb. 1, 2002, and issued Feb. 3, 2004.

Moreland, Kenneth, and Edward Angel. 2003. "The FFT on a GPU." In *Proceedings of the SIGGRAPH/Eurographics Workshop on Graphics Hardware 2003,* pp. 112–120.

Spitzer, John. 2003. "Implementing a GPU-Efficient FFT." NVIDIA course presentation, SIGGRAPH 2003.

Wright, J. Nelson. 1997. "Image Formation in Diagnostic Ultrasound." Course notes, IEEE International Ultrasonic Symposium.

The authors thank Mark Harris at NVIDIA Corporation for helpful discussions and feedback during the development of the FFT algorithm presented in this chapter.

Index

efficiency *(continued)*
    in soft-edged shadows, 274–277
    in stream programming model, 466
efficient tone mapping, 162
elevation angles in material acquisition, 179
elevation data for geometry clipmaps, 40
elevation maps
    in deferred shading, 163
    for geometry clipmaps, 30
emitters in ambient occlusion computations, 225–226
emitting modified draw calls, 443–444
emulators, 397
encoding indices for octrees, 602
environment maps
    dynamic irradiance. *See* dynamic irradiance environment maps
    in glass simulation, 303
environment shaders
    in Cg vertex program, 217–218
    and Phenomena, 202
equations
    for image panoramas, 658–660
    linear. *See* linear equations
erosion in conservative rasterization, 679
estimation for soft-edged shadows, 276–278
European options
    Black-Scholes model, 721–724
    exercising, 721
    lattice models, 726–730
exercise restrictions on options, 721
expansion operations in stream programming model, 464
expiration date of options, 720
exponential functions, 484
exponents in floating-point representation, 513–514
exterior regions in sketchy rendering, 246
extracting edges, 241
extraordinary points
    for surfaces, 110
    in tessellation performance, 122
extrapolation in octree texture conversions, 609–610
eye space in G-buffer optimization, 152–153

F

false-colored mipmaps, 437–439
Far Cry game, 295, 300

fast algorithms, 509
    computation emphasis in, 511–512
    download and readback in, 512–513
    memory performance in, 510–511
fast filtering schemes, 326
Fast Fourier Transform. *See* FFT (Fast Fourier Transform)
fast sorting, 735
fat-format encoding, 151
fat lines, drawing, 355
feature vectors for computer vision, 661–663
fetch instructions, latency of, 511
fetching data in GeForce 6 Series GPU, 475–476
FFT (Fast Fourier Transform), 765–767
    algorithm, 767–768
    benchmarking in, 775–776
    fragment processors for, 770–772
    implementing, 768–770
    load balancing in, 775
    in medical imaging, 776–780
    in ultrasonic imaging, 780–783
    vertex processors, rasterizers, and fragment processors for, 772–775
    in water rendering, 283
filters and filtering
    antialiasing in, 337–339, 423–427
    bicubic
        B-spline, 319–320
        reconstruction, 323
    bilinear. *See* bilinear filtering
    compaction for, 574–579
    for computer vision, 650, 653
    convolution, 395, 419–422
    cubic, 314–317
    deferred. *See* deferred filtering
    in deferred shading, 150, 155, 158–159
    digital image resampling for, 422–423
        antialiasing in, 423–427
        image reconstruction in, 427–430
    with distance functions, 132
    in GeForce 6 Series GPU, 477–478, 482, 490
    image samples for, 418–419
    implementing, 417–418, 433
    for lines, 351
    motion blur removal, 434
    performance of, 579
    shock, 430–432
    in stream programming model, 464

hair animation and rendering *(continued)*
 tessellation in, 364–365
 volumetric shadows in, 375–378
hand tracking in computer vision, 656–658
hard-edged shadows, blurring, 271–274
hardware
 in CPU performance, 463
 in deferred shading, 155
 in optimization, 152–153, 568
hardware occlusion queries, 91–92
 coherent hierarchical culling in. *See* coherent
  hierarchical culling
 hierarchical stop-and-wait function, 94–97
 occlusion culling in, 93–94
 optimizations in, 105–106
 scenes for, 92
harmonics in water surface models, 284
hashing
 for Perlin noise, 411
 for texture tile mapping, 195
haze
 atmospheric scattering from, 256
 refraction for, 295
HDR (high-dynamic-range) data
 in atmospheric scattering, 265–266
 blending, 483
 lookup tables for, 390–391
head, MRI for, 779–780
Heapsort algorithm, 734
heat haze, refraction for, 295
height maps for water
 in rendering, 286–287
 surface models, 284–285
hemispherical clustering of final gathering rays, 621
hemispherical projection for visibility, 639–641
Hermite polynomials, 412
Hero's Journey, 7–8, 14
hidden objects in occlusion culling, 93
hierarchical culling. *See* coherent hierarchical
  culling
hierarchical occlusion-culling systems, 148
 benefits of, 95
 naive algorithm for, 94–95
 stalls in, 96
hierarchy, memory, 524
high-dynamic-range (HDR) data
 in atmospheric scattering, 265–266
 blending, 483

 lookup tables for, 390–391
high-frequency components, shock filtering for,
  430–432
high-frequency limiting for prefiltered lines, 347
high-latency operations, 467
High-Level Shader Language (HLSL) vertex program, 37–38, 41
high-performance computing, 461
 communication efficiency in, 462–463
 computation efficiency in, 461–462
 CPUs, 463–464
high-precision storage, 405–406
higher-dimensional arrays, 534
higher-order filtering. *See* third-order texture
  filtering
highlights, lookup tables for, 384–385
HLSL (High-Level Shader Language) vertex program, 37–38, 41
holders of options, 720
Horner's rule, 723
HSV color space, 656
hue in HSV color space, 656
human head, MRI for, 779–780

I

I streams in multistreaming, 76–78, 84
`IDirect3DQuery9` interface, 91
illumination, global. *See* global illumination
image-based lighting, 629
image buffers in computer vision, 655–656
image panoramas, 658–660
image reconstruction, 427–430
images in Motion, 394
implicit surfaces, 538–539
in-scattering equation, 257
in-slice periodic boundary faces, 756
independent neighborhood operations, 395
index buffers
 for geometry clipmaps, 31, 33–34
 for grass layer, 12
index data and indices
 for attributes in Shader Model 3.0 programming,
  485
 in geometry packets, 49
 in multistreaming, 88–89
 for octrees, 602

largest numbers allowed, 514
Larmor frequency, 777
latency
    in CPU performance, 464
    in DRAM performance, 458
    in fetch instructions, 511
    in GeForce 6 Series GPU, 476
    in mipmap-level measurements, 444
    trends in, 459
Lattice Boltzmann Method (LBM), 747–749
    algorithm overview, 749–751
    packing in, 751–752
    streaming in, 752–753
lattices, 725
    binomial model, 725–727
    for European options, 726–730
    in LBM model. *See* Lattice Boltzmann Method
        (LBM)
    for lookup tables, 389–391
layering in deferred shading, 163
LBM (Lattice Boltzmann Method), 747–749
    algorithm overview, 749–751
    packing in, 751–752
    streaming in, 752–753
leaf cluster images, 19
leakage, shadow, 278
leather material, 184
leaves and leaf nodes
    in hierarchical stop-and-wait function, 96
    in octrees, 597–598
lens shaders, 202
less-than comparisons in sorts, 734–735, 740
level-of-detail (LOD)
    in geometry instancing, 55
    for tree and shrub layers, 18–19
    in water rendering, 287, 289–290
levels of indirection in structures, 536
levels of mipmapping in painting on meshes,
    606–607
Leviathan engine, mipmap levels with,
    442–444
light
    bending. *See* refraction simulation
    in Marschner reflectance models, 371–372
    scattering. *See* atmospheric scattering
light maps
    in deferred shading, 157
    in multistreaming, 86

light shaders
    in Cg vertex program, 211, 213–214
    and Phenomena, 203
    variables for, 212
lighting and light sources
    in Cg vertex program, 220
    in deferred shading, 146–150, 154
    environment maps for. *See* dynamic irradiance
        environment maps
    global. *See* global illumination
    for grass layer, 15–16
    indirect. *See* indirect lighting
    in material acquisition and rendering, 179,
        181
    for soft-edged shadows, 278
limit positions in subdivision tessellation algorithm,
    118
limit surfaces, 110
linear equations, 703–704
    operations in, 708
        conjugate gradient solver, 713–714
        matrix-vector products, 710–712
        vector arithmetic, 709
        vector reduce, 709–710
    partial differential equations, 714–717
    representation for, 704
        matrices, 706–708
        single float, 704
        vectors, 704–705
linear filtering, 314–315
linear interpolation
    in lookup tables, 385
    in painting on meshes, 605–606
linear mipmap filtering, 440
linear searches in relief mapping, 126
linear transformations
    in antialiasing, 425
    in recursive cubic convolution, 317
lines
    in GeForce 6 Series GPU, 475
    prefiltered. *See* prefiltered lines
liquid flowing simulation, 611–612
load balancing
    in FFT, 775
    in optimization, 568–570
loading
    fragment processor, 770–772
    kernel programs, 504

loading *(continued)*
    vertex processors, rasterizers, and fragment
        processors, 772–775
local frame-buffer memory, 474
local perturbations in water rendering, 292–293
LOD pools in painting on meshes, 607
LOD (level-of-detail) schemes
    in geometry instancing, 55
    for tree and shrub layers, 18–19
    in water rendering, 287, 289–290
lookup for octrees, 599–601
lookup tables (LUTs)
    basics, 381–382
    Cg shaders for, 386–388
    for color transformation, 381
    high-dynamic-range imagery with, 390–391
    interpolation for, 384–386
    mapping, 386
    in Marschner reflectance models, 373–375
    one-dimensional, 382–383
    optimization for, 387–388
    for precomputation, 564–565
    for prefiltered lines, 353–355
    system integration for, 388–390
    three-dimensional, 383–385
lookup textures, 317, 327–328
loop invariants, precomputation of, 563–564
loops
    data-dependent, 554–555
    for displaced values searches, 578
    in flow control, 548
    for rasterization, 562
low-pass filters
    in deferred shading, 158–159
    for prefiltered lines, 347–348, 351
    in Shannon-Nyquist signal reconstruction func-
        tion, 428
low-polygonal geometry in deferred shading, 157
LUTs. *See* lookup tables (LUTs)

M

magnetic resonance imaging (MRI), 765–766
    for human head, 779–780
    for mouse heart, 778–779
    operation of, 776–778
magnification filtering, 328

magnification in mipmap-level measurements, 445
main root shaders, 204
mantissas in floating-point representation,
    513–514
many-to-one mappings for feature vectors, 661
maps and mapping
    bump, 206, 216–217
    in deferred shading, 154, 157, 162–163
    depth, 379
    displacement, 109–110
        per-pixel with distance functions. *See* distance
            functions
        for subdivision surfaces, 119–121
        in water rendering, 283–284, 293
    dynamic irradiance. *See* dynamic irradiance
        environment maps
    for feature vectors, 661
    for geometry clipmaps, 30
    in glass simulation, 303
    height, 284–287
    lookup tables, 386
    in multistreaming, 86
    shadow. *See* shadow maps
    in stream programming, 464–465, 467
    texture
        lookup tables for, 564–565
        in multistreaming, 76
        tile-based. *See* tile-based texture mapping
    tone, 162
Marschner reflectance models, 369–375
masks and masking
    in deferred shading, 150, 154–155
    depth, 242–244
    in G-buffer optimization, 153
    for geometry clipmaps, 40
    in refraction simulation, 297–300
material shaders
    in Cg vertex program, 211
    and Phenomena, 203
materials
    acquisition of, 179–181
    in deferred shading, 146, 157–158
    discussion, 186–187
    in G-buffer optimization, 153
    in realistic images, 177
    rendering process, 181–184
    rendering results, 184–186
    variables for, 212

matrices in linear equations, 706
full, 706
sparse, 706–708
matrix-vector products, 710–712
medical image reconstruction
MRI, 765–766
for human head, 779–780
for mouse heart, 778–779
operation of, 776–778
ultrasonic imaging, 780–783
memory
in CPU performance, 463–464
in deferred shading, 155
in GeForce 6 Series GPU, 474, 477
hierarchy of, 524
kernel access to, 527–528
for lookups, 565
in mipmap-level measurements, 448
performance of, 510–511
stream types, 525–526
trends in, 458
memory clocks, 488
memory footprints
in geometry instancing, 55
texture, 322
memory-free terrain synthesis, 44
memory interface for GPUs, 472
mental images Phenomena renderer
implementing. *See* Cg vertex program
and shaders, 202–205
meshes
in distance-mapping algorithm, 129
in multistreaming, 76, 82–83
painting on. *See* painting on meshes
in refraction simulation, 299
mesostructure of materials, 177
meta-mipmaps, 321–323
METs (multi-element textures), 152
microprocessor performance, 463–464
midpoint shadow maps, 278
midtones, lookup tables for, 384–385
Mie scattering, 255–259
MIMD (multiple-instruction, multiple-data)
processors, 523, 548
mipmap-level measurements, 437–438
derivative instructions in, 447
emitting modified draw calls in, 443–444
magnification in, 445

mip-level velocity, 445–447
multiple, 440–441
overhead in, 444
pixel counting in, 439–443
results of, 441–443
samples, 447–448
mipmap pyramids for geometry clipmaps, 28
mipmapping
in antialiasing, 424
in painting on meshes, 606–607
in third-order texture filtering, 320–323
in tile-based texture mapping, 197–198
mixed derivatives, 325
Monte Carlo methods
for light sources, 630–632
for soft-edged shadows, 274
Moore, Gordon, 458
Moore's Law, 458
Motion, 393
alpha fringes in, 402–405
bilinear filtering in, 400–405
color transformations in, 394–395
conditional execution in, 395
CPU fallback in, 396–397
debugging in, 406–407
design for, 393–394
high-precision storage in, 405–406
independent neighborhood operations in, 395
languages in, 396
resource limits in, 397–399
sequential neighborhood operations in, 395
softening in, 400–402
vertex components in, 400
motion blur removal, 434
mouse heart, MRI for, 778–779
moving instances in geometry instancing, 56
moving light in deferred shading, 149
MRI (magnetic resonance imaging), 765–766
for human head, 779–780
for mouse heart, 778–779
operation of, 776–778
MRTs (multiple render targets)
for deferred shading, 146, 153
in hair generation, 377
multi-element textures (METs), 152
multidimensional arrays, 528–529
1D, 529–530
2D, 530–531

multidimensional arrays *(continued)*
  3D, 531–534
  higher dimensions, 534
multipass shadow algorithm, 226–228
multiple-instruction, multiple-data (MIMD)
      processors, 523, 548
multiple lines, compositing, 355–356
multiple parallel projection, 623–624
multiple render targets (MRTs)
  for deferred shading, 146, 153
  in hair generation, 377
multisample antialiasing, 481
multistreaming, 75–77
  with DirectX 9.0, 78–81
  implementing, 77–78
  rendering in, 89
  for resource management, 81–83
  vertices in, 76, 83–89
multisurface pbuffers, 542

N

N^3-trees. *See* octrees
Nalu demo. *See* hair animation and rendering
NaN value, 399
nature. *See* virtual botany
Navier-Stokes equations, 717
nearest-neighbor interpolation for lookup tables,
      385
nearest-neighbor sampling in texture filtering,
      314–315
nearest-neighborhood filtering in Motion, 401
neighbor textures in octrees, 611
neighborhood operations in Motion, 395
nested loops for rasterization, 562
next shooters in global illumination, 643
NMR (nuclear magnetic resonance) spectroscopy,
      695–696
nodes
  in coherent hierarchical culling, 102
  in hierarchical stop-and-wait() function, 95–96
  in octrees, 597–598
noise
  for alpha transparency, 14
  for geometry clipmaps, 42
  for grass layer, 17
  Perlin. *See* Perlin noise

in shadows, 274
in sketchy rendering, 246, 248–249
nonuniformly sampled lattices, 391
nonvisible edges, extracting, 241
normal buffers in G-buffer optimization, 152–153
normal maps
  for geometry clipmaps, 42, 44
  in refraction simulation, 296
  shading with, 120–121
normal shaders in tessellation algorithm, 118
normalization hardware, 487
normals
  in ambient occlusion computations, 225, 227
  in Cg vertex program, 206
nuclear magnetic resonance (NMR) spectroscopy,
      695–696
null records
  in filtering, 574
  in sum scans, 575–576
`NV_float_buffer` extension, 769
`NV_fragment_program2` extension, 553
`NV_occlusion_query` extension, 91, 93
`NV_texture_rectangle` extension, 769
NVPerfHUD tool, 569
NVShaderPerf tool, 569
nylon material, 184
Nyquist's rule, 423

O

object IDs in deferred shading, 146
obstacle boundaries, 757–759
occlusion, ambient. *See* ambient occlusion
occlusion culling, 93–94, 157
occlusion queries
  data-dependent looping with, 554–555
  in GeForce 6 Series GPU, 480, 482
  hardware. *See* hardware occlusion queries
oceans. *See* water rendering
octaves in water surface models, 284
octrees, 595–596
  accessing, 599–601
  converting into standard 2D textures, 607–610
  creating, 603–604
  definition, 597
  implementing, 598
  indices for, 602

Perlin noise *(continued)*
  optimizing, 415
  in sketchy rendering, 246, 248–249
  storage vs. computation for, 410–411
perturbations
  in refraction simulation, 296–298
  in sketchy rendering, 246–247
  in water rendering, 292–293
phase function in atmospheric scattering, 256
Phenomena renderer, 201–202
  implementing. *See* Cg vertex program
  and shaders, 202–205
Phong models
  diffuse environment maps for, 169
  in material rendering, 181–182
photon maps
  in deferred shading, 163
  in global illumination, 617–618
  as sparse structures, 537
photorealistic images, 177
piezoelectric elements, 780
ping-pong buffering, 698
pipelines
  branching in, 275, 549–550
  challenges in, 469
  in dynamic branching, 275
  flow control in, 548
  in GeForce 6 Series GPU, 476–477, 491
  in Motion, 404–405
  for rasterization, 562
  in Shader Model 3.0 programming, 487
  in stream programming, 465–467
pixel buffers (pbuffers), 541–543
pixel cells in conservative rasterization, 678–679
pixel counting in mipmap-level measurement,
    439–443
pixel engines, 478
pixel pipelines, 476
pixel-processing power, 125
pixel shaders, 497
  branching in, 269, 275–276
    implementation details, 277–280
    performance of, 278–280
    prediction and forecasts in, 276–277
  in dynamic irradiance environment maps, 174–175
  for geometry clipmaps, 28, 38–39, 41

in material rendering, 183–184
  for texture access, 125
plan views for architecture, 244
plants. *See also* virtual botany
  grids for, 8–9
  strategy for, 9–10
point illumination
  light shaders for, 213
  in material rendering, 181
pointers for octrees, 598
points
  in GeForce 6 Series GPU, 475
  rendering, 518
Poisson-pressure equation, 717
pollution, atmospheric scattering from, 256
polygon edges with hemispherical projection,
    641
polygons
  antialiasing, 357
  bounding, 679–686
  converting to surface elements, 223–225
  texture, 417, 438
popping in global illumination, 630–632
portal culling, 93
porting collision detection, 581–583
position encoding, 151–152
position parameters in Cg vertex program, 206
post-processing
  in deferred shading, 147
  in virtual botany, 22–24
post-projection space, 151–152
potentially visible sets (PVSs), 149
power, trends in, 460–461
power management challenges, 468–469
PPI (pulse plane-wave imaging), 780–781
precision in Shader Model 3.0 programming,
    485
precomputation
  for branching, 550
  lookup tables for, 564–565
  of loop invariants, 563–564
predication for flow control, 549
prediction in soft-edged shadows, 276–277
prefiltered lines, 345
  bandlimiting signals for, 347–349
  compositing, 355–356

rasterization *(continued)*
  computation efficiency in, 462
  conservative. *See* conservative rasterization
  CPU-GPU analogies, 501
  in GeForce 6 Series GPU, 481
  in global illumination. *See* global illumination
  in occlusion culling, 93
  pipelines for, 562
rasterization blocks, 476
rasterizers
  for FFT, 772–775
  in parallel processors, 498
Rational Quantify tool, 569
ray casts
  as multiple parallel projection, 623–624
  in virtual botany, 21
ray tracing
  in final gathering, 618–620
  in view-dependent displacement mapping,
    126
Rayleigh scattering, 255–259
reaction-diffusion model, 505–508
read-only vertex buffers, 30–31
readback in fast algorithms, 512–513
reads, dependent texture, 540–541
real spherical harmonic transforms, 170
real-time atmospheric scattering, 258–260
real-time computation of dynamic irradiance envi-
    ronment maps. *See* dynamic irradiance
    environment maps
real-time global illumination, 163–164
real-time optimization, 10
real-time rendering, 182–184
real-time volumetric shadows, 375–378
receivers in ambient occlusion computations,
    225–226
reconstruction
  in deferred filtering, 671–673
  derivative, 324–327
  in global illumination, 639
  image, 427–430
rectangle textures, 529
recursive cubic convolution, 315–320
reductions
  CPU-GPU analogies, 502–503
  in stream programming, 464
reflectance models for hair, 369–375
reflection maps, 303

reflections
  in deferred shading, 148
  in indirect lighting, 231
reflective surfaces and Phenomena, 203
refraction simulation, 295–296
  glass simulation, 303–305
  masks in, 297–300
  techniques, 296–297
  water simulation, 300–302
region-of-interest decoding, 42
regions
  for geometry clipmaps, 28–29
  in sketchy rendering, 246
registers
  in GeForce 6 Series GPU, 491
  in Shader Model 3.0 programming, 483
  swizzle operator for, 566
  VPOS, 173
relief mapping, 126
render contexts
  in geometry instancing, 50–51
  for pbuffers, 542
render phase in geometry instancing, 53
render targets in Shader Model 3.0 programming,
    484–485
render-to-texture feature, 499
  CPU-GPU analogies, 501
  for deferred filtering, 671
  in dynamic irradiance environment maps, 175
  in water rendering, 291
render-to-vertex arrays, 225
render-to-vertex-buffer operation, 525
rendering
  blueprints. *See* blueprints
  geometry clipmaps, 32–39, 43
  in global illumination. *See* global illumination
  hair, 220
  for materials, 181–184
  in multistreaming, 89
  painting on meshes, 604–607
  points, 518
  sketchy. *See* sketchy rendering
  terrain. *See* geometry clipmaps
  in tile-based texture mapping, 198
  water. *See* water rendering
repeated edges, 248
resampling
  images, 422–423

trilinear reconstruction filters, 324
trilinear texture lookups, 317
two-dimensional arrays, 530–531
two-dimensional isosurfaces, 538
two-dimensional packing, 193
two-dimensional reflection maps, 303
two-pass methods in gathering, 617–621
two-pass separable filters, 338–339

U

ultrasonic imaging, 780–783
ultrasonic scanning, 765
uncertainty in sketchy rendering, 245–249
under-tessellation, 111
underestimated conservative rasterization,
        678–680, 686
underlying assets of options, 720
undersampling, artifacts from, 423
uniform arguments, computational frequency of, 541
uniform tessellation, 113
unrolled cube-map faces in deferred shading, 154
update phase in geometry instancing, 53
update rate for geometry clipmaps, 43
updates
    for geometry clipmaps, 39–43
    in protein structure prediction, 698
upsampling for geometry clipmaps, 40–41

V

valences for vertices, 110
value functions, 504
value in HSV color space, 656
variation in grass layer, 15
VBO (vertex buffer object) routines, 343
vector-vector sums, 709
vectors
    for computer vision, 661–663
    in linear equations, 704–705, 709–710
    in Marschner reflectance models, 374
    for Perlin noise, 411
    in protein structure prediction, 699–700
Verlet integration, 366
vertex buffer object (VBO) routines, 343
vertex buffers
    binding to streams, 81

for geometry clipmaps, 30–31, 33–34
for geometry instancing, 58, 62
for grass layer, 12–13
in multistreaming, 85–88
vertex constants instancing, 57–61
vertex fetch units, 474
vertex processors
    characteristics of, 497–498
    for FFT, 772–775
    for fragment streams, 526
    in GPUs, 125, 475
vertex programs
    Cg. *See* Cg vertex program
    in GeForce 6 Series GPU, 475
    in stream programming model, 467
vertex shaders, 497
    in atmospheric scattering, 262–264
    for distance functions, 130
    in GeForce 6 Series GPU, 478
    for geometry clipmaps, 28, 36–38
    for geometry instancing, 60, 64
    for grass layer, 16
    in material rendering, 183–184
    in Shader Model 3.0 programming, 483–484
    in water rendering, 287
vertex shading units, 474–475
vertex streams, 525
    computational frequency of, 541
    in GeForce 6 Series GPU, 481
vertex texture fetch (VTF) feature, 498
vertex textures
    for geometry clipmaps, 44
    in Shader Model 3.0 programming, 484
    for water rendering. *See* water rendering
vertices
    in conservative rasterization, 682–683
    in CPU-GPU analogies, 502
    for feature vectors, 662
    in GeForce 6 Series GPU, 474
    in geometry instancing, 57–61
    in geometry packets, 49
    in Motion, 400
    in multistreaming, 76, 80, 83–89
    for subdivision, 111
    for surfaces, 110
    in tessellation algorithm, 118
    in voxelization, 755–756
VideoOrbits algorithm, 658–660

informIT